ESSENTIALS OF MARKETING RESEARCH

FOURTH EDITION

William G. Zikmund

Barry J. Babin
Louisiana Tech University

SOUTH-WESTERN
CENGAGE Learning

Australia • Brazil • Japan • Korea • Mexico • Singapore • Spain • United Kingdom • United States

SOUTH-WESTERN
CENGAGE Learning

Essentials of Marketing Research, **4th Edition**
William G. Zikmund, Barry J. Babin

VP/Editorial Director: Jack W. Calhoun

Executive Editor: Michael Roche

Editor-in-Chief: Melissa Acuña

Developmental Editor: Elizabeth Lowry

Editorial Assistant: Shanna Shelton

Executive Marketing Manager: Kimberly Kanakes

Senior Marketing Coordinator: Sarah Rose

Marketing Communications Manager: Sarah Greber

Director, Content and Media Production: Barbara Fuller-Jacobsen

Content Project Manager: Emily Nesheim

Media Editor: John Rich

Production Service: Macmillan Publishing Solutions

Senior Art Director: Stacy Jenkins Shirley

Internal Designer: Craig Ramsdell

Cover Designer: Craig Ramsdell

Cover Image: ©Getty Images/Digital Vision

Senior Permissions Manager, Text: Bob Kauser

Senior Permissions Manager, Images: Deanna Ettinger

Photo Permissions Researcher: Susan Lawson

Senior First Print Buyer: Miranda Klapper

To my family:
my wife Laurie, my dear daughter Amie,
and that awesome dude, James.

BRIEF CONTENTS

Preface, xii

Part 1: Introduction, 1

1. The Role of Marketing Research, 2
2. Information Systems and Knowledge Management, 24
3. The Marketing Research Process, 42
4. The Human Side of Marketing Research: Organizational and Ethical Issues, 64

Part 2: Designing Research Studies, 90

5. Qualitative Research, 91
6. Secondary Data Research in a Digital Age, 122
7. Survey Research, 145
8. Observation, 186
9. Conducting Marketing Experiments , 207

Part 3: Measurement, 236

10. Measurement and Attitude Scaling, 237
11. Questionnaire Design, 269

Part 4: Sampling and Statistical Theory, 299

12. Sampling Designs and Sampling Procedures, 300
13. Determination of Sample Size: A Review of Statistical Theory, 324

Part 5: Analysis and Reporting, 351

14. Basic Data Analysis, 352
15. Testing for Differences Between Groups and for Relationships Among Variables, 372
16. Communicating Research Results, 399

Part 6: Comprehensive Cases with Computerized Databases, 418

Endnotes, 424
Index, 431

CONTENTS

CONTENTS

Preface, xii

PART 1: INTRODUCTION

Chapter 1 The Role of Marketing Research, 2

Introduction, 3

Survey This!, 4

What Is Marketing Research?, 5
  Business and Marketing Research, 5
  Marketing Research Defined, 5

Research Snapshot Good Fat and Bad Fat , 6

Applied and Basic Marketing Research, 7
  Applied Marketing Research, 7
  Basic Marketing Research, 7
  The Scientific Method, 7

Marketing Research and Strategic Management Orientation, 8
  Customer Orientation, 8
  Long-Run Profitability, 9
  A Cross-Functional Effort, 10
  Keeping Customers and Building Relationships, 11
  Marketing Research: A Means for Implementing
     the Marketing Concept, 11

Research Snapshot Harley-Davidson Goes Abroad , 12
  Marketing Research and Strategic Marketing
     Management, 13

Planning and Implementing a Marketing Mix, 14
  Product Research, 15
  Pricing Research, 15
  Distribution Research, 16
  Promotion Research, 16
  The Integrated Marketing Mix, 17
  Analyzing Marketing Performance, 18

When Is Marketing Research Needed?, 18
  Time Constraints, 18
  Availability of Data, 19

Nature of the Decision, 19
  Benefits versus Costs, 19

Marketing Research in the Twenty-First Century, 20
  Communication Technologies, 20

Research Snapshot "Jacques" Daniels , 21
  Global Marketing Research, 21

Tips of the Trade, 22

Summary, 22
Key Terms and Concepts, 23
Questions for Review and Critical Thinking, 23
Research Activities, 23

Chapter 2 Information Systems
and Knowledge Management, 24

Introduction, 25

Data, Information, and Intelligence Equal Value, 25

Survey This!, 26

The Characteristics of Valuable Information, 26
  Data Characteristics, 26
  Global Information Systems, 27

**Research Snapshot RFID Technology Gets Cheaper—
Marketing Knowledge Grows, 28**

Decision Support Systems, 28
  Databases and Data Warehousing, 29
  Input Management, 29
  Computerized Data Archives, 32

Research Snapshot MySpace Means My Data, 33
  Networks and Electronic Data Interchange, 35

Predictive Analytics, 35

Research Snapshot How Did They Know That?, 36
How Is the Internet Useful in Research?, 36
Environmental Scanning, 37
Information Technology, 38
Intranets, 38

Tips of the Trade, 39

Summary, 39
Key Terms and Concepts, 40
Questions for Review and Critical Thinking, 40
Research Activities, 41

**Chapter 3 The Marketing
Research Process, 42**

Introduction, 43

Types of Marketing Research, 43
Exploratory Research, 44

**Research Snapshot Cute, Funny, or Sexy? What Makes
a Mascot Tick?, 45**
Descriptive Research, 45

Research Snapshot The Squeaky Wheel Gets … , 46
Causal Research, 47
Uncertainty Influences the Type of Research, 49

Stages in the Research Process, 50
Alternatives in the Research Process, 50
Defining the Research Objectives, 51

Research Snapshot Nothing So Practical As Theory?, 56
Planning the Research Design, 56
Sampling, 58
Gathering Data, 59
Processing and Analyzing Data, 59
Drawing Conclusions and Preparing a Report, 60

The Research Program Strategy, 60

Tips of the Trade, 60

Summary, 61
Key Terms and Concepts, 62

Questions for Review and Critical Thinking, 62
Research Activities, 63

**Chapter 4 The Human Side of
Marketing Research: Organizational
and Ethical Issues, 64**

Introduction, 65

Who Does the Research?, 65
Do It Yourself or Let Your Fingers Do the Walking?, 65

Survey This!, 66

Working in the Marketing Research Field, 67
Research Suppliers and Contractors, 67

Research Snapshot Finding Häagen-Dazs in China, 68
Limited Research Service Companies
and Custom Research, 69
Size of the Marketing Research Firm, 69
The Director of Marketing Research as a Manager, 71

Research Snapshot Marketing Research Pays, 73
Cross-Functional Teams, 73

Ethical Issues in Marketing Research, 74
Ethical Questions Are Philosophical Questions, 74
General Rights and Obligations of Concerned Parties, 74
Rights and Obligations of the Research Participant, 75
Rights and Obligations of the Client Sponsor (User), 79

**Research Snapshot Must Win Auction! Must
Win Auction!, 80**
Privacy, 81
Privacy on the Internet, 81
Rights and Obligations of the Researcher, 81

The Researcher and Conflicts of Interest, 85
A Final Note on Ethics, 86

Tips of the Trade, 86

Summary, 86
Key Terms and Concepts, 87
Questions for Review and Critical Thinking, 88
Research Activities, 88

PART 2: DESIGNING RESEARCH STUDIES

Chapter 5 Qualitative Research, 91

Introduction: What Is Qualitative Research?, 92
Describing Qualitative Research, 92

Survey This!, 93

Qualitative "versus" Quantitative Research, 93

Contrasting Qualitative with Quantitative Methods, 94

Research Snapshot My Friends at P&G, 95

Qualitative Research and Exploratory Research Designs, 95
Idea Generation, 96
Concept Testing, 96

Qualitative Research Orientations, 97
Phenomenology, 98

Research Snapshot "When Will I Ever Learn?", 99
Ethnography, 99
Grounded Theory, 100
Case Studies, 101

Common Techniques Used in Qualitative Research, 102
Focus Group Interview, 102
Depth Interviews, 107
Conversations, 109
Free-Association and Sentence Completion Methods, 110

Preparing a Focus Group Outline, 112

Modern Technology and Qualitative Research, 114
  Facilitating Interviewing, 114

Research Snapshot Research Knows Almost No Boundaries! , 116

Exploratory Research in Science and in Practice, 117
  Misuses of Exploratory Qualitative Research, 117

Tips of the Trade, 119

Summary, 119
Key Terms and Concepts, 120
Questions for Review and Critical Thinking, 120
Research Activities, 121

Chapter 6 Secondary Data Research in a Digital Age, 122

Introduction, 123

Using Secondary Data in Marketing Research, 123
  Advantages, 123

Survey This!, 124
  Disadvantages, 124

Typical Objectives for Secondary-Data Research Designs, 127
  Fact-Finding, 127

Research Snapshot New Trends—Music for Mobile Phones, 128
  Model Building, 129

Research Snapshot Mining Data from Blogs, 133

Sources of Internal Secondary Data, 133
  Internal and Proprietary Data, 134

External Secondary Data Sources, 134
  Information as a Product and Its Distribution Channels, 134

Research Snapshot Uncle Sam Finds You!, 135

Single-Source and Global Research Data, 140
  Single-Source Data-Integrated Information, 140
  Government Agencies, 140

Tips of the Trade, 142

Summary, 142
Key Terms and Concepts, 143
Questions for Review and Critical Thinking, 143
Research Activities, 143

Chapter 7 Survey Research, 145

Introduction, 146

The Types of Information Gathered Using Surveys, 146

Survey This!, 147

Advantages and Disadvantages of Surveys, 147
  Advantages of Survey Research, 147

Research Snapshot Blu-rays are Best's Rays, 148
  Disadvantages of Survey Research, 148

Sources of Error in Surveys, 148
  Random versus Systematic Sampling Error, 148
  Rule-of-Thumb Estimates for Systematic Error, 154
  What Can Be Done to Reduce Survey Error?, 154

Different Ways that Marketing Researchers Conduct Surveys, 154
  Interactive Survey Approaches, 155
  Noninteractive Media, 155

Conducting Personal Interviews, 155

Research Snapshot iPod, uPod, FMPod?, 156
  Advantages of Personal Interviews, 156

Research Snapshot Matters of Taste, 158
  Disadvantages of Personal Interviews, 158
  Door-to-Door Interviews and Shopping Mall Intercepts, 159
  Global Considerations, 160
  Telephone Interviews, 160
  Phone Interview Characteristics, 162
  Central Location Interviewing, 165
  Computer-Assisted Telephone Interviewing, 165
  Computerized Voice-Activated Telephone Interview, 166
  Global Considerations, 166

Surveys Using Self-Administered Questionnaires, 166
  Mail Questionnaires, 166
  Response Rates, 168
  Increasing Response Rates for Mail Surveys, 169
  Self-Administered Questionnaires Using Other Forms of Distribution, 172
  Fax Surveys, 172
  E-Mail Surveys, 172
  Internet Surveys, 174
  Text-Message Surveys, 178
  Choosing an Appropriate Survey Approach, 178

Pretesting Survey Instruments, 178

Ethical Issues in Survey Research, 180

Tips of the Trade, 181

Summary, 181
Key Terms and Concepts, 182
Questions for Review and Critical Thinking, 183
Research Activity, 184

Chapter 8 Observation, 186

Introduction, 187

Observation in Marketing Research, 187
  What Can Be Observed?, 187

Survey This!, 188
  The Nature of Observation Studies, 188

Research Snapshot This Trend Brought to You by DDB SignBank, 189
  Observation of Human Behavior, 189
  Complementary Evidence, 190

Direct and Contrived Observation, 191
  Direct Observation, 191
  Contrived Observation, 192

Research Snapshot Clean as We Say, or Clean as We Do?, 193

Ethical Issues in the Observation of Humans, 193

Observation of Physical Objects, 194
  Artifacts, 194
  Inventories, 195
  Content Analysis, 196

Mechanical Observation, 196
   Television and Radio Monitoring, 196
   Monitoring Web Site Traffic, 198
   Scanner-Based Research, 199
   Camera Surveillance, 199
   Neurological Devices, 200
Measuring Physiological Reactions, 200

Tips of the Trade, 202

Summary, 202
Key Terms and Concepts, 203
Questions for Review and Critical Thinking, 203
Research Activities, 204

Chapter 9 Conducting Marketing Experiments, 207

Introduction, 208
The Characteristics of Experiments, 208

Survey This!, 209
   Subjects, 209
   Experimental Conditions, 209
   Effects, 210
   Summary of Experimental Characteristics, 212

Basic Issues in Experimental Design, 212
   Manipulation of the Independent Variable, 212
   Selection and Measurement of the Dependent Variable, 214
   Selection and Assignment of Test Units, 214

Research Snapshot Goldfishing or Bluefishing?, 215

Demand Characteristics and Experimental Validity, 217
   What are Demand Characteristics?, 217

Experimenter Bias and Demand Effects, 218
   Reducing Demand Characteristics, 218
   Establishing Control, 219
   Basic versus Factorial Experimental Designs, 220
   Laboratory Experiments, 220
   Field Experiments, 221
   Advantages of Between-Subjects Designs, 222
   Internal Validity, 222
   External Validity, 224
   Trade-Offs Between Internal and External Validity, 225
Ethical Issues in Experimentation, 225

Using Test-Marketing, 226
   Forecasting New Product Success, 226
   Testing the Marketing Mix, 226
   Identifying Product Weaknesses, 227
   Projecting Test-Market Results, 228
   Estimating Sales Volume: Some Problems, 228
   Advantages of Test-Marketing, 229
   Disadvantages of Test-Marketing, 229

Research Snapshot All Fed Up!, 230

Research Snapshot The Hidden in Hidden Valley Ranch, 231
   Selecting a Test-Market Site, 231

Tips of the Trade, 233

Summary, 233
Key Terms and Concepts, 234
Questions for Review and Critical Thinking, 234
Research Activities, 235

PART 3: MEASUREMENT

Chapter 10 Measurement and Attitude Scaling, 237

Introduction, 238
What to Measure, 238

Survey This!, 239
   Concepts, 240
   Operational Definitions, 240

Levels of Scale Measurement, 241
   Nominal Scale, 241
   Ordinal Scale, 242
   Interval Scale, 244
   Ratio Scale, 244
   Mathematical and Statistical Analysis of
      Scales, 245

Reliable and Valid Index Measures, 246
   Indexes and Composites, 247
   Computing Scale Values, 247

Research Snapshot Recoding Made Easy, 248
   Reliability, 248

Validity, 250
   Establishing Validity, 250
   Reliability versus Validity, 251

What Is an Attitude?, 252

Attitudinal Rating Scales, 252
   Category Scales, 253
   The Likert Scale, 255
   Assessing Item and Scale Quality, 256
   Semantic Differential, 256
   Constant-Sum Scale, 257
   Graphic Rating Scales, 258

Research Snapshot Click, Click, Click, 259
   Ranking, 259
   Paired Comparisons, 259
   Direct Assessment of Consumer Attitudes, 260
   Ranking, Sorting, Rating, or Choice Technique?, 260
   Monadic or Comparative Scale?, 260
   What Type of Category Labels, If Any?, 261
   How Many Scale Categories or Response Positions?, 261
   Balanced or Unbalanced Rating Scale?, 261
   Forced-Choice Scales?, 262
   Single or Multiple Items?, 262

Attitudes and Intentions, 263
  Multi-attribute Attitude Score, 263
  Behavioral Intention, 264

Tips of the Trade, 265

Summary, 265
Key Terms and Concepts, 266
Questions for Review and Critical Thinking, 266
Research Activities, 267

Chapter 11 Questionnaire Design, 269

Survey This!, 270

Introduction, 270

Basic Considerations in Questionnaire Design, 270
  What Should Be Asked?, 271
  Questionnaire Relevancy, 271
  Questionnaire Accuracy, 271

Question Phrasing: Open- or Close-Ended Statements?, 272
  Open-Ended Response versus Fixed-Alternative
    Questions, 272
  Types of Fixed-Alternative Questions, 274
  Phrasing Questions for Self-Administered, Telephone,
    and Personal Interview Surveys, 275

Avoiding Mistakes, 276
  Avoid Complexity: Simpler Language is Better, 276
  Avoid Leading and Loaded Questions, 276
  Avoid Ambiguity: Be as Specific as Possible, 278
  Avoid Double-Barreled Items, 279

Research Snapshot Who's _Really_ Doing the Housework?, 280
  Avoid Making Assumptions, 280
  Avoid Burdensome Questions That May Tax
    the Respondent's Memory, 280
  Order Bias, 281

What Is the Best Layout?, 284
  Traditional Questionnaires, 284
  Internet Questionnaires, 287

Pretesting and Revising Questionnaires, 291

**Research Snapshot It's Not Always What You Ask,
but How You Ask It!, 292**
  Designing Questionnaires for Global Markets, 293

Tips of the Trade, 294

Summary, 294
Key Terms and Concepts, 295
Questions for Review and Critical Thinking, 295
Research Activity, 297

PART 4: SAMPLING AND STATISTICAL THEORY

Chapter 12 Sampling Designs and
Sampling Procedures, 300

Introduction, 301

Why Sample?, 301
  Pragmatic Reasons, 301

Survey This!, 302
  Accurate and Reliable Results, 302
  Destruction of Test Units, 303

Identifying a Relevant Population and Sampling Frame, 304
  Defining the Target Population, 304

**Research Snapshot George Gallup's Nation
of Numbers, 306**
  The Sampling Frame, 306
  Sampling Units, 307

Random Sampling and Nonsampling Errors, 308
  Random Sampling Error, 308
  Systematic Sampling Error, 308
  Less than Perfectly Representative Samples, 311

Probability versus Nonprobability Sampling, 311
  Convenience Sampling, 312
  Judgment Sampling, 312
  Quota Sampling, 312

Probability Sampling, 314
  Simple Random Sampling, 314
  Systematic Sampling, 315
  Stratified Sampling, 315
  Proportional versus Disproportional Sampling, 317
  Cluster Sampling, 318

**Research Snapshot Who's at Home? Different Ways
to Select Respondents, 319**
  Multistage Area Sampling, 319

What Is the Appropriate Sample Design?, 319
  Degree of Accuracy, 320
  Resources, 320
  Time, 320
  Advance Knowledge of the Population, 320
  National versus Local Project, 320

Tips of the Trade, 321

Summary, 321
Key Terms and Concepts, 322
Questions for Review and Critical Thinking, 322
Research Activity, 323

Chapter 13 Determination of Sample Size:
A Review of Statistical Theory, 324

Introduction, 325

Basic Descriptive and Inferential Statistics, 325
  What Are Sample Statistics and Population Parameters?, 325

Survey This!, 326
  Measures of Central Tendency, 328
  Measures of Dispersion, 329

Distinguish Between Sample and Sample Distribution, 333
  The Normal Distribution, 333
  Population Distribution and Sample Distribution, 336
  Sampling Distribution, 336

Central-Limit Theorem, 337

Estimation of Parameters and Confidence Intervals, 339

Research Snapshot Measuring Viewership . . . with Confidence, 340
Point Estimates, 340
Confidence Intervals, 340

Sample Size, 342
Random Error and Sample Size, 342

Research Snapshot Target and Wal-Mart Shoppers Really Are Different, 343
Factors in Determining Sample Size for Questions
  Involving Means, 343

Estimating Sample Size for Questions Involving
  Means, 344
Population Size and Sample Size, 345
Determining Sample Size for Proportions, 345
Determining Sample Size on the Basis of
  Judgment, 346

Tips of the Trade, 347

Summary, 347
Key Terms and Concepts, 348
Questions for Review and Critical Thinking, 348
Research Activities, 349

PART 5: ANALYSIS AND REPORTING

Chapter 14 Basic Data Analysis, 352

Introduction, 353

Coding Qualitative Responses, 353
Structured Qualitative Responses and Dummy
  Variables, 353

Survey This!, 354

The Nature of Descriptive Analysis, 354

Creating and Interpreting Tabulation, 355

Cross-Tabulation, 356
Contingency Tables, 356
Percentage Cross-Tabulations, 358
Elaboration and Refinement, 358
How Many Cross-Tabulations?, 359

Data Transformation, 359
Simple Transformations, 359
Problems with Data Transformations, 361

Research Snapshot Wine Index Can Help Retailers, 362
Index Numbers, 362
Tabular and Graphic Methods of Displaying Data, 362

Computer Programs for Analysis, 362
Statistical Packages, 362
Interpretation, 364

Hypothesis Testing Using Basic Statistics, 365
Hypothesis Testing Procedure, 365
Significance Levels and p-values, 366
Type I and Type II Errors, 366

Research Snapshot The Law and Type I and Type II Errors, 367
Type I Error, 367
Type II Error, 368

Tips of the Trade, 368

Summary, 368
Key Terms and Concepts, 369
Questions for Review and Critical Thinking, 369
Research Activities, 370

Chapter 15 Testing for Differences Between Groups and for Relationships Among Variables, 372

Introduction, 373

What Is the Appropriate Test Statistic?, 373

Survey This!, 374

Cross-Tabulation Tables: The χ^2 Test for Goodness-of-Fit, 375

The t-Test for Comparing Two Means, 378
Independent Samples t-Test, 378
Independent Samples t-test Calculation, 378
Practically Speaking, 380

Research Snapshot Expert "T-eeze", 381
Paired-Samples t-Test, 382

The Z-Test for Comparing Two Proportions, 383

One-Way Analysis of Variance (ANOVA), 384
Simple Illustration of ANOVA, 385
Partitioning Variance in ANOVA, 386
The F-Test, 387
Practically Speaking, 388

Research Snapshot More than One-Way, 389

General Linear Model, 390
GLM Equation, 390
Regression Analysis, 390

Tips of the Trade, 393

Summary, 393
Key Terms and Concepts, 394
Questions for Review and Critical Thinking, 394
Research Activities, 397

Chapter 16 Communicating Research Results, 399

Introduction, 400

What Is a Marketing Research Report?, 400
Report Format, 400

Survey This!, 401

Research Snapshot **Sloppy Numbers in the Crosshairs of Dow Jones Newspaper Fund's Director, 402**
    Tailoring the Format to the Project, 402
    The Parts of the Report, 402
    Basic Marketing Research Report, 405

Using Tables Effectively, 405
    Creating Tables, 405

Using Charts Effectively, 407
    Pie Charts, 408
    Line Graphs, 408
    Bar Charts, 409

The Oral Presentation, 410

Research Snapshot **Online Reports: Easy to Get, Easy to Ignore, 411**

Reports on the Internet, 412

The Research Follow-Up, 412

Tips of the Trade, 413

Summary, 413
Key Terms and Concepts, 414
Questions for Review and Critical Thinking, 414
Research Activity, 414
A Final Note on Marketing Research, 417

PART 6: COMPREHENSIVE CASES WITH COMPUTERIZED DATABASES

Case 1: Attiring Situation, 419
Case 2: Say It Ain't So! Is This the Real Thing?, 420

Case 3: TABH, INC., Automotive Consulting, 422

Endnotes, 424

Index, 431

Marketing research is a little like searching for a needle in a haystack. Researchers search for answers but forming the questions can be just as important. The "search" cannot be removed from "research." Following this analogy, the researcher must address questions such as these: How do you find the needle? Where does the search start? How do you translate recorded data into intelligence that can be used to answer managerial questions? Clearly, it would be helpful if you could discover better places to start searching and better techniques to help direct the search. When it works right, marketing research is a win–win proposition. The process enables a company to identify its customers and design products that maximize the value they receive from a purchase. In return, the company receives value as the customers spend their hard-earned money. The result: customers win and businesses win! All are better off.

Like searching for a needle in a haystack, imagine trying to find a single piece of market information on the Internet. This information may well be hidden beneath piles and piles of irrelevant stuff! Or how about trying to find a key piece of market information that may be hidden in the mind of a consumer or an employee who isn't consciously aware of all his or her reasons for some preference or behavior and, consequently, can't identify or talk about it? How do you go about finding this information that could be so crucial to making a good market decision?

Using an X-ray monitor would be a great way to find the needle. But your real-world success is probably more dependent on the ability to wield an effective research process than an X-ray monitor. And that's where this text comes in: *Essentials of Marketing Research* aquaints students with basic knowledge and skills involved in the research process.

Chapter 3 introduces this process, which includes six stages. Researchers must first work together with decision makers to decide why they are looking for that metaphorical needle; the next two stages plot out the way to go about finding the needle. Next are two stages that focus on the actual search for the needle. The process concludes when the market researcher communicates the benefits of finding "pointed" information that can help mend problems or create something really new and special to the decision maker. Success in this process usually merits the researcher a reward that is a bit more valuable than that needle!

New to *Essentials of Marketing Research*

To ensure that students are able to conduct market research with an understanding of all the latest theories and techniques available to them, the fourth edition is revised and updated. Certainly, the field of marketing research is dynamic both in terms of the demands placed on it by business and in terms of the technological advances that provide more tools for the researcher's toolbox.

The Internet is revolutionizing information systems, ways of gathering secondary data, survey processes, sampling, questionnaire design, qualitative analysis, and communication of results. The Survey This! feature is new to this edition and gets students and instructors directly involved with one important way that the Internet has changed research. This particular feature provides first-hand experience with the advantages and disadvantages of using online questionnaires. Additionally, students can then analyze data that they actually helped to provide.

In addition to greater currency and attention given to the Internet, key features added to the fourth edition include:

- Survey This!—Students respond to an online questionnaire using Qualtrics software. The questionnaire involves students' opinions, activities, and interests regarding numerous everyday behaviors ranging from study habits to involvement with social networking. The resulting data are made available to instructors and students. In the early chapters, this feature is useful for critiquing the way questionnaires are constructed and how research hypotheses are addressed in a questionnaire. In later chapters, students can use the data to respond to real research questions about other students. Students also get access to Qualtrics to design their own questionnaires.

- Tips of the Trade—Each chapter contains a useful list of important tips that correspond to the particular stage of the research process discussed in the chapter. The tips provide information addressing practical questions such as interview length, question wording, interviewer involvement, sample size requirements, and guides for data reliability and validity, as well as useful tips for testing hypotheses using inferential statistics.

- Chapter Vignettes—Each chapter opens with a story relevant to the material featured in that particular chapter. Some of these vignettes involve famous brands and companies, so the reader may well be familiar with some of the topics. Other vignettes involve "slice of life" stories describing a businessperson's struggle to make smart decisions and demonstrate how research is intertwined with this struggle. About half of the vignettes are new to this edition.

- A Simplified Approach and Style—The boxed material, chapter objectives, and end-of-chapter materials are now presented in a simplified form that allows greater focus on the truly important information. Boxed materials highlight Research Snapshots that cover ethical angles of research, provide illustrations of research in practice, and offer relevant tips or detailed examples. The chapter learning objectives ensure an important coherence and structure to the chapters that culminate with the end-of-chapter materials. Learning objectives are keyed to the major headings in each chapter. This facilitates organization around objectives that can be used to develop measurable assessment outcomes.

- Greater Attention to Qualitative Research—More and more companies are benefiting from qualitative research. In response to this important phenomenon, Chapter 5 was rewritten in the third edition to focus more exclusively on qualitative research. That emphasis has been increased further in this edition. Additionally, topics relevant to qualitative research are found throughout the text. In particular, several sections focus on technological advances that facilitate the collection and use of qualitative data. Phenomenology, grounded theory, ethnography, and case study approaches are now all covered. Qualitative research is dramatically being changed by the Internet as consumers leave more and more artifactual data behind on social networking Web sites, company chat rooms, blogs, micro-blogs (such as tweets left on Twitter), and more.

- More on analytics—Analytic tools are discussed throughout, but in particular, the closing chapters present an introduction to more analytic techniques than in the previous edition.

Organization of the Book

The organization of the fourth edition of *Essentials of Marketing Research* follows the logic of the marketing research process. The book is organized into six parts. Each part presents the basic research concepts for one of the stages in the research process and discusses how these concepts relate to decisions about conducting specific projects.

Part 1: Introduction begins the book by discussing the scope of marketing research. An overview of the problem definition and the entire marketing research process is provided. The interplay between research and business is emphasized throughout this discussion. Research is not equally important among all firms. The way that the importance and scope of research varies with the type of business orientation that characterizes some company is illustrated. An overview of computerized data management and information systems and an explanation of how all of this is changing due to the Internet follows. Without high ethical standards, no business is good. Thus, the introductory materials also include an emphasis on business ethics and the special ethical problems associated with marketing research.

Part 2: Designing Research Studies covers essentials that provide a starting place to studying business problems. In this context, Part 2 discusses the need for exploratory research and secondary data collection. Research proposals are covered in some detail, and the reader is encouraged to see these as the written agreement that helps put the decision maker and the researcher on the same page.

Chapter 5 emphasizes qualitative research applications. One role played by qualitative research is helping to separate business problem symptoms from true issues that can be attacked with marketing research. However, qualitative research is a topic extending far beyond problem definition by allowing greater potential for discovery and greater potential for deeper and potentially more meaningful explanations.

Part 2 includes a detailed discussion of secondary data and emphasizes its increasing importance in an increasingly data rich world. This part also examines some topics most closely associated with marketing research. For example, the chapters describe issues related to planning, conducting, and administering surveys. Surveys remain a mainstay for collecting consumer and employee opinion. Part 2 concludes with material dealing specifically with market experiments. As such, this part emphasizes test marketing, which to many is synonymous with marketing research.

Part 3: Measurement is critical to research. This part of the text discusses the basics of measurement theory. Two chapters offer practical explanations of measurement and questionnaire design. Key topics include descriptions of the different levels of scale measurement and how this affects the interpretation of results.

Part 4: Sampling and Statistical Theory examines sampling designs and sample size. These chapters explain the difference between a population and a sample. The reasons why sampling is needed and why it can be used to confidently allow predictions about larger numbers of people are covered. The fieldwork process also is discussed, including the importance of supervision of the work that goes on in the field.

Part 5: Analysis and Reporting covers important processes necessary in translating raw data into market intelligence. Included among these topics, the data must be edited and coded. The coded data are then ready for analysis. Some of the most commonly used methods for analyzing data also are presented. For instance, basic descriptive statistics are discussed as ways of portraying key results like central tendency. Inferential statistics also are discussed, including often-used univariate and bivariate approaches such as *t*-tests.

Part 6: Comprehensive Cases with Computerized Databases make up the last section of the book. These cases provide materials to challenge students to apply and integrate concepts learned. Instructors will find that these cases provide some flexibility either to expand or simplify the assignment to suit the demands of varying course assignments. The three cases provide more variety and involve analysis of internal marketing problems as well as an opportunity to use qualitative research. When quantitative data are included, they can be easily analyzed with basic statistical tools like SPSS. Excel files are also included with the same data. These files can be read directly by statistical programs like SAS or other programs.

For this edition of Essentials, the Appendix and Glossaries have been moved to the website.

Superior Pedagogy

More than other marketing research textbooks, the fourth edition of *Essentials of Marketing Research* addresses students' need to comprehend all aspects of the marketing research process. The following features facilitate learning throughout the book:

- **Learning Objectives.** Each chapter begins with a concise list of learning objectives that emphasize the major areas of competency the student should achieve before proceeding to the next chapter. The key is to avoid labeling everything a major learning objective and to provide the instructors with flexibility for emphasizing additional material from each chapter as they see fit.

- **Major Headings Keyed to Learning Objectives.** All first-level headings, with the exception of those labeled "Introduction," are keyed to learning objectives. This should be an aid in developing assessment rubrics and makes the book more user friendly in terms of identifying key material. Example assessment rubrics are available in the instructional resources.
- **Research Snapshots.** All of the box materials share a common title, Research Snapshots. Each chapter contains three Research Snapshots. The boxes explore marketing research processes in a variety of modern businesses situations, ranging from international considerations to research ethics. Some boxes also illustrate research techniques and applications in a step-by-step fashion. Every attempt is made to make the box material lively and relevant to the subject matter of the chapters.
- **Writing Style.** An accessible, interesting writing style continues as a hallmark of this book. With a careful balance between theory and practice and a sprinkling of interesting examples and anecdotes, the writing style clarifies and simplifies the market research process. In addition, the text offers a comprehensive treatment of important and current topics.
- **Statistical Approach.** A short review of statistical theory in Chapter 13 provides students with an overview of the basic aspects of statistics. Because this text stresses managerial applications more than statistical theory, students are given some basic tools to perform common data analysis. More sophisticated data analysis approaches are left for further reference. Thus, the readers can learn how to test simple hypotheses involving differences between means or relationships among variables. Cross-tabulation, *t*-tests, ANOVA, and regression are covered in sufficient depth to allow a student to use these techniques. The text includes screen shots to get students started running statistics using EXCEL, SAS, or SPSS, which is available with this text.

   In addition, easy-to-follow, click-through sequences can walk a student through a few of the most basic approaches to producing statistical results.
- **Key Terms.** Learning the vocabulary of marketing research is essential to understanding the topic, and *Essentials of Marketing Research* facilitates this with key terms. First, key concepts are boldfaced and completely defined when they first appear in the textbook. Second, all key terms and concepts are listed at the end of each chapter, and many terms are highlighted in a marginal glossary. Third, a glossary summarizing all key terms and definitions appears at the end of the book for handy reference. A glossary of frequently used symbols is also included.
- **Ethics Questions.** Identified by a special icon, ETHICS, ethics questions are included in most chapters. Among the compelling issues students are asked to explore is redefining the right to privacy in light of new technology. The ethical issues also provide a great opportunity for building critical thinking skills.
- **Internet Questions.** Internet questions also are identified by a special icon, 'NET. Nearly all chapters include multiple questions and research activities that illustrate advances in Internet applications common to marketing research.
- **Research Activities.** The end-of-chapter materials include a few real-world research activities intended to provide actual research experience for the student. Most provide an opportunity for the student to gain experience with multiple content areas. Some involve ethical aspects of research, and some involve Internet usage.
- **Cases.** Extensive cases taken from real-life situations illustrate marketing research concepts and build knowledge and research skills. These cases offer students the opportunity to participate actively in the decision-making process, one of the most effective forms of learning. Video cases are also available via the instructor section of the book's Web site (www.cengage.com/marketing/zikmund).

Comprehensive Instructor Resources

It is important for any text to develop comprehensive supplemental materials to support instructors in their vital teaching function. Because of this pedagogical philosophy, the extensive learning package provided with *Essentials of Marketing Research* includes a test bank, a computerized test bank (ExamView testing software), a comprehensive instructor's manual, PowerPoint presentation slides, data sets for several cases, a DVD, and online marketing resources (available on the Web at www.cengage.com/marketing/zikmund).

- The Instructor's Resource CD-ROM (ISBN: 0-324-59440-2) contains valuable instructor resources on one easy-to-use CD-ROM: the test bank, ExamView testing software, the instructor's manual (includes comprehensive lecture outlines, solutions to all assignments, and case solutions), PowerPoint presentation slides, and data sets for cases. The ancillary files were prepared by Laurie Babin of the University of Louisiana–Monroe.

- Data Sets are provided that match several end-of-chapter exercises and different case analyses. The data are provided both in EXCEL files, allowing great flexibility to be used with many programs, and in SPSS files, which are ready to use with either the student or full version of SPSS. Students may download the data sets at www.cengage.com/marketing/zikmund by clicking on the textbook and then on "Data Sets." Data sets are also available on the Instructor's Resource CD-ROM.

- Video DVD (ISBN: 1-439-08088-7). The video cases guide students through marketing research issues faced by a variety of well-known companies, such as Mercedes-Benz, Krispy Kreme, and the successful e-commerce business Wine.com.

- Web Resources at www.cengage.com/marketing/zikmund provide the latest information about what's new and what's cool in marketing research. The instructor's manual, test bank, PowerPoint slides, and video cases can also be found here.

- The Qualtrics Research Suite was built for researchers by researchers. Enclosed with each new copy of *Essentials of Marketing Research* is an access code that gives your students access to a tool that makes survey creation easy enough for a beginner while at the same time sophisticated enough for the most demanding academic or corporate researcher. Qualtrics allows your students to create and deploy surveys, and provides data for analysis. A survey included in the book in the Survey This! box on page 4 has your students fill out an initial survey. Then the survey data collected from adopters of *Essentials of Marketing Research* from around the globe are used throughout the rest of the book in a variety of ways, from critiquing questionnaire construction to using the data to respond to real research questions about other students. Qualtrics is a perfect solution for instructors who have students conduct a survey project as part of a term project. Students also get access to Qualtrics to design their own questionnaires. To learn more about Qualtrics, please go to http://www.qualtrics.com/essentials or contact your local Cengage Learning sales representative.

- WebTutor™ Toolbox. Preloaded with content and available free via PIN code when packaged with new texts, WebTutor ToolBox pairs all the content of the text's rich Book Companion Web Site with all the sophisticated course management functionality of a Blackboard or WebCT product. Instructors can assign materials (including online quizzes) and have the results flow automatically to their gradebooks.

Resources for Students

To promote learning and competency, it is also important to provide students with well-crafted resources. In addition to covering the latest information technology (described above), the fourth edition includes the following student resources:

- The Dedicated Web Site www.cengage.com/marketing/zikmund, developed especially for the new edition, includes chapter quizzes that allows you to test and retest student knowledge of chapter concepts. Each chapter has a quiz to encourage retesting. In addition, the Web site features downloadable flashcards of key terms, the very best online marketing research resources available, and much more.

- The Qualtrics Research Suite was built for researchers by researchers. Enclosed with each new copy of *Essentials of Marketing Research* is an access code that gives you access to a tool that makes survey creation easy enough for a beginner while at the same time sophisticated enough for the most demanding academic or corporate researcher. Qualtrics allows you to create and deploy surveys, and provides data for analysis. A survey included in the book in the Survey This! box on page 4 has you fill out an initial survey. Then the survey data collected from students using *Essentials of Marketing Research* around the globe are used throughout the rest of the book in a variety of ways, from critiquing questionnaire construction to using the data to respond to real research questions about other students. Access to Qualtrics requires an access code that is provided with each new copy of the book.

Acknowledgments

Certainly, no list of acknowledgments will be complete. So many people have assisted in this project. Chief among these would be to the late Bill Zikmund for carrying the weight of this project for the first editions. I am privileged to be able to carry the project along into hopefully many more editions as the premier marketing research text. Also, thanks go to some of my team. My graduate assistants Kevin James, David Shows, Melanie Gardner, and Christina Chung have helped with research for this text and helped share some of the workload on other endeavors, freeing up time for me to spend on this project. David was particularly helpful in getting the Survey This! feature underway. Thanks also to Julia Callaway for helping to manage my crazy schedule. I would be remiss not to also mention the support and patience of my family. All have contributed to the project, and my kids were particularly helpful in judging the relevance of vignettes and examples. Also, thanks go to all the great faculty who mentored me during my days in the Ph.D. program at LSU. Most notable among these are Joseph F. Hair, Jr. and the late William R. Darden.

Special thanks go to all the good people at Cengage Learning who helped make this project possible. Thanks to my publishers, Neil Marquardt and Mike Roche, for motivating the whole team to stay on schedule. Thanks to Kimberly Kanakes for creative inspirations and marketing support. Also, a special thanks to Elizabeth Lowry, Emily Nesheim, and Jill Traut. They provided tremendous support through the writing and production process, including assistance with proofing, permissions, photos, and exhibits.

Many colleagues contributed ideas for this book. They made many suggestions that greatly enhanced this book. For their insightful reviews of the manuscript for the fourth or previous editions of *Essentials of Marketing Research*, I would like to thank the following:

Karen Goncalves
Nichols College

Carol Bienstock
Radford University

Steven V. Cates
Averett University

Stephanie Noble
The University of Mississippi

Bob Lauman
Webster University

Natalie Wood
St. Joseph's University

Robert Jaross
Florida International University

Terry Paul
The Ohio State University

Mike Parent
Utah State University

Stephen Batory
Bloomsburg University

Michael R. Hyman
New Mexico State University

Rick Saucier
St. John's University

Xin Zhao
University of Utah

Gerald Albaum
University of Oregon

William Bearden
University of South Carolina

Joseph A. Bellizzi
Arizona State University–West

James A. Brunner
University of Toledo

F. Anthony Bushman
San Francisco State University

Thomas Buzas
Eastern Michigan University

Roy F. Cabaniss
Huston-Tillotson College

Michael d'Amico
University of Akron

Ron Eggers
Barton College

H. Harry Friedman
City University of New York–Brooklyn

Ron Goldsmith
Florida State University

Larry Goldstein
Iona College

David Gourley
Arizona State University

Jim Grimm
Illinois State University

Christopher Groening
University of Missouri

Al Gross
Robert Morris College

Don Heinz
University of Wisconsin

Craig Hollingshead
Texas A&M University–Kingsville

Victor Howe
University of Kentucky

Roy Howell
Texas Tech University

Rhea Ingram
Columbus State University–Georgia

P. K. Kannan
University of Maryland

Susan Kleine
Arizona State University

David B. Klenosky
Purdue University

C. S. Kohli
California State University–Fullerton

Jerome L. Langer
Assumption College

James H. Leigh
Texas A&M University

Larry Lowe
Bryant College

Karl Mann
Tennessee Technological University

Charles R. Martin
Wichita State University

Marlys Mason
Oklahoma State University

Tom K. Massey
University of Missouri–Kansas City

Sanjay Mishra
University of Kansas

G. M. Naidu
University of Wisconsin–Whitewater

Charles Prohaska
Central Connecticut State University

Alan Sawyer
University of Florida

Robert Schaffer
California State University–Pomona

Leon G. Schiffman
City University of New York–Baruch

David Shows
Louisiana Tech University

K. Sivakumar
Lehigh University

Mark Speece
Central Washington University

Harlan Spotts
Western New England College

Wilbur W. Stanton
Old Dominion University

Bruce L. Stern
Portland State University

James L. Taylor
University of Alabama

Gail Tom
California State University–Sacramento

Deborah Utter
Boston College

David Wheeler
Suffolk University

Richard Wilcox
Carthage College

Margaret Wright
University of Colorado

Clifford E. Young
University of Colorado–Denver

William Lee Ziegler
Bethune-Cookman College

Thanks also to all of the students who have inspired me and reinforced the fact that I made a great career decision about two decades ago. Thanks also to my close colleagues Mitch Griffin, Jon Carr, Dave Ortinau, and Jim Boles for their continued support and insight.

Barry J. Babin
Louisiana Tech University
March 2009

In Remembrance ◀

William G. Zikmund (1943–2002)

A native of the Chicago area, William G. Zikmund was a professor of marketing at Oklahoma State University and died shortly after completing the eighth edition of *Exploring Marketing Research*. He received a Ph.D. in business administration with a concentration in marketing from the University of Colorado.

Before beginning his academic career, Professor Zikmund worked in marketing research for Conway/Millikin Company (a marketing research supplier) and Remington Arms Company (an extensive user of marketing research). Professor Zikmund also has served as a marketing research consultant to several business and nonprofit organizations. During his academic career, Professor Zikmund published dozens of articles and papers in a diverse group of scholarly journals, ranging from the *Journal of Marketing* to the *Accounting Review* to the *Journal of Applied Psychology*. In addition to *Exploring Marketing Research*, Professor Zikmund authored *Essentials of Marketing Research, Business Research Methods, Marketing, Effective Marketing,* and a work of fiction, *A Corporate Bestiary*.

Professor Zikmund was a member of several professional organizations, including the American Marketing Association, the Academy of Marketing Science, the Association for Consumer Research, the Society for Marketing Advances, the Marketing Educators' Association, and the Association of Collegiate Marketing Educators. He served on the editorial review boards of the *Journal of Marketing Education, Marketing Education Review, Journal of the Academy of Marketing Science,* and *Journal of Business Research*.

Part 1
Introduction

© PHIL KNOTT/PYMCA/JUPITER IMAGES

CHAPTER 1
The Role of Marketing Research

CHAPTER 2
Information Systems and
Knowledge Management

CHAPTER 3
The Marketing Research Process

CHAPTER 4
The Human Side of Marketing
Research: Organizational
and Ethical Issues

CHAPTER 1
THE ROLE OF MARKETING RESEARCH

After studying this chapter, you should be able to

1. Know what marketing research is and what it does for business
2. Understand the differences between basic and applied marketing research
3. Understand how the role of marketing research changes when a firm is truly marketing oriented
4. Integrate marketing research results into the strategic planning process
5. Know when marketing research should and should not be conducted
6. Appreciate the way that technology and internationalization are changing marketing research

Chapter Vignette: "The Dude Looks Like a Lady"

Picture the typical car company. Now, picture the typical car customer. What do you see? Put those two images together and most people imagine one of the Big Three (GM, Ford, or Chrysler), selling an SUV to a middle-aged man. The idea of men selling cars to men may have once been accurate. But times change and many of the assumptions that underlie the car industry can be questioned. Perhaps one reason many car companies are struggling today is the failure to read these changes in the marketplace. Is the typical car customer a man? Is the typical car sold in the United States an SUV? Are men better at selling cars?

© AP PHOTO/ROBERT E. KLEIN

Toyota surpassed General Motors as the number one selling car brand in 2008. Toyota has earned this position by successfully selling to many types of customers, but they have been particularly successful in designing cars that appeal to women. Women buy about 6 out of every 10 Toyota cars sold in the United States. This is no accident. Toyota works hard to know their customers better than the competition.

Recently, Toyota placed an emphasis on conducting marketing research that addressed the key question: What features create the most value for female car consumers? The results were particularly revealing and helped Toyota make important design changes. For example, research revealed that women, in contrast to men, are more interested in the car interior and less interested in the car exterior. Women want a car that is easy to get in and out of, easy to put things like children's car seats into, and ergonomic controls that are easily adjustable even for a driver who is less than six feet tall. Safety and security are also key benefits that create relatively high value for women. Women also show more interest in fuel economy and the Toyota Prius appeals to this desire to save fuel! Although men generally find value in features like these too, men are still more often first concerned with exterior styling and power. Even the Toyota Yaris, Toyota's lowest-priced model, contains a driver's seat that can be adjusted not only forward and back, but up and down as well.

Toyota's status as the leading car company has other manufacturers playing catch-up. But, General Motors and Volvo, among others, are also gearing up by aiming marketing research more squarely at women. For example, General Motors made the decision to make its OnStar communication system standard on all vehicles. This added feature helps create a sense of security by automatically contacting help in the event of a crash. Volvo's research also suggests that women are more concerned than men with easy parking and a car that does not need frequent maintenance. Volvo has put an exclamation point on the emphasis on women in the marketplace by naming Anne Belec as president of Volvo Cars of North America. Now, research has put the "lady" squarely in the center of the auto industry and Aerosmith could say "the dude looks like a lady" for a good reason![1]

Introduction

Changes in the automobile industry like those discussed in the vignette clearly demonstrate how beneficial the right information can be in making informed marketing and managerial decisions. Consumers in today's economy need more than ever to be convinced that a car is really worth the expense. Marketing research can provide the information that shows the factors that will cause consumers to react favorably. Without the input that research provides, key business decisions including those shaping product and brand promotion, pricing, distribution, and product design are made in the dark.

Jelly Belly brand traditionally offered fifty official jelly bean flavors. However, research input from customers has helped that number grow and now Jelly Belly even has a variety of specialty beans. Consumers willingly submitted new flavor ideas as part of the Jelly Belly Dream Bean Contest (http://www.dreambeancontest.com). In return, the consumers received an opportunity to win prizes. The company receives some really off-the-wall flavor ideas.

Among the strangest are flavors such as Dill Pickle, Rotten Egg, Taco, Burned Bacon, and Cream of Wheat.[2] Top suggestions were put back on the Web so that people could vote for the flavor they most wanted to see introduced. In 2008, the winning flavor was Acai Berry which beat out other finalist flavors such as Sublime Chili Lime, Thai Iced Tea, and Mojito.

More recently, Jelly Belly is trying to capitalize on consumers' desires for sports performance products. Survey research suggests that consumers would respond favorably to food and drink products providing benefits that improve one's ability to exercise.[3] As a result, Jelly Belly has introduced Sport Beans. Sport Beans contain added electrolytes, carbohydrates, and vitamins designed to provide added energy and alertness. In addition, all the strange flavor suggestions also have spawned a new product offering for the entire jelly bean market. Bean-Boozled Jelly Beans combines a traditional flavor with an exotic flavor so consumers can decide if they really prefer a buttered-popcorn

Jelly Belly brand's market research has capitalized on consumers' desires to produce fifty varieties of jelly beans as well as recipes on how to create snacks with them.

jelly bean to a rotten egg. The product provides added value through the fun that comes with all the potential surprises. A Skunk Spray bean looks exactly like a Licorice bean. So, the bean lover never is sure when the bean will bamboozle! Successful companies are constantly scanning ideas in the hope of providing ways of adding value. Jelly Belly's Sports Beans and Bean-Boozled Beans offer two different ways of adding value.[4]

The coffee industry, after years of the "daily grind," has proved quite dynamic over the past decade. After years of steady decline, research on consumers' beverage purchases shows that

This book introduces the reader to the world of marketing research. Marketing research represents the eyes and the ears of a competitive business firm. The researcher's job includes determining what information is needed so that data can be analyzed and become intelligence. Consumers play a crucial role in this process.

They often are used as research participants and, with or without their knowledge, they provide the information. One way that consumers (and sometimes employees or managers) take part is by participating in surveys. Most readers have probably participated in surveys previously. Here is another chance to do so, only this time, you will first play the role of a research participant. Later, you will fill the role of a research analyst and even a key marketing decision maker as you try to make sense of data provided by the many users of this textbook.

Your first interaction with the "Survey This!" feature is simply to play the role of respondent and respond to the entire survey as honestly and completely as possible. Go to the URL provided in the preface and by your instructor, and simply participate. Your answers will be anonymously stored in the database. Once you've completed the survey, you can visit the course Web site and get a copy of the questions contained in the questionnaire.

coffee sales began rebounding around 1995. Telephone interviews with American consumers estimated that there were 80 million occasional coffee drinkers and 7 million daily upscale coffee drinkers in 1995. By 2001, estimates suggested there were 161 million daily or occasional U.S. coffee drinkers and 27 million daily upscale coffee drinkers.[5] By 2007, research indicates that although practically all coffee drinkers visit gourmet coffee shops, younger coffee consumers, particularly those under the age of 30, drink most of their coffee the *gourmet* way.[6]

Coffee drinking habits have also changed. In 1991 there were fewer than 450 coffeehouses in the United States. Today, places such as Starbucks, Second Cup, The Coffee Bean, Tea Leaf, and Gloria Jean's are virtually everywhere in the United States and Canada. There are more than 11,000 Starbucks stores alone today.[7] While locating these outlets requires significant formal research, Starbucks also is market testing new concepts aimed at other ways a coffee shop can provide value to consumers. One concept that has survived testing thus far is the addition of free, in-store high-speed wireless Internet access. Thus, you can have hot coffee in a hot spot! After Starbucks *barristas* began reporting that customers were asking clerks what music was playing in the stores, Starbucks began testing the sales of CDs containing their in-store music. The research that underlies the introduction of these value-added concepts could first include simply asking a consumer or a small group of consumers for their reaction to the concept. Survey research and then actual in-store tests may follow. However, had Starbucks simply asked consumers the question, "Are you willing to pay three dollars for a cup of coffee?" back in 1985, we would likely not be discussing them today. So, the research underlying such decisions can be multilayered.

The statistics about coffee demonstrate how research can track trends that may lead to new business opportunities. Also, it is clear to see how research can be used to examine new concepts in progressively more complex stages, setting the stage for a more successful product introduction. These are only the tip of the iceberg when it comes to the types of marketing research that are conducted every day. This chapter introduces basic concepts of marketing research and describes how research can play a crucial role in successful marketing and business success in general.

What Is Marketing Research?

Part of business involves studying the different things that come together to create a business environment. Marketing research would not exist if business didn't exist. Thus, understanding marketing research requires at least a cursory understanding of business.

Business and Marketing Research

In its essence, business is very simple. Companies need to produce benefits that people want to buy. That means that consumers view the company as providing valuable bundles of benefits. There are many factors that can affect perceived value, and successful companies are those that understand the value equation. With this in mind, there are several key questions, the answers to which help provide this understanding.

1. *What do we sell?*
   This includes not only the benefits that are easily seen, but also the more emotional benefits such as the comfort and relaxation of enjoying a cup of gourmet coffee in a pleasant atmosphere or the novelty of trying a rotten egg jelly bean.
2. *How do consumers view our company?*
   All too often, companies define themselves too narrowly based only on the physical *product* they sell. A key question involves whom the customers will do business with if they do not choose your company. For instance, how is Starbucks viewed relative to its competitors? Who are the competitors? Does Starbucks compete more directly with Maxwell House, Seattle Drip, or something completely outside the coffee arena like a local lounge? Are we viewed more or less favorably relative to the competition?
3. *What does our company/product mean?*
   What knowledge do people have of the company and its products? Do they know how to use them? Do they know all the different needs the company can address? What does the packaging and promotion communicate to consumers?
4. *What do consumers desire?*
   How can the company make the lives of its customers better, and how can it do this in a way that is not easily duplicated by another firm? Part of this lies in uncovering the things that customers truly desire, but which they can often not put into words.

Answering these questions requires information. Marketing research's function is to supply information that helps provide these answers, thereby leading to more informed and more successful decision making. Managers that use this information reduce the risk associated with decision making.

In a way, "every business issue ultimately boils down to an information problem":[8] Can the right information be obtained and delivered? Research thus seeks to deliver accurate and precise information that can make marketing strategy and management more effective.[9] Marketing research attempts to supply accurate information that reduces the uncertainty in decision making. Very often, decisions are made with little information for various reasons, including insufficient time to conduct research or management's belief that enough is already known. Relying on seat-of-the-pants decision making—decision making without research—is like betting on a long shot at the racetrack because the horse's name is appealing. Occasionally there are successes, but in the long run uninformed decision making is unwise. Marketing research helps decision makers shift from intuitive information gathering to systematic and objective investigating.

Marketing Research Defined

Marketing research is the application of the scientific method in searching for the truth about marketing phenomena. Research applications include defining marketing opportunities and problems, generating and evaluating marketing ideas, monitoring performance, and generally understanding the marketing process. Marketing research is more than conducting surveys.[10] This process includes

marketing research

The application of the scientific method in searching for the truth about marketing phenomena. These activities include defining marketing opportunities and problems, generating and evaluating marketing ideas, monitoring performance, and understanding the marketing process.

Good Fat and Bad Fat

American consumers can be seen every day scouring nutrition labels. Most likely, the item they show the most interest in recently is the amount of fat. The Food and Drug Administration (FDA) is concerned that consumers get information that is not only accurate, but that also conveys the proper message to achieve a healthy diet. But all fat is not created equal. In particular, dieticians warn of the dangers associated with excess amounts of trans fats; diet nutrition labels break fats into saturated and unsaturated fats. Among numerous factors that complicate the interpretation of the nutrition label, trans fat (hydrogenated) is technically a nonsaturated fat, but it acts more like a saturated fat when consumed. So, where should it be placed? The FDA cannot address this problem intelligently without marketing research addressing questions such as the following.

1. If trans fats are listed as saturated fats, would consumers' beliefs about their consumption become more negative?

© SUSAN VAN ETTEN

2. If the saturated fat amount includes a specific line indicating the amount of "saturated fat" that is really trans fat, would consumers become more confused about their diet?

3. If all amounts of fat are given equal prominence on the label, will consumer attitudes toward the different types of fats be the same?

4. Will consumers interpret foods free of trans fats as healthy?

Making this even more complicated is the fact that some consumer segments, such as teenagers in this case, may actually use the nutrition labels to select the brands that are least nutritious rather than most nutritious. So, they may actually seek out the one with the worst proportion of trans fats! The FDA specifically addressed trans fats in labeling regulations that took effect in 2006. Under these regulations, the FDA allows labels to claim zero trans fat as long as less than half a gram of hydrogenated oil per serving is contained. Simple?

Sources: "Health Labels are in the Eye of the Beholder," *Food Management*, 40 (January 2005), 80; Hunter, B. T., "Labeling Transfat is Tricky," *Consumers' Research Magazine*, 86 (July 2003), 8–10; Weise, E., "Food Labels Now Required to Mention Trans Fat, Allergens," *USA Today* (January 2, 2006), H1.

© GEORGE DOYLE & CIARAN GRIFFIN

idea and theory development, problem definition, searching for and collecting information, analyzing data, and communicating the findings and their implications.

This definition suggests that marketing research information is not intuitive or haphazardly gathered. Literally, *research* (re-search) means "to search again." The term connotes patient study and scientific investigation wherein the researcher takes another, more careful look to try and know more about the subject. Ultimately, all findings are tied back to marketing theory.

The definition also emphasizes, through reference to the scientific method, that any information generated should be accurate and objective. The researcher should be personally detached and free of bias attempting to find truth. Research isn't performed to support preconceived ideas but to test them. If bias enters into the research process, the value of the research is considerably reduced. We will discuss this further in a subsequent chapter.

Clearly, our definition makes it clear that marketing research is relevant to all aspects of the marketing mix. Research can facilitate managerial decision making in all aspects of the firm's marketing mix: product, pricing, promotion, and distribution. By providing the necessary information on which to base marketing mix decisions, marketing research can decrease the risk of making a wrong decision in each area.

Finally, this definition of marketing research is limited by one's definition of *marketing*. Although one could hardly argue that research aimed at designing better products for a for-profit corporation like Toyota is clearly marketing research, marketing research also includes efforts that assist nonprofit organizations such as the American Heart Association, the San Diego Zoo, or a parochial elementary school. Each of these organizations exists to satisfy societal needs, and each requires marketing skills to produce and distribute their products and services. The federal government performs many of the same functions as for-profit business organizations. Governments can use research in much the same way as managers at Starbucks or General Motors. For instance, the FDA is an important user of marketing research, employing it to address the way people view and use various food and drugs. The FDA commissioned and funded research to address the question of how consumers used the risk summaries that are included with all drugs sold in the United States.[11] The Research Snapshot above describes a typical FDA market research project. This book explores marketing research as it applies to all organizations and institutions engaging in some form of marketing activity.

Applied and Basic Marketing Research

One useful way to describe research is based on the specificity of its purpose. Is the research intended to address a very specific problem or is it meant to describe some overall marketing phenomenon?

Applied Marketing Research

Applied marketing research is conducted to address a specific marketing decision for a specific firm or organization. The opening vignette describes a situation in which companies like Toyota and General Motors use applied marketing research to decide how to best create knowledge leading to better-designed products for particular market segments. Applied research is quite specific and a big part of this research is identifying exactly what issue a business needs to address.

applied marketing research

Research conducted to address a specific marketing decision for a specific firm or organization.

Basic Marketing Research

Basic marketing research is conducted without a specific decision in mind, and it usually does not address the needs of a specific organization. It attempts to expand the limits of marketing knowledge in general, and as such it is not aimed at solving a particular pragmatic problem. Basic research can be used to test the validity of a general marketing theory (one that applies to all of marketing) or to learn more about some market phenomenon. For instance, a great deal of basic marketing research addresses the ways in which retail atmosphere influences consumers' emotions and behavior.[12] From such research, we can learn how much the physical place creates value for consumers relative to the actual product consumed. This basic research does not examine the problem from any single retail or service provider's perspective. However, Starbucks' management may become aware of such research and use it to design applied research studies examining questions about its store designs. Thus, the two types of research are not completely independent.

basic marketing research

Research conducted without a specific decision in mind that usually does not address the needs of a specific organization. It attempts to expand the limits of marketing knowledge in general and is not aimed at solving a particular pragmatic problem.

Sometimes researchers use different terms to represent the same distinction. Some reserve the term *marketing* research to refer to basic research. Then, the term *market* research is used to capture applied research addressing the needs of a firm within a particular market. While the distinction is very useful in describing research, there are very few aspects of research that apply to only basic or only applied research. In addition, we will use the term *marketing research* more generally to refer to either type of research.

The Scientific Method

All marketing research, whether basic or applied, involves the scientific method. **The scientific method** is the way researchers go about using knowledge and evidence to reach objective conclusions about the real world. The scientific method is the same in social sciences such as marketing and in physical sciences such as physics. In this case, it is the way we come to understand marketing phenomena.

the scientific method

The way researchers go about using knowledge and evidence to reach objective conclusions about the real world.

Exhibit 1.1 on the next page briefly illustrates the scientific method. In the scientific method, there are multiple routes to developing ideas. When the ideas can be stated in researchable terms, we reach the hypothesis stage. The next step involves testing the hypothesis against empirical evidence (facts from observation or experimentation). The results either support a hypothesis or do not support a hypothesis. From these results, new knowledge is acquired.

In basic research, testing these prior conceptions or hypotheses and then making inferences and conclusions about the phenomena leads to the establishment of general laws about the phenomena. Use of the scientific method in applied research ensures objectivity in gathering facts and testing creative ideas for alternative marketing strategies. The essence of research, whether basic or applied, lies in the scientific method. Much of this book deals with scientific methodology. Thus, the techniques of basic and applied research differ largely in application rather than in substance.

A Summary of the Scientific Method

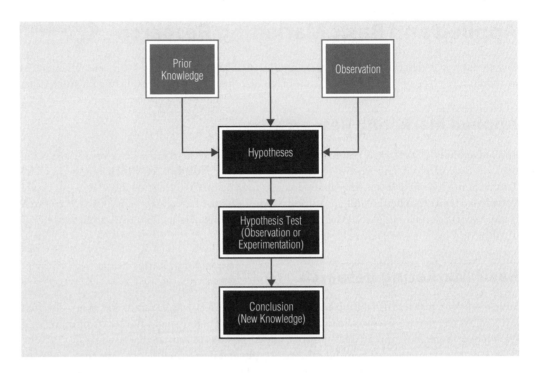

Marketing Research and Strategic Management Orientation

product-oriented

Describes a firm that prioritizes decision making in a way that emphasizes technical superiority in the product.

production-oriented

Describes a firm that prioritizes efficiency and effectiveness of the production processes in making decisions.

marketing concept

A central idea in modern marketing thinking that focuses on how the firm provides value to customers more than on the physical product or production process.

marketing orientation

The corporate culture existing for firms adopting the marketing concept. It emphasizes customer orientation, long-term profitability over short-term profits, and a cross-functional perspective.

customer-oriented

Describes a firm in which all decisions are made with a conscious awareness of their effect on the consumer.

In all of business strategy, there are only a few business orientations. A firm can be **product-oriented**. A product-oriented firm prioritizes decision making in a way that emphasizes technical superiority in the product. Thus, input from technicians and experts in the field are very important in making critical decisions. A firm can be **production-oriented**. Production orientation means that the firm prioritizes efficiency and effectiveness of the production processes in making decisions. Here, input from engineers and accounting becomes important as the firm seeks to drive costs down. Production-oriented firms are usually very large firms manufacturing products in very large quantities. In both of these orientations, marketing research may take a backseat.

In contrast, marketing research is a primary tool enabling implementation of a marketing orientation.[13] The **marketing concept** is a central idea in modern marketing thinking that focuses more on how the firm provides value to customers than on the physical product or production process. It has evolved over time as product- and production-oriented firms respond to changes in the competitive and economic environments. When a firm adapts the marketing concept, it develops a **marketing orientation**. A marketing-oriented firm exhibits several key aspects including:

1. Be **customer-oriented**—meaning that all firm decisions are made with a conscious awareness of their effect on the consumer
2. Emphasize long-run profitability rather than short-term profits or sales volume
3. Adopt a cross-functional perspective, meaning that marketing is integrated across other business functions

Customer Orientation

According to the marketing concept, the consumer is at the center of the operation, the pivot point about which the business moves to achieve the balanced best interests of all concerned. According to this philosophy, the firm creates products and services with consumers' needs in mind. Many marketing theorists and marketing managers believe that the creation of value for consumers is the justification for a firm's existence. Therefore, unlike the other two orientations, marketing research addressing consumer desires, beliefs, and attitudes becomes essential.

Yoplait Go-Gurt, yogurt packaged in a three-sided tube designed to fit in kids' lunchboxes, had more than $100 million in sales its first year on the market. The development of Go-Gurt clearly illustrates a consumer orientation. The company's consumer research about eating regular yogurt at school showed that moms and kids in their "tweens" wanted convenience and portability. Some brands, like Colombo Spoon in a Snap, offered the convenience of having a utensil as part of the packaging and delivery system. However, from what Yoplait marketers learned about consumers, they thought kids would eat more yogurts if they could "lose the spoon" and eat yogurt anywhere, anytime. Moms and kids participating in a taste test were invited to sample different brand-on-the-go packaging shapes—long tubes, thin tubes, fat tubes, and other shapes—without being told how to handle the packaging. One of the company's researchers said, "It was funny to see the moms fidget around, then daintily pour the product onto a spoon, then into their mouths. The kids instantly jumped on it. They knew what to do."[14] Squeezing Go-Gurt from the tube was a big plus. The kids loved the fact that the packaging gave them permission to play with their food, something parents always tell them not to do. Go-Gurt is a fun, convenient product that allows consumers the freedom to eat whenever and wherever they want. Yoplait realized that knowledge of consumers' needs, coupled with product research and development, leads to successful marketing strategies and that industry leadership—indeed, corporate survival—depends on satisfying consumers.

Long-Run Profitability

Customer orientation does not mean slavery to consumers' every fleeting whim. Implicit in the marketing concept is the assumption of the continuity of the firm. Thus, the firm must eventually experience profitability to survive (see Exhibit 1.2). High fuel prices have stifled the market for large SUVs and trucks. This has contributed to troubles at most automotive companies. GM is now carefully considering which brands should be part of its portfolio. Surprisingly, one of the brands that GM is considering dropping is Saturn. Saturn produces economy cars that generally get great gas mileage, are recognized as innovative by automotive experts, and that display among the highest average customer satisfaction among GM brands. However, Saturn has yet to become profitable.[15] Pricing the cars higher is not a good option because Saturn consumers show too much price sensitivity and thus, they would likely switch to other brands.

EXHIBIT 1.2
Long-Run Profitability

Goods
Gas
Corn
Tools

Services
Day Care
Spas
Internet Service Provider

Provide Benefits by Meeting Customers
Needs and Desires

Value

When the Firm Provides Benefits,
It Creates Value for Customers and Itself

The second aspect of the marketing concept argues against profitless volume or sales volume for the sake of volume alone. Sometimes, the best decision for a customer and the best decision in the long run for the firm is the sale that is not made. For instance, a parts supplier might be able to mislead a customer about the relative quality of the parts he or she sells and make an immediate sale. However, when the parts begin to fail sooner than expected, the customer will almost certainly not do business with this firm again. If instead the salesperson had been honest and suggested another supplier, he or she might have been able to find another opportunity to do business with that firm.

A Cross-Functional Effort

Marketing personnel do not work in a vacuum, isolated from other company activities. The actions of people in areas such as production, credit, and research and development may affect an organization's marketing efforts. Similarly, the work of marketers will affect activities in other departments. Problems are almost certain to arise from lack of an integrated, company-wide effort. The marketing concept stresses a cross-functional perspective to achieve consumer orientation and long-term profitability. The first panel of Exhibit 1.3 illustrates a firm in which every department works independently; it is not cross-functional and, consequently, not marketing-oriented. The second panel illustrates a firm in which marketing personnel work cross-functionally with other departments to achieve long-term profitability.

Problems occur when the marketing department views focusing on consumer needs as its sole responsibility. Indeed, other functional areas' goals may conflict with customer satisfaction or long-term profitability. For instance, the engineering department may want long lead times for product design, with simplicity and economy as major design goals. Marketing, however, may prefer short lead times and more complex designs with custom components and optional features for multiple models. The finance department may want fixed budgets, strict spending justifications, and prices that cover costs, whereas the marketing department may seek flexible budgets, liberal spending rationales, and below-cost prices to develop markets quickly.

Similar differences in outlook may be found in other functional areas of the organization, and these may be sources of serious conflicts. When a firm lacks organizational procedures for

EXHIBIT 1.3
Isolation versus Cross-functionality of Marketing in a Firm

Finance

Market Research

Finance

Distribution

Production

Distribution

Production

(a) Isolation

(b) Cross-functionality

communicating marketing information and coordinating marketing efforts, the effectiveness of its marketing programs will suffer. Marketing research findings produce some of the most crucial marketing information; thus, such research is management's key tool for finding out what customers want and how best to satisfy their needs. It is vital, then, that management conduct marketing research, that researchers produce valid and reliable results, and that those results be communicated to decision makers so that they can help shape the firm's marketing strategy.

Marketing-oriented firms visualize a chain of customers within the production and delivery system.[16] An accountant who prepares a report for a sales manager should view the manager as a customer who will use the information to make decisions that will benefit external customers who buy the company's products. Every employee should contribute to quality improvement and providing value to customers.

Keeping Customers and Building Relationships

Marketers often talk about getting customers, but keeping customers is equally important. Effective marketers work to build long-term relationships with their customers. The term **relationship marketing** communicates the idea that a major goal of marketing is to build long-term relationships with the customers contributing to the firm's success. Once an exchange is made, effective marketing stresses managing the relationships that will bring about additional exchanges. Effective marketers view making a sale not as the end of a process but as the start of the organization's relationship with a customer. Satisfied customers will return to a company that has treated them well if they need to purchase the same product in the future. If they need a related item, satisfied customers know the first place to look. Harley-Davidson is a company that over time has developed a familial type bond with its loyal customers. Now, they are seeking to expand their offering to new parts of the world. The Research Snapshot on the next page describes some of the issues arising from this investigation.

Total quality management is a business philosophy that has much in common with the marketing concept. It embodies the belief that the management process must focus on integrating customer-driven quality throughout the organization. The philosophy underlying the implementation of total quality management was clearly articulated by a Burger King executive: "The customer is the vital key to our success. We are now looking at our business through the customers' eyes and measuring our performance against their expectations, not ours."[17] A company that employs a total quality strategy must evaluate itself through the eyes of the customer.

When Ford Motor Company advertises that "Quality Is Job One," the production department must make sure that every automobile that comes off the assembly line will meet consumers' quality specifications. The notion that quality improvement is every employee's job must be integrated throughout the organization so that marketing and production will be in harmony. Chapter 10 discusses the measurement of important marketing concepts like attitude and value in detail. Throughout this book, however, we will explain how marketing research can help a company achieve the goal of creating valuable experiences for customers.

relationship marketing

Communicates the idea that a major goal of marketing is to build long-term relationships with the customers contributing to the firm's success.

total quality management

Total quality management is a business philosophy that has much in common with the marketing concept.

Marketing Research: A Means for Implementing the Marketing Concept

Home building used to be a business completely dominated by local construction contractors. If a customer wanted a home that would provide maximum satisfaction, a custom home at a custom price was the only option. Today, there is another option. Several home builders are going national. In doing so, they have implemented market-driven design processes that integrate research into the home designs. The research tracks consumers' actual living patterns to build homes with maximum livability. Thus, rather than "wasting space" on things like hallways that add little or even distract from a home's livability, that space is cannibalized, allowing more space allocated to the places where families really "live." In addition, research shows that consumers will

Harley-Davidson Goes Abroad

Before Harley-Davidson goes overseas, it must perform considerable research on that market. It may find that consumers in some countries, such as France or Italy, have a strong preference for more economical and practical motor bikes. There, people may prefer a Vespa Wasp to a Harley Hog! Other times, they may find that consumers have a favorable attitude toward Harley-Davidson and that it could even be a product viewed as very prestigious. Harley recently considered doing business in India based on trend analysis showing a booming economy. Favorable consumer opinion and a booming economy were insufficient to justify distributing Harleys in India. The problem? Luxury imports would be subject to very high duties which would make them cost-prohibitive to nearly all Indian consumers and India has strict emission rules for motor bikes. Thus, although research on the market was largely positive, Harley's research on the political operating environment eventually determined its decision. Even after considerable negotiation, India refused to budge on tariffs although they were willing to give on emission standards. Instead, Harley may direct its effort more toward the U.S. women's market for bikes. Research shows that motorcycle ownership among U.S. women has nearly doubled since 1990 to approximately 10 percent. Product research suggests that Harley may need to design smaller and sportier bikes to satisfy this market's desires. Perhaps these new products would also be easier to market in India. Research will tell.

Sources: "Harley Davidson Rules Out India Foray for Near Future," *Asia-Africa Intelligence Wire* (September 2, 2005); "Women Kick it Into Gear," *Akron Beacon Journal* (May 22, 2005); "No Duty Cut on Harley Davidson Bikes, India to US," *The Financial Express* (February 24, 2008), www.financialexpress.com/news/No-duty-cut-on-Harley-Davidson-bikes-India-to-US/276635, accessed July 7, 2008.

make use of outdoor living areas if they are properly designed. Thus, the homes often include covered porches or lanais in place of less used indoor space like a formal living room.[18]

Marketing research can also help prevent commercialization of products that are not consumer oriented. Sometimes ideas that look like technological breakthroughs in the laboratory fall flat when presented to consumers. For example, a powdered pain reliever was supposed to be a soothing remedy because it was to be mixed with milk. It did not soothe customers, however. Research showed that the public thought this great step forward was actually a step backward in convenience. Someone forgot to consider how consumers would actually use the product.

By improving efficiency, research also facilitates profitability. For instance, during the introduction of a new product, accurate forecasting of the product's potential sales volume is an essential basis for estimating its profitability. A firm considering the introduction of a cat snack that contains hairball medicine might rely on a test market experiment to determine the optimal price for this new concept. Extensive testing should be done to ensure that the marketing program is fine-tuned to maximize the firm's profitability while satisfying consumers.

Analysis of data may also be a form of marketing research that can increase efficiency. Marketing representatives from Exxon Chemical Company used laptop computers to present a complex set of calculations to sales prospects to show them the advantage of Exxon products over competitors' products. Such analysis of research data improves the salesperson's batting average and the firm's efficiency.

Because of the importance of integrating company efforts, a marketing researcher must be knowledgeable not only about marketing research but about the entire spectrum of marketing activities.

Fun in the snow depends on weather trends, equipment, and clothing—all subjects for a market researcher.

Marketing Research and Strategic Marketing Management

Effective marketing management requires research. DirectTV, the direct-broadcast satellite television service, uses marketing research to determine which kinds of programming to add to its lineup of channels. A company executive says, "Research has driven every aspect of our business decisions."[19] At Ford Motor Company, research is so fundamental that the company hardly makes any significant decision without the benefit of some kind of marketing research. The prime managerial value of marketing research comes from the reduced uncertainty that results from information and facilitates decision making about marketing strategies and tactics to achieve an organization's strategic goals.

Developing and implementing a marketing strategy involves four stages:

1. Identifying and evaluating market opportunities
2. Analyzing market segments and selecting target markets
3. Planning and implementing a marketing mix that will provide value to customers and meet organizational objectives
4. Analyzing firm performance

Exhibit 1.4 illustrates the integration of research and marketing strategy and the way they come together to create value in the marketplace.

TO THE POINT

The secret of success is to know something nobody else knows.

—Aristotle Onassis

EXHIBIT 1.4
Marketing Research Cuts Decision Risk with Input that Leads to Value

Marketing Research

Identify and Evaluate Market Opportunities

Analyze Market Segments and Select Target Markets

Plan and Implement Marketing Mix

Value

Firm Performance

■ IDENTIFYING AND EVALUATING MARKET OPPORTUNITIES

One job that marketing research can perform is monitoring the competitive environment for signals indicating a business opportunity. A mere description of some social or economic activity, such as trends in consumer purchasing behavior, may help managers recognize problems and identify opportunities for enriching marketing efforts. In some cases, this research can motivate a firm to take action to address consumer desires to the benefit of both the customers and the firm.

At times, evaluating opportunities may involve something as mundane as tracking weather trends. Consumers have a physical need to maintain some degree of physical comfort. Thus, changes in the temperature patterns may create business opportunities for utility companies, appliance companies, and even beverage companies as more consumers will select a hot beverage like hot chocolate when the weather is cold and dreary. Companies can also adjust their logistic distribution patterns based on the weather. When Hurricane Katrina hit the Gulf Coast of the United States, several chainsaw companies (such as Poulan) and companies that manufacture generators (such as Honda) began directing inventory toward those areas even before the hurricane actually struck. As a result, many home supply stores like Home Depot and Lowe's were able to maintain inventories of these vital products despite an increase in demand of over 1,000 percent! Thus, the misfortune of a hurricane created a business opportunity that also provided real value to consumers. In this case, the businesses and the consumers all benefited from the fact that firms scan the environment for opportunities.

Another opportunity was presented by a research study on running shoes was to investigate the occasions or situations associated with product use—that is, when individuals wore running shoes. The researchers found that most owners of running shoes wore the shoes while walking, not running. Also, most of this walking was part of a normal daily activity like shopping or commuting to work. Many of the people who wore running shoes for routine activities considered the shoes an alternative to other casual shoes. This research ultimately led to a shift in design and production toward walking shoes designed for comfortable, everyday walking and casual wear.[20]

Market opportunities may be evaluated using many performance criteria. For example, the performance criterion of market demand typically is estimated using marketing research techniques. Estimates of market potential or predictions about future environmental conditions allow managers to evaluate opportunities. Accurate sales forecasts are among the most useful pieces of planning information a marketing manager can have. Complete accuracy in forecasting the future is not possible, because change is constantly occurring in the marketing environment. Nevertheless, objective forecasts of demand or changing environments may be the foundations on which marketing strategies are built.

■ ANALYZING AND SELECTING TARGET MARKETS

The second stage of marketing strategy development is to analyze market segments and select target markets. Marketing research is a major source of information for determining which characteristics of market segments distinguish them from the overall market. Such research can help "locate" or describe a market segment in terms of demographic and characteristics. Geo-demographics can be important to study and track in this effort. **Geo-demographics** refers to information describing the demographic profile of consumers in a particular geographic region. The company may learn that consumers in a particular postal code within a region tend to be middle-aged, have multiple children over the age of twelve, and have college degrees and white-collar jobs. Once the company knows the geo-demographics of a market segment, it can effectively communicate with those customers by choosing media that reach that particular profile. For example, *Architectural Digest* is a magazine that is read predominantly by consumers with very high social status in the most exclusive zip codes in the United States.

geo-demographics

Refers to information describing the demographic profile of consumers in a particular geographic region.

Planning and Implementing a Marketing Mix

Using the information obtained in the two previous stages, marketing managers plan and execute a marketing-mix strategy. Marketing research may be needed to support specific decisions about any aspect of the marketing mix. For instance, the research can evaluate an alternative course of action. For example, advertising research might investigate whether an actress like Julia Roberts or a singer like Mariah Carey would make a better spokesperson for a specific brand of hair coloring. Research might be conducted involving test ads with each celebrity examining questions such as whether or not consumer attitudes toward the brand are higher for Julia or for Mariah and how much each celebrity is liked, but also, perhaps not as obviously, how much credibility each celebrity would have based on the beliefs consumers have about whether or not each would really use the product.

It is essential that an overall research plan involve all elements of marketing strategy. In other words, once the research identifies a target market and media that can be used in promotion, it needs to determine what benefits are required to create value for the customers, what price is most appropriate and, not to be overlooked, what channels of distribution will best reach the consumer. The integration of all of this research leads to effective brand management.[21] The following examples highlight selected types of research that might be conducted for each element of the marketing mix.

Product Research

Product research takes many forms and includes studies designed to evaluate and develop new products and to learn how to adapt existing product lines. Concept testing exposes potential customers to a new product idea to judge the acceptance and feasibility of the concept. Product testing reveals a product prototype's strengths and weaknesses or determines whether a finished product performs better than competing brands or according to expectations. Brand-name evaluation studies investigate whether a name is appropriate for a product. Package testing assesses size, color, shape, ease of use, and other attributes of a package. Product research encompasses all applications of marketing research that seek to develop product attributes that will add value for consumers.

Before Cheetos became the first major brand of American snack food to be made and marketed in China, product taste tests revealed that traditional cheese-flavored corn puffs Cheetos did not appeal to Chinese consumers. So the company conducted consumer research with 600 different flavors to learn which flavors would be most appealing. Among the flavors Chinese consumers tested and disliked were ranch dressing, nacho, Italian pizza, Hawaiian barbecue, peanut satay, North Sea crab, chili prawn, coconut milk curry, smoked octopus, caramel, and cuttlefish. Research did show that consumers liked other flavors. So, when Cheetos were introduced in China, they came in two flavors: savory American cream and zesty Japanese steak.[22] So, the result was essentially cheeseless Cheetos.

Pricing Research

In many ways, pricing research represents typical marketing research. Many test markets address the question of how consumers will respond to a product offering two different prices. **Pricing** involves finding the amount of monetary sacrifice that best represents the value customers perceive in a product after considering various market constraints. Most organizations conduct pricing research. Starbucks may seem expensive now, but if the price doubled, would Starbucks lose many customers? How much more are Toyota customers willing to pay for each extra mile per gallon? How much is too much to pay for gas? Pricing research also investigates the way people respond to pricing tactics. How do consumers respond to price reductions in one form or another? How much are people willing to pay for some critical product attribute? Do consumers view prices and/or quantity discounts as fair in a given category?[23] Do price gaps among national brands, regional brands, and private labels exist?[24] Most importantly, research also addresses the way consumers determine perceived value.

Pricing research addresses consumer quality perceptions by its very nature. A great deal of research addresses consumer reactions to low prices and documents the fact that, in quite a few instances, prices can actually be too low. In other words, sales can actually decrease with lower prices instead of increasing.[25]

pricing

Involves finding the amount of monetary sacrifice that best represents the value customers perceive in a product after considering various market constraints.

Wal-Mart test marketed a Starbucks-type coffee shop called Medina's Kicks.[26] A Kicks coffee shop was set up in a Texas Wal-Mart store. They are testing prices relative to the nearby Starbucks. At prices 25 percent below Starbucks, sales remain relatively low while Starbucks remains popular. By lowering the price, they may also have lowered the perceived product quality. By raising the price, might quality perceptions improve and get consumers to think the coffee may be more similar to Starbucks? These are typical pricing questions.

Distribution Research

marketing channel

A network of interdependent institutions that perform the logistics necessary for consumption to occur.

supply chain

Another term for a channel of distribution, meaning the link between suppliers and customers.

Distribution involves the marketing channels that will physically "distribute" products from a producer to a consumer. A **marketing channel** is a network of interdependent institutions that perform the logistics necessary for consumption to occur. Some channels are very short and involve only a producer and a consumer, and some are very long involving much transportation and wholesale and retail firms. It may be somewhat obvious why the term **supply chain** is sometimes used to refer to a channel of distribution. Distribution is necessary to remove the physical separations between buyers and sellers.

Distribution research is typified by studies aimed at selecting retail sites or warehouse locations. A survey of retailers or wholesalers may be conducted because the actions of one channel member can greatly affect the performance of other channel members. Distribution research often is needed to gain knowledge about retailers' and wholesalers' operations and to learn their reactions to a manufacturer's marketing policies. It may also be used to examine the effect of just-in-time ordering systems or exclusive distribution on product quality. Research focused on developing and improving the efficiency of marketing channels is extremely important.

Golden Books traditionally distributed its small hardcover children's books with golden spines to book retailers like Waldenbooks or B. Dalton Booksellers. When it researched where its customers would prefer to purchase Golden Books, the company learned that mass merchandisers, grocery stores, and drug stores would be just as popular as the upscale stores as distribution channels. Today, publishing companies like Golden Books face the possibility of new and shorter marketing channels that would allow home delivery via the Internet. Not only does this mean reduced time from production to consumption, but it also allows the books to come alive through interactivity. Should Golden Book abandon its more traditional marketing channels and focus its resources on this new delivery option?

Prescription drugs can now be purchased via the Internet. For the consumer, this marketing channel bypasses the traditional doctor's visit and local pharmacy. For the pharmaceutical firm, is it wise to take advantage of this channel? By removing the family doctor from the channel of distribution, does the drug seem to be less effective, and if so, is the brand's reputation harmed? Marketing research is needed to examine related issues including whether or not the product is equally effective through both the new and traditional marketing channel. Research results may both help firms make the distribution decision and help policy makers decide on the limits that should be placed on prescription drug distribution options.

Promotion Research

promotion

The communication function of the firm responsible for informing and persuading buyers.

promotion research

Investigates the effectiveness of advertising, premiums, coupons, sampling, discounts, public relations, and other sales promotions.

Promotion is the communication function of the firm responsible for informing and persuading buyers. **Promotion research** investigates the effectiveness of advertising, premiums, coupons, sampling, discounts, public relations, and other sales promotions. However, among all of these, firms spend more time, money, and effort on advertising research.

The marketing research findings of Zales, a large jewelry retailer, helped in the creation of advertising with large, one-word headlines that simply asked, "Confused?," "Nervous?," or "Lost?" The advertisements overtly acknowledged the considerable emotional and financial risks that consumers face in jewelry purchases. Research had shown that typical consumers felt unable to determine the relative quality of various jewelry items, believed jewelry purchases were expensive, and needed reassurance about their purchases, especially because they often purchased jewelry for someone else. This promotion helped communicate an effective message of empathy with the consumer.

Similarly, a business in transition must effectively communicate its meaning. As AT&T's business shifts from that of a pure long-distance provider into that of a distanceless cable, Internet, and wireless communication specialist, it is trying to make sure its image changes too. But research showed its brand name still conjured up the image of an old-fashioned telephone company.[27] Marketing research also indicates great familiarity with the blue-and-white striped globe that served as AT&T's logo. A survey found 75 percent unaided recognition among the broad consumer market, 77 percent recognition among 18- to 24-year-olds, and 80 percent recognition among "high-value, active networkers"—consumers spending seventy-five dollars or more per month on long-distance and wireless services. Because of this high level of recognition, AT&T produced numerous TV commercials featuring an animation of the logo bouncing around, giving fun, high-intensity demonstrations of the various ways the company is transforming itself in the broadband-enabled world, accompanied by voice-over explanations of these new services. Future research may even consider placing the logo on iPod sites or even as a product placement in video games as a way of further transforming AT&T's image from "Ma Bell" into a modern technology service provider.[28]

Media research helps businesses make decisions about whether television, newspapers, magazines, or other media alternatives are best suited to convey the intended message. Choices among media alternatives may be based on research that shows the proportion of consumers in each market segment that a particular advertising vehicle can reach.

The Integrated Marketing Mix

Marketing today focuses increasingly on the fact that different promotional decisions should not be made in isolation. Instead, the concept of **integrated marketing communication** is adopted, meaning that all promotional efforts (advertising, public relations, personal selling, event marketing, and so forth) should be coordinated to communicate a consistent image. Likewise, marketing firms realize that the elements of the marketing mix itself must work together. For instance, a change in price can affect the quality of the product, which may also influence decisions about distribution. From a research standpoint, the **integrated marketing mix** means that research studies often investigate effects of various combinations of marketing mix elements on important outcomes like sales and image. Research suggests that consumer-oriented firms are particularly oriented toward integrating all aspects of their marketing into a single message.[29]

Best Buy, a U.S.-based electronic and appliance retailer, recently showed the success of integrating sales and service with promotion. You'll find a Geek in every Best Buy. The Geeks are technology experts (i.e., "computer geeks") that provide knowledgeable sales advice and technical service. To be a Geek, you have to look like a Geek! Their attire is carefully coordinated: white socks with black shoes, black pants that are just a little too short, a white sport shirt, and a narrow black tie. Today, the Geeks have become prominent in Best Buy

integrated marketing communication

All promotional efforts (advertising, public relations, personal selling, event marketing, and so forth) should be coordinated to communicate a consistent image.

integrated marketing mix

The effects of various combinations of marketing-mix elements on important outcomes.

Best Buy has reinvented the traditional Geek image and made it work for them.

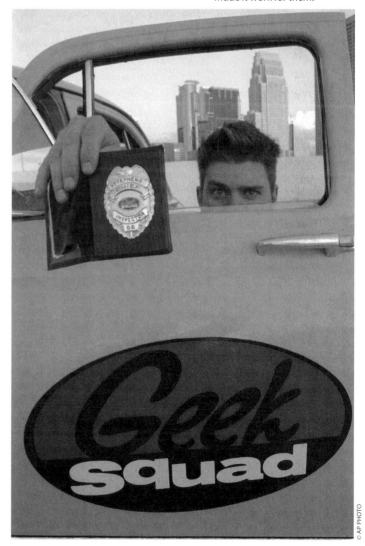

television ads, and they even provide in-home setup and technical service. The Geeks transformed Best Buy in the minds of consumers.[30] Companies that integrate the use of consistent spokespeople, such as the Geeks, across marketing elements enjoy more favorable brand images among consumers and are better able to communicate relevant information.[31] Competitors like Circuit City tried to copy with experts with names like Fire Dog, but they failed to effectively integrate it with their message.

Analyzing Marketing Performance

After a marketing strategy has been implemented, marketing research may serve to inform managers whether planned activities were properly executed and are accomplishing what they were expected to achieve. In other words, marketing research may be conducted to obtain feedback for evaluation and control of marketing programs. This aspect of marketing research is especially important for successful **total value management**, which attempts to manage the entire process by which a consumer receives benefits from a company.

Performance-monitoring research refers to research that regularly, sometimes routinely, provides feedback for evaluation and control of marketing activity. For example, most firms continuously monitor wholesale and retail activity to ensure early detection of sales declines and other anomalies. In the grocery and drug industries, sales research may use Universal Product Codes (UPCs) on packages read by electronic cash registers and computerized checkout counters to provide valuable market-share information to store and brand managers interested in the retail sales volumes of their products. Market-share analysis and sales analysis are the most common forms of performance-monitoring research. Almost every organization compares its current sales with previous sales and with competitors' sales. However, analyzing marketing performance is not limited to the investigation of sales figures.

Marketing metrics refer to quantitative ways of monitoring and measuring marketing performance. Research is needed to determine marketing metrics that allow a firm to know whether the resources invested in marketing activities have met their quantitative business goals. Marketing metrics allow the firm to assess the return on investment (ROI) associated with marketing activities. Performance monitoring research conducted by the ACNielsen firm suggests that only 18 percent of television commercials return a positive ROI for the companies advertised.[32]

total value management

The management and monitoring the entire process by which consumers receive benefits from a company.

performance-monitoring research

Refers to research that regularly, sometimes routinely, provides feedback for evaluation and control of marketing activity.

marketing metrics

Quantitative ways of monitoring and measuring marketing performance.

When Is Marketing Research Needed?

The need to make intelligent, informed decisions ultimately motivates marketing research. Not every decision requires marketing research. Thus, when confronting a key decision, a marketing manager must initially decide whether or not to conduct marketing research. The determination of the need for marketing research centers on (1) time constraints, (2) the availability of data, (3) the nature of the decision to be made, and (4) the value of the research information in relation to costs.

Time Constraints

Systematic research takes time. In many instances management believes that a decision must be made immediately, allowing no time for research. Decisions sometimes are made without adequate information or thorough understanding of market situations. Although making decisions without researching a situation is not ideal, sometimes the urgency of a situation precludes the use of research. The urgency with which managers often want to make decisions often conflicts with the marketing researchers' desire for rigor in following the scientific method.

Availability of Data

Often managers already possess enough information to make sound decisions without additional marketing research. When they lack adequate information, however, research must be considered. This means that data need to be collected from an appropriate source. If a potential source of data exists, managers will want to know how much it will cost to get the data.

If the data cannot be obtained, or it cannot be obtained in a timely fashion, this particular research project should not be conducted. For example, many African nations have never conducted a population census. Organizations engaged in international business often find that data about business activity or population characteristics that are readily available in the United States are nonexistent or sparse in developing countries. Imagine the problems facing marketing researchers who wish to investigate market potential in places like Uzbekistan, Yugoslavian Macedonia, and Rwanda.

Nature of the Decision

The value of marketing research will depend on the nature of the managerial decision to be made. A routine tactical decision that does not require a substantial investment may not seem to warrant a substantial expenditure for marketing research. For example, a computer company must update its operator's instruction manual when it makes minor product modifications. The research cost of determining the proper wording to use in the updated manual is likely to be too high for such a minor decision. The nature of the decision is not totally independent of the next issue to be considered: the benefits versus the costs of the research. In general, however, the more strategically or tactically important the decision, the more likely it is that research will be conducted.

Benefits versus Costs

There are both costs and benefits to conducting marketing research. Earlier we discussed some of the managerial benefits of marketing research. Of course, conducting research to obtain these benefits requires an expenditure of money. In any decision-making situation, managers must identify alternative courses of action and then weigh the value of each alternative against its cost. Marketing research can be thought of as an investment alternative. When deciding whether to make a decision without research or to postpone the decision in order to conduct research, managers should ask three questions:

1. Will the payoff or rate of return be worth the investment?
2. Will the information gained by marketing research improve the quality of the marketing decision enough to warrant the expenditure?
3. Is the proposed research expenditure the best use of the available funds?

For example, *TV-Cable Week* was not test-marketed before its launch. Although the magazine had articles and stories about television personalities and events, its main feature was program listings, channel by channel, showing the exact programs a particular subscriber could receive. To produce a custom magazine for each individual cable television system in the country required developing a costly computer system. Because that development necessitated a substantial expenditure, one that could not be scaled down for research, conducting research was judged to be an unwise investment. The value of the research information was not positive because its cost exceeded its benefits. Unfortunately, pricing and distribution problems became so compelling after the magazine was launched that the product was a marketing failure. Nevertheless, without the luxury of hindsight, managers made a reasonable decision not to conduct research. They analyzed the cost of the information (that is, the cost of test-marketing) relative to the potential benefits of the information. Exhibit 1.5 on the next page outlines the criteria for determining when to conduct marketing research.

EXHIBIT 1.5 **Determining When to Conduct Marketing Research**

Time Constraints	Availability of Data	Nature of the Decision	Benefits versus Costs	
Is sufficient time available before a decision will be made? Yes →	Can the decision be made with what is already known? Yes →	Is the decision of considerable strategic or tactical importance? Yes →	Does the value of the research information exceed the cost of conducting research? Yes →	Conduct Marketing Research
No ↓	No ↓	No ↓	No ↓	

Do Not Conduct Marketing Research

Marketing Research in the Twenty-First Century

Marketing research, like all business activity, continues to change. Changes in communication technologies and the trend toward an ever more global marketplace have played a large role in many of these changes.

Communication Technologies

Virtually everyone is "connected" today. Increasingly, many people are "connected" nearly all the time. Within the lifetime of the typical undergraduate college senior, the way information is exchanged, stored, and gathered has been revolutionized completely. Today, the amount of information formally contained in an entire library can rest easily in a single personal computer.

The speed with which information can be exchanged has also increased tremendously. During the 1970s, exchanging information overnight from anywhere in the continental United States was heralded as a near miracle of modern technology. Today, we can exchange information from nearly anywhere in the world to nearly anywhere in the world almost instantly. Internet connections are now wireless, so one doesn't have to be tethered to a wall to access the World Wide Web. Our mobile phones and handheld data devices can be used not only to converse, but also as a means of communication that can even involve marketing research data. In many cases, technology also has made it possible to store or collect data for lower costs than in the past. Electronic communications are usually less costly than regular mail—and certainly less costly than a face-to-face interview—and cost about the same amount no matter how far away a respondent is from a researcher. Thus, the expressions "time is collapsing" and "distance is disappearing" capture the tremendous revolution in the speed and reach of our communication technologies.

Changes in computer technology have made for easier data collection and data analysis. As we discuss in a later chapter, many consumer household panels now exist and can be accessed via the Internet. Thus, there is less need for the time and expense associated with regular mail survey approaches. Furthermore, the computing power necessary to solve complicated statistical problems is now easily accessible. Again, as recently as the 1970s, such computer applications required expensive mainframe computers found only in very large corporations, major universities, and large governmental/military institutions. Researchers could expect to wait hours or even longer to get results from a statistical program involving 200 respondents. Today, even the most basic laptop computers can solve complicated statistical problems involving thousands of data points in practically a nanosecond.

"Jacques" Daniels

Sales of U.S. distilled spirits declined over the last 10 to 15 years as more Americans turn to wine or beer as their beverage of choice. As a result, companies like Bacardi and Brown-Forman, producers of Jack Daniels, pursued market development strategies involving increased efforts to expand into international markets. The Brown-Forman marketing budget for international ventures includes a significant allocation for marketing research. By doing research before launching the product, Brown-Forman can learn product usage patterns within a particular culture. Some of the findings from this research are indicated as follows.

1. Japanese consumers use Jack Daniels (JD) as a dinner beverage. A party of four or five consumers in a restaurant will order and drink a bottle of "JD" with their meal.
2. Australian consumers mostly consume distilled spirits in their homes. Also in contrast to Japanese consumers, Australians prefer to mix JD with soft drinks or other mixers. As a result of this research, JD launched a mixture called "Jack and Cola" sold in 12-ounce bottles all around Australia. The product has been very successful.

3. British distilled spirit consumers also like mixed drinks, but they usually partake in bars and restaurants.
4. In China and India, consumers more often chose counterfeits or "knock-offs" to save money. Thus, innovative research approaches have addressed questions related to the way the black market works and how they can better educate consumers about the differences between the real thing and the knock-offs.
5. Chinese consumers enjoy JD mixed with green tea.

The result is that more than half of all Jack Daniels made is now consumed outside of the United States. The global sales increase has contributed to impressive sales growth of over 40 percent since 2002. Indeed, sales of Jack Daniels are looking up as of 2009.

Sources: Swibel, Mathew, "How Distiller Brown-Forman Gets Rich by Exploiting the Greenback's Fall—and Pushing its Brands Abroad," *Forbes*, 175, no. 8 (2005), 152–155. Kiley, D. "Jack Daniel's International Appeal," *Businessweek* (October 10, 2007), accessed at http://www.businessweek.com/innovate/content/oct2007/id20071010_651037.htm, September 14, 2008.

Global Marketing Research

Marketing research has become increasingly global as more and more firms take advantage of markets that have few, if any, geographic boundaries. Some companies have extensive international marketing research operations. Upjohn conducts marketing research in 160 different countries. ACNielsen International, known for its television ratings, is the world's largest marketing research company. Two-thirds of its business comes from outside the United States.[33] Starbucks can now be found in nearly every developed country on the earth. Toyota offers its products on all continents and truly represents today's global corporation.

Companies that conduct business in foreign countries must understand the nature of those particular markets and judge whether they require customized marketing strategies. For example, although the fifteen nations of the European Union share a single formal market, marketing research shows that Europeans do not share identical tastes for many consumer products. Marketing researchers have found no such thing as a typical European consumer; language, religion, climate, and centuries of tradition divide the nations of the European Union. Scantel Research, a British firm that advises companies on color preferences, found inexplicable differences in Europeans' preferences in medicines. The French prefer to pop purple pills, but the English and Dutch favor white ones. Consumers in all three countries dislike bright red capsules, which are big sellers in the United States. This example illustrates that companies that do business in Europe must research throughout Europe to adapt to local customs and buying habits.[34]

Even companies that produce brands that are icons in their own country are now doing research internationally. The Research Snapshot above discusses how Brown-Forman, the parent company of Jack Daniels (the classic American "Sour Mash" or Bourbon Whiskey), are now interviewing consumers in the far corners of the world.[35] The internationalization of research places greater demands on marketing researchers and heightens the need for research tools that allow us to **culturally cross-validate** research results, meaning that the empirical findings from one culture also exist and behave similarly in another culture. The development and application of these international research tools are an important topic in basic marketing research.

culturally cross-validate

To verify that the empirical findings from one culture also exist and behave similarly in another culture.

- Throughout this text, a Tips of the Trade section is provided to give hints for using and doing marketing research. The first tip is to pay attention to these sections as helpful references.
- Customers and employees are valuable sources for input that leads to innovation in the marketplace and in the workplace.
- Business problems ultimately boil down to information problems because with the right information, the business can take effective action.
- Good marketing research is as rigorous as good research in other fields, including the physical sciences.

- Research plays a role before, during, and after key marketing decisions.
    - Research helps design marketing strategies and tactics before action is taken.
    - Once a plan is implemented, research monitors performance with key metrics providing valuable feedback.
    - After a plan is implemented, research assesses performance against benchmarks and seeks explanations for the failure or success of the action.
- Research that costs more than it could ever return should not be conducted.

© GEORGE DOYLE & CIARAN GRIFFIN

Summary

There were six learning objectives in this chapter. After reading the chapter, the student should be competent in each area described by a learning objective.

1. Know what marketing is and what it does for business. Marketing research is is the application of the scientific method in searching for the truth about marketing phenomena. Thus, it is the intelligence-gathering function in business. The intelligence includes information about customers, competitors, economic trends, employees, and other factors that affect marketing success. This intelligence assists in decisions ranging from long-range planning to near-term tactical decisions. While many business decisions are made "by the seat of the pants" or based on a manager's intuition, this type of decision making carries with it a large amount of risk. By first researching an issue and gathering intelligence on customers, competitors, and the market, a company can make a more informed decision. The result is less risky decision making.

2. Understand the differences between basic and applied marketing research. Applied marketing research seeks to facilitate managerial decision making. Basic or pure research seeks to increase knowledge of theories and concepts. Both are important. Applied research examples are emphasized in this text although practically all of the tools and techniques that are discussed are appropriate to either type of research. Some use the term market research to refer to applied research and marketing research to refer to basic research.

3. Understand how the role of marketing research changes when a firm is truly marketing oriented. Every company has a particular operating orientation. Production-oriented companies emphasize producing outputs as efficiently as possible. Generally, this leads to an emphasis on low-cost production and low-cost positioning in the marketplace. Product-oriented companies emphasize producing a sophisticated product that is also technologically advanced. Firms that are oriented around the marketing concept become very consumer oriented. Consumer-oriented companies have to have close contact with customers on a regular basis because providing a high value experience is the central focus of the entire firm. On the other hand, a low-cost orientation typical to a production orientation does not require a great deal of consumer-oriented research. Marketing oriented companies, therefore, tend to do more marketing research and emphasize marketing research more than do other firms.

4. Integrate marketing research results into the strategic planning process. Marketing research is a means of implementing the marketing concept, the most central idea in marketing. The marketing concept says that a firm must be oriented both toward consumer satisfaction and toward long-run profitability (rather than toward short-run sales volume). Organizations need to focus both on creating and on keeping customers. Marketing research can help implement the marketing concept by identifying consumers' problems and needs, improving efficiency, and evaluating the effectiveness of marketing strategies and tactics. The development and implementation of a marketing strategy consist of four stages: (1) identifying and evaluating opportunities, (2) analyzing market segments and selecting target markets, (3) planning and implementing a marketing mix that will provide value to customers and meet the objectives of the organization, and (4) analyzing firm performance. Marketing research helps in each stage by providing information for strategic decision making. In particular, marketing research aimed at the marketing mix seeks information useful in marking better decisions about product design, promotion, distribution, and pricing.

5. Know when marketing research should and should not be conducted. Marketing managers determine whether marketing research should be conducted based on (1) time constraints, (2) availability of data, (3) the nature of the decision to be made, and (4) the benefit of the research information versus its cost. Research should only be conducted when time is available, data can be found, the decision can be shaped by information, and the benefits outweigh the cost of doing the research.

6. Appreciate the way that technology and internationalization are changing marketing research. Technology has changed almost every aspect of marketing research. Modern computer and communications technology makes data collection, study design, data analysis, data reporting, and practically all other aspects of research easier and better. Furthermore, as more companies do business outside their own borders, companies are doing research in an international marketplace. This places a greater emphasis on research that can assess the degree to which research tools can be applied and interpreted the same way in difference cultures. Thus, research techniques often must cross-validate results.

Key Terms and Concepts

applied marketing research, 7
basic marketing research, 7
culturally cross-validate, 21
customer-oriented, 8
geo-demographics, 14
integrated marketing communication, 17
integrated marketing mix, 17
marketing channel, 16

marketing concept, 8
marketing metrics, 18
marketing orientation, 8
marketing research, 5
performance-monitoring research, 18
pricing, 15
product-oriented, 8
production-oriented, 8

promotion, 16
promotion research, 16
relationship marketing, 11
the scientific method, 7
supply chain, 16
total quality management, 11
total value management, 18

Questions for Review and Critical Thinking

1. Is it possible to make sound marketing decisions without marketing research? What advantages does research offer to the decision maker over seat-of-the-pants decision making?
2. Define a marketing orientation and a product orientation. Under which strategic orientation is there a greater need for marketing research?
3. Name some products that logically might have been developed with the help of marketing research.
4. Define *marketing research* and describe its task.
5. Which of the following organizations are likely to use marketing research? Why? How?
   a. Manufacturer of breakfast cereals
   b. Manufacturer of nuts, bolts, and other fasteners
   c. The Federal Trade Commission
   d. A hospital
   e. A company that publishes marketing textbooks
6. An automobile manufacturer is conducting research in an attempt to predict the type of car design consumers will desire in the year 2020. Is this basic or applied research? Explain.

7. What is the definition of an *integrated marketing mix*? How might this affect the research a firm conducts?
8. Comment on the following statements:
   a. Marketing managers are paid to take chances with decisions. Marketing researchers are paid to reduce the risk of making those decisions.
   b. A marketing strategy can be no better than the information on which it is formulated.
   c. The purpose of research is to solve marketing problems.
9. List the conditions that help a researcher decide when marketing research should or should not be conducted.
10. How have technology and internationalization affected marketing research?
11. **'NET** How do you believe the Internet has facilitated research? Try to use the Internet to find the total annual sales for Starbucks and for Toyota. You might start by using a general search engine like ask.com. University libraries also generally have access to business resources that may contain industry level data.
12. What types of tools does the marketing researcher use more given the ever increasing internationalization of marketing?

Research Activities

1. **'NET** Suppose you owned a jewelry store in Denton, Texas. You are considering opening a second store just like your current store. You are undecided on whether to locate the new store in another location in Denton, Texas, or in Birmingham, Alabama. Why would you decide to have some marketing research done before making the decision? Should the research be conducted? Go to http://www.census.gov. Do you think any of this information would be useful in the research?

2. Use the Internet to find recent examples of news articles involving the use of marketing research in making decisions about each element of the marketing mix.
3. Find an article illustrating an example of an applied marketing research study involving some aspect of technology. How does it differ from a basic research study also focusing on a similar aspect of technology?

CHAPTER 2
INFORMATION SYSTEMS AND KNOWLEDGE MANAGEMENT

After studying this chapter, you should be able to

1. Know why concepts like data, information, and intelligence represent value
2. Understand the four characteristics that describe data
3. Know what a decision support system is and does
4. Describe marketing research's role in predictive analytics
5. Recognize the major categories of databases

Chapter Vignette: That Ding Is Lifting Me Higher!

In just over a decade, online technologies have dramatically changed the way we shop for airline tickets. Most transactions can be conducted without any person-to-person contact. These changes mean that airline consumers spend a lot of time online. At any given time, a major airline is serving approximately 1,000 customers through its Web site. In a typical day, that means over 1 million customers have *touched* the company. Each touch leaves behind a record that researchers and managers can use to guide decision making.

Even occasional flyers probably know that airline prices can be difficult to predict. A roundtrip flight from Atlanta to Tampa may well cost more than a roundtrip flight from Tampa to San Francisco! A direct flight from New York to Paris may cost less than an indirect flight from New York to Paris with a two-hour layover in Houston! Airline pricing doesn't always make sense to consumers, but does make sense to managers interested in the bottom line. Pricing like this takes a great deal of research on who is flying to where. At times, the airline's attempt to maximize yield can lead to very attractive price offers to consumers. In fact, airline travel can sometimes compete with or even beat the price of driving, particularly when a consumer is targeted by an airline with a special fare between specific locations.

Airlines use sophisticated yield management systems which try to maximize the revenue realized on any given flight and by the airline overall. An empty seat is the worst thing for a positive yield. However, how can an airline predict how many consumers will be on each flight? When someone books a flight online, a lot of information is recorded beyond the fact that one more seat is unavailable on a particular flight. Information can be taken from the consumer's Web cookies so that the company knows what cities the consumer searched for, how long it took for a decision to be made, how the ticket was paid for and much more. All of which may be useful to yield management. Empty seats can be minimized by offering price promotions on specific flights for which a lot of unsold seats remain beyond some date determined by patterns of purchasing.

Southwest Airlines prices often ring a bell! Consumers can opt to download Southwest's Ding software, which uses information input into a questionnaire along with customer patterns of behavior to trigger special offers tailored specifically to a particular consumer. For example, a college student in College Station, Texas may wish to visit parents in Orange County, California. The student has flexibility to visit on any of a number of weekends. Ding retains this information and integrates it with anticipated load. When Ding anticipates flights from Houston, Texas to Orange County Airport that will not be at full load, the student is notified with an audible "ding" on her computer which is followed up with an e-mail containing a link showing very low fares for that customer. From a profitability standpoint, allowing someone to fly for a ridiculously low price is better than having an empty seat on the airplane. Although it may seem strange to consumers, the results of yield management systems like these show that airlines actually increase profits when the disparity between the lowest prices and highest prices that passengers pay is greatest.

Now, why are some airlines charging you to check a bag and charging you several hundred dollars to make small changes in your reservations? Remember, these systems are designed to maximize profits, not customer value![1]

Introduction

Southwest Airlines' use of Ding to manage its pricing illustrates the sophisticated way in which modern marketing firms often integrate real-time data into their decision processes. Many of the decisions that used to be made with guesswork are now supplemented with intelligence either automatically delivered by computer software or drawn from a data warehouse.

Airlines aren't alone in this effort. Imagine all the information that passes through a single Home Depot store each day. Every customer transaction, every empty shelf, every employee's work schedule—right down to the schedule to clean restrooms—creates potentially valuable information that can be used by researchers and decision makers. Considering that Home Depot operates thousands of stores, obviously, Home Depot needs a data depot!

Like many firms, Home Depot has outsourced the storage and management of data inventories. In this case, IBM manages the data, allowing it to be integrated into management strategy and tactics. Data from cash registers, time clocks, shelf counts, and much more are all compiled, analyzed, and either fed automatically into management systems or supplied in the form of a research report. In a way, this type of marketing research is automatic![2]

This chapter discusses knowledge management and the role decision support systems and predictive analytics play in helping firms make informed marketing decisions. The chapter also introduces the concept of global information systems that exist beyond the walls of any business. Marketing research plays an important role in making sense out of the glut of data now available. Today, data technology allows businesses to more easily integrate research findings into marketing strategy and operations.

Data, Information, and Intelligence Equal Value

In everyday language, terms like *information* and *data* are often used interchangeably. Researchers use these terms in specific ways that emphasize how useful each can be. Marketing managers may not be as intimately involved in finding and analyzing data; however, the decisions that they make based on the input received from research will make or break the firm. In this way, data, information, and intelligence all have the potential to create value to the firm through better decision making. One way in which these terms are not interchangeable lies in how closely linked they are to creating value for consumers and businesses.

Data are simply facts or recorded measures of certain phenomena (things or events). **Information** is data formatted (structured) to support decision making or define the relationship between two facts. **Market intelligence** is the subset of data and information that actually has some explanatory power enabling effective decisions to be made. So, there is more data than information, and more information than intelligence. Most data are irrelevant to any specific decision making situation and therefore not always valuable. When data becomes information, its relevance is examined more closely through some analytical procedure. Conclusions are drawn from the structured data or information to actually shape marketing decisions. The result is market intelligence and this should enable better decision making, better value provided to customers in that their desires are more closely met and thereby, more value for the firm in the form of improved performance.[3]

data

Facts or recorded measures of certain phenomena (things).

information

Data formatted (structured) to support decision making or define the relationship between two facts.

market intelligence

The subset of data and information that actually has some explanatory power enabling effective decisions to be made.

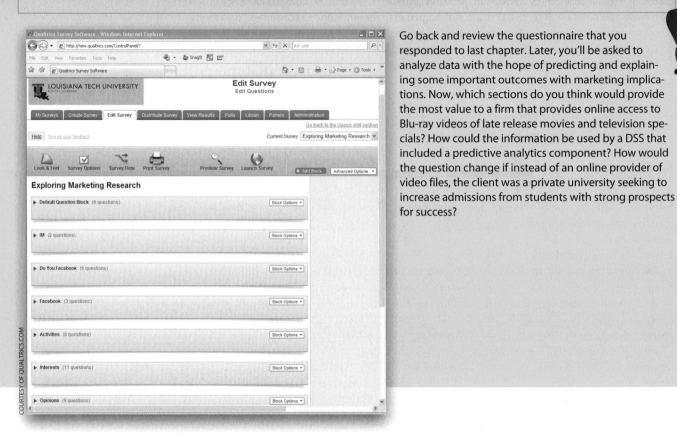

Go back and review the questionnaire that you responded to last chapter. Later, you'll be asked to analyze data with the hope of predicting and explaining some important outcomes with marketing implications. Now, which sections do you think would provide the most value to a firm that provides online access to Blu-ray videos of late release movies and television specials? How could the information be used by a DSS that included a predictive analytics component? How would the question change if instead of an online provider of video files, the client was a private university seeking to increase admissions from students with strong prospects for success?

The chapter vignette revealed the tremendous amount of data recorded through airline customers' interactions with airline Web sites. Think again about the thousands upon thousands of unsummarized facts recorded by Home Depot each day. Each time a product is scanned at checkout, that fact is recorded and becomes data. Each customer's transactions are simultaneously entered into the store's computerized inventory system. The inventory system structures the data in such a way that a stocking report can be generated and orders for that store can be placed. Thus, the automated inventory system turns data into information. Further, the information from each store's sales and inventory records may be harvested by analysts tracking sales trends. The analysts may analyze the trends and prepare reports that help Home Depot buyers get the right products into each store or to even suggest places for new Home Depot locations. Thus, the analyst has now completed the transformation of data into intelligence.

The Characteristics of Valuable Information

Not all data are valuable to decision makers. Useful data become information and help a marketing manager make decisions. Useful data can also become intelligence. Altogether, data, information, and intelligence can create knowledge.

Data Characteristics

Two important characteristics that do much to determine the value of information are relevance and completeness.

■ RELEVANCE

Relevance is the characteristics of data reflecting how pertinent these particular facts are to the situation at hand. Put another way, the facts are logically connected to the situation. Unfortunately, irrelevant data and information often creep into decision making. One particularly useful way to distinguish relevance from irrelevance is to think about how things change. Relevant data are facts about things that will materially alter the situation if they change. So, this simple question becomes important:

> *Will a change in the data coincide with a change in some important outcome?*

American consumers' dietary trends are relevant to Krispy Kreme Doughnuts. If American diets become more health-conscious, then it can be expected that sales of doughnuts will be affected. This may lead Krispy Kreme to rethink its product offering. However, information on the height of Mount Washington is irrelevant because it isn't going to change any time soon and even if it did, it would not affect U.S. doughnut preferences.

relevance

The characteristics of data reflecting how pertinent these particular facts are to the situation at hand.

■ COMPLETENESS

Information completeness refers to having the right amount of information. Marketing managers must have sufficient information about all aspects of their decisions. For example, a researcher investigating Eastern European markets may plan to analyze four former Soviet-bloc countries. Population statistics and information on inflation rates may be available on all four countries. However, information about disposable personal income may be available for only three of the countries. If information about disposable personal income or other economic characteristics cannot be obtained, the information is incomplete. Often incomplete information leads decision makers to conduct marketing research.

information completeness

Having the right amount of information.

global information system

An organized collection of computer hardware, software, data, and personnel designed to capture, store, update, manipulate, analyze, and immediately display information about worldwide business activity.

Global Information Systems

Increased global competition and technological advances in interactive media have given rise to global information systems. A **global information system** is an organized collection of computer hardware, software, data, and personnel designed to capture, store, update, manipulate, analyze, and immediately display information about worldwide business activities. A global information system is a tool for providing past, present, and projected information on internal operations and external activity. Using satellite communications, high-speed microcomputers, electronic data interchanges, fiber optics, data storage devices, and other technological advances in interactive media, global information systems are changing the nature of business.

Consider a simple example. At any moment, United Parcel Service (UPS) can track the status of any shipment around the world. UPS drivers use handheld electronic clipboards called delivery information acquisition devices (DIADs) to record appropriate data about each pickup or delivery. The data are then entered into the company's main computer for record-keeping and analysis. A satellite telecommunications system allows UPS to track any shipment for a customer. Consumers also can get near real time information on the status of a delivery as information from the DIADs is eventually made available through www.ups.com.

RFID stands for radio frequency identification. This relatively new technology is in a tiny chip, which can be woven onto a fabric, placed in packaging, or otherwise attached to virtually any product, allowing it to be tracked anywhere in the world. This can provide great insight into the different distribution channels around the world and, potentially, to the different ways consumers acquire and use products. The U.S. military uses RFID technology to assist in its logistics, and Wal-Mart is one of the leading proponents of the technology as it can greatly assist in its global information system.[5] The Research Snapshot on the next page describes in more detail how RFID technology is used by the United States Marine Corps and by Wal-Mart.

TO THE POINT

An immense and ever-increasing wealth of knowledge is scattered about the world today; knowledge that would probably suffice to solve all the mighty difficulties of our age, but it is dispersed and unorganized. We need a sort of mental clearing house for the mind: a depot where knowledge and ideas are received, sorted, summarized, digested, clarified and compared.[4]

—H. G. Wells

RFID Technology Gets Cheaper—Marketing Knowledge Grows

Radio frequency identification (RFID) tags have been used by large organizations for several years now. The U.S. military makes great use of RFIDs in tracking the whereabouts of virtually all kinds of products both big and small. Logistics officers can instantly track the whereabouts of Humvees and MREs (Meals Ready to Eat). Information from the tag is transmitted to computer servers and then directly into a GTN (Global Tracking Network). Equipment and supplies can then be ordered and dispatched to needed locations with a minimal of human contact. Product consumption (ammunition, food, water, computer printers, and so forth) can also be tracked in real time. The Marines can know in real time if personnel in a desert use more food and water than personnel in a jungle.

COURTESY: DIVISION OF PUBLIC AFFAIRS, UNITED STATES MARINE CORPS, DEPARTMENT OF DEFENSE, USA

Wal-Mart is pushing suppliers to adopt the technology. Not only can Wal-Mart use them in logistical operations, but the potential exists to "go into" consumers' homes and track how much and the way consumers actually consume products. Potentially, decision support systems (DSS) could tie ordering to customer consumption. However, the costs of RFIDs make it impractial for many suppliers.

Alien Technology Corporation recently announced a drop in the price of RFID tags. Now, when a company orders a million or more, the unit cost for an RFID is 12.9 cents and can be as low as 7 cents. Although this is a "basic" RFID tag, it still can store up to one kilobyte of information. Analysts predict that the price of RFID tags will continue to drop, opening up the avenue for more and more applications. RFID technology is even contributing to a drop in shoplifting around the USA due to the ability to better track product whereabouts both in and out of the store.

Sources: Clark, Don, "Alien Cuts Radio ID Tag Price to Spur Adoption by Retailiners," *The Wall Street Journal* (September 12, 2005), D4; Fergueson, R. B., "Marines Deploy RFID," *e-Week*, 21 (November 15, 2004), 37. *Business Wire*, "Correcting and Replacing Shoplifting and Retail Loss Continue Six Year Decline According to Survey," (June 24, 2008), Retrieved July 14, 2008, from ABI/INFORM Dateline database (document ID: 1500093791).

© GEORGE DOYLE & CIARAN GRIFFIN

Decision Support Systems

Marketing research can be described in many ways. One way is to categorize research based on the four possible functions it serves in business:

1. Foundational—answers basic questions such as what consumer segments should be served and with what types of products.
2. Testing—addresses things like new product concepts or promotional ideas. How effective will they be?
3. Issues—examines how specific issues impact the firm. The way organizational structure impacts employee outcomes or the impacts of advertising spending are issues that can be researched.
4. Performance—this type of research monitors specific metrics including financial statistics like profitability and delivery times. They are critical in real-time management and in "what-if" and sensitivity types of analyses examining the potential impact of a change in policy.

The performance category is most relevant in decision support systems. The metrics that are monitored can be fed into automated decision-making systems, or they can trigger reports that are delivered to managers. These form the basis of a decision support system and best typify the way marketing research assists managers with day-to-day operational decisions.

decision support system (DSS)

A computer-based system that helps decision makers confront problems through direct interaction with databases and analytical software programs.

A marketing **decision support system (DSS)** is a system that helps decision makers confront problems through direct interaction with computerized databases and analytical software programs. The purpose of a decision support system is to store data and transform them into organized information that is easily accessible to marketing managers. Doing so saves managers countless hours so that decisions that might take days or even weeks otherwise can be made in minutes using a DSS.

customer relationship management (CRM)

Part of the DSS that addresses exchanges between the firm and its customers.

Modern decision support systems greatly facilitate **customer relationship management (CRM)**. A CRM system is the part of the DSS that addresses exchanges between the firm and its customers. It brings together information about customers including sales data, market trends, marketing promotions and the way consumers respond to them, customer preferences, and more. A CRM system describes customer relationships in sufficient detail so that managers, salespeople, customer service representatives, and perhaps the customers themselves can access information directly, match customer needs with satisfying product offerings, remind customers of service requirements, and know what other products a customer has purchased.

Casinos track regular customers' behavior via "player's cards" that are swiped each time a consumer conducts a transaction. This information is fed automatically into a CRM system that creates tailor-made promotional packages. The promotion may be unique to a specific customer's preferences as tracked by their own pattern of behavior. You may notice when visiting certain Web sites that they seem to be able to predict your behavior. Casino customers arrive to the resort and are greeted with their favorite beverage and coupons for their favorite restaurants. This information is found in the CRM system and is based on behavior tracked on previous visits.

Exhibit 2.1 illustrates a decision support system. Raw, unsummarized data are input to the DSS. Data collected in marketing research projects are a major source of this input, but the data may be purchased or collected by accountants, sales managers, production managers, or company employees other than marketing researchers. Effective marketers spend a great deal of time and effort collecting information for input into the decision support system. Useful information is the output of a DSS. A decision support system requires both databases and software. For firms operating across national borders, the DSS becomes part of its global information system.

EXHIBIT 2.1
Decision Support System

Databases and Data Warehousing

A **database** is a collection of raw data arranged logically and organized in a form that can be stored and processed by a computer. A customer mailing list is one type of database. Population characteristics may be recorded by state, county, and city in another database. Modern computer technology makes both the storage and retrieval of this information easy and convenient. The population data needed to do a retail site analysis may have meant days, possibly weeks, in a library. Today, the information is just a few clicks away.

Data warehousing is the process allowing important day-to-day operational data to be stored and organized for simplified access. More specifically, a **data warehouse** is the multitiered computer storehouse of current and historical data. Data warehouse management requires that the detailed data from operational systems be extracted, transformed, placed into logical partitions (for example, daily data, weekly data, etc.), and stored in a consistent and secure manner. Organizations with data warehouses may integrate databases from both inside and outside the company. Managing a data warehouse effectively requires considerable computing power and expertise. As a result, data warehouse companies exist that provide this service for companies in return for a fee.[6] Data warehousing allows for sophisticated analysis, such as data mining, discussed in Chapter 6.

database

A collection of raw data arranged logically and organized in a form that can be stored and processed by a computer.

data warehousing

The process allowing important day-to-day operational data to be stored and organized for simplified access.

data warehouse

The multitiered computer storehouse of current and historical data.

Input Management

How does data end up in a data warehouse where it can be used by a decision support system? In other words, how is the input managed? Input includes all the numerical, text, voice, and image data that enter the DSS. Systematic accumulation of pertinent, timely, and accurate data is essential to the success of a decision support system.

DSS managers, systems analysts, and programmers are responsible for the decision support system as a whole, but many functions within an organization provide input data. Marketing researchers, accountants, corporate librarians, sales personnel, production managers, and many others within the organization help to collect data and provide input for the DSS. Input data can also come from external sources.

Exhibit 2.2 shows six major sources of data input: internal records, proprietary marketing research, salesperson input, behavioral tracking, Web tracking, and outside vendors and external distributors of data. Each source can provide valuable input.

■ INTERNAL RECORDS

Internal records, such as accounting reports of sales and inventory figures, provide considerable data that may become useful information for marketing managers. An effective data collection

EXHIBIT 2.2 **Six Major Sources of Marketing Input for Decision Support Systems**

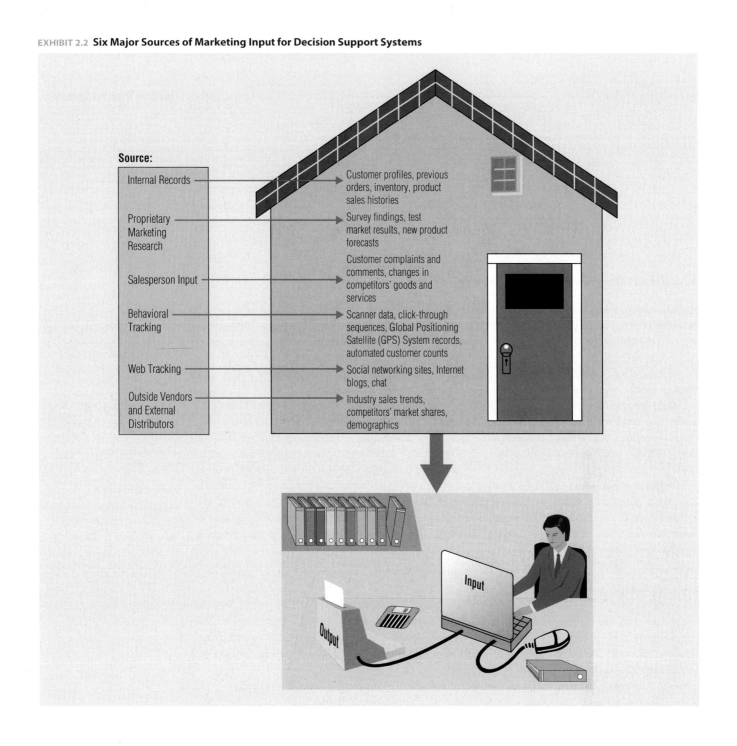

system establishes orderly procedures to ensure that data about costs, shipments, inventory, sales, and other aspects of regular operations are routinely collected and entered into the computer.

■ PROPRIETARY MARKETING RESEARCH

Marketing research has already been defined as a broad set of procedures and methods. To clarify the DSS concept, consider a narrower view of marketing research. **Proprietary marketing research** emphasizes the company's gathering of new data. Few proprietary marketing research procedures and methods are conducted regularly or continuously. Instead, research projects conducted to study specific company problems generate data; this is proprietary marketing research. Providing managers with nonroutine data that otherwise would not be available is a major function of proprietary marketing research. Earlier, we discussed four categories of research. Proprietary marketing research may involve either or both of the "testing" and "issues" types of research.

proprietary marketing research

The gathering of new data to investigate specific problems.

■ SALESPERSON INPUT

Salespeople work in firms' external environments, so they commonly provide essential marketing data. Sales representatives' reports frequently alert managers to changes in competitors' prices and new product offerings. It also may involve the types of complaints salespeople are hearing from customers. As trends become evident, this data may become marketing intelligence, leading to a change in product design or service delivery.

■ BEHAVIORAL TRACKING

Modern technology provides new ways of tracking human behavior. Global positioning satellite (GPS) systems allow management to track the whereabouts of delivery personnel at all times. This is the same system that provides directions through an automobile's navigation system. For example, if your delivery person takes a quick break for nine holes of golf or decides to stop at Neil's Bar for a couple of beers mid-afternoon, management can spot these as deviations from the appropriate delivery route are noted. Thus, it can help track which employees are doing their jobs well.

GPS devices, like those used in automobile navigation systems, allow management to track delivery personnel or even actual customer behavior.

© CREATAS IMAGES/JUPITER IMAGES

Technology also allows firms to track actual customer behavior. While it's possible that GPS tracking data of customers is also sometimes possible, as the photograph suggests, the Internet also greatly facilitates customer behavior tracking. For instance, Google tracks the "click-through" sequence of customers. Therefore, if a customer is searching for information on refrigerators, and then goes to BestBuy.com, Google can track this behavior and use the information to let BestBuy know how important it is to advertise on Google and even automate pricing for advertisers.[7]

scanner data

The accumulated records resulting from point of sale data recordings.

Purchase behavior can also be tracked at the point of sale. **Scanner data** refers to the accumulated records resulting from point of sale data recordings. In other words, each time products are scanned at a checkout counter, the information can be stored. The term *single-source* data refers to a system's ability to gather several types of interrelated data, such as type of purchase, use of a sales promotion, or advertising frequency data, from a single source in a format that will facilitate integration, comparison, and analysis.

■ WEB TRACKING

Little did the original inventors of the Internet probably foresee back in the 1960s, but the Internet has become perhaps the most important communication vehicle for the latest generations of teens. Web tracking is performed by marketing researchers to monitor trends and information posted by consumers that pertains to the company's brand or products. MySpace.com logged nearly 70 million unique visitors in December 2007 and is one of the top 10 most visited web sites in America.[8] Marketing researchers monitor postings and create vehicles such as contests which invite consumers to leave ideas and feedback about the brand. The Research Snapshot on the next page demonstrates how publishing and production companies use input from social networking sites. Other sources for information include Internet blogs and chat rooms where consumers share information about their own experiences, including complaints that serve as a type of warning to other consumers.

■ OUTSIDE VENDORS AND EXTERNAL DISTRIBUTORS

Outside vendors and external distributors market information as their products. Many organizations specialize in the collection and publication of high-quality information. One outside vendor, the ACNielsen Company, provides television program ratings, audience counts, and information about the demographic composition of television viewer groups. Other vendors specialize in the distribution of information. Public libraries have always purchased information, traditionally in the form of books, and they have served as distributors of this information.

Media representatives often provide useful demographic and lifestyle data about their audiences. *Advertising Age, The Wall Street Journal, Sales and Marketing Management,* and other trade- and business-oriented publications are important sources of information. These publications keep managers up-to-date about the economy, competitors' activities, and other aspects of the marketing environment.

Companies called *data specialists* record and store certain marketing information. Computer technology has changed the way many of these organizations supply data, favoring the development of computerized databases.

Computerized Data Archives

Historically, collections of organized and readily retrievable data were available in printed form at libraries. The *Statistical Abstract of the United States,* which is filled with tables of statistical facts, is a typical example. In recent years, the *Statistical Abstract* has become available electronically. Users can purchase it via CD-ROM or access it via the Internet. The entire 2000 census as well as projections through the current year are available in print, CD-ROM, and via the Internet at http://www.census.gov. More and more data are available in digitized form every day.

Numerous computerized search and retrieval systems and electronic databases are available as subscription services or in libraries. Just as a student can query the school library to find information for a term paper without leaving home, data acquisition for businesses has also become far more convenient in recent years. Today, business people access online information search and

MySpace Means My Data

Social networking sites have become perhaps the most important marketing tool for companies wanting to reach youth markets. Information gathered from these Web sites has become input into product designs including music, movies, and books aimed at teen markets. The publishers of the Clique series of teen books such as Twilight Saga create MySpace pages and encourage fans to visit the sites and leave input. Fans can even give input that will shape the content of the novels. The publishers set up polls asking questions such as who Bella should choose. The polls record thousands of votes and the publishers use the information to help keep authors in tune with the teen markets.

Another benefit of Web tracking is international access. For example, nearly 1 million Indian consumers have a Facebook account. The popularity of Facebook over more regional networking sites like Hi5 or Orkut is thought to lie in a simple fact—Indian consumers find Facebook fun! By creating entertaining activities and experiences, consumers become practically addicted. The more time consumers spend, the more information they leave behind. Thus, social networking is an inexpensive way to take in data from international sources.

Sources: Sellers, J., "Teen Marketing 2.0," *Publishers' Weekly*, 254, no. 35 (2007), 27; Srivasta, P., "The Gregarious Web: What Are Senior Indian Execs Doing Hanging Around at Social Networking Site, Facebook.com?" *Business Today*, (October 21, 2007), 226.

retrieval services, such as Dow Jones News Retrieval and Bloomberg Financial Markets, without leaving their offices. In fact, some information services can be accessed from remote locations via digital wireless devices.

Modern library patrons can command a computer to search indexes and retrieve databases from a range of vendors. Just as wholesalers collect goods from manufacturers and offer them for sale to retailers who then provide them to consumers, many information firms serve as data wholesalers. **Data wholesalers** put together consortia of data sources into packages that are offered to municipal, corporate, and university libraries for a fee. Information consumers then access the data through these libraries. Some of the better known *databases* include Wilson Business Center, Hoovers, PROQUEST, INFOTRAC, DIALOG (Dialog Information Services, Inc.), LEXIS-NEXIS, and Dow Jones News Retrieval Services. These databases provide all types of information including recent news stories and data tables charting statistical trends.

DIALOG, for example, maintains more than 600 databases. A typical database may have a million or more records, each consisting of a one- or two-paragraph abstract that summarizes the major points of a published article along with bibliographic information. One of the DIALOG databases, ABI/INFORM, abstracts significant articles in more than 1,000 current business and management journals. Many computerized archives provide full-text downloads of published articles about companies and various research topics.

Exhibit 2.3 on the next page illustrates the services provided by two popular vendors of information services that electronically index numerous databases. For a more extensive listing, see the *Gale Directory of Databases*.[9]

Several types of databases from outside vendors and external distributors are so fundamental to decision support systems that they deserve further explanation. The following sections discuss statistical databases, financial databases, and video databases in slightly more detail.

data wholesalers

Companies that put together consortia of data sources into packages that are offered to municipal, corporate, and university libraries for a fee.

■ STATISTICAL DATABASES

Statistical databases contain numerical data for market analysis and forecasting. Often demographic, sales, and other relevant marketing variables are recorded by geographical area. Geographic information systems use these *geographical databases* and powerful software to prepare computer maps of relevant variables. Companies such as Claritas, Urban Decision Systems, and CACI all offer geographic or demographic databases that are widely used in industry.

One source for these huge data warehouses is scanner data. Substituting mechanized record-keeping like optical scanners for human record-keeping results in greater accuracy and more rapid feedback about store activity.

EXHIBIT 2.3
**Vendors of Information
Services and Electronic
Indexing**

Vendors	Selected Databases	Type of Data
DIALOG	ABI/INFORM	Summaries and citations from over 1,000 academic management, marketing, and general business journals with full text of more than 500 of these publications
	ASI (American Statistics Index)	Abstracts and indexes of federal government statistical publications
	PROMT (The Predicast Overview of Markets and Technologies)	Summaries and full text from 1,000 U.S. and international business and trade journals, industry newsletters, newspapers, and market research studies; information about industries and companies, including the products and technologies they develop and the markets in which they compete
	Investext	Full text of over 2 million company, industry, and geographic research reports written by analysts at more than 600 leading investment banks, brokerage houses, and consulting firms worldwide
Dow Jones News Retrieval	Business Newsstand	Articles from *New York Times*, *Los Angeles Times*, *Washington Post*, and other leading newspapers and magazines
	Historical Market Data Center	Historical data on securities, dividends, and exchange rates
	Web Center	Information obtained from searches of corporate, industry, government, and news Web sites

One weakness of scanner data is that not all points of sale have scanner technology. For instance, many convenience stores lack scanner technology, as do most vending machines. Thus, those purchases go unrecorded. The Universal Product Code, or UPC, contains information on the category of goods, the manufacturer, and product identification based on size, flavor, color, and so on. This is what the optical scanner actually reads. If a large percentage of a brand's sales occur in environments without the ability to read the UPC code, the marketer should be aware that the scanner data may not be representative.

■ FINANCIAL DATABASES

Competitors' and customers' financial data, such as income statements and balance sheets, may interest managers. These are easy to access in financial databases. CompuStat publishes an extensive financial database on thousands of companies, broken down by industry and other criteria. To illustrate the depth of this pool of information, CompuStat's Global Advantage offers extensive data on approximately 7,000 companies in more than thirty countries in Europe, the Pacific Rim, and North America.

■ VIDEO DATABASES

Video databases and streaming media are having a major impact on the marketing of many goods and services. For example, movie studios provide clips of upcoming films and advertising agencies put television commercials on the Internet (see AdCritic at http://www.creativity-online.com, for example). McDonald's maintains a digital archive of television commercials and other video footage to share with its franchisers around the world. The video database enables franchisers and their advertising agencies to create local advertising without filming the same types of scenes already archived. Videos on practically every type of product consumption or brand can be found on YouTube.com. In 2008, both major political campaigns produced advertisements meant solely for distribution through YouTube and other Web video sources. Just imagine the potential value of digital video databases to advertising agencies' support systems as firms can monitor the number of hits on different videos and even know for how long most people view a video. They can also monitor the buzz (Internet chatter) created by provocative videos.

Networks and Electronic Data Interchange

Electronic data interchange (EDI) systems integrate one company's computer system directly with

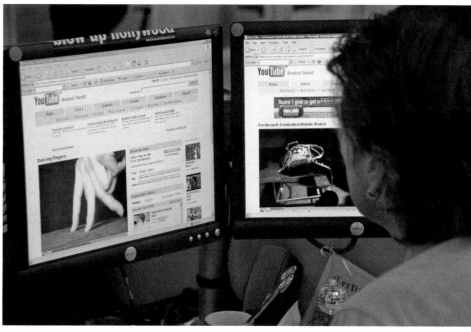

YouTube provides a digital archive that can be mined for data or used as a vehicle to test ideas and concepts.

another company's system. Much of the input to a company's decision support system may come through networks from other companies' computers. Companies such as Computer Technology Corporation and Microelectronics market data services that allow corporations to exchange business information with suppliers or customers. For example, every evening Wal-Mart transmits millions of characters of data about the day's sales to its apparel suppliers. Wrangler, a supplier of blue jeans, for instance, shares the data and a model that interprets the data. Wrangler also shares software applications that act to replenish stock in Wal-Mart stores. This DSS lets Wrangler's managers know when to send specific quantities of specific sizes and colors of jeans to specific stores from specific warehouses. The result is a learning loop that lowers inventory costs and leads to fewer stockouts.

electronic data interchange (EDI)

Type of exchange that occurs when one company's computer system is integrated with another company's system.

Predictive Analytics

The term predictive analytics did not exist prior to the widespread usage of the Internet. In fact, no other facet of business better illustrates how the Internet can be leveraged for business success than predictive analytics. Broadly speaking, **predictive analytics** refers to linking computerized data sources to statistical tools that can search for predictive relationships and trends which allow more accurate forecast of consumers' opinions and actions. Predictive analytics also eliminates manual scanning of data. Software companies like SPSS and SAS offer products that both look for data and then use statistical tools to reveal key predictive relationships. We'll learn more about SPSS and specific statistical tools later in the book.

predictive analytics

A system linking computerized data sources to statistical tools allowing more accurate forecasts of consumers' opinions and actions.

The airline systems described in the opening vignette represent a type of predictive analytics. Information taken from consumers' actual archived behavior along with preference data provided by direct input from the consumer is used to model sales levels that can be achieved with various amounts of discounts. Airlines may be expected to use the latest research technologies like predictive analytics, but other industries including some that are much smaller and seemingly less significant are taking advantage of this new tool. Monterey Mushrooms, the nation's leading mushroom producer, used to arm its salesforce with volumes of paper reports showing sales data for hundreds and hundreds of vendors over several quarters.[10] Spotting trends was much like finding a needle in a hastack! The company now integrates information about vendors and cost information including shipping and packaging cost to predict which sales calls will be most profitable. The company can allocate resources accordingly (see the Research Snapshot on next page for an illustration). Beats finding a needle in a haystack!

How Did They Know That?

Major state universities have thousands and thousands of alumni. But, typically, the university has limited resources to personally call on alumni to financially support the university. Historically, only one out of every hundred or so alumni would provide gifts sufficient to balance the average unit costs of marketing to all alums. What if the university could improve the hit ratio and better target relatively expensive marketing approaches like personal meetings to those who are 50 percent likely to give a major gift instead of 5 percent likely. This is exactly what modern predictive analytic tools can do. Using all the information on alumni, much of it gathered through various touchpoints with the university, a statistical model can be built which predicts responsiveness to appeals and places a potential donor value on each alumnus. So, perhaps an alum with football season tickets who also attends at least three orchestra performances and who majored in marketing becomes registered as a donor with high value. More marketing efforts can be directed their way and in this way, marketing is made much more efficient.

Similarly, pharmaceutical firms use data mining approaches based on volumes of input on physicians in their directories to better predict the types of drugs each doctor is likely to prescribe. When a doctor switches prescriptions for a patient, the program identifies a probable reason such as side effects, insurance coverage, cost, and so on; and this feedback allows them to adjust production and marketing accordingly. In this manner, they can design products that doctors are more likely to prescribe. Predictive outcomes of programmed research of this type truly represent win-win propositions. The physicians (customers) get products that more closely match their desires and the company performs better through increased sales. Modern technology enhances firms' ability to be opportunistic in their relationships in a good way.

Sources: Crosno, J. L. and R. Dahlstrom, "A Meta-Analytic Review of Opportunism in Exchange Relationships," *Journal of the Academy of Marketing Science*, 36 (June 2008), 191–201; Goldman, L., "Web 2.0 Brings Web Analytics 2.0," *DM Review*, 17 (March 2007), 28; "SAS Helps ImpactRX Provide Real Time Marketing Intelligence to Pharma Companies," *Business Wire*, (March 17, 2008), retrieved July 14, 2008 from ABI/INFORM Dateline database (document ID: 1447327611); "SPSS Text Mining Reveals Greater Customer Insights as Organizations Worldwide Tap into Unstructured Data," *Business Wire*, (June 16, 2008), retrieved July 15, 2008 from ABI/INFORM Dateline database (document ID: 1495884601).

The marketing researchers' job in predictive analytics is twofold. First, identify the key sources of information that may create predictive intelligence and second, use analytic tools to build predictive models. Although the information can come from many varied places, the Internet is a prime source for key information. In the following pages we discuss the World Wide Web and how to use the Internet for research. However, keep in mind that the Internet is constantly changing.

TOTHEPOINT

The Net is 10.5 on the Richter scale of economic change.

—Nicholas Negroponte

How Is the Internet Useful in Research?

The Internet is useful to researchers in many ways. In fact, more and more applications become known as the technology grows and is adopted by more and more users. The Internet is particularly useful as a source of available data and as a way of collecting data.

■ NAVIGATING THE INTERNET

content providers

Parties that furnish information on the World Wide Web.

Parties that furnish information on the World Wide Web are called **content providers**. Content providers maintain Web sites. A Web site consists of one or more Web pages with related information about a particular topic; for example, a university Web site might include pages about its mission, courses, and faculty (see http://www.gsu.edu, for example). The introductory page or opening screen is called the home page because it provides basic information about the purpose of the document along with a menu of selections or links that lead to other screens with more specific information. Thus, each page can have connections, or hyperlinks, to other pages, which may be on any computer connected to the Internet. People using the World Wide Web may be viewing information that is stored on a host computer or on a machine halfway around the world.

Uniform Resource Locator (URL)

A Web site address that Web browsers recognize.

Most Web browsers also allow the user to enter a **Uniform Resource Locator (URL)** into the program. The URL is really just a Web site address that Web browsers recognize. Many Web sites allow any user or visitor access without previous approval. However, many commercial sites require that the user have a valid account and password before access is granted.

One of the most basic research tools available via the Internet is a search engine. A **search engine** is a computerized directory that allows anyone to search the World Wide Web for information based on a keyword search. A **keyword search** takes place as the search engine searches through millions of Web pages for documents containing the keywords. Some of the most comprehensive and accurate search engines are.

Ask Jeeves	http://www.ask.com
Yahoo!	http://www.yahoo.com
Dogpile	http://www.dogpile.com
Google	http://www.google.com
Hotbot	http://www.hotbot.com
Go network	http://go.com
Excite	http://www.excite.com
Lycos	http://www.lycos.com
WebCrawler	http://www.webcrawler.com

Google revolutionized search engines by changing the way the search was actually conducted. It searches based on a mathematical theory known as *graph theory*.[11] Google greatly improved the accuracy and usefulness of the search results obtained from a keyword search. For instance, if one clicks on Google Scholar, a search of basic research papers on any given topic indicated by the keywords can be performed.

A Boolean search is a search that combines relevant key words by operators that refine the search. The operators include words like and, or, and not. So, a search of Churchill will bring up thousands of hits. For example, Churchill Downs the home of the Kentucky Derby will surface. However, enter "war" and "Churchill" and the search becomes quickly limited to sites that contain both words. As a result, a student doing a paper on Winston Churhill's leadership during WWII has just become easier. Modern data mining approaches can actually automate Web searches using Boolean operators. Researchers may wish to monitor negative information about a brand.

Environmental Scanning

The Internet is an especially useful source for scanning many types of environmental changes. **Environmental scanning** entails all information gathering designed to detect changes in the external operating environment of the firm. Even things beyond the control of the firm can have a significant impact on firm performance.

Ford Motor Company maintains an Internet-based relationship marketing program that, among other things, helps the automaker scan its environment using the Internet. Its dealer Web site creates a centralized communication service linking dealers via an Internet connection. Its buyer Web site allows prospective buyers to visit a virtual showroom and to get price quotes and financial information. Its owner Web site allows an owner who registers and supplies pertinent vehicle information to get free e-mail and other ownership perks. A perk might be a free Hertz

search engine

A computerized directory that allows anyone to search the World Wide Web for information using a keyword search.

keyword search

Takes place as the search engine searches through millions of Web pages for documents containing the keywords.

environmental scanning

Entails all information gathering designed to detect changes in the external operating environment of the firm.

Here is the result of a Boolean search for "Ford and Feedback." The URL is shown but can be reached by navigating to ask.com and then searching the key phrase.

pull technology

Consumers request information from a Web page and the browser then determines a response; the consumer is essentially asking for the data.

push technology

Sends data to a user's computer without a request being made; software is used to guess what information might be interesting to consumers based on the pattern of previous responses.

smart agent software

Software capable of learning an Internet user's preferences and automatically searching out information in selected Web sites and then distributing it.

cookies

Small data files that a content provider can save onto the computer of someone who visits its Web site.

The iPod offers one example of how modern technology makes it possible to store and deliver information. Various models can capture, store, and deliver hundreds of songs to their owners.

upgrade or an autographed photo of one of the Ford-sponsored NASCAR drivers. In return, Ford collects data at all levels, which allows managers to scan for trends and apply what they learn at a local level.

Information Technology

Data and information can be delivered to consumers or other end users via either **pull technology** or **push technology**. Conventionally, consumers request information from a Web page and the browser then determines a response. Thus, the consumer is essentially asking for the data. In this case, it is said to be pulled through the channel. The opposite of pull is push. Push technology sends data to a user's computer without a request being made. In other words, software is used to guess what information might be interesting to consumers based on the pattern of previous responses. Push technology allows personalized information to be delivered to consumers without the need for them to even be physically at their Internet device.[12] When airline customers go to a Web site to search for flights from Columbus to Riverside, they are pulling information. When those same customers get "Dinged" with a special on flights from Columbus to Riverside, they have had the information pushed to them based on their previous behavior.

Today's information technology uses "smart agents" or "intelligent agents" to deliver customized content to a viewer's desktop. **Smart agent software** is capable of learning an Internet user's preferences and automatically searching out information and distributing the information to a user's computer. My Yahoo! and MyExcite are portal services that personalize Web pages. Users can get stock quotes relevant to their portfolios, news about favorite sports teams, local weather, and other personalized information. Users can customize the sections of the service they want delivered. With push technology, pertinent content is delivered to the viewer's desktop without the user having to do the searching.

© VICKI BEAVER

Cookies, in computer terminology, are small data files that record a user's Web usage history. If a person looks up a weather report by keying in a zip code into a personalized Web page, the fact that the user visited the Web site and the zip code entered are recorded in the cookie. This is a clue that tells where the person lives (or maybe where he or she may be planning to visit). Web sites can then direct information to that consumer based on information in the cookie. So, someone in College Station, Texas, may receive pop-up ads for restaurants in College Station. Information technology is having a major impact on the nature of marketing research. We will explore this topic in several places throughout this book.

Intranets

An **Intranet** is a company's private data network that uses Internet standards and technology.[13] The information on an Intranet—data, graphics, video, and voice—is available only inside the organization or to those individuals whom the organization deems as appropriate participants. Thus, a key difference between the Internet and an Intranet is that security software programs, or "firewalls," are installed to limit access to only those employees authorized to enter the system. Intranets then serve as secure knowledge portals that contain substantial amounts of organizational memory and can integrate it with information from outside sources. The challenge in designing an Intranet is making sure that it is capable of delivering relevant data to decision makers. Research suggests that relevance is a key in getting knowledge workers to actually make use of company Intranets.[14]

- Researchers should focus on relevance as the key characteristic of useful data. Do so by asking, "Will knowledge of some fact change some important outcome?"
- Focus more on getting managers the right data than the most data.

- The Internet is a valuable source of data. The Internet is:
  - A useful information collection vehicle
  - An exhaustive information repository
  - A great place for data mining

The Intranet can be extended to include key consumers as a source of valuable research. Their participation in the Intranet can lead to new product developments. Texas Instruments has successfully established an Intranet that integrates communications between customers and researchers leading to the introduction and modification of its calculators.[15] An Intranet lets authorized users, possibly including key customers, look at product drawings, employee newsletters, sales figures, and other kinds of company information.

Intranet

A company's private data network that uses Internet standards and technology.

Summary

1. Know why concepts like data, information, and intelligence represent value. Increased global competition and technological advances in interactive media have spurred development of global information systems. A global information system is an organized collection of computer hardware, software, data, and personnel designed to capture, store, update, manipulate, analyze, and immediately display information about worldwide business activity.

From a research perspective, there is a difference between data, information, and intelligence. Data are simply facts or recorded measures of certain phenomena (things); information is data formatted (structured) to support decision making or define the relationship between two facts. Market intelligence is the subset of data and information that actually has some explanatory power enabling effective decisions to be made. The proper use of data, information, and intelligence means better decision making and better decision making means greater value for the firm.

2. Understand the four characteristics that describe data. The usefulness of data to management can be described based on four characteristics: relevance, quality, timeliness, and completeness. Relevant data have the characteristic of pertinence to the situation at hand. The information is useful. The quality of information is the degree to which data represent the true situation. High-quality data are accurate, valid, and reliable. High-quality data represent reality faithfully and present a good picture of reality. Timely information is obtained at the right time. Computerized information systems can record events and present information soon after a transaction takes place, improving timeliness. Complete information is the right quantity of information. Marketing managers must have sufficient information to relate all aspects of their decisions together.

3. Know what a decision support system is and does. A database is a collection of raw data arranged logically and organized in a form that can be stored and processed by a computer. Marketing data come from four major sources: internal records, proprietary marketing research, marketing intelligence, and outside vendors and external distributors. Each source can provide valuable input. Because most companies compile and store many different databases, they often develop data warehousing systems. Data warehousing is the process allowing important day-to-day operational data to be stored and organized for simplified access. More specifically, a data warehouse is the multitiered computer storehouse of current and historical data. Data warehouse management requires that the detailed data from operational systems be extracted, transformed, and stored (warehoused) so that the various database tables from both inside and outside the company are consistent. All of this feeds into the decision support system that automates or assists business decision making.

4. Describe marketing research's role in predictive analytics. Predictive analytics refers to linking computerized data sources to statistical tools that can search for relationships and trends which allow more accurate prediction of consumers' opinions and actions. Thus, it combines automated data mining with multivariate statistical tools to enhance prediction. The marketing researcher's job in predictive analytics is twofold. First, identify the key sources of information that may create predictive intelligence and second, use analytic tools to build predictive models.

5. Recognize the major categories of databases. The Internet is a worldwide network of computers that allows users access to information and documents from distant sources. It is a combination of a worldwide communication system and the world's largest public library. The World Wide Web is a system of thousands of interconnected pages, or documents, that can be easily accessed with Web browsers and search engines.

An Intranet is a company's private data network that uses Internet standards and technology. The information on an Intranet—data, graphics, video, and voice—is available only inside the organization. Thus, a key difference between the Internet and an Intranet is that "firewalls," or security software programs, are installed to limit access to only those employees authorized to enter the system.

A company uses Internet features to build its own Intranet. Groupware and other technology can facilitate the transfer of data, information, and knowledge. In organizations that practice knowledge management, Intranets function to make the knowledge of company experts more accessible throughout their organizations.

Key Terms and Concepts

content providers, *36*	decision support system (DSS), *28*	predictive analytics, *35*
cookies, *38*	electronic data interchange (EDI), *35*	proprietary marketing research, *31*
customer relationship management (CRM), *28*	environmental scanning, *37*	pull technology, *38*
data, *25*	global information system, *27*	push technology, *38*
database, *29*	information, *25*	relevance, *27*
data warehouse, *29*	information completeness, *27*	scanner data, *32*
data warehousing, *29*	Intranet, *39*	search engine, *37*
data wholesalers, *33*	keyword search, *37*	smart agent software, *38*
	market intelligence, *25*	Uniform Resource Locator (URL), *36*

Questions for Review and Critical Thinking

1. What is the difference between data, information, and intelligence?
2. What are the characteristics of useful information?
3. What is the key question distinguishing relevant data from irrelevant data?
4. Define *knowledge management*. What is its purpose within an organization?
5. What types of databases might be found in the following organizations?
   a. Holiday Inn
   b. A Major University Athletic Department
   c. Anheuser-Busch
6. What type of operational questions could a delivery firm like FedEx expect to automate with the company's decision support system?

7. What makes a decision support system successful?
8. What is data warehousing?
9. **'NET** How does data warehousing assist decision making? Visit http://www.kbb.com. While there, choose two cars that you might consider buying and compare them. Which do you like the best? What would you do now? What are at least three pieces of data that should be stored in a data warehouse somewhere based on your interaction with *Kelly Blue Book*?
10. **'NET** Give three examples of computerized databases that are available at your college or university library.
11. **'NET** What is predictive analytics? Think about the three Web sites that you interact with most. List at least 10 pieces of information that you exchange with these Web sites that you believe have potential to become useful data that can be made into intelligence through predictive analytics.

12. Suppose a retail firm is interested in studying the effect of lighting on customer purchase behavior. Which of the following pieces of information is the least relevant and why?
    a. Amount of natural light in the store
    b. The compensation system for store salespeople
    c. The color of the walls in the store
    d. The type of lighting: fluorescent or incandescent
13. **'NET** Imagine the data collected by eBay each day. List at least five types of data that are collected through the daily operations. Describe how each type illustrates in it data, information, or intelligence. Make sure you list at least one example of each.
14. How could New Balance, a maker of athletic shoes, use RFID technology to collect data?
15. **'NET** The Spider's Apprentice is a Web site that provides many useful tips about using search engines. Go to http://www.monash.com/spidap.html to learn the ins and outs of search engines.

Research Activities

1. **'NET** To learn more about data warehousing, go to http://www.dwinfocenter.org. How could a company that provides music and video files via the Internet use a data warehouse?
2. **'NET** Use the Internet to see if you can find information to answer the following questions:
    a. What is the weather in Denver today?
    b. What are four restaurants in the French Quarter in New Orleans?
    c. What is the most popular novel among teenage girls age 14–16?

Case 2.1 Harvard Cooperative Society

© GETTY IMAGES/ PHOTODISC GREEN

From his office window overlooking the main floor of the Harvard Cooperative Society, CEO Jerry Murphy can glance down and see customers shopping.[16] They make their way through the narrow aisles of the crowded department store, picking up a sweatshirt here, trying on a baseball cap there, checking out the endless array of merchandise that bears the Harvard University insignia.

Watching Murphy, you can well imagine the Co-op's founders, who started the store in 1882, peering through the tiny windowpanes to keep an eye on the shop floor. Was the Harvard Square store attracting steady traffic? Were the college students buying enough books and supplies for the Coop to make a profit? Back then, it was tough to answer those questions precisely. The owners had to watch and wait, relying only on their gut feelings to know how things were going from minute to minute.

Now, more than a hundred years later, Murphy can tell you, down to the last stock-keeping unit, how he's doing at any given moment. His window on the business is the PC that sits on his desk.

All day long it delivers up-to-the-minute, easy-to-read electronic reports on what's selling and what's not, which items are running low in inventory and which have fallen short of forecast. In a matter of seconds, the computer can report gross margins for any product or supplier, and Murphy can decide whether the margins are fat enough to justify keeping the supplier or product on board. "We were in the 1800s, and we had to move ahead," he says of the $55 million business.

Questions

1. What is a decision support system? What advantages does a decision support system have for a business like the Harvard Cooperative Society?
2. How would the decision support system of a business like the Harvard Cooperative Society differ from that of a major corporation?
3. Briefly outline the components of the Harvard Cooperative Society's decision support system.

CHAPTER 3
THE MARKETING RESEARCH PROCESS

LEARNING OUTCOMES

After studying this chapter, you should be able to

1. Classify marketing research as either exploratory research, descriptive research, or causal research
2. List the major stages of the marketing research process and the steps within each
3. Understand the concepts of theory and hypothesis and the critical role they play in research
4. Know the difference between a research project and a research program

Chapter Vignette: Changing for Wired Students

It has been said that today's students are wired differently than their predecessors. Well, in today's high-tech world, students don't even need a wire to be different.[1] The changing educational technologies and environment mean today's students enjoy many more choices than did their parents. Universities offer new degree programs in varied and specific fields including areas like sports marketing and gaming management, and graduate degrees can be obtained without ever physically stepping foot on an actual university campus. Options for nontraditional students who have difficulty attending day classes or devoting years of study to obtaining a degree have grown exponentially. The University of Phoenix, Strayer University, and Nova Southeast typify institutions that specifically cater to those seeking a nontraditional degree program. These competitive pressures have led even the most traditional universities to rethink the traditional "sage on the stage" approach and conventional academic calendars.

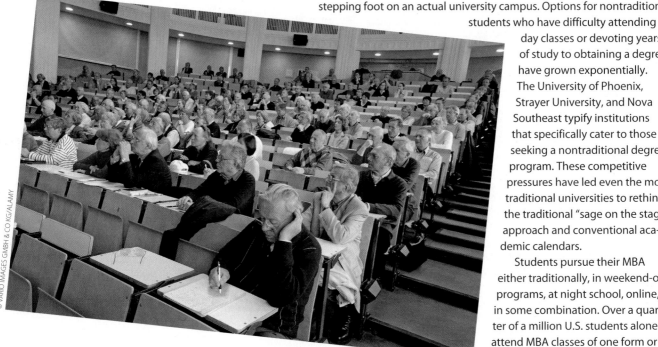

© VARIO IMAGES GMBH & CO KG/ALAMY

Students pursue their MBA either traditionally, in weekend-only programs, at night school, online, or in some combination. Over a quarter of a million U.S. students alone attend MBA classes of one form or another at any given time. In urban areas, such as the Dallas-Fort Worth, Texas area, there are sometimes a dozen or more institutions offering an MBA. It is clear that the market for the MBA degree is particularly competitive and the fact is that those universities that offer a market-oriented program are most attractive to students. Marketing research can help accomplish this by addressing questions such as the following:

- How do consumers trade off convenience with quality perceptions?
- Will offering courses online expand the pool of MBA program applicants?
- Who are the key sources of competition?
- When is the best time to offer classes? Should schools offer a weekend program?

- Where is the best place to hold classes? Should classes be offered in multiple locations? Should a program be offered overseas?
- How are nontraditional vis-à-vis traditional MBA programs viewed in terms of value, quality, and prestige?
- Is demand sufficient? That is, are there enough potential students to make this financially feasible?
- How can a particular MBA program be differentiated from competing schools?
- Can a business school better accomplish the mission of the university with an online MBA program?

The competitive MBA market typifies the landscape of many marketing firms. Clearly, universities could benefit from marketing research addressing some of these key questions. Each university maintains its own academic standard while still trying to attract enough students to make its MBA program feasible. The competitive landscape is filled with both potential opportunities and potential problems. Decisions made by university faculty and administrators will determine how successfully each school deals with the changing marketplace.

Introduction

This chapter focuses on the relationship between business decisions and marketing research. Business success is determined directly by the quality of decisions made by key personnel. Researchers contribute to decision making in several key ways. These include

1. Helping to better define the current situation
2. Defining the firm—determining how consumers, competitors, and employees view the firm
3. Providing ideas for product improvements or possible new product development
4. Testing ideas that will assist in implementing the marketing mix strategy for the firm
5. Examining how correct a certain marketing theory is in a given situation

The chapter introduces the types of research that allow researchers to provide input to key decision makers. Product design is also discussed because effective design depends on marketing research. Last but not least, the chapter discusses stages in the marketing research process.

Types of Marketing Research

Marketing research can reduce uncertainty. It also helps focus decision making. Sometimes marketing researchers know exactly what their marketing problems are and can design careful studies to test specific hypotheses. A university may face a problem with an out-of-date curriculum. Awareness of this problem could be based on input from employers, students, and alumni. The problem could even be contributing to low enrollment. How should the faculty and administration decide to address this problem? They may devise a careful test exploring which of three new curricula can be implemented to improve this perception. This type of research is problem-oriented and seems relatively unambiguous. The marketing research may culminate with researchers preparing a report suggesting the relative effect of each alternative curriculum on enrollment. The decision should follow relatively directly from the research.

In more ambiguous circumstances, management may be totally unaware of a marketing problem. Alternatively, the company may be scanning the environment for opportunities. For example, a small undergraduate university in a mid-sized Colorado town may consider adding an online MBA program. University administrators may have little idea as to how this would affect the image of their school among current students, employers, alumni, or faculty. They also may not know exactly what programs would be most desired by its current or potential customer bases. Some preliminary research may be necessary to gain insights into the nature of such a situation. Without it, the situation may remain too ambiguous to make more than a seat-of-the-pants decision. Marketing research is almost certainly needed.

Marketing research can be classified on the basis of either technique or purpose. Experiments, surveys, and observational studies are just a few common research techniques. Classifying research by its purpose shows how the nature of a decision situation influences the research methodology. The following section introduces the three types of marketing research:

1. Exploratory
2. Descriptive
3. Causal

Matching the particular decision situation with the right type of research is important in obtaining useful research results.

Exploratory Research

exploratory research

Conducted to clarify ambiguous situations or discover ideas that may be potential business opportunities.

Exploratory research is conducted to clarify ambiguous situations or discover ideas that may be potential business opportunities. Exploratory research is *not* intended to provide conclusive evidence from which to determine a particular course of action. In this sense, it is not an end unto itself. Researchers usually undertake exploratory research with the full expectation that more research will be needed to provide more conclusive evidence. Using exploratory research can sometimes also make the difference in determining the relevance of follow-up research. Rushing into detailed surveys before it is clear exactly what decisions need to be made can waste time, money, and effort by providing irrelevant information.

■ INNOVATION AND EXPLORATORY RESEARCH

Exploratory research is particularly useful in new product development.[2] Sony and Honda have each been instrumental in developing robot technology.[3] Making a functional robot that can move around, perform basic functions, carry out instructions, and even carry on a conversation isn't really a problem. What Sony and Honda have to research is what market opportunities may exist based on robot technology. Research can allow consumers to interact with robots as a form of exploratory research. The observational research suggest that consumers interact much more when the robot has human qualities, including the ability to walk on two legs. Researchers noticed that people will actually talk to the robot (which can understand basic oral commands) more when it has human qualities. In addition, consumers do seem entertained by a walking, talking, dancing robot. Thus, this has allowed each company to form more specific research questions focusing on the relative value of a robot as an entertainment device or as a security guard.

■ EXPLORATORY RESEARCH AND PROBLEM SOLVING

In our university example, it could be that exploratory research is needed to help identify concerns about nontraditional course delivery for business classes. This exploratory research should include open-ended interviews with faculty, students, and alumni. By doing so, specific hypotheses can be developed that test the relative attractiveness of alternative curricula to students and the effect of online instruction on job satisfaction and on alumni quality perceptions.[4] These hypotheses may be tested by either or both of the remaining two research types. The Research Snapshot on the next page describes how exploratory research helps companies understand what a mascot like the Aflac duck or a pair of M&Ms can do for their performance.

Exploratory research can be useful in helping to better define a marketing problem or identify a market opportunity. Problems are usually not as obvious as they may seem. In fact, they usually are not easily observable. Instead, problems are inferred from **symptoms**, which are observable cues that serve as a signal of a problem because they are caused by that problem. A drop in market share is generally only a symptom of a market problem and not the problem itself. Research may help identify what is causing this symptom so that decision makers can actually attack the problem, not just the symptom. Patients don't usually go to the doctor and point out their problem (like an ulcer). Instead, they point out symptoms (upset stomach). Similarly, decision makers usually hear about symptoms and often need help from research to identify and attack problems. Whether facing an opportunity or a problem, businesses need quality information to deal effectively with these situations. Decision situations are also characterized by how much certainty or ambiguity exists.

symptoms

Observable cues that serve as a signal of a problem because they are caused by that problem.

Cute, Funny, or Sexy? What Makes a Mascot Tick?

Has the Pillsbury Doughboy ever changed? How old should the Brawny (paper towel) man be? What should the M&Ms characters be named? Why is Aflac synonymous with a duck? Does a country need a mascot? In truth, a lot of research goes into these kinds of questions beginning with exploratory research. For instance, focus groups involving female consumers revealed a considerable amount of intimate discussion about the Brawny man. Thus, it seemed that a sexy Brawny man would yield a better response than a humorous or intelligent Brawny man. When England developed an official mascot in conjunction with the World Cup, the desire to cultivate children's affinity led to more of a cute Sir George.

Mr. Peanut, the icon for Planter's Peanuts, has actually changed very little since his introduction in the 1920s. He looks good for his age. Again, exploratory research suggests generally positive comments about Mr. Peanut, so only minor changes

in the color scheme have been introduced. A few years ago, exploratory research led to some further tests of a Mr. Peanut in Bermuda shorts, but the tests proved overwhelmingly negative, sending Planters back to a more original peanut!

Similarly, simple exploratory research merely asked a few consumers for their reactions to the Mars M&M characters. Mars was interested in discovering names for the characters. They found that most consumers simply referred to them by their colors. This piece of information became useful in shaping future research and marketing strategy.

Sources: Voight, Joan, "Mascot Makeover: The Risky Business of Tampering with Brand Icons," *Adweek* (July 7, 2003), 20–26; Elliot, Stuart, "Updating a venerable character, or tarnishing a sterling reputation?" *The New York Times*, (March 19, 2004), C5; "A Mascot for All Seasons: Arise, Sir George," *License! Europe*, (January 31, 2006).

Descriptive Research

Descriptive research, as the name implies, describes characteristics of objects, people, groups, organizations, or environments. Put more simply, descriptive research tries to "paint a picture" of a given situation. Marketing managers frequently need to determine who purchases a product, portray the size of the market, identify competitors' actions, and so on. Descriptive research addresses *who, what, when, where, why,* and *how* questions.

Descriptive research often helps describe market segments. For example, marketing researchers used simple descriptive surveys to describe consumers who are heavy consumers (buy a lot) of organic food products. The resulting report showed that these consumers tend to live in coastal cities with populations over 500,000, with the majority residing on the West Coast. The most frequent buyers of organic foods are affluent men and women ages 45–54 (36 percent) and 18–34 (35 percent).[5] Interestingly, consumers who buy organic foods are not very brand-oriented—81 percent of them cannot name a single organic brand. Research such as this helps high-quality supermarkets such as Whole Foods make location decisions. Over half of Whole Foods' food products are organic.

Similarly, the university considering the addition of an online MBA program might benefit from descriptive research profiling the market and the potential customers. Online customers are not identical to the traditional

descriptive research

Describes characteristics of objects, people, groups, organizations, or environments; tries to "paint a picture" of a given situation.

Descriptive research about consumers who buy organic food has paid off for the Whole Foods chain of stores.

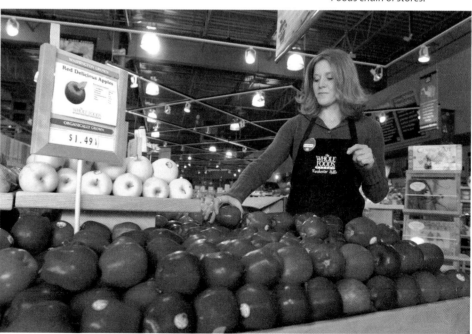

The Squeaky Wheel Gets ...

Marketing problems are often people problems. Disgruntled marketing employees can lack creativity and lose the motivation that drives a strong work ethic. What appears to be a marketing problem can reallly be an internal people problem. With this in mind, what kind of things do coworkers do that irritate other coworkers? Several descriptive research studies address this by surveying employees and having them rate potentially problematic behaviors based on how annoying they actually are. Perhaps the resulting list isn't surprising, but some of the most problematic coworker habits and practices include the following.

- Slacking—the perception that a coworker is simply not pulling his or her share of the work is one of the most frequently mentioned annoying behaviors.
- Abusing the printer or copier—printing things unnecessarily, wasting paper, occupying the printer or copier or both with personal documents and slowing down the work.
  - Leaving used tea bags in the office sink.
  - Currying favor with the boss.

- Constantly eating and leaving behind crumbs and warming things in the microwave that leave behind strong odors (i.e., pickled cabbage, fish, popcorn, etc.)
- Over air-conditioning the office making it cold as a meat locker.
- Being fortunate enough to have a window and then keeping the shade closed all day.
- Coming in late but leaving on time.
- Noisiness—squeaky chairs, loud laughter, loud phone calls, annoying body noises.

The question becomes how these annoying habits should be dealt with. Should employees confront each other or should management create policies that restrict all possible annoying behavior? Is that possible? Maybe this calls for more research.

Sources: "What Your Workers Find Most Annoying," *Legal Alert for Supervisors*, 3, no. 64 (2008) 3; Piccolo, C. "Irritating Coworkers," *Medhunters.com*, (2008), http://www.medhunters.com/articles/irritatingCoworkers.html, accessed July 20, 2008; "Xerox Survey Reveals Environmental Pet Peeves Among Office Workers," *Graphic Arts Online* (April 17, 2008), www.graphicartsonline.com, accessed June 18, 2008; Nudd, T., "Pet Peeves," *Adweek*, 46 (September 26, 2005), 33.

MBA student. They tend to be older than the average 24-year-old traditional student, instead averaging about 30 years of age. Also, they tend to live in rural communities, be more introverted, and expect a higher workload than traditional students. Another key statistic is that the dropout rate for online students is significantly higher than for traditional MBA students. Nearly 14 percent of online students drop before completing a course as compared to 7.2 percent for traditional in-class students. For this and other reasons, online students are much more costly to serve.[6] What makes a coworker irritating? The Research Snapshot above describes this phenomenon using descriptive research results.

Accuracy is critically important in descriptive research. If a descriptive study misestimates a university's demand for its MBA offering by even a few students, it can mean the difference between the program sustaining itself or being a drain on already scarce resources. For instance, if a cohort group of twenty-five students is predicted, but only fifteen students actually sign up, the program will likely not generate enough revenue to sustain itself. Therefore, it is easy to see that descriptive research forecasting sales revenue and costs or describing consumer attitudes, satisfaction, and commitment must be accurate or decision making will suffer.

Unlike exploratory research, descriptive studies are conducted with a considerable understanding of the situation being studied. This understanding, which may have been developed in part from exploratory research, directs the study toward specific issues. Later, we will discuss the role of research questions and hypotheses. These statements help greatly in designing and implementing a descriptive study. Without these, the researcher would have little or no idea of what questions to ask.

Survey research typifies a descriptive study. Many surveys try to answer questions such as "Why are brand A's sales lower than brand B's sales?" In other words, a **diagnostic analysis** seeks to diagnose reasons for market outcomes and focuses specifically on the beliefs and feelings consumers have about and toward competing products. A research study trying to diagnose slumping French wine sales might ask consumers their beliefs about the taste of French, Australian, and American wines. The results might indicate a deficiency in taste, suggesting that consumers do not believe French wines taste as fruity as do the others. Descriptive research can sometimes provide an explanation by diagnosing differences among competitors, but descriptive research does not provide direct evidence of causality.

diagnostic analysis

Seeks to diagnose reasons for market outcomes and focuses specifically on the beliefs and feelings consumers have about and toward competing products.

Causal Research

If a decision maker knows what causes important outcomes like sales and employee satisfaction, then he or she can shape firm decisions in a positive way. Causal inferences are very powerful because they lead to greater control. **Causal research** allows causal inferences to be made. That is, causal research seeks to identify cause-and-effect relationships to show that one event actually makes another happen. Rain causes grass to get wet. Rain is the cause and wet grass is the effect.

Exploratory and/or descriptive research usually precedes causal research. In causal studies, researchers typically have a good understanding of the phenomena being studied. Because of this, the research can make an educated prediction about the cause and effect relationships that will be tested. Although greater knowledge of the situation is a good thing, it doesn't come without a price. Causal research designs can take a long time to implement. Also, they often involve intricate designs that can be very expensive. Thus, even though managers may often want the assurance that causal inferences can bring, they are not always willing to spend the time and money it takes to get them.

causal research
Allows causal inferences to be made; seeks to identify cause-and-effect relationships.

■ CAUSALITY

Ideally, managers want to know how a change in one event (say, using a new product logo) will change another event of interest, like sales. Causal research attempts to establish that when we do one thing, another thing will follow. A **causal inference** is just such a conclusion. While we use the term "cause" all the time in everyday language, scientifically establishing something as a cause is not so easy and even researchers sometimes confuse causality with correlation. A causal inference can only be supported when very specific causal evidence exists. Three critical pieces of causal evidence are

1. Temporal Sequence
2. Concomitant Variance
3. Nonspurious Association

causal inference
A conclusion that when one thing happens, another specific thing will follow.

Temporal Sequence

Temporal sequence deals with the time order of events. In other words, having an *appropriate causal order of events,* or temporal sequence, is one criterion for causality. The cause must occur before the effect. It would be difficult for a restaurant manager to blame a decrease in sales on a new chef if the drop in sales occurred before the new chef arrived. If advertising causes sales, the advertising must appear before the change in sales.

temporal sequence
One of three criteria for causality; deals with the time order of events—the cause must occur before the effect.

Concomitant Variation

Concomitant variation occurs when two events "covary," meaning they vary systematically. In causal terms, concomitant variation means that when a change in the cause occurs, a change in the outcome also is observed. Correlation, which we discuss in a later chapter, is often used to represent concomitant variation. Causality cannot possibly exist when there is no systematic variation between the variables. For example, if a retail store never changes its employees' vacation policy, then the vacation policy cannot possibly be responsible for a change in customer satisfaction. There is no correlation between the two events. On the other hand, if two events vary together, one event may be causing the other. If a university increases its number of online MBA course offerings and experiences a decrease in enrollment in its traditional in-class MBA offerings, the online course offerings may be causing the decrease. But, the systematic variation alone doesn't guarantee it.

concomitant variation
One of three criteria for causality; occurs when two events "covary," meaning they vary systematically.

Nonspurious Association

Nonspurious association means any covariation between a cause and an effect is indeed due to the cause and not simply due to some other variable. A spurious association is one that is not true. Often, a causal inference cannot be made even though the other two conditions exist because both the cause and effect have some common cause; that is, both may be influenced by a third variable. For instance, a city worker notices an alarming trend. On days when a large number of ice cream cones are sold at Virginia Beach, more people drown. So, when ice cream sales go up, so does drowning. Should the city decide to ban ice cream? This would be silly because the concomitant variation observed between

nonspurious association
One of three criteria for causality; means any covariation between a cause and an effect is true and not simply due to some other variable.

ice cream consumption and drowning is spurious. On days when the beach is particularly crowded, more ice cream is sold and more people drown. So, the number of people at the beach, being associated with both, may cause both. Exhibit 3.1 illustrates the concept of spurious association.

EXHIBIT 3.1 **Ice Cream is a Spurious Cause of Drowning**

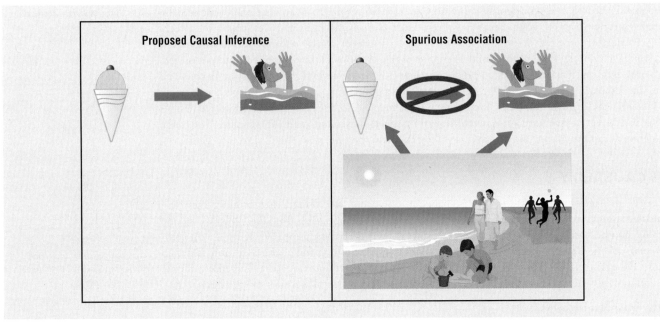

Establishing evidence of nonspuriousness can be difficult. If a researcher finds a third variable that is related to both the cause and effect, causing a significant drop in the correlation between the cause and effect, then a causal inference becomes difficult to support. Although the researcher would like to rule out the possibility of any alternative causes, it is impossible to observe the effect of all variables on the correlation between the cause and effect. Therefore, the researcher must use theory to identify the most likely "third" variables that would relate significantly to both the cause and effect. The research must control for these variables in some way, as we will see in Chapter 9. In addition, the researcher should use theory to make sure that the cause-and-effect relationship truly makes sense.

In summary, causal research should do all of the following:

1. Establish the appropriate causal order or sequence of events
2. Measure the concomitant variation (relationship) between the presumed cause and the presumed effect
3. Examine the possibility of spuriousness by considering the presence of alternative plausible causal factors

■ EXPERIMENTS

experiment

A carefully controlled study in which the researcher manipulates a proposed cause and observes any corresponding change in the proposed effect.

experimental variable

Represents the proposed cause which the researcher controls by manipulating its value

manipulation

Means that the researcher alters the level of the variable in specific increments.

Marketing *experiments* hold the greatest potential for establishing cause-and-effect relationships. An **experiment** is a carefully controlled study in which the researcher manipulates a proposed cause and observes any corresponding change in the proposed effect. An **experimental variable** represents the proposed cause and is controlled by the researcher who manipulates its value. **Manipulation** means that the researcher alters the level of the variable in specific increments. So, managers often want to make decisions about the price and distribution of a new product. In other words, both price and the type of retail outlet in which a product is placed are considered potential causes of sales. A study can be designed which manipulates both the price and distribution.

Suppose a company produces a new video game console called the Wee Station. They may manipulate price by offering it for $100 among some consumers and $300 among others. Retail distribution may be manipulated by selling the Wee Station at discount stores in some consumer markets and at specialty electronic stores in others. The retailer can examine whether price and distribution cause sales by comparing the sales results in each of the four conditions created. Exhibit 3.2 illustrates this study. We will say much more about manipulations and experimental designs in Chapter 9.

EXHIBIT 3.2
Testing for Causes with an Experiment

	Wee Station Sales by Condition	
	High Price	**Low Price**
Specialty Distribution	Peoria, Illinois: Retail Price: $300 Retail Store: Best Buy	Des Moines, Iowa: Retail Price: $100 Retail Store: Best Buy
General Distribution	St. Louis, Missouri: Retail Price: $300 Retail Store: Big Cheap-Mart	Kansas City, Missouri: Retail Price: $100 Retail Store: Big Cheap-Mart

Assuming that Wee Station consumers are the same in each of these cities, the extent to which price and distribution cause sales can be examined by comparing the sales results in each of these 4 conditions.

Most basic scientific studies in marketing (for example, the development of consumer behavior theory) ultimately seek to identify cause-and-effect relationships. One often associates science with experiments. To predict a relationship between, say, price and perceived quality of a product, causal studies often create statistical experiments with controls that establish contrast groups.

Uncertainty Influences the Type of Research

The most appropriate type and the amount of research needed are determined in part by how much uncertainty surrounds the marketing situation motivating the research. Exhibit 3.3 contrasts the types of research and illustrates that exploratory research is conducted during the early stages of decision making. At this point, the decision situation is usually highly ambiguous and management is very uncertain about what actions should be taken. When management is aware of the problem but lacks some knowledge, descriptive research is usually conducted. Causal research requires sharply defined problems.

Each type of research also produces a different type of result. In many ways, exploratory research is the most productive since it should yield large numbers of ideas. It is discovery-oriented and as such, unstructured approaches can be very successful. Too much structure in this type of

EXHIBIT 3.3 **Characteristics of Different Types of Marketing Research**

	Exploratory Research	**Descriptive Research**	**Causal Research**
Amount of Uncertainty Characterizing Decision Situation	Highly ambiguous	Partially defined	Clearly defined
Key Research Statement	Research question	Research question	Research hypothesis
When Conducted?	Early stage of decision making	Later stages of decision making	Later stages of decision making
Usual Research Approach	Unstructured	Structured	Highly structured
Examples	"Our sales are declining for no apparent reason" "What kinds of new products are fast-food customers interested in?"	"What kind of people patronize our stores compared to our primary competitor?" "What product features are most important to our customers?"	"Will consumers buy more products in a blue package?" "Which of two advertising campaigns will be more effective?"
Nature of Results	Discovery oriented, productive, but still speculative. Often in need of further research.	Can be confirmatory although more research is sometimes still needed. Results can be managerially actionable.	Confirmatory oriented. Fairly conclusive with managerially actionable results often obtained.

research may lead to more narrowly focused types of responses that could stifle creativity. Thus, although it is productive, its results usually need further testing and evaluation before they can be made actionable. At times, managers do take managerial action based only on exploratory research results. Sometimes, management may not be able to or may not care to invest the time and resources needed to conduct further research. Decisions made based only on exploratory research can be more risky since exploratory research does not test ideas among a scientific sample.[7] For instance, a business school professor may ask a class of current MBA students for ideas about an online program. Although the students may provide many ideas that sound very good, even the best of them has not been tested on a sample of potential online MBA students.

Descriptive research is usually focused around one or more fairly specific research questions. It is usually much more structured, and for many common types of marketing research, it can yield managerially actionable results. For example, descriptive research is often used to profile a market segment both demographically and psychographically. Results like this can greatly assist firms in deciding when and where to offer their goods or services for sale.

Causal research is usually very tightly focused around a small number of research hypotheses. Experimental methods require tight control of research procedures. Thus, causal research is highly structured to produce specific results. Causal research results are often managerially actionable since they suggest that if management changes the value of a "cause," some desirable effect will come about. So, by changing a package's color, i.e., the cause, from orange to blue, higher sales occur.

Stages in the Research Process

Marketing research, like other forms of scientific inquiry, involves a sequence of highly interrelated activities. The stages of the research process overlap continuously, and it is somewhat of an oversimplification to state that every research project has exactly the same ordered sequence of activities. Nevertheless, marketing research often follows a general pattern. The stages are

1. Defining the research objectives
2. Planning a research design
3. Planning a sample
4. Collecting the data
5. Analyzing the data
6. Formulating the conclusions and preparing the report

Exhibit 3.4 portrays these six stages as a cyclical or circular-flow process. The circular-flow concept is used because conclusions from research studies can generate new ideas and knowledge that can lead to further investigation. Thus, there is a dashed connection between *conclusions and reporting* and *defining the research objectives*. Notice also, though, that management is in the center of the process. The research objectives cannot be properly defined without managerial input. After all, it is the manager who ultimately has to make the decision. It is also the manager who may ask for additional research once a report is given.

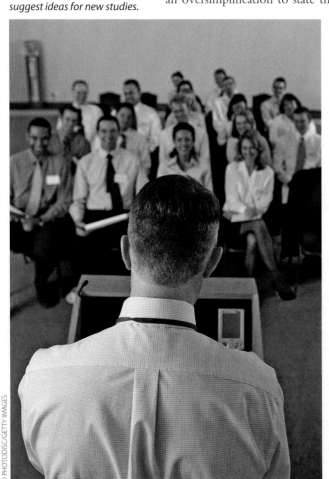

Research is sometimes directly actionable. The results may also suggest ideas for new studies.

Alternatives in the Research Process

The researcher must choose among a number of alternatives during each stage of the research process. The research process can be compared to a map. There is no single right or best path for all journeys. The road one takes depends on where one wants to go and the resources (money, time, labor, and so on) available for the trip. The map analogy is useful for the marketing

EXHIBIT 3.4
Stages of the Research Process

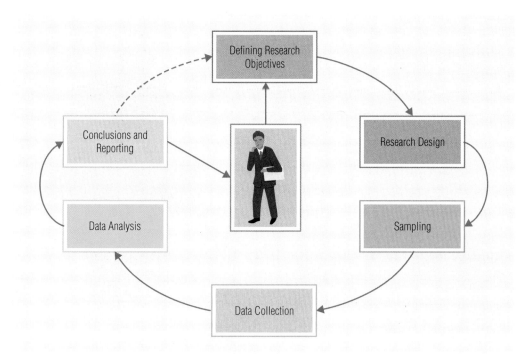

researcher because there are several paths that can be followed at each stage. When there are severe time constraints, the quickest path may be most appropriate. When money and human resources are plentiful, the appropriate path may be quite different.

The following sections briefly describe the six stages of the research process. (Each stage is discussed in greater depth in later chapters.) Exhibit 3.5 on the next page shows the decisions that researchers must make in each stage. This discussion of the research process begins with research objectives, because most research projects are initiated to remedy managers' uncertainty about some aspect of the firm's marketing program.

Defining the Research Objectives

Exhibit 3.5 shows that the research process begins with **research objectives**. Research objectives are the goals to be achieved by conducting research. In consulting, the term **deliverables** is often used to describe the objectives to a research client. The genesis of the research objectives lies in the type of decision situation faced. The objectives may involve exploring some new product within a new market. Alternatively, they may involve testing the effect of some policy change on service quality. Different types of objectives lead to different types of research designs.

In applied or market research, the objectives cannot be listed until there is an understanding of the decision situation. This understanding must be shared between the actual decision maker and the lead researcher. We often describe this understanding as a problem statement. In general usage, the word *problem* suggests that something has gone wrong. This isn't always the case before research gets started. Actually, the research objective may be to simply clarify a situation, define an opportunity, or monitor and evaluate current operations. The research objectives cannot be developed until managers and researchers have agreed on the actual business "problem" that will be addressed by the research. Thus, they set out to "discover" this problem through a series of interviews and through a document called a research proposal.

It should be noted that this process is oriented more toward *discovery* than *confirmation*. Managers and researchers alike may not have a clear-cut understanding of the situation at the outset of the research process. Managers may only be able to list symptoms that could indicate a problem. Sales may be declining, but management may not know the exact nature of the problem. Thus, the problem statement often is made only in general terms; what is to be investigated is not yet specifically identified.

research objectives

The goals to be achieved by conducting research.

deliverables

The term used often in consulting to describe research objectives to a research client.

EXHIBIT 3.5 **Flowchart of the Marketing Research Process**

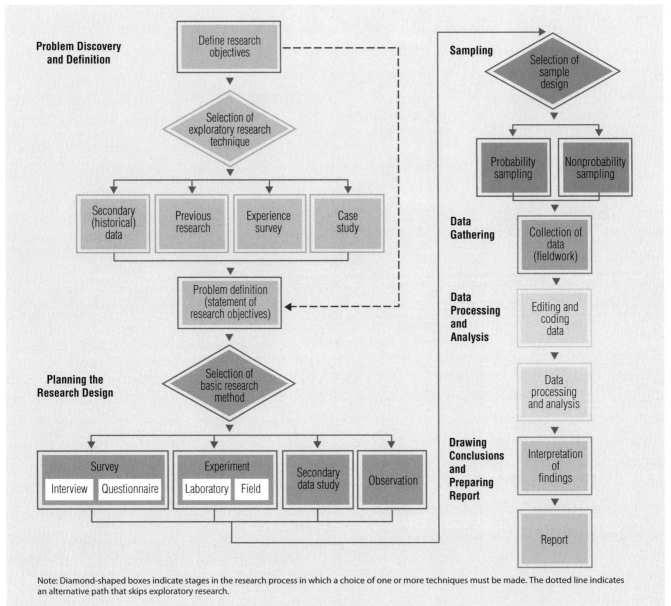

Note: Diamond-shaped boxes indicate stages in the research process in which a choice of one or more techniques must be made. The dotted line indicates an alternative path that skips exploratory research.

■ DEFINING THE MANAGERIAL DECISION SITUATION

In marketing research, the adage "a problem well defined is a problem half solved" is worth remembering. This adage emphasizes that an orderly definition of the research problem lends a sense of direction to the investigation. Careful attention to problem definition allows the researcher to set the proper research objectives. If the purpose of the research is clear, the chances of collecting necessary and relevant information and not collecting surplus information will be much greater.

Albert Einstein noted that "the formulation of a problem is often more essential than its solution."[8] This is good advice for marketing managers. Managers naturally concentrate on finding the right answer rather than asking the right question. They also want one solution quickly rather than having to spend time considering many possible solutions. Properly defining a problem can be more difficult than solving it. In marketing research, if data are collected before the nature of the marketing problem is carefully thought out, they probably will not allow useful results.

Marketing research must have clear objectives and definite designs. Unfortunately, little or no planning goes into the formulation of many research problems. Consider the case of the Ha-Pah-Shu-Tse brand of Indian fried bread mix (the name "Ha-Pah-Shu-Tse" comes from the Pawnee

Indian word for red corn). The owner of the company, Mr. Ha-Pah-Shu-Tse, thought that his product, one of the few Native American food products available in the United States, was not selling because it was not widely advertised. He wanted a management consulting group to conduct some research concerning advertising themes. However, the management consultants pointed out to the Ha-Pah-Shu-Tse family that using the family name on the bread mix might be a foremost source of concern. They suggested that consumer behavior research investigating the brand image might be a better initial starting point rather than advertising copy research. Family management agreed.

Defining the decision situation must precede the research objectives. Frequently the marketing researcher will not be involved until line management has discovered that some information about a particular aspect of the marketing mix is needed. Even at this point the exact nature of the situation may be poorly defined. Once a problem area has been discovered, the marketing researcher and management together can begin the process of precisely defining it.

Frequently, research is conducted without a clear definition of the research's objectives. Too many researchers forget that the best place to begin a research project is at the end. Knowing what is to be accomplished determines the research process. An error or omission in problem objectives is likely to be a costly mistake that cannot be corrected in later stages of the process. Chapter 5 discusses problem objectives in greater detail.

■ EXPLORATORY RESEARCH

Exploratory research can be used to help identify the decisions that need to be made. The preliminary activities undertaken can yield results that place the situation into a more easily researched context. Exploratory research can progressively narrow the scope of the research topic and help transform ambiguous problems into well-defined ones that yield specific research objectives. By investigating any existing studies on the subject, talking with knowledgeable individuals, and informally investigating the situation, the researcher can progressively sharpen the concepts. After such exploration, the researcher should know exactly which data to collect during the formal phases of the project and how to conduct the project. Exhibit 3.5 indicates that researchers must decide whether to use one or more exploratory research techniques or bypass this stage altogether.

The marketing researcher can employ techniques from four basic categories to obtain insights and gain a clearer idea of the problem: previous research, pilot studies, case studies, and experience surveys. This section will briefly discuss previous research and pilot studies interviews, the most popular type of pilot study.

literature review

A directed search of published works, including periodicals and books, that discusses theory and presents empirical results that are relevant to the topic at hand.

The library contains a wealth of information. Studies forming a literature review can be found in the library.

■ PREVIOUS RESEARCH

As a general rule, researchers should first investigate previous research to see whether or not others may have addressed the same research problems previously. Previous research reports should be searched within the company's archives. In addition, some firms specialize in providing various types of research reports, such as economic forecasts. The *Census of Population* and the *Survey of Current Business* are each examples of previous research conducted by an outside source.

Literature Review

Previous research may also exist in the public domain. A **literature review** is a directed search of published works, including periodicals and books, that discusses theory and presents empirical results that are relevant to the topic at hand. A literature survey is common in applied market research studies but it is a fundamental requirement of a basic (i.e., marketing) research report.

© DIGITAL VISION/GETTY IMAGES

A business endeavor this big is best done with a lot of research. Luckily, there is a lot of previous research in the form of previous literature and reports to provide a start.

Literature reviews are conducted using traditional Internet and library research tools. Modern electronic search engines available in most university libraries have made literature reviews simpler and faster.

Suppose a real estate developer is interested in developing a piece of commercial property. In particular, the site has been identified as a location for a lifestyle center containing places for people to shop, be entertained, dine, work and live—all in one location. Success will depend on attracting people to this place and creating the right feel. The decision to move forward with the project involves many dimensions including the location, tenant mix, the physical design or atmosphere of the place, which is affected by things like color, scents, and architecture. Obviously, prudence calls for more than a cursory study of the feasibility of this project and the implications for different types of designs. Before launching an exhaustive study, the researcher can first look through research journals and find hundreds of studies that address the different decision dimensions.[9] This may, for example, give some idea on what type of architecture will work best to create the right atmosphere and enable a smaller set of possibilities to be studied further.

Pilot Studies

Almost all consumers take a test drive before buying a car. A pilot study serves a similar purpose for the researcher. A **pilot study** is a small-scale research project that collects data from respondents similar to those that will be used in the full study. It can serve as a guide for a larger study or examine specific aspects of the research to see if the selected procedures will actually work as intended. Pilot studies are critical in refining measures and reducing the risk that the full study will be fatally flawed. This is particularly true for experimental research, which depends critically on valid manipulations of experimental variables.[10] Pilot studies also often are useful in fine-tuning research objectives. Pilot studies are sometimes referred to as pretests. A **pretest** is a very descriptive term indicating a small-scale study in which the results are only preliminary and intended only to assist in design of a subsequent study.

Focus group interviews are sometimes used as a pilot study. A **focus group** interview brings together six to twelve people in a loosely structured format. The technique is based on the assumption that individuals are more willing to talk about things when they are able to do so within a group discussion format. Focus group respondents sometimes feed on each other's comments to develop ideas that would be difficult to express in a different interview format. Focus groups are discussed much more in Chapter 5.

For example, suppose a consultant is hired by Carrefour to research the way consumers react to sales promotions. Carrefour is second in size only to Wal-Mart, operating nearly 11,000 stores in twenty-nine countries (**www.carrefour.fr**). Carrefour began in France over forty-five years ago and pioneered the discount hypermarket format. More specifically, the researcher may be asked to help management decide whether or not the size of promotions should vary with national culture. In other words, the basic research question is whether or not culture influences consumer perceptions of sales promotions.[11] A pretest may be needed to examine whether or not differences in currency might interfere with these perceptions, or whether or not the different terms that refer to promotions and discounts can be translated into the languages of each culture. For example, is

pilot study

A small-scale research project that collects data from respondents similar to those to be used in the full study.

pretest

A small-scale study in which the results are only preliminary and intended only to assist in design of a subsequent study.

focus group

A small group discussion about some research topic led by a moderator who guides discussion among the participants.

a discount expressed in Korean won interpreted the same way as a discount expressed in euros? Using mid 2008 exchange rates, each euro equals about $1.60, whereas a single dollar is worth about 1,020 won.[12] As a result, a €1 (1 Euro) discount means a savings of over 1,600 won!

Exploratory research need not always follow a structured design. Because the purpose of exploratory research is to gain insights and discover new ideas, researchers may use considerable creativity and flexibility. Some companies perform exploratory research routinely as part of environmental scanning. If the conclusions made during this stage suggest marketing opportunities, the researcher is in a position to begin planning a formal, quantitative research project.

■ STATING RESEARCH OBJECTIVES

After identifying and clarifying the problem, with or without exploratory research, the researcher must formally state the research objectives. This statement delineates the type of research that is needed and what intelligence may result that would allow the decision maker to make informed choices. The statement of research objectives culminates the process of clarifying the managerial decision into something actionable.

A written decision statement expresses the business situation to the researcher. The research objectives try to directly address the decision statement or statements, as the case may be. As such, the research objectives represent a contract of sorts that commits the researcher to producing the needed research. This is why they are expressed as deliverables in applied market research. Research objectives drive the rest of the research process. Indeed, before proceeding, the researcher and managers must agree that the objectives are appropriate and will produce relevant information.

■ WHAT IS A THEORY?

Ultimately, theory plays a role in determining the appropriate research objectives. A **theory** is a formal, logical explanation of some events that includes descriptions of how things relate to one another. A theory is built through a process of reviewing previous findings of similar studies, simple logical deduction, and knowledge of applicable theoretical areas. For example, if a web designer is trying to decide what color the background of the page should be, the researcher may first consult previous studies examining the effects of color on package design and retail store design. He or she may also find theories that deal with the wavelength of different colors or theories that explain retail atmospherics. This may lead to specific predictions that predict blue as a good background color.[13]

theory
A formal, logical explanation of some events that includes predictions of how things relate to one another.

While it may seem that theory is only relevant to academic or basic marketing research, theory plays a role in understanding practical research as well. Before setting research objectives, the researcher must be able to describe the business situation in some coherent way. Without this type of explanation, the researcher would have little idea of where to start. Ultimately, the logical explanation helps the researcher know what variables need to be included in the study and how they may relate to one another. The Research Snapshot on the next page illustrates how theory and practice come together in marketing research.

■ WHAT IS A HYPOTHESIS?

A **hypothesis** is a formal statement explaining some outcome. Hypotheses (pl.) must be testable. In other words, when one states a hypothesis, it should be written as a proposition. For example, using our opening vignette as an example, the researcher may use theoretical reasoning to develop the following hypothesis:

hypothesis
A formal statement explaining some outcome.

H1: The more hours per week a prospective MBA student works, the more favorable the attitude toward online MBA class offerings.

In its simplest form, a hypothesis is a guess. A sales manager may hypothesize that the salespeople who are highest in product knowledge will be the most productive. An advertising manager may hypothesize that if consumers' attitudes toward a product change in a positive direction, there will be an increase in consumption of the product.

Nothing So Practical As Theory?

Theory and marketing practice do come together. First, students learn theory in their formal education. Business professors consider it good practice to blend theory and practice in their teaching. Business professionals use these theories to help shape their thinking about different business situations.

Neurology, psychobiology, anthropology, economics, and social psychology all offer relevant theories that can help explain marketing problems.

Recently, structuration theory has been proposed as a way of explaining marketing communication outcomes. The theory suggests that more focus should be placed on the communication exchanges between buyers and sellers and that if one can understand the goals of the buyer and seller involved in a communication interaction, then the outcome of the interaction can be predicted. Studies using theory of this type may assist electronic communication design in better placements of pop-up ads and hyperlinks and can also assist face-to-face sales exchanges in better predicting when a consumer is actually ready to buy.

Sources: Green, Paul E., "Theory, Practice Both Have Key MR Roles," *Marketing News*, 38 (September 15, 2004), 40–44; Schultz, Don, "Accepted Industry Truths Not Always Acceptable," *Marketing News*, 39 (October 15, 2005), 6; Stewart, D. T., "Traditional Ad Research Overlooks Interactions," *Marketing News*, 39 (November 15, 2005), 26–29.

---

empirical testing

Means that something has been examined against reality using data.

We often apply statistics to data to empirically test hypotheses. **Empirical testing** means that something has been examined against reality using data. When the data are consistent with a hypothesis, we say the hypothesis is *supported*. When the data are inconsistent with a hypothesis, we say the hypothesis is *not supported*. We are often tempted to say that we prove a hypothesis when the data conform to the prediction; this isn't really true. Because our result is based on statistics, there is always the possibility that our conclusion is wrong. Now, at times we can be very, very confident in our conclusion, but from an absolute perspective, statistics cannot prove a hypothesis is true.

Exhibit 3.6 illustrates how decision statements are linked to research objectives, which are linked to research hypotheses. Although the first two objectives each have one hypothesis, notice that the third has two. In reality, most research projects will involve more than one research objective, and each of these may often involve more than one hypothesis. Think about how you might go about trying to test the hypotheses listed in Exhibit 3.6.

Planning the Research Design

research design

A master plan that specifies the methods and procedures for collecting and analyzing the needed information.

After the researcher has formulated the research problem, he or she must develop the research design as part of the research design stage. A **research design** is a master plan that specifies the methods and procedures for collecting and analyzing the needed information. A research design provides a framework or plan of action for the research. Objectives of the study determined during

EXHIBIT 3.6

Example Decision Statements, Research Objectives, and Research Hypotheses

Decision Statement	Research Objectives	Hypotheses
What should be the retail price for product X?	Forecast sales for product X at three different prices.	Sales will be higher at $5.00 than at $4.00 or at $6.99.
In what ways can we improve our service quality?	Identify the top factors that contribute to customers' perceptions.	Cleanliness is related positively to customers' service quality service perceptions.
		Crowding is related negatively to customers' service quality perceptions.
Should we invest in a training program to reduce employee role conflict among our employees?	Determine how much role conflict influences employee job satisfaction.	Role conflict is related positively to job satisfaction.

the early stages of research are included in the design to ensure that the information collected is appropriate for solving the problem. The researcher also must determine the sources of information, the design technique (survey or experiment, for example), the sampling methodology, and the schedule and cost of the research.

■ SELECTION OF THE BASIC RESEARCH METHOD

Here again, the researcher must make a decision. Exhibit 3.5 shows four basic design techniques for descriptive and causal research: surveys, experiments, secondary data, and observation. The objectives of the study, the available data sources, the urgency of the decision, and the cost of obtaining the data will determine which method should be chosen. The managerial aspects of selecting the research design will be considered later.

The most common method of generating primary data is the survey. Most people have seen the results of political surveys by Gallup or Harris Online, and some have been respondents (members of a sample who supply answers) to marketing research questionnaires. A **survey** is a research technique in which a sample is interviewed in some form or the behavior of respondents is observed and described in some way. The term *surveyor* is most often reserved for civil engineers who describe some piece of property using a transit. Similarly, marketing researchers describe some market segment using a questionnaire. The task of writing a list of questions and designing the format of the printed or written questionnaire is an essential aspect of the development of a survey research design.

Research investigators may choose to contact respondents by telephone or mail, on the Internet, or in person. An advertiser spending nearly $3 million for thirty seconds of commercial time during the Super Bowl may telephone people to quickly gather information concerning their responses to the advertising. A forklift truck manufacturer trying to determine a cause for low sales in the wholesale grocery industry might choose a mail questionnaire because the appropriate executives are hard to reach by telephone. A manufacturer of a birth control device for men might determine the need for a versatile survey method wherein an interviewer can ask a variety of personal questions in a flexible format. While personal interviews are expensive, they are valuable because investigators can use visual aids and supplement the interviews with observations. Each of these survey methods has advantages and disadvantages. A researcher's task is to find the most appropriate way to collect the needed information.

The objective of many research projects is merely to record what can be observed—for example, the number of automobiles that pass by a proposed site for a gas station. This can be mechanically recorded or observed by humans. Research personnel known as mystery shoppers may act as customers to observe actions of sales personnel or do comparative shopping to learn prices at competing outlets. A mystery shopper is paid to pretend to be a customer and gather data about the way employees behave and the way they are treated in general. How often are store policies followed? How often are they treated courteously? Mystery shoppers can be valuable sources for observational data.

The main advantage of the observation technique is that it records behavior without relying on reports from respondents. Observational data are often collected unobtrusively and passively without a respondent's direct participation. For instance, the ACNielsen Company uses a "people meter" attached to television sets to record the programs being watched by each household member. This eliminates the possible bias of respondents stating that they watched the president's State of the Union address rather than a situation comedy on another station.

Observation is more complex than mere "nose counting," and the task is more difficult than the inexperienced researcher would imagine. Several things of interest, such as attitudes, opinions, motivations, and other intangible states of mind, simply cannot be observed.

survey

A research technique in which a sample is interviewed in some form or the behavior of respondents is observed and described in some way.

■ THE "BEST" RESEARCH DESIGN

It is argued that there is no single best research design. As such, the researcher often has several alternatives that can accomplish the stated research objectives. Consider the researcher who must forecast sales for the upcoming year. Some commonly used forecasting methods are surveying executive opinion, collecting sales force composite opinions, surveying user expectations, projecting trends, and analyzing market factors. Any one of these may yield a reliable forecast.

The ability to select the most appropriate research design develops with experience. Inexperienced researchers often jump to the conclusion that a survey methodology is usually the best design because they are most comfortable with this method. When Chicago's Museum of Science and Industry wanted to determine the relative popularity of its exhibits, it could have conducted a survey. Instead, a creative researcher familiar with other research designs suggested a far less expensive alternative: an unobtrusive observation technique. The researcher suggested that the museum merely keep track of the frequency with which the floor tiles in front of the various exhibits had to be replaced, indicating where the heaviest traffic occurred. When this was done, the museum found that the chick-hatching exhibit was the most popular. This method provided the same results as a survey but at a much lower cost.

TO THE POINT

You cannot put the same shoe on every foot.

—Publius Syrus

Sampling

Although the sampling plan is outlined in the research design, the sampling stage is a distinct phase of the research process. For convenience, however, we will treat the sample planning and the actual sample generation processes together in this section.

sampling

Involves any procedure that draws conclusions based on measurements of a portion of the population.

If you take your first bite of a steak and conclude that the entire steak needs salt to taste good, you have just conducted a sample. **Sampling** involves any procedure that draws conclusions based on measurements of a portion of the entire population. In other words, a sample is a subset from a larger population. In the steak analogy, the first bite is the sample and the entire steak is the population. If certain statistical procedures are followed, a researcher need not select every item in a population because the results of a good sample should have the same characteristics as the population as a whole. Of course, when errors are made, samples do not give reliable estimates of the population. So, should the first bite come from the edge or the center of a steak?

A famous example of error due to sampling is the 1936 *Literary Digest* fiasco. The magazine conducted a survey and predicted that Republican Alf Landon would win over Democrat Franklin D. Roosevelt by a landslide in that year's presidential election. This prediction was wrong—and the error was due to sample selection. The post-mortems showed that *Literary Digest* had sampled its readers as well as telephone subscribers. In 1936, these people were not a representative cross-section of voters, because a disproportionate number of them were Republicans.

In 2004, early "exit polls" led many to believe that John Kerry would win the U.S. Presidential election.[14] The "exit polls" were performed early on election day and done mostly in highly urban areas in the Northeast, areas that are predominantly democratic. The resulting sample of voters responding to the early exit polls did not represent the entire U.S. population, and Kerry lost to Bush by over 3 million votes, or about 3 percent of all votes cast. Thus, the accuracy of predictions from research depends on getting a sample that really matches the population.

The first sampling question to ask is "Who is to be sampled?" The answer to this primary question requires the identification of a *target population*. Defining this population and determining the sampling units may not be so easy. If, for example, a savings and loan association surveys people who already have accounts for answers to image questions, the selected sampling units will not represent *potential* customers. Specifying the target population is a crucial aspect of the sampling plan.

The next sampling issue concerns sample size. How big should the sample be? Although management may wish to examine every potential buyer of a product or service, doing so may be unnecessary as well as unrealistic. Typically, larger samples are more precise than smaller ones, but proper probability sampling can allow a small proportion of the total population to give a reliable measure of the whole. A later discussion will explain how large a sample must be in order to be truly representative of the universe or population.

The final sampling decision is how to select the sampling units. Simple random sampling may be the best known type, in which every unit in the population has an equal and known chance of being selected. However, this is only one type of sampling. For example, a cluster-sampling procedure may reduce costs and make data gathering procedures more efficient. If members of the population are found in close geographical clusters, a sampling procedure that selects area clusters rather than individual units in the population will reduce costs. Rather than selecting 1,000 individuals throughout the United States, it may be more economical to first select twenty-five counties and then sample within those counties. This will substantially reduce travel, hiring, and training costs. In determining the appropriate sampling plan, the researcher will have to select the most appropriate sampling procedure for meeting the established study objectives. Chapter 12 provides a full discussion of sampling.

Gathering Data

The data gathering stage begins once the sampling plan has been formalized. Data gathering is the process of gathering or collecting information. Data may be gathered by human observers or interviewers, or they may be recorded by machines as in the case of scanner data.

Obviously, the many research techniques involve many methods of gathering data. Surveys require direct participation by research respondents. This may involve filling out a questionnaire or interacting with an interviewer. In this sense, they are obtrusive. **Unobtrusive methods** of data gathering are those in which the subjects do not have to be disturbed for data to be collected. They may even be unaware that research is going on at all. For instance, a simple count of motorists driving past a proposed franchising location is one kind of data gathering method. However the data are collected, it is important to minimize errors in the process. For example, the data gathering should be consistent in all geographical areas. If an interviewer phrases questions incorrectly or records a respondent's statements inaccurately (not verbatim), major data collection errors will result.

unobtrusive methods

Methods in which research respondents do not have to be disturbed for data to be gathered.

Processing and Analyzing Data

■ EDITING AND CODING

After the fieldwork has been completed, the data must be converted into a format that will answer the marketing manager's questions. This is part of the data processing and analysis stage. Here, the information content will be mined from the raw data. Data processing generally begins with editing and coding the data. Editing involves checking the data collection forms for omissions, legibility, and consistency in classification. The editing process corrects problems such as interviewer errors (an answer recorded on the wrong portion of a questionnaire, for example) before the data are transferred to the computer.

Before data can be tabulated, meaningful categories and character symbols must be established for groups of responses. The rules for interpreting, categorizing, recording, and transferring the data to the data storage media are called codes. This coding process facilitates computer or hand tabulation. If computer analysis is to be used, the data are entered into the computer and verified. Computer-assisted (online) interviewing is an example of the impact of technological change on the research process. Telephone interviewers, seated at computer terminals, read survey questions displayed on the monitor. The interviewer asks the questions and then types in the respondents' answers. Thus, answers are collected and processed into the computer at the same time, eliminating intermediate steps that could introduce errors.

■ DATA ANALYSIS

Data analysis is the application of reasoning to understand the data that have been gathered. In its simplest form, analysis may involve determining consistent patterns and summarizing the relevant details revealed in the investigation. The appropriate analytical technique for data analysis will be determined by management's information requirements, the characteristics of the research design, and the nature of the data gathered. Statistical analysis may range from portraying a simple frequency distribution to more complex multivariate analyses approaches, such as multiple regression. Later chapters will discuss three general categories of statistical analysis: univariate analysis, bivariate analysis, and multivariate analysis.

data analysis

The application of reasoning to understand the data that have been gathered.

- Extra effort spent distinguishing symptoms from problems usually pays off. Tracking symptoms to root causes proves very difficult in many cases. Managers generally are focused on symptoms. Make sure the managers are interviewed with the thought in mind that the research should focus on relevant issues. Here are two tips to keep in mind.
  - Use exploratory research tools in the interviews with managers. Later in the text, we'll discuss ways to probe during an interview that may help get the discussion beyond symptoms.
  - A diagnostic analysis can be helpful at sorting relevant issues from symptoms.
- Vague research questions usually call for exploratory research. Very specific research questions usually call for a causal design. For example:
  - In what ways can Oracle leverage its brand name into new industries? Because this is a broad and relatively vague question, some exploratory research addressing the way consumers view the Oracle brand is a potential starting place for research.
  - The use of an animated character in a pop-up help window will lead consumers to be more satisfied with the information they receive from the www.edmunds.com Web site than will the use of a videotaped person. This is actually stated in hypotheses form and is very specific. It is relatively easy for the researcher to visualize the details of the study needed to test this question. A causal design seems appropriate.
- Don't overlook the first stage of the research process—defining research objectives. The deliverables are in many ways the most important part of a research proposal. Make sure that management agrees with the deliverables by securing official approval prior to moving forward with the research. Just as importantly, do not promise deliverables that cannot be fulfilled. Researchers should try to state deliverables in terms of research outcomes not in terms of decision outcomes:
  - Good deliverable: Provide a measure of consumer shopping value perceptions for Anthopolgie consumers (both store and online shoppers) and its major competitor, Urban Outfitters.
  - Poor deliverable: Increase profitability at Anthropologie by luring customers from Urban Outfitters.

Drawing Conclusions and Preparing a Report

One of the most important jobs that a researcher performs is communicating the research results. This is the final stage of the research project, but it is far from the least important. The conclusions and report preparation stage consists of interpreting the research results, describing the implications, and drawing the appropriate conclusions for managerial decisions. These conclusions should fulfill the deliverables promised in the research proposal. In addition, it's important that the researcher consider the varying abilities of people to understand the research results. The report shouldn't be written the same way to a group of PhDs as it would be to a group of line managers.

All too many applied market research reports are overly complicated statements of technical aspects and sophisticated research methods. Frequently, management is not interested in detailed reporting of the research design and statistical findings, but wishes only a summary of the findings. If the findings of the research remain unread on the marketing manager's desk, the study will have been useless. The importance of effective communication cannot be overemphasized. Research is only as good as its applications.

Now that we have outlined the research process, note that the order of topics in this book follows the flowchart of the research process presented in Exhibit 3.3. Keep this flowchart in mind while reading later chapters.

The Research Program Strategy

Our discussion of the marketing research process began with the assumption that the researcher wished to collect data to achieve a specific marketing objective. When the researcher has only one or a small number of research objectives that can be addressed in a single study, that study is referred to as a **research project**. We have emphasized the researcher's need to select specific techniques for solving one-dimensional problems, such as identifying market segments, selecting the best packaging design, or test-marketing a new product.

research project

A single study that addresses one or a small number of research objectives.

However, if you think about a firm's marketing mix activity in a given period of time (such as a year), you'll realize that marketing research is not a one-shot activity—it is a continuous process. An exploratory research study may be followed by a survey, or a researcher may conduct a specific research project for each aspect of the marketing mix. If a new product is being developed, the different types of research might include market potential studies to identify the size and characteristics of the market; product usage testing to record consumers' reactions to prototype products; brand name and packaging research to determine the product's symbolic connotations; and test-marketing the new product. Thus, when numerous related studies come together to address issues about a single company, we refer to this as a **research program**. Because research is a continuous process, management should view marketing research at a strategic planning level. The program strategy refers to a firm's overall plan to use marketing research. It is a planning activity that places a series of marketing research projects in the context of the company's marketing plan.

The marketing research program strategy can be likened to a term insurance policy. Conducting marketing research minimizes risk and increases certainty. Each research project can be seen as a series of term insurance policies that makes the marketing manager's job a bit safer.

research program

Numerous related studies that come together to address multiple, related research objectives.

Summary

1. Classify marketing research as either exploratory research, descriptive research, or causal research. Exploratory, descriptive, and causal research are three major types of marketing research projects. The clarity with which the decision situation is defined determines whether exploratory, descriptive, or causal research is most appropriate. When the decision is very ambiguous, or the interest is on discovering ideas, exploratory research is most appropriate. Descriptive research attempts to paint a picture of the given situation by describing characteristics of objects, people, or organizations. Causal research identifies cause-and-effect relationships. Or, in other words, what change in "Y" will occur when there is some change in "X"? Three conditions must be satisfied to establish evidence of causality: 1) temporal sequence—the cause must occur before the effect; 2) concomitant variation—a change in the cause is associated with a change in the effect; and 3) nonspurious association—the cause is true and not eliminated by the introduction of another potential cause.

2. List the major stages of the marketing research process and the steps within each. The six major stages of the research process are 1) defining the research objectives, 2) planning the research design, 3) sampling, 4) data gathering, 5) data processing and analysis, and 6) drawing conclusions and report preparation. Each stage involves several activities or steps. For instance, in planning the research design, the researchers must decide which type of study will be done and, if needed, recruit participants and design and develop experimental stimuli. Quite often research projects are conducted together as parts of a research program. Such programs can involve successive projects that monitor an established product or a group of projects undertaken for a proposed new product to determine the optimal form of various parts of the marketing mix.

3. Understand the concepts of theory and hypothesis and the critical role they play in research. A *hypothesis* is a formal statement explaining some outcome. It is stated in a way that it is testable. A *theory* is a formal, logical explanation of some events that includes predictions of how things relate to one another. A theory is built through a process of reviewing previous findings of similar studies, simple logical deduction, and knowledge of applicable theoretical areas. The explanations in a theory are often in the form of hypotheses. They are extremely useful in research because they give the research an idea of what to expect prior to testing. As such, they also help to identify the variables that need to be included in the study. Often, certain types of hypotheses point to the need for a specific type of research design.

4. Know the difference between a research project and a research program. A *research project* addresses one of a small number of research objectives that can be included in a single study. In contrast, a *research program* represents a series of studies addressing multiple research objectives. Many marketing activities require an ongoing research task of some type.

Key Terms and Concepts

causal inference, *47*

causal research, *47*

concomitant variation, *47*

data analysis, *59*

deliverables, *51*

descriptive research, *45*

diagnostic analysis, *46*

empirical testing, *56*

experiment, *48*

experimental variable, *48*

exploratory research, *44*

focus group, *54*

hypothesis, *55*

literature review, *53*

manipulation, *48*

nonspurious association, *47*

pilot study, *54*

pretest, *54*

research design, *56*

research objectives, *51*

research program, *61*

research project, *60*

sampling, *58*

survey, *57*

symptoms, *44*

temporal sequence, *47*

theory, *55*

unobtrusive methods, *59*

Questions for Review and Critical Thinking

1. List five ways that marketing research can contribute to effective business decision making.
2. Define *market symptoms*. Give an example as it applies to a university business school.
3. Consider the following list, and indicate and explain whether each best fits the definition of a problem, opportunity, or symptom:
   a. A 12.5 percent decrease in store traffic for a children's shoe store in a medium-sized city mall.
   b. FedEx's fuel costs increase 200 percent between 2005 and 2009.
   c. A furniture manufacturer and retailer in North Carolina reads a research report indicating consumer trends toward Australian Jara and Kari wood. The export of these products is very limited and very expensive.
   d. Marlboro reads a research report written by the U.S. FDA. It indicates that the number of cigarette smokers in sub-Saharan Africa is expected to increase dramatically over the next decade.
   e. The Starwood Hotel group faces exchange rates between the US and Europe, Great Britain, and Canada that have changed dramatically between 2004 and 2009.
4. What are the three types of marketing research? Indicate which type each item in the list below illustrates. Explain your answers.
   a. Establishing the relationship between advertising and sales in the beer industry
   b. Identifying target market demographics for a shopping center located in Omaha, Nebraska
   c. Estimating the 5-year sales potential for Cat-Scan machines in the Ark-La-Tex (Arkansas, Louisiana, and Texas) region of the United States
   d. Testing the effect of the inside temperature of a clothing store on sales of outerwear
   e. Discovering the ways that people who live in apartments actually use vacuum cleaners, and identifying cleaning tasks for which they do not use a vacuum
5. Describe the type of research evidence that allows one to infer causality.
6. What is an experimental manipulation? A marketing researcher is hired by a specialty retail firm. The retailer is trying to decide what level of lighting and what temperature it should maintain in its stores. How can the researcher manipulate these experimental variables within a causal design?
7. Describe how a literature search is useful in marketing research.
8. Do the stages in the research process seem to follow the scientific method?
9. Why is the "define research objectives" of the research process probably the most important stage?
10. Suppose Auchan (http://www.auchan.fr), a hypermarket chain based out of France, was considering opening three hypermarkets in the midwestern United States. What role would theory play in designing a research study to track how the shopping habits of consumers from the United States differ from those in France and from those in Japan? What kind of hypothesis might be examined in a study of this topic?
11. Define research project and research program. Referring to the question immediately above, do you think a research project or a research program is needed to provide useful input to the Auchan decision makers?
12. What type of research design would you recommend in the situations below? For each applied market research project, what might be an example of a "deliverable"? Which do you think would involve actually testing a research hypothesis?
   a. The manufacturer and marketer of flight simulators and other pilot training equipment wish to forecast sales volume for the next five years.
   b. A local chapter of the American Lung Association wishes to identify the demographic characteristics of individuals who donate more than $500 per year.
   c. A major petroleum company is concerned with the increased costs of producing and marketing regular leaded gasoline and is considering dropping this product.
   d. A food company researcher wishes to know what types of food are carried in brown-bag lunches to learn if the company can capitalize on this phenomenon.
   e. A researcher wishes to explore the feasibility of a casino in a community where gaming had previously been banned.

Research Activities

1. **'NET** Look up information about the online MBA programs at the University of Phoenix.(http://business.phoenix.edu/business/graduate.aspx). Compare it to the traditional MBA program at your university. Suppose each was looking to expand the numbers of students in their programs. How might the research design differ for each?
2. **'NET** Use a web browser to go to the Gallup Organization's home page (http://www.gallup.com). The Gallup home page changes regularly. However, it should provide an opportunity to read the results of a recent poll. For example, a poll might break down Americans' sympathies toward Israel or the Palestinians based on numerous individual characteristics such as political affiliation or religious involvement. After reading the results of a Gallup poll of this type, learn how polls are conducted (hint: see "About Gallup" for "FAQs"). You may need to click on the Frequently Asked Questions List (FAQ) to find this information. List the various stages of the research process and how they were (or were not) followed in Gallup's project.
3. Any significant business decision requires input from a research project. Write a brief essay either defending this statement or refuting it.

Case 3.1 A New "Joe" on the Block

© GETTY IMAGES/
PHOTODISC GREEN

Joe Brown is ready to start a new career. After spending 30 years as a market researcher and inspired by the success of Starbucks, he is ready to enter the coffee shop business. However, before opening his first shop, he realizes that a great deal of research is needed. He has some key questions in mind.

- What markets in the United States hold the most promise for a new coffee shop?
- What type of location is best for a coffee shop?
- What is it that makes a coffee shop popular?
- What coffee do Americans prefer?

A quick trip to the Internet reveals more previous research on coffee, markets, and related materials than he expected. Many studies address taste. For example, he finds several studies that in one way or another compare the taste of different coffee shop coffees. Most commonly, they compare the taste of coffee from Starbucks against coffee from McDonald's, Dunkin' Donuts, Burger King, and sometimes a local competitor. However, it becomes difficult to draw a conclusion as the results seem to be inconsistent.

- One study had a headline that poked fun at Starbucks' high-priced coffee. The author of this study personally purchased coffee to go at four places, took them to his office, tasted them, made notes and then drew conclusions. All the coffee was tasted black with no sugar. Just cups of joe. He reached the conclusion that McDonald's Premium Coffee (at about $1.50 a cup), tasted nearly as good as Starbucks House Blend (at about $1.70 a cup), both of which were much better than either Dunkin' Donuts (at about $1.20) or Burger King (less than $1). This study argued that McDonald's was best, all things considered.
- Another study was written up by a good critic who was simply interested in identifying the best-tasting coffee. Again, he tasted them all black with nothing added. Each cup of coffee was consumed in the urban location near the inner city center in which he lived. He reached the conclusion that Starbucks' coffee had the best flavor although it showed room for improvement. McDonald's premium coffee was not as good, but better than the other two. Dunkin' Donuts coffee had reasonably unobjectionable taste but was very weak and watery. The Burger King coffee was simply not very good.
- Yet another study talked about Starbucks becoming a huge company and how it has lost touch with the common coffee shop coffee customer. The researchers stood outside a small organic specialty shop and interviewed 100 consumers as they exited the shop.

They asked, "Which coffee do you prefer?" The results showed a preference for a local coffee, tea, and incense shop, and otherwise put Starbucks last behind McDonald's, Burger King, and Dunkin' Donuts.

- Still another study compared the coffee-drinking experience. A sample of 50 consumers in St. Louis, Missouri were interviewed and asked to list the coffee shop they frequented most. Starbucks was listed by more consumers than any other place. A small percentage listed Dunkin' Donuts but none listed McDonald's, despite their efforts at creating a premium coffee experience. The study did not ask consumers to compare the tastes of the coffee across the different places.

Joe also wants to find data showing coffee consumption patterns and the number of coffee shops around the United States, so he spends time looking for data on the Internet. His searches don't reveal anything satisfying.

As Joe ponders how to go about starting "A Cup of Joe," he wonders about the relevance of this previous research. Is it useful at all? He even questions whether he is capable of doing any primary research himself and considers hiring someone to do a feasibility study for him. Maybe doing research is easier than using research.

Sources: Shiver, J., "Taste Test: The Little Joes Take on Starbucks," *USA Today*, (March 26, 2008), http://www.usatoday.com/money/industries/food/2006-03-26-coffee_x. htm, accessed July 20, 2008; Associated Press, "McDonald's Coffee Beats Starbucks, Says Consumer Reports," *The Seattle Times*, (February 2, 2007), http://seattletimes.nwsource. com/html/businesstechnology/2003553322_webcoffeetest02.html, accessed July 20, 2008; "Coffee Wars: Starbucks v McDonald's," *The Economist* 386, (January 10, 2008), 58.

Questions

1. What are the top three key decisions faced by Joe?
2. What are the key deliverables that an outside researcher should produce to help Joe with the key decisions?
3. How relevant are the coffee taste studies cited above? Explain.
4. What flaws in the coffee taste studies should Joe consider in trying to weigh the merits of their results?
5. Briefly relate this situation to each of the major stages of the marketing research process.
6. Try to do a quick search to explore the question: "Are American consumer preferences the same all across the United States?"
7. Would it be better for Joe to do the research himself or have a consultant perform the work?
8. If a consultant comes in to do the job, what are three key deliverables that would likely be important to Joe in making a decision to launch the Cup of Joe coffee shop?

CHAPTER 4
THE HUMAN SIDE OF MARKETING RESEARCH: ORGANIZATIONAL AND ETHICAL ISSUES

After studying this chapter, you should be able to

1. Know when research should be conducted externally and when it should be done internally
2. Be familiar with the types of jobs, job responsibilities, and career paths available within the marketing research industry
3. Define ethics and understand how it applies to marketing research
4. Appreciate the rights and obligations of a) research respondents—particularly children, b) research clients or sponsors, and c) marketing researchers
5. Avoid situations involving a conflict of interest in performing marketing research

Chapter Vignette: The Longest Drive or the Tallest Tale?

Pick up a golf magazine, watch the Golf Channel, or view some golf-related Web sites, and no doubt you will see a lot of claims by companies who say they can help golfers lower their scores. Even a golf novice can see how a longer golf shot is usually better than a shorter golf shot. Thus, the claims include slogans such as Callaway's "designed to be the longest ball in all of golf," Bridgestone's "distance technology," and balls with names such as Precept Distance iQ, and Nike Juice with "Ginormous Hugantic Distance!" Obviously, these companies do a great deal of product research to produce golf balls that will conform to the rules of golf while gaining a yard or two over the competitors. Perhaps not quite as obviously, they do equal amounts of marketing research to understand just what it is that makes a golfer believe they have the longest ball in the game.

Now, imagine a young marketing researcher who leaves her job as a research analyst for a mid-sized firm to start a small firm of her own. The mid-sized firm that she worked for previously had been involved in a project for Maxfli so she had some insight into how consumers perceive golf technology. Her first big break comes when a polymer company that wants to leverage their brand into the golf ball business approaches her about a research project. The project is related to golfer perceptions of the technological advantage and perceived distance of golf balls and how this would relate to sales. The owner of the company is adamant that he wants to know how to make golfers "think they are hitting the longest drives of their lives." The company has invested millions of dollars in new polymer coatings that enhance the energy of the ball when struck at high speeds. From her previous project, she knows that perceived distance is the number one concern of golfers when purchasing golf balls. She also knows that the company has already gone forward with plans to build a production facility. The only deliverable the owner is interested in is "how to make people believe this is the longest ball."

Golf ball companies traditionally have tested golf ball performance with mechanical robots called Iron Byron and by surveying actual golfers about the golf balls they use. In this case, the robot tests reveal two things: (1) the top 10 or so longest golf balls all go approximately the same distance, and (2) the golf balls that deliver the longest drives for professional golfers do not deliver the longest drives for average golfers. The young researcher really needs the business and would like to deliver a report that the owner will like and do so with the least cost. Based on her research with Maxfli, she believes that this new technology will be best suited to weaker golfers with slower swing speeds (who cannot swing a club as fast as others). She thinks about a possible study. She can get a sample of golfers with slower swing speeds, tell them that the golf ball they will be testing will be the most expensive on the market, and have them compare it to a Maxfli ball that she knows is best for golfers with a high swing speed. The group should both really hit and believe that the new ball goes further than the Maxfli. Then, she would be able to deliver the results the owner of the company wants and have a successful big break.

Sources: For information on golf ball testing and research, see "Flying High and Far," Golf.com, http://www.golf.com/golf/features/flash/ballguide3.html, accessed July 21, 2008; Sauerhaft, R., "How We Did It: The Best Golf Ball for You," *Golf Magazine*, (February 1, 2008), http://www.golf.com/golf/equipment/article/0,28136,1695805,00.html, accessed July 21, 2008; Tannar, K., "The Longest Golf Ball Testing for 2007 Balls," http://probablegolfinstruction.com/longest_golf_ball.htm, accessed July 21, 2008.

Introduction

The vignette describes a situation that involves marketing research and in particular, the human side. A company is looking for research to help sell a new product, in this case a golf ball. Rather than doing the research itself, an outside agency is hired. The owner, given this is a small agency, is faced with a number of dilemmas. Some of these introduce business ethic into the arena of marketing research. This chapter focuses on the social element of marketing research by discussing the people who do use and participate in research and the situations that they sometimes find themselves in.

Who Does the Research?

The vignette described in this chapter involves one company hiring an outside company to conduct and provide results from a research project. Although this is very typical, many companies have their own employees perform research projects and research programs. Thus, research is sometimes performed in-house, meaning that employees of the company that will benefit from the research project actually perform the research. In other cases, the research is performed by an **outside agency**, meaning that the company that will benefit from the research results hires an independent, outside firm to perform a research project. While it would seem that **in-house research** would usually be of higher quality because of the increased knowledge of the researchers conducting the studies, there are several reasons why employees of the firm may not always be the best people to do the job.

Do It Yourself or Let Your Fingers Do the Walking?

When the firm facing a decision encounters one of the following situations, they should consider having the research performed by an outside agency.

- An outside agency often can provide a fresh perspective. Creativity is often hindered by too much knowledge. When a firm is seeking new ideas, particularly in discovery-oriented research, an outsider is not constrained by the groupthink that often affects a company employee. In other words, employees who spend so much time together in their day-to-day work activities begin to act and think alike to a large degree. History is filled with stories of products that remained unsuccessful commercially for years until someone from outside the company discovered a useful application. The technology for a microwave oven was invented in the 1940s by a company called Raytheon. Raytheon worked on radar systems for the Allied military in World War II. Not until someone from another company, Amana, tested the concept of using microwaves in a kitchen appliance did it become a commercial success.

outside agency

An independent research firm contracted by the company that actually will benefit from the research.

in-house research

Research performed by employees of the company that will benefit from the research.

TO THE POINT

To manage a business is to manage its future; and to manage the future is to manage information.

—Marion Harper

By now, you are becoming familiar with the student questionnaire that accompanies this book. Examine the items in the questionnaire and the questionnaire overall for the following issues.

1. Were you required to identify yourself by name in completing the survey?

2. Can the results (you can access the results through your instructor) be linked to respondents by name?
3. Do any items need to be tied to a name to be useful to the researcher?
4. Consider the portion of the survey shown below. What if another instructor asked for the results from this particular section of the survey but was only interested in them if the names of the students also can be provided? The instructor believes that he can use the results to encourage particular students to change their study habits. Take the role of the researchers who implemented this research. Should you provide the information this instructor is asking for? Why or why not?

Please read each of the following statements. After reading each, click on the the circle that best describes how much you agree with each statement.	Strongly Agree	Agree	Neutral	Disagree	Strongly Disagree
I make time to study every day.	○	○	○	○	○
I know the material better after I study.	○	○	○	○	○
I can't study when it's quiet.	○	○	○	○	○
I prefer to not be around others when I study.	○	○	○	○	○
I can study the night before and be ready for a test.	○	○	○	○	○
I like to study with others.	○	○	○	○	○
I arrange time to study with others.	○	○	○	○	○

COURTESY OF QUALTRICS.COM

© GEORGE DOYLE

- An outside agency often can be more objective. When a firm is facing a particularly sensitive situation that may even impact a large number of jobs within the company, it may be difficult for researchers to be objective. Alternatively, if a particular chief executive within the firm is in love with some new idea, researchers may feel a great deal of pressure to present results that are supportive of the concept. In these cases, outside researchers may be a good choice. Since they don't have to work for the company and interact with the players involved on a daily basis, they are less concerned about presenting results that may not be truly welcome.

- An outside agency may have special expertise. When a firm needs research requiring a particular expertise that some outside agency specializes in, it may be a good idea to use that firm to conduct the research. For example, if a company is searching for new ideas about how to use its Web site, an online focus group interview may be needed. While this is a skill that may not be prevalent within the company, there are several research firms that specialize in this particular type of research. Thus, the outside agency may have greater competency in this specific area.

- An outside agency will have local knowledge and expertise and may specialize in research from its home area. When a company needs consumer research from that particular country or even from a particular part of a country, the outside agency becomes advantageous because of its knowledge of customs and values in that particular area plus the acceptable ways with which to get information from consumers. For example, a research agency based here in the United States would probably not strongly consider a door–to–door survey for consumer research. However, in other parts of the world, particularly with less developed communication infrastructure, this may be a viable and accepted option.

Likewise, there are conditions that make in-house research more attractive as well, as in the following situations.

- If the research project needs to be completed very quickly, chances are that in-house researchers can get started more quickly and get quicker access to internal resources that can help get the project done in short order.
- If the research project will require the close collaboration of many other employees from diverse areas of the organization, then in-house research may be preferable. The in-house

research firms can usually gain cooperation and can more quickly ascertain just who needs to be interviewed and where those people can be found.

- A third reason for doing a project in-house has to do with economy. In house research can almost always be done more cheaply than that done by an outside research firm.
- If secrecy is a major concern, then the research is best done in-house. Even though the outside firm might be trusted, it may take slightly less care in disguising its research efforts. Thus, other companies may pick up on signals in the marketplace that suggest the area of research for a firm.

Working in the Marketing Research Field

About three-fourths of all U.S. organizations have a department or individual responsible for marketing research. Consumer products companies, manufacturers, service firms, health-care organizations and retailers are most likely to have an in-house marketing research department. Marketing research clearly has a presence and this is particularly true for larger firms. The amount of companies doing research is likely increasing because as times get tough or as competition increases, firms actually become more attuned to marketing research. The insurance industry has been tuned into marketing research in a big way as competition increased over the last decade. A large research company may well be staffed with dozens or even hundreds of people involved with marketing research in some way. MetLife has been singled out as a role model for exemplary performance and integration of its marketing research team into decision making. The marketing research team has helped MetLife:[1]

- Build stronger relationships with customers
- Integrate customer and competitor information into decision processes
- Have better working relationships with vendors
- Become more entrepeneurial and marketing oriented

The placement of marketing research within a firm's organizational structure and the structure of the research department itself vary substantially, depending on the firm's degree of marketing orientation and research sophistication. A marketing research department can easily become isolated with poor organizational placement. Researchers may lack a voice in executive committees when they have no continuous relationship with marketing management. This can occur when the research department is positioned at an inappropriately low level. Given the critically important nature of the intelligence coming out of a research department, it should be placed relatively high in the organizational structure to ensure that senior management is well informed. Research departments should also be linked with a broad spectrum of other units within the organization. Thus, they should be positioned to provide credible information both upstream and downstream within the marketing organization—as is the case at MetLife.

Research departments that perform a staff function must wait for management to request assistance. Often the term "client" is used by the research department to refer to line management for whom services are being performed. The research department responds to clients' requests and is responsible for the design and execution of all research.

Thousands of people work for large global research firms like Nielsen. Marketing research truly presents a world of opportunity for careers. [http:// www2.acnielsen.com/careers/]

Research Suppliers and Contractors

As mentioned in the beginning of the chapter, sometimes obtaining marketing research from an outside organization makes good sense. In these cases, marketing

Finding Häagen-Dazs in China

Ice cream lovers needn't worry if they are sent on a business trip to China. Häagen-Dazs ice cream shops first appeared in Shanghai, China, in 1996 and now there are dozens of Häagen-Dazs ice cream shops in coastal China, with plans for many more. Clearly, many firms would like to follow Häagen-Dazs into China. China is expected to be the world's largest consumer market by 2020. However, where should an ice cream shop be located in China? While location decisions can be difficult enough within the borders of one's own country, imagine trying to decide where to put a shop in a huge, unfamiliar country.

Fortunately, standardized research companies like Retail Forward have resources deployed all around the world that can synthesize Geographic Information Systems (GIS) information with survey research and other information to assist firms with location decisions

in China and in other developing countries. Since U.S.-based retail firms may lack the necessary connections and knowledge (expertise) to efficiently conduct research in faraway places, the use of an outside research provider not only saves time and money, but also yields higher quality results than an in-house study. Imagine how difficult language barriers could be when dealing with the Chinese consumer market.

And, as difficult as identifying good retail locations seems in China, other top emerging retail nations include India, Russia, and the Ukraine. As in China, American and European firms may find that using a research supplier to help with retail location issues in these countries is wiser than doing the research themselves.

Sources: "Häagen-Dazs in China," *China Business Review*, 31 (July/August 2004), 22; Hall, Cecily, "Spanning the Retail Globe," *WWD: Women's Wear Daily*, 190 (July 21, 2005), 11. www.haagen-dazs.com, accessed September 15, 2008.

---

research suppliers

Commercial providers of marketing research services.

managers must interact with **research suppliers**, who are commercial providers of marketing research services. Marketing research is carried out by firms that may be variously classified as marketing research consulting companies, such as Burke or the Walker Information Research Company; advertising agencies, such as JWT Worldwide; suppliers of syndicated research services, such as The Nielsen Company; as well as interviewing agencies, universities, and government agencies, among others. Research suppliers provide varied services which can be classified into several types.

■ SYNDICATED SERVICE

syndicated service

A marketing research supplier that provides standardized information for many clients in return for a fee.

No matter how large a firm's marketing research department is, some projects are too expensive to perform in-house. A **syndicated service** is a marketing research supplier that provides standardized information for many clients in return for a fee. They are a sort of supermarket for standardized research results. For example, J. D. Power and Associates sells research about customers' ratings of automobile quality and their reasons for satisfaction. Most automobile manufacturers and their advertising agencies subscribe to this syndicated service because the company provides important industry-wide information it gathers from a national sample of thousands of car buyers. By specializing in this type of customer satisfaction research, J. D. Power gains certain economies of scale.

Syndicated services can provide expensive information economically to numerous clients because the information is not specific to one client but interests many. Such suppliers offer standardized information to measure media audiences, wholesale and retail distribution data, and other forms of data. The world's largest marketing research company, The Nielsen Company, is a leader in providing standardized data across many industries including retailing, consumer behavior, and media. They also provide services beyond syndicated information, but this is a core of their business. Nearly 40,000 people work for The Nielsen Company worldwide.

■ STANDARDIZED RESEARCH SERVICES

standardized research service

Companies that develop a unique methodology for investigating a business specialty area.

Standardized research service providers develop a unique methodology for investigating a business specialty area. Several research firms, such as Retail Forward (http://www.retailforward.com), provide location services for retail firms. The Research Snapshot above illustrates an interesting application for which an outside location service company may be particularly useful. Research suppliers conduct studies for multiple individual clients using the same methods.

The Nielsen Company (http://www2.acnielsen.com) collects information throughout the new-product development process, from initial concept screening through test-marketing. The BASES system can evaluate initiatives relative to other products in the competitive environment. For example, a client can compare its Day-After Recall scores with average scores for a product category.

Even when a firm could perform the research task in-house, research suppliers may be able to conduct the project at a lower cost, faster, and relatively more objectively. A company that wishes to quickly evaluate a new advertising strategy may find an ad agency's research department is able to provide technical expertise on copy development research that is not available within the company itself. Researchers may be well advised to seek outside help with research when conducting research in a foreign country in which the necessary human resources and knowledge to effectively collect data are lacking. The Research Snapshot on the previous page illustrates this situation.

Limited Research Service Companies and Custom Research

Limited-service research suppliers specialize in particular research activities, such as syndicated service, field interviewing, data warehousing, or data processing. Full-service research suppliers sometimes contract these companies for ad hoc marketing research projects. The client usually controls these marketing research agencies or management consulting firms, but the research supplier handles most of the operating details of **custom research** projects. These are projects that are tailored specifically to a client's unique needs. A custom research supplier may employ individuals with titles that imply relationships with clients, such as *account executive* or *account group manager,* as well as functional specialists with titles such as *statistician, librarian, director of field services, director of tabulation and data processing,* and *interviewer.*

Exhibit 4.1 on the next page lists the top twenty suppliers of global research. Most provide multiple services ranging from designing activities to fieldwork. The services they can provide are not covered in detail here because they are discussed throughout the book, especially in the sections on fieldwork. Clearly, the exhibit reveals that research is big business. Its growth will continue as data availability increases and as businesses desire more precision in their decision making. Therefore, attractive career opportunities are numerous for those with the right skills and desires.

A look at the top 20 shows that marketing research also is a global enterprise. Marketing research is conducted all around the world although given roots within the United States; American firms are numerous. Other large firms based in the United States that don't make the top 20 global list include:

Burke, Inc. with revenue of nearly $50 million.
Walker Research (Information) at just over $20 million in revenue.
Savitz Research with revenue of about $15 million.

Each of these firms is within the top 50 largest market research firms in the United States.

Size of the Marketing Research Firm

Marketing research organizations themselves consist of layers of employees. Each employee has certain specific functions to perform based on his or her area of expertise and experience. A look at these jobs not only describes the potential structure of a research organization, but it also provides insight into the types of careers available in marketing research.

Doing research in a foreign country is often better done by an outside agency with resources in those places.

custom research

Research projects that are tailored specifically to a client's unique needs.

EXHIBIT 4.1 **The Largest Research Firms in the World**

Rank	Company	Home Country	Web site	Number of Employees	Approximate Revenue (millions)
1	The Nielsen Company	USA	www.nielsen.com	39,500	3,696
2	IMS Health Inc.	USA	www.imshealth.com	7,400	2,000
3	TNS	UK	www.tns-global.com	14,600	1,850
4	The Kantar Group	UK	www.kantargroup.com	6900	1400
5	GfK AG	Germany	www.gfk.com	9000	1400
6	Ipsos Group	France	www.ipsos.com	6500	1100
7	Synovate	UK	www.synovate.com	6000	750
8	IRI	USA	www.infores.com	3600	700
9	Westat Inc.	USA	www.westat.com	2000	425
10	Arbitron	USA	www.arbitron.com	1050	350
11	INTAGE Inc	Japan	www.intage.co.jp	1600	265
12	JD Power	USA	www.jdpa.com	850	230
13	Harris Interactive Inc	USA	www.harrisinteractive.com	1100	220
14	Maritz Research	USA	www.maritzresearch.com	800	215
15	The NPD Group	USA	www.npd.com	950	190
16	Video Research	Japan	www.videor.co.jp	400	175
17	Opinion Research Corp.	USA	www.opinionresearch.com	675	155
18	IBOPE	Brazil	www.ibope.com.br	1700	105
19	Lieberman Research Worldwide	USA	www.lrwonline.com	300	80
20	Telephia Inc	USA	www.telephia.com	250	70

Sources: "Top 50 US Market Research Firms," *Marketing News*, (June 15, 2008), H4; "Top 25 Global Research Organizations," *Marketing News*, August 15, 2007), H4.

■ SMALL FIRMS

While it is difficult to precisely define the boundaries between small firms, mid-sized firms, and large firms, generally speaking, government statistics usually consider firms with fewer than 100 employees to be small. In small firms, the vice president of marketing may be in charge of all significant marketing research. This officer generally has a sales manager collect and analyze sales histories, trade association statistics, and other internal data. Small marketing companies usually have few resources and special competencies to conduct large-scale, sophisticated research projects. An advertising agency or a firm that specializes in marketing research will be contracted if a large-scale survey is needed. Small businesses will generally have fewer than five employees regularly involved in marketing research.

Some small firms are small marketing research firms. Small marketing research firms are less likely to have major corporate clients, rather, they will probably work for other small firms and in particular, start-up firms. Typical studies involve feasibility studies and assessing consumer attitudes and the relationship between customer satisfaction and customer loyalty.[2] A small firm can be a good place to start a career or to start your own business. Researchers working for a small firm will probably have to be involved in many, if not all, of the stages of research.

■ MID-SIZED FIRMS

Mid-sized firms can be thought of as those with between 100 and 500 employees. In a mid-sized marketing research firm, someone usually holds the position of **director of marketing research**. This person provides leadership in research efforts and integrates all staff-level research activities.

A **research analyst** is responsible for client contact, project design, preparation of proposals, selection of research suppliers, and supervision of data collection, analysis, and reporting activities. Normally, the research analyst is responsible for several projects simultaneously covering a wide spectrum of the firm's organizational activities. He or she works with product or division management and makes recommendations based on analysis of collected data.

Research assistants (or associates) provide technical assistance with questionnaire design, data analyses, and so forth. Another common name for this position is *junior analyst*. The **manager of decision support systems** supervises the collection and analysis of sales, inventory, and other periodic customer relationship management (CRM) data. Sales forecasts for product lines usually are developed using analytical and quantitative techniques. Sales information is provided to satisfy the planning, analysis, and control needs of decision makers. The manager of decision support systems may be assisted by a **forecast analyst** who provides technical assistance, such as running computer programs and manipulating data to forecast sales.

Personnel within a planning department may perform the marketing research function in a mid-sized firm. At times, they may outsource some research functions. The planner may design research studies and then contract with outside firms that supply research services such as interviewing or data processing. They can combine the input from these outside agencies with their own work to write research reports.

■ LARGE FIRMS

As marketing research departments grow, they tend to specialize by product or strategic business unit. Major firms can be thought of as those with over 500 employees. Marriott Corporation has a director of marketing research for lodging (for example, Marriott Hotels and Resorts, Courtyard by Marriott, and Fairfield Inn) and a director of marketing research for contract services (for example, Senior Living Services). Each business unit's research director reports to the vice president of corporate marketing services. Many large organizations have managers of customer quality research who specialize in conducting surveys to measure consumers' satisfaction with product quality.

Exhibit 4.2 on the next page illustrates the organization of a major firm's marketing research department. Within this organization, the centralized marketing research department conducts research for all the division's product groups. This is typical of a large research department that conducts much of its own research, including fieldwork. The director of marketing research reports to the vice president of marketing.

The Director of Marketing Research as a Manager

A director of marketing research plans, executes, and controls the firm's marketing research function. This person typically serves on company executive committees that identify competitive opportunities and formulate marketing strategies. The various directors from each functional area generally make up this committee (such as finance, sales, production, and so forth).

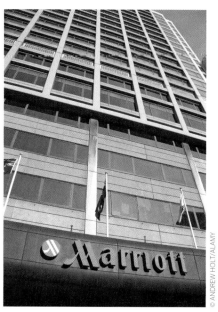

© ANDREW HOLT/ALAMY

When market research departments grow, they begin to specialize by product or business unit. This happened in the Marriott Corporation, which now has a specific director of marketing research for its lodging facilities.

director of marketing research

This person provides leadership in research efforts and integrates all staff-level research activities into one effort. The director plans, executes, and controls the firm's marketing research function.

research analyst

A person responsible for client contact, project design, preparation of proposals, selection of research suppliers, and supervision of data collection, analysis, and reporting activities.

research assistants

Research employees who provide technical assistance with questionnaire design, data analyses, and similar activities.

manager of decision support systems

Employee who supervises the collection and analysis of sales, inventory, and other periodic customer relationship management (CRM) data.

forecast analyst

Employee who provides technical assistance such as running computer programs and manipulating data to generate a sales forecast.

EXHIBIT 4.2 Organization of the Marketing Research Department in a Large Firm

```
                              ┌─────────────┐
                              │  Director   │
                              │  Marketing  │
                              │  Research   │
                              └──────┬──────┘
         ┌──────────────────────────┼──────────────────────────┐
    ┌────┴─────┐              ┌──────┴─────┐             ┌───────┴────┐            ┌───────┴────┐
    │ Manager  │              │  Manager   │             │  Manager   │            │  Manager   │
    │ Market/  │              │  Customer  │             │ Marketing  │            │  Decision  │
    │   New    │              │Satisfaction│             │  Research   │            │  Support   │
    │ Product  │              │    and     │             │            │            │  Systems   │
    │ Research │              │   Total    │             │            │            │            │
    │          │              │  Quality   │             │            │            │            │
    └────┬─────┘              └──────┬─────┘             └─────┬──────┘            └─────┬──────┘
```

| Supervisor Product Research | Supervisor Product Research | Supervisor Customer Satisfaction Research | Supervisor Employee Research[a] | Supervisor Marketing Practice Research[b] | Supervisor Promotion Research[c] | Supervisor Fundamental Research[d]/ Environmental Research | Supervisor Marketing Statistics | Supervisor Marketing Information from Syndicated Services |

(by product groupings)

[a]Conducts research to improve total quality management in production.
[b]Conducts research that cuts across product lines or involves competitive marketing practices or characteristics of customer groups.
[c]Conducts research that cuts across product lines to measure the effectiveness of promotional activities.
[d]Conducts research aimed at gaining a basic understanding of various elements of the marketing process.

The director of marketing research provides the research perspective during meetings. For instance, the researcher can provide input as to what types of market intelligence can be feasibly obtained given the decision being discussed. Marketing research directors typically face problems like these:

- Skilled research professionals like conducting research better than managing people. They pride themselves on being hands-on researchers. However, a director is a manager and spends more time in meetings and managing than actually conducting research.
- The research management role often is not formally recognized.
- Outstanding research professionals often have trouble delegating responsibility. The pride that comes with being a knowledgeable researcher makes it difficult to give up control. They may genuinely feel "I can do it better myself." As a result, they delegate only elementary or tedious tasks to subordinates. The subordinates can sometimes become disenchanted and thus become unhappy with their work.
- Finally, research is often seen as a hodgepodge of techniques available to answer individual, unrelated questions. According to this view, a research operation encompasses an array of more or less equal projects, each handled by a project director. Hence, many firms view a full-time director as unnecessary.[3]

Marketing research jobs range across a large spectrum of activities and salaries. Jobs are available practically all over the world. The Research Snapshot on the next page gives a rough idea of what marketing research salaries are like internationally.

Marketing Research Pays

Marketing research can pay! Careers in marketing research can be very lucrative. This is particularly true if one has the right attributes. These attributes include being a good people person as well as having good quantitative skills and a good education. The fastest career tracks in marketing research are for those with at least a master's degree.

The prospects of finding a job remain good. Marketing researchers have long been in greater demand than the supply can address. The salaries also can be very lucrative. The 2006 U.S. Department of Labor Salary Survey suggests that marketing research analysts' salaries are generally between $40,000 and $85,000 although some analysts have salaries well over $100,000 per year. These are for actual research analysts and not research directors. Beginning research employees, with little or no experience, generally enter the firm as a survey researcher. Those salaries are considerably less, generally between $22,500 and $45,000. However, they require no significant work experience.

Job opportunities in marketing research exist outside the United States as well. The salaries also are lucrative in other countries. The chart in next column shows typical salary ranges for non-managerial marketing research positions in the United States, Australia, Japan, and the United Kingdom. For comparison purposes, salaries for non-managerial sales employees also are provided. The salaries are expressed in thousands of U.S. dollars and reflect the latest available statistics. As can be seen, research jobs compare very favorably. In addition, researchers that move into research director positions see a substantial increase in pay. Perhaps you'll give marketing research a try?

Common Currency ($)	Australia	UK	Japan	United States
Sales Executive				
High	97.32	89.88	74.89	55.00
Low	38.92	49.93	46.81	35.00
Marketing Research				
High	116.78	89.88	93.59	85.76
Low	38.92	37.95	46.81	41.23

Sources: Enright, A., "Carve out a Niche," *Marketing News* (November 15, 2005), 17; "Occupational Employment and Wages," U.S. Department of Labor, (2008), http://www.bls.gov/oes/current/oes193021.htm accessed September 15, 2008; Walters, Robert, "Market Research Search Results," (2008), http://www.robertwalters.com, accessed July 20, 2008.

© GEORGE DOYLE & CIARAN GRIFFIN

© PHOTODISC/GETTY IMAGES

Cross-Functional Teams

In a truly marketing-oriented organization, all employees are involved in the intelligence-gathering and dissemination process. Therefore, employees from different areas of the organization are more likely to communicate and act on marketing information in marketing-oriented firms.

Thus, employees are more likely to discuss market information between different functional areas in a marketing-oriented firm. **Cross-functional teams** are composed of individuals from various functional areas such as engineering, production, finance, and marketing who share a common purpose. Cross-functional teams help organizations focus on a core business process, such as customer service or new-product development. Working in teams reduces the tendency for employees to focus single-mindedly on an isolated functional activity. Cross-functional teams help employees increase customer value since communication about their specific desires and opinions are better communicated across the firm.

At trendsetting organizations, many marketing research directors are members of cross-functional teams. New-product development, for example, may be done by a cross-functional team of engineers, finance executives, production personnel, marketing managers, and marketing researchers who take an integrated approach to solve a problem or exploit opportunities. In the old days, marketing research may not have been involved in developing new products until long after many key decisions about product specifications and manufacturing had been made. Now marketing researchers' input is part of an integrated team effort. Researchers act both as business consultants and as providers of technical services. Researchers working in teams are more likely to understand the broad purpose of their research and less likely to focus exclusively on research methodology.

The effective cross-functional team is a good illustration of the marketing concept in action. It reflects an effort to satisfy customers by using all the organization's resources. Cross-functional teams are having a dramatic impact on views of the role of marketing research within the organization.

cross-functional teams

Employee teams composed of individuals from various functional areas such as engineering, production, finance, and marketing who share a common purpose.

Ethical Issues in Marketing Research

As in all human interactions, ethical issues exist in marketing research. This book considers various ethical issues concerning fair business dealings, proper research techniques, and appropriate use of research results in other chapters. The remainder of this chapter introduces ethical issues with an emphasis on societal and managerial concerns.

Ethical Questions Are Philosophical Questions

Ethical questions are philosophical questions. There are several philosophical theories that address how one develops a moral philosophy and how behavior is affected by morals. These include theories about cognitive moral development, the bases for ethical behavioral intentions, and opposing moral values.[4] While ethic remains a somewhat elusive topic, what is clear is that not everyone involved in business, or in fact involved in any human behavior, comes to the table with the same ethical standards or orientations.[5]

marketing ethics

The application of morals to behavior related to the exchange environment.

moral standards

Principles that reflect beliefs about what is ethical and what is unethical.

ethical dilemma

Refers to a situation in which one chooses from alternative courses of actions, each with different ethical implications.

Marketing ethics is the application of morals to business behavior related to the exchange environment. Generally, good ethic conforms to the notion of "right," and a lack of ethic conforms to the notion of "wrong." Highly ethical behavior can be characterized as being fair, just, and acceptable.[6] Ethical values can be highly influenced by one's moral standards. **Moral standards** are principles that reflect beliefs about what is ethical and what is unethical. More simply, they can be thought of as rules distinguishing right from wrong. The Golden Rule, "Do unto others as you would have them do unto you," is one such ethical principle.

An **ethical dilemma** simply refers to a situation in which one chooses from alternative courses of actions, each with different ethical implications. Each individual develops a philosophy or way of thinking that is applied to resolve the dilemmas they face. Many people use moral standards to guide their actions when confronted with an ethical dilemma. Others adapt an ethical orientation that rejects absolute principles. Their ethics are based more on the social or cultural acceptability of behavior. If it conforms to social or cultural norms, then it is ethical.

■ RELATIVISM

relativism

A term that reflects the degree to which one rejects moral standards in favor of the acceptability of some action. This way of thinking rejects absolute principles in favor of situation-based evaluations.

Relativism is a term that reflects the degree to which one rejects moral standards in favor of the acceptability of some action. This way of thinking rejects absolute principles in favor of situation-based evaluations. Thus, an action that is judged ethical in one situation can be deemed unethical in another.

■ IDEALISM

idealism

A term that reflects the degree to which one bases one's morality on moral standards.

In contrast, **idealism** is a term that reflects the degree to which one bases one's morality on moral standards. Someone who is an ethical idealist will try to apply ethical principles like the Golden Rule in all ethical dilemmas.

For example, a student may face an ethical dilemma when taking a test. Another student may arrange to exchange multiple choice responses to a test via electronic text messages. This represents an ethical dilemma because there are alternative courses of action each with differing moral implications. An ethical idealist may apply a rule that cheating is always wrong and therefore would not be likely to participate in the behavior. An ethical relativist may instead argue that the behavior is acceptable because a lot of the other students will be doing the same. In other words, the consensus is that this sort of cheating is acceptable, so this student would be likely to go ahead and participate in the behavior. Marketing researchers, marketing managers, and even consumers face ethical dilemmas practically every day. The following sections describe how this can occur.

General Rights and Obligations of Concerned Parties

Everyone involved in marketing research can face an ethical dilemma. For this discussion, we can divide those involved in research into three parties:

1.   The people actually performing the research, who can also be thought of as the "doers"

2. The research client, sponsor, or the management team requesting the research, who can be thought of as "users" of marketing research
3. The research participants, meaning the actual research respondents or subjects

Each party has certain rights and obligations toward the other parties. Exhibit 4.3 diagrams these relationships.

EXHIBIT 4.3
Interaction of Rights and Obligations Informed

Like the rest of business, research works best when all parties act ethically. Each party depends on the other to do so. A client depends on the researcher to be honest in presenting research results. The researcher depends on the client to be honest in presenting the reasons for doing the research and in describing the business situation. Each is also dependent on the research participant's honesty in answering questions during a research study. Thus, each is morally obligated toward the other. Likewise, each also has certain rights. The following section elaborates on the obligations and rights of each party.

Rights and Obligations of the Research Participant

Most marketing research is conducted with the research participant's consent. In other words, the participation is active. Traditional survey research requires that a respondent voluntarily answer questions in one way or another. This may involve answering questions on the phone, responding to an e-mail request, or even sending a completed questionnaire by regular mail. In these cases, **informed consent** means that the individual understands what the researcher wants him or her to do and consents to the research study. In other cases, research participants may not be aware that they are being monitored in some way. For instance, a research firm may monitor superstore purchases via an electronic scanner. The information may assist in understanding how customers respond to promotions. However, no consent is provided since the participant is participating passively. The ethical responsibilities vary depending on whether participation is active or passive.

informed consent

When an individual understands what the researcher wants him or her to do and consents to the research study.

■ THE OBLIGATION TO BE TRUTHFUL

When someone willingly consents to participate actively, it is generally expected that he or she will provide truthful answers. Honest cooperation is the main obligation of the research participant. In return for being truthful, the subject has the right to expect confidentiality. **Confidentiality** means that information involved in the research will not be shared with others. When the respondent truly believes that confidentiality will be maintained, then it becomes much easier to respond truthfully, even about potentially sensitive topics. Likewise, the researcher and research sponsor also may expect the respondent to maintain confidentiality. For instance, if the research involves a new food product from Nabisco, then they may not want the respondent to discuss the idea for fear that the idea may fall into the competition's hands. Thus, confidentiality is a tool to help ensure truthful responses.

confidentiality

The information involved in a research will not be shared with others.

■ PARTICIPANT'S RIGHT TO PRIVACY

Active Research

Americans relish their privacy. Hence, the right to privacy is an important issue in marketing research. This issue involves the participant's freedom to choose whether to comply with the investigator's request. Traditionally, researchers have assumed that individuals make an informed choice. However, critics have argued that the old, the poor, the poorly educated, and other underprivileged individuals may be unaware of their right to choose. They have further argued that an interviewer may begin with some vague explanation of a survey's purpose, initially ask questions that are relatively innocuous, and then move to questions of a highly personal nature. It has been suggested that subjects be informed of their right to be left alone or to break off the interview at any time. Researchers should not follow the tendency to "hold on" to busy respondents. However, this view definitely is not universally accepted in the research community.

The privacy issue is illustrated by these questions:

- "Is a telephone call that interrupts family dinner an invasion of privacy?"
- "Is an e-mail requesting response to a 30-minute survey an invasion of privacy?"

Generally, interviewing firms practice common courtesy by trying not to interview late in the evening or at other inconvenient times. However, the computerized random phone number interview has stimulated increased debate over the privacy issue. As a practical matter, respondents may feel more relaxed about privacy issues if they know who is conducting the survey. Thus, it is generally recommended that field interviewers indicate that they are legitimate researchers and name the company they work for as soon as someone answers the phone. For in-person surveys, interviewers should wear official name tags and provide identification giving their name and the names of their companies.

do-not-call legislation
Restricts any telemarketing effort from calling consumers who either register with a no-call list or who request not to be called.

Research companies should adhere to the principles of the "do-not-call" policy and should respect consumers' "Internet privacy." **Do-not-call legislation** restricts any telemarketing effort from calling consumers who either register with a no-call list in their state or who request not to be called. Legislators aimed these laws at sales-related calls. However, legislation in several states, including California, Louisiana, and Rhode Island, has extended this legislation to apply to "those that seek marketing information." Thus, the legislation effectively protects consumers' privacy from researchers as well as salespeople.[7]

Consumers often are confused about the difference between telemarketing efforts and true marketing research. Part of this is because telemarketers sometimes disguise their sales efforts by opening the conversation by saying they are doing research. The resulting confusion contributes to both increased refusal rates and lower trust. In 1980, a public opinion poll found that 19 percent of Americans reported having refused to participate in a marketing survey within the past year. Today, that number approaches 50 percent. In 2001, only 40 percent of Americans either agreed or strongly agreed that marketers will protect their privacy. That number is down from 50 percent in 1995.[8]

Companies using the Internet to do marketing research also face legislative changes. Much of this legislation is aimed at making sure consumers are properly notified about the collection of data and to whom it will be distributed. Researchers should make sure that consumers are given a clear and easy way to either consent to participation in active research or to easily opt out. Furthermore, companies should ensure that the information consumers send via the Internet is secure.[9]

Passive Research

Passive research involves different types of privacy issues. Generally, it is believed that unobtrusive observation of public behavior in places such as stores, airports, and museums is not a serious invasion of privacy. This belief is based on the fact that the consumers are indeed anonymous in that they are never identified by name nor is any attempt made to identify them. They are "faces in the crowd." As long as the behavior observed is typical of behavior commonly conducted in public, then there is no invasion of privacy. In contrast, recording behavior that is not typically conducted in public would be a violation of privacy. For example, hidden cameras recording people (without consent) taking showers at a health club, even if ultimately intended to gather information to help improve the shower experience, would be considered inappropriate.

Technology has also created new ways of collecting data passively that have privacy implications. Researchers are very interested in consumers' online behavior. For instance, the paths that consumers take while browsing the Internet can be extremely useful in understanding what kinds of information are most valued by consumers. Much of this information can be harvested and entered into a data warehouse. Researchers sometimes have legitimate reasons to use this data, which can improve consumers' ability to make wise decisions. In these cases, the researcher should gain the consumers' consent in some form before harvesting information from their Web usage patterns. Furthermore, if the information will be shared with other companies, a specific consent agreement is needed. This can come in the form of a question to which consumers respond yes or no, as in the following example:

From time to time, the opportunity to share your information with other companies arises and this could be very helpful to you in offering you desirable product choices. We respect your privacy, however, and if you do not wish us to share this information, we will not. Would you like us to share your information with other companies?

- *Yes, you can share the information*
- *No, please keep my information private*

Not all of these attempts are legitimate. Most readers have probably encountered spyware on their home computer. **Spyware** is software that is placed on your computer without consent or knowledge while using the Internet. This software then tracks your usage and sends the information back through the Internet to the source. Then, based on these usage patterns, the user will receive push technology advertising, usually in the form of pop-up ads. Sometimes, the user will receive so many pop-up ads that the computer becomes unusable. The use of spyware is illegitimate when it is done without consent, thus violating the right to privacy and confidentiality.

spyware

Software placed on a computer without consent or knowledge of the user.

Kid's Stuff Is Complicated

Children are involved in at least half of all spending in the United States. Thus, researchers need input from them to be able to deliver high-value products. However, legislators rightly have special concern for privacy when business interacts with children in some way. Researchers have a special obligation to ensure the safety of children. COPPA, the Children's Online Privacy Protection Act, defines a child as anyone under the age of thirteen. Anyone engaging in contact with a child through the Internet is obligated to obtain parental consent and notification before any personal information or identification can be provided by a child. Therefore, a researcher collecting a child's name, phone number, or e-mail address without parental consent is violating the law. While the law and ethic do not always correspond, in this case, it is probably pretty clear that a child's personal information shouldn't be collected.

Issues involving consent and confidentiality are complicated by a child's increased vulnerability. For instance, should a child be allowed to consent to participating in research without parental consent? Even something as innocuous as offering a child a cupcake for participating in research might not meet all parents' approval. Clearly, children under a certain age should only be interviewed in the presence of a parent. However, will the child respond the same way when a parent is present as when alone? Imagine asking a fourteen-year-old if he or she enjoys smoking cigarettes. How might a parent's presence change the response?[10] The age of consent for marketing research isn't clear even when research is within the guidelines of COPPA. To be safe, most standard research conducted with children under the age of sixteen should only be

© DAVID KATZENSTEIN/CORBIS

done with parental consent. When the research involves matters that are for "mature audiences," such as human sexuality or alcohol consumption, then parental consent should be sought for anyone under the age of eighteen.

Doing research with children can yield extremely useful information. However, it is also more risky than doing research with adults. When in doubt, researchers should consider how they would like to see their own child treated and then go even further to make sure that there are no ethical problems with the use of children in research.

■ DECEPTION AND THE RIGHT TO BE INFORMED

Experimental Designs

Experimental manipulations often involve some degree of deception. In fact, without some deception, a researcher would never know if a research subject was responding to the actual manipulation or to their perception of the experimental variable. This is why researchers sometimes use a placebo.

placebo

A false experimental effect used to create the perception that some effect has been administered.

A **placebo** is a false experimental effect used to create the perception of a true effect. Imagine two consumers, each participating in a study of the effect of a new herbal supplement on hypertension. One consumer receives a packet containing the citrus-flavored supplement, which is meant to be mixed in water and drunk with breakfast. The other also receives a packet, but in this case the packet contains a mixture that will simply color the water and provide a citrus flavor. The second consumer also believes he or she is drinking the actual supplement. In this way, the psychological effect is the same on both consumers, and any actual difference in hypertension must be due to the actual herbs contained in the supplement. Interestingly, experimental subjects often display some placebo effect in which the mere belief that some treatment has been applied causes some effect.

This type of deception can be considered ethical. Primarily, researchers conducting an experiment must generally (1) gain the willful cooperation of the research subject and (2) fully explain the actual experimental variables applied following the experiment's completion. Every experiment should include a **debriefing** session in which research subjects are fully informed and provided a chance to ask any questions that they may have about the experiment.

debriefing

Research subjects are fully informed and provided with a chance to ask any questions they may have about the experiment.

Mystery Shopper Research

Researchers sometimes will even withhold the actual research questions from respondents in simple descriptive research. A distinction can thus be made between deception and discreet silence. For instance, sometimes providing the actual research question to respondents is simply providing them more information than they need to give a valid response. A researcher may ask questions about the perceived price of a product when his or her real interest is in how consumers form quality impressions.

Research aimed at marketing employees also sometimes involves deception. For instance, employees are sometimes passive respondents in observational research involving a mystery shopper. **Mystery shoppers** are employees of a research firm that are paid to "pretend" to be actual shoppers. A mystery shopper would rarely identify him- or herself as anything other than a customer. However, since most employees perform their jobs in public, and perform behaviors that are easily observable, research using mystery shoppers is not considered an invasion of an employee's privacy. Mystery shoppers are used in nearly all areas of retailing and in most typical consumer services including the hotel, restaurant and tourism industries.

mystery shoppers

Employees of a research firm that are paid to pretend to be actual shoppers.

■ PROTECTION FROM HARM

Researchers should do everything they can to make sure that research participants are not harmed by participating in research. Most marketing research does not expose participants to any harm. However, the researcher should consider every possibility. For example, if the research involves tasting food or drink, the possibility exists that a research participant could have a severe allergic reaction. Similarly, researchers studying retail and workplace atmospherics often manipulate odors by injecting certain scents into the air.[11] The researcher is sometimes in a difficult situation. He or she has to somehow find out what things the subject is allergic to, without revealing the actual experimental conditions. One way this may be done is by asking the subjects to provide a list of potential allergies ostensibly as part of a separate research project.

Other times, research may involve some potential psychological harm. This may come in the form of stress or in the form of some experimental treatment that questions some strongly held conviction. For instance, a researcher studying helping behavior may lead a subject to believe that another person is being harmed in some way. In this way, the researcher can see how much a subject can withstand before doing something to help another person. In reality, the other person is usually a research confederate simply pretending to be in pain. Three key questions that can determine whether a research participant is being treated unethically as a result of experimental procedures are:

1. Has the research subject provided consent to participate in an experiment?
2. Is the research subject subjected to substantial physical or psychological trauma?
3. Can the research subject be easily returned to his or her initial state?

The issue of consent is tricky in experiments because the researcher cannot reveal exactly what the research is about ahead of time or the validity of the experiment will be threatened. In addition, experimental research subjects are usually provided some incentive to participate. We will have more on this later in the book, but ethically speaking, the incentives should always be noncoercive. In other words, a faculty member seeking volunteers should not withhold a student's grade if he or she does not participate in an experiment. Thus, the volunteer should provide consent without fear of harm for saying no and with some idea about any potential risk involved.

If the answer to the second question is yes, then the research should not be conducted. If the answer to the second question is no and consent is obtained, then the manipulation does not present an ethical problem, and the researcher can proceed.

The third question is really helpful in understanding how far one can go in applying manipulations to a research subject. If the answer to the third question is no, then the research should not be conducted. The Research Snapshot on the next page discussed the use of hypnosis in marketing research. If the hypnotic state would cause the participant severe trauma, or if he or she cannot be easily returned to the prehypnotic state, then the research procedure should not be used. If, for instance, the consumer makes a large number of purchases under hypnosis, going deeply into debt, returning him or her to the original state may be difficult. If so, the application of hypnosis is probably inappropriate. If the answer to this question is yes, then the manipulation is ethical.

Many research companies and practically all universities now maintain a **human subjects review committee**. This is a committee that carefully reviews a proposed research design to try to make sure that no harm can come to any research participant. A side benefit of this committee is that it can also review the procedures to make sure no legal problems are created by implementing the particular design. Sometimes, the name **Institutional Review Board** (IRB) is used to refer to this committee.

Rights and Obligations of the Client Sponsor (User)

■ ETHICAL BEHAVIOR BETWEEN BUYER AND SELLER

The general business ethic expected between a purchasing agent and a sales representative should hold in a marketing research situation. For example, if a purchasing agent has already decided to purchase a product from a friend, it would be unethical for that person to solicit competitive bids from others because they have no chance of being accepted. Similarly, a client seeking research should only seek bids from firms that have a legitimate chance of actually doing the work. In addition, any section on the ethical obligation of a research client would be remiss not to mention that the user is obligated to pay the provider the agreed-upon wage and pay within the agreed-upon time.

■ AN OPEN RELATIONSHIP WITH RESEARCH SUPPLIERS

The client sponsor has the obligation to encourage the research supplier to objectively seek out the truth. To encourage this objectivity, a full and open statement of the decision situation, a full disclosure of constraints in time and money, and any other insights that assist the researcher should be provided. This means that the researcher will be provided adequate access to key decision makers. These decision makers should agree to openly and honestly discuss matters related to the situation. Finally, this means that the client is open to actually using the research results. Time is simply too valuable to ask a researcher to perform a project when the results will not be used.

human subjects review committee

Carefully reviews proposed research design to try to make sure that no harm can come to any research participant. Otherwise known as an Institutional Review Board or IRB.

Institutional Review Board

Another name for a human subjects review committee.

Must Win Auction! Must Win Auction!

Auctions are certainly not new. However, auctions are no longer relegated to estate sales, livestock yards, or art sales; eBay and competing Web sites have brought the consumer auction to the masses. Consumers can bid on practically any product imaginable. The NCAA BCS Football Championship Game is sold out each year. But, you can always bid for tickets on eBay. A lucky owner of tickets for this game can sell tickets to the highest bidder. In 2004, loyal Louisiana State University Tiger fans were willing to bid and pay more than $600 for a ticket with a face value of about $60. Four years later, some of those same fans paid over $1,000 for a ticket to watch the Tigers win the national championship again.

Recently, there has been considerable interest in understanding why consumers have flocked to online auctions in such large numbers. The research can help Web designers and online auction companies decide how to design their sites to enhance the experience for consumers. When questioned, consumers often talk about how they can get a good price by participating in an auction, or they can get something they might not be able to otherwise. However, could it be that emotional reasons involved in competing to "win" the auctions are equally as important?

When consumers are unable or unwilling to voice their emotional or psychological reasons for behavior, some researchers have turned to hypnosis. Hypnosis relaxes the inhibitions of consumers and can get them to behave in a manner that may more accurately reflect their true thoughts, emotions, and behavior. A researcher may consider using hypnosis to study online auctions. Research participants could be recruited and asked to participate in a real online auction on eBay. Half of the participants will participate in the auction while a researcher looks on. The other half will do the same thing, but only after being induced into a hypnotic state by a member of the research team.

When preparing the report, the researcher notices that, indeed, those in the hypnotic state reported experiencing more emotions and more feelings of competitiveness than did other participants. Hypnotized respondents also placed more bids, purchased more goods, and had higher average price offers than did the others. Although the results appear to be valuable to the client, the researcher is beginning to have some reservations about the research approach used. Is the use of hypnosis ever ethical marketing research? If so, would this situation qualify as one in which there are no ethical issues in the use of hypnosis? Questions like these continue to plague the researcher. Compounding this problem is the fact that the research client wanted the research report completed by yesterday. The researcher suspects that the company already has a tactical plan for redesigning their Web operations. It isn't clear that the research results would ever be used anyway.

Sources: Wood, Charles M. and Tracy A. Suter, "Making Marketing Principles Tangible: Online Auctions as Living Case Studies," *Journal of Marketing Education*, 26 (August 2004), 137–144; Weinberg, Bruce D. and Lenita Davis, "Exploring the WOW in Online-Auction Feedback," *Journal of Business Research*, 58 (November 2005), 1609–1621. Fellman, M. W., "Mesmerizing Method Gets Results," *Marketing News*, 32 (July 20 1998), 1–38; McDonald, W. J., "Consumer Decision Making and Altered States of Consciousness: A Study of Dualities," *Journal of Business Research*, 42 (July 1998), 287–294; Handerson, Naomi R., "Good Research Tools Never Go Out of Style and Don't Shift in the Winds of Whatever Is New and Trendy," *Marketing Research*, 17 (Spring 2005), 39–40.

■ AN OPEN RELATIONSHIP WITH INTERESTED PARTIES

Conclusions should be based on data—not conjecture. Users should not knowingly disseminate conclusions from a research project in a manner that twists them into a position that cannot be supported by the data. Twisting the results in a self-serving manner or to support some political position poses serious ethical questions. A user may also be tempted to misrepresent results while trying to close a sale. Obviously, this is also morally inappropriate.

advocacy research

Research undertaken to support a specific claim in a legal action or represent some advocacy group.

Advocacy research—research undertaken to support a specific claim in a legal action or to represent some advocacy group—puts a client in a unique situation. Researchers often conduct advocacy research in their role as an expert witness. For instance, a researcher may be deposed to present evidence showing that a "knock-off" brand diminishes the value of a better known name brand. In conventional research, attributes such as sample size, profile of people actually interviewed, and number of questions asked are weighed against cost in traditional research. However, a court's opinion on whether research results are reliable may be based exclusively on any one specific research aspect. Thus, the slightest variation from technically correct procedures may be magnified by an attorney until a standard marketing research project no longer appears adequate in a judge's eyes. How open should the client be in the courtroom?

The ethic of advocacy research presents a number of serious issues that can lead to an ethical dilemma:

- Lawyers' first responsibility is to represent their clients. Therefore, they might not be interested as much in the truth as they are in evidence that supports their client's position. Presenting accurate research results may harm the client.

- A researcher should be objective. However, he or she runs the risk of conducting research that does not support the desired position. In this case, the lawyer may ask the researcher if the results can somehow be interpreted in another manner.
- Should the lawyer (in this case a user of research) ask the researcher to take the stand and present an inaccurate picture of the results?

Ethically, the attorney should certainly not put the researcher on the stand and encourage an act of perjury. The attorney may hope to ask specific questions that are so limited that taken alone, they may appear to support the client. However, this is risky because the opposing attorney likely also has an expert witness that can suggest questions for cross-examination. Returning to our branding example, if the research does not support an infringement of the known brand's name, then the brand name's attorney should probably not have the researcher take the stand.

Advocacy researchers do not necessarily bias results intentionally. However, attorneys rarely submit advocacy research evidence that does not support their clients' positions.

The question of advocacy research is one of objectivity: Can the researcher seek out the truth when the sponsoring client wishes to support its position at a trial? The ethical question stems from a conflict between legal ethic and research ethic. Although the courts have set judicial standards for marketing research methodology, perhaps only the client and individual researcher can resolve this question.

Privacy

People believe the collection and distribution of personal information without their knowledge is a serious violation of their privacy. The privacy rights of research participants create a privacy obligation on the part of the research client. Suppose a database marketing company is offering a mailing list compiled by screening millions of households to obtain brand usage information. The information would be extremely valuable to your firm, but you suspect those individuals who filled out the information forms were misled into thinking they were participating in a survey. Would it be ethical to purchase the mailing list? If respondents have been deceived about the purpose of a survey and their names subsequently are sold as part of a user mailing list, this practice is certainly unethical. The client and the research supplier have the obligation to maintain respondents' privacy.

Consider another example. Sales managers know that a marketing research survey of their business-to-business customers' buying intentions includes a means to attach a customer's name to each questionnaire. This confidential information could be of benefit to a sales representative calling on a specific customer. A client wishing to be ethical must resist the temptation to identify those accounts (that is, those respondents) that are the hottest prospects.

Privacy on the Internet

Privacy on the Internet is a controversial issue. A number of groups question whether Web site questionnaires, registration forms, and other means of collecting personal information will be kept confidential. Many marketers argue that their organizations don't need to know who the user is because the individual's name is not important for their purposes. However, they do want to know certain information (such as demographic characteristics or product usage) associated with an anonymous profile. For instance, a Web advertiser could reach a targeted audience without having access to identifying information. Of course, unethical companies may violate anonymity guidelines. Research shows that consumers are sensitive to confidentiality notices before providing information via a Web site. Over 80 percent of consumers report looking for specific privacy notices before they will exchange information electronically. In addition, over half believe that companies do not do enough to ensure the privacy of personal information.[12] Thus, research users should not disclose private information without permission from the consumers who provided that information.

Rights and Obligations of the Researcher

Marketing research firms and marketing research departments should practice good business ethic. Researchers are often the focus of discussions of business ethic because of the necessity that they interact with the public. Several professional organizations have written and adopted codes of ethic for their researchers, including the American Marketing Association, the European Society for Opinion and Market Research, and the Marketing Research Society.[13] Many of these codes are lengthy and the full contents can be found at the associations' Web sites. Key code components, most of which are described further in this chapter, directly relevant to marketing research prohibit:

- Representing a sales pitch as marketing research
- Providing the name of respondents who were promised anonymity for some purpose other than the research
- Breaching the confidentiality of the research client or research participant
- Doing research for multiple firms competing in the same market
- Disseminating false or misleading results
- Plagiarizing the work of other researchers
- Violating the integrity of data gathered in the field

In addition, the researchers have rights. In particular, once a research consulting firm is hired to conduct some research, they have the right to cooperation from the sponsoring client. Also, the researchers have the right to be paid for the work they do as long as it is done professionally. Sometimes, the client may not like the results. But not liking the results is no basis for not paying. The client should pay the researcher for competent work in full and in a timely manner.

■ THE PURPOSE OF RESEARCH IS RESEARCH

Mixing Sales and Research

Consumers sometimes agree to participate in an interview that is purported to be pure research, but it eventually becomes obvious that the interview is really a sales pitch in disguise. This is unprofessional at best and fraudulent at worst. The Federal Trade Commission (FTC) has indicated that it is illegal to use any plan, scheme, or ruse that misrepresents the true status of a person seeking admission to a prospect's home, office, or other establishment. No research firm or basic marketing researcher should engage in any sales attempts. Applied market researchers working for the sponsoring company should also avoid overtly mixing research and sales. However, the line is becoming less clear with increasing technology.

Research That Isn't Research

Consider the following typical exchange between a product manager and a marketing researcher. The manager wants to hire the firm to do a test-market for a new product:

Researcher:	*What if the test results are favorable?*
Product manager:	*Why, we'll launch the product nationally, of course.*
Researcher:	*And if the results are unfavorable?*
Product manager:	*They won't be. I'm sure of that.*
Researcher:	*But just suppose they are.*
Product manager:	*I don't think we should throw out a good product just because of one little market test.*
Researcher:	*Then why test?*
Product manager:	*Listen, Smith, this is a major product introduction. It's got to have some research behind it.*

It's probably pretty easy to see what is actually going on here. The product manager really wants research that will justify a decision that already has been made. If the test-market's results contradict the decision, the product manager will almost certainly disregard the research. This isn't really research so much as it is **pseudo-research** because it is conducted not to gather information for marketing decisions but to bolster a point of view and satisfy other needs.

The most common type of pseudo-research is performed to justify a decision that has already been made or that management is already strongly committed to. A media company may wish to sell advertising space on Internet search sites. Even though they strongly believe that the ads will be worth the rates they will charge advertisers, they may not have the hard evidence to support this view. Therefore, the advertiser's sales force may provide feedback indicating customer resistance to moving their advertising from local radio to the Internet. The advertising company may then commission a study for which the only result they care to find is that the Internet ads will be effective. In this situation, a researcher should walk away from the project if it appears that management strongly desires the research to support a predetermined opinion only. While it

pseudo-research

Conducted not to gather information for marketing decisions but to bolster a point of view and satisfy other needs.

is a fairly easy matter for an outside researcher to walk away from such a job, it is another matter for an in-house researcher to refuse such a job. Thus, avoiding pseudo-research is a right of the researcher but an obligation for the manager.

Occasionally, marketing research is requested simply to pass blame for failure to another area. A product manager may deliberately request a research study with no intention of paying attention to the findings and recommendations. The manager knows that the particular project is in trouble but plays the standard game to cover up for his or her mismanagement. If the project fails, marketing research will become the scapegoat. The ruse may involve a statement something like this: "Well, research should have identified the problem earlier!"

Push Polls

Politicians have concocted and specialize in a particular type of pseudo-research as a means of damaging opposing candidates' reputations and protecting their own. A **push poll** is telemarketing under the guise of research. Its name derives from the fact that the purpose of the poll is to push consumers into a pre-determined response. For instance, thousands of potential voters can be called and asked to participate in a survey. The interviewer then may ask loaded questions that put a certain spin on a candidate. "Do you think that candidate X, who is involved with people known to be linked to scandal and crime, can be trusted with the responsibility of office?" This is a push poll. An honest question may simply ask how much candidate X can be trusted.

push poll
Telemarketing under guise of research.

Push polling has pushed beyond politics. For example, during the summer of 2008, famous Green Bay Packer quarterback Brett Favre, who had announced his retirement earlier in the year, changed his mind and expressed a desire to play the 2008–09 season. However, the Packers were less than receptive. Several polls on the Internet and even via the telephone were conducted. Most of the polls were intended to get the Packers to welcome Brett back more than they were intended to provide a true picture of the population. The questions were often phrased in a leading fashion such as: "Do you believe that a proven, experienced quarterback who has led his team to the Super Bowl in the past gives the Packers the best chance of winning this year?" Obviously, this is a leading question because it frames the choice so that a yes response is very likely.

Service Monitoring

Occasionally, the line between research and customer service isn't completely clear. For instance, Toyota may survey all of its new car owners after the first year of ownership. While the survey appears to be research, it may also provide information that could be used to correct some issue with the customer. For example, if the research shows that a customer is dissatisfied with the way the car handles, Toyota could follow up with the specific customer. The follow-up could result in changing the tires of the car, resulting in a smoother and quieter ride, as well as a more satisfied customer. Should a pattern develop showing other customers with the same opinion, Toyota may need to switch the original equipment tires used on this particular car.

Push polls are often used to sway public opinion rather than measure it. Were they helpful to Brett Favre in 2008? Not really! He turned up as a Jet!

In this case, both research and customer service are involved. Since the car is under warranty, there would be no selling attempt. Researchers are often asked to design satisfaction surveys. These may identify the customer so they may be contacted by the company. Such practice is acceptable as long as the researcher allows the consumer the option of either being contacted or not being contacted. In other words, the customer should be asked whether it is okay for someone to follow up in an effort to improve their satisfaction. There are actually situations in which a customer could be made more satisfied by purchasing some product.

Push polls, selling under the guise of research, and pseudo-research are all misrepresentations of the true purpose of research and should be avoided. It is important that researchers understand the difference between research and selling.

■ OBJECTIVITY

The need for objective scientific investigation to ensure accuracy is stressed throughout this book. Researchers should maintain high standards to be certain that their data are accurate. Furthermore, they must not intentionally try to prove a particular point for political purposes. The conclusions should be based on the data not the desires of the researchers, the clients/managers or even the participants.

■ MISREPRESENTATION OF RESEARCH

It should go without saying, but research results should not be misrepresented. This means, for instance, that the statistical accuracy of a test should be stated precisely and the meaning of findings should not be understated or overstated. Both the researcher and the client share this obligation. There are many ways that research results can be reported in a less than full and honest way. For example, a researcher may present results showing a relationship between advertising spending and sales. However, the researcher may also discover that this relationship disappears when the primary competitors' prices are taken into account. In other words, the relationship between advertising spending and sales is made spurious by the competitors' prices (see Chapter 3). Thus, it would be questionable to say the least to report a finding suggesting that sales could be increased by increasing ad spending without also mentioning the spurious nature of this finding.

Honesty in Presenting Results

Misrepresentation can also occur in the way results are presented. For instance, charts can be created that make a very small difference appear very big. Likewise, they can be altered to make a meaningful difference seem small. Exhibit 4.4 illustrates this effect. Each chart presents exactly the same data. The data represent consumer responses to service quality ratings and satisfaction ratings. Both quality and satisfaction are collected on a 5-point strongly-disagree-to-strongly-agree scale. In frame A, the chart appears to show meaningful differences between men and women, particularly for the service-quality rating. However, notice that the scale range is shown as 4 to 5. In frame B, the researcher presents the same data but shows the full scale range (1 to 5). Now, the differences are reported as trivial.

All charts and figures should reflect fully the relevant range of values reported by respondents. If the scale range is from 1 to 5, then the chart should reflect a 1 to 5 range unless there is some value that is simply not used by respondents. If no or only a very few respondents had reported a 1 for their service quality or satisfaction rating, then it may be appropriate to show the range as 2 to 5. However, if there is any doubt, the researcher should show the full scale range.

The American Marketing Association's marketing Code of Ethic states that "a user of research shall not knowingly disseminate conclusions from a given research project or service that are inconsistent with or not warranted by the data." A dramatic example of a violation of this principle occurred in an advertisement of a cigarette smoker study. The advertisement compared two brands and stated that "of those expressing a preference, over 65 percent preferred" the advertised brand to a competing brand. The misleading portion of this reported result was that most of the respondents did *not* express a preference; they indicated that both brands tasted about the same. Thus, only a very small percentage of those studied actually revealed a preference, and the results were somewhat misleading. Such shading of results violates the obligation to report accurate findings.

■ HONESTY IN REPORTING ERRORS

Likewise, any major error that has occurred during the course of the study should not be kept secret from management or the sponsor. Hiding errors or variations from the proper procedures tends to distort or shade the results. Similarly, every research design presents some limitations. For instance, the sample size may be smaller than ideal. The researcher should point out the key limitations in the research report and presentation. In this way, any factors that qualify the findings can be understood. The decision maker needs this information before deciding on any risky course of action.

■ CONFIDENTIALITY

Confidentiality comes into play in several ways. The researcher must abide by any confidentiality agreement with research participants. For instance, a researcher conducting a descriptive

EXHIBIT 4.4
How Results Can Be Misrepresented in a Report or Presentation

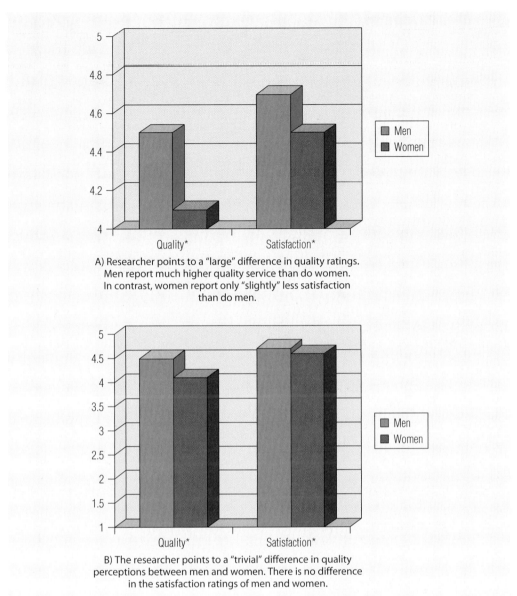

A) Researcher points to a "large" difference in quality ratings. Men report much higher quality service than do women. In contrast, women report only "slightly" less satisfaction than do men.

B) The researcher points to a "trivial" difference in quality perceptions between men and women. There is no difference in the satisfaction ratings of men and women.

research survey may have identified each participant's e-mail address in the course of conducting the research. After seeing the results, the client may ask for the e-mail addresses as a logical prospect list. However, as long as the researcher assured each participant's confidentiality, the e-mail addresses cannot ethically be provided to the firm. Indeed, a commitment of confidentiality also helps build trust among survey respondents.[14]

The marketing researcher often is obligated to protect the confidentiality of the research sponsor. In fact, business clients value marketing researchers' confidentiality more than any other attribute of a research firm.[15] Researchers must honor all implied and expressed promises of confidentiality whether they are made to a research participant or research client. This brings us to the topic of conflicts of interest which should be avoided, but doing so isn't always as easy as it may seem.

The Researcher and Conflicts of Interest

Imagine a researcher conducting a test market for a new high-tech Apple iPhone device that allows interactive video. Just after conducting the research, the same researcher is contacted by Samsung. Samsung, who has yet to develop video capability, wants research that addresses whether or not there

- A good way to get started in the marketing research industry is to target either a large marketing research firm or a local research firm with offers to serve as an intern. An internship will provide insight and experience that can provide a leg up on others in getting the job.
- When a company faces a very emotional decision, it is usually better to have the research needed to address the related research questions done by an outside firm.
- Those involved in research should consider the position of others involved in the process. When considering conducting or using research in some manner, one way to help ensure fair treatment of others involved in research is to consider whether you would like to be treated in this manner or whether you would like someone to treat a close member of your family in such a manner.
- Research with particularly vulnerable segments such as children involves special care. When doing research with children under the age of 16, parental consent is nearly always needed.
- Even the appearance of a conflict of interest can taint the research and the researcher. So, the wise researchers stay away from such appearances.

is a market for iPhone interactive video. The researcher is now in a difficult position. Certainly, an ethical dilemma exists presenting multiple choices to the researcher, including the following.

- Agreeing to do the research for Samsung and using some results from the Apple study to prepare a report and recommendation for Samsung
- Agreeing to sell the new concept to Samsung without doing any additional research. In other words, provide Apple's company secrets to Samsung
- Conducting an entirely new project for Samsung without revealing any of the results or ideas from the Apple study
- Turning down the chance to do the study without revealing any information about Apple to Samsung

Which is the best choice? Obviously, both of the first two options violate the principle of maintaining client confidentiality. Thus, both are unethical. The third choice, conducting an entirely new study, may be an option. However, it may prove nearly impossible to do the entire project as if the Apple study had never been done. Even with the best of intentions, the researcher may inadvertently violate confidentiality with Apple. The last choice is the best option from a moral standpoint. It avoids any potential **conflict of interest**. In other words, actions that would best serve one client, Samsung, would be detrimental to another client, Apple. Generally, it is best to avoid working for two direct competitors.

conflict of interest

Occurs when one researcher works for two competing companies.

This would be a good time to revisit the opening chapter vignette. Does the situation present the researcher with any potential conflicts of interest? How can they be addressed?

A Final Note on Ethics

Certainly, there are researchers who would twist results for a client or who would fabricate results for personal gain. However, these are not professionals. When one is professional, one realizes that one's actions not only have personal implications, but also implications for one's field. Indeed, just a few unscrupulous researchers can give the field a bad name. Thus, researchers should maintain the highest integrity in their work to protect our industry. Research participants should also play their role, or else the data they provide will not lead to better products for all consumers. Finally, the research users must also follow good professional ethic in their treatment of researchers and research results. When all three parties participate with integrity, consumers in general, and society overall, gain the most benefit from professional marketing research.

Summary

1. Know when research should be conducted externally and when it should be done internally. The company who needs the research is not always the best company to actually perform the research. Sometimes it is better to use an outside supplier of some form. An outside agency is better when a fresh perspective is needed, when it would be difficult for inside researchers to be objective, and when the outside firm has some special expertise. In contrast, it is better to do the research in-house when it needs to be done very quickly, when the project requires close collaboration of many employees within the company, when the budget for the project is limited, and when secrecy is a major concern. The decision to go outside or stay inside for research depends on these particular issues.

2. Be familiar with the types of jobs, job responsibilities, and career paths available within the marketing research industry. A marketing research function may be organized in any number of ways depending on a firm's size, business, and stage of research sophistication. Marketing research managers must remember they are managers, not just researchers. Marketing research offers many career opportunities. Entry-level jobs may involve simple tasks such as data entry or performing survey research. A research analyst may be the next step on the career path. This position may involve project design, preparation of proposals, data analysis, and interpretation. Whereas there are several intermediate positions that differ depending on whether one works for a small or large firm, the director of marketing research is the chief information officer in charge of marketing information systems and research projects. The director plans, executes, and controls the marketing research function.

3. Define ethics and understand how it applies to marketing research. Marketing ethic is the application of morals to behavior related to the exchange environment. Generally, good ethic conforms to the notion of "right" and a lack of ethic conforms to the notion of "wrong." Those involved in marketing research face numerous ethical dilemmas. Researchers serve clients or, put another way, the doers of research serve the users. It is often easy for a doer to compromise professional standards in an effort to please the user. After all, the user pays the bills. Given the large number of ethical dilemmas involved in research, ethic is highly applicable to marketing research.

4. Appreciate the rights and obligations of (a) research respondents—particularly children, (b) research clients or sponsors, and (c) marketing researchers. Each party involved in research has certain rights and obligations. These are generally interdependent in the sense that one party's right often leads to an obligation for another party. While the rights and obligations of all three parties are important, the obligation of the researcher to protect research participants is particularly important. Experimental manipulations can sometimes expose subjects to some form of harm or involve them in a ruse. The researcher must be willing to fully inform the subjects of the true purpose of the research during a debriefing. The researcher must also avoid subjecting participants to undue physical or psychological trauma. In addition, it should be reasonably easy to return an experimental subject to his or her original, pre-experiment condition.

5. Avoid situations involving a conflict of interest in performing marketing research. A marketing research conflict of interest occurs when a researcher is faced with doing something to benefit one client at the expense of another client. One situation where this occurs is when a researcher could use results obtained in a study done for Brand A to prepare a report for its primary competitor Brand B. The researcher might consider recollecting the data anew for Brand B, but even this opens up the researcher to the appearance of a conflict of interest. The best way to avoid a conflict of interest is to avoid getting involved with multiple projects involving competing firms within some market.

Key Terms and Concepts

advocacy research, 80

confidentiality, 75

conflict of interest, 86

cross-functional teams, 73

custom research, 69

debriefing, 78

director of marketing research, 71

do-not-call legislation, 76

ethical dilemma, 74

forecast analyst, 72

human subjects review committee, 79

idealism, 74

informed consent, 75

in-house research, 65

Institutional Review Board, 79

manager of decision support systems, 72

marketing ethics, 74

moral standards, 74

mystery shoppers, 78

outside agency, 65

placebo, 78

pseudo-research, 82

push poll, 83

relativism, 74

research analyst, 71

research assistants, 72

research suppliers, 68

spyware, 77

standardized research service, 68

syndicated service, 68

Questions for Review and Critical Thinking

1. What are the conditions that make in-house research preferable? What are the conditions that make outside research preferable? Would the company in the opening vignette have been better off to do the marketing research desired in-house rather than out-house?

2. Read a recent news article from *The Wall Street Journal* or other key source that deals with a new-product introduction. Would you think it would be better for that firm to do research in-house or to use an outside agency? Explain.

3. What might the organizational structure of the research department be like for the following organizations?
   a. A large advertising agency
   b. A founder-owned company that operates a 20-unit restaurant chain
   c. Your university
   d. An industrial marketer with four product divisions
   e. A large consumer products company

4. What problems do marketing research directors face in their roles as managers?

5. **NET** Search Internet job sites like www.monster.com. Try to gather 3 to 5 ads that are for marketing research positions of some type. Comment on the salary ranges and expected qualifications listed in these ads.

6. What is a cross-functional team? How is it relevant to marketing research?

7. What is the difference between research and pseudo-research? Cite several examples of each.

8. **ETHICS** What are marketing ethics? How are marketing ethics relevant to research?

9. **ETHICS** What is the difference between ethical relativism and ethical idealism? How might a person with an idealist ethical philosophy and a person with a relativist ethical philosophy differ with respect to including a sales pitch at the end of a research survey?

10. **ETHICS** What obligations does a researcher have with respect to confidentiality?

11. How should a marketing researcher help top management better understand the functions and limitations of research?

12. **ETHICS** List at least one research obligation for researcher participants (respondents), marketing researchers, and research clients (sponsors).

13. **ETHICS** What is a conflict of interest in a research context? How can such conflicts of interest be avoided?

14. **ETHICS** What key questions help resolve the question of whether or not research participants serving as subjects in an experiment are treated ethically?

15. Identify a research supplier in your area and determine what syndicated services and other functions are available to clients.

16. **'NET** Use the internet to find at least five marketing research firms that perform survey research. List and describe each firm briefly.

17. What actions might the marketing research industry take to convince the public that marketing research is a legitimate activity and that firms that misrepresent their intentions and distort findings to achieve their aims are not true marketing research companies?

18. **ETHICS** Comment on the ethic of the following situations.
    a. A food warehouse club advertises "savings up to 30 percent" after a survey showed a range of savings from 2 to 30 percent below average prices for selected items.
    b. A radio station broadcasts the following message during a syndicated rating service's rating period: "Please fill out your diary" [which lists what media the consumer has been watching or listening to].
    c. A sewing machine retailer advertises a market test and indicates that the regular price will be cut to one-half for three days only.
    d. A researcher tells a potential respondent that an interview will last ten minutes rather than the thirty minutes he or she actually anticipates.
    e. A respondent tells an interviewer that she wishes to cooperate with the survey, but her time is valuable and, therefore, she expects to be paid for the interview.
    f. When you visit your favorite sports team's home page on the Web, you are asked to fill out a registration questionnaire before you enter the site. The team then sells your information (team allegiance, age, address, and so on) to a company that markets sports memorabilia via catalogs and direct mail.

19. **ETHICS** Comment on the following interview:

Interviewer:	*Good afternoon, sir. My name is Mrs. Johnson, and I am with Counseling Services. We are conducting a survey concerning Memorial Park. Do you own a funeral plot? Please answer yes or no.*
Respondent:	*(pauses)*
Interviewer:	*You do not own a funeral plot, do you?*
Respondent:	*No.*
Interviewer:	*Would you mind if I sent you a letter concerning Memorial Park? Please answer yes or no.*
Respondent:	*No.*
Interviewer:	*Would you please give me your address?*

20. **ETHICS** Try to participate in a survey at a survey Web site such as http://www.mysurvey.com or http://www.themsrgroup.com. Write a short essay response about your experience with particular attention paid to how the sites have protections in place to prevent children from providing personal information.

Research Activities

1. **'NET** Find the mission statement of at least 3 of the top research firms described earlier in the chapter (see Exhibit 4.1). What career opportunities exist at these firms? Would you consider each firm a small, mid-sized, or large firm? How might a job with one of these firms differ from starting your own research business?

2. **'NET—ETHICS** One purpose of the United Kingdom's Market Research Society is to set and enforce the ethical standards to be observed by research practitioners. Go to its Web site at http://www.mrs.org.uk. Click on its code of conduct and evaluate it.

Case 4.1 Global Eating

© GETTY IMAGES/
PHOTODISC GREEN

Barton Boomer, director of marketing research for a large research firm, has a bachelor's degree in marketing from Michigan State University. He joined the firm nine years ago after a one-year stint as a marketing research trainee at the corporate headquarters of a western packing corporation. Barton has a wife and two children. He earns $60,000 a year and owns a home in the suburbs. He is typical of a marketing research analyst. He is asked to interview an executive with a local restaurant chain, Eats-R-Wee. Eats-R-Wee is expanding internationally. The logical two choices for expansion are either to expand first to other nations that have values similar to those in the market area of Eats-R-Wee or to expand to the nearest geographical neighbor. During the initial interviews, Mr. Big, Vice President of Operations for Eats-R-Wee, makes several points to Barton.

- "Barton, we are all set to move across the border to Ontario and begin our international expansion with our neighbor to the north, Canada. Can you provide some research that will support this position?"
- "Barton, we are in a hurry. We can't sit on our hands for weeks waiting to make this decision. We need a comprehensive research project completed by the end of the month."
- "We are interested in how our competitors will react. Have you ever done research for them?"
- "Don't worry about the fee; we'll pay you top money for a 'good' report."

Marla Madam, Barton's Director of Marketing Research, encourages Barton to get back in touch with Mr. Big and tell him that the project will get underway right away.

Question

Critique this situation with respect to Barton's job. What recommendations would you have for him? Should the company get involved with the research? Explain your answers.

Case 4.2 Big Brother is Watching?

© GETTY IMAGES/
PHOTODISC GREEN

Technology is making our behavior more and more difficult to keep secret. Right at this very moment, there is probably some way that your location can be tracked in a way that researchers could use the information. Do you have your mobile phone with you? Is there an RFID (sometimes pronounced Rfid) tag in your shirt, your backpack, or some other personal item? Are you in your car, and does it have a GPS (Global Positioning Satellite) device? All of these are ways that your location and movements might be tracked.

For instance, rental cars can be tracked using GPS. Suppose a research firm contracts with an insurance firm to study the way people drive when using a rental car. A customer's every movement is then tracked. So, if the customer stops at a fast-food restaurant, the researcher knows. If the customer goes to the movie when he or she should be on a sales call, the researcher knows. If the customer is speeding, the researcher knows.

Clearly, modern technology is making confidentiality more and more difficult to maintain. While legitimate uses of this type of technology may assist in easing traffic patterns and providing better locations for service stations, shopping developments, and other retailers, at what point does the collection of such information become a concern? When would you become concerned about having your whereabouts constantly tracked?

Question

Suppose a GIS (Geographic Information Systems) research firm is approached by the state legislature and asked to provide data about vehicle movement within the state for all cars with a satellite tracking mechanism. Based on the movement of the cars over a certain time, the police can decide when a car was speeding. They intend on using this data to send speeding tickets to those who moved too far, too fast. If you are the research firm, would you supply the data? Discuss the ethical implications of the decision.

Part 2
Designing
Research Studies

CHAPTER 5
Qualitative Research

CHAPTER 6
Secondary Data Research
in a Digital Age

CHAPTER 7
Survey Research

CHAPTER 8
Observation

CHAPTER 9
Conducting Marketing Experiments

CHAPTER 5
QUALITATIVE RESEARCH

After studying this chapter, you should be able to

1. Contrast qualitative research with quantitative research
2. Know the role of qualitative research in exploratory research designs
3. Describe the basic orientations of qualitative research
4. Recognize common qualitative research tools and know the advantages and limitations of their use
5. Prepare a focus group interview outline
6. Recognize technological advances in the application of qualitative research approaches
7. Appreciate the role of exploratory qualitative research in scientific decision making

Chapter Vignette: What's in the Van?

Is this shoe too cool? That was really the question asked by VF Corporation when they acquired Vans, the company that makes the shoe shown here.[1] Vans traditionally are synonymous with skateboarding and skateboard culture. Readers that are unfamiliar with skateboarding may well have never heard of the company. However, a reader that is part of the skateboard culture is probably looking down at his or her Vans right now!

Former Vans CEO Gary Schoenfeld points out that a decade before the acquisition (a $396 million deal), Vans was practically a dead brand.[2] However, he hoped to capitalize on a revival in skateboard interest that began in the 1990s. If Vans could remain the number one skateboard shoe provider, the shoe segment of their business would grow with this trend. Beyond this, the incoming management team was given the task of deciding how to raise Vans sales to $500 million per year.

Where would the growth come from? The trend in skateboard growth alone cannot support this goal. Should the company define itself as a "skateboard footwear" company, a "lifestyle" company, or as the icon for the skate culture? How would a core customer react to seeing Vans products in department stores like JCPenney? Answering this question requires a deeper interpretation of the meaning of the "Van."

Skateboarding is a dynamic activity. A study by Board-Trac suggests that today over one in four skateboarders is female, as opposed to fewer than one in ten as recently as 2000.[3] So, what exactly is in the mind and heart of a "boarder"? In 2008, the first "Goofy versus Regular" Skateboarding Competition was held and illustrates the carefree attitude of skaters.[4] In contrast, some of the growth is attributable to both men and women who simply find skateboarding a good alternative to more mundane exercise routines. Two important research questions involve "What is the meaning of a pair of Vans?" and "What things define the skateboarding experience?"

Questions like these call for qualitative research methods.[5] Not just any researcher is "fit" for this job. One way to collect this data is to hire young, energetic research employees to become "boarders" and immerse themselves into the culture.

They may have to "Kasper" like a "flatland techer" while probing for meaning among the discussion and activities of the other boarders. Here, Vans may find that their brand helps identify a boarder and make them feel unique in some ways. If so, Vans may want to investigate increasing their product line beyond shoes and simple apparel. The Vans Web site is much more than a place to find a pair of shoes (http://www.vans.com). Here, the lifestyle of the Vans fan is epitomized.

Depth interviews of Vans wearers can describe in detail why a consumer wears Vans. Vans shouldn't be surprised if they find a significant portion of their shoes are sold to people like Mr. Samuel Teel, a retired attorney from Toledo, Ohio. Sam is completely unaware of the connection between Vans and skateboarding. He likes Vans because he doesn't have to bend to tie his shoes! Maybe there are some secondary segments that could bring growth to Vans. Distribution through more general merchandisers like Kohl's and JCPenney provides ready access to secondary markets like these. But, will openly marketing to them complicate things? Time will tell.

Introduction: What Is Qualitative Research?

qualitative marketing research

Research that addresses marketing objectives through techniques that allow the researcher to provide elaborate interpretations of market phenomena without depending on numerical measurement; its focus is on discovering true inner meanings and new insights.

researcher-dependent

Research in which the researcher must extract meaning from unstructured responses such as text from a recorded interview or a collage representing the meaning of some experience.

Qualitative researchers can learn about the skating experience by becoming immersed in the culture.

Chemists sometimes use the term *qualitative analysis* to mean research that determines what some compound is made of. In other words, the focus is on the inner meaning of the chemical—its *qualities*. As the word implies, qualitative research is interested more in *qualities* than quantities. Therefore, qualitative research is not about applying specific numbers to measure variables or using statistical procedures to numerically specify a relationship's strength.

Describing Qualitative Research

Qualitative marketing research is research that addresses marketing objectives through techniques that allow the researcher to provide elaborate interpretations of market phenomena without depending on numerical measurement. Its focus is on discovering true inner meanings and new insights. Qualitative research is very widely applied in practice. There are many research firms that specialize in qualitative research.

Qualitative research is less structured than most quantitative approaches. Unlike the marketing research that most people are most familiar with, qualitative research does not rely on self-response questionnaires containing structured response formats. Instead, a qualitative approach is more **researcher-dependent** in that the researcher must extract meaning from unstructured responses, such as text from a recorded interview or a collage representing the meaning of some experience, such as skateboarding. The researcher interprets the data to extract its meaning and converts it to information.

■ USES OF QUALITATIVE RESEARCH

Mechanics can't use a hammer to fix everything that is broken. Instead, the mechanic has a toolbox from which a tool is matched to a problem. Marketing research is the same. The researcher has many tools available and the research design should try to match the best tool to the research objective. Also, just as a mechanic is probably not an expert with every tool, each researcher usually has special expertise with a small number of tools. Not every researcher has expertise with tools that would comprise qualitative research.

Generally, the less specific the research objective, the more likely that qualitative research tools will be appropriate. Also, when the emphasis is on a deeper understanding of motivations or on developing novel concepts, qualitative research is very appropriate. The following list represents common situations that often call for qualitative research.[6]

1. When it is difficult to develop specific and actionable decision statements or research objectives. For instance, if after several interviews with the research client the researcher still can't determine what needs to be measured, then qualitative research approaches may help with problem definition. Perhaps several previous studies of the same topic have not proven particularly useful.

© SKY BONILLO/PHOTOEDIT

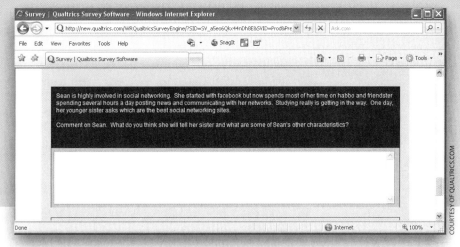

Although we most often think of surveys as ways of collecting quantitative data, we can also use them to collect qualitative data. Take a look at the question that was part of the in-class survey at left in the screenshot. Find at least three responses from students in the data and try to interpret the results. What approach best fits your attempt to interpret this data? What do you think (what theory) can be learned from the responses to this question? Compare your interpretation to those of other students. How much do you agree with other students and what do you think is the source of disagreement if any?

© GEORGE DOYLE & CIARAN GRIFFIN

COURTESY OF QUALTRICS.COM

2. When the research objective is to develop an understanding of some phenomena in great detail and in much depth. Qualitative research tools are aimed at discovering the primary themes indicating human motivations and the documentation of activities is usually very complete.

3. When the research objective is to learn how consumers use a product in its natural setting or to learn how to express some concept in colloquial terms. A survey can probably ask many useful questions, but watching how someone actually experiences a product will usually be more insightful. Qualitative research produces many product improvement ideas.

4. When some behavior the researcher is studying is particularly context-dependent—meaning the reasons something is liked or some behavior is performed depends very much on the particular situation surrounding the event. Understanding why Vans are liked so much is probably difficult to understand properly outside the skating environment.

5. When a fresh approach to studying some problem is needed. This is particularly the case when quantitative research has been less than satisfying. Qualitative tools can yield unique insights, many of which may lead to new product ideas.

Each situation also describes a situation that may require an exploratory orientation. In Chapter 3, we defined exploratory research as appropriate in ambiguous situations or when new insight is needed. We also indicated that exploratory research approaches are sometimes needed just to reach the appropriate decision statement and research objectives. While equating qualitative research with exploratory research is an oversimplification, the application of qualitative tools can help clear up ambiguity and provide innovative ideas.

Qualitative "versus" Quantitative Research

In social science, one can find many debates about the superiority of qualitative research over quantitative research or vice versa.[7] We'll begin by saying that this is largely a superfluous argument in either direction. The truth is that qualitative research can accomplish research objectives that quantitative research cannot. Similarly truthful, but no more so, quantitative research can accomplish objectives that qualitative research cannot. The key to successfully using either is to match the right approach to the right research context.

Many good research projects combine both qualitative and quantitative research. For instance, developing valid survey measures requires first a deep understanding of the concept to be measured and a description of the way these ideas are expressed in everyday language. Both of these are tasks best suited for qualitative research. However, validating the measure formally to make sure it can reliably capture the intended concept will likely require quantitative research.[8] Also, qualitative research may be needed to separate symptoms from problems and then quantitative research may follow to test relationships among relevant variables. The Research Snapshot on the next page describes one such situation.[9]

quantitative marketing research

Marketing research that addresses research objectives through empirical assessments that involve numerical measurement and analysis.

Quantitative marketing research can be defined as marketing research that addresses research objectives through empirical assessments that involve numerical measurement and analysis approaches. Qualitative research is more apt to stand on its own in the sense that it requires less interpretation. For example, quantitative research is quite appropriate when a research objective involves a managerial action standard. For example, a salad dressing company considered changing its recipe.[10] The new recipe was tested with a sample of consumers. Each consumer rated the product using numeric scales. Management established a rule that a majority of consumers rating the new product higher than the old product would have to be established with 90 percent confidence before replacing the old formula. A project like this can involve both quantitative measurement in the form of numeric rating scales and quantitative analysis in the form of applied statistical procedures.

Contrasting Qualitative with Quantitative Methods

Exhibit 5.1 illustrates some differences between qualitative and quantitative research. Certainly, these are generalities and exceptions may apply. However, it covers some of the key distinctions.

Quantitative researchers direct a considerable amount of activity toward measuring concepts with scales that either directly or indirectly provide numeric values. The numeric values can then be used in statistical computations and hypothesis testing. As will be described in detail later, this

EXHIBIT 5.1
Comparing Qualitative and Quantitative Research

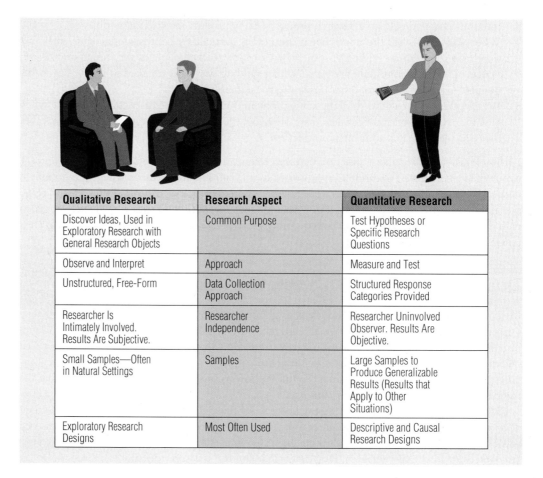

Qualitative Research	Research Aspect	Quantitative Research
Discover Ideas, Used in Exploratory Research with General Research Objects	Common Purpose	Test Hypotheses or Specific Research Questions
Observe and Interpret	Approach	Measure and Test
Unstructured, Free-Form	Data Collection Approach	Structured Response Categories Provided
Researcher Is Intimately Involved. Results Are Subjective.	Researcher Independence	Researcher Uninvolved Observer. Results Are Objective.
Small Samples—Often in Natural Settings	Samples	Large Samples to Produce Generalizable Results (Results that Apply to Other Situations)
Exploratory Research Designs	Most Often Used	Descriptive and Causal Research Designs

My Friends at P&G

With literally thousands of products to manage, Procter & Gamble (P&G) finds itself in the situation to conduct qualitative research almost daily. P&G doesn't introduce a product that hasn't been reviewed from nearly every possible angle. In-depth input on all aspects of business is part of the recipe for success. Before taking a product to a new country, P&G combines qualitative research techniques to discover potential problems or opportunities for marketing the product. So we can be sure that a product modification like Tide Kick or a laundry detergent made just for the French market, Le Croix Plus, has been "focus grouped." Today, P&G takes advantage of the Internet and the social networking phenomenon with a MySpace page dedicated to collecting qualitative research input. Here, they can float ideas about new products and collect criticisms and praise for their old products. Interestingly, P&G is among the companies actively blocking social networking Web sites in the workplace out of concerns for productivity and computer security.

At times, P&G seeks outside help to conduct research. Such was the case when P&G wanted a study of its marketing problems. The selected researchers began by applying qualitative research techniques including depth interviews, observational techniques (shadowing), and focus groups on P&G managers and marketing employees. These interviews gave the researchers the idea that perhaps P&G was suffering more from a management problem than from a marketing problem. It helped form a general research question that asked whether any marketing problems were really due to low morale among the marketing employees. After a lot of qualitative interviews with dozens and dozens of P&G employees, a quantitative study followed up these findings and supported this idea and led to suggestions for improving marketing morale! P&G quality begins with qualitative research.

Sources: Cornwell, L., "P&G Launches Two Social Networking Sites," *Marketing News*, 41 (February 1, 2007), 21; Nelson, Emily, "Focus Groupies: P&G Keeps Cincinnati Busy with all its Studies," *The Wall Street Journal* (Eastern Edition), 239 (January 24 2002), A1; Stengel, J. R., A. L. Dixon, and C. T. Allen, "Listening Begins at Home," *Harvard Business Review* (November 2003), 106–116; Lynch, C., "More Companies Ban Social Networks," *CIO*, 21 (April 15, 2008), 14.

© GEORGE DOYLE & CIARAN GRIFFIN

© AMY ETRA/PHOTOEDIT

process involves comparing numbers in some way. In contrast, qualitative researchers are more interested in observing, listening, and interpreting. As such, the researcher is intimately involved in the research process and in constructing the results. For these reasons, qualitative research is said to be more **subjective**, meaning that the results are researcher-dependent. Different researchers may reach different conclusions based on the same interview. In contrast, when a survey respondent provides a commitment score on a quantitative scale, it is thought to be more objective because the number will be the same no matter what researcher is involved in the analysis.

Qualitative research seldom involves samples with hundreds of respondents. Instead, a handful of consumers are usually the source of qualitative data. This is perfectly acceptable in discovery-oriented research. All ideas would still have to be tested before adopted. Does a smaller sample mean that qualitative research is cheaper than quantitative? Perhaps not. Although fewer respondents have to be interviewed, the greater researcher involvement in both the data collection and analysis can drive up the costs of qualitative research.

Given the close relationship between qualitative research and exploratory designs, it should not be surprising that qualitative research is most often used in exploratory designs. Small samples, interpretive procedures that require subjective judgments, and the unstructured interview format all make traditional hypotheses testing difficult with qualitative research. Thus, these procedures are not best suited for drawing definitive conclusions such as results from causal designs involving experiments. These disadvantages for drawing inferences, however, become advantages when the goal is to draw out potential explanations because the researcher spends more time with each respondent and is able to explore much more ground due to the flexibility of the procedures.

subjective

Results are researcher-dependent, meaning different researchers may reach different conclusions based on the same interview.

Qualitative Research and Exploratory Research Designs

When researchers have limited experience or knowledge about a research issue, exploratory research is a useful step. Exploratory research, which often involves qualitative methods, can be an essential first step to a more rigorous, conclusive, confirmatory study by reducing the chance of beginning with an inadequate, incorrect, or misleading set of research objectives.

Philosophically, research can be considered as either exploratory or confirmatory. Confirmatory research tests hypotheses. The results of these tests help decision making by suggesting a specific course of action. Exploratory research, on the other hand, takes a different approach. For instance, exploratory research may well be needed to develop the ideas that lead to research hypotheses in the first place.

qualitative data

Data that are not characterized by numbers, and instead are textual, visual, or oral; focus is on stories, visual portrayals, meaningful characterizations, interpretations, and other expressive descriptions.

Most exploratory research designs produce **qualitative data**. These data are not characterized by numbers and instead are textual, visual, or oral. The focus of qualitative research is not on numbers but on stories, visual portrayals, meaningful characterizations, interpretations, and other expressive descriptions. Exploratory designs do not usually produce **quantitative data**, which represent phenomena by assigning numbers in an ordered and meaningful way.

quantitative data

Represent phenomena by assigning numbers in an ordered and meaningful way.

For example, a quantitative researcher may search for numbers that indicate economic trends. This may lead to hypothesis tests concerning how much the economy influences movie consumption. An exploratory researcher is more likely to adopt a qualitative approach that might involve trying to develop a deeper understanding of how families are impacted by changing economic times and why people suffering economically spend scarce resources on movie consumption. This may lead to the development of a hypothesis, but would not test one.

Some types of qualitative studies can be conducted very quickly. Others take a very long time. For example, a single focus group analysis involving a large bottling company's sales force can likely be conducted and interpreted in a matter of days. This would provide faster results than most descriptive or causal designs. However, other types of qualitative research, such as a participant-observer study aimed at understanding skateboarding, could take months to complete. A qualitative approach can, but does not necessarily, save time.

Idea Generation

Exploratory research plays a big role in new product development, including developing and screening new product ideas. Exploratory research is particularly useful in idea generation and screening by producing multiple ideas and then narrowing the choices down to a small number of alternatives. In this process, exploratory research may indicate that some new product ideas are unworkable.

Qualitative research can generate ideas for new products, advertising copy, promotional ideas, and product improvements in numerous ways. Researchers using qualitative approaches can ask consumers to describe their product experiences in great detail. This data can reveal the consumer needs that a product can truly address. For example, a consumer may be asked to describe their dog food experiences. When a customer is asked what he or she wants in a dog food, the reply likely will be "Something that is good for the dog." Once the consumer is encouraged to continue, however, we may learn that the dog food "smells bad in the refrigerator" and "is messy to clean up." Thus, the interview reveals that needs related to dog food are not entirely centered on the dog.

Technology can also assist in this effort. For example, automobile marketers have consumers design their dream cars using computerized design systems similar to those used by automotive designers. This exploratory research might generate ideas that would never have occurred to the firm's own designers.[11]

Concept Testing

concept testing

A frequently performed type of exploratory research representing many similar research procedures all having the same purpose: to screen new, revised, or repositioned ideas.

Research's main role in idea screening is concept testing. **Concept testing** is a frequently performed type of exploratory research representing many similar research procedures all having the same purpose: to screen new, revised, or repositioned ideas. Although the term *testing* is used, concept testing approaches are largely qualitative. Typically, respondents are presented with a written statement, pictorial representation, or some other idea description form and asked for comments. The questions almost always include whether the idea is likable, whether it would be useful, and whether it seems new. Respondents then are provided an opportunity to elaborate on the idea orally, in writing, or through some visual communication. Concept testing allows an initial evaluation prior to the commitment of any additional research and development, manufacturing, or other company resources. Perhaps just as importantly, the qualitative analysis of respondent comments provides themes that can be used to improve the product.

Concept testing processes work best when they not only identify ideas with the most potential, but they also lead to important refinements. Beiersdorf, the German company that produces Nivea skin care products (http://www.beiersdorf.com, http://www.nivea.com), like all consumer product firms, is constantly developing and screening new product ideas. One idea included a blemish-hiding skin crème that worked by reflecting light from the blemish causing it to "disappear." During concept testing, most consumers were interested but asked questions about its moisturizing abilities. As a result, the product was introduced by emphasizing both its ability to hide blemishes and to moisturize the skin.[12]

Likewise, if Vans introduces snowboarding and biking products as a way of increasing sales revenues, those products will have to undergo concept screening. Will consumers respond favorably to the ideas of a Vans Cushioned Snowboard or Vans Biking Shoes? What does the Vans idea mean to snowboarders or bikers? Clearly, concept testing including probing interview techniques will be helpful in this effort.

Exhibit 5.2 shows excellent concept statements for two new alternative chain restaurant concepts. Each is being floated by a national franchise that operates various chain restaurants that compete with the likes of Hooters and Outback Steakhouse. The statements portraying the intangibles (brand image, product appearance, name, and price) and a description of the product simulate reality. The product idea is clearly conveyed to the research participant who is then asked to respond in some way. Their comments become the key information gleaned from the study.

EXHIBIT 5.2

Testing New Product Concepts

| | Concept | |
Component	Havana's	Bekkah
Brand Image	Family oriented, Cuban themed, with generous portions of modestly priced food	Upscale hangout for on-the-go individuals looking for a change of pace
Atmosphere	Bright colors, Cuban music all day and every day with every restaurant built around a bar featuring genuine '57 Chevys	Muted colors and stone walls giving the appearance of an oasis in an arid climate
Product Assortment	Traditional Cuban slow-cooked meats with generous sides like black beans and fried plantains. Cuban sangria and a wide assortment of beer are featured.	Lebanese meats sliced very thin with traditional Middle Eastern seasonings, a variety of pita breads, feta cheese, and yogurt relishes. Lebanese wines are featured and supplement an otherwise domestic collection.
Price Points	Average ticket per customer is projected to be around $14.	Average ticket per customer is projected to be around $26.
Location	Suburban location around the top 10 largest metropolitan areas in the United States and Canada	Major SMSAs (standard metropolitan statistical areas) across the southern United States from San Diego, CA to Jacksonville, FL

Qualitative Research Orientations

Qualitative research can be performed in many ways using many techniques. Orientations to qualitative research are very much influenced by the different fields of study involved in research. These orientations are each associated with a category of qualitative research. The major categories of qualitative research include

1. Phenomenology—originating in philosophy and psychology
2. Ethnography—originating in anthropology

3. Grounded theory—originating in sociology
4. Case studies—originating in psychology and in business research

Precise lines between these approaches are difficult to draw and a particular qualitative research study may involve elements of two or more approaches. However, each category does reflect a somewhat unique approach to human inquiry and approaches to discovering knowledge. Each will be described briefly, followed by a description of some of the more common qualitative techniques used to generate qualitative data.

Phenomenology

■ WHAT IS A PHENOMENOLOGICAL APPROACH TO RESEARCH?

phenomenology

A philosophical approach to studying human experiences based on the idea that human experience itself is inherently subjective and determined by the context in which people live.

Phenomenology represents a philosophical approach to studying human experiences based on the idea that human experience itself is inherently subjective and determined by the context in which people live.[13] The phenomenological researcher focuses on how a person's behavior is shaped by the relationship he or she has with the physical environment, objects, people, and situations. Phenomenological inquiry seeks to describe, reflect upon, and interpret experiences.

Researchers with a phenomenological orientation rely largely on conversational interview tools. When conversational interviews are face to face, they are recorded either with video- or audiotape and then interpreted by the researcher. The phenomenological interviewer is careful to avoid asking direct questions when at all possible. Instead, the research respondent is asked to tell a story about some experience. In addition, the researcher must do everything possible to make sure a respondent is comfortable telling his or her story. One way to accomplish this is to become a member of the group (for example, becoming a skateboarder in the scenario described earlier in this chapter). Another way may be to avoid having the person use his or her real name. This might be particularly necessary in studying potentially sensitive topics including smoking, shoplifting, or employee theft.

Therefore, a phenomenological approach to studying the meaning of Vans may require considerable time. The researcher may first spend weeks or months fitting in with the person or group of interest to establish a comfort level. During this time, careful notes of conversations are made. If an interview is sought, the researcher would likely not begin by asking a skateboarder to describe his or her shoes. Rather, asking for favorite skateboard incidents or talking about what makes a skateboarder unique may generate productive conversation. Generally, the approach is very unstructured as a way of avoiding leading questions and to provide every opportunity for new insights.

■ WHAT IS HERMENEUTICS?

hermeneutics

An approach to understanding phenomenology that relies on analysis of texts through which a person tells a story about him- or herself.

The term hermeneutics is important in phenomenology. **Hermeneutics** is an approach to understanding phenomenology that relies on analysis of texts in which a person tells a story about him- or herself.[14] Meaning is then drawn by connecting text passages to one another or to themes expressed outside the story. These connections are usually facilitated by coding the key meanings expressed in the story. While a full understanding of hermeneutics is beyond the scope of this text, some of the terminology is used when applying qualitative tools. For instance, a **hermeneutic unit** refers to a text passage from a respondent's story that is linked with a key theme from within this story or provided by the researcher.[15] These passages are an important way in which data are interpreted.

hermeneutic unit

Refers to a text passage from a respondent's story that is linked with a key theme from within this story or provided by the researcher.

Computerized software exists to assist in coding and interpreting texts and images. ATLAS.ti is one such software package that adopts the term hermeneutic unit in referring to groups of phrases that are linked with meaning. Hermeneutic units and computerized software are also very appropriate in grounded theory approaches. One useful component of computerized approaches is a word counter. The word counter will return counts of how many times words were used in a story or recorded interview. Often, frequently occurring words suggest a key

"When Will I Ever Learn?"
A hermeneutic approach can be used to provide insight into car shopping experiences. The approach involves a small number of consumers providing relatively lengthy stories about recent car shopping experiences. The goal is trying to discover particular reasons why certain car models are eliminated from consideration. The consumer tells a story of comparing a Ford and a GM (General Motors) minivan. She describes the two vehicles in great detail and ultimately concludes, "We might have gone with the Ford instead because it was real close between the Ford and the GM." The Ford was cheaper, but the way the door opened suggested difficulties in dealing with kids and groceries and the like, and so she purchased the GM model. The researcher in this story goes on to interpret the plotline of the story as having to do with her responsibility for poor consumption outcomes. Consider the following passage.

"It has got GM defects and that is really frustrating. I mean the transmission had to be rebuilt after about 150 miles . . . and it had this horrible vibration problem. We took a long vacation where you couldn't go over sixty miles an hour because the thing started shaking so bad. . . . I told everybody, 'Don't buy one of these things.' We should have known because our Buick—the Buick that is in the shop right now—its transmission lasted about 3,000 miles. My husband's parents are GM people and they had one go bad. I keep thinking, When I am going to learn? I think this one has done it. I don't think I will ever go back to GM after this."

The research concludes that a hermeneutic link exists between the phrase "When I am going to learn?" and the plot of self-responsibility. The resulting behavior including no longer considering GM products and the negative word-of-mouth behavior are ways of restoring esteem given the events.

Source: *Journal of Marketing Research* by/Winer, Russ. Copyright 1997 by Am Marketing assn (AMA) (CHIC). Reproduced with permission of Am Marketing Assn (AMA) (CHIC) in the format Textbook via Copyright Clearance Center; Thompson, Craig J., "Interpreting Consumers: A Hermeneutical Framework for Deriving Marketing Insights from the Tests of Consumers' Consumption Stories," *Journal of Marketing Research*, 34 (November 1997), 438–455 (see pp. 443–444 for quotation).

theme and greatly assist the researcher in developing an interpretation. Additionally, qualitative software provides an easy way to record field notes and remove the clerical tasks of transcribing or otherwise manually recording large volumes of text or other qualitative input.[16] The Research Snapshot above demonstrates the use of hermeneutics in interpreting a story about a consumer shopping for a car.

Ethnography

■ WHAT IS ETHNOGRAPHY?

Ethnography represents ways of studying cultures through methods that involve becoming highly active within that culture. **Participant-observation** typifies an ethnographic research approach. Participant-observation means the researcher becomes immersed within the culture that he or she is studying and draws data from his or her observations. A *culture* can be either a broad culture, like American culture, or a narrow culture, like urban gangs or skateboarding enthusiasts.[17]

Organizational culture would also be relevant for ethnographic study.[18] At times, researchers have actually become employees of an organization for an extended period of time. In doing so, they become part of the culture and over time other employees come to act quite naturally around the researcher. The researcher may observe behaviors that the employee would never reveal otherwise. For instance, a researcher investigating the ethical behavior of salespeople may have difficulty getting a car salesperson to reveal any potentially deceptive sales tactics in a traditional interview. However, ethnographic techniques may result in the salesperson letting down his or her guard, resulting in more valid discoveries about the car-selling culture.

■ OBSERVATION IN ETHNOGRAPHY

Observation plays a key role in ethnography. Researchers today sometimes ask households for permission to place video cameras in their home. In doing so, the ethnographer can study the

ethnography
Represents ways of studying cultures through methods that involve becoming highly active within that culture.

participant-observation
Ethnographic research approach where the researcher becomes immersed within the culture that he or she is studying and draws data from his or her observations.

Ethnographic (participant-observation) approaches may be useful to understanding how children obtain value from their experiences with toys.

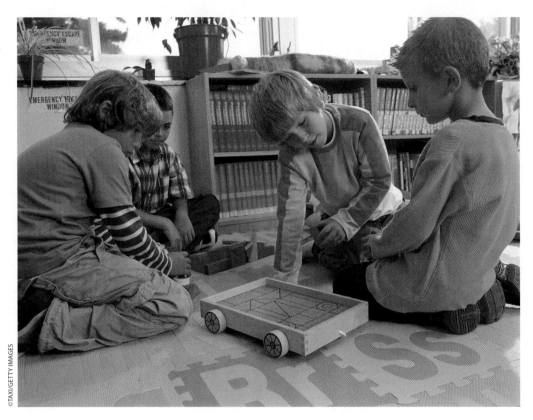

©TAXI/GETTY IMAGES

consumer in a "natural habitat" and use the observations to test new products, develop new product ideas, and develop marketing strategies in general.[19]

Ethnographic study can be particularly useful when a certain culture is comprised of individuals who cannot or will not verbalize their thoughts and feelings. For instance, ethnography has advantages for discovering insights among children since it does not rely largely on their answers to questions. Instead, the researcher can simply become part of the environment, allow the children to do what they do naturally, and record their behavior.[20]

The opening vignette describing a participant-observer approach to learning about skateboarding culture represents an ethnographic approach. Here, the researcher would draw insight from observations and personal experiences with the culture. Kodak used in-home ethnographic research in developing the "Pass Along" advertisement campaign.[21] The research revealed that consumers, particularly younger consumers, enjoyed passing disposable cameras around to friends and these images became a prominent part of the campaign.

Grounded Theory

■ WHAT IS GROUNDED THEORY?

Grounded theory is probably applied less often in business research than is either phenomenology or ethnography.[22]

Grounded theory represents an inductive investigation in which the researcher poses questions about information provided by respondents or taken from historical records. The researcher asks the questions to him- or herself and repeatedly questions the responses to derive deeper explanations. Grounded theory is particularly applicable in highly dynamic situations involving rapid and significant change. Two key questions asked by the grounded theory researcher are "What is happening here?" and "How is it different?"[23] The distinguishing characteristic of grounded theory is that it does not begin with a theory but instead extracts one from whatever emerges from an area of inquiry.

grounded theory

Represents an inductive investigation in which the researcher poses questions about information provided by respondents or taken from historical records; the researcher asks the questions to him- or herself and repeatedly questions the responses to derive deeper explanations.

■ HOW IS GROUNDED THEORY USED?

Consider a company that approaches a researcher to study whether or not its sales force is as effective as it has been over the past five years. The researcher uses grounded theory to discover a potential explanation. A theory is inductively developed based on text analysis of dozens of sales meetings that had been recorded over the previous five years. By questioning the events discussed in the sales interviews and analyzing differences in the situations that may have led to the discussion, the researcher is able to develop a theory. The theory suggests that with an increasing reliance on e-mail and other technological devices for communication, the salespeople do not communicate with each other informally as much as they did five years previously. As a result, the salespeople had failed to bond into a close-knit "community."[24]

Computerized software also can be useful in developing grounded theory. In our Vans example, the researcher may interpret skateboarders' stories of good and bad skating experiences by questioning the events and changes described. These may yield theories about the role that certain brands play in shaping a good or bad experience. Alternatively, grounded theorists often rely on visual representations. Thus, the skateboarder could develop collages representing good and bad experiences. Just as with the text, questions can be applied to the visuals in an effort to develop theory.

Case Studies

■ WHAT ARE CASE STUDIES?

Case studies simply refer to the documented history of a particular person, group, organization, or event. Typically, a case study may describe consumers' acceptance or rejection of a particular product. Alternatively, case studies may describe the events of a specific company introducing a new product or dealing with some management crisis. Textbook cases typify this kind of case study. Clinical interviews of individual consumers can represent a case study. These may focus on their experiences with certain brands or products.

The case studies can then be analyzed for important themes. **Themes** are identified by the frequency with which the same term (or a synonym) arises in the narrative description. The themes may be useful in discovering variables that are relevant to potential explanations.

■ HOW ARE CASE STUDIES USED?

Case studies are commonly applied in business. For instance, case studies of brands that sell "luxury" products helped provide insight into what makes up a prestigious brand. A marketing researcher carefully conducted case studies of higher-end wine labels (such as Penfold's Grange) including the methods of production and marketing. This analysis suggested that a key ingredient to a prestige brand may well be authenticity. When consumers know something is authentic, they attach more esteem to that product or brand.[25]

A primary advantage of the case study is that an entire organization or entity can be investigated in depth with meticulous attention to detail. This highly focused attention enables the researcher to carefully study the order of events as they occur or to concentrate on identifying the relationships among functions, individuals, or entities. Conducting a case study often requires the cooperation of the party whose history is being studied. This freedom to search for whatever data an investigator deems important makes the success of any case study highly dependent on the alertness, creativity, intelligence, and motivation of the individual performing the case analysis.

case studies

The documented history of a particular person, group, organization, or event.

themes

Identified by the frequency with which the same term (or a synonym) arises in the narrative description.

Qualitative research reveals that products that are perceived as "authentic" offer more value for consumers.

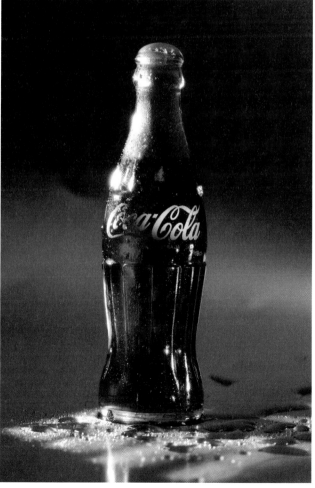

©PHOTO CUISINE/CORBIS

Common Techniques Used in Qualitative Research

Qualitative researchers apply a nearly endless number of techniques. These techniques overlap more than one of the categories previously discussed, although each category may display a preference for certain techniques. Exhibit 5.3 lists characteristics of some common qualitative research techniques. Each is then described.

Focus Group Interview

The focus group interview is so widely used that many advertising and research agencies do nothing but focus group interviews. In that sense, it is wrongly synonymous with qualitative

EXHIBIT 5.3 **Common Qualitative Research Tools**

Tool	Description	Type of Approach (Category)	Key Advantages	Key Disadvantages
Focus Group Interviews	Small group discussions led by a trained moderator	Ethnography, Case Studies	• Can be done quickly • Gain multiple perspectives • Flexibility	• Results do not generalize to larger population • Difficult to use for sensitive topics • Expensive
Depth Interviews	One-on-one, probing interview between a trained researcher and a respondent	Ethnography, Grounded Theory, Case Studies	• Gain considerable insight from each individual • Good for understanding unusual behaviors	• Results not meant to generalize • Very expensive per each interview
Conversations	Unstructured dialogue recorded by a researcher	Phenomenology, Grounded Theory	• Gain unique insights from enthusiasts • Can cover sensitive topics • Less expensive than depth interviews or focus groups	• Easy to get off course • Interpretations are very researcher-dependent
Semi-Structured Interviews	Open-ended questions, often in writing, that ask for short essay-type answers from respondents	Grounded theory, ethnography	• Can address more specific issues • Results can be easily interpreted • Cost advantages over focus groups and depth interviews	• Lack the flexibility that is likely to produce truly creative or novel explanations
Word Association/ Sentence Completion	Records the first thoughts that come to a consumer in response to some stimulus	Grounded theory, case studies	• Economical • Can be done quickly	• Lack the flexibility that is likely to produce truly creative or novel explanations
Observation	Recorded notes describing observed events	Ethnography, grounded theory, case studies	• Can be inobtrusive • Can yield actual behavior patterns	• Can be very expensive with participant-observer series
Collages	Respondent assembles pictures that represent their thoughts/feelings	Phenomenology, Grounded theory	• Flexible enough to allow novel insights	• Highly dependent on the researcher's interpretation of the collage
Thematic Apperception/ Cartoon Tests	Researcher provides an ambiguous picture and respondent tells about the story	Phenomenology, Grounded theory	• Projective, allows to get at sensitive issues • Flexible	• Highly dependent on the researcher's interpretation

research. A **focus group interview** is an unstructured, free-flowing interview with a small group of people, usually between six and ten. Focus groups are led by a trained moderator who follows a flexible format encouraging dialogue among respondents. Common focus group topics include employee programs, brand meanings, problems with products, advertising themes, or new-product concepts.

The group meets at a central location at a designated time. Participants may range from consumers talking about hair coloring, petroleum engineers talking about problems in the "oil patch," children talking about toys, or employees talking about their jobs. A moderator begins by providing some opening statement to broadly steer discussion in the intended direction. Ideally, discussion topics emerge at the group's initiative, not the moderator's. Consistent with phenomenological approaches, moderators should avoid direct questioning unless absolutely necessary.

■ ADVANTAGES OF FOCUS GROUP INTERVIEWS

Focus groups allow people to discuss their true feelings, anxieties, and frustrations, as well as the depth of their convictions, in their own words. While other approaches may also do much the same, focus groups offer several advantages.

1. Relatively fast
2. Easy to execute
3. Allow respondents to piggyback off each other's ideas
4. Provide multiple perspectives
5. Flexibility to allow more detailed descriptions
6. High degree of scrutiny

Speed and Ease

In an emergency situation, three or four group sessions can be conducted, analyzed, and reported in a week or so. The large number of research firms that conduct focus group interviews makes it easy to find someone to conduct the research. Practically every state in the United States contains multiple research firms that have their own focus group facilities. Companies with large research departments likely have at least one qualified focus group moderator so that they need not outsource the focus group.

Piggybacking and Multiple Perspectives

Furthermore, the group approach may produce thoughts that would not be produced otherwise. The interplay between respondents allows them to **piggyback** off of each other's ideas. In other words, one respondent stimulates thought among the others and, as this process continues, increasingly creative insights are possible. A comment by one individual often triggers a chain of responses from the other participants. The social nature of the focus group also helps bring out multiple views as each person shares a particular perspective.

Flexibility

The flexibility of focus group interviews is advantageous, especially when compared with the more structured and rigid survey format. Numerous topics can be discussed and many insights can be gained, particularly with regard to the variations in consumer behavior in different situations. Responses that would be unlikely to emerge in a survey often come out in group interviews: "*If* it is one of the three brands I sometimes use and *if* it is on sale, I buy it; otherwise, I buy my regular brand" or "*If* the day is hot and I have to serve the whole neighborhood, I make Kool-Aid; otherwise, I give them Dr Pepper or Coke."

If a researcher is investigating a target group to determine who consumes a particular beverage or why a consumer purchases a certain brand, situational factors must be included in any interpretations of respondent comments. For instance, in the situation above, the fact that a particular beverage is consumed must be noted. It would be inappropriate to say that Kool-Aid is preferred in general. The proper interpretation is situation-specific. On a hot day the whole neighborhood

focus group interview

An unstructured, free-flowing interview with a small group of around six to ten people. Focus groups are led by a trained moderator who follows a flexible format encouraging dialogue among respondents.

piggyback

A procedure in which one respondent stimulates thought among the others; as this process continues, increasingly creative insights are possible.

Focus group facilities typically include a comfortable room for respondents, recording equipment, and a viewing room via a two-way mirror.

gets Kool-Aid. When the weather isn't hot, the kids may get nothing, or if only a few kids are around, they may get lucky and get Dr Pepper. Thus, Kool-Aid can be interpreted as appropriate for satisfying large numbers of hot kids while Dr Pepper is a treat for a select few.

Scrutiny

A focus group interview allows closer scrutiny in several ways. First, the session can be observed by several people, as it is usually conducted in a room containing a two-way mirror. The respondents and moderator are on one side, and an invited audience that may include both researchers and decision makers is on the other. If the decision makers are located in another city or country, the session may be shown via a live video hookup. Either through live video or a two-way mirror, some check on the eventual interpretations is provided through the ability to actually watch the research being conducted. Second, focus group sessions are generally recorded on audio- or videotape. Later, detailed examination of the recorded session can offer additional insight and help clear up disagreements about what happened.

■ FOCUS GROUP ILLUSTRATION

Focus groups often are used for concept screening and concept refinement. The concept may be continually modified, refined, and retested until management believes it is acceptable. While RJR's initial attempts at smokeless cigarettes failed in the United States, Philip Morris is developing a smokeless cigarette for the U.K. market. Focus groups are being used to help understand how the product will be received and how it might be improved.[26] The voluntary focus group respondents are presented with samples of the product and then they discuss it among themselves. The interview results suggest that the key product features that must be conveyed are the fact that it produces no ashes, no side smoke, and very little odor. These beliefs are expected to lead to a positive attitude. Focus group respondents show little concern about how the cigarette actually functioned. Smokers believe they will use the product if nonsmokers are not irritated by being near someone using the "electronic cigarette." Thus, the focus groups are useful in refining the product and developing a theory of how it should be marketed.

■ FOCUS GROUP RESPONDENTS

What is a research supplier's responsibility when recruiting individuals to participate in a focus group? Practically every focus group interview requires that respondents be screened based on some

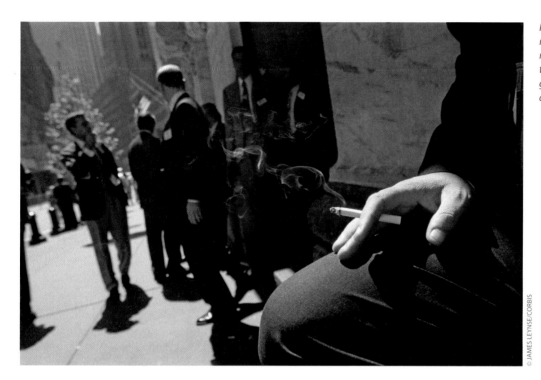

Imagine the differences in reactions to legislation further restricting smoking behavior that would be found among a group of smokers compared to a group of nonsmokers.

relevant characteristic. For example, if the topic involves improving parochial school education, the group should probably not include non-parents or parents with no plans of having children. The respondents in this case should be parents who are likely to put or are currently putting a child through school.

Even after careful screening, some consumers that fit the desired profile make poor focus group participants because they are unwilling to express their views or from the other extreme, because they are overbearing. When a researcher finds good focus group participants, he or she may be tempted to use them over and over again. Is this appropriate? Should respondents be recruited because they will freely offer a lot of discussion without being overbearing or because they have the desired characteristics given the focus group topic? This is a question the focus group planner may well face. Consider a research client viewing videotapes of a series of six focus groups conducted about new kitchen appliance designs. The client realizes that four respondents appeared in more than one of the six focus group interviews and that ten respondents appeared in focus groups performed by the same researcher on another topic six months previous. Whenever diversity of opinion is needed, relying on what essentially become professional focus group respondents is not likely appropriate. The researcher should take the extra effort to find new respondents rather than relying on conveniently available and appropriately talkative respondents.

Group Composition

The ideal size of the focus group is six to ten people. If the group is too small, one or two members may intimidate the others. Groups that are too large may not allow for adequate participation by each group member.

Homogeneous groups seem to work best because they allow researchers to concentrate on consumers with similar lifestyles, experiences, and communication skills. This lessens the chance for an overly confrontational focus group but it also matches the fact that so much marketing is directed toward market segments than to all consumers. From an ethnographic perspective, qualitative research respondents should all be members of a unique and identifiable culture. Vans may benefit from a focus group interview comprised only of skateboard enthusiasts. Perhaps participants can be recruited from a local skate park.

When the Center for Disease Control and Prevention tested public service announcements about AIDS through focus groups, it discovered that single-race groups and racially diverse groups reacted differently. By conducting separate focus groups, the organization was able to gain important insights about which creative strategies were most appropriate for targeted versus broad audiences.

Researchers who wish to collect information from different types of people should conduct several focus groups. A diverse overall sample may be obtained by using different groups even though each group is homogeneous. For instance, in discussing household chores, four groups might be used.

1. Married Men
2. Married Women
3. Single Men
4. Single Women

Although each group is homogenous, by using four groups, researchers obtain opinions from a wide degree of respondents. Similarly, a rule of thumb is that four focus group sessions, each in a different city, can satisfy exploratory research needs dealing with common consumer product or possible employee development issues.

■ ENVIRONMENTAL CONDITIONS

A focus group session may typically take place at the research agency in a room specifically designed for this purpose. Research suppliers that specialize in conducting focus groups operate from commercial facilities that have videotape cameras in observation rooms behind two-way mirrors and microphone systems connected to tape recorders and speakers to allow greater scrutiny as discussed above. Refreshments are provided to help create a more relaxed atmosphere conducive to a free exchange of ideas. More open and intimate reports of personal experiences and sentiments can be obtained under these conditions.

■ THE FOCUS GROUP MODERATOR

moderator

A person who leads a focus group interview and ensures that everyone gets a chance to speak and contribute to the discussion.

During a focus group interview, a **moderator** ensures that everyone gets a chance to speak and he or she also contributes to the discussion.

There are several qualities that a good moderator must possess.

1. The moderator must develop rapport with the group to promote interaction among all participants. The moderator should be someone who is really interested in people, who listens carefully to what others have to say, and who can readily establish rapport, gain people's confidence, and make them feel relaxed and eager to talk.
2. The moderator must be a good listener. Careful listening is especially important because the group interview's purpose is to stimulate spontaneous responses. Without good listening skills, the moderator may direct the group in an unproductive direction.
3. The moderator must try not to interject his or her own opinions. Good moderators usually say less rather than more. They can stimulate productive discussion with generalized follow-ups such as, "Tell us more about that incident," or "How are your experiences similar or different from the one you just heard?" The moderator must be particularly careful not to ask leading questions such as "You do like cornflakes, don't you?"
4. The moderator must be able to control discussion without being overbearing. The moderator's role is also to focus the discussion on the areas of concern. When a topic is no longer generating fresh ideas, the effective moderator changes the flow of discussion. The moderator does not give the group total control of the discussion, but he or she normally has prepared questions on topics that concern management. However, the timing of these questions in the discussion and the manner in which they are raised are left to the moderator's discretion. The term *focus group* thus stems from the moderator's task. He or she starts out by asking for a general discussion but usually *focuses* in on specific topics during the session.

■ FOCUS GROUPS AS DIAGNOSTIC TOOLS

Focus groups are perhaps the predominant means by which marketing researchers implement exploratory research designs. Focus groups also can be helpful in later stages of a research project, particularly when the findings from surveys or other quantitative techniques raise more questions than they answer. Managers who are puzzled about the meaning of survey research results may use focus groups to better understand what consumer surveys indicate. In such a situation, the focus group supplies diagnostic help after quantitative research has been conducted.

Focus groups are also excellent diagnostic tools for spotting problems with ideas. For instance, idea screening is often done with focus groups. An initial concept is presented to the group and then they are allowed to comment on it in detail. This usually leads to lengthy lists of potential product problems and some ideas for overcoming them. Mature products can also be "focused-grouped" in this manner.

Depth Interviews

An alternative to a focus group is a depth interview. A **depth interview** is a one-on-one interview between a professional researcher and a research respondent. Depth interviews are much the same as a psychological, clinical interview, but with a different purpose. The researcher asks many questions and follows up each answer with probes for additional elaboration. An excerpt from a depth interview is given in Exhibit 5.4. The interviews allowed the reserachers to develop a theory of the way children react to product advertisements. In each case, the child was elaborating on their reactions to or memories of advertisements.

depth interview

A one-on-one interview between a professional researcher and a research respondent conducted about some relevant business or social topic.

Like focus group moderators, the interviewer's role is critical in a depth interview. He or she must be a highly skilled individual who can encourage the respondent to talk freely without influencing the direction of the conversation. Probing questions are critical.

Laddering is a term used for a particular approach to probing, asking respondents to compare differences between brands at different levels. A repertory grid interview is an approach developed in the mid-twentieth century to conduct interviews that drew out the way people distinguished concepts. Laddering is derived from the repertory grid approach and is very useful in identifying the potential meaning of brand names. What usually results with laddering is that respondents first distinguish things using attribute-level distinctions, second are benefit-level distinctions, and third are distinctions at the value or motivation level. Laddering, for example, can then distinguish two brands of skateboarding shoes based on a) the materials they are made of, b) the comfort they provide, and c) the excitement they create.

laddering

A particular approach to probing asking respondents to compare differences between brands at different levels that produces distinctions at the attribute level, the benefit level, and the value or motivation level. Laddering is based on the classical repertory grid approach.

EXHIBIT 5.4 **Example Results from a Depth Interview**

Respondent Comments	Interpreted Meaning
"I like to watch [Barbie ads] because I like to see how pretty the Barbies are and if there is going to be, like, a new kind of Barbie. There is one Barbie . . . that comes with some little lipstick-type thing on a towel. You dip it in water and put the lipstick on the Barbie. The Barbie's lipstick turns darker."	Children look forward to seeing some advertisements and take value from viewing them.
"It's like a fairy tale on the commercial, I mean people can't really be thin. And they can't just pop out of it like that. That's not real."	Children are not detached from reality when viewing the ads.
"The Honey Comb commercial has never left my head because it's got all those details in it. It's got bright colors, and music and kids with interesting things in it. That's what makes it stay in my head. I don't like that kind of cereal or the new kinds. I don't like sweet cereal. I just like the commercials though."	Children appreciate the hedonic value aspects of viewing advertisements.
"I don't like that one (Chip's Ahoy ad) because it made me too hungry. Cookies are my favorite. And we're not allowed to have snacks."	Signifies the role of parents in facilitating the consumption of children.

© ELENA ELISSEEVA/SHUTTERSTOCK

Source: Adapted from Moore, E. S. and R. J. Lutz, "Children, Advertising, and Product Experiences: A Multimethod Inquiry," *Journal of Consumer Research*, 27 (June 2000), 31–48.

■ DEPTH INTERVIEW PROCEDURE

Each depth interview may last more than an hour. Thus, it is a time-consuming process if multiple interviews are conducted. Not only does the interview have to be conducted, but each interview produces about the same amount of text as does a focus group interview. This has to be analyzed and interpreted by the researcher. A third major issue stems from the necessity of recording both surface reactions and subconscious motivations of the respondent. Analysis and interpretation of such data are highly subjective, and it is difficult to settle on a true interpretation.

Depth interviews provide more insight into a particular individual than do focus groups. In addition, since the setting isn't really social, respondents are more likely to discuss sensitive topics than are those in a focus group. Depth interviews are particularly advantageous when some unique or unusual behavior is being studied. For instance, depth interviews have been usefully applied to reveal characteristics of adolescent behavior, ranging from the ways they get what they want from their parents to shopping, smoking, and shoplifting.[27]

Depth interviews are similar to focus groups in many ways. The costs are similar if only one to two interviews are conducted. However, if a dozen or more interviews are included in a report, the costs are higher than focus group interviews due to the increased interviewing and analysis time.

■ PROBING

Researchers often feel the need for the respondent to provide deeper explanations during qualitative research. In fact, the interviews between researchers and decision makers often resemble a depth interview. Interviews with key decision makers also can be one of the best ways to identify key problem symptoms. Recall that all problems have symptoms just as human disease is diagnosed through symptoms. Once symptoms are identified, then the researcher must probe to identify possible causes of these changes. **Probing** is an interview technique that tries to draw deeper and more elaborate explanations from the discussion. This discussion may involve potential problem causes. This probing process will likely be very helpful in identifying key variables that are prime candidates for study. Applications of qualitative research tools in probing can be very helpful.[28] Probing should take place along several key dimensions.

probing

An interview technique that tries to draw deeper and more elaborate explanations from the discussion.

1. Clarification—ask the decision maker to explain exactly what certain phrases or terms mean.
2. Free form thinking—ask for top of the mind associations by saying "What does __ make you think of."
3. Pause—the researcher can sometimes pause and not say anything. The silence may motivate the decision maker to elaborate in a meaningful way.
4. Contrast—ask the decision maker to describe how events discussed are similar or different to other events.
5. Meaning—ask the decision maker to "tell me something," or elaborate on an interesting point.
6. Most important, the researcher should ask, "What has changed?" Then, the researcher should probe more deeply to identify potential causes of the change.

At the risk of seeming repetitive, it is important that the researcher repeatedly probe to make sure that some important change has not been left out.

In addition, the researcher should look for changes in company documents, including financial statements and operating reports. Changes may also be identified by tracking down news about competitors and customers. Exhibit 5.5 provides a summary of this approach.

Almost any situation can be framed by probing from different perspectives. A pricing problem may be rephrased as a brand image problem. People expect high quality products to have higher prices. A quality problem may be rephrased as a packaging problem. For example, a potato chip company thought that a quality differential between their potatoes and their competitors was the cause for the symptom showing sliding market share. However, one of the research questions that eventually resulted dealt with consumer preferences for packaging. In the end, research suggested that consumers prefer a foil package because it helps the chips stay fresher longer. Thus, the key gap turned out to be a package gap![29]

Question: What changes have occurred recently?

Probe: Tell me about this change.

Probe: What has brought this about?

Problem: How might this be related to your problem?

Question: What other changes have occurred recently (i.e., competitors, customers, environment, pricing, promotion, suppliers, employees, etc.)?

Continue Probing

EXHIBIT 5.5
What Has Changed?

Conversations

Holding **conversations** in qualitative research is an informal data-gathering approach in which the researcher engages a respondent in a discussion of the relevant subject matter. This approach is almost completely unstructured and the researcher enters the conversation with few expectations. The goal is to have the respondent produce a dialogue about his or her lived experiences. Meaning will be extracted from the resulting dialogue.

A conversational approach to qualitative research is particularly appropriate in phenomenological research and for developing grounded theory. In our Vans experience, the researcher may simply tape-record a conversation about becoming a "skater." The resulting dialogue can then be analyzed for themes and plots. The result may be some interesting and novel insight into the consumption patterns of skaters, for example, if the respondent said,

"I knew I was a real skater when I just had to have Vans, not just for boarding, but for wearing."

This theme may connect to a rite-of-passage plot and show how Vans play a role in this process.

Technology is also influencing conversational research. Online communications such as the reviews posted about book purchases at http://www.barnesandnoble.com can be treated as a conversation. Companies may discover product problems and ideas for overcoming them by analyzing these computer-based consumer dialogues.[30]

A conversational approach is advantageous because each interview is usually inexpensive to conduct. Unlike depth interviews or focus groups, respondents need not be paid because they are enthusiasts in a product area. Often, the conversation takes place spontaneously, with little set up or with little need for any formal setting such as a focus group studio. They are relatively effective at getting at sensitive issues once the researcher establishes a rapport with them. Conversational approaches, however, are prone to produce little relevant information since little effort is made to steer the conversation. Additionally, the data analysis is very much researcher-dependent.

conversations

An informal qualitative data-gathering approach in which the researcher engages a respondent in a discussion of the relevant subject matter.

■ SEMI-STRUCTURED INTERVIEWS

Semi-structured interviews usually come in written form and ask respondents for short essay responses to specific open-ended questions. Respondents are free to write as much or as little as they want. The questions would be divided into sections, typically, and within each section, the opening question would be followed by some probing questions. When these are performed face to face, there is room for less structured follow-ups.

The advantages to this approach include an ability to address more specific issues. Responses are usually easier to interpret than other qualitative approaches. Since the researcher can simply prepare the questions in writing ahead of time, and if in writing, the questions are administered without the presence of an interviewer, semi-structured interviews can be relatively cost-effective.

Some researchers interested in studying car salesperson stereotypes used qualitative semi-structured interviews to map consumers' cognitions (memory). The semi-structured interview began with a free-association task.

List the first five things that come into your mind when you think of a "car salesman."

This was followed up with a probing question.

Describe the way a typical "car salesman" looks.

This was followed with questions about how the car salesperson acts and how the respondent feels in the presence of a car salesperson. The results led to research showing how the information that consumers process differs in the presence of a typical car salesperson, as opposed to a less typical car salesperson.[31]

Free-Association and Sentence Completion Methods

free-association techniques
Record respondents' first (top-of-mind) cognitive reactions to some stimulus.

Free-association techniques simply record a respondent's first cognitive reactions (top-of-mind) to some stimulus. The Rorschach or inkblot test typifies the free-association method. Respondents view an ambiguous figure and are asked to say the first thing that comes to their mind. Free-association techniques allow researchers to map a respondent's thoughts or memory.

The sentence completion method is based on free-association principles. Respondents simply are required to complete a few partial sentences with the first word or phrase that comes to mind. For example:

People who drink beer are _____.
A man who drinks a dark beer is _____.
Imported beer is most liked by _____.
The woman in the phone commercial _____.

Answers to sentence-completion questions tend to be more extensive than responses to word-association tests. Although the responses lack the ability to probe for meaning as in other qualitative techniques, they are very effective in finding out what is on a respondent's mind. They can also do so in a quick and very cost-effective manner. Free-association and sentence-completion tasks are sometimes used in conjunction with other approaches. For instance, they can sometimes be used as effective icebreakers in focus group interviews.

■ OBSERVATION

Field notes
The researcher's descriptions of what actually happens in the field; these notes then become the text from which meaning is extracted.

Throughout this chapter, we have described how observation can be a very important qualitative tool. The participant-observer approach typifies how observation can be used to explore various issues. Meaning is extracted from field notes. **Field notes** are the researchers' descriptions of what actually happens in the field. These notes then become the text from which meaning is extracted.

Observation may also take place in visual form. Researchers may observe consumers in their home, as mentioned above, or try to gain knowledge from photographic records of one type or another. Observation can either be very inexpensive, such as when a research associate sits and simply observes behavior, or it can be very expensive, as in most participant-observer studies. Observational research is keenly advantageous for gaining insight into things that respondents cannot or will not verbalize.

■ COLLAGES

Marketing researchers sometimes have respondents prepare a collage to represent their experience with some good, service, or brand. The collages are then analyzed for meaning much in the same manner as text dialogues are analyzed. Computer software can even be applied to help develop potential grounded theories from the visual representations.

Harley-Davidson commissioned research in which collages depicting feelings about Harley-Davidson were compared based on whether the respondent was a Harley owner or an owner of a competitor's brand. The collages of "Hog" owners revealed themes of artwork and the freedom of the great outdoors. These themes did not emerge in the non-Hog groups. This led to confirmatory research which helped Harley continue its growth, appealing more specifically to its diverse market segments.[32]

Like sentence completion and word association, collages are often used within some other approach, such as a focus group or a depth interview. Collages offer the advantage of flexibility but are also very much subject to the researcher's interpretations.

■ THEMATIC APPERCEPTION TEST (TAT)

A **thematic apperception test (TAT)** presents subjects with an ambiguous picture(s) in which consumers and products are the center of attention. The investigator asks the subject to tell what is happening in the picture(s) now and what might happen next. Hence, themes (*thematic*) are elicited on the basis of the perceptual-interpretive (*apperception*) use of the pictures. The researcher then analyzes the contents of the stories that the subjects relate.

> **thematic apperception test (TAT)**
>
> A test that presents subjects with an ambiguous picture(s) in which consumers and products are the center of attention; the investigator asks the subject to tell what is happening in the picture(s) now and what might happen next.

The picture or cartoon stimulus must be sufficiently interesting to encourage discussion but ambiguous enough not to disclose the nature of the research project. Clues should not be given to the character's positive or negative predisposition. A pretest of a TAT investigating why men might purchase chainsaws used a picture of a man looking at a very large tree. The research respondents were homeowners and weekend woodcutters. They almost unanimously said that they would get professional help from a tree surgeon to deal with this situation. Thus, early in pretesting, the researchers found out that the picture was not sufficiently ambiguous. The tree was too large and did not allow respondents to identify with the tree-cutting task. If subjects are to project their own views into the situation, the environmental setting should be a well-defined, familiar problem, but the solution should be ambiguous.

Frequently, the TAT consists of a series of pictures with some continuity so that stories may be constructed in a variety of settings. The first picture might portray two people discussing a product in a supermarket; in the second picture, a person might be preparing the product in the kitchen; the final picture might show the product being served at the dinner table. A TAT might include several ambiguous pictures of a skateboarder and then show him or her heading to the store. This might reveal ideas about the brands and products that fit the role of skateboarder.

A **picture frustration** version of the TAT uses a cartoon drawing in which the respondent suggests a dialogue in which the characters might engage. Exhibit 5.6 on the next page is a purposely ambiguous illustration of an everyday occurrence. The two office workers are shown in a situation and the respondent is asked what the woman might be talking about. This setting could be used for discussions about products, packaging, the display of merchandise, store personnel, and so on.

> **picture frustration**
>
> A version of the TAT using a cartoon drawing in which the respondent suggests a dialogue in which the characters might engage.

■ PROJECTIVE RESEARCH TECHNIQUES

A TAT represents a projective research technique. A **projective technique** is an indirect means of questioning enabling respondents to project beliefs and feelings onto a third party, an inanimate object, or a task situation. Projective techniques usually encourage respondents to describe a situation in their own words with little prompting by the interviewer. Individuals are expected to interpret the situation within the context of their own experiences, attitudes, and personalities and to express opinions and emotions that may be hidden from others and possibly themselves. All projective techniques are particularly useful in studying sensitive issues.

> **projective technique**
>
> An indirect means of questioning enabling respondents to project beliefs and feelings onto a third party, an inanimate object, or a task situation.

There is an old story about asking a man why he purchased a Mercedes. When asked directly why he purchased a Mercedes, he responds that the car holds its value and does not depreciate much, that it gets better gas mileage than you'd expect, or that it has a comfortable ride. If you ask the same person why a neighbor purchased a Mercedes, he may well answer, "Oh, that status seeker!" This story illustrates that individuals may be more likely to give true answers (consciously or unconsciously) to disguised questions, and a projective technique provides a way of disguising just who is being described.

EXHIBIT 5.6
**Picture Frustration Version
of TAT**

EXHIBIT 5.6
**Picture Frustration Version
of TAT**

Preparing a Focus Group Outline

discussion guide

A focus group outline that
includes written introductory
comments informing the group
about the focus group purpose
and rules and then outlines topics or questions to be addressed
in the group session.

Focus group researchers use a discussion guide to help control the interview and guide the discussion
into product areas. A **discussion guide** includes written introductory comments informing the group
about the focus group purpose and rules and then outlines topics or questions to be addressed in
the group session. Thus, the discussion guide serves as the focus group outline. Some discussion
guides will have only a few phrases in the entire document. Others may be more detailed. The
amount of content depends on the nature and experience of the researcher and the complexity
of the topic.

A marketing researcher conducting a focus group interview for a cancer center had the following objectives in mind when preparing the guide for the interview and conducting the interview:

- The first question was very general, asking that respondents describe their feelings about being
  out in the sun. This opening question aimed to elicit the full range of views within in the
  group. Some individuals might view being out in the sun as a healthful practice, whereas others view the sun as deadly. The hope is that by exposing the full range of opinions, respondents
  would be motivated to fully explain their own position. This was the only question asked
  specifically of every respondent. Each respondent had to give an answer before free discussion
  began. In this way, individuals experience a nonthreatening environment encouraging their
  free and full opinion. A general question seeking a reaction serves as an effective icebreaker.
- The second question asks whether participants could think of any reason they should be
  warned about sunlight exposure. This question was simply designed to introduce the idea of a
  warning label.
- Subsequent questions were asked and became increasingly specific. They were first asked about
  possible warning formats that might be effective. Respondents are allowed to react to any
  formats suggested by any other respondent. After this discussion, the moderator will introduce
  some specific formats the cancer center personnel have in mind.
- Finally, the "bottom-line" question is asked: "What format would be most likely to induce people to take protective measures?" There would be probing follow-ups of each opinion so that a

respondent couldn't simply say something like "the second one." All focus groups finish up with a catch-all question asking for any comments including any thoughts they wanted passed along to the sponsor (which in this case was only then revealed as the Houston-based cancer center).

Researchers who planned the outline established certain objectives for each part of the focus group. The initial effort was to break the ice and establish rapport within the group. The logical flow of the group session then moved from general discussion about sunbathing to more focused discussion of types of warnings about danger from sun exposure.

In general, the following steps should be used to conduct an effective focus group discussion guide.

1. Welcome and introductions should take place first. Respondents begin to feel more comfortable after introducing themselves.
2. Begin the interview with a broad icebreaker that does not reveal too many specifics about the interview. Sometimes, this may even involve respondents providing some written story or their reaction to some stimulus like a photograph, film, product, or advertisement.
3. Questions become increasingly more specific as the interview proceeds. However, the moderator will notice that a good interview will cover the specific question topics before they have to be asked. This is preferable as respondents are clearly not forced to react to the specific issue; it just emerges naturally.
4. If there is a very specific objective to be accomplished, such as explaining why a respondent would either buy or not buy a product, that question should probably be saved for last.
5. A debriefing statement should provide respondents with the actual focus group objectives and answer any questions they may have. This is also a final shot to gain some insight from the group.

■ DISADVANTAGES OF FOCUS GROUPS

Focus groups offer many advantages. Like practically every other research technique, the focus group has some limitations and disadvantages too. Problems with focus groups include those discussed as follows.

First, focus groups require objective, sensitive, and effective moderators. It is very difficult for a moderator to remain completely objective about most topics. In large research firms, the moderator may be provided only enough information to effectively conduct the interview, no more. The focus group interview shouldn't reduce to only the moderator's opinion. Also, without a good moderator, one or two participants may dominate a session, yielding results that are really the opinion of one or two people, not the group. The moderator has to try very hard to make sure that all respondents feel comfortable giving their opinions and even a timid respondent's opinion is given due consideration. While many people, even some with little or no background to do so, conduct focus groups, good moderators become effective through a combination of good people skills (which cannot be taught), training (in qualitative research), and experience.

Second, some unique sampling problems arise with focus groups. Researchers often select focus group participants because they have similar backgrounds and experiences or because screening indicates that the participants are more articulate or gregarious than the typical consumer. Such participants may not be representative of the entire target market. Thus, focus group results are not intended to be representative of a larger population.

Third, although not so much an issue with online formats where respondents can remain anonymous, traditional face-to-face focus groups may not be useful for discussing sensitive topics. A focus group is a social setting and usually involves people with little to no familiarity with each other. Therefore, issues that people normally do not like to discuss in public may also prove difficult to discuss in a focus group.

Fourth, focus groups do cost a considerable amount of money, particularly when they are not conducted by someone employed by the company desiring the focus group. As research projects go, there are many more expensive approaches, including a full-blown mail survey using a national random sample. This may costs thousands of dollars to conduct and thousands of dollars to analyze and disseminate. Focus group prices vary regionally, but the following figures provide a rough guideline.

Renting Facilities and Equipment	$ 700
Paying Respondents ($100/person)	$ 1,000

Researcher Costs
- Preparation $ 800
- Moderating $ 1,000
- Analysis and Report Preparation $ 1,500
Miscellaneous Expenses $ 300

Thus, a client can expect a professional focus group to cost around $5,000 or more. However, most marketing topics will call for multiple focus groups. There is some cost advantage in this, as some costs will not change proportionately just because there are multiple interviews. Preparation costs may be the same for one or more interviews; the analysis and report preparation will likely only increase slightly because two or three interviews are included instead of one.

Modern Technology and Qualitative Research

Technological advances have greatly improved researchers ability to perform all aspects of marketing research. Modern statistical packages and easy to use software packages enable quantitative analyses to be easily and quickly conducted. Technological advances are perhaps changing qualitative marketing research even more. The Internet and data warehouses make volumes and volumes of data available, only a small portion of which is numerical. Software is increasingly able to identify text data and group it in some way. This section focuses on how technology enables and facilitates modern qualitative research.

Facilitating Interviewing

■ VIDEOCONFERENCING AND STREAMING MEDIA

The videoconferencing industry has grown dramatically in recent years. As our ability to communicate via telecommunications and videoconferencing links has improved in quality, the number of companies using these systems to conduct focus groups has increased. With videoconference focus groups, marketing managers can stay home and watch on television rather than having to take a trip to a focus group facility.

Focus Vision Network of New York is a marketing research company that provides videoconferencing equipment and services. The Focus Vision system is modular, allowing for easy movement and an ability to capture each group member close up. The system operates via a remote keypad that allows observers in a far-off location to pan the focus group room or zoom in on a particular participant. Managers viewing at remote locations can even send the moderator messages during the interview. For example, while new product names were being tested in one focus group, an observant manager contacted the moderator with an idea and the moderator then asked respondents for a reaction to the new name on the spot.[33]

streaming media

Consist of multimedia content such as audio or video that is made available in real time over the Internet or a corporate Intranet.

Streaming media consist of multimedia content such as audio or video that is made available in real time over the Internet or a corporate Intranet. This new technology for digital media delivery allows researchers to "broadcast" focus groups that can be viewed online. Offsite managers view the focus group using a media player like Microsoft Media Player. Like videoconferencing, this saves a trip to a focus group facility. Traditionally, the quality of streaming video has been far lower than videoconferencing. However, the quality difference is fast disappearing as streaming technology improves.

■ INTERACTIVE MEDIA AND ONLINE FOCUS GROUPS

online focus group

A qualitative research effort in which a group of individuals provides unstructured comments by entering their remarks into an electronic Internet display board of some type.

Internet applications of qualitative exploratory research are growing rapidly and involve both formal and informal applications. Formally, the term **online focus group** refers to a qualitative research effort in which a group of individuals provides unstructured comments by entering their remarks into an electronic, Internet display board of some type. Participants use a keyboard and mouse to make their remarks during a chat-room session or in the form of a blog. Because respondents enter their comments into the computer, transcripts of verbatim responses are available immediately after the group session. Online groups can be quick and cost-efficient. However, because there is less interaction between participants, group synergy and snowballing of ideas may be diminished.

Several companies have established a form of informal, "continuous" focus group by establishing an Internet blog for that purpose.[34] We might call this technique a **focus blog** when the intention is to mine the site for business research purposes. General Motors, P&G, American Express, Fandango and Lego all have used ideas harvested from their focus blogs. Lego blogs can be found at http://www.thenxtstep.blogspot.com and http://www.legoblog.co.uk. While real life, in-person focus group respondents are generally paid $100 or more to show up and participate for ninety minutes, bloggers and online focus group respondents often participate for absolutely no fee at all! Thus, technology provides some cost advantages over traditional focus group approaches.[35]

focus blog

A type of informal, "continuous" focus group established as an Internet blog for the purpose of collecting qualitative data from participant comments.

■ ONLINE VERSUS FACE-TO-FACE FOCUS GROUP TECHNIQUES

A research company can facilitate a formal online focus group by setting up a private, electronic chat room for that purpose. Participants in formal and informal online focus groups feel that their anonymity is very secure. Often respondents will say things in this environment that they would never say otherwise. For example, a lingerie company was able to get insights into how it could design sexy products for larger women. Online, these women freely discussed what it would take "to feel better about being naked."[36] One can hardly imagine how difficult such a discussion might be face to face. Increased anonymity can be a major advantage for a company investigating sensitive or embarrassing issues.

Because participants do not have to be together in the same room at a research facility, the number of participants in online focus groups can be larger than in traditional focus groups. Twenty-five participants or more is not uncommon for the simultaneous chat-room format. Participants can be at widely separated locations, even in different time zones, because the Internet does not have geographical restrictions. Of course, a major disadvantage is that often the researcher does not exercise as much control in precisely who participates. In other words, a person could very easily not match the desired profile or even answer screening questions in a misleading way simply to participate.

A major drawback with online focus groups is that moderators cannot see body language and facial expressions (bewilderment, excitement, interest, and so forth). Thus, they cannot fully interpret how people are reacting. Also, moderators' ability to probe and ask additional questions on the spot is reduced in online focus groups. Research that requires focus group members to actually touch something (such as a new easy-opening packaging design) or taste something is not generally suitable for an online format.

TO THE POINT

Necessity, mother of invention.

—William Wycherley

■ SOCIAL NETWORKING

Social networking is one of the most impactful trends in recent times. For many consumers, particularly younger generations, social networking sites like MySpace, Second Life, Zebo, and others, have become the primary tool for communicating with friends both far and near and known and unknown. Social networking has replaced large volumes of e-mail and many would say, face–to-face communications as well. While the impact that social networking will eventually have on society is an interesting question, what is most relevant to marketing research is the large portion of this information that discusses marketing and consumer-related information.

Companies can assign research assistants to monitor these sites for information related to their particular brands. The information can be coded as either positive or negative. When too much negative information is being spread, the company can try to react to change the opinions. In addition, many companies like P&G (see the Research Snapshot on page 95) and Ford maintain their own social networking sites for the purpose of gathering research data (see the Research Snapshot on the next page). In a way, these social networking sites are a way that companies can eavesdrop on consumer conversations and discover key information about their products.

Research Knows Almost No Boundaries!

Qualitative research knows *almost* no boundaries! Well, at least not for Ford. Large companies like Ford are increasingly using qualitative research including phenomenology, ethnography, and grounded theory. Ford now relies on qualitative input to help with ideas for product design, marketing campaign design, concept testing and even relationships with suppliers. The advances in technologies have helped make automakers more willing to base decisions on consumer input. Some feel that, for perhaps the first time, companies like Ford may now place consumer input above cost cutting in making key decisions.

Ford used information posted online, in-home ethnography, and traditional focus groups to refine a global marketing campaign centered around the Ford Mustang. Marketing researchers interpreted all of this input in a way that placed great emphasis on the feelings associated with driving a Mustang. As a result, Ford developed a slogan and campaign built around "No boundaries!" However, early concept testing showed that this slogan did not create a positive impression in some Asian cultures. Thus, after a few adjustments and further testing, they settled on "Make Every Day Exciting!" Additionally, grounded theory approaches are helping companies better see into the future by building predictive theories about what characteristics might create value for consumers into the future.

Sources: Flint, D. and B. Woodruff, "The Initiators of Changes in Customers' Desired Values: Results from a Theory Building Study," *Industrial Marketing Management*, 30 (2008), 321–330; "Market Research Drives Product Development at Ford," *RP News Wire* (2008), www.reliableplant.com/article.asp?articleid=3802, accessed June 30, 2008; "Changan Ford's Focus Finishes First and Second at China Circuit Championship Beijing Race," *Ford Motor Company Press Release* (2006), http://media.ford.com/newsroom/release_display.cfm?release=24292, accessed August 4, 2008.

© TRANSTOCK/JUPITER IMAGES

© GEORGE DOYLE & CIARAN GRIFFIN

■ SOFTWARE DEVELOPMENT

Interpretive Software

Computerized qualitative analysis is now commonly used. Two commonly used programs are ATLAS.ti and NVivo. These can save a lot of time by helping to identify themes and connections within text. In fact, today's programs can even assist in interpreting videotapes and photographs for meaning.

Computerized analysis of depth interviews with service providers and their customers revealed interesting key themes dealing with the friendship or bond that forms between them. Some of the themes that emerged included the feeling that meetings were more like get-togethers with a friend, the feeling that the service provider wants to give something back to a client, and the belief that one can share one's true thoughts and feelings with a client. On the not-so-positive side, a theme that also emerged was that sometimes the friendships are not mutual. Comments like, "I thought she would never leave" or "Won't he give me a break?" would be consistent with that theme.[37]

There are many other software programs that can assist with basic qualitative interpretation. Some are available as freeware. AnSWR is available from the U.S. Centers for Disease Control and Prevention (http://www.cdc.gov/hiv/software/answr.htm) as is EZ-Text (http://www.cdc.gov/hiv/software/ez-text.htm). Transana will read video and audio tape data and is available from the Wisconsin Center for Education Research (http://www.transana.org). Commercial programs will normally have a student or trial version available free of charge or at reduced rates.

Text Mining

Generally, when managers think of data mining capabilities, they think of statistical analyses of large volumes of quantitative data. However, modern predictive analytic software enables text data to be mined from various sources including social networking sites, recorded conversations from call centers, e-mail contacts, and many more sources. Large companies including Sikorsky Aircraft, one of the largest helicoptor companies in the world, and Cablecom, a Swiss telecommunications firm, have used text mining software to help reveal and interpret issues related to customer churn.[38] Leading statistical analysis companies such as SAS and SPSS offer advanced text mining capabilities. Although these programs can be expensive, they offer companies the ability to extract meaning from the tremendous amounts of verbal information generated by their customers, partners and competitors.

Exploratory Research in Science and in Practice ◀━━━━━

Any research tool, qualitative or quantitative, can be misapplied. Some people believe that a good statistician can support practically any argument. Well, this may be part urban legend but certainly statistics can be misleading. For instance, a statistician may leave a key variable out of an analysis as a way of not presenting the entire picture. Qualitative research and exploratory research also can be used improperly and produce misleading results. Hopefully, the researcher has simply errored when this occurs. Intentionally misleading others with research results is blatantly unprofessional. A big part of correctly applying any tool is knowing when to use it.

Misuses of Exploratory Qualitative Research

Exploratory research, whether qualitative or quantitative, cannot take the place of conclusive, confirmatory research. Because many qualitative tools are applied in exploratory design, they are likewise limited in the ability to draw conclusive inferences—test hypotheses. One of the biggest drawbacks is the subjectivity that comes along with "interpretation." In fact, the term *interpretive* research is sometimes used synonymously with qualitative research. When only one researcher interprets the meaning of what a single person said in a depth interview or similar technique, one should be very cautious before major marketing decisions are made based only on these results. Is the result **replicable**, meaning the same conclusion is intersubjectively certifiable—another researcher's interpretation would match (or they would get the same result by conducting the same research procedures)? The temptation is to act on one interpretation because having other researchers interpret things like depth interviews takes resources that are not always readily available.

replicable

Something is intersubjectively certifiable meaning the same conclusion would be reached based on another researcher's interpretation of the research or by independently duplicating the research procedures.

Indeed, some qualitative methodologies were generally frowned upon for years based on a few early and public misapplications during what became known as the "motivational research" era. While many of the ideas produced during this time had some merit, as can sometimes be the case, too few researchers did too much interpretation of too few respondents. Compounding this, marketers were quick to act on the results, believing that the results peaked inside one's subliminal consciousness and therefore held some type of extra power. Thus, often the research was flawed based on poor interpretation, and the decision process was flawed because the deciders acted prematurely. Projective techniques and depth interviews were frequently used in the late 1950s and early 1960s, producing some interesting and occasionally bizarre reasons for consumers' purchasing behavior:

- A woman is very serious when she bakes a cake because unconsciously she is going through the symbolic act of giving birth.
- A man buys a convertible as a substitute mistress and a safer (and potentially cheaper) way of committing adultery.
- Men who wear suspenders are reacting to an unresolved castration complex.[39]

Decades later, researchers for McCann-Erickson and other advertising agencies interviewed women about roaches. Among other qualitative techniques, a form of TAT involving story completion regarding attitudes toward insecticides is often used in understanding the meanings of insects in consumers' lives. Research like this revealed themes including:

- The joy of victory over roaches (watching them die or seeing them dead)
- Using the roach as a metaphor through which women can take out their hostility toward men (women generally referred to roaches as "he" instead of "she" in their stories).
- A pervasive fear and hatred of roaches. When Orkin tested ads depicting roaches running on the television screen, viewers actually threw things at the screen before even thinking about whether the bugs were real. Although viewers felt real fear during the ads, Orkin decided to run the ads and even started a contest for people who could tell stories about damaging a television during the ad.[40]

Certainly, some useful findings resulted. Even today, we have the Pillsbury Doughboy as evidence that useful ideas were produced. In many of these cases, interpretations were either misleading or too ambitious (taken too far). However, many companies became frustrated when decisions based upon motivational research approaches proved poor. Thus, marketing researchers moved away from qualitative tools during the late 1960s and 1970s. Today, however, qualitative tools have won acceptance once again as researchers realize they have greater power in discovering insights that would be difficult to capture in typical survey research (which is limited as an exploratory tool).

■ SCIENTIFIC DECISION PROCESSES

Objectivity and replicability are two characteristics of scientific inquiry. Are focus groups objective and replicable? Would three different researchers all interpret focus group data identically? How should a facial expression or nod of the head be interpreted? Have subjects fully grasped the idea or concept behind a nonexistent product? Have respondents overstated their interest because they tend to like all new products? Many of these questions reduce to a matter of opinion that may vary from researcher to researcher and from one respondent group to another. Therefore, a focus group, or a depth interview, or TAT alone does not best represent a complete scientific inquiry.

However, if the thoughts discovered through these techniques survive preliminary evaluations and are developed into research hypotheses, they can be further tested. These tests may involve survey research or an experiment testing an idea very specifically (for example, if Diet Cherry Dr. Pepper is liked better than Diet Pepsi, and so forth). Thus, exploratory research approaches using qualitative research tools are very much a *part* of *scientific* inquiry.

An exploratory research design is the most productive design, meaning the tools used produce more discoveries than do other research designs. A company cannot determine the most important product benefits until all benefits obtained from consuming the product are known.

Before making a *scientific* decision, a research project should include a confirmatory study using objective tools and an adequate sample in terms of both size and how well it represents a population. But, is a *scientific* decision approach always used or needed?

In practice, many marketing decisions are based solely on the results of focus group interviews or some other exploratory result. Given that some decisions involve relatively small risk, a scientific decision process is not always justified. However, as risk increases, the confidence that comes along with a rigorous research and decision process becomes well worth the investment. The primary barriers to scientific decisions are (1) time, (2) money, and (3) emotion.

■ TIME

Sometimes, researchers simply are not given enough time to follow up on exploratory research results. Marketing companies feel an increasingly urgent need to get new products to the market faster. Thus, a seemingly good idea generated in a focus group (like Diet, Vanilla, or Cherry Dr Pepper) is simply not tested with a more conclusive study. The risk of delaying a decision may be seen as greater than the risk of proceeding without completing the scientific process. Thus, although the researcher may wish to protest, there may be logical reasons for such action. The decision makers should be aware, though, that the conclusions drawn from exploratory research designs are just that—exploratory. Thus, there is less likelihood of good results from the decision than if the research process had involved further testing.

■ MONEY

Similarly, researchers sometimes do not follow up on exploratory research results because they believe the cost is too high. Realize that thousands of dollars may have already been spent on qualitative research. Managers who are unfamiliar with research will be very tempted to wonder, "Why do I need yet another study?" and "What did I spend all that money for?" Thus, they choose to proceed based only on exploratory results. Again, the researcher has fulfilled the professional obligation as long as the tentative nature of any ideas derived from exploratory research has been relayed through the research report.

Again, this isn't always a bad approach. If the decision itself does not involve a great deal of risk or if it can be reversed easily, the best course of action may be to proceed to implementation instead of investing more money in confirmatory research. Remember, research shouldn't be performed if it will cost more than it will return.

- Qualitative research tools are most helpful when
  - Research questions are not very specific
  - Some specific behavior needs to be studied in depth
  - When the value of a product changes dramatically from situation to situation or consumer to consumer
  - When exploring a research area with the intent of studying it further
  - Concept testing
- The focus group moderator is key to a successful interview. Not just anyone can moderate a focus group. Generally speaking, a good moderator can get more out of a respondent by saying less.
  - Focus group questions should start with more general questions and work to the more specific.

- Don't be afraid to use props such as advertisements, photos, or actual products to get respondents talking.
- Modern technology makes a tremendous amount of qualitative information available via the Internet. Formal interviews can sometimes be replaced by data pulled from blogs and social networking sites. Consumers can also be interviewed using Internet video technology.
- Exploratory research designs do not lend themselves well to hypothesis testing or scientifically concluding that one alternative is better than another.
- The overall value of a research tool is not determined by whether it is quantitative or qualitative but by the value that it produces. Qualitative tools are irreplacable for many, many marketing research situations.

© GEORGE DOYLE & CIARAN GRIFFIN

■ EMOTION

Time, money, and emotion are all related. Decision makers sometimes become so anxious to have something resolved, or they get so excited about some novel discovery resulting from a focus group interview, they may act rashly. Perhaps some of the ideas produced during the motivational research era sounded so enticing that decision makers got caught up in the emotion of the moment and proceeded without the proper amount of testing. Thus, as in life, when we fall in love with something, we are prone to act irrationally. The chances of emotion interfering in this way are lessened, but not eliminated, by making sure multiple decision makers are involved in the decision process.

Summary

1. Contrast qualitative research with quantitative research. The chapter emphasized that any argument about the overall superiority of qualitative versus quantitative research is misplaced. Rather, each approach has advantages and disadvantages that make it appropriate in certain situations. The most noticeable difference is the relative absence of numbers in qualitative research. Qualitative research relies more on researchers' subjective interpretations of text or other visual material. In contrast, the numbers produced in quantitative research are objective in the sense that they don't change simply because someone else computed them. Qualitative research involves small samples while quantitative research usually uses large samples. Qualitative procedures are generally more flexible and produce deeper and more elaborate explanations than quantitative research.

2. Know the role of qualitative research in exploratory research designs. The high degree of flexibility that goes along with most qualitative techniques makes it very useful in exploratory research designs. Therefore, exploratory research designs most often involve some qualitative research technique. Many of the things that some criticize qualitative research for, such as lack of structure, actually are advantageous in an exploratory design.

3. Describe the basic orientations of qualitative research. Phenomenology is a philosophical approach to studying human experiences based on the idea that human experience itself is inherently subjective and determined by the context within which a person experiences something. It lends itself well to conversational research. Ethnography represents ways of studying cultures through methods that include high involvement with that culture. Participant-observation is a common ethnographic approach. Grounded theory represents inductive qualitative investigation in which the researcher continually poses questions about a respondent's discourse in an effort to derive a deep explanation of their behavior. Collages are sometimes used to develop grounded theory. Case studies simply are documented histories of a particular person, group, organization, or event.

4. Recognize common qualitative research tools and know the advantages and limitations of their use. Two of the most common qualitative research tools include the focus group interview and the depth interview. The focus group has some cost advantage per respondent because it would take ten times as long to conduct the interview portion(s) of a series of depth interviews compared to one focus group. However, the depth interview is more appropriate for discussing sensitive topics. Researchers today though have a wide variety of tools at their disposal aside from the focus group and depth interview. Exhibit 5.3 describes many of these approaches.

5. Prepare a focus group interview outline. A focus group outline should begin with introductory comments followed by a very general opening question that does not lead the respondent. More specific questions should be listed until a blunt question directly pertaining to the study objective is included. It should conclude with debriefing comments and a chance for question-and-answers with respondents.

6. Recognize technological advances in the application of qualitative research approaches. Videoconferencing and online chat rooms are more economical ways of trying to do much the same as traditional focus group interviews. Some companies have even established a focus blog that is a source for continuous commentary on a company. Others have their own social networking sites intended to collect information about their brand and products. While they are certainly cost advantageous, there is less control over who participates. Modern software also enables much more power to mine and aid in the interpretation of non-numeric data.

7. Appreciate the role of exploratory qualitative research in scientific decision making. Qualitative research has a rightful place in scientific discovery and the idea that qualitative research is somehow lacking in rigor because it is not quantitative is simply misplaced. Risks do come with using exploratory research procedures in general to make scientific decisions. While not all decisions require a scientific decision process, companies sometimes do make major decisions using only exploratory research. There are several explanations for this behavior that involve time, money and emotion. A lack of time, a lack of money and strong emotions to move on all represent barriers to a scientific decision process. Ultimately, the researcher's job is to make sure that decision makers understand the increased risk that comes along with basing a decision only on exploratory research results.

Key Terms and Concepts

case studies, *101*
concept testing, *96*
conversations, *109*
depth interview, *107*
discussion guide, *112*
ethnography, *99*
field notes, *110*
focus blog, *115*
focus group interview, *103*
free-association techniques, *110*
grounded theory, *100*

hermeneutic unit, *98*
hermeneutics, *98*
laddering, *107*
moderator, *106*
online focus group, *114*
participant-observation, *99*
phenomenology, *98*
picture frustration, *111*
piggyback, *103*
probing *108*
projective technique, *111*

qualitative data, *96*
qualitative marketing research, *92*
quantitative data, *96*
quantitative marketing research, *94*
replicable, *117*
researcher-dependent, *92*
streaming media, *114*
subjective, *95*
thematic apperception test (TAT), *111*
themes, *101*

Questions for Review and Critical Thinking

1. Define *qualitative* and *quantitative* research. Compare and contrast the two approaches.
2. Why do exploratory research designs rely so much on qualitative research techniques?
3. Why do causal designs rely so much on quantitative research techniques?
4. What are the basic categories (orientations) of qualitative research?

5. Of the four basic categories of qualitative research, which do you think is most appropriate for a qualitative approach designed to better define a marketing situation prior to conducting confirmatory research?
6. How might ethnography be used in concept testing?

7. What type of exploratory research would you suggest in the following situations?
   a. A product manager suggests development of a non-tobacco cigarette blended from wheat, cocoa, and citrus.
   b. A research project has the purpose of evaluating potential brand names for a new insecticide.
   c. A manager must determine the best site for a convenience store in an urban area.
   d. An advertiser wishes to identify the symbolism associated with cigar smoking.
8. What are the key differences between a focus group interview and a depth interview?
9. **'NET** Visit some Web sites for large companies like Honda, Qantas Airlines, Target, Tesco, and Marriot. Is there any evidence that they are using their Internet sites in some way to conduct a continuous online focus blog or intermittent online focus groups?
10. What is *laddering*? How might it be used in trying to understand which fast-food restaurant different segments of customers prefer?
11. How is a focus group outline used by an effective focus group moderator?
12. List at least four ways that recent technological advances have advanced the use of qualitative research. Explain your choices. Do you know any even newer ways that technological advancements could provide data in the form of text or picture messages? Can you think of a way that SMS text messages or MMS messages might provide qualitative input?
13. Comment on the following remark by a marketing consultant: "Qualitative exploration is a tool of marketing research and a stimulant to thinking. In and by itself, however, it does not constitute market research."
14. **ETHICS** A researcher tells a manager of a wine company that he has some "cool focus group results" suggesting that respondents like the idea of a screw-cap to top wine bottles. Even before the decision maker sees the report, the manager begins purchasing screw-caps and the new bottling equipment. Comment on this situation.
15. A packaged goods manufacturer receives many thousands of customer letters a year. Some are complaints, some are compliments. They cover a broad range of topics. Are these letters a possible source for exploratory research? Why or why not?

Research Activities

1. **'NET** How might the following organizations use an Internet social networking site for exploratory research? Can you find any such attempts on your favorite social networking site?
   a. A zoo
   b. A computer software manufacturer
   c. A video game manufacturer
2. Go back to the opening vignette. What if Vans approached you to do a focus group interview that explored the idea of offering casual attire (off-board) aimed at their primary segment (skateboarders) and offering casual attire for male retirees like Samuel Teel? How would you recommend the focus group(s) proceed? Prepare a focus group outline(s) to accomplish this task.
3. Interview two people about their exercise behavior. In one interview, try to use a semi-structured approach by preparing questions ahead of time and trying to have the respondent complete answers for these questions. With the other, try a conversational approach. What are the main themes that emerge in each? Which approach do you think was more insightful? Do you think there were any "sensitive" topics that a respondent was not completely forthcoming about?

Case 5.1 Disaster and Consumer Value

After September 11, 2001, U.S. consumers showed a desire to tone down their consumer activities. They ordered simpler foods in restaurants and spent more time at home. Therefore, a lot of marketing campaigns began emphasizing down-home themes.

At some point after a disaster, it is time to get back to business. But, major catastrophic events are likely to leave permanent changes on consumers and employees in those areas. Suppose you are approached by the owner of several delicatessens and full-service wine stores in the Gulf Coast area. It is January 2006, and they want to get back to business. But they are uncertain about whether they should simply maintain the same positioning they had previous to Hurricane Katrina and Hurricane Rita. They would like to have a report from you within eighty days.

1. How could each classification of qualitative research be used here?
2. What qualitative research tool(s) would you recommend be used and why?
3. Where would you conduct any interviews and with whom would you conduct them?
4. **ETHICS** Are there ethical issues that you should be sensitive to in this process? Explain.
5. What issues would arise in conducting a focus group interview in this situation?
6. Prepare a focus group outline.

CHAPTER 6
SECONDARY DATA RESEARCH IN A DIGITAL AGE

After studying this chapter, you should be able to

1. Discuss the advantages and disadvantages of secondary data

2. Understand the types of objectives that can be achieved using secondary data

3. Identify various internal and proprietary sources of secondary data

4. Give examples of various external sources of secondary data

5. Describe the impact of single-source data and globalization on secondary data research

Chapter Vignette: Every (Virtual) Move You Make

So, do you like *Big Brother*? This television concept has been copied and altered many times since its advent in Europe a decade or so ago. Do people like to eavesdrop on others? Do people like to be eavesdropped upon? Considering the information conveyed via social networking sites like MySpace, Bebo, Facebook, and others, perhaps some do! But, nonetheless, a wealth of information is left behind. Many researchers would like to eavesdrop to address the research questions they face. Today, the fact that many of the "moves" that people make are done online means that these people are easier to watch than ever before.

Researchers with different motives are watching. All of these parties are very interested in the electronic records of behavior that are left behind when we do things online.

- A marketing research firm hired by a mobile phone service company is trying to find the appropriate target market for different types of products including pay as you go media devices.
- An online university is looking for target markets expressing dissatisfaction with their life situations. They want to test to see if these segments will be more receptive to marketing appeals to attend the online university than segments identified through more traditional methods.
- Employers hire a research firm to identify employees who have serious issues in their personal lives as evidenced by messages posted on their social networking sites or who are shirking on–the-job based on the amount of time they spend logged in to different Web sites.
- Security officials at the Pentagon and MI6 (British intelligence service) mine material posted on social networking sites looking for potential security theats.
- Political candidates have researchers mine data from blogs and social networks to identify potential targets for significant donations.

These efforts have led to successful marketing appeals, dismissal of employees, and security opera-tions that may have prevented terrorist acts. One company in the U.K. identified an employee who spent 35 hours a week logged into a social networking site when he was supposed to be working. So, 35 out of 40 hours were spent logged in. The employee had no idea that the amount of time spent on the site could be monitored.

The information that we leave behind in our online behaviors can become stored as secondary data. Advances in technology, particularly something called Resource Description Framework or RDF, are enabling better communication across different Web-based interfaces so that once an individual is identified, information taken from different sources about different aspects of the individual's life can all be gathered together in a single record.

Obviously, the sheer volume of secondary data available reveals how important information that is collected and stored as a matter of routine or for some purpose other than a specific research purpose can be. But, perhaps questions about the morality or ethics of using this data are worth debating. Nonetheless, for marketing researchers who specialize in analyzing secondary data, this is a very good time to watch every virtual move consumers make.[1]

Introduction

Market researchers are always working under budget constraints. So, they are wise to ask if the data that will be needed to examine the research question already exist. If so, the analysis can pro-ceed quickly and efficiently. If not, a much more laborious process lies ahead. This chapter focuses on instances where the data may indeed already exist in some usable format.

Using Secondary Data in Marketing Research

Research projects often begin with **secondary data**, which are gathered and recorded by someone else prior to (and for purposes other than) the current project. Secondary data usually are histori-cal and already assembled. They require no additional access to research respondents or subjects. Secondary data is often thought of as quantitative, but many sources of qualitative secondary data also exist.

secondary data

Data that have been previously collected for some purpose other than the one at hand.

Advantages

The primary advantage of secondary data is their availability. Obtaining secondary data is almost always faster and less expensive than acquiring primary data. This is particularly true when research-ers use electronic retrieval to access data stored digitally. In many situations, collecting secondary data is instantaneous.

Consider the money and time saved by researchers who obtained updated population esti-mates for a town during the interim between the 2000 and 2010 censuses. Instead of doing the fieldwork themselves, researchers could acquire estimates from a firm dealing in demographic information or from sources such as Claritas or PCensus. As in this example, the use of secondary data eliminates many of the activities normally associated with primary data collection, such as sampling and data processing.

Secondary data are essential in instances when data cannot be obtained using primary data collection procedures. For example, a manufacturer of farm implements could not duplicate the information in the *Census of Agriculture* because much of the information there (for example, amount of taxes paid) might not be accessible to a private firm.

TO THE POINT

If I have seen farther than others, it is because I have stood on the shoulders of giants.

—Isaac Newton

Key Terms and Concepts

cross-checks, *125*

customer discovery, *132*

data conversion, *125*

data mining, *132*

database marketing, *133*

external data, *134*

index of retail saturation, *131*

internal and proprietary data, *133*

market-basket analysis, *132*

market tracking, *128*

model building, *129*

neural network, *132*

secondary data, *123*

single-source data, *140*

site analysis techniques, *131*

Questions for Review and Critical Thinking

1. Secondary data have been called the first line of attack for marketing researchers. Discuss this description.

2. Suppose you wish to learn about the size of the soft-drink market, particularly root beer sales, growth patterns, and market shares. Indicate probable sources for these secondary data.

3. What is *push technology?*

4. Identify some typical research objectives for secondary-data studies.

5. How might a marketing researcher doing a job for a company such as Pulte Homes (http://www.pultehomes.com) or David Weekley Homes (http://www.davidweekley.com) use secondary data and data mining?

6. What would be a source for the following data?
   a. Population, average income, and employment rates for Oregon
   b. Maps of U.S. counties and cities
   c. Trends in automobile ownership
   d. Divorce trends in the United States
   e. Median weekly earnings of full-time, salaried workers for the previous five years
   f. Annual sales of the top ten fast-food companies
   g. Top ten Web sites ranked by number of unique visitors
   h. Attendance at professional sports events

7. Suppose you are a marketing research consultant and a client comes to your office and says, "I must have the latest information on the supply of and demand for Maine potatoes within the next 24 hours." What would you do?

8. Find the following data in the *Survey of Current Business:*
   a. U.S. gross domestic product for the first quarter of 2004
   b. Exports of goods and services for the fourth quarter of 2004
   c. Imports of goods and services for the fourth quarter of 2004

9. **ETHICS** A newspaper reporter finds data in a study that surveyed children that reports that a high percentage of children can match cartoon characters with the products they represent. For instance, they can match cereal with Captain Crunch and Ronald McDonald with a Big Mac. The reporter used this to write a story about the need to place limits on the use of cartoon characters. However, the study also provided data suggesting that matching the cartoon character and the product did not lead to significantly higher consumption. Would this be a proper use of secondary data?

10. **ETHICS** Go back to the opening chapter vignette. Do you believe it is ethical for an employer to mine social networking sites for personal information about employees? Does it matter if the information refers to behavior solely away from work or that is somehow tied to things done while at work? Address the same issue for a marketing research firm that distributes entertainment to mobile appliances (movies, music, games). Is it ethical for them to search for relationships and market segments using information people post about themselves on the Internet?

Research Activities

1. Use secondary data to learn the size of the U.S. golf market and to profile the typical golfer.

2. **'NET** Where could a researcher working for the U.S. Marine Corps (http://www.marines.com) find information that would identify the most productive areas of the United States in which to recruit? What would you recommend?

3. **'NET** POPClocks estimate the U.S. and world populations. Go to the Census Bureau home page (http://www.census.gov), navigate to the population section, and find today's estimate of the U.S. and world populations.

4. **'NET** Try to find the U.S. market share for the following companies within thirty minutes:
   a. Home Depot
   b. Burger King
   c. Marlboro

   d. Was this a difficult task? If so, why do you think it is this difficult?

5. **'NET** Use the Internet to learn what you can about Indonesia.
   a. Check the corruption index for Indonesia at http://www.transparency.org.
   b. What additional kinds of information are available from the following sources?
   - Go to http://freetheworld.com/member.html and view info for Indonesia.
   - Visit the CIA's World Factbook *at* https://www.cia.gov/library/publications/the-world-factbook.
   - Go to Google, Yahoo! Search, or another search engine, and use "Indonesia" as a search word.

6. **'NET** Go to Statistics Norway at http://www.ssb.no. What data, if any, can you obtain in English? What languages can be used to

search this Web site? What databases might be of interest to the business researcher?

7. **'NET** Go to Statistics Canada at http://www.statcan.ca. What languages can be used to search this Web site? What databases might be of interest to the business researcher?

8. **'NET** Suppose you were working for a company that wanted to start a business selling handmade acoustic guitars that are reproductions of classic vintage guitars. Pricing is a big part of the decision. Secondary information is available via the Internet. Use eBay (http://ebay.com) to identify four key brands of acoustic guitars by studying the vintage acoustic guitars listed for sale. Since the company wishes to charge premium prices, they will model after the most expensive brand. What brand seems to be associated with the highest prices?

9. **'NET** Visit a social networking site (assuming you can log into a site). Search for information about Starbucks. Is there anything useful that turns up in your search that could be used by Starbucks to improve their sales and overall business operations? Explain.

Case 6.1   Demand for Gas Guzzlers

In fall 2005, Hurricanes Katrina and Rita churning in the Gulf of Mexico damaged oil rigs and refineries, contributing to a spike in oil prices. Many observers expressed confidence that those events were the long-expected trigger that would kill off demand for SUVs and other gas-guzzling vehicles.[18] They were only partly right.

In the months leading up to the hurricanes, sales of SUVs had already been falling, according to data from *Automotive News*. Automakers had been shifting ad dollars away from these products. CNW Market Research said that in August 2005, consumers had for the first time placed fuel economy ahead of performance when ranking factors for choosing a new vehicle. When gas prices approached three dollars a gallon in September 2005, marketers felt sure that fuel economy would remain a top concern. Advertisers began creating more ads featuring vehicles' gas mileage.

But by the end of the year, attitudes were shifting again. The National Automobile Dealers Association surveyed consumers visiting its Web site for information about car purchases, and it learned they ranked price as most important, followed by make and model, then performance. Fuel economy ranked last, with 3 percent considering it most important and 11 percent considering it least important. What's a carmaker to do? General Motors gathers data from the shoppers who visit Web sites such as www.kbb.com to look up information, and it is analyzing the data to identify the price of fuel at which car buyers adjust their priorities.

Questions

1. From the standpoint of an automobile company, what sources of information in this article offer secondary data?

2. Suggest two or three other sources of data that might be of interest to auto companies interested in forecasting demand.

3. Online or at your library, look for information about recent trends in SUV purchases. Report what you learned, and forecast whether SUV sales are likely to recover or continue their decline. What role do gas prices play in your forecast?

CHAPTER 7
SURVEY RESEARCH

After studying this chapter, you should be able to

1. Define surveys and describe the type of information that may be gathered in a survey
2. Explain the advantages and disadvantages of surveys
3. Identify sources of error in survey research
4. Summarize the ways researchers gather information through personal interviews
5. Know the advantages and disadvantages of conducting surveys using personal interviews via door-to-door, mall intercept, landline telephone, or mobile-phone interviews
6. Appreciate the importance of pretesting questionnaires
7. Describe ethical issues that arise in survey research

Chapter Vignette: TLK 2 U L8TR

Sometimes it's not what you ask, but how you ask it that determines the quality of the answers you get. Researchers continue to have more options for asking questions. A researcher working for a 2008 Olympics advertiser wanted instant feedback on whether or not 30-second television spots during the Olympics were being viewed and understood. In this way, they could help their client understand if the investment in an Olympics commercial was worth the high price they paid. The firm eventually decided to send a text message to implement this survey. Wise decision?

In 2006, a British research firm used a text message survey to assess U.K. consumers' attitudes toward the World Cup. In contrast, research firms in the United States still rely heavily on day-after telephone surveys to assess consumer reactions to Super Bowl advertising. Does the method by which one asks a question affect the quality of responses? You betcha!

First, although text messaging has become commonplace among a wide cross section of consumers in many parts of the world, particularly in Japan and South Korea, text message usage is dominated by the youth culture in the United States and many parts of Europe. Additionally, each country has different rules and regulations that govern different media that can be used to implement a survey. Different cultures also respond differently to requests made through different technologies. For example, in the U.K., estimates suggest about 2 percent of consumers are generally receptive to surveys conducted through electronic media. However, in Japan and South Korea, consumers do not find such requests bothersome. So, if the manner of asking questions can be made interesting in some way, the odds of getting responses are improved. If the survey is intended to span different countries, then there are also issues of compatibility across countries. Not only might compatibility affect the likelihood of a questionnaire reaching a recipient in a useful manner, but it can also affect the researcher's ability to know just who responded.

© ANDRESR/SHUTTERSTOCK

Bottom line, know the population you want to represent. If your market resides in a place where sending text message survey requests is prohibited unless the consumer has opted in (as in the United States), or if your market is not in a demographic that is unreceptive to text messaging, and if your survey is sufficiently short and contains questions that can be answered in a text message format, then maybe a text message survey is for you. For example, contacting college students in Chong-buk, Korea to assess how much they have watched the Olympic games could be useful. Even better if the questions are asked in a form that contains some type of game involving flying gymnasts or divers doing impossible acrobatics.[1]

Introduction

respondents

People who verbally answer an interviewer's questions or provide answers to written questions.

survey

A method of collecting primary data based on communication (questions and answers) with a representative sample of respondents.

sample survey

A more formal term for a survey.

Marketing research focuses on human behavior. So, the marketing researcher needs input from or about people. One way to obtain input is to simply ask people questions in the form of an interview. The people who answer the questions are referred to as **respondents**. These interviews are conducted via e-mail, on the telephone, through a Web interface, text messaging or even through an actual face-to-face question and answer discussion. Thus, a **survey** is defined as a method of collecting primary data based on communication with a representative sample of individuals. Surveys provide a snapshot at a given point in time. More precisely, a survey is a **sample survey** because the respondents are of interest because their answers are presumed to be a sample of the way the larger target population would respond.

Surveys indicate that 40 percent of consumers select the electronics brand only after deciding on what store to shop in. As a result, Sony felt the need to redesign its brand image in a way that attracted more attention and made an emotional connection with consumers.[2] Sony followed up this key finding with a variety of research projects, both qualitative and quantitative, which helped them identify changes to their logo and packaging that not only enabled them to be more prominent in stores, but also helped sell the brand and not just the product.

The Types of Information Gathered Using Surveys

Information gathered in a survey varies considerably depending on its objectives. Typically, surveys attempt to describe what is happening, what people believe, what they are like or to learn the reasons for a particular marketing activity. Marketers can make decisions about what products to sell, what the prices should be, where they should be sold, or other elements of the marketing mix. The Research Snapshot on page 148 illustrates how retailers can adjust merchandising with technological advances based on survey input.

More specifically, surveys gather information to assess consumer knowledge and awareness of products, brands, or issues and to measure consumer attitudes and feelings. Additionally, surveys describe consumer characteristics including purchasing patterns, brand usage, and descriptive characteristics including demographics and lifestyle. Thus, psychographic research involves surveys.

Most marketing surveys have multiple objectives; few gather only a single type of factual information. Questions about product use and desirable features help with product development and advertising messages. Demographic information and information on media exposure might also be collected in the survey to help plan a market segmentation strategy. A survey commissioned by eBay learned that almost 60 percent of respondents receive unwanted gifts, and 15 percent of them had sold an unwanted gift online, suggesting a possible source of demand for eBay's auction services.[3] In addition, the survey indicated that selling unwanted gifts online was twice as common among 25- to 34-year-olds. Although consumer surveys are a common form of marketing research, not all survey research is conducted with the ultimate consumer. Frequently, studies focus on wholesalers, retailers, or industrial buyers.

Because most survey research is descriptive research, the term *survey* is most often associated with quantitative findings. Although most surveys are conducted to quantify certain factual information, some aspects of surveys may also be qualitative. In new-product development, a survey often has a qualitative objective of refining product concepts. Stylistic, aesthetic, or functional changes may be made on the basis of respondents' suggestions. Evaluating the qualitative nature of advertising may also be an objective of survey research, as in the following story told to advertiser Michael Arlen about testing a rough commercial for AT&T.

We called it "Fishing Camp." The idea was this: These guys go off to a fishing camp in the north woods, somewhere far away, where they're going to have a terrific time together and do all this great fishing, only what happens is that it rains all the time and the fishing is a bust. Mind you, this was a humorous ad. The emphasis was on the humor. Anyway, the big moment occurs when the fishing guys are talking on the phone to their jealous friends back home—who naturally want to know how great the fishing is—and what you see are the fishing guys, huddled in this cabin, with the rain pouring down outside, and one of the guys is staring at a frying pan full of hamburgers sizzling on the stove while he says into the phone, "Boy, you should see the great trout we've got cooking here."[4]

However, much to the advertisers' astonishment, when they tested the advertisement and gave subjects a questionnaire, respondents recalled that what was cooking was trout. To counteract this misimpression, said the advertiser, "We ended up making it, but what we had to do was, when we came to that segment, we put the camera almost *inside* the frying pan, and in the frying pan we put huge, crude chunks of hamburger that were so raw they were almost red."

Advantages and Disadvantages of Surveys

No data source is perfect. All present opportunities for error from different sources. However, the sheer number of survey applications suggests that the advantages often outweigh the disadvantages of performing survey research.

Advantages of Survey Research

Survey research presents numerous advantages. Surveys provide a quick, often inexpensive, efficient, and accurate means of assessing information about a population. Researchers also can apply fairly straightforward statistical tools in analyzing sample survey results. The examples given earlier illustrate that surveys are quite flexible and, when properly conducted, extremely valuable to the manager.

As we discussed in Chapter 1, marketing research has proliferated among companies adopting the marketing concept. One simple way to understand what consumers think is to ask them questions. The consumer orientation that goes along with adopting the marketing concept forces companies to exchange ideas with customers and a survey is a primary tool for doing so.

Blu-rays are Best's Rays

LCD, HDTV, CD, DVD, and now Blu-ray. Truly, consumers just seem to get used to one technology when we are faced with another. HDTVs, which were novel ten years ago, are now mainstream and account for the majority of television purchases. Not all technologies succeed, however, and they are often produced and marketed without a sufficient understanding of whether consumers will indeed adopt the technology.

Blu-ray technology has now been around for several years. However, DVDs and even CDs have far from disappeared. Given the almost certain technological superiority of Blu-ray (associated with Sony), what seems to make Blu-ray discs so apparently slow to diffuse? Part of the problem lies in competition from HD DVD (associated with Panasonic) and part from the distribution channel.

Survey research suggests that consumers prefer Blu-ray technology to HD DVD. A sample of over one thousand consumers suggests that 58 percent prefer Blu-ray Discs while only 16 percent preferred HD DVD technology. The surveys also asked what electronic format consumers would next purchase. Sixty-six percent of consumers expressed intentions to purchase Blu-ray as opposed to 15 percent who expressed intentions to purchase HD DVD. Nineteen percent reported being undecided. The surveys also suggested consumers saw Blu-ray as more flexible (able to be played in a wider range of appliances), better for gaming, having better company support, and able to store more.

As a result, Best Buy has bet that Blu-ray is the way to go and Wal-Mart has decided to stock Blu-ray products exclusively rather than HD DVD. A chain reaction has started as in-home movie companies such as Netflix switch from other HD formats to Blu-ray only. Certainly, the survey research eventually led to changes in the distribution channel that will speed the diffusion of Blu-ray technology through the marketplace. The Blu-ray is the best way, for now!

Sources: Lee, D., "Blu-ray Wins, So What?" *Marketing Magazine*, 113 (March 10, 2008), 12; LeClaire, J., "Survey Shows Consumers Favor Blu-ray Over HD DVD Format," TechNews-World, (July 14, 2005), http://www.technewsworld.com, accessed August 12, 2008.

Disadvantages of Survey Research

Over the last 50 years and particularly during the last two decades, survey research techniques and standards have become quite scientific and accurate. When properly conducted, surveys offer managers many advantages. However, they can also be ineffective or misleading when researchers do not follow basic research principles, such as taking care in designing both the survey instrument and the sampling frame. Sometimes even a well-designed and carefully executed survey is not helpful because the results are delivered too late or because they measure the wrong thing. Surveys are also an additional source of error when the researchers intend to study actual behavior because the respondent may error answering questions about what they have done or what they will do. Low response rates can also be a problem with many types of surveys.

Each survey tool also introduces some unique disadvantages. However, errors are common to all forms of surveys, so it is appropriate to describe them generally. Then, the researcher can hopefully better match a survey data collection approach with a given situation in the hope of mitigating ill effects due to error.

Sources of Error in Surveys

A manager who is evaluating the quality of a survey must estimate its accuracy. Exhibit 7.1 outlines the various forms of survey error. They have two major sources: random sampling error and systematic error.

Random versus Systematic Sampling Error

Most surveys try to portray a representative cross-section of a particular target population. Even with technically proper random probability samples, however, statistical errors will occur because of chance variation in the elements selected for the sample. These statistical problems are

EXHIBIT 7.1 **Categories of Survey Errors**

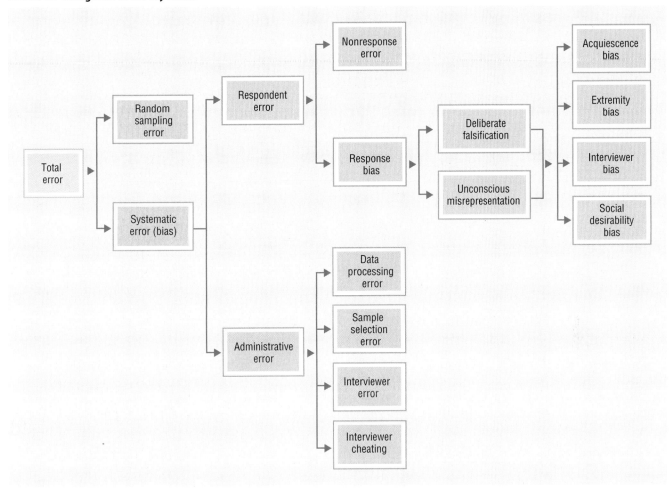

unavoidable without very large samples (>400). However, the extent of **random sampling error** can be estimated. This topic is discussed in later chapters in more detail.

The other major source of survey error, **systematic error**, results from some imperfect aspect of the research design or from a mistake in the execution of the research. Because systematic errors include all sources of error other than those introduced by the random sampling procedure, these errors or biases are also called *nonsampling errors*. A **sample bias** exists when the results of a sample show a persistent tendency to deviate in one direction from the true value of the population parameter. The many sources of error that in some way systematically influence answers can be divided into two general categories: respondent error and administrative error.

■ RESPONDENT ERROR

Surveys ask people for answers. If people cooperate and give truthful answers, a survey will likely accomplish its goal. If these conditions are not met, nonresponse error or response bias, the two major categories of **respondent error**, may cause sample bias.

Nonresponse Error

Few surveys have 100 percent response rates. But a researcher who obtains a 1 percent response to a five-page e-mail questionnaire concerning various brands of spark plugs may face a serious problem. To use the results, the researcher must believe that consumers who responded to the questionnaire are representative of consumers who did not respond. The statistical differences between a survey that includes only those who responded and a survey that also included those

random sampling error

A statistical fluctuation that occurs because of chance variation in the elements selected for a sample.

systematic error

Error resulting from some imperfect aspect of the research design that causes respondent error or from a mistake in the execution of the research.

sample bias

A persistent tendency for the results of a sample to deviate in one direction from the true value of the population parameter.

respondent error

A category of sample bias resulting from some respondent action or inaction such as nonresponse or response bias.

nonresponse error

The statistical differences between a survey that includes only those who responded and a perfect survey that would also include those who failed to respond.

nonrespondents

People who are not contacted or who refuse to cooperate in the research.

no contacts

People who are not at home or who are otherwise inaccessible on the first and second contact.

refusals

People who are unwilling to participate in a research project.

self-selection bias

A bias that occurs because people who feel strongly about a subject are more likely to respond to survey questions than people who feel indifferent about it.

Many e-mail addresses are actually inactive. Inactive e-mails contribute to low response rates.

© YURI ARCURS/SHUTTERSTOCK

who failed to respond are referred to as **nonresponse error**. This problem is especially acute in mail and Internet surveys, but nonresponse also threatens telephone and face-to-face interviews. Of course, knowing exactly how big this error truly is becomes practically impossible because nonrespondents, by definition, have not provided input. People who are not contacted or who refuse to cooperate are called **nonrespondents**.

Survey approaches present researchers with the opportunity to ask consumers questions. However, getting consumers to respond can prove difficult. Those who do not respond can be placed into categories.

A nonresponse occurs if no one answers the phone at the time of both the initial call and a subsequent callback. The number of **no contacts** in survey research has been increasing because of the proliferation of answering machines, mobile phones, and the growing use of caller ID to screen telephone calls.[5] A parent who must juggle the telephone and a half-diapered child and refuses to participate in the survey because he or she is too busy also is a nonresponse. An e-mail request sent to a potential respondent via an old unused e-mail address likewise is a nonresponse.

Refusals occur when people are unwilling to participate in the research. A research team reviewed 50 mail surveys of pediatricians conducted by the American Academy of Pediatrics (AAP) and found that response rates declined through the first decade of the 21st century. In the early years of the study period, an average 70 percent of pediatricians returned completed surveys; the response rate fell to an average 63 percent in the second half of the period.[6] No contacts and refusals can seriously bias survey data. In the case of the pediatricians, the researchers found little difference in the response rates attributable to differences in such easy-to-measure variables as age, sex, and type of membership in the AAP, leaving them to wonder whether the cause of refusals was some unknown but important difference among these doctors.

Because of this problem, researchers investigate the causes of nonresponse. For example, a study analyzed a large database collected by AT&T and found that the effort required to participate in an ongoing study contributes to the problem.[7] People tend not to respond to questions that are difficult to answer. When they are asked to participate in a long-term panel, the rate of nonresponse to individual items grows over time, and eventually some people stop participating altogether. However, eventually it becomes easier to keep answering the same kinds of panel questions, and nonresponse rates level off.

Comparing the demographics of the sample with the demographics of the target population is one means of inspecting for possible biases in response patterns. If a particular group, such as older citizens, is underrepresented or if any potential biases appear in a response pattern, additional efforts should be made to obtain data from the underrepresented segments of the population. For example, personal interviews may be used instead of telephone interviews for the underrepresented segments.

After receiving a refusal from a potential respondent, an interviewer can do nothing other than be polite. The respondent who simply is not at home when called or visited can be scheduled to be interviewed at a different time of day or on a different day of the week.

With a mail survey, the researcher never really knows whether a nonrespondent has refused to participate or is just indifferent. Researchers know that those who are most involved in an issue are more likely to respond to a mail survey. **Self-selection bias** is a problem that frequently plagues self-administered questionnaires. In a restaurant, for example, a customer on whom a waiter spilled soup, a person who was treated to a surprise dinner, or others who feel strongly about the service are more likely to complete a self-administered questionnaire left at the table than individuals who are indifferent about the restaurant. Self-selection biases distort surveys because they overrepresent extreme positions while underrepresenting responses from those who are indifferent. Several techniques will be discussed later for encouraging respondents to reply to mail and Internet surveys.

Response Bias

A **response bias** occurs when respondents tend to answer questions with a certain slant. People may consciously or unconsciously misrepresent the truth. If a distortion of measurement occurs because respondents' answers are falsified or misrepresented, either intentionally or inadvertently, the resulting sample bias will be a response bias. When researchers identify response bias, they should include a corrective measure.

Deliberate Falsification. Occasionally people deliberately give false answers. It is difficult to assess why people knowingly misrepresent answers. A response bias may occur when people misrepresent answers to appear intelligent, conceal personal information, avoid embarrassment, and so on. For example, respondents may be able to remember the total amount of money spent grocery shopping, but they may forget the exact prices of individual items that they purchased. Rather than appear ignorant or unconcerned about prices, they may provide their best estimate and not tell the truth—namely, that they cannot remember. Sometimes respondents become bored with the interview and provide answers just to get rid of the interviewer. At other times respondents try to appear well informed by providing the answers they think are expected of them. On still other occasions, they give answers simply to please the interviewer.

Unconscious Misrepresentation. Even when a respondent is consciously trying to be truthful and cooperative, response bias can arise from the question format, the question content, or some other stimulus. For example, bias can be introduced by the situation in which the survey is administered. The results of two in-flight surveys concerning aircraft preference illustrate this point. Passengers flying on B-747s preferred B-747s to L-1011s (74 percent versus 19 percent), while passengers flying on L-1011s preferred L-1011s to B-747s (56 percent versus 38 percent). The difference in preferences appears to have been largely a function of the aircraft the respondents were flying on when the survey was conducted.[8] Respondent's in this case may have little awareness of the differences between the planes and be responding more to the overall flying experience including the airline he or she is flying.

Respondents who misunderstand questions may unconsciously provide biased answers. Or, they may be willing to answer but unable to do so because they have forgotten the exact details. Asking "When was the last time you attended a concert?" may result in a best-guess estimate because the respondent has forgotten the exact date.

A bias may also occur when a respondent has not thought about an unexpected question. Many respondents will answer questions even though they have given them little thought. For example, in most investigations of consumers' buying intentions, the predictability of the intention scales depends on how close the subject is to making a purchase. The intentions of subjects who have little knowledge of the brand or the store alternatives being surveyed and the intentions of subjects who have not yet made any purchase plans cannot be expected to predict purchase behavior accurately.

In many cases consumers cannot adequately express their feelings in words. The cause may be questions that are vague or ambiguous. Researchers may ask someone to describe his or her frustration when using a computer. The problem is, the researcher may be interested in software problems while the respondent is thinking of hardware issues. Language differences also may be a source of misunderstanding. A survey in the Philippines found that, despite seemingly high toothpaste usage, only a tiny percentage of people responded positively when asked, "Do you use toothpaste?" As it turned out, people in the Philippines tend to refer to toothpaste by using the brand name Colgate. When researchers returned and asked, "Do you use Colgate?" the positive response rate soared.

As the time following a purchase or a shopping event increases, people become more likely to underreport information about that event. Time lapse influences people's ability to precisely remember and communicate specific factors.

Unconscious misrepresentation bias may also occur because consumers unconsciously avoid facing the realities of a future buying situation. Housing surveys record that Americans overwhelmingly continue to aspire to own detached, single-family dwellings (preferably single-level, ranch-type structures that require two to five times the amount of land per unit required for attached homes). However, builders know that *attached* housing purchases by first buyers are more common than respondents expect.

Types of Response Bias

Response bias falls into four specific categories: acquiescence bias, extremity bias, interviewer bias, and social desirability bias. These categories overlap and are not mutually exclusive. A single biased answer may be distorted for many complex reasons, some distortions being deliberate and some being unconscious misrepresentations.

Acquiescence Bias. Some respondents are very agreeable. They seem to agree to practically every statement they are asked about. A tendency to agree with all or most questions is known as **acquiescence bias**. This bias is particularly prominent in new-product research. Questions about a new-product idea generally elicit some acquiescence bias because respondents give positive connotations to most new ideas. For example, consumers responded favorably to survey questions about pump baseball gloves (the pump inserts air into the pocket of the glove providing more cushioning). However, when these expensive gloves hit the market, they sat on the shelves. When conducting new-product research, researchers should recognize the high likelihood of acquiescence bias.

Another form of acquiescence is evident in some people's tendency to disagree with all questions. Thus, acquiescence bias is a response bias due to the respondents' tendency to concur with a particular position.

Extremity Bias. Some individuals tend to use extremes when responding to questions; others consistently avoid extreme positions and tend to respond more neutrally. Response styles vary from person to person, and extreme responses may cause an **extremity bias** in the data.[9]

Interviewer Bias. Response bias may arise from the interplay between interviewer and respondent. If the interviewer's presence influences respondents to give untrue or modified answers, the survey will be marred by **interviewer bias**. Sometimes, respondents may give answers they believe will please the interviewer rather than the truthful responses. Respondents may wish to appear intelligent and wealthy—of course they read *Scientific American* rather than *Playboy*.

Interviewer characteristics including age, sex, style of dress, tone of voice, facial expressions, or other nonverbal characteristics may have some influence on a respondent's answers. If an interviewer smiles and makes a positive statement after a respondent's answers, the respondent will be more likely to give similar responses. In a research study on sexual harassment against saleswomen, male interviewers might not obtain as candid responses from saleswomen as female interviewers would. Thus, interviewer techniques in which the interviewer remains unseen have an advantage of preventing this particular type of interviewer bias.

Many interviewers, contrary to instructions, shorten or rephrase questions to suit their needs. A researcher doing survey research for major U.S. newspapers asked a question about the Nazi holocaust in the following fashion:

> "Do you believe it seems possible or does it seem impossible to you that the Nazi Extermination of the Jews never happened?"[10]

Obviously, this question is confusing and yielded a result that should be meaningless, but instead could be interpreted as suggesting that nearly 1 in 4 respondents doubted that the holocaust ever occurred.

This potential influence on responses can be avoided to some extent if interviewers receive training and supervision that emphasize the necessity of appearing neutral. Also, researchers with strong opinions may be

acquiescence bias
A tendency for respondents to agree with all or most questions asked of them in a survey.

extremity bias
A category of response bias that results because some individuals tend to use extremes when responding to questions.

interviewer bias
A response bias that occurs because the presence of the interviewer influences respondents' answers.

The more people are susceptible to interpersonal influence, the more likely a response bias will occur. One example of this can be found in adolescents' buying behavior.

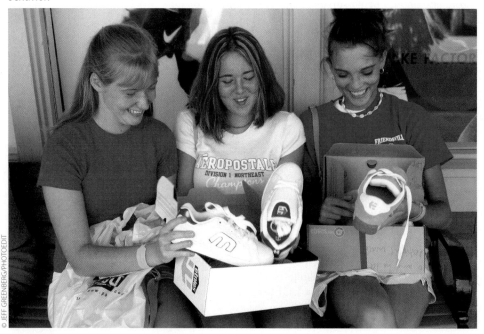

steered toward other projects or be made aware that misleading results are unethical and likely do not further their cause in the long run.

The interviewer may also encourage error if a survey takes too long to complete. If interviews go on too long, respondents may feel that time is being wasted. They may answer as abruptly as possible with little forethought.

Social Desirability Bias. A **social desirability bias** may occur either consciously or unconsciously because the respondent wishes to create a favorable impression or save face in the presence of an interviewer. Incomes may be inflated, education overstated, or perceived respectable answers given to gain prestige. In contrast, answers to questions that seek factual information or responses about matters of public knowledge (zip code, number of children, and so on) usually are quite accurate. An interviewer's presence may increase a respondent's tendency to give inaccurate answers to sensitive questions such as "Did you vote in the last election?," "Do you have termites or roaches in your home?," or "Do you color your hair?"

The social desirability bias is especially significant in the case of research that addresses sensitive or personal topics, including respondents' sexual behavior. A group of researchers recently evaluated responses to questions about homosexual sexual activity, collected by NORC's long-running General Social Survey.[11] The researchers found that over time, as attitudes toward homosexual conduct have softened, the frequency of repeated female-female sexual contacts increased dramatically, suggesting the possibility that reporting levels have been subject to social desirability bias. However, the researchers noted that rates of male-male sexual contact were fairly steady over the period and that the rate of change for female-female sexual contact persisted even when adjusted for measures of greater tolerance. This evidence suggests that the data reflect more phenomena than mere social desirability bias.

■ ADMINISTRATIVE ERROR

The result of improper administration or execution of the research task is called an **administrative error**. Administrative errors are caused by carelessness, confusion, neglect, omission, or some other blunder. Four types of administrative error are data-processing error, sample selection error, interviewer error, and interviewer cheating.

Data-Processing Error

Processing data by computer, like any arithmetic or procedural process, is subject to error because data must be edited, coded, and entered into the computer by people. The accuracy of data processed by computer depends on correct data entry and programming. **Data-processing error** can be minimized by establishing careful procedures for verifying each step in the data-processing stage.

Sample Selection Error

Many kinds of error involve failure to select a representative sample. **Sample selection error** is systematic error that results in an unrepresentative sample because of an error in either the sample design or the execution of the sampling procedure. Executing a sampling plan free of procedural error is difficult. A firm that selects its sample from the phone book will have some systematic error, because unlisted numbers

social desirability bias

Bias in responses caused by respondents' desire, either conscious or unconscious, to gain prestige or appear in a different social role.

administrative error

An error caused by the improper administration or execution of the research task.

data-processing error

A category of administrative error that occurs because of incorrect data entry, incorrect computer programming, or other procedural errors during data analysis.

sample selection error

An administrative error caused by improper sample design or sampling procedure execution.

One problem with Web-based surveys is that there is no way of knowing who exactly responded to the questionnaire.

are not included. Stopping respondents during daytime hours in shopping centers excludes working people who shop by mail, Internet, or telephone. In other cases, researchers interview the wrong person. Consider a political pollster who uses random-digit dialing to select a sample, rather than a list of registered voters. Unregistered 17-year-olds may be willing to give their opinions, but they are the wrong people to ask because they cannot vote.

Interviewer Error

interviewer error

Mistakes made by interviewers failing to record survey responses correctly.

Interviewers' abilities vary considerably. **Interviewer error** is introduced when interviewers record answers but check the wrong response or are unable to write fast enough to record answers verbatim. Also, selective perception may cause interviewers to misrecord data that do not support their own attitudes and opinions.

Interviewer Cheating

interviewer cheating

The practice of filling in fake answers or falsifying questionnaires while working as an interviewer.

Interviewer cheating occurs when an interviewer falsifies entire questionnaires or fills in answers to questions that have been intentionally skipped. Some interviewers cheat to finish an interview as quickly as possible or to avoid questions about sensitive topics.

If interviewers are suspected of faking questionnaires, they should be told that a small percentage of respondents will be called back to confirm whether the initial interview was actually conducted. This practice should discourage interviewers from cheating. The term *curb-stoning* is sometimes used to refer to interviewers filling in responses for respondents that do not really exist.

Rule-of-Thumb Estimates for Systematic Error

The techniques for estimating systematic, or nonsampling, error are less precise than many sample statistics. Researchers have established experience-based, conservative rules of thumb based on experience to estimate systematic error. In the case of consumer research, experienced researchers might determine that only a certain percentage of people who say they will definitely buy a new product actually do so. Evidence for a mere-measurement effect suggests that in some situations, researchers might conclude that respondents' own buying behavior will exaggerate overall sales. Thus, researchers often present actual survey findings *and* their interpretations of estimated purchase response based on estimates of nonsampling error. For example, one pay-per-view cable TV company surveys geographic areas it plans to enter and estimates the number of people who indicate they will subscribe to its service. The company knocks down the percentage by a "ballpark 10 percent" because experience in other geographic areas has indicated that there is a systematic upward bias of 10 percent on this intentions question.

What Can Be Done to Reduce Survey Error?

Now that we have examined the sources of error in surveys, you may have lost some of your optimism about survey research. Don't be discouraged! The discussion emphasized the bad news because it is important for marketing managers to realize that surveys are not a panacea. There are, however, ways to handle and reduce survey errors. For example, Chapter 11 on questionnaire design discusses the reduction of response bias; Chapter 12 discusses the reduction of sample selection and random sampling error. Indeed, much of the remainder of this book discusses various techniques for reducing bias in marketing research. The good news lies ahead!

Different Ways that Marketing Researchers Conduct Surveys

When two people engage in a conversation, human interaction takes place. Human interactive media are a personal form of communication. One human being directs a message to and interacts with another individual (or a small group). When most people think of interviewing, they envision two people engaged in a face-to-face dialogue or a conversation on the telephone. However, people don't always communicate in a two-way fashion. Sometimes, communication is one-way with little chance for spontaneous interaction. For example, traditional print advertisements are considered one-way communications because they are noninteractive in the sense that a consumer who views the ad has no immediate way of talking back to the ad designer. Likewise, we can summarize all the ways that marketing researchers communicate with survey respondents broadly into interactive and noninteractive media.

Interactive Survey Approaches

Interactive survey approaches are those that allow spontaneous two-way interaction between the interviewer and the respondent. These can be either personal or electronic. Either way, these approaches try to capture the dynamic exchange that is possible through face-to-face interviews. Survey respondents need not be passive audience members. Today's interactive approaches allow respondents to be involved in two-way communication using electronic media such as mobile phones or Web sites. More detail on various electronic options is provided later in this chapter.

Noninteractive Media

Noninteractive survey approaches are those that do not facilitate two-way communications and are thus largely a vehicle by which respondents give answers to static questions. The traditional questionnaire received by mail, completed by a respondent, and mailed back to the researcher, does not allow a dialogue or an exchange of information providing immediate feedback. So, from this perspective, self-administered questionnaires printed on paper are noninteractive. This fact does not mean that they are without merit, just that this type of survey is less flexible than surveys using interactive communication media. In fact, noninteractive media can be the best approach in some situations. Simple opinion polls, awareness studies and even surveys assessing consumer attitudes can generally be collected adequately via one-way communication.

Each technique for conducting surveys has merits and shortcomings. The purpose of this chapter is to explain when researchers should use different types of surveys. We will begin with a discussion of surveys that use live interviews. Then we turn to noninteractive, self-administered questionnaires. Finally, we explain how the Internet and digital technology are dramatically changing survey research. The Research Snapshot on the next page provides an example of how survey research can provide market intelligence.

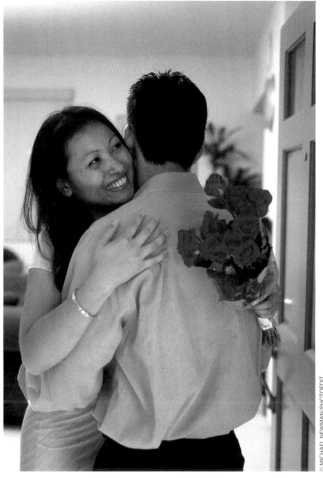

Electronic dating services have become a popular, successful example of electronic interactive media.

interactive survey approaches

Communication that allows spontaneous two-way interaction between the interviewer and the respondent.

noninteractive survey approaches

Two-way communication by which respondents give answers to static questions.

Conducting Personal Interviews

A **personal interview** is a form of direct communication in which an interviewer asks respondents questions face-to-face. This versatile and flexible method is a two-way conversation between interviewer and respondent. Personal interviews are truly interactive. The researcher can communicate with individuals in person by going door-to-door or intercepting them in shopping malls, or interviews may take place over the phone. Traditionally, researchers have recorded interview results using paper and pencil, by reading questions and recording answers. Today, computers are increasingly supporting survey research by automatically recording responses. In

personal interview

Face-to-face communication in which an interviewer asks a respondent to answer questions.

iPod, uPod, FMPod?

Apple has revolutionized the way consumers listen to music by providing portability for personalized high-fidelity listening. The iPod is a fraction of the size of the old Sony Walkman and allows the user to store a virtually unlimited number of songs. Of course, the iPod owner can also store movies and even class lectures in the form of a podcast. Nothing is perfect, however, and Apple and other companies that offer MP3 players are constantly searching for ways to improve their products. So, what's the best method of survey to communicate with this market?

In 2007, a survey of iPod owners asked respondents what one thing they would most like added to their iPod. The number one choice was an FM radio tuner; 40 percent of respondents indicated that an FM tuner would be desirable. However, when an FM tuner was offered to iPod users as an accessory for about $50, the sell through rate proved far under 40 percent. Follow-up surveys studying the lack of success revealed several issues that may have made the 40 percent figure inflated.

- The survey was implemented through a noninteractive format that did not allow any elaboration on behalf of the respondent. Thus, Apple overlooked the fact that an integrated FM tuner would have produced far better results than an add-on accessory. As a result, Apple may have missed an opportunity to get consumers to upgrade to a newer iPod had the company simply introduced and emphasized new models with built-in FM tuners.
- The noninteractive survey also took advantage of a mailing list used by a group of FM radio stations that may have not represented the entire iPod population very well.
- The survey failed to ask questions about how the iPod was actually used. Follow-up Internet surveys suggest that the ability to easily use the iPod in the automobile was probably a more attractive improvement option that appealed to a large number of users.

Sources: Withers, S., "Do iPod Users Really Want FM Tuners?" *The Wire* (April 4, 2008), www.itwire.com, accessed June 16, 2008; Harris Interactive (2006), "Two-Thirds of Adult Automobile Owners Who Own MP3/iPod Players Use the Device in Their Vehicles," www.marketresearchworld.net, accessed June 15, 2008; Elliott, A.M., "iPod Use Sees Increase with under 10-year-olds," *Pocket-Lint* (2008), accessed at www.pocket-lint.co.uk on June 15, 2008.

this section, we examine the general characteristics of face-to-face personal interviews, then compare the characteristics of door-to-door personal interviews and personal interviews conducted in shopping malls. The next section examines telephone interviews.

Although the history of marketing research is sketchy, gathering information through face-to-face contact with individuals goes back many years. Periodic censuses were used to set tax rates and aid military conscription in the ancient empires of Egypt and Rome.[12] During the Middle Ages, the merchant families of Fugger and Rothschild prospered in part because their far-flung organizations enabled them to get information before their competitors could.[13] Today, survey researchers typically present themselves in shopping centers and train stations and announce, "Good afternoon, my name is _____. I am with _____ Marketing Research Company, and we are conducting a survey on _____."

Advantages of Personal Interviews

Marketing researchers find that personal interviews offer many unique advantages. One of the most important is the opportunity for feedback.

■ OPPORTUNITY FOR FEEDBACK

Personal interviews provide the opportunity for feedback and clarification. For example, if a consumer is reluctant to provide sensitive information, the interviewer may offer reassurance that his or her answers will be strictly confidential. Personal interviews offer the lowest chance that respondents will misinterpret questions, because an interviewer who senses confusion can clarify the instruction or questions. Circumstances may dictate that at the conclusion of the interview, the respondent be given additional information concerning the purpose of the study. This clarification is easily accomplished with a personal interview. If the feedback indicates that some question or set of questions is particularly confusing, the researcher can make changes that make the questionnaire easier to understand.

■ PROBING COMPLEX ANSWERS

Another important characteristic of personal interviews is the opportunity to follow up by probing. If a respondent's answer is too brief or unclear, the researcher may request a more comprehensive or clearer explanation. In probing, the interviewer asks for clarification with standardized questions such as "Can you tell me more about what you had in mind?" (See the chapter on qualitative research for an expanded discussion of probing.) Although interviewers are expected to ask questions exactly as they appear on the questionnaire, probing allows them some flexibility. Depending on the research purpose, personal interviews vary in the degree to which questions are structured and in the amount of probing required. The personal interview is especially useful for obtaining unstructured information. Skilled interviewers can handle complex questions that cannot easily be asked in telephone or mail surveys.

■ LENGTH OF INTERVIEW

If the research objective requires an extremely lengthy questionnaire, personal interviews may be the only option. A general rule of thumb on mail and e-mail surveys is that they should not take more than 12 minutes to complete and telephone interviews typically should take less than 10 minutes. In contrast, a personal interview can be much longer, perhaps an hour or even more. However, the longer the interview, no matter what the form, the more the respondent should be compensated for their time and participation. Researchers should also be clear about how long participation should take in the opening dialogue requesting participation. Online surveys should include a completion meter that shows the progress a respondent has made toward completing the task.

■ COMPLETENESS OF QUESTIONNAIRE

The social interaction between a well-trained interviewer and a respondent in a personal interview increases the likelihood that the respondent will answer all the items on the questionnaire. The respondent who grows bored with a telephone interview may terminate the interview at his or her discretion simply by hanging up the phone. Self-administration of a mail questionnaire requires even more effort by the respondent. Rather than write lengthy responses, the respondent may fail to complete some of the questions. **Item nonresponse**—failure to provide an answer to a question—is least likely to occur when an experienced interviewer asks questions directly.

item nonresponse

Failure of a respondent to provide an answer to a survey question.

■ PROPS AND VISUAL AIDS

Interviewing respondents face-to-face allows the investigator to show them new product samples, sketches of proposed advertising, or other visual aids. When Lego Group wanted to introduce new train model sets for its famous building bricks, the company targeted adults who build complex models with its product. The company invited adults who were swapping ideas at the Lego Web site to visit the New York office, where they viewed ideas and provided their opinions. The respondents wound up rejecting all the company's ideas, but they suggested something different: the Santa Fe Super Chief set, which sold out within two weeks, after being advertised only by enthusiastic word of mouth.[14] This research could not have been done in a telephone interview or mail survey.

Marketing research that uses visual aids has become increasingly popular with researchers who investigate film concepts, advertising problems, and moviegoers' awareness of performers. Research for movies often begins by showing respondents videotapes of the prospective cast. After the movie has been produced, film clips are shown and interviews conducted to evaluate the movie's appeal, especially which scenes to emphasize in advertisements. The Research Snapshot on the next page demonstrates how respondents can even taste new products—a real advantage for examining new products—at least until the virtual tongue takes over.

■ HIGH PARTICIPATION RATE

Although some people are reluctant to participate in a survey, the presence of an interviewer generally increases the percentage of people willing to complete the interview. People are often

Matters of Taste

Asking an opinion is easy to do over the phone or online, but not if you want people's reactions to a new food, wine, or perfume. For those opinions, you probably want people to sample the new product first, so a face-to-face interview seems to be the only option. But, researchers have some creative options.

Sometimes researchers simply want to know whether consumers like the product, but in other situations they are trying to meet objectives such as maintaining the same taste after substituting a new ingredient. Sartori Foods uses a chart it calls the Italian Cheese Flavor Wheel to ask consumers to describe various cheeses. The chart matches consumer-friendly terms like *nutty, buttery,* and *creamy* with terms useful in the industry (for example, *aromatic amino acids* and *sulfur compounds*). Researchers can use an alternative to face-to-face interviews by sending both a sample of the product to potential respondents along with a color wheel. A phone interview can then have the respondent use the wheel to describe the taste.

Better yet, scientists have developed a virtual tongue. That's right! A synthetic surface absorbs foods and identifies certain tastes by feeding information into a computer. This may eliminate the need for a respondent altogether. For instance, the virtual tongue has quite a wine palate. It can tell Chardonnay from Malvasia and it can tell a 2005 vintage from a 2007 vintage. Well, this may be reliable, but many consumers are willing to stand in line to verify the wine's characteristics by tasting it for themselves!

Sources: Based on Claudia D. O'Donnell, "Tips for Sensory Tests," *Prepared Foods* (January 2005), downloaded from InfoTrac at http://www.galenet.com; Fran LaBell, "International Sensory Tests: When in Rome," *Prepared Foods* (February 2002), downloaded from Business & Company Resource Center, http://galenet.galegroup.com; Abend, L., "E-Tongue Passes Wine Taste Test," *Time* (August 12, 2008), http://www.time.com/time/business/article/0,8599,1831413,00.html, accessed August 1, 2008.

more hesitant to tell a person "no" face-to-face than they are over the phone, in a mail request, or through some other impersonal contact. Respondents typically are required to do no reading or writing—all they have to do is talk. A personable interviewer can also do much to improve response rates. Many people enjoy sharing information and insights with friendly and sympathetic interviewers.

Disadvantages of Personal Interviews

Personal interviews also have some disadvantages. Respondents are not anonymous and as a result may be reluctant to provide confidential information to another person. Suppose a survey asked top executives, "Do you see any major internal instabilities or threats (people, money, material, and so on) to the achievement of your marketing objectives?" Many managers may be reluctant to answer this sensitive question honestly in a personal interview in which their identities are known.

■ INTERVIEWER INFLUENCE

Some evidence suggests that demographic characteristics of the interviewer influence respondents' answers. For example, one research study revealed that male interviewers produced larger amounts of interviewer variance than female interviewers in a survey in which 85 percent of the respondents were female. Older interviewers who interviewed older respondents produced more variance than other age combinations, whereas younger interviewers who interviewed younger respondents produced the least variance.

Differential interviewer techniques may be a source of bias. The rephrasing of a question, the interviewer's tone of voice, and the interviewer's appearance may influence the respondent's answer. Consider the interviewer who has conducted 100 personal interviews. During the next one, he or she may lose concentration and either selectively perceive or anticipate the respondent's answer. The interpretation of the response may differ somewhat from what the respondent intended. Typically, the public thinks of the person who does marketing research as a dedicated scientist. Unfortunately, some interviewers do not fit that ideal. Considerable interviewer variability exists. Cheating is possible; interviewers cut corners to save time and energy or fake parts of their reports by dummying up part or all of the questionnaire. Control over interviewers is important to ensure that difficult, embarrassing, or time-consuming questions are handled properly.

■ LACK OF ANONYMITY OF RESPONDENT

Because a respondent in a personal interview is not totally anonymous, he or she may be reluctant to provide confidential information to the interviewer. Researchers take care to phrase sensitive questions to avoid social desirability bias. For example, the interviewer may show the respondent a card that lists possible answers and ask the respondent to read a category number rather than be required to verbalize sensitive answers.

■ COST

Personal interviews are expensive, generally substantially more costly than mail, e-mail, Internet, or phone surveys. The geographic proximity of respondents, the length and complexity of the questionnaire, and the number of people who are nonrespondents because they could not be contacted (not-at-homes) will all influence the cost of the personal interview.

Door-to-Door Interviews and Shopping Mall Intercepts

Personal interviews can be conducted through several different media. The next sections provide an overview of the options for personal interviews.

Personal interviews may be conducted at the respondents' homes or offices or in many other places. Increasingly, personal interviews are being conducted in shopping malls. Mall intercept interviews allow many interviews to be conducted quickly. Respondents can be intercepted in public areas of shopping malls and then asked to come to a permanent research facility to taste new food items or to view advertisements. The locale for the interview generally influences the participation rate, and thus the degree to which the sample represents the general population.

■ DOOR-TO-DOOR INTERVIEWS

The presence of an interviewer at the door generally increases the likelihood that a person will be willing to complete an interview. Because **door-to-door interviews** increase the participation rate, they provide a more representative sample of the population than mail questionnaires. For example, response rates to mail surveys are substantially lower among Hispanics whether the questionnaire is printed in English or Spanish.[15] People who do not have telephones, who have unlisted telephone numbers, or who are otherwise difficult to contact may be reached using door-to-door interviews. However, door-to-door interviews may underrepresent some groups and overrepresent others based on the geographic areas covered.

door-to-door interviews
Personal interviews conducted at respondents' doorsteps in an effort to increase the participation rate in the survey.

Door-to-door interviews may exclude individuals who live in multiple-dwelling units with security systems, such as high-rise apartment dwellers, or executives who are too busy to grant personal interviews during business hours. Other people, for security reasons, simply will not open the door when a stranger knocks. Telephoning an individual in one of these subgroups to make an appointment may make the total sample more representative. However, obtaining a representative sample of this security-conscious subgroup based on a listing in the telephone directory may be difficult. For these reasons, door-to-door interviews are becoming a thing of the past.

■ CALLBACKS

When a person selected to be in the sample cannot be contacted on the first visit, a systematic procedure is normally initiated to call back at another time. **Callbacks**, or attempts to recontact individuals selected for the sample, are the major means of reducing nonresponse error. Calling back a sampling unit is more expensive than interviewing the person the first time around, because subjects who initially were not at home generally are more widely dispersed geographically than the original sample units. Callbacks in door-to-door interviews are important because not-at-home individuals (for example, working parents) may systematically vary from those who *are* at home (nonworking parents, retired people, and the like).

callbacks
Attempts to recontact individuals selected for a sample who were not available initially.

■ MALL INTERCEPT INTERVIEWS

Personal interviews conducted in shopping malls are referred to as **mall intercept interviews**, or *shopping center sampling*. Interviewers typically intercept shoppers at a central point within the shopping center or at a main entrance. Mall intercept interviews are conducted because their costs are lower. No travel is required to the respondent's home; instead, the respondent comes to the interviewer, and many interviews can be conducted quickly in this way.

A major problem with mall intercept interviews is that individuals usually are in a hurry to shop, so the incidence of refusal is high—typically around 50 percent. Yet, the commercial marketing research industry conducts many more personal interviews in shopping malls or shoping centers than it conducts door-to-door.

In a mall interview, the researcher must recognize that he or she should not be looking for a representative sample of the total population. Each mall has its own target market's characteristics, and there is likely to be a larger bias than with careful household probability sampling. However, personal interviews in shopping malls are appropriate when the target group is a special market segment such as the parents of children of bike-riding age. If the respondent indicates that he or she has a child of this age, the parent can then be brought into a rented space and shown several bikes. The mall intercept interview allows the researcher to show large, heavy, or immobile visual materials, such as a television commercial. A mall interviewer can give an individual a product to take home to use and obtain a commitment that the respondent will cooperate when recontacted later by telephone. Mall intercept interviews are also valuable when activities such as cooking and tasting of food must be closely coordinated and timed to follow each other. They may also be appropriate when a consumer durable product must be demonstrated. For example, electronics manufacturers often do not want to test new appliances in consumers homes because they can be bulky or difficult to properly set up. Thus, bringing respondents to the appliances is a better option.

Global Considerations

Willingness to participate in a personal interview varies dramatically around the world. For example, in some Arab nations, women would never consent to be interviewed by a man. And in many countries the idea of discussing grooming behavior and personal-care products with a stranger would be highly offensive. Few people would consent to be interviewed on such topics.

The norms about appropriate business conduct also influence businesspeople's willingness to provide information to interviewers. For example, conducting business-to-business interviews in Japan during business hours is difficult because managers, strongly loyal to their firm, believe that they have an absolute responsibility to oversee their employees while on the job. In some cultures when a businessperson is reluctant to be interviewed, a reputable third party may be asked to intervene so that an interview may take place.

Telephone Interviews

In days past, a telephone was a telephone. Today however, phones can actually be any one of a number of appliances. The question to the researcher who wishes to do a phone interview returns to this: Do all types of phones produce identical survey results?

■ LANDLINE PHONES

For several decades, landline **telephone interviews** have been the mainstay of commercial survey research. The quality of data obtained by telephone is potentially comparable to the quality of data collected face-to-face. Respondents are more willing to provide detailed and reliable information on a variety of personal topics over the phone while in the privacy of their own homes than when answering questions face-to-face.

In-home phone surveys are still considered capable of providing fairly representative samples of the U.S. population. However, the "no-call" legislation dating back to the mid-2000s has limited this capability somewhat. Marketing researchers cannot solicit information via phone numbers listed on the do-not-call registry. Thus, to the extent that consumers who place their numbers on these lists share something in common, such as a greater desire for privacy, a representative sample of the general population cannot be obtained. Marketers and marketing researchers can obtain the do-not-call lists of phone numbers from the FTC for $62 per area code. The entire registry can be obtained for $17,050. This information can be obtained from the FTC do-not-call Web site at http://www.ftc. gov/donotcall. Although this may seem expensive, the FTC levies fines on the order of $10,000 per violation (per call), so obtaining the registry is a wise investment for those wishing to contact consumers via the telelphone. AT&T faced fines of over three-quarters of a million dollars for making 78 unwanted calls to 29 consumers listed on the do-not-call list. The Feds do take violations very seriously.

Information about do-not-call lists for each state can be found at the Direct Marketing Association's Web site at http://www.the-dma.org/government/donotcalllists.shtml.

Likewise, the Canadian government has instituted a nearly identical do-not-call program. The Canadian Radio-television and Telecommunications Commission imposes fines up to $11,000 per call for calls made to people on the Canadian do-not-call list. Other countries in Europe and elsewhere are also considering such legislation. The advantages of privacy simply make phones less capable of obtaining representative samples than they once were. Often however, a landline phone call is still the researcher's best option.

Inevitably though, even when calls do get through, an all too often outcome for the researcher is something like this:

> Good evening, I'm with a nationwide marketing research company. Are you watching television tonight?
> A: Yes.
> Did you see 60 minutes on CBS?
> A: "Click"

■ MOBILE PHONE INTERVIEWS

Mobile phone interviews differ from landline phones most obviously because they are directed toward a mobile (i.e., cell) phone number. However, there are other less obvious distinctions.

- In the United States, no telemarketing can be directed toward mobile phone numbers by law. The primary reason for enacting this law was because respondents would often have to pay to receive the call. A respondent would have to "opt in" before their phone number would be made available for such calls.
- The recipient of a mobile phone call is even more likely to be distracted than the recipient of a home or office call. In fact, the respondent may be driving a car, on a subway train, or walking down a noisy street. Factors such as this are not conducive to a high-quality interview.
- The area codes for mobile phones are not necessarily tied to geography. For instance, a person who moves from Georgia to Arizona can choose to keep his or her old phone number. Therefore, a researcher may be unable to determine whether or not a respondent fits into the desired geographic sampling population simply by taking note of the area code.
- The phones have varying abilities for automated responses and differing keypads. Some requests, such as "hit pound sign," may be more difficult to do on some keypads than on others.

We'll discuss the relative advantages and disadvantages of mobile phone interviews in the following sections. However, suffice it to say at this point, interviewing people via a landline phone is not the same as interviewing people via a mobile phone. Exhibit 7.2 on the next page provides a summary of potential differences in surveying by landline or mobile phones.

EXHIBIT 7.2
**Landline and Mobile Phone
Pros and Cons**

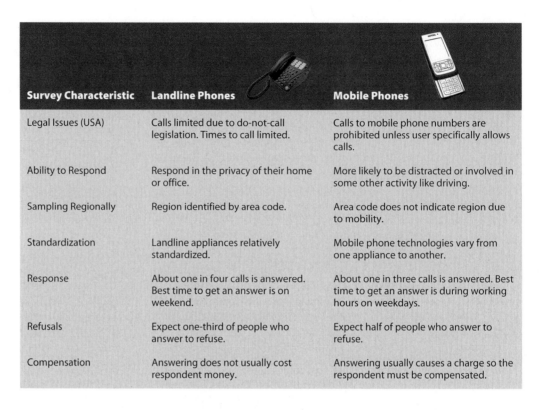

Survey Characteristic	Landline Phones	Mobile Phones
Legal Issues (USA)	Calls limited due to do-not-call legislation. Times to call limited.	Calls to mobile phone numbers are prohibited unless user specifically allows calls.
Ability to Respond	Respond in the privacy of their home or office.	More likely to be distracted or involved in some other activity like driving.
Sampling Regionally	Region identified by area code.	Area code does not indicate region due to mobility.
Standardization	Landline appliances relatively standardized.	Mobile phone technologies vary from one appliance to another.
Response	About one in four calls is answered. Best time to get an answer is on weekend.	About one in three calls is answered. Best time to get an answer is during working hours on weekdays.
Refusals	Expect one-third of people who answer to refuse.	Expect half of people who answer to refuse.
Compensation	Answering does not usually cost respondent money.	Answering usually causes a charge so the respondent must be compensated.

Phone Interview Characteristics

Phone interviews have several distinctive characteristics that set them apart from other survey techniques. These characteristics present significant advantages and disadvantages for the researcher.

■ REPRESENTATIVE SAMPLES

Practically every consumer over the age of 18 in developed nations around the world has a phone. In some of these countries, including the U.S. and countries throughout Europe, children often have their own mobile phone beginning around the age of 12 or 13. The widespread diffusion of phones through the population makes them attractive for trying to represent all different types of populations. Landline phone directories remain widely available and easy to access. Although a growing number of consumers are choosing not to have a landline phone, it's safe to say that about 90 percent of households in the U.S. can be reached via a traditional in-home telephone call. The less than 10 percent without a landline do cause some problems with obtaining a random sample. However, the desire for privacy causes many people to have an unlisted phone number and other consumers have recently moved and have a number that is too new to be in directories. The inaccuracy of directories is an even greater problem than the small percentage of people with no landline phone.

Individuals whose phone numbers are unlisted differ slightly from those with published numbers. Recent movers tend to be younger, more urban, and less likely to own their own home. Households that maintain unlisted phone numbers by choice tend to have higher incomes and live in the suburbs. In either case, the fact that these potential respondents are removed from the entire population means that they will be underrepresented in any sample that relies on landline phone directories. Researchers who wish to draw inferences about the entire U.S. population must be willing to accept the error due to this problem if they decide to sample in this way.

Random Digit Dialing

random digit dialing

Use of telephone exchanges and a table of random numbers to contact respondents with unlisted phone numbers.

The problem of unlisted phone numbers can be partially resolved through the use of random digit dialing. **Random digit dialing** eliminates the counting of names in a list (for example, calling every fiftieth name in a column) and subjectively determining whether a directory listing is a business, institution, or legitimate household. In the simplest form of random digit dialing, telephone exchanges (prefixes) for the geographic areas in the sample are obtained. Using a table of random numbers, the last four digits of the telephone number are selected. Telephone directories can be ignored entirely or used in combination with the assignment of one or several random digits. By law, mobile phone numbers must be excluded as should numbers on the do-not-call list. Random digit dialing also helps overcome the problem due to new listings and recent changes in numbers. Unfortunately, the refusal rate in commercial random digit dialing studies is higher than the refusal rate for telephone surveys that use only listed telephone numbers.

Additionally, although most American households still have landline phones, some predictions suggest this is changing quickly. Some estimates suggest that within the next 5 years, the number of households that have only mobile phones may approach 40 percent.[16] Should this prediction be true, this will have a dramatic effect on polling and marketing research in the United States. The consumer movement toward solely mobile phones may have less effect on research in Europe and other nations where mobile phone numbers can be included in samples alongside landline phone numbers.

Landline versus Mobile Phone Results

People do not use mobile phones the same way they use landline phones. Additionally, those with high mobile-phone usage are not entirely the same as those with low or no mobile-phone usage and perhaps high landline-phone usage. Researchers should not be surprised to observe differences in the characteristics of both sets of respondents. For example, the chances of getting someone to answer a phone vary across these two types. For instance, compared to mobile phone users:[17]

- Calls to mobile phone numbers are more likely to result in someone answering the phone on weekdays during working hours than are landline numbers. About one in three calls to mobile phones will be answered as opposed to about one in four calls to landline numbers.
- Calls to mobile phone numbers are less likely to result in someone answering the phone on weekends than are landline numbers. Less than one in three calls to mobile phones are answered on the weekends as opposed to nearly four in ten calls to landline numbers.
- Refusals are higher for calls to mobile phone numbers than for calls to landline numbers. About half of mobile phone calls result in refusals to participate in the survey whereas landline refusals average around 30 percent.
- Mobile phone users should be duly compensated for their responses given the potential costs involved and the calls should be kept to a short duration given that a mobile phone user is more likely in a situation involving attention to some other activity.

These factors all affect the equality of data and samples obtained from landline and mobile-phone sampling. Researchers should consider these factors before making a quick decision that any type of phone interviewing will satisfy the data needs at hand.

■ SPEED

One advantage of telephone interviewing is the relative speed of data collection. Data collection with mail or personal interviews can take weeks. In contrast, hundreds of telephone interviews can be conducted within a few hours. When an interviewer enters a respondent's answers directly into a computerized system, data processing speeds up even more relative to mail interviews or any other approach that would involve manual data coding and entry.

■ COST

As the cost of personal interviews continues to increase, phone interviews are becoming relatively inexpensive. The cost of telephone interviews is estimated to be less than 25 percent of the cost of door-to-door personal interviews. Travel time and costs are eliminated. However, the typical Internet survey is even less expensive than a phone-based survey.

■ ABSENCE OF FACE-TO-FACE CONTACT

Telephone interviews are more impersonal than face-to-face interviews. Respondents may answer embarrassing or confidential questions more willingly in a telephone interview than in a personal interview. However, mail and Internet surveys, although not perfect, are better media for gathering extremely sensitive information because they seem more anonymous. Some evidence suggests that people provide information on income and other financial matters only reluctantly, even in telephone interviews. Such questions may be personally threatening for a variety of reasons, and high refusal rates for this type of question occur with each form of survey research.

Although telephone calls may be less threatening because the interviewer is not physically present, the absence of face-to-face contact is more often a liability than an asset. When the interviewer isn't physically present, for instance, a respondent cannot see when the interviewer is still writing down the previous comment and may continue to elaborate on an answer. Thus, some important information may not get recorded. Likewise, the inability of the interviewer to see the respondent causes problems. If a respondent pauses to think about an answer, the interviewer may simply interpret the pause as "no response" and go on to the next question. Hence, there is a greater tendency for interviewers to record no answers and incomplete answers in telephone interviews than in personal interviews.

■ COOPERATION

One trend is very clear. In the last few decades, telephone response rates have fallen. Analysis of response rates for the long-running Survey of Consumer Attitudes conducted by the University of Michigan found that response rates fell from a high of 72 percent to 67 percent during the period from 1979 to 1996 and then even faster after 1996, dropping to 60 percent.[18] Lenny Murphy of the data collection firm Dialtek says he has observed a decline in survey response rates from a typical range of 30 to 40 percent in the past down to below 20 percent.[19] Fewer calls are answered because more households are using caller ID and answering machines to screen their calls, and many individuals do not pick up the phone when the display reads "out of area" or when an unfamiliar survey organization's name and number appear on the display. Also, more phone lines are dedicated to fax machines and computers. However, the University of Michigan study found that the rate of refusal actually grew faster in the more recent period than the rate of not answering researchers' calls. Getting someone to answer the phone does not mean that the battle for a meaningful response is won.

One way researchers can try to improve response rates is to leave a message on the household's telephone answering machine or voice mail. However, many people will not return a call to help someone conduct a survey. Using a message explicitly stating that the purpose of the call is not sales related may improve responses. Other researchers simply hope to reach respondents when they call back, trying callbacks at different times and on different days.

Despite the restrictions in the United States, other countries may not adopt laws restricting calls to mobile phones. In addition, consumers in other countries are more open to responding to research delivered by voice or by text messaging. Thus, the mobile phone may be a better interview tool outside of the United States than in the United States.

Refusal to cooperate with interviews is directly related to interview length. A major study of survey research found that interviews of 5 minutes or less had a refusal rate of 21 percent; interviews of between 6 and 12 minutes had 41 percent refusal rates; and interviews of 13 minutes or more had 47 percent rates. In unusual cases, a few highly interested respondents will put up with longer interviews. A good rule of thumb is to keep telephone interviews approximately 10 minutes long. In general, 30 minutes is the maximum amount of time most respondents will spend unless they are highly interested in the survey subject.

Another way to encourage participation is to send households an invitation to participate in a survey. The invitation can describe the purpose and importance of the survey and the likely duration of the survey. The invitation can also encourage subjects to be available and reassure them that the caller will not try to sell anything. In a recent study comparing response rates, the rates were highest among households that received an advance letter, somewhat lower when the notice came on a postcard, and lowest when no notice was sent.[20]

■ INCENTIVES TO RESPOND

Respondents should receive some incentive to respond. Research addresses different types of incentives. For telephone interviews, test-marketing involving different types of survey introduction suggests that not all introductions are equally effective. A financial incentive or some significant chance to win a desirable prize will produce a higher telephone response rate than a simple assurance that the research is not a sales pitch, a more detailed description of the survey, or an assurance of confidentiality.[21]

■ CALLBACKS

An unanswered call, a busy signal, or a respondent who is not at home requires a callback. Telephone callbacks are much easier to make than callbacks in personal interviews. However, as mentioned, the ownership of telephone answering machines and the use of voice mail is widespread, and their effects on callbacks are not well understood. However, if a respondent decides not to answer a number the first time, one has to wonder why they would decide to answer it on a callback.

■ LIMITED DURATION

Respondents who run out of patience with the interview can merely hang up. To encourage participation, interviews should be relatively short. The length of the telephone interview is definitely limited. The shorter the better and seldom longer than 10 minutes. Interviewers should also inform the respondent at the start of the interview of the maximum time the interview will take.

■ LACK OF VISUAL MEDIUM

Because visual aids cannot be used in telephone interviews, this method is not appropriate for packaging research, copy testing of television and print advertising, and concept tests that require visual materials. Likewise, certain attitude scales and measuring instruments, such as the semantic differential (discussed more in a later chapter), require the respondent to see a graphic scale, so they are difficult to use over the phone.

Central Location Interviewing

Research agencies or interviewing services typically conduct all telephone interviews from a central location. Such **central location interviewing** allows firms to hire a staff of professional interviewers and to supervise and control the quality of interviewing more effectively. When telephone interviews are centralized and computerized, an agency or business can benefit from additional cost economies. Some of the cost economies are realized by outsourcing interviews to call centers where labor costs are low including centers in other countries.

Computer-Assisted Telephone Interviewing

Advances in computer technology allow responses to telephone interviews to be entered directly into the computer in a process known as **computer-assisted telephone interviewing (CATI)**. Telephone interviewers are seated at computer terminals. Monitors display the questionnaires, one question at a time, along with precoded possible responses to each question. The interviewer reads each question as it appears on the screen. When the respondent answers, the interviewer enters the response directly into the computer, and it is automatically stored in the computer's memory. The computer then displays the next question on the screen. Computer-assisted telephone interviewing requires that answers to the questionnaire be highly structured. If a respondent gives an unacceptable answer (that is, one not precoded and programmed), the computer will reject it.

Computer-assisted telephone interviewing systems include telephone management systems that select phone numbers, dial the numbers automatically, and perform other labor-saving functions. These systems can automatically control sample selection by randomly generating names or fulfilling a sample quota. A computer can generate an automatic callback schedule. A typical call management system might schedule recontact attempts to recall unanswered calls after two hours

central location interviewing

Telephone interviews conducted from a central location allowing firms to hire a staff of professional interviewers and to supervise and control the quality of interviewing more effectively.

computer-assisted telephone interviewing (CATI)

Technology that allows answers to telephone interviews to be entered directly into a computer for processing.

and busy numbers after 10 minutes and allow the interviewer to enter a more favorable time slot (day and hour) when a respondent indicates that he or she is too busy to be interviewed. Software systems also allow researchers to request daily status reports on the number of completed interviews relative to quotas. CATI interviews can also be conducted by a pre-recorded voice with the respondent answering by punching buttons on the phone.

Computerized Voice-Activated Telephone Interview

Technological advances have combined computerized telephone dialing and voice-activated computer messages to allow researchers to conduct telephone interviews without human interviewers. However, researchers have found that computerized voice-activated telephone interviewing works best with very short, simple questionnaires. One system includes a voice-synthesized module controlled by a microprocessor. With it the sponsor is able to register a caller's single response such as "true/false," "yes/no," "like/dislike," or "for/against." This type of system has been used by television and radio stations to register callers' responses to certain issues. One system, Telsol, begins with an announcement that the respondent is listening to a recorded message. The computer then asks questions, leaving blank tape in between to record the answers. If respondents do not answer the first two questions, the computer disconnects and goes to the next call. With this process, the entire data collection process can be automated because a recorded voice is used to ask the questions and responses are recorded automatically.

Global Considerations

Different cultures often have different norms about proper telephone behavior. For example, business-to-business researchers have learned that Latin American businesspeople will not open up to strangers on the telephone. So, researchers in Latin America usually find personal interviews more suitable than telephone surveys. In Japan, respondents consider it ill-mannered if telephone interviews last more than 20 minutes. Laws governing researchers ability to call via landline or mobile phones also vary based on factors such as do-not-call laws and the legality of calling mobile phone numbers. Calling mobile phones is generally prohibited in the United States but allowed in Europe, for instance.

Surveys Using Self-Administered Questionnaires

Many noninteractive surveys can be implemented without an interviewer. Marketing researchers distribute questionnaires to consumers through the mail and in many other ways (see Exhibit 7.3). They insert questionnaires in packages and magazines. They may place questionnaires at points of purchase or in high-traffic locations in stores or malls. They may even fax questionnaires to individuals. Questionnaires can be printed on paper, but they may be posted on the Internet or sent via e-mail. No matter how the **self-administered questionnaires** are distributed, they are different from interviews because the respondent takes responsibility for reading and answering the questions.

Self-administered questionnaires present a challenge to the marketing researcher because they rely on the clarity of the written word rather than on the skills of the interviewer. The nature of self-administered questionnaires is best illustrated by explaining mail questionnaires.

self-administered questionnaires

Surveys in which the respondent takes the responsibility for reading and answering the questions.

Mail Questionnaires

A traditional **mail survey** is a self-administered questionnaire sent to respondents through a postal service, or as it is more frequently referred to today, snail mail. This paper-and-pencil method has several advantages and disadvantages.

mail survey

A self-administered questionnaire sent to respondents through the mail.

EXHIBIT 7.3 **Self-Administered Questionnaires Can Be Either Printed or Electronic**

GEOGRAPHIC FLEXIBILITY

Mail questionnaires can reach a geographically dispersed sample simultaneously because interviewers are not required. Respondents (such as farmers) who are located in isolated areas or those (such as executives) who are otherwise difficult to reach can easily be contacted by mail. For example, a pharmaceutical firm may find that doctors are not available for personal or telephone interviews. However, a mail survey can reach both rural and urban doctors who practice in widely dispersed geographic areas.

COST

Mail questionnaires are relatively inexpensive compared with personal interviews, though they are not cheap. Most include follow-up mailings, which require additional postage and printing costs. And it usually isn't cost-effective to try to cut costs on printing—questionnaires photocopied on low-grade paper have a greater likelihood of being thrown in the wastebasket than those prepared with more expensive, high-quality printing. The low response rates contribute to the high cost.

RESPONDENT CONVENIENCE

Mail surveys and other self-administered questionnaires can be filled out when the respondents have time, so respondents are more likely to take time to think about their replies. Many hard-to-reach respondents place a high value on convenience and thus are best contacted by mail. In some situations, particularly in business-to-business marketing research, mail questionnaires allow respondents to collect facts, such as sales statistics, that they may not be able to recall without checking. Being able to check information by verifying records or, in household surveys, by consulting with other family members should provide more valid, factual information than either personal or telephone interviews would allow. A catalog retailer may use mail surveys to estimate sales volume for catalog items by sending a mock catalog as part of the questionnaire. Respondents would be asked to indicate how likely they would be to order selected items. Using the mail allows respondents to consult other family members and to make their decisions within a reasonable timespan.

ANONYMITY OF RESPONDENT

In the cover letter that accompanies a mail or self-administered questionnaire, marketing researchers almost always state that the respondents' answers will be confidential. Respondents are more likely to provide sensitive or embarrassing information when they can remain anonymous. For example, personal interviews and a mail survey conducted simultaneously asked the question "Have you borrowed money at a regular bank?" Researchers noted a 17 percent response rate for the personal interviews and a 42 percent response rate for the mail survey. Although random sampling error may have accounted for part of this difference, the results suggest that for research on personal and sensitive financial issues, mail surveys are more confidential than personal interviews.

Anonymity can also reduce social desirability bias. People are more likely to agree with controversial issues, such as extreme political candidates, when completing self-administered questionnaires than when speaking to interviewers on the phone or at their doorsteps.

■ ABSENCE OF INTERVIEWER

Although the absence of an interviewer can induce respondents to reveal sensitive or socially undesirable information, this lack of personal contact can also be a disadvantage. Once the respondent receives the questionnaire, the questioning process is beyond the researcher's control. Although the printed stimulus is the same, each respondent will attach a different personal meaning to each question. Selective perception operates in research as well as in advertising. The respondent does not have the opportunity to question the interviewer. Problems that might be clarified in a personal or telephone interview can remain misunderstandings in a mail survey. There is no interviewer to probe for additional information or clarification of an answer, and the recorded answers must be assumed to be complete.

Respondents have the opportunity to read the entire questionnaire before they answer individual questions. Often the text of a later question will provide information that affects responses to earlier questions.

■ STANDARDIZED QUESTIONS

Mail questionnaires typically are highly standardized, and the questions are quite structured. Questions and instructions must be clear-cut and straightforward. Ambiguous questions only create additional error. Interviewing allows for feedback from the interviewer regarding the respondent's comprehension of the questionnaire. An interviewer who notices that the first 50 respondents are having some difficulty understanding a question can report this fact to the research analyst so that revisions can be made. With a mail survey, however, once the questionnaires are mailed, it is difficult to change the format or the questions.

■ TIME IS MONEY

If time is a factor in management's interest in the research results, or if attitudes are rapidly changing (for example, toward a political event), mail surveys may not be a good communication medium. A minimum of two or three weeks is necessary for receiving the majority of the responses. Follow-up mailings, which usually are sent when the returns begin to trickle in, require an additional two or three weeks. The time between the first mailing and the cut-off date (when questionnaires will no longer be accepted) normally is six to eight weeks. In a regional or local study, personal interviews may even be conducted more quickly.

■ LENGTH OF MAIL QUESTIONNAIRE

Mail questionnaires vary considerably in length, ranging from extremely short postcard questionnaires to multipage booklets that require respondents to fill in thousands of answers. A general rule of thumb is that a paper questionnaire should not exceed six pages in length. When a questionnaire requires a respondent to expend a great deal of effort, an incentive is generally required to induce the respondent to return the questionnaire. The following sections discuss several ways to pursue higher response rates even when questionnaires are relatively long.

Response Rates

response rate

The number of questionnaires returned or completed divided by the number of eligible people who were asked to participate in the survey.

All questionnaires that arrive via bulk mail are likely to get thrown away. Questionnaires that are boring, unclear, or too complex are even more likely to get thrown in the wastebasket. A poorly designed mail questionnaire often is returned by fewer than 5 percent of those sampled (that is, a 5 percent response rate). The basic calculation for obtaining a **response rate** is to count the number of questionnaires returned or completed, then divide the total by the number of eligible people who were contacted or requested to participate in the survey. Typically, the number in the denominator is adjusted for faulty addresses and similar problems that reduce the number of eligible participants

The major limitations of mail questionnaires relate to response problems. Respondents who complete the questionnaire may not be typical of all people in the sample. Individuals with a special interest in the topic are more likely to respond to a mail survey than those who are indifferent.

A researcher has no assurance that the intended subject is the person who fills out the questionnaire. The wrong person answering the questions may be a problem when surveying corporate executives, physicians, and other professionals, who may pass questionnaires on to subordinates to complete. This probably is not unique to mail surveys since electronic surveying suffers similarly.

Evidence suggests that cooperation and response rates rise as home value increases. Conversely if the sample has a high proportion of retired households, response rates will be lower. Mail survey respondents tend to be better educated than nonrespondents. If they return the questionnaire at all, poorly educated respondents who cannot read and write well may skip open-ended questions to which they are required to write out their answers. Rarely will a mail survey have a 50 percent or greater response rate. However, the use of follow-up mailings and other techniques may increase the response rate to an acceptable percentage. The lower the response rate, the greater the concern that the resulting sample will not adequately represent the population.

Increasing Response Rates for Mail Surveys

Nonresponse error is always a potential problem with mail surveys. Individuals who are interested in the general subject of the survey are more likely to respond than those with less interest or little experience. Thus, people who hold extreme positions on an issue are more likely to respond than individuals who are largely indifferent to the topic. To minimize this bias, researchers have developed a number of techniques to increase the response rate to mail surveys. For example, almost all surveys include postage-paid return envelopes. Using a stamped return envelope instead of a business reply envelope increases response rates even more.[22] Designing and formatting attractive questionnaires and wording questions so that they are easy to understand also help ensure a good response rate. However, special efforts may be required even with a sound questionnaire. Several of these methods are discussed in the following subsections.

■ COVER LETTER

A **cover letter** that accompanies a questionnaire or is printed on the first page of the questionnaire booklet is an important means of inducing a reader to complete and return the questionnaire. Exhibit 7.4 on the next page illustrates a cover letter and some of the points considered by a marketing research professional to be important in gaining respondents' attention and cooperation. The first paragraph of the letter explains why the study is important. The basic appeal alludes to the social usefulness of responding. Two other frequently used appeals are asking for help ("Will you do us a favor?") and the egotistical appeal ("Your opinions are important!"). Most cover letters promise confidentiality, invite the recipient to use an enclosed postage-paid reply envelope, describe any incentive or reward for participation, explain that answering the questionnaire will not be difficult and will take only a short time, and describe how the person was scientifically selected for participation.

A personalized letter addressed to a specific individual shows the respondent that he or she is important. Including an individually typed cover letter on letterhead rather than a printed form is an important element in increasing the response rate in mail surveys.[23]

cover letter
Letter that accompanies a questionnaire to induce the reader to complete and return the questionnaire.

■ MONEY HELPS

The respondent's motivation for returning a questionnaire may be increased by offering monetary incentives or premiums. Although pens, lottery tickets, and a variety of premiums have been used, monetary incentives appear to be the most effective and least biasing incentive. Money attracts

EXHIBIT 7.4
A Cover Letter Requesting Participation in a Survey

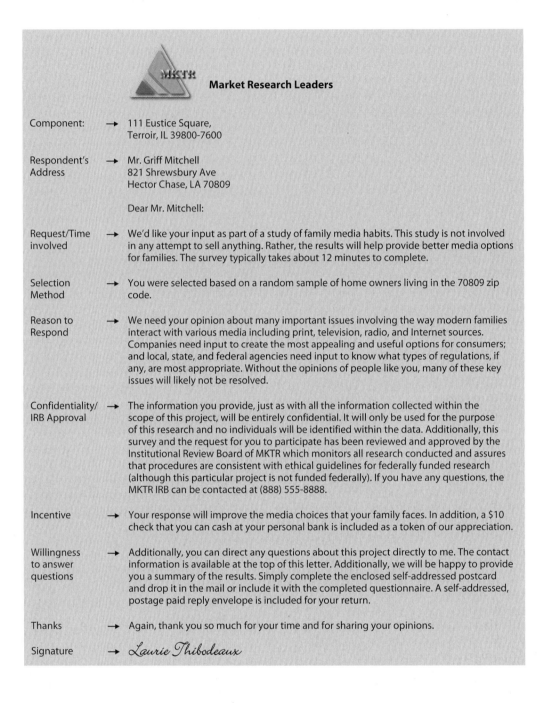

EXHIBIT 7.4
A Cover Letter Requesting Participation in a Survey

attention and creates a sense of obligation. Perhaps for this reason, monetary incentives work for all income categories. Often, cover letters try to boost response rates with messages such as "We know that the attached dollar cannot compensate you for your time but please accept it as a token of our appreciation." Response rates increase dramatically when a monetary incentive can be sent to a charity of the respondent's choice rather than directly to the respondent.

■ INTERESTING QUESTIONS

The topic of the research—and thus the point of the questions—cannot be manipulated without changing the definition of the marketing problem. However, certain interesting questions can be added to the questionnaire, perhaps at the beginning, to stimulate respondents' interest and to induce cooperation. By including questions that are of little concern to the researchers but that the respondents want to answer, the researchers may give respondents who are indifferent to the major questions a reason for responding.

■ FOLLOW-UPS

Most mail surveys generate responses in a pattern. The response rates are relatively high for the first two to three weeks (as indicated by the steepness of each curve), then the rates gradually taper off.

After responses from the first wave of mailings begin to trickle in, most studies use a follow-up letter or postcard reminder, which requests that the questionnaire be returned because a 100 percent return rate is important. A follow-up may include a duplicate questionnaire or may merely be a reminder to return the original questionnaire. Multiple contacts almost always increase response rates. The more attempts made to reach people, the greater the chances of their responding.[24]

■ ADVANCE NOTIFICATION

Advance notification that a questionnaire will be arriving can increase response rates in some situations. ACNielsen has used this technique to ensure a high cooperation rate in filling out diaries of television watching. Advance notices that go out closer to the questionnaire mailing time produce better results than those sent too far in advance. The optimal lead time for advance notification is three days before the mail survey is to arrive. Advanced notification can come in the form of a postcard, a phone call, or even an e-mail.

■ SURVEY SPONSORSHIP

Sometimes, response quality is enhanced when the survey sponsor remains anonymous. Respondents may, perhaps unintentionally, provide biased results when the survey sponsor is known. One business-to-business marketer wished to conduct a survey of its wholesalers to learn their stocking policies and their attitudes concerning competing manufacturers. A mail questionnaire sent on corporate letterhead very likely would have received a much lower response rate than the questionnaire actually sent, which used the letterhead of a commercial marketing research firm.

Sponsorship by well-known and prestigious organizations such as universities or government agencies may significantly improve response rates. A mail survey sent to members of a consumer panel will receive an exceptionally high response rate because panel members have already agreed to cooperate as part of membership.

■ KEYING MAIL QUESTIONNAIRES WITH CODES

A marketing researcher planning a follow-up letter, postcard, or e-mail should not disturb respondents who already have completed and returned the questionnaire. The expense of mailing questionnaires to those who already have responded is usually avoidable. One device for eliminating those who have already responded from the follow-up mailing list is to mark the questionnaires so that they may be keyed to identify members of the sampling frame who are nonrespondents. Blind keying of questionnaires on a return envelope (systematically varying the job number or room number of the marketing research department, for example) or a visible code number on the

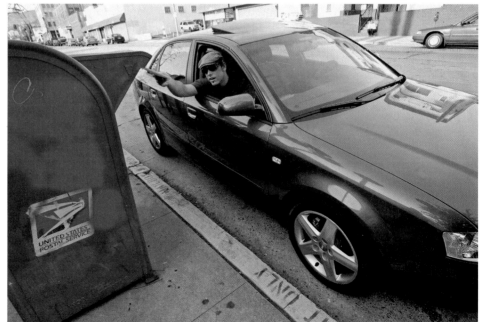

Mail surveys can reach a geographically dispersed sample and are relatively inexpensive. One disadvantage is the length of time involved in getting responses back. Response rates themselves also offer a challenge to surveyors.

© AP PHOTO

questionnaire has been used for this purpose. Visible keying is indicated with statements such as "The sole purpose of the number on the last page is to avoid sending a second questionnaire to people who complete and return the first one." E-mail surveys will be discussed later. But, electronic questionnaires can sometimes allow identification using computer Internet protocols (IP addresses) or with other electronic identification methods as a way of noting which respondents have participated in a questionnaire. Ethical researchers key questionnaires only to increase response rates, thereby preserving respondents' anonymity.

Self-Administered Questionnaires Using Other Forms of Distribution

Many forms of self-administered, printed questionnaires are very similar to mail questionnaires. Airlines occasionally pass out questionnaires to passengers during flights. Restaurants, hotels, and other service establishments print short questionnaires on cards so that customers can evaluate the service. *Tennis Magazine, Advertising Age, Wired,* and many other publications have used inserted questionnaires to survey current readers inexpensively, and often the results provide material for a magazine article.

Many manufacturers use their warranty or owner registration cards to collect demographic information and data about where and why products were purchased. Using owner registration cards is an extremely economical technique for tracing trends in consumer habits. Again, problems may arise because people who fill out these self-administered questionnaires differ from those who do not.

Extremely long questionnaires may be dropped off by an interviewer and then picked up later. The **drop-off method** sacrifices some cost savings because it requires traveling to each respondent's location. However, the response rate is generally improved. In the U.S., drop-offs are more commonly applied when the sample involves businesspeople who can best be reached at their place of work.

drop-off method

A survey method that requires the interviewer to travel to the respondent's location to drop off questionnaires that will be picked up later.

Fax Surveys

With fax surveys, potential survey respondents receive and/or return questionnaires via fax machines.[25] A questionnaire inserted in a magazine may instruct the respondent to clip out the questionnaire and fax it to a certain phone number. In a mail survey, a prepaid-postage envelope places little burden on the respondent. But faxing a questionnaire to a long-distance number may require a respondent to pay for the transmission of the fax. Thus, a disadvantage of the **fax survey** is that only respondents with fax machines who are willing to exert the extra effort will return questionnaires. Again, people with extreme opinions will be more likely to respond.

fax survey

A survey that uses fax machines as a way for respondents to receive and return questionnaires.

To address this disadvantage, marketers may use faxing as one of several options for replying to a survey. The journal *American Family Physician* carried a reader survey that gave respondents the option of either returning the reply by fax or visiting the journal's Web site to answer the same questions online.[26] For busy physicians who likely have access to office equipment, this approach would improve the response rate.

The use of fax survey approaches though is largely being replaced by other electronic communication options.

E-Mail Surveys

e-mail surveys

Surveys distributed through electronic mail.

E-mail surveys involve making the questionnaire available to a potential respondent via e-mail. Today, more questionnaires are distributed by e-mail in one way or another than by any other means. E-mail surveys can put a respondent together with a questionnaire in one of three ways.

■ USING E-MAIL

Three ways to contact respondents via e-mail include the following.

- A questionnaire can be included in the body of an e-mail. In this case, the questionnaire should be very short (no more than 10 questions). These are likely to receive the highest response rate.

- Questionnaires can also be distributed as an attachment to an e-mail. The respondent may be asked to open the questionnaire and respond via radio boxes. **Radio boxes** (buttons) allow a respondent to enter a mark such as an "X" or a check mark as a way of making a response. As might be expected, response rates drop when a person is asked to open an attachment and perhaps save it to his or her computer or even print it before the response is complete. Researchers can use common software such as Microsoft Word or Adobe Acrobat to create these files. After completing the questionnaire, the respondent has the burden of reattaching and returning by e-mail. Alternatively, the respondent may have the option of marking the questionnaire with a pen or pencil and returning via fax or mail. Obviously, the last approach should be avoided because of the burden placed on the respondent.

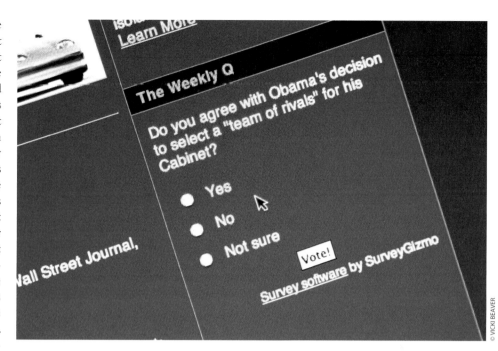

© VICKI BEAVER

radio boxes (buttons)

A small box character (box or button) that can be inserted into a word-processing or JavaScript document that allows a respondent to indicate a choice with a check mark or X.

- A third option is to include a hyperlink within the body of an e-mail that will direct the respondent to a Web site that contains the questionnaire. The person can then complete the response directly on that Web site. This approach is fast becoming the most common way of soliciting responses via e-mail. In essence, the e-mail survey becomes an Internet survey at this point.

■ SAMPLING AND E-MAIL

Like phone surveys, most, but not all, people in developed countries have access to e-mail. Researchers must remember that some individuals cannot be reached this way. In particular, researchers targeting senior citizens may wish to avoid this approach if a true cross section of their opinion is desired. For many segments, researchers can reliably count on potential respondents having access to e-mail. Businesspeople are probably more reliably reached via e-mail than mail. Younger consumers between the ages of 15 and 45 almost certainly use e-mail on a regular basis. E-mail is now considered a viable alternative for contacting research respondents and soon will perhaps match or surpass the landline telephone as a vehicle useful for contacting a wide cross section of the population.

■ ADVANTAGES AND DISADVANTAGES OF E-MAIL

The benefits of incorporating a questionnaire in an e-mail include the speed of distribution, lower distribution and processing costs, faster turnaround time, more flexibility, and less handling of paper questionnaires. The speed of e-mail distribution and the quick response time can be major advantages for surveys dealing with time-sensitive issues.

Some researchers also believe that respondents are more candid in e-mail than in person or on the telephone. One caveat would exist when dealing with research directed at employers using company e-mail addresses. Employees often believe that their e-mails are not secure and "eavesdropping" by a supervisor could possibly occur. The belief that a response is not secure is particularly strong when the questionnaire is contained in the e-mail itself and a reply e-mail is needed to return a completed questionnaire. Researchers designing e-mail surveys in this way need to work especially hard to assure respondents that their answers will be confidential. Better yet, if any confidential subject matter is being exchanged, the respondent should be allowed to respond via a questionnaire accessed through a hyperlink rather than a reply e-mail. Thus, the ability to get candid responses remains an advantage.

One potential disadvantage is that not all e-mail systems have the same capacity. Some handle color and graphics well; others are limited to text. The extensive differences in the capabilities of respondents' computers and e-mail software limit the types of questions and the layout of the e-mail questionnaire. For example, the display settings for computer screens vary widely, and wrap-around of lines may put the questions and the answer choices into strange and difficult-to-read patterns.[27] Many novice e-mail users find it difficult to mark answers in brackets on an e-mail questionnaire and/or to send a completed questionnaire using the e-mail reply function. For very simple questionnaires, this is generally not a problem. Otherwise, the researcher can avoid these problems by using a hyperlinked survey approach.

In general, the guidelines for printed mail surveys apply to e-mail surveys. For example, delivering the material in the cover letter is more difficult because people generally do not like e-mails that are more than two or three lines. Thus, a traditional cover letter may need to be made as brief as possible if it is contained in the e-mail request itself. Another option is to move some of the cover letter material, such as the assurances of confidentiality and IRB approval, to the actual questionnaire introduction. Also, if the e-mail lists more than one address in the "to" or "CC" field, all recipients will see the entire list of names. This lack of anonymity has the potential to cause response bias and nonresponse error. When possible, the e-mail should be addressed to a single person. Alternatively, the blind carbon copy, or BCC, field can be used if the same message must be sent to an entire sample. A drawback to this approach is that some spam filters will identify any message addressed to a large number of respondents as junk e-mail. Bulk-mailing programs exist that attempt to work around this problem by e-mailing potential respondents a few at a time. As can be seen, the problems associated with successful delivery to respondents remain a disadvantage of e-mail surveys.

Internet Surveys

Internet survey

A self-administered questionnaire posted on a Web site.

An **Internet survey** is a self-administered questionnaire posted on a Web site. Respondents provide answers to questions displayed onscreen by highlighting a phrase, clicking an icon, or actually typing in a response. Response rates remain an issue with Internet surveys. Typically, repondents are made aware of the existence of an Internet survey either by simply coming across it while browsing, through a pop-up notification, or via an e-mail containing a hyperlink as described above.

With Internet surveys, we can track both click rate, which assesses the portion of potential respondents who actually take a look at the questionnaire, and actual response rates. Of course, response rates will be no higher than the click rate. Generally, except for very long questionnaires, the vast majority of respondents who click through to view the questionnaire also respond to it. Like every other type of survey, Internet surveys have both advantages and disadvantages.

■ SPEED AND COST-EFFECTIVENESS

Internet surveys allow marketers to reach a large audience (possibly a global one), personalize individual messages, and secure confidential answers quickly and cost-effectively. These computer-to-computer self-administered questionnaires eliminate the costs of paper, postage, and data entry, as well as other administrative costs. Once an Internet questionnaire has been developed, the incremental cost of reaching additional respondents is minimal. So, samples can be larger than with interviews or other types of self-administered questionnaires. Even with large samples, surveys that used to take many weeks can be conducted in a week or less.

■ VISUAL APPEAL AND INTERACTIVITY

Surveys conducted on the Internet can have limted interactivity. The questionnaire can actually change based on the specific responses provided. The researcher can then use more sophisticated lines of questioning based on a respondent's prior answers. Many of these interactive surveys utilize color, sound, and animation, which may help to increase respondents' cooperation and willingness to spend time answering the questionnaires. The Internet is an excellent medium for the presentation of visual materials, such as photographs or drawings of product prototypes, advertisements, and movie trailers. Innovative measuring instruments that take advantage of the ability to adjust backgrounds, fonts, color, and other features have been designed and applied with considerable success.

■ RESPONDENT PARTICIPATION AND COOPERATION

Internet survey respondents can be highly involved in a particular issue when they intentionally click through to a particular questionnaire that they come across while browsing. For example, Ticketmaster quickly obtained more than 10,000 responses based on a survey invitation placed on their home page. The responses helped Ticketmaster better understand its customer purchase patterns and evaluate visitor satisfaction with the site. A response like this is possible only when consumers are involved and believe their cooperation will help make the experience better. Lacking involvement, and when participation is voluntary, Internet survey response rates can be very low.

Today, respondents are typically initially contacted via e-mail. Often they are members of consumer panels who have previously indicated their willingness to cooperate. When panel members receive an e-mail invitation to participate, they are given logon instructions and a password. This security feature prevents access by individuals who are not part of the scientifically selected sample. Requiring a login better enables the researcher to identify whether or not an invitee has already responded.

Panel members also need an incentive to respond. A study of German consumers showed that nothing beats financial incentives. In other words, the best way to get responses was to simply pay consumers for participating in surveys.[28] This may sound easy enough, although perhaps expensive, professional respondents could be an end result. Professional respondents may only be participating for the incentive and may even be giving bogus responses simply to finish each survey quickly. Such patterns are likely detectable as we discuss in a later chapter. Researchers using panel surveys need to be particularly vigilant in screening responses for authenticity.

■ ACCURATE REAL-TIME DATA CAPTURE

The computer-to-computer nature of Internet surveys means that each respondent's answers are entered directly into the researcher's computer as soon as the questionnaire is submitted. In addition, the questionnaire software may be programmed to reject improper data entry. For example, on a paper questionnaire a respondent might incorrectly check two responses even though the instructions call for a single answer. In an Internet survey, this mistake can be interactively corrected as the survey is taking place. Thus, the data capture is more accurate than when humans are involved.

Real-time data capture allows for real-time data analysis. A researcher can review up-to-the-minute sample size counts and tabulation data from an Internet survey in real time.

■ CALLBACKS

When the sample for an Internet survey is drawn from a consumer panel, those who have not completed the survey questionnaire can be easily recontacted. Computer software can simply automatically send e-mail reminders to panel members who did not visit the welcome page. Computer software can sometimes identify respondents who completed only a portion of the questionnaire and send those people customized messages. Sometimes such e-mails offer additional incentives to those individuals who terminated the questionnaire with only a few additional questions to answer, so that they are motivated to comply with the request to finish the questionnaire. On occasions when respondents are assured of complete anonymity and no individual tracking of computer identification takes place, the only callback option would be a reminder to the entire sample qualified by an "excuse me" message for those who may have already responded.

■ PERSONALIZED AND FLEXIBLE QUESTIONING

Computer-interactive Internet surveys are programmed in much the same way as computer-assisted telephone interviews. That is, the software that is used allows questioning to branch off into two or more different lines depending on a respondent's answer to a filtered question. The difference is that there is no interviewer. The respondent interacts directly with software on a Web site. In other words, the computer program asks questions in a sequence determined by the respondent's previous answers. The questions appear on the computer screen, and answers are recorded by simply pressing a key, clicking an icon, or typing a response, thus immediately entering the data into an electronic file. Of course, these methods avoid labor costs associated with data collection and processing of paper-and-pencil questionnaires.

This ability to sequence questions based on previous responses is a major advantage of computer-assisted surveys. The computer can be programmed to skip from question 6 to question 9 if the answer to question 6 is no. Furthermore, responses to previous questions can lead to questions that can be personalized for individual respondents (for example, "When you cannot buy your favorite brand, Revlon, what brand of lipstick do you prefer?"). Often the respondent's name appears in questions to personalize the questionnaire. Fewer and more relevant questions speed up the response process and increase the respondent's involvement with the survey.

A related advantage of using a Web survey is that it can prompt respondents when they skip over a question. In a test comparing telephone and Internet versions of the same survey, the rate of item nonresponse was less for the Internet version, which issued a prompt for each item that was left blank.[29] This was likely not a simple matter of motivation, because the rate of respondents who actually took the Web version was less than for the telephone version, even though the researchers offered a larger incentive to those who were asked to go online. (An earlier telephone screening had verified that everyone who was asked to participate had a computer.)

The ability to customize questions and the low cost per recipient also help researchers keep surveys short, an important consideration for boosting responses.[30] Jakob Nielsen, a consultant on Internet usability with the Nielsen Norman Group, emphasizes that "quick and painless" surveys generate the highest response and urges researchers to keep surveys as short as possible. He suggests that if the research objectives call for a long survey, the questions can be divided among several questionnaires, with each version sent to a different group of respondents.

■ RESPONDENT ANONYMITY

Respondents are more likely to provide sensitive or embarrassing information when they can remain anonymous. The anonymity of the Internet encourages respondents to provide honest answers to sensitive questions.

■ IMPROVING RESPONSE RATES

The methods for improving response rates for an Internet survey are similar to those for other kinds of survey research. A personalized invitation may be important. In many cases, the invitation is delivered via e-mail. The respondents may not recognize the sender's address, so the message's subject line is critical.[31] The subject line should refer to a topic likely to interest the audience, and legal as well as ethical standards dictate that it may not be deceptive. Thus, the line might be worded in a way similar to the following: "Please give your opinion on [subject matter of interest]." Researchers should avoid gimmicks like dollar signs and the word *free,* either of which is likely to alert the spam filters installed on most computers.

As mentioned earlier, with a password system, people who have not participated in a survey in a predetermined period of time can be sent a friendly e-mail reminder asking them to participate before the study ends. This type of follow-up, along with preliminary notification, interesting early questions, and variations of most other techniques for increasing response rates to mail questionnaires, is recommended for Internet surveys.

Unlike mail surveys, Internet surveys do not offer the opportunity to send a physical incentive, such as a dollar bill, to the respondent. Incentives to respond to a survey must be in the form of a coupon or a promise of a future reward. A coupon can be included that contains a discount code which can be applied at a retail Web site or even in a store. For example, a respondent might receive a $10 coupon good at www.target.com or in any Target store as a thanks for participating. Otherwise, a promise can be offered: "As a token of appreciation for completing this survey, the sponsor of the survey will make a sizable contribution to a national charity. You can vote for your preferred charity at the end of the survey." Although some researchers have had success with promising incentives, academic research about Internet surveys is sparse, and currently there are few definitive answers about the most effective ways to increase response rates.

A Web survey invitation or prenotification can also be sent via mail. The research firm can send postcards or letters informing potential respondents that an e-mail will be arriving in their inbox containing the hyperlink to the questionnaire. This is an alternative to sending a notification by e-mail only. For example, researchers studying why students enroll in the universities that they attend could be conducted by contacting recent college applicants. They might first receive a letter indicating that a survey invitation will arrive via e-mail. Alternatively, they may receive only the e-mail invitation. With a study like this, one might expect about 20 percent of potential respondents to click through to the questionnaire, and all but 1 or 2 percent of these would respond, for a final response rate of just under 20 percent. The response rate is relatively high when the respondent has shown some behavior indicative of involvement in the subject matter. In this case, applying to a university.

A mail notification has several potential advantages. Spammers do not send notifications via mail so the survey may end up having a little more legitimacy. Additionally, the prenotification establishes the potential for a relationship and can even include a request to put the sender on the recipient's safe sender list. However, research suggests that mail notifications offer little advantage in click and response rates. Response rates for respondents who were notified via mail respond in practically the same proportion as those receiving an e-mail prenotification.[32] Any advantage that the mail approach would have is likely countered by the additional costs of sending a mail notification. Thus, prenotifications do not appear very useful in increasing response rates.

Internet surveys, even those not associated with a panel, are often directed toward a finite population. For example, all members of the Atlanta area Sales and Marketing Executives Association might comprise a population of interest for researchers studying attitudes toward customer relationship management programs. What kind of response rate might be expected in this case? Recent research shows that a combination of pop-up notification on a software user forum's home page plus a single e-mail notification (to all members of the forum) yields a response rate of just about 14 percent.[33] While this does not seem very high, a response rate of this type is also common in mail surveys.

■ SECURITY CONCERNS

Many organizations worry that hackers or competitors may access Web sites to discover new product concepts, new advertising campaigns, and other top-secret ideas. Respondents may worry whether personal information will remain private. So may the organizations sponsoring the research. Recently, McDonald's conducted quality-control research in England and Scotland, automating the transmittal of data with a system in which consultants used handheld devices and sent the numbers to headquarters as e-mail messages. The system saved hours of work, but the company worried that confidential information could be compromised. McDonald's therefore purchased software that encrypted the data and allowed the handhelds to be remotely wiped clean of data if they were lost or stolen.[34]

As in the experience of McDonald's, no system can be 100 percent secure, but risks can be minimized. Many research service suppliers specializing in Internet surveying have developed password-protected systems that are very secure. One important feature of these systems restricts access and prevents individuals from filling out a questionnaire over and over again.

■ RESPONSE QUALITY

Internet surveys are still in their infancy in many ways. However, the prospects for a bright future are good. Surveys asking potential respondents questions that can be compared with known population demographics can be used to compare the response quality of different survey media. For instance, basic demographic information for each U.S. zip code is available through http://www. census.gov. Random samples taken from zip codes asking respondents to report these basic statistics should produce results that match the census data with allowance for a small amount of error. Thus far, indications are that Web-based survey approaches produce data that is as good as or better in quality than traditional phone surveys.[35]

Text-Message Surveys

Yes, surveys are even being sent via text messages. These may use the SMS (short-message service) or MMS (Multi-Media Service). This technique is perhaps the newest survey approach. It has all the advantages of mobile-phone surveys in terms of reach and it also shares the disadvantages in terms of reaching respondents who have not opted in via a mobile phone. However, text-message surveys are catching on in other countries and are ideal for surveys involving only a few very short questions. Additionally, MMS messages can include graphic displays or even short videos. This technology is likely to see more applications in the near future.

Choosing an Appropriate Survey Approach

Earlier discussions of research design and problem definition emphasized that many research tasks may lead to similar decision-making information. There is no best form of survey; each has advantages and disadvantages. A researcher who must ask highly confidential questions may use a mail survey, thus sacrificing speed of data collection to avoid interviewer bias. If a researcher must have considerable control over question phrasing, central location telephone interviewing may be appropriate.

To determine the appropriate technique, the researcher must ask several questions: Is the assistance of an interviewer necessary? Are respondents interested in the issues being investigated? Will cooperation be easily attained? How quickly is the information needed? Will the study require a long and complex questionnaire? How large is the budget? The criteria—cost, speed, anonymity, and so forth—may differ for each project.

Exhibit 7.5 summarizes some major advantages and disadvantages of different survey approaches. It emphasizes typical types of surveys. For example, a creative researcher might be able to design highly versatile and flexible mail questionnaires, but most researchers use standardized questions. An elaborate mail survey may be far more expensive than a short personal interview, but generally this is not the case.

Pretesting Survey Instruments

A researcher who is surveying 3,000 consumers does not want to find out after the questionnaires have been completed or returned that most respondents misunderstood a particular question, skipped a series of questions, or misinterpreted the instructions for filling out the questionnaire. Problems such as these can be made less likely by various screening procedures, or *pretesting*. **Pretesting** involves a trial run with a group of colleagues or actual respondents to iron out fundamental problems in the instructions or design of a questionnaire. Researchers benefit by spotting problems in the pretest and rightly inferring that a problem with this very small sample will likely be a problem in the full sample once data collection actually begins.

Broadly speaking, researchers choose from three basic ways of pretesting. The first two involve screening the questionnaire with other research colleagues, and the third—the one most often called pretesting—is a trial run with an actual group of respondents. When screening the questionnaire with other research professionals, the investigator asks them to look for such problems as

pretesting

Screening procedure that involves a trial run with a group of respondents to iron out fundamental problems in the survey design.

EXHIBIT 7.5 **Advantages and Disadvantages of Typical Survey Methods**

	Door-to-Door Personal Interview	Mall Intercept Personal Interview	Telephone Interview	Mail Survey	Internet Survey
Speed of data collection	Moderate to fast	Fast	Very fast	Slow; researcher has no control over return of questionnaire	Instantaneous; 24/7
Geographic flexibility	Limited to moderate	Confined, possible urban bias	High	High	High (worldwide)
Respondent cooperation	Excellent	Moderate to low	Good	Moderate; poorly designed questionnaire will have low response rate	Varies depending on website; high from consumer panels
Versatility of questioning	Quite versatile	Extremely versatile	Moderate	Not versatile; requires highly standardized format	Extremely versatile
Questionnaire length	Long	Moderate to long	Moderate	Varies depending on incentive	Moderate; length customized based on answers
Item non-response rate	Low	Medium	Medium	High	Software can assure none
Possibility for respondent misunderstanding	Low	Low	Average	High; no interviewer present for clarification	High
Degree of interviewer influence on answers	High	High	Moderate	None; interviewer absent	None
Supervision of interviewers	Moderate	Moderate to high	High, especially with central-location interviewing	Not applicable	Not applicable
Anonymity of respondent	Low	Low	Moderate	High	Respondent can be either anonymous or known
Ease of callback or follow-up	Difficult	Difficult	Easy	Easy, but takes time	Difficult, unless e-mail address is known
Cost	Highest	Moderate to high	Low to moderate	Lowest	Low
Special features	Visual materials may be shown or demonstrated; extended probing possible	Taste tests, viewing of TV commercials possible	Fieldwork and supervision of data collection are simplified; quite adaptable to computer technology	Respondent may answer questions at own convenience; has time to reflect on answers	Streaming media software allows use of graphics and animation

Note: The emphasis is on *typical* surveys. For example, an elaborate mail survey may be far more expensive than a short personal interview, but this generally is not the case.

difficulties with question wording, leading questions, and bias due to question order. An alternative type of screening might involve a client or the research manager who ordered the research. Often, managers ask researchers to collect information, but when they see the questionnaire, they find that it does not really meet their needs. Only by checking with the individual who has requested the questionnaire does the researcher know for sure that the information needed will be provided. Additionally, other research experts may sometimes be asked to judge the content of survey items as a way of trying to verify that the items are measuring what the researcher intended. Later, we return to this idea under the heading of validity.

The third form is basically a trial run of the entire research project. Once the researcher has decided on the final questionnaire, data should be collected with a small number of respondents (perhaps as many as 100 but at least three dozen) to determine whether the questionnaire needs refinement. These particular respondents also may be asked to indicate specifically any items that are difficult to understand. The researcher can analyze these data for suspicious patterns that may indicate a problem. For example, in some cases the researcher may be surpised to find that all respondents have indicated the same answer to a specific question. Such a result is highly unlikely when more than a handful of respondents are included. Thus, a response like this probably indicates a problem.

Unfortunately, although the value of a pretest is readily apparent, this step is often skipped. The researcher may feel too much time pressure or pressure to produce the entire project within a certain budget. The risk of collecting some items that end up not being very helpful increases without a pretest. Needless to say, pretests are highly recommended in almost all types of primary data collection efforts.

Ethical Issues in Survey Research

Chapter 4 mentioned that codes of ethics express researchers' obligation to protect the public from misrepresentation and exploitation under the guise of marketing research. Thou shall not disguise selling as research! Many ethical issues apply to survey research, such as respondents' right to privacy, the use of deception, respondents' right to be informed about the purpose of the research, the need for confidentiality, the need for honesty in collecting data, and the need for objectivity in reporting data. You may wish to reexamine Chapter 4's coverage of these issues now that various survey research techniques have been discussed.[36]

At this time, a few points can be emphasized. Researchers should not ask for information in a misleading way. Also, researchers must be careful to guard the resulting data carefully. For instance, a researcher may end up with data that identifies children's responses to several different new products. The data may also contain demographics and other material. Once that data becomes stored on a laptop, it is vulnerable to theft or misplacement. The researcher should follow good security procedures in protecting the data stored on various storage mediums.

Additionally, technology brings new issues to the forefront. Although e-mail is an extremely useful tool, researchers should avoid needlessly contributing to spam volume by sending unsolicited e-mails seeking survey respondents. While at times, this may be the only way to reach a population, whenever possible, e-mail requests for responses should be sent to individuals who in some way may have indicated that the e-mail may not be so unwanted. For example, members of consumer response panels have opted in and have given their explicit approval to receive such e-mails. Additionally, consumers who query about certain information may end up being good research respondents. Consider someone who has sought information about new hybrid cars from a Web site like Kelley Blue Book (www.kbb.com). A Web site like this may even include a place where a consumer can register and indicate whether they are open to being contacted in the future. If they appear to be open to responding to research that may be tied to new automobiles or environmentally sensitive products, sending a survey about attitudes toward new car features may not be an imposition. On the other hand, phoning someone during dinner or filling up a busy executive's in-box with requests to participate in irrelevant surveys pushes the boundaries of good ethics. Certainly, as technology continues to evolve, marketing researchers will be faced with even more challenges.

- Standard survey research works best for implementing a descriptive research design. In particular, survey research is very useful for describing:
  - Consumer beliefs
  - Consumer attitudes
  - Consumer opinions—particularly of a nonsensitive nature
  - Characteristics of respondents such as demographics and lifestyles
- The extent to which respondents will actually behave as they describe in survey research is often overstated. When measuring future behavior such as purchase intentions, some researchers routinely apply a rule of thumb that subtracts 10 percent from the stated probability.
- Interpretative research involving a survey generally requires an interactive approach. On occasion, respondents may simply be asked to write a story without any elaboration, but generally, particularly with phenomenology, the researcher and the respondent are actively engaged.
- The longer the questionnaire, the lower the response rate.

- When long questionnaires are absolutely necessary, the researcher should:
  - Look for respondents who are essentially a captive audience; like students in a class
  - Offer a nontrivial incentive to respond
  - Try to target the survey toward individuals who are highly involved in the topic
  - Use a survey research panel
- Mobile-phone survey calls are slightly more likely to be answered, particularly on weekdays, but mobile-phone users are more likely to refuse to participate than are landline phone users.
- E-mail surveys and Internet surveys are good approaches for most types of surveys.
  - When a panel or special interest group provides responses, the researcher should be extra vigilant for bogus response patterns.
  - Good response rates with no true special considerations such as a very high incentive or extreme levels of involvement can be expected to be between 10 and 15 percent.
- A short pretest is better than no pretest at all.

© GEORGE DOYLE & CIARAN GRIFFIN

Summary

1. Define surveys and describe the type of information that may be gathered in a survey. A *survey* is defined as a method of collecting primary data based on communication with a representative sample of individuals. Members of the representative sample are known as respondents. The term *sample survey* is often used because a survey is expected to obtain a representative sample of the target population. The typical survey is part of a descriptive research design with the objective of measuring awareness, product knowledge, brand usage behavior, opinions, attitudes, purchasing behavior, and identifying characteristics of target markets.

2. Explain the advantages and disadvantages of surveys. The survey is a common tool for asking respondents questions. When executed properly, surveys provide quick, inexpensive, and accurate information for a variety of objectives. When executed improperly, surveys can provide misleading information that can precipitate poor decision making. Each survey data collection tool has unique disadvantages that lead to different types of error. However, surveys are particularly disadvantageous when the researcher is interested in actual behavior. While behavior can be observed directly with little error, the error introduced by respondents having to remember what they've done or being unwilling to report what they've done is a significant source of error.

3. Identify sources of error in survey research. Two major forms of error are common in survey research. The first, random sampling error, is caused by chance variation and results in a sample that is not absolutely representative of the target population. Such errors are inevitable, but they can be predicted using the statistical methods discussed in later chapters on sampling. The second major category of error, systematic error, takes several forms. Nonresponse error is caused by subjects' failing to respond to a survey. This type of error can be reduced by comparing the demographics of the sample population with those of the target population and making a special effort to contact underrepresented groups. In addition, response bias occurs when a response to a questionnaire is falsified or misrepresented, either intentionally or inadvertently. There are four specific categories of response bias: acquiescence bias, extremity bias, interviewer bias, and social desirability bias. An additional source of survey error comes from administrative problems such as inconsistencies in interviewers' abilities, cheating, coding mistakes, and so forth.

4. Summarize the ways researchers gather information through personal interviews. Interviews can be categorized based on the medium used to communicate with respondents. A primary classification of survey approaches can be developed based on interactivity. An interactive approach facilitates two-way communication. Thus, the respondent and interviewer truly can have a dialogue. A face-to-face personal interview typifies this approach but other media including mobile phones and landline phones allow two-way communication. Noninteractive media primarily allow a way for respondents to give answers to predetermined questions with no opportunity for interactive two-way communication. Typical mail or e-mail questionnaires represent noninteractive media well. Both approaches have advantages and disadvantages.

5. Know the advantages and disadvantages of conducting surveys using personal interviews via door-to-door, mall intercept, landline telephone, or mobile-phone interviews. Door-to-door personal interviews can get high response rates, but they are more costly to administer than other types of surveys. Additionally, security issues make them increasingly rare today. Mall intercept interviews reduce costs and also provide the flexibility of a personal interview. The researcher has to be aware of the limitations of representing an entire consumer population from mall intercepts conducted in only one or a few locations. Phone interviewing has the advantage of providing data quickly and at a lower cost per personal interview. Phone interviews need to be shorter than other types of personal interviews. Although they are still considered fairly capable of producing a representative sample, they are not perfect. Do-not-call legislation also has provided challenges for traditional landline survey approaches. More and more consumers are choosing to own only a mobile phone. In the United States, mobile phones cannot be cold-called for research purposes. Thus, representativeness is limited because only consumers who opt in can be part of the sample.

6. Appreciate the importance of pretesting questionnaires. Pretesting a questionnaire on a small sample of respondents is a useful way to discover problems while they can still be corrected. Pretests may involve screening the questionnaire with other research professionals or conducting a trial run with a set of respondents.

7. Describe ethical issues that arise in survey research. Researchers must protect the public from misrepresentation and exploitation. This obligation includes honesty about the purpose of a research project and protection of subjects' right to refuse to participate or to answer particular questions. Researchers also should protect the confidentiality of participants and record responses honestly. Lastly, as technology evolves, researchers should be mindful of not needlessly contributing to unwanted electronic or personal communications. Thus, both the reason for and the method of contact should be carefully scrutinzed.

Key Terms and Concepts

acquiescence bias, *152*
administrative error, *153*
callbacks *159*
central location interviewing *165*
computer-assisted telephone interviewing
    (CATI) *165*
cover letter *169*
data-processing error, *153*
door-to-door interviews *159*
drop-off method *172*
e-mail surveys *172*
extremity bias, *152*
fax survey *172*
Internet survey *174*
interactive survey approaches *155*

interviewer bias, *152*
interviewer cheating, *154*
interviewer error, *154*
item nonresponse *157*
mail survey *166*
mall intercept interviews *160*
no contacts, *150*
noninteractive survey approaches *155*
nonrespondents, *150*
nonresponse error, *150*
personal interview *155*
pretesting *178*
radio boxes *173*
random digit dialing *162*
random sampling error, *149*

refusals, *150*
respondent error, *149*
respondents, *146*
response bias, *151*
response rate *168*
sample bias, *149*
sample selection error, *153*
sample survey, *146*
self-administered questionnaires *166*
self-selection bias, *150*
social desirability bias, *153*
survey, *146*
systematic error, *149*
telephone interviews *160*

Questions for Review and Critical Thinking

1. Name several nonbusiness applications of survey research.
2. What is *self-selection bias?*
3. Do surveys tend to gather qualitative or quantitative data? What types of information are commonly measured with surveys?
4. Give an example of each type of error listed in Exhibit 7.1.
5. In a survey, chief executive officers (CEOs) indicated that they would prefer to relocate their businesses to Atlanta (first choice), San Diego, Tampa, Los Angeles, or Boston. The CEOs who said they were going to build the required office space in the following year were asked where they were going to build. They indicated they were going to build in New York, Los Angeles, San Francisco, or Chicago. Explain the difference.
6. What potential sources of error might be associated with the following situations?
   a. In a survey of frequent fliers age 50 and older, researchers concluded that price does not play a significant role in airline travel because only 25 percent of the respondents check off price as the most important consideration in determining where and how they travel, while 35 percent rate price as being unimportant.
   b. A survey of voters finds that most respondents do not like negative political ads—that is, advertising by one political candidate that criticizes or exposes secrets about the opponent's "dirty laundry."
   c. Researchers who must conduct a 45-minute personal interview decide to offer $10 to each respondent because they believe that people who will sell their opinions are more typical than someone who will talk to a stranger for 45 minutes.
   d. A company's sales representatives are asked what percentage of the time they spend making presentations to prospects, traveling, talking on the telephone, participating in meetings, working on the computer, and engaging in other on-the-job activities.
   e. A survey comes with a water hardness packet to test the hardness of the water in a respondent's home. The packet includes a color chart and a plastic strip to dip into hot water. The respondent is given instructions in six steps on how to compare the color of the plastic strip with the color chart that indicates water hardness.
7. A sample of 14-year-old schoolchildren is asked if they have ever smoked a cigarette. The students are asked to respond orally in the presence of other students. What types of error might enter into this process?
8. A survey conducted by the National Endowment for the Arts asked, "Have you read a book within the last year?" What response bias might arise from this question?
9. Name some common objectives of cross-sectional surveys.
10. ETHICS A researcher sends out 2,000 questionnaires via e-mail. Fifty are returned because the addresses are inaccurate. Of the 1,950 delivered questionnaires, 100 are completed and e-mailed back. However, 40 of these respondents wrote that they did not want to participate in the survey. The researcher indicates the response rate was 5.0 percent. Is this the right thing to do?
11. Why is it so important today for researchers to take advantage of new technologies in finding new ways to communicate with respondents?
12. Define interactive and noninteractive survey approaches. Why might a researcher choose an interactive survey approach over a noninteractive survey approach?
13. A publisher offers teenage boys (aged 14–17 years old) one of four best-selling famous rock posters as an incentive for filling out a 10-page mail questionnaire about guitars. What are the pros and cons of offering this incentive? Yes or no, should the incentive be offered?
14. What do you think should be the maximum length of a self-administered e-mail questionnaire?
15. A survey researcher reports that "205 usable questionnaires out of 942 questionnaires delivered in our mail survey converts to a 21.7 percent response rate." What are the subtle implications of this statement?
16. What is do-not-call legislation? What effect has it had on survey research?
17. Agree or disagree with this statement: Landline and mobile-phone surveys are essentially the same and can be used in the same situations with the same results.
18. What are the advantages and disadvatanges of e-mail surveys? What are situations when they may not be appropriate?
19. Evaluate the following survey designs:
   a. A text message survey asking the potential respondent to indicate with yes or no responses whether they are driving or not, whether they are alone, whether they believe the roads in their area can adequately handle traffic, whether more money should be devoted to better roadways, whether or not traffic is adequately policed, and whether or not automatic cameras should be used to issue speeding tickets. The sample is drawn from people who have agreed to be contacted via mobile phone regarding their new Toyota.
   b. A shopping mall that wishes to evaluate its image places packets including a questionnaire, cover letter, and stamped return envelope in the mall where customers can pick them up if they wish.
   c. An e-mail message is sent asking respondents to complete a questionnaire on a Web site. Respondents answer the questions and then have the opportunity to play a slot-machine game on the Web site. Each respondent is guaranteed a monetary incentive but has the option to increase it by repeatedly playing the slot-machine game.
   d. A mall intercept interviewing service is located in a regional shopping center. The facility contains a small room for television and movie presentations. Shoppers are used as sampling units. However, mall intercept interviewers recruit additional subjects for television commercial experiments by offering them several complimentary tickets for special sneak previews. Individuals contacted at the mall are allowed to bring up to five guests. In some cases the complimentary tickets are offered through ads in a local newspaper.

e.   *Time* magazine opts to conduct a mobile-phone survey rather than mail survey for a study to determine the demographic characteristics and purchasing behavior of its subscribers in the U.K. and in France.

20. What type of survey approach is most likely to yield the highest reponse rate? What approach(es) will yield the lowest reponse rate? What can be done to improve response rates in e-mail and Internet surveys?

21. **ETHICS** Comment on the ethics of the following situations:

a.   A researcher plans to use invisible ink to code questionnaires to identify respondents in a mail survey designed to get honest opinions from people who have filed to run for political office. The code will allow their identities to be known by the researcher.

b.   A political action committee conducts a survey about its cause. At the end of the questionnaire, it includes a request for a donation.

c.   A telephone interviewer calls at 1 p.m. on Sunday and asks the person who answers the phone to take part in an interview.

d.   An industrial marketer wishes to survey its own distributors. It invents the name "Mountain States Marketing Research" and sends out an e-mail questionnaire under this name.

e.   A questionnaire is printed on the back of a warranty card included inside the package of a food processor. The questionnaire includes a number of questions about shopping behavior, demographics, and customer lifestyles. At the bottom of the warranty card is a short note in small print that says "Thank you for completing this questionnaire. Your answers will be used for marketing studies and to help us serve you better in the future. You will also benefit by receiving important mailings and special offers from a number of organizations whose products and services relate directly to the activities, interests, and hobbies in which you enjoy participating on a regular basis. Please indicate if there is some reason you would prefer not to receive this information."

22. **ETHICS** How might the marketing research industry take action to ensure that the public believes that landline phone surveys and door-to-door interviews are legitimate activities and that firms that misrepresent and deceive the public using marketing research as a sales ploy are not true marketing researchers?

23. **'NET** Go to the Pew Internet and American Life page at http://www.pewinternet.org. Several reports based on survey research will be listed. Select one of the reports. What were the research objectives? What were the first three questions on the survey?

Research Activity

1. Ask a small sample of students at your local university to report their GPA. Then, try to find the average GPA of students at your school. If you have to, ask several professors to give their opinion. Does it seem that the student data are subject to error? Explain.

Case 7.1 SAT and ACT Writing Tests

The SAT and ACT college entrance exams once were completely multiple-choice, but both tests recently began including an essay portion (which is optional for the ACT). Some researchers have investigated how the essay tests are used by one group they serve: the admissions offices of the colleges that look at test results during the selection process.[37]

Early survey research suggests that some admissions officers harbor doubts about the essay tests. ACT, Inc. reported that among the schools it surveyed, only about one-fifth are requiring that applicants take the writing portion of the exam. Another one-fifth merely recommend (but don't require) the essay.

Kaplan, Inc., which markets test preparation services, conducted surveys as well. Kaplan asked 374 colleges whether they would be using the SAT writing test in screening candidates. Almost half (47 percent) said they would not use the essay at all. Another 22 percent said they would use it but give it less weight than the math and verbal SAT scores.

Kaplan also surveys students who take the exams for which it provides training. On its Web site, the company says, "More than 25 percent of students ran out of time on the essay!"

Questions

1. What survey objectives would ACT have in asking colleges how they use its essay test? What objectives would Kaplan have for its survey research?

2. If you were a marketer for the College Board (the SAT's company) or ACT, Inc., what further information would you want to gather after receiving the results described here?

3. What sources of error or response bias might be present in the surveys described here?

Case 7.2 National Do Not Call Registry

Citizens' annoyance with phone calls from salespeople prompted Congress to pass a law setting up a National Do Not Call Registry. The registry was soon flooded with requests to have phone numbers removed from telemarketers' lists. By law, salespeople may not call numbers listed on this registry. The law makes exceptions for charities and researchers. However, a recent poll suggests that even though phone calls from researchers may be legal, they are not always well received.[38]

In late 2005, Harris Interactive conducted an Internet survey in which almost 2,000 adults answered questions about the National Do Not Call Registry. About three-quarters of the respondents said they had signed up for the registry, and a majority (61 percent) said they had since received "far less" contact from telemarketers. In addition, 70 percent said that since registering, they had been contacted by someone "who was doing a poll or survey" and wanted them to participate. But apparently respondents weren't sure whether this practice was acceptable. Only one-fourth (24 percent) of respondents said they knew that researchers "are allowed to call," and over half (63 percent) weren't sure about researchers' rights under the law.

Questions

1. Was an online survey the best medium for a poll on this subject? What were some pros and cons of conducting this poll online?
2. How might the results have differed if this poll had been conducted by telephone?
3. As a researcher, how would you address people's doubts about whether pollsters may contact households listed on the Do Not Call Registry?

CHAPTER 8
OBSERVATION

LEARNING OUTCOMES

After studying this chapter, you should be able to

1. Discuss the role of observation as a marketing research method
2. Describe the use of direct observation and contrived observation
3. Identify ethical issues particular to research using observation
4. Explain the observation of physical objects and message content
5. Describe major types of mechanical observation
6. Summarize techniques for measuring physiological reactions

Chapter Vignette: Neuroco Peers into the Consumer's Brain

When Hewlett-Packard was developing advertisements for its digital photography products, the firm wanted to ensure its ad images would evoke the desired response. For guidance, the company turned to Neuroco and its high-tech research method, known as neuromarketing.[1] Neuroco researchers showed subjects a pair of photos of the same woman, and about half of them preferred each picture. Then Neuroco measured the electrical activity in the brains of subjects looking at the same images, and the analysis showed a definite preference for one of the pictures in which the woman's smile was a little warmer.

Neuroco's approach uses a technology called *quantified electroencephalography (QEEG)*. Subjects wear light and portable EEG equipment that records brain activity; software presents the data in computer maps that display activity levels in areas of the brain. Researchers can then evaluate whether the person is attentive and whether brain activity signifies emotional involvement or analytical thinking. QEEG is more flexible than the better-known use of functional magnetic resonance imaging (fMRI), which has provided many advances in brain research but requires all subjects to lie still in a large, noisy machine. With QEEG, the measuring equipment can travel with subjects as they walk around a store or watch advertisements.

Consider a young woman demonstrating a Neuroco study by shopping with electrodes discreetly attached to her head. Neuroco chief scientist David Lewis observes a computer screen showing a map of her brain waves in red and green, with the colors signaling levels of alpha-wave activity. The zigzag pattern tells Lewis that this shopper is alert but not engaged in making purchase decisions. As the woman walks into a store's shoe department, however, the pattern changes when she picks up a pair of stiletto heels. An explosion of brain activity occurs, then the woman heads for the cash register, decision made.

As this example illustrates, observation can provide significant insights to marketers, and advances in observation technology are literally providing a view of what is happening in customers' brains. This chapter introduces the observation method of data gathering in marketing research.

Introduction

Scientists rely heavily on observation. This is true today, it will be true tomorrow, and it certainly was true in the past. Simple observation has played a key role in scientific discoveries for as long as people have pursued knowledge. Bernoulli developed the laws of buoyancy and fluid dynamics by observing what happened to his bath water when he entered the tub; it went up in proportion to his mass. What a simple observation! According to legend, Newton developed the laws of gravitation by observing (and feeling) the way an apple fell onto his head while he rested under the tree. Observation like this is how inductive learning begins. Researchers also deductively develop theories that require observation of some specific phenomena to empirically test them. This chapter focuses especially on observing marketing behavior directly. Like with surveys, modern technology has greatly enhanced marketing researchers ability to observe the actual behavior of consumers in the marketplace and marketing employees on their jobs.

Observation in Marketing Research

In marketing research, **observation** is a systematic process of recording actual behavioral patterns of people, objects, and events as they happen. No questioning or communicating with people is needed. Researchers who use observation method data collection either witness and record information while watching events take place or take advantage of some tracking system such as checkout scanners or Internet activity records. These tracking systems can observe and provide data such as whether or not a specific consumer purchased more products on discount or at regular price or how much time a consumer spent viewing a particular Web page before either exiting or clicking through to the next page.

Observation can be a useful part of either qualitative or quantitative research. Additionally, actual observations of behavioral patterns can be part of an exploratory, descriptive, or even a causal design. For instance, researchers studying compliance with a diet program might manipulate different features of the program and then observe actual eating and exercise habits. These observations would play a key role as a dependent variable in a causal design. More often, however, observation is associated with qualitative research and with exploratory research designs. Observation is nearly synonymous with ethnographic research as researchers often try to blend into the environment and simply scrutinize the germane behavior. Callaway Golf may plant ethnographic researchers as caddies (who carry clubs for golfers) on nice golf courses to observe the actual behavior of golfers on the golf course. The caddies blend into the environment in a manner traditional to ethnographic research. Scientific observation is scarcely distinguished from simple observation. However, scientific observation is motivated by some research question aimed at discovering or testing market knowledge.

observation

The systematic process of recording the behavioral patterns of people, objects, and occurrences as they are witnessed.

Retailers can learn a great deal about merchandising, store design, and promotion simply by watching their customers.

What Can Be Observed?

Observational studies gather a wide variety of information about behavior. Exhibit 8.1 on the next page lists eight kinds of observable phenomena: physical actions, such as shopping patterns (in-store or via a Web interface) or television viewing; verbal behavior, such as sales

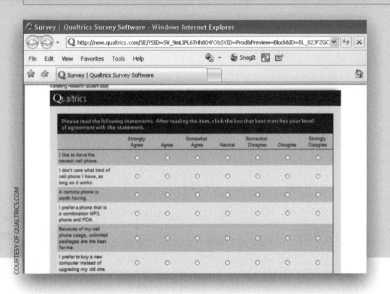

COURTESY OF QUALTRICS.COM

Perhaps you recall answering these questions about opinions and preferences for technological products. Take a look at the results from this section of the survey. In what way has behavioral observation been used to collect additional data—if at all? How might this information be useful to companies that sell small electronic appliances? Are there other places in the survey where behavioral observation has been combined with this traditional survey approach?

© GEORGE DOYLE

TO THE POINT

Where observation is concerned, chance favors only the prepared mind.

—Louis Pasteur

conversations; expressive behavior, such as tone of voice or facial expressions; spatial relations and locations, such as traffic patterns; temporal patterns, such as amount of time spent shopping or driving; physical objects, such as the amount of newspapers recycled; verbal and pictorial records, such as the content of advertisements; and neurological activity such as brain activity in response to marketing stimuli.

The observation method may be used to describe a wide variety of behavior, but cognitive phenomena such as attitudes, motivations, and preferences cannot be observed. As a result, observation research cannot provide an explanation of why a behavior occurred or what actions were intended. Another limitation is that the observation period generally is short. Observing behavior patterns that occur over a period of several days or weeks generally is too costly or even impossible. The Research Snapshot on the next page illustrates a way that trends are tracked with observations.

The Nature of Observation Studies

Marketing researchers can observe people, objects, events, or other phenomena using either human observers or machines designed for specific observation tasks. Human observation best

EXHIBIT 8.1 **What Are Things that People Do and Marketing Researchers Observe?**

Phenomenon	Example
Physical activities	The way a shopper moves through a store, patterns of motion and interaction with objects
Verbal behavior	Statements made by consumers at the Wal-Mart checkout either to each other or to a Wal-Mart employee
Expressive behavior and physiological reactions	Facial expressions of consumers in a restaurant or the body language of consumers visiting a day spa; measures of how much sweat a person is producing
Spatial relations and locations	How close shoppers stand to service providers while getting advice about fashion
Temporal patterns	How long patients in a doctor's office will wait before approaching the counter to inquire or complain
Physical objects	What brand of shoes, clothing, and skateboards teens at a skate park own and use
Verbal and pictorial records	Photographs or videos of early childhood Christmas experiences; comments left on Internet blogs
Neurological events	Brain activity in response to a consumer experiencing joy or disgust or perhaps while reading nutrition information

This Trend Brought to You by DDB SignBank

Extending the practice of observation beyond what can clearly be done scientifically, such as counting the number of tomato soup cans in a pantry or measuring the time spent watching television, some researchers have tried to catalog behaviors that may signal the beginning of important trends. This practice, called *trend spotting*, is controversial because the observations are subjective and unsystematic. In spite of the criticism, marketers are increasingly turning to trend spotters, so researchers have an incentive to develop this method's capabilities.

Starting in its office in Copenhagen, Denmark, giant ad agency DDB Worldwide has created a service called DDB Sign-Bank, which invites all of DDB's staff throughout the world, plus other targeted groups such as members of youth organizations, to submit their observations to managers appointed as SignBankers. Staff members are directed to identify consumer behaviors, rather than comments gathered from other research methods, that might signal a new trend in the society or culture. The Sign-Bankers classify the observations and enter them into a corporate database. The database is updated each day, and account teams at the agency can search it for signs related to their clients' advertising objectives.

The idea behind SignBank, developed by sociologist Eva Steensig, is that the size of the database (which contained thirty thousand signs at a recent count) will allow patterns to emerge in the sheer number of observations. The data may be most useful as a source of ideas to test more rigorously. Anthon Berg, a Scandinavian brand of chocolate, used SignBank data to identify new occasions for which to promote chocolate and new uses for chocolate in health and beauty treatments.

Source: Based on Matthew Creamer, "DDB Collects 'Signs' to Identify Trends," *Advertising Age* (December 5, 2005), downloaded from http://www.adage.com, June 16, 2006; Eric Pfanner, "On Advertising: Do I Spot a Trend?" *International Herald Tribune* (January 1, 2006), www.iht.com; and DDB Worldwide, "DDB Worldwide Introduces DDB SignBank, a New Consumer Knowledge Model," news release (November 29, 2005), http://www.ddbneedham.dk.

suits a situation or behavior that is not easily predictable in advance of the research. Mechanical observation, as performed by supermarket scanners or traffic counters, can very accurately record situations or types of behavior that are routine, repetitive, or programmatic. Sophisticated machines that assess biological reactions such as a lie detector or neurological activities such as brain activation are also considered mechanical.

Human or mechanical observation is often **unobtrusive**, meaning no communication with a respondent takes place. For example, rather than asking customers how much time they spend shopping in the store, a supermarket manager might observe and record the intervals between when shoppers enter and leave the store. The unobtrusive nature of observational data collection often generates data without a subject's knowledge. A situation in which an observer's presence, or the mechanical device doing the recording, is easily known to the subject involves **visible observation**. A situation in which a subject is unaware that any observation is taking place is **hidden observation**. Hidden, unobtrusive observation minimizes respondent error. Asking subjects to participate in research is not generally required when they are unaware that they are being observed. A consumer who is asked to wash his or her hair in front of a video camera is visibly observed while a consumer observed by security cameras while shopping for shampoo is captured by hidden observation.

The major advantage of gathering data through unobtrusive observation over surveys, which obtain self-reported data from respondents, is that the data are free from distortions, inaccuracies, or other response biases due to memory error, social desirability bias, and so on. The data are recorded when and as the actual event takes place.

unobtrusive observation

No communication with the person being observed is necessary so that he or she is unaware that he or she is an object of research

visible observation

Observation in which the observer's presence is known to the subject.

hidden observation

Observation in which the subject is unaware that observation is taking place.

Observation of Human Behavior

Whereas surveys emphasize verbal responses, observation studies emphasize and allow for the systematic recording of nonverbal behavior. Toy manufacturers such as Fisher Price use the observation technique because children often cannot express their reactions to products. By observing children at play with a proposed toy, doll, or game, marketing researchers may be able to identify the elements of a potentially successful product. Toy marketing researchers might observe play to answer the following questions:

- How long does the child's attention stay with the product?

- Does the child put the toy down after two minutes or twenty minutes?
- Are the child's peers equally interested in the toy?

Behavioral scientists have recognized that nonverbal behavior can be a communication process by which meanings are exchanged among individuals. Head nods, smiles, raised eyebrows, and other facial expressions or body movements have been recognized as communication symbols. Observation of nonverbal communication may hold considerable promise for the marketing researcher. For example, a hypothesis about customer-salesperson interactions is that the salesperson would signal status based on the importance of each transaction. In low-importance transactions, in which potential customers are plentiful and easily replaced (say, a shoe store), the salesperson may show definite nonverbal signs of higher status than the customer. When customers are scarce, as in big-ticket purchase situations (real estate sales), the opposite should be true, with the salesperson showing many nonverbal indicators of deference. One way to test this hypothesis would be with an observation study using the nonverbal communication measures shown in Exhibit 8.2. Each row in the table indicates an aspect of nonverbal communication that might be observed in a common market situation.

Of course, researchers would not ignore verbal behavior. In fact, in certain observation studies, verbal expression is very important.

Complementary Evidence

The results of observation studies may amplify the results of other forms of research by providing *complementary evidence* concerning individuals' "true" feelings. Focus group interviews often are conducted behind two-way mirrors from which marketing executives observe as well as listen to what is occurring. This additional source allows for interpretation of nonverbal behavior such as facial expressions or head nods to supplement information from interviews.

For example, in one focus group session concerning women's use of hand lotion, researchers observed that all the women's hands were above the table while they were casually waiting for the session to begin. Seconds after the women were told that the topic was to be hand lotion, all their

EXHIBIT 8.2 **Observing and Interpreting Nonverbal Communication**

Behavior		Description	Example
Facial expressions		Expressions of emotion such as surprise (eyes wide open, mouth rounded and slightly open, brow furrowed)	A consumer reacts to the price quoted by a salesperson.
Body language		Posture, placement of arms and legs	A consumer crosses arms as salesperson speaks, possibly indicating a lack of trust.
Eye activity		Eye contact, staring, looking away, dilated pupils. In U.S. culture, not making eye contact is indicative of a deteriorating relationship. Dilated pupils can indicate emotion or degree of honesty.	A consumer avoids making eye contact with a salesperson knowing that he or she will not make a purchase.
Personal space		Physical distance between individuals; in the United States, people like to be about eight feet apart to have a discussion.	A consumer may back away from a salesperson who is viewed to be violating one's personal space.
Gestures		Responses to certain events with specific body reactions or gestures	A consumer who wins something (maybe at the casino or a sports contest) lifts arms, stands tall, and sticks out chest.
Manners		Accepted protocol for given situations	A salesperson may shake a customer's hand, but should not touch a customer otherwise.

hands were placed out of sight. This observation, along with the group discussion, revealed the women's anger, guilt, and shame about the condition of their hands. Although they felt they were expected to have soft, pretty hands, their housework required them to wash dishes, clean floors, and do other chores that were hard on their hands.

Some research studies combine visible observation with personal interviews. During or after in-depth observations, individuals are asked to explain their actions.[2] Direct observation of women applying hand and body lotion identified two kinds of users. Some women slapped on the lotion, rubbing it briskly into their skin. Others caressed their skin as they applied the lotion. When the women were interviewed about their behavior, the researchers were able to interpret this finding. Women who slapped the lotion on were using the lotion as a remedy for dry skin. Those who caressed their skin were more interested in making their skin smell nice and feel soft.

When focus group behavior is videotaped, observation of the nonverbal communication symbols can add even more to marketers' knowledge of the situation. Observations of customers in a shopping center may also be followed with survey research to follow up on some observed behavior. For example, if customers are observed looking into the window of a store for more than 30 seconds but then moving on without going in, researchers may intercept them with a few questions potentially revealing reasons for this behavior.

Recording the decision time necessary to make a choice is a relatively simple, unobtrusive task easily accomplished through direct observation; it is also an example of complementary evidence. Survey responses can be combined with information on how long the respondent took to make a choice. This recorded choice time is a measure of **response latency**. This measure is based on the hypothesis that the longer a decision maker takes, the more difficult that decision was and the more thought the respondent put into the choice. A quick decision presumably indicates an easy or obvious choice. Computer-administered surveys can incorporate an automatic measure of response latency and thereby offer a big advantage over paper and pencil approaches.

response latency

The amount of time it takes to make a choice between two alternatives; used as a measure of the strength of preference.

Direct and Contrived Observation

Researchers always are faced with a decision of how much they should interject themselves into the situation being studied. In a phenomenological approach, the researcher is often very much within the research situation. Consider the case where restaurant employees might be asked to talk about working in a restaurant and to explain how much emphasis is placed on hygiene and general concern for customer safety. The researcher has to ask questions and may even provide some prop or stimulus for the respondent to react to. On the other hand, hidden cameras might be placed within the restaurants so that data can be gathered with no researcher present. Alternatively, an ethnographer may actually take a job in the restaurant and perform certain acts to see how other employees react. This brings us to the difference between direct and contrived observation.

Direct Observation

Direct observation can produce detailed records of what people actually do during an event. The observer plays a passive role, making no attempt to control or manipulate a situation, instead merely recording what occurs. Every effort is made for the interviewer not to interject him- or herself into the situation. For example, recording traffic counts and traffic flows within a supermarket can help managers design store layouts that maximize a typical customer's exposure to the merchandise offered while also facilitating search efforts. This data can be more accurately gathered simply by observing consumers rather than by asking consumers about their movement in the store. A manufacturer can then better determine shelf locations, the arrangement of departments and merchandise within those departments, the location of checkout facilities, and other characteristics that improve the shopping value consumers obtain from visiting a store. If directly questioned in a survey, most shoppers would be unable to accurately portray the time they spent in each department.

With the direct observation method, the data consist of records of events made as they occur. An observation form often helps keep researchers' observations consistent and ensures that they record all relevant information. A respondent is not required to recall—perhaps inaccurately—an

direct observation

A straightforward attempt to observe and record what naturally occurs; the investigator does not create an artificial situation.

event after it has occurred; instead, the observation is instantaneous. For instance, a response latency measure embedded in an online survey will "observe" how long a respondent took to answer a question without the respondent ever knowing the measure was taken. Will this provide more accurate information than if the respondent was asked to report how many seconds it took him or her to respond? Almost certainly the answer is yes!

■ WHY USE DIRECT OBSERVATION?

In many cases, direct observation is the most straightforward form of data collection—or the only form possible. A produce manager for Auchan (a France-based hypermart firm) may periodically gather competitive price information from Carrefour (also a France-based hypermart firm) stores within competing areas. Both Carrefour and Auchan can monitor each other's promotions by observing advertisements posted on the competitor's Web site (see http://www.auchan.fr and http://www.carrefour.fr), for example. In other situations, observation is the most economical technique. In a common type of observation study, a shopping center manager may observe the license plate (tag) numbers on cars in its parking lot. These data, along with automobile registration information, provide an inexpensive means of determining where customers live.

Certain data may be obtained more quickly or easily using direct observation than by other methods—gender, race, and other respondent characteristics can simply be observed. Researchers investigating a diet product may use observation when selecting respondents in a shopping mall. Overweight people may be prescreened by observing pedestrians, thus eliminating a number of screening interviews. Direct observation is used because it often is the simplest, quickest and most accurate way to gather data. On the other hand, direct observation has limited flexibility because not all phenomena are observable.

■ ERRORS ASSOCIATED WITH DIRECT OBSERVATION

Although direct observation involves no interaction with the subject, the method is not error-free; the observer may record events subjectively. The same visual cues that may influence the interplay between interviewer and respondent (e.g., the subject's age or sex) may come into play in some direct observation settings, such as when the observer subjectively attributes a particular economic status or educational background to a subject. A distortion of measurement resulting from the cognitive behavior or actions of the witnessing observer is called **observer bias**. For example, in a research project using observers to evaluate whether salesclerks are rude or courteous, fieldworkers may be required to rely on their own interpretations of people or situations during the observation process.

Also, accuracy may suffer if the observer does not record every detail that describes the persons, objects, and events in a given situation. Generally, the observer should record as much detail as possible. However, the pace of events, the observer's memory, the observer's writing speed, and other factors will limit the amount of detail that can be recorded.

Interpretation of observation data is another potential source of error. Facial expressions and other nonverbal communication may have several meanings. Does a smile always mean happiness? Does the fact that someone is standing or seated next to the president of a company necessarily indicate the person's status?

observer bias

A distortion of measurement resulting from the cognitive behavior or actions of a witnessing observer.

TO THE POINT

What we see depends mainly on what we look for.

—Sir John Lubbock

Contrived Observation

Most observation takes place in a natural setting, but sometimes the investigator intervenes to create an artificial environment to test a hypothesis. This approach is called **contrived observation**. Contrived observation can increase the frequency of occurrence of certain behavior patterns, such as employee responses to complaints. An airline passenger complaining about a meal or service from the flight attendant may actually be a researcher recording that person's reactions. If situations were not contrived, the research time spent waiting and observing would expand considerably. A number of retailers use observers called *mystery shoppers* to visit a store and pretend to be interested in a particular product or service. After leaving the store, the "shopper" evaluates the salesperson's performance.

contrived observation

Observation in which the investigator creates an artificial environment in order to test a hypothesis.

Clean as We Say, or Clean as We Do?

People know that hand washing is a fundamental way to stay healthy, not to mention simple good manners. So, when you ask them, most people say they faithfully wash their hands. But according to observational research, what people say about this behavior is not what they necessarily do.

The American Society for Microbiology and the Soap and Detergent Association together arranged for a nationwide study of hand washing by U.S. adults. In an online survey by Harris Interactive, 91 percent of adults said they always wash their hands after using a public restroom. Men were somewhat less likely to make this claim—88 percent, versus 94 percent of women. The researchers followed up on the survey results by observing adults in public restrooms in Atlanta, Chicago, New York City, and San Francisco. A 2007 tally of the percentage who washed their hands found that only 77 percent did so. About 66 percent of men were observed washing their hands after going to the restroom while women washed their hands 88 percent of the time. The difference between reporting of hand washing and actual hand washing was greater for the men (about a 22 percent difference) than for the women (6 percent). The numbers also vary geographically across the United States. Among major cities, Chicago has the cleanest hands as 81 percent of people can be observed washing after a toilet break while San Francisco scored lowest at 73 percent overall. Additionally, handwashing is down 6 percent since 2005.

This research showing a divide between what individuals believe they should be doing, what they say they do, and what they actually do could be useful in helping agencies craft messages aimed at improving citizens' health. In addition, soap marketers may want to learn more about what keeps individuals from washing their hands (is it inconvenient? are public sinks a turnoff?), even while being prepared for some response bias.

The study was conducted by having observers discreetly watch and record the frequency of the number of people using a public toilet facility and the number of people who washed their hands. Observers pretended to be grooming themselves while watching the visitors. Over 6,000 people were observed in four U.S. cities. Do you think a hidden camera would reveal different results?

Source: Based on "Hygiene Habits Stall: Public Handwashing Down," Cleaning 101, www.cleaning101.com/newsroom/09-17-07.cfm; Harris Interactive, "Many Adults Report Not Washing Their Hands When They Should, and More People Claim to Wash Their Hands than Who Actually Do," news release (December 14, 2005); "Hand Washing Survey Fact Sheet" (2005), http://www.cleaning101.com, accessed February 24, 2006; and Harris Interactive, "A Survey of Hand Washing Behavior (2005 Findings)" (September 2005), accessed at "2005 ASM/SDA Hand Hygiene Survey Results," http://www.cleaning101.com (SDA Web site), February 24, 2006.

© GEORGE DOYLE & CIARAN GRIFFIN

© M. THOMSEN/ZEFA/CORBIS

The Research Snapshot above discusses direct observation of hand washing in public restrooms. Similarly, a study compared results from self-reported questionnaire data, focus group data, and observational data concerning hygiene among restaurant employees. The questionnaires suggested that 95 percent of employees washed their hands thoroughly after handling raw chicken, that number averaged about 82 percent in the face–to-face condition, but when observation was used, 75 percent of the restaurant employees did not wash their hands adequately after handling raw chicken.[3] This direct observation could be turned into a contrived situation if a participant observer, pretending to be a new employee, asked another employee to assist by in some way handling raw chicken, and then observed the other employee's behavior. In the latter case, the researcher has interjected him- or herself into a situation, but perhaps for a very good reason. This may allow a hypothesis stating that interruptions will be associated with less hand washing compared to a no interruption condition.

Ethical Issues in the Observation of Humans

Observation methods introduce a number of ethical issues. Hidden observation raises the issue of the respondent's right to privacy. Suppose a research firm is approached by a company interested in acquiring information about how women put on their bras by observing behavior in a spa dressing area. The researcher considers approaching spas in several key cities about placing small cameras inconspicuously to observe women getting dressed. Obviously, such a situation raises an ethical question. While to some extent the dressing room is an area where women often do dress where others can observe them, women do not expect to have their dressing behavior recorded. Therefore, unless a way can be found to have some women consent to such observation, this observational approach is unethical.

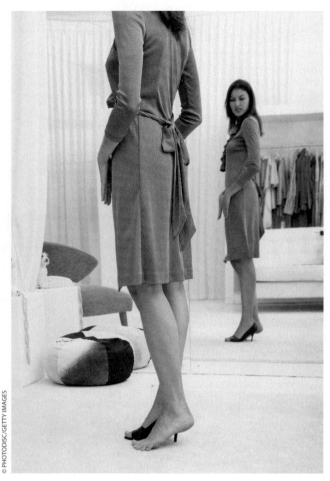

Even if fashion companies could learn a lot about the types of problems consumers typically have when purchasing and wearing clothes, would observation through two-way mirrors (also referred to as one-way mirrors) be appropriate?

artifacts

The things that people made and consumed within a culture that signal something meaningful about the behavior taking place at the time of consumption

If the researcher obtains permission to observe someone, the subject may not act naturally. So, at times there is a strong temptation to observe without obtaining consent or gaining input from an IRB (Institutional Review Board). Many times, such as monitoring people walking through and waiting in an airport, obtaining consent from individual respondents is impractical if not impossible. Further, asking for consent just before the actual observation will likely change the behavior.

So, when should researchers feel comfortable collecting observational data? While exceptions exist to every rule, here are three questions that can help address this question:

1. Is the behavior being observed commonly performed in public where it is expected that others can observe the behavior?
2. Is the behavior performed in a setting in which the anonymity of the person being observed is assured (meaning there is no way to identify individuals)?
3. Has the person agreed to be observed?

If the answer to the first two questions is yes, then there is not likely a violation of privacy in collecting observational research data. If the answer to the third question is yes, then gathering the data also is likely to be ethical. Otherwise, the researcher should carefully consider input from an IRB or other authority before proceeding with the research.

Also, some might see contrived observation as unethical based on the notion of entrapment. To *entrap* means to deceive or trick into difficulty, which clearly is an abusive action. For instance, in the hand washing example above, when the experimenter interrupts the real employee, he/she may entrap the employee into a lower probability of washing hands thoroughly. In this instance, if the employee was caused or caused harm to others (by getting in trouble with a superior or making someone ill) then clearly the intrusion is unethical. However, if no possibility of harm exists, then the researcher can likely proceed although this particular instance should be done under the auspices of an IRB.

Observation of Physical Objects

Physical phenomena may be the subject of observation study. Physical-trace evidence is a visible mark of some past event or occurrence. For example, the wear on library books indirectly indicates which books are actually read (handled most) when checked out. A classic example of physical-trace evidence in a nonprofit setting was erosion on the floor tiles around the hatching-chick exhibit at Chicago's Museum of Science and Industry. These tiles had to be replaced every six weeks; tiles in other parts of the museum did not need to be replaced for years. The selective erosion of tiles, indexed by the replacement rate, was a measure of the relative popularity of exhibits.

Artifacts

Clearly, a creative marketing researcher has many options for determining the solution to a problem. The story about Charles Coolidge Parlin, generally recognized as one of the founders of commercial marketing research, examining garbage cans at the turn of the twentieth century illustrates another study of physical traces. Physical traces often involve artifacts. **Artifacts** are things that people made and consumed within a culture that signal something meaningful about the behavior taking place at the time of consumption. Ethnographers are particularly interested in examining artifacts and Parlin's garbage can escapades illustrate how a marketing researcher can apply an ethnographic approach involving observation of artifacts.

Parlin designed an observation study to persuade Campbell's Soup Company to advertise in the *Saturday Evening Post*. Campbell's was reluctant to advertise because it believed that the *Post* was read primarily by working people who would prefer to make soup from scratch, peeling the potatoes and scraping the carrots, rather than paying ten cents for a can of soup. To

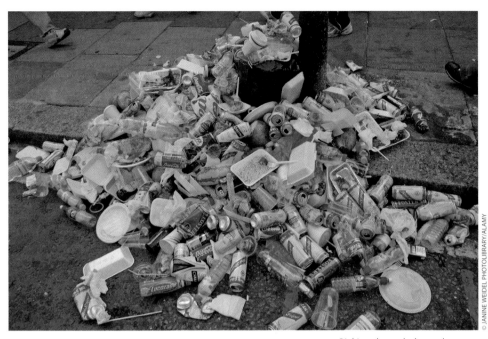

Picking through the garbage on the side of the road can reveal behaviors of fast-food customers.

demonstrate that rich people weren't the target market, Parlin selected a sample of Philadelphia garbage routes. Garbage from each specific area of the city that was selected was dumped on the floor of a local National Guard Armory. Parlin had the number of Campbell's soup cans in each pile counted. The results indicated that the garbage from the rich people's homes didn't contain many cans of Campbell's soup. Although they may not have made soup from scratch themselves, their housekeepers may have. The garbage piles from the blue-collar area showed a larger number of Campbell's soup cans. This observation study was enough evidence for Campbell's. They advertised in the *Saturday Evening Post*.[4]

The method used in this study has since been used in a scientific project at the University of Arizona in which aspiring archaeologists have sifted through garbage for over thirty years. They examine soggy cigarette butts, empty milk cartons, and half-eaten Big Macs in an effort to understand modern life. Like other research involving observation, observations can be compared with the results of surveys about food consumption—and garbage does not lie. This type of observation can correct for potential overreporting of healthful item consumption and underreporting of, say, cigarettes or fast food.

Inventories

Another application of observing physical objects is to count and record physical inventories through retail or wholesale audits. This method allows researchers to investigate brand sales on regional and national levels, market shares, seasonal purchasing patterns, and so on. Marketing research suppliers offer audit data at both the retail and the wholesale levels.

An observer can record physical-trace data to discover information a respondent could not recall accurately. For example, measuring the number of ounces of liquid bleach used during a test provides precise physical-trace evidence without relying on the respondent's memory. The accuracy of respondents' memories is not a problem for the firm that conducts a pantry audit. The pantry audit requires an inventory of the brands, quantities, and package sizes in a consumer's home rather than responses from individuals. The problem of untruthfulness or some other form of response bias is avoided. For example, the pantry audit prevents the possible problem of respondents erroneously claiming to have purchased prestige brands. However, gaining permission to physically check consumers' pantries is not easy, and the fieldwork is expensive. In addition, the brand in the pantry may not reflect the brand purchased most often if consumers substituted it because they had a coupon, the usual brand was out of stock, or another reason.

Content Analysis

content analysis

The systematic observation and quantitative description of the manifest content of communication.

Besides observing people and physical objects, researchers may use **content analysis**, which obtains data by observing and analyzing the contents or messages of advertisements, newspaper articles, television programs, letters, and the like. This method involves systematic analysis as well as observation to identify the specific information content and other characteristics of the messages. Content analysis studies the message itself and involves the design of a systematic observation and recording procedure for quantitative description of the manifest content of communication. This technique measures the extent of emphasis or omission of a given analytical category. For example, content analysis of advertisements might evaluate their use of words, themes, characters, or space and time relationships. Content analysis often counts the frequency of themes or occurences within the hermeneutic unit being studied. For instance, the frequency with which women, African-Americans, Hispanics, or Asians appear in advertising displayed on a cable network can be studied with content analysis.

Content analysis might be used to investigate questions such as whether some advertisers use certain themes, appeals, claims, or deceptive practices more than others or whether recent consumer-oriented actions by the Federal Trade Commission have influenced the contents of advertising. A cable television programmer might do a content analysis of network programming to evaluate its competition. Every year researchers analyze the Super Bowl telecast to see how much of the visual material is live-action play and how much is replay, or how many shots focus on the cheerleaders and how many on spectators. Content analysis also can explore the information content of television commercials directed at children, the company images portrayed in ads, and numerous other aspects of advertising.

Study of the content of communications is more sophisticated than simply counting the items; it requires a system of analysis to secure relevant data. After one employee role-playing session involving leaders and subordinates, researchers analyzed videotapes to identify categories of verbal behaviors (e.g., positive reward statements, positive comparison statements, and self-evaluation requests). Trained coders, using a set of specific instructions, then recorded and coded the leaders' behavior into specific verbal categories. Ideally, two or three coders perform the task allowing for an assessment of rater reliability or how replicable are the results.

Mechanical Observation

In many situations, the primary—and sometimes the only—means of observation is mechanical rather than human. Video cameras, traffic counters, and other machines help observe and record behavior. Some unusual observation studies have used motion-picture cameras and time-lapse photography. An early application of this observation technique photographed train passengers and determined their levels of comfort by observing how they sat and moved in their seats. Another time-lapse study filmed traffic flows in an urban square and resulted in a redesign of the streets. Similar techniques may help managers design store layouts and resolve problems in moving people or objects through spaces over time.

Television and Radio Monitoring

television monitoring

Computerized mechanical observation used to obtain television ratings.

Perhaps the best-known marketing research project involving mechanical observation and computerized data collection is ACNielsen's **television monitoring** system for estimating national television audiences. Nielsen Media Research uses a consumer panel and a monitoring device called a PeopleMeter to obtain ratings for television programs nationwide.[5] The Nielsen PeopleMeter gathers data on what each television in a household is playing and who is watching it at the time. Researchers attach electronic boxes to television sets and remote controls to capture information on program choices and the length of viewing time. Nielsen matches the signals captured through these devices with its database of network broadcast and cable program schedules so that it can identify the specific programs being viewed.

When a television in the panel household is turned on, a red light on the PeopleMeter periodically flashes to remind viewers to indicate who is watching. The viewer then uses a remote control to record who is watching. One button on the control is assigned to each member of the household and a separate visitor button is used for potential guests. The household member presses his or her button to indicate the sex and age of the person who is watching. Knowing who in the family is watching allows executives to match television programs with demographic profiles.

Each night, Nielsen's computers automatically retrieve the data stored in the PeopleMeter's recording box. In this way, Nielsen gathers daily estimates of when televisions are in use, which channels are used, and who is viewing each program. The panel includes more than five thousand households, selected to be representative of the U.S. population. For local programming, Nielsen uses additional panels equipped with recording devices but not PeopleMeters to record viewer demographics. (Nielsen uses surveys to record demographic data for local programming.)

Traffic cameras that monitor speeding on major highways are becoming commonplace in Europe, Australia, and even in some parts of the United States. Would car companies learn anything from the observed behavior?

Critics of the PeopleMeter argue that subjects in Nielsen's panel grow bored over time and do not always record when they begin or stop watching television. Arbitron, best known for measuring radio audiences, has attempted to answer this objection with its own measuring system, which it calls the Portable People Meter.[6] Each participant is awarded points for the amount of time the meter is on. Total points are displayed in the base station and used to determine the size of the incentive paid to each participant. Arbitron's meter simplifies the participants' role and collects data on exposure to radio and television programming outside the home. However, the device records only signals that the radio or television system embeds using Arbitron's equipment.

Other devices gather data about the viewing of advertisements. The TiVo digital television recorder collects detailed viewing data, such as what commercials people skip by using fast-forward. The PreTesting Company sets up contrived observational studies in which viewers equipped with a remote control are invited to watch any of three prerecorded channels playing different programs and advertisements, including the client's ads to be tested.[7] The system records the precise points at which the viewer changes the channel. By combining the results from many participants, the company arrives at a Cumulative Zapping Score, that is, the percentage of viewers who had exited the client's advertisement by each point in the ad. So that viewing behavior will be more natural, subjects are told they are evaluating the programming, not the ads.

Mobiltrak, a research firm based in Herndon, Virginia, uses a device that can observe what is playing on cars' stereos. The company installs observation equipment the size of a shoebox on towers located at heavily traveled intersections. Sensors on the equipment measure the level of electronic radiation emitted by the radio of each car as it passes by. The data describe the volume of traffic listening to each station, not the stations being played by individual vehicles or any demographic data about the vehicles' drivers or passengers.[8] By paying a subscription fee to Mobiltrak, radio stations in the company's service areas can obtain data about their listeners. They can use the data to sell advertising time to businesses located where the most listeners are driving. In addition, advertisers can pay for data collected at particular locations. For example, Home Depot, which has used Mobiltrak, can find out which stations people are listening to as they travel on roads leading past one of the company's stores.

Monitoring Web Site Traffic

Computer technology makes gathering detailed data about online behavior easy and inexpensive. The greater challenges are to identify which measures are meaningful and to interpret the data correctly. For instance, most organizations record the level of activity at their Web sites. They may count the number of *hits*—mouse clicks on a single page of a Web site. If the visitor clicks on many links, that page receives multiple hits. Similarly, they can track *page views*, or single, discrete clicks to load individual pages of a Web site. Page views more conservatively indicate how many users visit each individual page on the Web site and may also be used to track the path or sequence of pages that each visitor follows.

■ CLICK-THROUGH RATES

click-through rate

Proportion of people who are exposed to an Internet ad who actually click on it's hyperlink to enter the Web site; click-through rates are generally very low.

A **click-through rate** (CTR) is the percentage of people who are exposed to an advertisement who actually click on the corresponding hyperlink which takes them to the company's Web site. Counting hits or page views can suggest the amount of interest or attention a Web site is receiving, but these measures are flawed. First, hits do not differentiate between a lot of activity by a few visitors and a little activity by many visitors. In addition, the researcher lacks information about the meaning behind the numbers. If a user clicks on a site many times, is the person finding a lot of useful or enjoyable material, or is the user trying unsuccessfully to find something by looking in several places? Additionally, some hits are likely made by mistake. The consumers may have had no intention of clicking through the ad or may not have known what they were doing when they clicked on the ad.

A more refined count is the number of *unique visitors* to a Web site. This measurement counts the initial access to the site but not multiple hits on the site by the same visitor during the same day or week. Operators of Web sites can collect the data by attaching small files, called *cookies*, to the computers of visitors to their sites and then tracking those cookies to see whether the same visitors return. Some marketing research companies, notably Jupiter Research and Nielsen//NetRatings, specialize in monitoring this type of Internet activity. A typical approach is to install a special tracking program on the personal computers of a sample of Internet users who agree to participate in the research effort. Nielsen//NetRatings has its software installed in thirty thousand computers in homes and workplaces. Internet monitoring enables these companies to identify the popularity of Web sites. The information that remains stored in cookies and other system files can also help researchers know about the habits of Internet usage for consumers. In recent years, accurate measurement of unique visitors and Web surfing behavior is becoming more difficult because over half of computer users routinely delete cookies and many users keep cookies turned off to help them remain *virtually* anonymous.[9] Computer security systems are also limiting the extent to which this information is transferred from the user's machine to the server.

■ CTR AND ONLINE ADVERTISING

As online advertising has become more widespread, marketing research has refined methods for measuring the effectiveness of the advertisements. The companies that place these ads can keep count of the click-through rate (CTR). Applying the CTR to the amount spent on the advertisement gives the advertiser a *cost per click*. These measures have been hailed as a practical way to evaluate advertising effectiveness. However, marketers have to consider that getting consumers to click on an ad is rarely the ad's objective. Companies are more often advertising to meet short- or long-term sales goals.

Google has benefited from CTR research indicating that the highest click-through rates tend to occur on pages displaying search results. (Not surprisingly, someone who searches for the term *kayaks* is more likely to be interested in an advertisement offering a good deal on kayaks.) The company showed Vanguard, for example, that its banner ads cost the financial firm less than fifty cents per click and generated a 14 percent click-through rate. That CTR is far above typical response rates for direct-mail advertising, but it does not indicate whether online clicks are as valuable in terms of sales.[10]

Scanner-Based Research

Lasers performing optical character recognition and bar code technology like the universal product code (UPC) have accelerated the use of mechanical observation in marketing research. Chapter 6 noted that a number of syndicated services offer secondary data about product category movement generated from retail stores using scanner technology.

This technology allows researchers to investigate questions that are demographically or promotionally specific. Scanner research has investigated the different ways consumers respond to price promotions and the effects of those differences on a promotion's profitability. One of the primary means of implementing this type of research is through the establishment of a **scanner-based consumer panel** to replace consumer purchase diaries. In a typical scanner panel, each household is assigned a bar-coded card, like a frequent-shopper card, which members present to the clerk at the register. The household's code number is coupled with the purchase information recorded by the scanner. In addition, as with other consumer panels, background information about the household obtained through answers to a battery of demographic and psychographic survey questions can also be coupled with the household code number.

Aggregate data, such as actual store sales as measured by scanners, are available to clients and industry groups. Data may also be aggregated by product category. To interpret the aggregated data, researchers can combine them with secondary research and panel demographics. For instance, data from Information Resources Inc. (IRI) have indicated a downward trend in sales of hair-coloring products. Demographic data suggest that an important reason is the aging of the population; many consumers who dye their hair reach an age at which they no longer wish to cover their gray hair. A smaller segment of the population is at an age where consumers typically begin using hair coloring.[11]

Data from scanner research parallel data provided by a standard mail diary panel, with some important improvements:

1. The data measure observed (actual) purchase behavior rather than reported behavior (recorded later in a diary).
2. Substituting mechanical for human record-keeping improves accuracy.
3. Measures are unobtrusive, eliminating interviewing and the possibility of social desirability or other bias on the part of respondents.
4. More extensive purchase data can be collected, because all UPC categories are measured. In a mail diary, respondents could not possibly reliably record all items they purchased. Because all UPC-coded items are measured in the panel, users can investigate many product categories to determine loyalty, switching rates, and so on for their own brands as well as for other companies' products and locate product categories for possible market entry.
5. The data collected from computerized checkout scanners can be combined with data about advertising, price changes, displays, and special sales promotions. Researchers can scrutinize them with powerful analytical software provided by the scanner data providers.

Advances in bar-code technology have led to **at-home scanning systems** that use handheld wands to read UPC symbols. Consumer panelists perform their own scanning *after* they have taken home the products. This advance makes it possible to investigate purchases made at stores that lack in-store scanning equipment.

scanner-based consumer panel

A type of consumer panel in which participants' purchasing habits are recorded with a laser scanner rather than a purchase diary.

at-home scanning systems

Systems that allow consumer panelists to perform their own scanning after taking home products, using handheld wands that read UPC symbols.

Camera Surveillance

Cameras are increasingly used in modern society to keep tabs on all sorts of behaviors. In 2005, London's famous tube (subway) system was rocked by multiple terrorist attacks. Within just a few hours of the attacks, London's video surveillance recordings were analyzed and potential suspects had begun to be identified. On a typical day, a Londoner's behavior is recorded automatically hundreds of times. Likewise, cameras planted inconspicuously in places can be useful in marketing research. Shopping center security video can help identify problems with merchandising and the types of things that attract consumers to come into and remain in an environment. However, cameras have many more applications.

Researchers sometimes ask and get permission to place cameras inconspicuously in consumers' homes, offices, or even cars.[12] If Microsoft Vista fails, it is not because of a lack of research.

Microsoft commissioned research involving the observation of 50 homes via inconspicuous, in-home cameras. As consumers encountered problems using the operating system in their homes, Microsoft was able to study the consumer behavior involved and try to find a way to avoid the problems in the future. Other companies including Kimberly-Clark, Sony, and Old Spice have also successfully applied observational research using cameras. The Old Spice research involved videos of guys taking showers in their homes (with permission and swimsuits) and the Kimberly-Clark research involved young parents wearing small hat cams while changing a baby's diaper. This type of research allows close inspection of activities in places and at times when having an actual observer present would not work.

Marketing researchers are also using something dubbed a Mindcam to understand various aspects of consumer activity, such as shopping.[13] A small camera and microphone combination is placed on the consumer's person. All of their sights and sounds are recorded. Typically, this is followed up with an interview where the consumer tries to explain his or her behavior and any purchases made. Small cameras and other recording devices make these types of developments possible.

Neurological Devices

The chapter's opening vignette described a technology that observed brain activity as a person went about everyday behaviors. More and more, we are able to observe what goes on in the consumer's mind. Neurological activity can reveal how much thought takes place and what types of feelings a person is probably experiencing. Similar processes involve things such as magnetic resonance imaging or transcranial magnetic simulation.[14] If these things sound complicated, it's because they are. These have the potential of allowing researchers to actually directly observe what is going on in the mind of a respondent as they perform an activity. Thus, these techniques may revolutionize research on information processing. We may still be several years away from widespread marketing applications of these approaches; researchers also will have to be concerned about the ethical implications of looking into someone's mind.

Measuring Physiological Reactions

Marketing researchers have used a number of other mechanical devices to evaluate consumers' physical and physiological reactions to advertising copy, packaging, and other stimuli. Researchers use such means when they believe consumers are unaware of their own reactions to stimuli such as advertising or that consumers will not provide honest responses. Four major categories of mechanical devices are used to measure physiological reactions: (1) eye-tracking monitors, (2) pupilometers, (3) psychogalvanometers, and (4) voice-pitch analyzers.

A magazine or newspaper advertiser may wish to grab readers' attention with a visual scene and then direct it to a package or coupon. Or a television advertiser may wish to identify which selling points to emphasize. Eye-tracking equipment records how the subject reads a print ad or views a television commercial and how much time is spent looking at various parts of the stimulus. In physiological terms, the

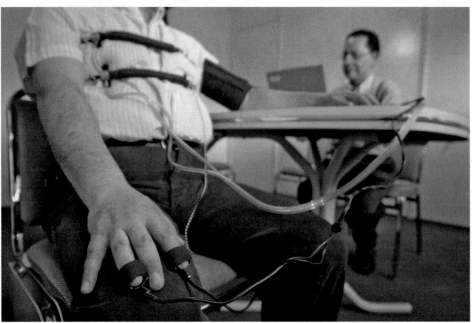

Physiological responses to advertising can be recorded with a device like this one.

© AP PHOTO

gaze movement of a viewer's eye is measured with an **eye-tracking monitor**, which measures unconscious eye movements. Originally developed to measure astronauts' eye fatigue, modern eye-tracking systems need not keep a viewer's head in a stationary position. The devices track eye movements with invisible infrared light beams that lock onto a subject's eyes. The light reflects off the eye, and eye-movement data are recorded while another tiny video camera monitors which magazine page is being perused. The data are analyzed by computer to determine which components in an ad (or other stimuli) were seen and which were overlooked. Eye-tracking monitors have recently been used to measure the way subjects view e-mail and Web marketing messages. OgilvyOne has used this technology to learn that people often skip over more than half of the words in e-mail advertising, especially words on the right side of the message. Interestingly, consumers generally ignore the word *free*.[15]

Other physiological observation techniques are based on a common principle: that adrenaline is released when the body is aroused. This hormone causes the heart to enlarge and to beat harder and faster. These changes increase the flow of blood to the fingers and toes. The blood vessels dilate, and perspiration increases, affecting the skin's electrical conductivity. Other physical changes following the release of adrenaline include dilation of the pupils, more frequent brain wave activity, higher skin temperature, and faster breathing. Methods that measure these and other changes associated with arousal can apply to a variety of marketing questions, such as subjects' reactions to advertising messages or product concepts.

A **pupilometer** observes and records changes in the diameter of a subject's pupils. A subject is instructed to look at a screen on which an advertisement or other stimulus is projected. When the brightness and distance of the stimulus from the subject's eyes are held constant, changes in pupil size may be interpreted as changes in cognitive activity that result from the stimulus, rather than from eye dilation and constriction in response to light intensity, distance from the object, or other physiological reactions to the conditions of observation. This method of research is based on the assumption that increased pupil size reflects positive attitudes toward and interest in advertisements.

A **psychogalvanometer** measures galvanic skin response (GSR), a measure of involuntary changes in the electrical resistance of the skin. This device is based on the assumption that physiological changes, such as increased perspiration, accompany emotional reactions to advertisements, packages, and slogans. Excitement increases the body's perspiration rate, which increases the electrical resistance of the skin. The test is an indicator of emotional arousal or tension and can be used to help detect dishonest responses as a lie detector.

Voice-pitch analysis is a relatively new physiological measurement technique that gauges emotional reactions as reflected in physiological changes in a person's voice. Abnormal frequencies in the voice caused by changes in the autonomic nervous system are measured with sophisticated, audio-adapted computer equipment. Computerized analysis compares the respondent's voice pitch during warm-up conversations (normal range) with verbal responses to questions about his or her evaluative reaction to television commercials or other stimuli. This technique, unlike other physiological devices, does not require the researcher to surround subjects with mazes of wires or equipment.

All of these devices assume that physiological reactions are associated with persuasiveness or predict some cognitive response. This assumption has not yet been clearly demonstrated. No strong theoretical evidence supports the argument that such a physiological change is a valid measure of future sales, attitude change, or emotional response. Another major problem with physiological research is the *calibration,* or sensitivity, of measuring devices. Identifying arousal is one thing, but precisely measuring *levels* of arousal is another. In addition, most of these devices

eye-tracking monitor

A mechanical device used to observe eye movements; some eye monitors use infrared light beams to measure unconscious eye movements.

pupilometer

A mechanical device used to observe and record changes in the diameter of a subject's pupils.

psychogalvanometer

A device that measures galvanic skin response, a measure of involuntary changes in the electrical resistance of the skin.

voice-pitch analysis

A physiological measurement technique that records abnormal frequencies in the voice that are supposed to reflect emotional reactions to various stimuli.

Companies like Visiontrack specialize in research that tracks how the eye moves during an activity. Think about how useful this might be to companies considering product placements within video games or in designing more efficient instrument panels for airplanes.

- Generally, observations have the most validity when the actual observations are performed unobtrusively. The big reason for this is that social influences such as may occur from an interviewer's presence or the knowledge that one is being observed are eliminated.
- Marketing research often involves information processing. Researchers should strongly consider using measures of response latency when studying information processing. Computer-aided survey technology makes observing response latency easy and accurate.

- Artifacts are great ways to put together a physical trace of human activities and to understand the value of those objects to the individuals involved.
- To avoid ethical issues, the anonymity of people whose behavior is captured using observational data collection should be protected at all times unless consent has been obtained to identify the person.

are expensive. However, as a prominent researcher points out, physiological measurement is coincidental: "Physiological measurement isn't an exit interview. It's not dependent on what was remembered later on. It's a live blood, sweat, and tears, moment-by-moment response, synchronous with the stimulus."[16]

Each of these mechanical devices has another limitation: The subjects are usually placed in artificial settings, such as watching television in a laboratory rather than at home, and they know they are being observed.

Summary

1. Discuss the role of observation as a marketing research method. Observation is a powerful tool for the marketing researcher. Scientific observation is the systematic process of recording the behavioral patterns of people, objects, and occurrences as they are witnessed. Questioning or otherwise communicating with subjects does not occur. A wide variety of information about the behavior of people and objects can be observed. Seven kinds of phenomena are observable: physical actions, verbal behavior, expressive behavior, spatial relations and locations, temporal patterns, physical objects, and verbal and pictorial records. Thus, both verbal and nonverbal behavior may be observed. Observation may not, however, be used for cognitive phenomena. Attitudes, motivations, expectations, intentions, and preferences are not observable; only overt behavior of short duration can be observed.

2. Describe the use of direct observation and contrived observation. Human observation, whether direct or contrived, is commonly used when the situation or behavior to be recorded is not easily predictable in advance of the research. The most advantageous observational data techniques are unobstrusive, meaning the observation is done without the knowledge of the person being watched. It may be unobtrusive, and many types of data can be obtained more accurately through direct observation than by questioning respondents. Direct observation involves watching and recording what naturally occurs, without creating an artificial situation. For some data, observation is the most direct or the only method of collection. For example, researchers can measure response latency, the time it takes individuals to choose between alternatives. Observer bias may be a problem in correctly perceiving the behaviors being observed. Observation can also be contrived by creating the situations to be observed. This can reduce the time and expense of obtaining reactions to certain circumstances.

3. Identify ethical issues particular to research using observation. Contrived observation, hidden observation, and other observation research designs have the potential to involve deception. For this reason, these methods often raise ethical concerns about subjects' right to privacy and right to be informed. The chapter includes a short checklist that can be useful in determining the morality of an observational data gathering approach.

4. Explain the observation of physical objects and message content. Physical-trace evidence serves as a visible record of past events. Researchers may examine whatever evidence provides such a record, including inventory levels, the contents of garbage cans, or the items in a consumer's pantry. Researchers can take advantage of artifacts that are left behind to try and explain the behavior associated with that particular object. Content analysis obtains data by observing and analyzing the contents of the messages in written or spoken communications.

5. Describe major types of mechanical observation. Mechanical observation uses a variety of devices to record behavior directly. It may be an efficient and accurate choice when the situation or behavior to be recorded is routine, repetitive, or programmatic. National television audience ratings are based on mechanical observation (for example, PeopleMeters) and computerized data collection. Web site traffic may be measured electronically. Scanner-based research provides product category sales data recorded by laser scanners in retail stores. Many syndicated services offer secondary data collected through scanner systems. Additionally, cameras can be used to study consumers in their homes and employees at their workplace. Small cameras can even be placed on people as they go about their daily activities. These cameras record the sights and sounds they experience. Additionally, new approaches exist to perform neural imaging which provide a more direct insight into the mind of the consumers or employees being studied.

6. Summarize techniques for measuring physiological reactions. Physiological reactions, such as arousal or eye movement patterns, may be observed using a number of mechanical devices. Eye-tracking monitors identify the direction of a person's gaze, and a pupilometer observes and records changes in the diameter of the pupils of subjects' eyes, based on the assumption that a larger pupil signifies a positive attitude. A psychogalvanometer measures galvanic skin response as a signal of a person's emotional reactions. Voice-pitch analysis measures changes in a person's voice and associates the changes with emotional response.

Key Terms and Concepts

artifacts, *194*
at-home scanning systems, *199*
click-through rate, *198*
content analysis, *196*
contrived observation, *192*
direct observation, *191*

eye-tracking monitor, *201*
hidden observation, *189*
observation, *187*
observer bias, *192*
psychogalvanometer, *201*
pupilometer, *201*

response latency, *191*
scanner-based consumer panel, *199*
television monitoring, *196*
unobtrusive observation, *189*
visible observation, *189*
voice-pitch analysis, *201*

Questions for Review and Critical Thinking

1. Yogi Berra, former New York Yankee catcher, said, "You can observe a lot just by watching." How does this fit in with the definition of scientific observation?
2. What are the major advantages of unobtrusive observation over other types of data collection?
3. Under what conditions are observation studies most appropriate and what situations may make them inappropriate?
4. ETHICS The chapter showed a photograph of a traffic monitoring camera. Do you think the use of these cameras to issue speeding tickets is ethical? What types of behavior might cameras like these capture that would help automobile designers produce products that better match our needs as drivers?
5. A multinational fast-food corporation plans to locate a restaurant in La Paz, Bolivia. Secondary data for this city are sketchy and outdated. How might you determine the best location using observational data collection?
6. Discuss how an observation study might be combined with a personal interview.
7. 'NET Click-through rates for advertisements placed in Web sites are usually very, very low (1 percent or less). What types of error might exist in using click-through rate data as a measure of an advertisement's success?
8. Outline a research design using observation for each of the following situations:
   a. A bank wishes to collect data on the number of customer services and the frequency of customer use of these services.
   b. A state government wishes to determine the driving public's use of seat belts.
   c. A researcher wishes to know how many women have been featured on *Time* covers over the years.
   d. A fast-food franchise wishes to determine how long a customer entering a store has to wait for his or her order.
   e. A magazine publisher wishes to determine exactly what people look at and what they pass over while reading one of its magazines.

f. A food manufacturer wishes to determine how people use diet foods in their homes.

g. An overnight package delivery service wishes to observe delivery workers beginning at the moment when they stop the truck, continuing through the delivery of the package, and ending when they return to the truck.

h. A political consulting agency would like to study the thought patterns of consumers as they view national candidates' political commercials on television.

9. What is an artifact to a marketing researcher? How might one use artifacts to study the types of things that fans at major sporting events might be willing to purchase when attending an event? Can artifacts also be used to study ergonomics in the office? If so, how?

10. What is a scanner-based consumer panel?

11. What are the major types of mechanical observation? What types of observations might eBay potentially have access to that would be of interest to basic marketing researchers?

12. How can a marketing researcher determine if an observational data collection involving hidden cameras is ethical?

13. **ETHICS** Comment on the ethics of the following situations:

a. During the course of telephone calls to investors, a stockbroker records respondents' voices when they are answering sensitive investment questions and then conducts a voice-pitch analysis. The respondents do not know that their voices are being recorded.

b. A researcher plans to invite consumers to be test users in a simulated kitchen located in a shopping mall and then to videotape their reactions to a new microwave dinner from behind a two-way mirror (one that an observer behind the mirror can see through but the person looking into the mirror sees only the reflection).

c. A marketing researcher arranges to purchase the trash from the headquarters of a major competitor. The purpose is to sift through discarded documents to determine the company's strategic plans.

14. What is a psychogalvanometer?

15. Look back to the chapter on qualitative research and find the definition for ethnography. Why is observation such a big part of this important qualitative research approach?

16. What is a contrived observational approach? Are contrived observational approaches ethical? Would they be considered unobtrusive?

Research Activities

1. **'NET** William Rathje, a researcher at the University of Arizona, Department of Anthropology, has become well-known for the "Garbage Project." The project involves observational research. Use http://www.ask.com to find information about the garbage project at the University of Arizona. What is the name of the book that describes some of the key findings of the Garbage Project? How do you think it involves observational research?

2. **'NET** The Internet is filled with webcams. For example, Pebble Beach Golf Club has several webcams (http://www.pebblebeach.com). How could a researcher use webcams like these to collect behavioral data? In your short time viewing these web cams, are there any research questions that you think might be addressed based on behaviors that can be observed in these views? If so, what might one or two be?

Case 8.1   Mazda and Syzygy

© GETTY IMAGES/ PHOTODISC GREEN

When Mazda Motor Europe set out to improve its Web site, the company wanted details about how consumers were using the site and whether finding information was easy. Mazda hired a research firm called Syzygy to answer those questions with observational research.[17] Syzygy's methods include the use of an eye-tracking device that uses infrared light rays to record what areas of a computer screen a user is viewing. For instance, the device measured the process computer users followed in order to look for a local dealer or arrange a test drive. Whenever a process seemed confusing or difficult, the company looked for ways to make the Web site easier to navigate.

To conduct this observational study, Syzygy arranged for sixteen subjects in Germany and the United Kingdom to be observed as they used the Web site. The subjects in Germany were observed with the eye-tracking equipment. As the equipment measured each subject's gaze, software recorded the location on the screen and graphed the data. Syzygy's results included three-dimensional contour maps highlighting the "peak" areas where most of the computer users' attention was directed.

Questions

1. What could Mazda learn from eye-tracking software that would be difficult to learn from other observational methods?

2. What are the shortcomings of this method?

3. Along with the eye-tracking research, what other research methods could help Mazda assess the usability of its Web site? Summarize your advice for how Mazda could use complementary methods to obtain a complete understanding of its Web site usability.

Case 8.2 Tulsa's Central Business District

The metropolitan Tulsa Chamber of Commerce recognized that there was a critical gap between the availability of timely information about the central business district (CBD) and the need for this information for investment decision making, commercial marketing efforts, and the continued pursuit of the goal of downtown revitalization. The Chamber of Commerce undertook four separate research projects to gather information about the CBD. One project was a physical inventory of the existing downtown commercial base. The objectives of the study were to determine what types of establishments were operating in the CBD and the number of vacancies there and to generally profile the commercial geography of the CBD. The researchers found that the central business district was based on the U.S. Bureau of the Census classification scheme. The CBD was identified as the area encompassed by the inner dispersal loop (a system of expressways), which corresponded identically with census tract 25 (see Case Exhibit 8.2–1).

A team of ten pedestrian fieldworkers covered each block in the inner dispersal loop. The fieldworkers used the observation form in Case Exhibit 8.2–2 to record the company name, address, primary business activity, estimated frontage, and other relevant information about each building site or office. Fieldworkers recorded Standard Industrial Classification (SIC) codes for retailers. SIC codes for all other establishments were recorded by research assistants after the data were collected. All the data were identified by census block.

Questions
1. Evaluate this research design.
2. What changes, if any, would you make in the observation form?
3. What problems would you expect in the data collection stage?
4. What techniques would you use to analyze the data?

CASE EXHIBIT 8.2–1 **Census Blocks in Census Tract 25**

Source: U.S. Bureau of the Census.

CASE EXHIBIT 8.2–2 **Observation Study Recording Form**

Company Name _____

_____

Address: _____

Tulsa, Oklahoma

Activities: ___ 1 Vacant ___ 2 Retail ___ 3 Wholesale ___ 4 Manufacturing

___ 5 Service ___ 6 Other (Specify) _____

Retail SIC: ___ 52 ___ 53 ___ 54 ___ 55 ___ 56 ___ 57 ___ 58 ___ 59 ___ 60

Other Activities (describe): _____

_____

Is the Building: ___ 1 For Sale? ___ 2 For Rent?

Leasable Space: _____

Realtor's Name: _____

Realtor's Phone: _____

Rent (per sq. foot)

Is the Building Being: ___ 1 Restored? ___ 2 Remodeled?

Estimated Frontage (Feet): _____

Estimated Number of Stories: _____

Comments: _____

_____

_____

CHAPTER 9
CONDUCTING MARKETING EXPERIMENTS

After studying this chapter, you should be able to

1. Know the basic characteristics of research experiments
2. Design an experiment using the basic issues of experimental design
3. Know ways of maximizing the validity of experiments, including the minimization of demand characteristics
4. Avoid unethical experimental practices
5. Weigh the trade-off between internal and external validity
6. Recognize the appropriate uses of test-marketing

Chapter Vignette: Warning! This Product May Cause . . .

"What cigarette do you smoke, Doctor?" This was the question posed in a 1949 ad for Camel cigarettes. Not surprisingly, the result stated in the ad was that more doctors smoked Camels than any other cigarette. The intended inference here is obvious—if doctors choose Camels, then they must not cause as many harmful effects as those of other cigarettes! The whole question of smoking has advanced a great deal since that time. Inevitably, debates about smoking involve questions of cause.

- Does smoking cause cancer?
- Does smoking cause death?
- Does advertising cause people to smoke?

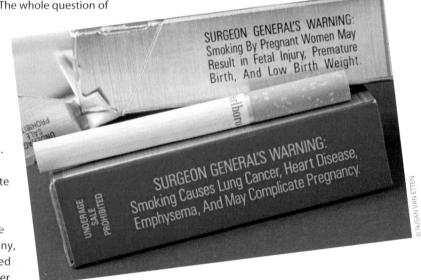

Warning labels say things like "Smoking causes lung cancer, heart disease, and emphysema." In U.S. courts, plaintiffs' attorneys and in some cases state governments have successfully argued that cigarette companies are responsible for the health problems and even deaths associated with long-term smoking.[1] As a result, tobacco companies have paid huge settlements. However, a U.K.-based tobacco company, Imperial Tobacco, faced with a £500,000 law suit filed on behalf of a cancer patient who had smoked Player Cigarettes for 40 years, is basing a legal defense on the notion that a lack of certainty remains over whether or not cigarettes cause cancer. They claim that the only evidence for this is statistical association and that many other factors are also statistically associated with the occurrence of cancer including a patient's socioeconomic status, childhood experiences (orientation toward healthy behaviors like exercise and diet), ethnicity, personality, and diet.

The defense is based on Imperial Tobacco's claim that no experimental evidence isolates the extent to which smoking truly causes cancer.[2] Further, they argued that advertising could not have caused the plaintiff to begin smoking. The Imperial defense was successful as the court ruled in their favor stating that the causal evidence was insufficient to hold the company responsible.

Nonetheless, many lawsuits in U.S. courts name the brand that a smoker first started smoking even if the person smoked many brands of cigarettes in the years and decades that followed. This tactic is based on the assumption that the branding and advertising efforts initially caused a person to smoke. The research evidence on this point is mixed, but researchers now are turning their attention toward experiments testing hypotheses related to the effectiveness of anti-smoking advertisements—particularly those aimed at adolescents. Typically, these experiments involve multiple groups of individuals, each subjected to a different set of conditions, and then each measured on variables related to their actual smoking behavior or favorableness toward smoking.[3] For instance, a set of four groups are given magazines with different types of ads.

- Group 1 views a magazine with several actual ads for cigarettes.
- Group 2 views a magazine with several anti-smoking ads which emphasize negative effects on health.
- Group 3 views a magazine with several anti-smoking ads which emphasize negative effects on one's social life.
- Group 4 views a magazine with no cigarette or anti-smoking ads.

The differences in responses across groups can then be analyzed to examine the effectiveness of the ads. In this case, groups 2 and 3 should be less favorably inclined toward smoking than either group 1 or group 4 if anti-smoking ads are effective. Then, the results from groups 2 and 3 can be compared to each other to see whether teens are more affected by fear of becoming ill or becoming less popular! The extent to which the researchers can truly establish causal evidence eventually will boil down to control.

Introduction

Most students are familiar with scientific experiments from studying physical sciences like physics and chemistry. The term *experiment* typically conjures up an image of a chemist surrounded by bubbling test tubes and Bunsen burners. Behavioral and physical scientists have used experimentation far longer than have marketing researchers. Nevertheless, both social scientists and physical scientists use experiments for much the same purpose.

Experiments are widely used in causal research designs. Experimental research allows a researcher to control the research situation so that *causal* relationships among variables may be evaluated. The marketing experimenter manipulates one or more independent variables and holds constant all other possible independent variables while observing effects on dependent variables. Variables may be controlled in an experiment to a degree not possible in a survey.

A simple example would be thinking about how changes in price might cause changes in sales. Price would be an independent variable and sales would be a dependent variable. The marketing research can experimentally control price by setting it at different levels and then study this problem by examining consumer reactions to each level.

A famous marketing experiment investigated the influence of brand name on consumers' taste perceptions. An experimenter manipulated whether consumers preferred the taste of beer in labeled or unlabeled bottles. One week respondents were given a six-pack containing bottles labeled only with letters (A, B, C). The following week, respondents received another six-pack with brand labels (like Budweiser, Coors, Miller, and so forth). The experimenter measured reactions to the beers after each tasting. In every case, the beer itself was the same. So, every person involved in the experiment drank the very same beer. Therefore, the differences observed in taste, the key dependent variable, could only be attributable to the difference in labeling. When the consumers participating in the experiment expressed a preference for the branded beer, the conclusion is that brand name does influence consumers' taste perceptions.

The Characteristics of Experiments

Marketing experiments often can best be illustrated through examples. Here, we illustrate the characteristics of experiments by describing a study aimed at testing hypotheses inferring the potential causal effects of color. We will refer back to this example throughout this chapter. Key characteristics of experiments are described in the sections that follow.

By now, perhaps you've had an opportunity to explore the editing features of the Qualtrics survey platform. As the name implies, the tool edits a "survey." Typically, surveys are thought of in association with descriptive research designs. Consider the following points in trying to understand the role such tools may play in causal designs.

1. What types of variables can be measured using survey items created with Qualtrics?
2. Would it be possible to implement an experimental manipulation within or in conjunction with a Qualtrics survey application?
3. Is it possible to create a manipulation check with a Qualtrics survey item?

4. How might computer technology assist in randomly assigning subjects to experimental conditions?

Subjects

Here, let's take a look at an experiment investigating how color and lights might influence shoppers. This particular research is highly relevant for those involved in retail management and design. The key decisions center around ways color and lighting can be changed to produce favorable consumer reactions. A corresponding research question is, "What is the effect of color and lighting on shopper patronage (meaning how much someone would shop in the store)?"[4]

Over two hundred female consumers were recruited to participate in the experiment. Participants in experimental research are referred to as **subjects** rather than respondents. This is because the experimenter subjects them to some experimental treatment. Each subject in this experiment was simply asked to provide responses to a "new fashion store" concept. The store would sell women's clothing and accessories to the fashion-minded professional woman.

subjects
The sampling units for an experiment, usually human respondents who provide measures based on the experimental manipulation.

Experimental Conditions

Perhaps the characteristic that most differentiates experimental research from survey research is the manner in which independent variables are created rather than simply measured. The illustration experiment involves two relevant independent variables. Fictitious store environments were created for the experiment. Four different hypothetical store environments were created corresponding to

An experiment can capture whether or not store color can cause differences in consumer preference for products.

different combinations of the independent variable values. Thus, the only thing differing between the four is combination of the predominant store color and the type of lighting.

The color independent variable was created by variously describing the new store as either predominantly blue or predominantly orange. Similarly, the lighting independent variable was created by describing the store as either having bright or soft lights. Exhibit 9.1 illustrates the four different experimental conditions created by combining the two possible values for each independent variable. An **experimental condition** refers to one of the possible levels of an experimental variable manipulation.

experimental condition

One of the possible levels of an experimental variable manipulation.

EXHIBIT 9.1

Experimental Conditions in Color and Lighting Experiment

		Color	
		Blue	**Orange**
Lighting:	Soft	¼ of Participants	¼ of Participants
	Bright	¼ of Participants	¼ of Participants

Subjects were assigned to one of these four condition groups. Each group was assigned a store with one of the four color and lighting combinations as shown in the exhibit. Thus, all participants within a group received the same description. Subjects in different groups received different descriptions. By analyzing differences between the groups, the researcher can see what effects occur due to the two experimentally controlled independent variables.

Independent variables that are not experimental conditions can also be included as a means of statistical control in the analysis of experiments. Researchers refer to these as either blocking variables or covariates. **Blocking variables** are categorical variables like a subject's gender or ethnicity. For example, researchers may group results based on whether respondents are male or female. On the other hand, a continuous variable that is expected to show a statistical relationship with the dependent variables is known as a **covariate**. Once statistical analysis begins, blocking variables are treated in much the same way as experimental variables and covariates are treated like a regression variable. We'll cover the statistical analysis of experiments later in the text.

blocking variables

Categorical variables included in the statistical analysis of experimental data as a way of statistically controlling or accounting for variance due to that variable.

covariate

A continuous variable included in the statistical analysis as a way of statistically controlling for variance due to that variable.

Effects

The key outcome, or dependent variable, in this example is a subject's perception of how much he or she would patronize the store. In this case, a rating scale asking how much each participant thought they would actually visit and buy things at the store was created. The possible scores ranged from 0 to 300. A higher score means higher patronage. Effects are the characteristics of experiments that allow hypotheses to be tested. They can be classified several ways. Here, we will focus on the difference between main effects and interaction effects.

■ MAIN EFFECTS

main effect

The experimental difference in dependent variable means between the different levels of any single experimental variable.

A **main effect** refers to the experimental difference in means between the different levels of any single experimental variable. In this case, there are potential main effects for color and for lighting. Main effects are examined by taking a look at the differences between the experimental variable levels for each experimental variable.

Exhibit 9.2 shows the average patronage score for each experimental condition. The results show that among experimental subjects who rated a blue store, an average patronage score of 153.8 was reported, which is considerably higher than the average of 131.8 reported by subjects who rated an orange store. The lighting experimental variable, however, doesn't seem to make much difference. Subjects in the soft lighting condition reported an average of 144.7 and subjects in the bright lighting condition reported only a slightly lower average of 140.4.

Thus, the conclusion at this point seems to be that changing a store's color can change consumer patronage. A blue store is better than an orange store! On the other hand, lighting doesn't seem to make much difference. Or does it?

EXHIBIT 9.2
**Consumer Average
Patronage Scores in Each
Condition**

		Color		
		Blue	**Orange**	
Lighting:	Soft	148.5	140.1	144.7
	Bright	159.1	122.6	**140.4**
		153.8	131.8	

EXHIBIT 9.2
**Consumer Average
Patronage Scores in Each
Condition**

■ INTERACTIONS

An **interaction effect** is due to a specific combination of independent variables. In this case, it's possible that the combination of color and lighting creates effects that are not clearly represented in the two main effects.

Experimental results are often shown with a line graph as shown in Exhibit 9.3. Main effects are illustrated when the lines are at different heights as is the case here. Notice the blue line is higher than the orange line. The midpoints of the lines correspond to the means of 153.8 and 131.8 for the blue and orange condition, respectively. A lighting main effect is less obvious because the difference between the midpoint between the two soft points (144.7) is not too different than the corresponding height of the two bright points (140.4). When the lines have very different slopes, an interaction is likely present. In this case, the combination of lights and color is presenting an interaction leading to the following interpretation.

interaction effect

Differences in dependant variable means due to a specific combination of independent variables.

EXHIBIT 9.3
**Experimental Graph
Showing Results within Each
Condition**

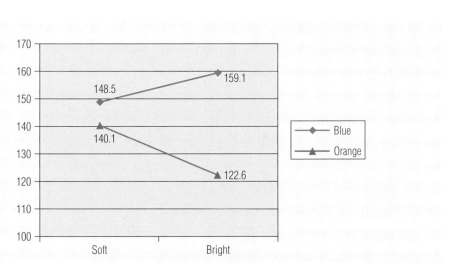

The best possible reaction occurs when the store has a blue color with bright lights and the worst combination occurs when the store is orange with bright lights. In contrast, the means are essentially the same for either color when the lights are soft. So, lights may indeed matter. When the lights are soft, there is little difference in patronage between a blue and orange store. But, when the lights are bright, there is quite a difference between blue and orange.

The pattern of results depicted in Exhibit 9.3 can be contrasted with those from another experiment shown in Exhibit 9.4 on the next page. Here, researchers conducted an experiment to see how different promotions offered by a nightclub might affect the amount of drinks a college student would have during the promotion.[5] The researchers were also interested in potential differences between men and women—a blocking variable. Notice that the line for men is higher than the line for women, suggesting a main effect of sex; men have more drinks than women. Also, the mean number of drinks is higher for the fifty-cent drink promotion than for either of the other two. But, in contrast to our illustration above, the lines are parallel to each other, suggesting that no interaction effect has occurred. In other words, men and women respond to the promotions in the same way.

EXHIBIT 9.4
**Results from Nightclub
Promotion Experiment**

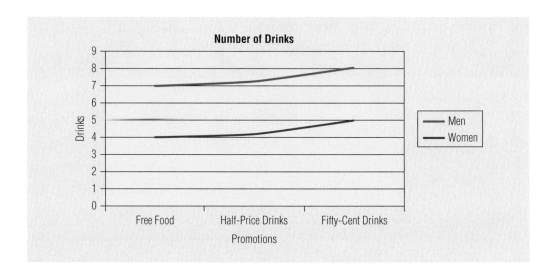

EXHIBIT 9.4
**Results from Nightclub
Promotion Experiment**

Summary of Experimental Characteristics

Experiments differ from ordinary survey research. The differences can be understood by identifying characteristics of experiments. These characteristics include the following:

- Experiments use subjects instead of respondents.
- Experimental variables become the key independent variables. The researcher creates the experimental variables rather than simply measuring them. Measured independent variables are called blocking variables or covariates in experiments.
- Experimental effects are determined by differences between groups formed in the experiment. Main effects are differences in the means based on a single variable. Interaction effects are differences in means based on combinations of two or more variables.

Basic Issues in Experimental Design

Experimental design is a major research topic. In fact, there are courses and books devoted only to that topic.[6] Here, an introduction into experimental design is provided. The terminology introduced in describing experimental characteristics will be helpful in learning how to implement a simple experimental design. Fortunately, most experimental designs in marketing are relatively simple.

Experimental designs involve no less than four important design elements:

1. manipulation of the independent variable
2. selection and measurement of the dependent variable
3. selection and assignment of experimental subjects
4. control over extraneous variables

Manipulation of the Independent Variable

Recall from Chapter 3, the thing that makes independent variables special in experimentation is that the researcher can actually create its values. This is how the researcher manipulates, and therefore controls, independent variables. In our color experiment, the researcher manipulated the values of the color independent variable by assigning it a value of either blue or orange. Experimental independent variables are hypothesized to be causal influences. Therefore, experiments are very appropriate in causal designs.

An **experimental treatment** is the term referring to the way an experimental variable is manipulated. For example, the illustration manipulates the store environment experimental treatment by assigning consumers to evaluate either a blue or orange store. Thus, there were two levels (or values) of the color variable. A medical researcher may manipulate an experimental variable by treating some subjects with one drug and the other subjects with a separate drug. Experimental variables often

experimental treatment

The term referring to the way an experimental variable is manipulated.

involve treatments with more than two levels. For instance, prices of $229, $269, and $299 might represent treatments in a pricing experiment examining how price causes sales for a small under-counter LCD television.

Experimental variables like these can not only be described as independent variables, but they also can be described as a *categorical variable* because they take on a value to represent some classifiable or qualitative aspect. Color, for example, is either orange or blue. Advertising copy style is another example of a categorical or classificatory variable that might be manipulated in an experiment. In other situations, an independent variable may truly exist as a *continuous variable*. When this is the case, the researcher must select appropriate levels of that variable as experimental treatments. For example, lighting can actually be varied over any level from no brightness onward. Price can take on any value but the researcher will only include levels representing relevant distinctions in price in an experiment. Before conducting the experiment, the researcher decides on levels that would be relevant to study. The levels should be noticeably different and realistic.

Marketing research sometimes involves experiments that manipulate different elements of physical environments.

■ EXPERIMENTAL AND CONTROL GROUPS

In perhaps the simplest experiment, an independent variable is manipulated over two treatment levels resulting in two groups, an experimental group and a control group. An **experimental group** is one in which experimental treatment is administered. A **control group** is one in which no experimental treatment is administered. For example, consider an experiment studying how advertising affects sales. In the experimental group, the advertising budget may be set at $200,000. In the control condition, advertising may remain at zero or may not change from its current level. By holding conditions constant in the control group, the researcher controls potential sources of error in the experiment. Sales (the dependent variable) in the two treatment groups are compared at the end of the experiment to determine whether the level of advertising (the independent variable) had any effect. Note that this simple experiment can only produce a main effect. Multiple independent variables are necessary for an interaction to occur.

experimental group

A group of subjects to whom an experimental treatment is administered.

control group

A group of subjects to whom no experimental treatment is administered.

■ SEVERAL EXPERIMENTAL TREATMENT LEVELS

The advertising/sales experiment with one experimental and one control group may not tell the advertiser everything he or she wishes to know. If the advertiser wished to understand the functional nature of the relationship between sales and advertising at several treatment levels, additional experimental groups with advertising expenditures of $250,000, $500,000, and $1 million might be studied. This experiment may still involve a control variable. By analyzing more groups, each with a different treatment level, a more precise result may be obtained than in the simple experimental group–control group experiment described above. This design also can produce only a main effect.

■ MORE THAN ONE INDEPENDENT VARIABLE

An experiment can also be made more complicated by including the effect of another experimental variable. Our extended example involving retail atmosphere would typify a still relatively simple

TOTHEPOINT

A magician pulls rabbits out of a hat. Experimental psychologists pull habits out of rats.

—Unknown

We are never deceived; we deceive ourselves.

—Johann Wolfgang Von Goethe

cell

Refers to a specific treatment combination associated with an experimental group.

two-variable experiment. Since there are two variables, each with two different levels, four experimental groups are obtained. Often, the term **cell** is used to refer to a treatment combination within an experiment. The number of cells involved in any experiment can be easily computed as follows:

$$K = (T_1)(T_2)..(T_m)$$

where K = the number of cells, T_1 = the number of treatment levels for experimental group number one, T_2 = the number of treatment levels for experimental group number two, and so forth through the mth experimental group (T_m). In the illustration experiment, there are two variables each with two levels so the computation is quite simple:

$$K = 2 \text{ (color levels)} \times 2 \text{ (lighting levels)} = 4 \text{ } cells$$

Including multiple variables allows a comparison of experimental treatments on the dependent variable. Since there are more than two experimental variables, this design involves both main effects and interactions.

Selection and Measurement of the Dependent Variable

Selecting dependent variables is crucial in experimental design. Unless the dependent variables are relevant and truly represent an outcome of interest, the experiment will not be useful. Sometimes, the logical dependent variable is fairly obvious. If researchers introduce a new cinnamon, pink grapefruit tea mix in a test-market, sales volume is most likely to be a key dependent variable. However, if researchers are experimenting with different forms of advertising copy appeals, defining the dependent variable may be more difficult. For example, measures of advertising awareness, recall, changes in brand preference, or sales might be possible dependent variables. In the retail atmosphere example, retail patronage was the key dependent variable. However, other potential dependent variables might include perceived product quality, excitement, or price perceptions.

Choosing the right dependent variable is part of the problem definition process. Like the problem definition process in general, it sometimes is considered less carefully than it should be. The experimenter's choice of a dependent variable determines what type of answer is given to assist managers in decision making.

The introduction of the original Crystal Pepsi illustrates the need to think beyond consumers' initial reactions. When Crystal Pepsi, a clear cola, was introduced, the initial trial rate was high, but only a small percentage of customers made repeat purchases. The brand never achieved high repeat sales within a sufficiently large market segment. Brand awareness, trial purchase, and repeat purchase are all possible dependent variables in an experiment. The dependent variable therefore should be considered carefully and more than one can be included in an experiment. Thorough problem definition will help the researcher select the most important dependent variable(s).

Selection and Assignment of Test Units

test units

The subjects or entities whose responses to the experimental treatment are measured or observed.

Test units are the subjects or entities whose responses to the experimental treatment are measured or observed. Individual consumers, employees, organizational units, sales territories, market segments, brands, stores, or other entities may be the test units. People are the most common test units in most marketing and consumer behavior experiments. In our unit retail atmospherics example, individual consumers are the test units as in the Research Snapshot on the next page.

■ SAMPLE SELECTION AND RANDOM SAMPLING ERRORS

As in other forms of marketing research, random sampling errors and sample selection errors may occur in experimentation. For example, experiments sometimes go awry even when a geographic area is specially chosen for a particular investigation. A case in point is an experiment testing a new lubricant for outboard motors by Dow Chemical Company. The lubricant was tested in Florida. Florida was chosen because researchers thought the hot, muggy climate would provide the most demanding test. In Florida the lubricant was a success. However, the story was quite different

Goldfishing or Bluefishing?

Food marketers are often claiming that their brand tastes better than the competitors. When a claim like this is made, it has to be supported somehow or else the company making the claim is liable and risks being sued for making a false or unsubstantiated claim. Thus, research is often needed to produce evidence supporting such claims. Marketers need to be very careful, however, that this type of research is conducted in a rigorous fashion.

Sea Snapper brand gourmet frozen fish products claimed in advertising that their fish sticks are preferred more than two to one over the most popular brand, Captain John's.[7] The advertisements all included a definitive statement indicating that research existed that substantiated this claim. Captain John's sued Sea Snapper over the claim and based the suit on the fact that the research was faulty. Sea Snapper managers conducted taste tests involving four hundred consumers who indicated that they regularly ate frozen food products. Two hundred tasted Sea Snapper premium fish sticks and the other two hundred tasted Captain

John's premium fish sticks. Results showed a main effect with an average preference score for Sea Snapper of 78.2 compared to 39.0 for Captain John's. Case closed? Not hardly. Captain John's attorney hired a marketing research firm to assist in the lawsuit.

The research firm was unable to duplicate the result. After intense questioning of subjects involved in the original research, it turned out that Sea Snapper fish sticks were always presented to consumers on a blue plate while Captain John's were always presented to consumers on a goldfish-colored (a sort of orangish gold) plate. Therefore, the Sea Snapper results could be attributable to a variable other than taste and Captain John's came out as the winner of this legal action—with the help of marketing research.

when the product was sold in Michigan. Although the lubricant sold well and worked well during the summer, the following spring Dow discovered the oil had congealed, allowing the outboard motors, idle all winter, to rust. The rusting problem never came to light in Florida, where the motors were in year–round use. Thus, sample selection error occurs because of flaws in procedures used to assign experimental test units. Here, testing units in Florida created error if the goal was understanding how the product worked in Michigan.

Systematic or nonsampling error may occur if the sampling units in an experimental cell are somehow different than the units in another cell, and this difference affects the dependent variable. For example, suppose some professors are interested in testing the effect of providing snacks during exams on students' scores. The experimental variable is snacks, manipulated over three levels: (1) fruit, (2) cookies, and (3) chocolate. The test units in this case are individual students. When the professors conduct the experiment, for convenience, they decide to give all of the 8 a.m. classes chocolate for a snack, all of the 1 p.m. classes get fruit, and all of the 7 p.m. classes get cookies. While this type of procedure is often followed, if our tastes and digestive systems react differently to different foods at different times of the day, systematic error is introduced into the experiment. Furthermore, because the night classes contain students who are older on average, the professors may reach the conclusion that students perform better when they eat cookies, when it may really be due to the fact that students who are older perform better no matter what they are fed.

■ RANDOMIZATION

Randomization—the random assignment of subject and treatments to groups—is one device for equally distributing the effects of extraneous variables to all conditions. The presence of nuisance variables will not be eliminated, but they will be controlled because they are likely to exist to the same degree in every experimental cell. Thus, all cells would be expected to yield similar average scores on the dependent variables if it were not for the experimental treatments administered in a particular cell. In other words, the researcher would like to set up a situation where everything

systematic or nonsampling error

Occurs if the sampling units in an experimental cell are somehow different than the units in another cell, and this difference affects the dependent variable.

randomization

The random assignment of subject and treatments to groups; it is one device for equally distributing the effects of extraneous variables to all conditions.

Although experiments are often administered in groups, if all groups are not the same, then systematic error is introduced.

in every cell is the same except for the experimental treatment. Random assignment of subjects allows the researcher to make this assumption, thereby reducing the chance of systematic error.

■ MATCHING

Random assignment of subjects to the various experimental groups is the most common technique used to prevent test units from differing from each other on key variables; it assumes that all characteristics of the subjects have been likewise randomized. Matching the respondents on the basis of pertinent background information is another technique for controlling systematic error by assigning subjects in a way that their characteristics are the same in each group. This is best thought of in terms of demographic characteristics. If a subject's sex is expected to influence dependent variable responses, as in a taste test, then the researcher may make sure that there are equal numbers of men and women in each experimental cell. In general, if a researcher believes that certain extraneous variables may affect the dependent variable, he or she can make sure that the subjects in each group are the same on these characteristics.

For example, in a taste test experiment for a dog food, it might be important to match the dogs in various experimental groups on the basis of age or breed. That way, the same number of basset hounds and Dobermans will test formula A, formula B, and formula C. While matching can be a useful approach, the researcher can never be sure that sampling units are matched on all characteristics. Here, for example, even though breeds can be matched, it is difficult to know if all dogs live in the same type of environment (indoors, outdoors, spacious, cramped, with table scraps or without, and so on).

■ REPEATED MEASURES

repeated measures

Experiments in which an individual subject is exposed to more than one level of an experimental treatment.

Experiments in which an individual subject is exposed to more than one level of an experimental treatment are referred to as **repeated measures** designs. Although this approach has advantages, including being more economical since the same subject provides more data than otherwise, it has several drawbacks that can limit its usefulness. We will discuss these in more detail later.

■ EXTRANEOUS VARIABLES

The fourth decision about the basic elements of an experiment concerns control over extraneous variables. This is related to the various types of experimental error. Earlier we classified total survey error into two basic categories: random sampling error and systematic error. The same dichotomy applies to all research designs, but the terms *random (sampling) error* and *systematic error* are more frequently used when discussing experiments.

Experimental Confounds

confound

An experimental confound means that there is an alternative explanation beyond the experimental variables for any observed differences in the dependent variable.

We have already discussed how systematic error can occur when the extraneous variables or the conditions of administering the experiment are allowed to influence the dependent variables. When this occurs, the results will be confounded because the extraneous variables have not been controlled or eliminated. The results can be confounded by an extraneous cause. A **confound** in an experiment means that there is an alternative explanation beyond the experimental variables for any observed differences in the dependent variable. Once a potential confound is identified, the validity of the experiment is severely questioned.

Recall from the Research Snapshot on page 215 that the experimental procedures involved a taste test. The Research Snapshot illustrates how a confound can ruin an experiment. Sea Snapper fish sticks were always presented on a blue plate and Captain John's fish sticks were always presented on a goldish-colored plate. The plate's color is confounding the explanation that the difference in brands is responsible for the difference in liking. Is the difference in liking due to the color or the product quality?

In a simple experimental group–control group experiment aimed at employee task efficiency, if subjects in the experimental group are always administered a treatment (an energy drink) in the morning and then have their efficiency measured also in the morning, and the control group always has their efficiency measured in the afternoon, a constant error has been introduced. In other words, the results will show a difference not only due to the treatment, but also due to the added efficiency that naturally occurs in the morning. In such a situation, time of day represents a confound. On the other hand, other types of error are random and not constant. For example, the natural fluctuations in efficiency that occur from day to day. Random errors are less of a problem for experiments than are contant errors because they do not cause systematic changes in outcomes.

Identifying Extraneous Variables

Most students of marketing realize that the marketing mix variables—price, product, promotion, and distribution—interact with uncontrollable forces in the market, such as competitors' activities and consumer trends. Thus, marketing experiments are subject to the effect of extraneous variables. Since extraneous variables can produce confounded results, they must be identified before the experiment if at all possible.

The chapter vignette illustrates how important isolating causes can be in developing theoretical explanations. Does cigarette advertising cause young people to smoke? One of the primary reasons for the inconclusiveness of this debate is the failure for most of the research to control for extraneous variables.[8] For instance, consider a study in which two groups of U.S. high school students are studied over the course of a year. One is exposed to a greater percentage of foreign television media in which American cigarettes are more often shown in a flattering and glamorous light. In fact, the programming includes cigarette commercials. The other group is a control group in which their exposure to media is not controlled. At the end of the year, the experimental group reports a greater frequency and incidence of cigarette smoking. Did the increased media exposure involving cigarettes cause smoking behavior?

While the result seems plausible at first, the careful researcher may ask the following questions:

- Was the demographic makeup of the two groups the same? While it is clear that the ages of the two groups are likely the same, it is well known that different ethnic groups have different smoking rates. Approximately 28 percent of all high school students report smoking, but the rate is higher among Hispanic teens, for example.[9] Therefore, if one group contained more Hispanics or Asians, we might expect it to report different smoking rates than otherwise.
- How did the control group fill the time consumed by the experimental group in being exposed to the experimental treatment? Could it be that it somehow dissuaded them from smoking? Perhaps they were exposed to media with more anti-smoking messages?
- Were the two groups of the same general achievement profiles? Those who are high in the need for achievement may be less prone to smoke than are other students.
- Although it is a difficult task to list all possible extraneous factors, some that even sound unusual can sometimes have an effect. For example, did the students have equally dispersed birthdays? Researchers have even shown that smoking rates correspond to one's birthday, meaning that different astrological groups have different smoking rates.[10]

Because an experimenter does not want extraneous variables to affect the results, he or she must control or eliminate such variables. It is always better to spend time thinking about how to control for possible extraneous variables before the experiment since often there is nothing that can be done to salvage results after a confounding effect is identified.

Demand Characteristics and Experimental Validity

What are Demand Characteristics?

The term **demand characteristic** refers to an experimental design element that unintentionally provides subjects with hints about the research hypothesis. Researchers cannot reveal the research hypotheses to subjects before the experiment or else they can create a confounding effect. Think about the retail atmospherics experiment. If the subjects were told before they participated that they were going to be involved in an experiment to see if they liked stores that were predominantly orange or predominantly blue, the researcher would never be sure if their responses to the

demand characteristic

Experimental design element or procedure that unintentionally provides subjects with hints about the research hypothesis.

dependent variable were really due to the differences in the experimental stimuli or due to the fact that the subjects were trying to provide a "correct" response. In addition, once subjects know the hypotheses, there is little hope that they will respond naturally.

So, knowledge of the experimental hypothesis creates a confound. This particular type of confound is known as a **demand effect**. Demand characteristics make demand effects very likely.

demand effect

Occurs when demand characteristics actually affect the dependent variable.

Experimenter Bias and Demand Effects

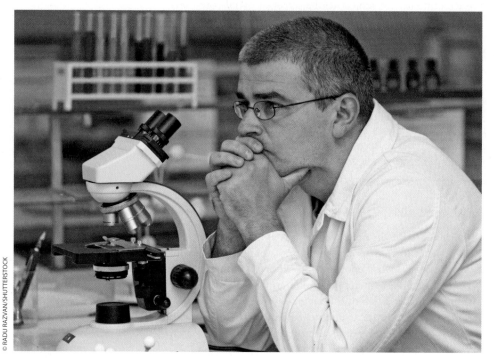

© RADU RAZVAN/SHUTTERSTOCK

The experimenter unintentionally can create a demand effect by smiling, nodding, or frowning at the wrong time.

Demand characteristics are aspects of an experiment that *demand* (encourage) that the subjects respond in a particular way. Hence, they are a source of systematic error. If participants recognize the experimenter's expectation or demand, they are likely to act in a manner consistent with the experimental treatment. Even slight nonverbal cues may influence their reactions.

Prominent demand characteristics are often presented by the person administering experimental procedures. If an experimenter's presence, actions, or comments influence the subjects' behavior or sway the subjects to slant their answers to cooperate with the experimenter, the experiment has introduced *experimenter bias*. When subjects slant their answers to cooperate with the experimenter, they are exhibiting behaviors that might not represent their behavior in the marketplace. For example, if subjects in an advertising experiment understand that the experimenter is interested in whether they changed their attitudes in accord with a given advertisement, they may answer in the desired direction. Acting in this manner reflects a demand effect rather than a true experimental treatment effect.

Reducing Demand Characteristics

Although it is practically impossible to eliminate demand characteristics from experiments, there are steps that can be taken to reduce them. Many of these steps make it difficult for subjects to know what the researcher is trying to find out. Some or all of these may be appropriate in a given experiment.

1. Use an experimental disguise.
2. Isolate experimental subjects.
3. Use a "blind" experimental administrator.
4. Administer only one experimental treatment level to each subject.

■ EXPERIMENTAL DISGUISE

Subjects participating in the experiment can be told that the purpose of the experiment is somewhat different than the actual purpose. Most often, they are simply told less than the complete "truth" about what is going to happen. For instance, in the retail atmosphere study above, subjects were told that they would be asked to react to a new retail store concept. This really is true, but they were not told anything about color, lighting, or any other potential experimental effect.

In other cases, more deceit may be needed. Psychologists studying how much pain one person may be willing to inflict on another might use a ruse telling the subject that they are actually interested in the effect of pain on human performance. The researcher tells the actual subject to administer a series of questions to another person (who is actually a research assistant) and to provide the person with an increasingly strong electric shock each time an incorrect answer is given. In reality, the real dependent variable has something to do with how long the actual subject will continue to administer shocks before stopping.

A **placebo** is an experimental deception involving a false treatment. A **placebo effect** refers to the corresponding effect in a dependent variable that is due to the psychological impact that goes along with knowledge that a treatment has been administered. A placebo is particularly important when the experimental variable involves physical consumption of some product. The placebo should not be different in any manner that is actually noticeable by the research subject. If someone is told that a special food additive will suppress appetite, and they are supposed to sprinkle it on their dinner before eating as part of an experiment, another group should receive a placebo that looks exactly like the actual food additive but actually is some type of inert compound. Both groups are likely to show some difference in consumption compared to someone undergoing no effect. The difference in the actual experimental group and the placebo group would represent the true effect of the additive.

Placebo effects exist in marketing research. For example, when subjects are told that an energy drink is sold at a discount price, they believe it is significantly less effective than when it is sold at the regular, non-discounted price.[11] Later, we will return to the ethical issues involved in experimental deception.

placebo

A false experimental treatment disguising the fact that no real treatment is administered.

placebo effect

The effect in a dependent variable associated with the psychological impact that goes along with knowledge of some treatment being administered.

■ ISOLATE EXPERIMENTAL SUBJECTS

Researchers should minimize the extent to which subjects are able to talk about the experimental procedures with each other. Although it may be unintentional, discussion among subjects may lead them to guess the experimental hypotheses. For instance, it could be that different subjects received different treatments. The experimental integrity will be higher when each only knows enough to participate in the experiment.

■ USE A "BLIND" EXPERIMENTAL ADMINISTRATOR

When possible, the people actually administering the experiment may not be told the experimental hypotheses. The advantage is that if they do not know what exactly is being studied, then they are less likely to give off clues that result in demand effects. Like the subjects, when there is some reason to expect that their knowledge may constitute a demand characteristic, administrators best know only enough to do their job.

■ ADMINISTER ONLY ONE EXPERIMENTAL CONDITION PER SUBJECT

When subjects know more than one experimental treatment condition, they are much more likely to guess the experimental hypothesis. So, even though there are cost advantages to administering multiple treatment levels to the same subject, it should be avoided when possible. For example, in the retail atmospherics example, if subjects responded first to a blue retail store concept, and then saw the same store that was exactly the same except the walls had become orange, then he or she is very likely to know that the researcher is interested in color.

Establishing Control

The major difference between experimental research and descriptive research is an experimenter's ability to control variables by either holding conditions constant or manipulating the experimental variable. If the color of beer causes preference, a brewery experimenting with a new clear beer must determine the possible extraneous variables other than color that may affect an experiment's results and attempt to eliminate or control those variables. Marketing theory tells us that brand image and packaging design are important factors in beer drinkers' reactions. Therefore, the researcher may wish to control the influence of these variables. He or she may eliminate these two extraneous variables by packaging the test beers in plain brown packages without any brand identification.

When extraneous variables cannot be eliminated, experimenters may strive for **constancy of conditions**. This means that subjects in all experimental groups are exposed to identical conditions except for the differing experimental treatments. The principle of matching discussed earlier helps make sure that constancy is achieved.

A supermarket experiment involving four test products shows the care that must be taken to hold all factors constant. The experiment required that all factors other than shelf space be kept constant throughout the testing period. In all stores the shelf level that had existed before the tests began was to be maintained throughout the test period. Only the *amount* of shelf space (the treatment) was changed. One problem involved store personnel accidentally changing shelf level when stocking the test products. This deviation from the constancy of conditions was minimized by auditing each store four times a week. In this way, any change could be detected in a minimum amount of time. The experimenter personally stocked as many of the products as possible, and the cooperation of stock clerks also helped reduce treatment deviations.

If an experimental method requires that the same subjects be exposed to two or more experimental treatments, an error may occur due to the *order of presentation*. For instance, if subjects are examining the effects of different levels of graphical interface on video game enjoyment, and they are asked to view each of four different levels, the order in which they are presented may influence enjoyment. Subjects might perform one level simply because it follows a very poor level. **Counterbalancing** attempts to eliminate the confounding effects of order of presentation by requiring that one fourth of the subjects be exposed to treatment A first, one fourth to treatment B first, one fourth to treatment C first, and finally one fourth to treatment D first. Likewise, the other levels are counterbalanced so that the order of presentation is rotated among subjects.

Basic versus Factorial Experimental Designs

In *basic experimental designs* a single independent variable is manipulated to observe its effect on a single dependent variable. However, we know that complex marketing dependent variables such as sales, product usage, and preference are influenced by several factors. The simultaneous change in independent variables such as price and advertising may have a greater influence on sales than if either variable is changed alone. *Factorial experimental designs* are more sophisticated than basic experimental designs and allow for an investigation of the interaction of two or more independent variables.

Laboratory Experiments

A marketing experiment can be conducted in a natural setting (a field experiment) or in an artificial or laboratory setting. In social sciences, the actual laboratory may be a behavioral lab, which is somewhat like a focus group facility. However, it may simply be a room or classroom dedicated to collecting data, or it can even take place in one's home.

In a **laboratory experiment** the researcher has more complete control over the research setting and extraneous variables. For example, subjects are recruited and brought to an advertising agency's office, a research agency's office, or perhaps a mobile unit designed for research purposes. They are exposed to a television commercial within the context of a program that includes competitors' ads among the commercials shown. They are then allowed to purchase either the advertised product or one of several competing products in a simulated store environment. Trial purchase measures are thus obtained. A few weeks later, subjects are contacted again to measure their satisfaction and determine repeat purchasing intention.

---

constancy of conditions

Means that subjects in all experimental groups are exposed to identical conditions except for the differing experimental treatments.

counterbalancing

Attempts to eliminate the confounding effects of order of presentation by requiring that one fourth of the subjects be exposed to treatment A first, one fourth to treatment B first, one fourth to treatment C first, and finally one fourth to treatment D first.

laboratory experiment

The researcher has more complete control over the research setting and extraneous variables.

Facilities like this one can break down the food that companies sell and tell them exactly what it should taste like. Is this a good way to test the taste of new products?

PHOTO COURTESY OF VICKI BEAVER

This laboratory experiment gives the consumer an opportunity to "buy" and "invest." In a short timespan, the marketer is able to collect information on decision making. Our retail atmospheric experiment also illustrates a laboratory experiment.

Other laboratory experiments may be more controlled or artificial. For example, a **tachistoscope** allows a researcher to experiment with the visual impact of advertising, packaging, and so on by controlling the amount of time a subject is exposed to a visual image. Each stimulus (for example, package design) is projected from a slide to the tachistoscope at varying exposure lengths (1/10 of a second, 2/10, 3/10, and so on). The tachistoscope simulates the split-second duration of a customer's attention to a package in a mass display.

The naturally occurring noise that exists in the field can interfere with experimental manipulations.

tachistoscope

Device that controls the amount of time a subject is exposed to a visual image.

field experiments

Research projects involving experimental manipulations that are implemented in a natural environment.

Field Experiments

Field experiments are research projects involving experimental manipulations that are implemented in a natural environment. They can be useful in fine-tuning marketing strategies and determining sales forecasts for different marketing mix designs.

McDonald's conducted a field experiment testing the Triple Ripple, a three-flavor ice cream product. The product was dropped because the experiment revealed that distribution problems reduced product quality and limited customer acceptance. In the distribution system the product would freeze, defrost, and refreeze. Solving the problem would have required each McDonald's city to have a local ice cream plant with special equipment to roll the three flavors into one. A naturalistic setting for the experiment helped McDonald's executives realize the product was impractical.

Experiments vary in their degree of artificiality and control. Exhibit 9.5 shows that as experiments increase in naturalism, they begin to approach a pure field experiment. As they become more artificial, they approach a pure laboratory experiment.

Generally, subjects know when they are participating in a laboratory experiment. Performance of certain tasks, responses to questions, or some other form of active involvement is characteristic of laboratory experiments. In field experiments, as in test-markets, subjects do not even know they have taken part in an experiment. Ethically, consent should be sought before having

EXHIBIT 9.5

The Artificiality of Laboratory versus Field Experiments

Laboratory experiments — Artificial environmental setting — Natural environmental setting — Field experiments

someone participate in an experiment. However, with field experiments the consent is implied since subjects are not asked to do anything departing from their normal behavior to participate in the experiment. All precautions with respect to safety and confidentiality should be maintained.

Advantages of Between-Subjects Designs

A basic question faced by the researchers involves how many treatments a subject should receive. For economical reasons, the researcher may wish to apply multiple treatments to the same subject. For instance, in the retail atmosphere experiment, each subject could rate each combination of colors and lighting. Thus, four observations on the dependent variable can be obtained from a single subject. Such a design is called a **within-subjects design**. Within-subjects designs involve repeated measures because with each treatment the same subject is measured.

In contrast, the researcher could decide that each person will receive only one treatment combination. This is referred to as a **between-subjects design**. Each dependent variable is measured only once for every subject.

Between-subjects designs are usually advantageous although they are usually more costly. The validity of between-subjects designs is usually higher because by applying only one treatment combination to one subject, demand characteristics are greatly reduced. When a subject sees multiple conditions, he or she is more likely to guess what the study is about. In addition, as we will see later, statistical analyses of between subjects designs are simpler than within-subjects designs. This also means the results are easier to report and explain to management.

Internal Validity

Internal validity exists to the extent that an experimental variable is truly responsible for any variance in the dependent variable. In other words, does the experimental manipulation truly cause changes in the specific outcome of interest? If the observed results were influenced or confounded by extraneous factors, the researcher will have problems making valid conclusions about the relationship between the experimental treatment and the dependent variable.

Thus, a lab experiment enhances internal validity because it maximizes control of outside forces. If we wish to know whether a certain odor causes increased productivity among service workers, we may set up a task in a room with a tightly controlled airflow so we can be sure that the specific odor exists in the air in the amount and intensity desired. We can also control temperature, lighting, density, sounds, and many other factors that would be difficult or impossible to control outside of a lab environment. If the only thing that varies from subject to subject is the odor, then we can safely say that any differences in performance must be attributable to human reactions to the scent.

■ MANIPULATION CHECKS

Internal validity depends in large part on successful manipulations. Manipulations should be carried out in a way that varies the experimental variable over meaningfully different levels. If the levels are too close together, the experiment may lack the power necessary to observe differences in the dependent variable. In a pricing experiment, it may be that manipulating the price of an automobile over two levels, $24,800 and $24,600, would not be successful in creating truly different price categories.

The validity of manipulations can often be checked with a **manipulation check**. If a drug is administered in different dosages that should affect blood sugar levels, the researcher could actually measure blood sugar level after administering the drug to make sure that the dosages were different enough to produce a change in blood sugar. In marketing, the manipulation check is often conducted by asking a survey question or two. In the pricing example above, subjects may be asked a question about how low they believe the price of the car to be. A valid manipulation would produce substantially different average responses to that question in a "high" and "low" price group. Manipulation checks

---

within-subjects design

Involves repeated measures because with each treatment the same subject is measured.

between-subjects design

Each subject receives only one treatment combination.

internal validity

Exists to the extent that an experimental variable is truly responsible for any variance in the dependent variable.

manipulation check

A validity test of an experimental manipulation to make sure that the manipulation does produce differences in the independent variable.

should always be administered after dependent variables in self-response format experiments. This keeps the manipulation check item from becoming a troublesome demand characteristic.

Extraneous variables can jeopardize internal validity. The six major ones are *history, maturation, testing, instrumentation, selection,* and *mortality.*

■ HISTORY

A **history effect** occurs when some change other than the experimental treatment occurs during the course of an experiment that affects the dependent variable. A common history effect occurs when competitors change their marketing strategies during a test marketing experiment. History effects are particularly prevalent in repeated measures experiments that take place over an extended time. If we wanted to assess how much a change in recipe improves individual subjects' consumption of a food product, we would first measure their consumption and then compare it with consumption after the change. Since several weeks may pass between the first and second measurement, there are many things that could occur that would also influence subjects' diets.

Although it may sound extreme, examining the effect of some dietary supplement on various health-related outcomes may require that a subject be confined during the experiment's course. This may take several weeks. Without confining the subject in something like a hospital setting, there would be little way of controlling food and drink consumption, exercise activities, and other factors that may also affect the dependent variables.

A special case of the history effect is the **cohort effect**, which refers to a change in the dependent variable that occurs because members of one experimental group experienced different historical situations than members of other experimental groups. For example, two groups of managers used as subjects may be in different cohorts because one group encountered different experiences over the course of an experiment. If the experimental manipulation involves different levels of financial incentives and performance is the dependent variable, one group may be affected by an informative article appearing in a trade magazine during the experiment. Since the other group participated prior to this group, members of that group could not benefit from the article. Therefore, the possibility exists that the article rather than the change in incentive is truly causing differences in performance.

■ MATURATION

A **maturation effect** is a function of time and the naturally occurring events that coincide with growth and experience. Experiments taking place over longer timespans may see lower internal validity as subjects simply grow older or experienced. Suppose an experiment were designed to test the impact of a new compensation program on sales productivity. If this program were tested over a year's time, some of the salespeople probably would mature as a result of more selling experience or perhaps gain increased knowledge. Their sales productivity might improve because of their knowledge and experience rather than the compensation program.

■ TESTING

Testing effects are also called *pretesting effects* because the initial measurement or test alerts or primes subjects in a way that affects their response to the experimental treatments. Testing effects only occur in a before-and-after study. A before-and-after study is one requiring an initial baseline measure be taken before an experimental treatment is administered. So, before-and-after experiments are a special case of a repeated measures design. For example, students taking standardized achievement and intelligence tests for the second time usually do better than those taking the tests for the first time. The effect of testing may increase awareness of socially approved answers, increase attention to experimental conditions (that is, the subject may watch more closely), or make the subject more conscious than usual of the dimensions of a problem.

■ INSTRUMENTATION

A change in the wording of questions, a change in interviewers, or a change in other procedures used to measure the dependent variable causes an **instrumentation effect**, which may jeopardize internal validity. If the same interviewers are used to ask questions for both before and after

---

history effect

Occurs when some change other than the experimental treatment occurs during the course of an experiment that affects the dependent variable.

cohort effect

Refers to a change in the dependent variable that occurs because members of one experimental group experienced different historical situations than members of other experimental groups.

maturation effect

A function of time and the naturally occurring events that coincide with growth and experience.

testing effects

A nuisance effect occurring when the initial measurement or test alerts or primes subjects in a way that affects their response to the experimental treatments.

instrumentation effect

A nuisance that occurs when a change in the wording of questions, a change in interviewers, or a change in other procedures causes a change in the dependent variable.

measurement, some problems may arise. With practice, interviewers may acquire increased skill in interviewing, or they may become bored and decide to reword the questionnaire in their own terms. To avoid this problem, new interviewers are hired, but different individuals are also a source of extraneous variation due to instrumentation variation. There are numerous other sources of instrument decay or variation. Again, instrumentation effects are problematic with any type of repeated measures design.

■ SELECTION

The selection effect is a sample bias that results from differential selection of respondents for the comparison groups, or sample selection error, discussed earlier.

■ MORTALITY

mortality effect (sample attrition)

Occurs when some subjects withdraw from the experiment before it is completed.

If an experiment is conducted over a period of a few weeks or more, some sample bias may occur due to the **mortality effect (sample attrition)**. Sample attrition occurs when some subjects withdraw from the experiment before it is completed. Mortality effects may occur if subjects drop from one experimental treatment group disproportionately from other groups. Consider a sales training experiment investigating the effects of close supervision of salespeople (high pressure) versus low supervision (low pressure). The high-pressure condition may misleadingly appear superior if those subjects who completed the experiment did very well. If, however, the high-pressure condition caused more subjects to drop out than the other conditions, this apparent superiority may be due to the fact that only very determined and/or talented salespeople stuck with the program.

External Validity

external validity

Is the accuracy with which experimental results can be generalized beyond the experimental subjects.

External validity is the accuracy with which experimental results can be generalized beyond the experimental subjects. External validity is increased when the subjects comprising the sample truly represent some population and when the results extend to market segments or other groups of people. The higher the external validity, the more researchers and managers can count on the fact that any results observed in an experiment will also be seen in the "real world" (marketplace, workplace, sales floor, and so on).

For instance, to what extent would results from our retail atmosphere experiment, which represents a simulated shopping experiment, transfer to a real-world retail store in a shopping mall, downtown mall, or lifestyle center? Can one extrapolate the results from a tachistoscope to an in-store shopping situation? Lab experiments are associated with low external validity because the limited set of experimental conditions, holding all else constant, do not adequately represent all the influences existing in the real world. In other words, the experimental situation may be too artificial. When a study lacks external validity, the researcher will have difficulty repeating the experiment with any change in subjects, settings, or time.

■ STUDENT SURROGATES

Basic researchers often use college students as experimental subjects.[12] Convenience, time, money, and a host of other practical considerations often lead to using students as research subjects. This practice is widespread in academic studies. Some evidence shows that students are quite similar to household consumers, but other evidence indicates that they do not provide sufficient external validity to represent most consumer or employee groups. This is particularly true when students are used as substitutes or surrogates for businesspeople.

The issue of external validity should be seriously considered because the student population is likely to be atypical. Students are easily accessible, but they often are not representative of the total population. This is not always the case, however, and when behaviors are studied for which students have some particular expertise, then they are certainly appropriate. For instance, when researchers are only interested in whether or not some effect might exist at all under any situation, students are as good as any other human subjects. This places the emphasis predominantly on internal validity with no consideration of generalizability. Additionally, students sometimes are very relevant. For example, research directed at understanding how young adults react to mobile phone promotions or how different studying techniques affect test performance can have a great deal of internal and external validity using students. This is because students fit within the population of interest. However, researchers wishing to conduct an experiment addressing a research question aimed at understanding how renovating church facilities affects clergy members' job satisfaction would probably not benefit much from using typical undergraduate business students as subjects. Why would anyone expect these students to behave like clergy?

Trade-Offs Between Internal and External Validity

Naturalistic field experiments tend to have greater external validity than artificial laboratory experiments. Marketing researchers often must trade internal validity for external validity. A researcher who wishes to test advertising effectiveness by manipulating treatments via a split-cable experiment has the assurance that the advertisement will be viewed in an externally valid situation, the subjects' homes. However, the researcher has no assurance that some interruption (for example, a telephone call) will not have some influence that will reduce the internal validity of the experiment. Laboratory experiments with many controlled factors usually are high in internal validity, while field experiments generally have less internal validity, but greater external validity. Ideally, results from lab experiments would be followed up with some type of field test.

Ethical Issues in Experimentation

Ethical issues with experimentation were discussed in Chapter 4 so we touch on them lightly here. The question of deception was raised as a key ethical dilemma in experimentation. Although deception is necessary in most experiments, when subjects can be returned to their prior condition through debriefing, then the experiment is probably consistent with high moral standards. When subjects have been injured significantly or truly psychologically harmed, debriefing will not return them to their formal condition and the experiment should not proceed. Therefore, some additional commentary on debriefing is presented.

Researchers should debrief experimental subjects following an experimental procedure. In fact, many academic researchers, such as those conducting basic marketing research, are required to debrief subjects by their university IRB procedures. Debriefing experimental subjects by communicating the purpose of the experiment and the researcher's hypotheses about the nature of consumer behavior is expected to counteract negative effects of deception, relieve stress, and provide an educational experience for the subject.

> *Proper debriefing allows the subject to save face by uncovering the truth for himself. The experimenter should begin by asking the subject if he has any questions or if he found any part of the experiment odd, confusing, or disturbing. This question provides a check on the subject's suspiciousness and effectiveness of manipulations. The experimenter continues to provide the subject cues to the deception until the subject states that he believes there was more to the experiment than met the eye. At this time the purpose and procedure of the experiment [are] revealed.*[13]

Debriefing therefore is critical because it allows us to return subjects to normal. If this cannot be done through a simple procedure like debriefing, the experiment is likely to be unethical. If an experimenter, for example, took 100 nonsmokers, divided them into 4 groups of 25, and had them smoke 20 or 40 cigarettes a day for 5 years (one experimental variable) that were either called Nicky's or BeFrees (another experimental variable), no debriefing could restore them to normal and therfore, this experiment would likely never be conducted.

Additionally, there is the issue of test-markets and efforts extended toward interfering with a competitor's test-market. When a company puts a product out for public consumption, they should be aware that competitors may also now freely consume the product. When attempts to interfere with a test-market are aimed solely at invalidating test results or they are aimed at infringing on some copyright protection, those acts are ethically questionable.

Using Test-Marketing

The most common type of field marketing experiment is the test market. Test-marketing has three broad primary uses in marketing research. Each use can be broken down more specifically to look at some issue in close detail. The three broad uses are as follows:

1. Forecasting the success of a newly developed product.
2. Testing hypotheses about different options for marketing mix elements.
3. Identifying weaknesses in product designs or marketing strategies.

Forecasting New Product Success

Test-markets have long been used as a pilot test for a new product introduction. While test-markets can be complicated to implement, the basic idea is simple. A product can be marketed on a small scale under actual market conditions and the results used to forecast the success or failure once the product is introduced on a large scale. The opening vignette described how Heineken used a test-market to forecast the success of Heineken Premium Light (HPL) beer. Not to be outdone, Miller is test-marketing very low calorie, amber beer to appeal to health-conscious segments of the population.[14]

Companies using test-markets should realize that a new product concept also involves issues like advertising, pricing, supply chains, and retail placement. These issues may also be manipulated within a test-market. Estimates can then be made about the optimal advertising level, the need for product sampling, retail channel fit, or perhaps even advertising and retail channel selection interaction. Test-marketing permits evaluation of the entire new product concept, not just the physical good itself.

A marketing manager for Life Savers candies vividly portrays this function of experimentation in the marketplace:

> *A market test may be likened to an orchestra rehearsal. The violinists have adjusted their strings, the trumpeters have tested their keys, and the drummer has tightened his drums. Everything is ready to go. But all these instruments have not worked in unison. So a test-market is like an orchestra rehearsal where you can practice with everything together before the big public performance.*[15]

A researcher conducting a test-market may evaluate not only new products' sales as a dependent variable, but also existing products' sales as relevant dependent variables, as seen in the HPL vignette. In this way, test-marketing allows a firm to determine whether a new offering will cannibalize sales from existing products, meaning that consumers are choosing the new offering as a replacement for another product offered by the same company.

For example, Nabisco's cracker business is mature. The company has many brands, and to add positively to overall sales, a new product must tap just the right market segment. Concept testing may suggest that a new cheese flavored saltine is a great concept. But a test-market may show that the consumers who are actually buying the new product are already Nabisco Cheese Nips fans. Rather than buying more Nabisco products, they are actually substituting the lower priced cheese saltines for the old product. Thus, Nabisco may decide not to proceed with the new product. Test-marketing provides the most effective examination of cannibalization prior to full-scale production.

Testing the Marketing Mix

Test-markets are not confined to studying new products or product modifications. They also are equally useful as a field experiment manipulating different marketing plans for existing products. Any element of the marketing mix can be examined with a test-market.

As we all know, retailers rely heavily on weekly flyers distributed through newspapers or through direct mail. This is particularly true in France, where retail advertising is restricted by law in many ways, including the ability to advertise on television. In France, the average

French household receives over 12 kg (26.4 lbs) of retail flyers annually[16] Yet, many have little idea about the effectiveness of different approaches. Should the flyers simply promote low price, or should they emphasize products related to a specific theme? In fact, different flyer styles can significantly affect not only sales, but retailer image too.[17]

The most effective distribution channel may also be indicated in a test-market. DVDs are facing increased competition from other technologies that allow consumers to access movies. Paramount recently test-marketed a different channel for the distribution of a motion picture.[18] In December of 2007, Paramount released *Jackass 2.5*, actually the third in the *Jackass* series of films, for online distribution at the same time the movie was released to theaters. The online version was free, but contained embedded advertisements. Paramount was testing to see how consumers would warm up to this novel method of distribution.

Test-marketing can be used to determine the impact of different promotional approaches on sales and brand image.

Identifying Product Weaknesses

Test-market experimentation also allows identification of previously undetected product or marketing plan weaknesses. The weaknesses can then be dealt with before the company commits to the actual sales launch. Although often this use of test-markets is accidental, in the sense that it isn't the reason for conducting the test-markets, huge sums of resources can be saved by spotting problems before the full-scale marketing effort begins. Often, this use of test-marketing occurs when a product underperforms in at least one location. Researchers can then follow up with other research approaches to try and reveal the reason for the lack of performance. Once identified, product modifications can be made that address these reasons specifically.

McDonald's test-marketed pizza periodically for years. The first test-market provided lower than expected sales results. The reasons for the underperformance included a failure to consider competitors' reactions and problems associated with the small, single portion pizza, which was the only way McPizza was sold. Additionally, McPizza didn't seem to bring any new customers to McDonald's. In the next round of test-marketing, the marketing strategy repositioned the pizza, shifting to a 14-inch pizza that was only sold from about 4 p.m. until closing. With still underwhelming results, McDonald's test-marketed "Pizza Shoppes" within the test McDonald's where employees could be seen assembling ingredients on ready-made pizza dough. Although the concept is still alive, McDonald's has shied away from pizza for the U.S. adult market. A McPizza Happy Meal remains as a sole pizza concept with promise for American stores. Pizza-like products, however, exist and succeed at many McDonald's locations in other nations.

Note that just because a product fails its market test, the test-market can't be considered a failure. In most cases, this represents an important *research success*. Encountering problems in a test-market either properly leads the company to introduce the new product or to make the planned change in marketing strategy. Thus, a huge mistake is likely avoided. In addition, test-market results may lead management to make adjustments that will turn the poor test-market results into a market success. The managerial experience gained in test-marketing can be extremely valuable, even when the performance results are disappointing.

Projecting Test-Market Results

Notice that in all of the uses of test-marketing there is an emphasis on generalizing the results. In other words, researchers do a trial test on a small scale with the hope that the results conducted on that small scale will be equally true when a product is introduced on a larger scale. Therfore, external validity is a key consideration in designing a test-market. Test-markets are not appropriate for research questions that require very rigorous control of internal validity. These latter tests are better done in a lab experiment. However, the fundamental reason that test-markets are conducted is the hope that results can be accurately projected from the sample to the entire market or population of customers. Researchers take several steps to try to make these projections as accurate as they possibly can.

Most researchers support sales data with consumer survey data during test-markets. These help monitor consumer awareness and attitudes toward the test-marketed product as well as the repeat-purchase likelihood. Frequently this information is acquired via consumer panels.

Estimating Sales Volume: Some Problems

Test-marketing is all about estimating how well some product will do in the marketplace. This means that sales projections must be made based on how well a product performs in a test-market. Numerous methodological factors cause problems in estimating national sales results based on regional tests. Often, these problems result from mistakes in the design or execution of the test-market itself.

■ OVERATTENTION

If too much attention is paid to testing a new product, the product may be more successful than it would be under more normal marketing conditions. In the test-market, the firm's advertising agency may make sure that the test-markets have excellent television coverage (which may or may not be representative of the national television coverage). If salespeople are aware that a test is being conducted in their territory, they may spend unusual amounts of time making sure the new product is available or displayed better. This also means that managers should avoid any added incentives that would encourage extra sales efforts to sell the test-marketed product.

■ UNREALISTIC STORE CONDITIONS

Store conditions may be set at the level of the market leader rather than at the national level. For example, extra shelf facings, eye-level stocking, and other conditions resulting from artificial distribution may be obtained in the test-market.

This situation may result from research design problems or overattention, as previously described. For example, if retailers are made aware that someone is paying more attention to their efforts with a given product, they may give it artificially high distribution and extra retail support.

■ READING THE COMPETITIVE ENVIRONMENT INCORRECTLY

Another common mistake is to assume that the competitive environment will be the same nationally as in the test-market. If competitors are unaware of a test-market, the results will not measure competitors' reactions to company strategy. Competitors' responses after a national introduction may differ substantially from the way they reacted in the test-market. On the other hand, competitors may react to a test-market by attempting to undermine it. If they know that a firm is testing, they may attempt to disrupt test-market results with increased promotions and lower prices for their own products, among other potential acts of **test-market sabotage**.

test-market sabotage
Intentional attempts to disrupt the results of a test-market being conducted by another firm.

When Starbucks test-marketed its supermarket brand coffee in Chicago, Procter & Gamble broadcast television commercials touting Millstone coffee's victory over Starbucks in taste tests. The commercials lampooned Starbucks for being more interested in selling T-shirts and novelties than coffee. P&G also offered free samples of Millstone to disrupt the result of Starbucks' test-market.[19]

■ TIME LAPSE

One relatively uncontrolled problem results from the time lapse between the test-market experiment and the national introduction of the product. Often, the time period between the test-market and national introduction is a year or more. Given the time needed to build production capacity, develop channels of distribution, and gain initial sales acceptance, this may be unavoidable. However, the longer the time between the test-market and the actual selling market, the less accurate one should expect the results to be.

Advantages of Test-Marketing

This discussion of test-marketing should make it clear that test-markets are advantageous in ways that are very difficult to match with other research approaches. The key advantage of test-marketing is the real-world setting in which the experiment is performed. Although focus groups and surveys also can be useful in describing what people may like in a new product, the actual behavior of consumers in a real test-market location is far more likely to lead to accurate projections.

A second advantage of test-marketing is that the results are usually easily communicated to management. Although the experiment itself can be difficult to implement for a host of reasons, most of which are related to small-scale or temporary marketing, the data analysis is usually very simple. Very often, the same procedures used in any simple experiment can be used with test-markets. As we will see, this relies heavily on comparing means in some way. Researchers find marketing managers much more receptive to these types of results than they may be to results drawn from complicated mathematical models or qualitative approaches relying on deep subjective interpretation. Many consumer industries depend heavily on test market results for help in decision making. The Research Snapshot on the next page illustrates how marketing managers in the fast-food industry can use test marketing.

Disadvantages of Test-Marketing

Test-markets also have disadvantages. While the power of test-markets in providing accurate predictions are apparently such that companies would use test-markets for all major marketing changes, this is hardly the case. The disadvantages are such that test-markets are used less frequently than one might think.

■ COST

Test-marketing is very expensive. Consider that for most new products, companies have to actually create production facilities on a small scale, develop distribution within selected test-market cities, arrange media coverage specific to those locations, and then have systems and people in place to carefully monitor market results. All of this leads to high cost overall and very high unit costs. Heineken was faced with all these issues in test-marketing HPL. As a result, each six-pack could cost several times over the actual selling price. However, when HPL was introduced throughout the United States, the economies of scale that come with full-scale marketing left unit costs below the selling price.

Test-marketing a packaged-goods product typically costs millions. As with other forms of marketing research, the value of the information must be compared with the research costs. The expense of test-marketing certainly is a primary reason why marketing managers refuse to use the approach. Although they do reduce error in decision making, they are not perfect and certainly some risk

All Fed Up!

Are consumers all fed up? Fast-food companies are among the leaders in test-marketing. Wendy's has had some of the most successful new sandwich launches ever, including the Big Bacon Classic. However, many fast-food restaurants have tried so many variations of food products, that they end up simply recycling old ideas. Marketing managers at these fast-food restaurants are more and more turning toward beverage items as a way of boosting sales and popularity. After all, Starbucks grew from one to over 10,000 locations in just over two decades—and they did it with drinks!

Which fast-food restaurant has the most locations? Well, it turns out the Subway in the subway station is just one of about 30,000 Subway stores making it the most prolific of fast-food franchises. Subway is eyeing the coffee market. So how should they enter this market? Should they offer Starbucks-style coffee drinks in their current locations? Or, should they open stand-alone coffee shops? Subway turned to marketing research to answer this question and test-marketed five Subway Café coffee shops, all in the Washington D.C. area. Many of the fast-food players offer coffee, but the long run strategy is to take advantage of convenient locations in topping the others.

Test-marketing is dynamic in part because of competitve pressures. McDonald's is also trying to capitalize on coffee and other drinks. They too are trying out McCafé stores that are aimed at directly competing with Starbucks. Additionally though, they are test-marketing different types of beverages for their normal menus. Ideally, they would steer people toward fountain beverages that don't conflict with their current soft drink contracts, but they also are test-marketing green tea and diet green tea as well as different soft drinks like Diet Mountain Dew. Considering the relatively high profit margin on drinks relative to food products, Subway, McDonald's, and others focusing on beverages may be glad to have consumers drink up whether they are fed up or not!

Sources: Zmuda, N., "McD's Tries to Slake Consumer Thirst for Wider Choice of Drinks," *Advertising Age*, 79 (June 9, 2008), 1–45; Young, E. B., "Drink Fresh? Subway Tests Out Coffee Concept," *Advertising Age*, 79 (July 14, 2008), 4–26.

remains in basing decisions on test-market results. If they were risk-free, managers would use them far more frequently. Because they are not risk-free and are so expensive, managers may decide to make go or no-go decisions based on less expensive techniques that are often less accurate.

■ TIME

Test-markets cost more than just money. Test-markets cannot be put together overnight. Simply planning a test-market usually takes months. Actually implementing one takes much longer. On top of the time for planning and implementation, researchers also must decide how long is long enough. In other words, when is the amount of data collected sufficient to have confidence in drawing valid conclusions?

The appropriate time period for a test-market varies depending on the research objectives. Sometimes, as in Procter & Gamble's testing of its unique new products Febreze, Dryel, and Fit Fruit & Vegetable Wash, the research takes several years. In other situations, as in P&G's testing of Encaprin pain reliever (a product that ultimately failed in national distribution), the time period may be shorter. HPL's test-markets lasted less than a year, relatively short by most standards.

Thus, even a quickly planned and implemented test-market can cost the firm a year or more in time. During this time, competitors are also trying to gain competitive advantage. The fear that competitors may make a big move first puts added pressure on marketing managers to move quickly. For this reason, the time costs associated with test-markets are a primary reason for forgoing them.

How long should a test-market be? Test-markets should be long enough for consumers to become aware of the product, have a chance to purchase it, consume it, and repurchase it at least one more time. Thus, it must be longer than the average purchase cycle for that particular product. A test-market that is too short may overestimate sales, because typically the early adopters are heavy users of the product. Thus, projections are based on consumers who are far from average.

Time must be allowed for sales to settle down from their initial honeymoon level. In addition, the share and sales levels must be allowed to stabilize. After the introduction of a product, peaks and troughs will inevitably stem from initial customer interest and curiosity as well as from competitive product retaliation.[20]

The Hidden in Hidden Valley Ranch

A few years ago, Hidden Valley Ranch (HVR) conducted a field market experiment to examine how effective three new flavors of salad dressings would be in the marketplace. Thus, there were three levels of the experimental variable, each representing a different flavor. HVR had to produce small batches of each flavor, get them bottled, and ship them to their sales representatives, who then had to stock the dressings in the participating retail stores. All of this was very expensive and the costs to produce each bottle used in a test-market were almost $20.

So, the first day of the test was consumed with sales reps placing the products in the salad dressing sections of retail stores. The second day, each rep went back to each store to record the number of sales for each flavor. By the third day, all of the bottles of all flavors had sold!! Amazing! Was every flavor a huge success??

Actually, one of HVR's competitors had sent their sales reps around beginning on the second day of the test to buy every bottle of the new HVR dressings in every store it had been placed in. Thus, HVR was unable to produce any sales data (the dependent variable) and the competitor was able to break down the dressing in their labs and determine the recipe.

This illustrates one risk that comes along with field tests. Once a product is available for sale, there are no secrets. Also, you risk espionage of this type that can render the experiment invalid.

© GEORGE DOYLE & CIARAN GRIFFIN

© SUSAN VAN ETTEN

■ LOSS OF SECRECY

As pointed out in the Research Snapshot above, one drawback to actual field experimentation is that the marketplace is a public forum. Therefore, secrets no longer exist. In the case of a new product, not only does the competition know about the new product, but a competitor can sometimes benefit from the test-market by monitoring the same dependent variables as is the sponsoring firms. This may cause them to launch a competing product. In some cases, the competitor can even beat the originating company to the national marketplace.

Selecting a Test-Market Site

Selecting test-markets is, for the most part, a sampling problem. The researcher seeks a sample of test-market cities that is representative of the population comprised of all consumers in the relevant marketing area. If a new product is being launched throughout Australia, for example, the researcher must choose cities that are typical of all Australians.

Thus, test-market cities should represent the entire competitive marketplace. For companies wishing to market a product through the United States, there is no single ideal test-market city. Nevertheless, the researcher must usually avoid cities that are not representative of the nation. Regional or urban differences, atypical climates, unusual ethnic compositions, or different lifestyles may dramatically affect a marketing program. Sometimes, although the researchers may wish to sell a product throughout the entire region of the United States, they may have a certain benefit segment in mind. Food companies may introduce a product that is intended for segments that enjoy spicy food, for example. In this case, they may choose cities known to favor spicier, more flavor-filled foods, such as New Orleans and San Antonio. In this case, those test-market cites have populations that fit the benefit segment to which the product is aimed.

Because of the importance of having representative markets for comparisons, certain cities are used repeatedly for test-market operations. Whereas some larger cities like Tampa; Peoria, Illinois; and San Antonio are attractive test-markets, many test-markets are conducted in smaller cities. Exhibit 9.6 on the next page lists several of the most popular U.S. test-markets.[21] Their popularity lies in how close they come to duplicating the average U.S. demographic profile.

Americans and Canadians are similar in many respects. However, one shouldn't assume that a product that is successful in the United States will be successful in Canada. Thus, even after

EXHIBIT 9.6
Popular test-markets and Selected Demographic Characteristics

City	2000 Population	Median Age	Percent of Households w/Children	Hispanic Proportion (Percent)
Cedar Rapids, IA	191,701	35.2	31.8	1.4
Eau Claire, WI	148,337	34.7	31.4	0.8
Grand Junction, CO	116,255	38.1	31.4	10.0
Odessa-Midland, TX	237,132	33.0	38.4	35.8
Pittsfield, MA	84,699	40.6	27.6	1.7
Wichita Falls, TX	140,518	33.6	33.8	11.8
Entire U.S.	281,000,000	35.3	32.8	12.5
Wichita, KS	344,284	34.1	34.6	7.4

a successful American launch, a company may wish to conduct a test-market in Canada. In addition, even if a new product is liked by the Canadian market, a unique marketing approach may be in order. Generally, Calgary, Alberta, is considered a prime test-market location for the Canadian market. When Italy's Podere Castorani Winery wished to expand to Canada, the product was tested in Calgary. Likewise, when Shell introduced a fast-pay charge system, Calgary again proved a suitable test-market. Edmonton also is frequently used to test-market products. Imperial Tobacco selected Edmonton for a test market of SNUS, a smokeless, spitless tobacco product, positioned as a safe alternative relative to smoking cigarettes.[22]

Like the United States, Canada is comprised of many different ethnic segments. Companies should also be aware that French Canada is quite different from the rest of the country. Edmonton may represent Canadians well enough but not French Canadians. Thus, companies may consider a test-market in Quebec City, Quebec, to see how French Canadian consumers will react.

Test-marketing in Europe can be particularly difficult. While companies can test their products country by country, the sheer costs involved with test-marketing motivate firms to look for cities more representative of large parts of Europe. Copenhagen, Denmark, is one such city. While the population is somewhat homogenous demographically, it is also multilingual and receptive to new ideas.[23] Copenhagen is particularly representative of northern Europe. Other cities to be considered include Frankfurt, Germany, Birmingham, England, and Madrid, Spain.

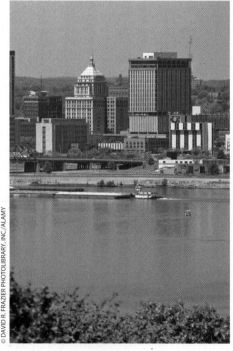

Peoria is considered more representative of the general US population than is Miami.

- Experiments are used to establish causal evidence and represent the primary tool for causal research designs.
  - Experimental manipulations in marketing research should have the following characteristics:
    - Distinct categories or magnitudes of effects
    - Two, three or, at most, four treatment levels per experimental variable. This is particularly true when multiple experimental variables are used in a single study.
    - Randomly applied across the experimental subjects
- Experimental graphs are useful in displaying results, particularly when interactions are involved.
- Laboratory experiments maximize internal validity.

- Field experiments increase external validity at the cost of internal validity.
- Test-markets clearly illustrate the trade-off of internal validity for external validity.
  - They remain one of the best tools for forecasting marketing success prior to implementing an idea full scale.
  - Test-markets remain expensive. Technology offers some virtual alternatives.
- Two big disadvantages of test-markets involve the time they take and the loss of secrecy.
  - When a product can easily be duplicated by competitors simply because they can obtain an actual product, then a test-market may not be wise.
  - Once a competitor knows a test-market is occurring, the risk of sabotage becomes real.

Summary

1. Know the basic characteristics of research experiments. Independent variables are created through manipulation in experiments rather than through measurement. The researcher creates unique experimental conditions that represent unique levels of an independent variable. Experiments are also distinguished from other research in that human sampling units are referred to as subjects rather than respondents. This is because they are subjected to the experimental manipulations. Experimental manipulations are examined for the extent to which they affect outcomes. Main effects are due to differences in observed outcomes based on any single experimental variable. Interaction effects are due to combinations of independent variables.

2. Design an experiment using the basic issues of experimental design. Systematic experimental error occurs because sampling units (research subjects) in one experimental cell are different from those in another cell in a way that affects the dependent variable. In an experiment involving how people respond to color, the researcher would not want to have all males in one color group and all females in another. Randomization is an important way of minimizing systematic experimental error. If research subjects are randomly assigned to different treatment combinations, then the differences among people that exist naturally within a population should also exist within each experimental cell. Additionally, the researcher must try to control for all possible extraneous variables. Extraneous variables can render any causal inference as spurious. Control is possible by holding nonexperimental variables constant across experimental conditions. In this way, the researcher can also help prevent confounds.

3. Know ways of maximizing the validity of experiments including the minimization of demand characteristics. Demand characteristics are experimental procedures that somehow inform the subject about the actual research purpose. Demand effects can result from demand characteristics. When this happens, the results are confounded. Demand characteristics can be minimized by following these simple rules: using an experimental disguise, isolating experimental subjects, using a "blind" experimental administrator, and administering only one experimental treatment combination to each subject. A between-subjects design means that every subject receives only one experimental treatment combination. The main advantages of between-subjects designs are the reduced likelihood of demand effects and simpler analysis and presentation, all of which can improve validity.

4. Avoid unethical experimental practices. Experiments involve deception. Additionally, research subjects are sometimes exposed to stressful or possibly dangerous manipulations. Every precaution should be made to ensure that subjects are not harmed. Debriefing subjects about the true purpose of the experiment following its conclusion is important for the ethical treatment of subjects. If debriefing can restore subjects to their preexperimental condition, the experimental procedures are likely consistent with ethical practice. If subjects are affected in some way that makes it difficult to return them to their prior condition, then the experimental procedures probably go beyond what is considered ethical.

5. **Weigh the trade-off between internal and external validity.** Lab experiments offer higher internal validity because they maximize control of extraneous variables. High internal validity is a good thing because we can be more certain that the experimental variable is truly the cause of any variance in the dependent variable. Field experiments maximize external validity because they are conducted in a more natural setting meaning that the results are more likely to generalize to the actual business situation. The increased external validity comes at the expense of internal validity.

6. **Recognize the appropriate uses of test-marketing.** Major uses of test-marketing include forecasting the success of a newly developed product, testing hypotheses about different options for marketing mix elements, and identifying weaknesses in product designs or marketing strategies. Whereas the first two reasons are usually intentional results in that they are the reason a test-market is implemented in the first place, the last reason often occurs when results from a test-market are less favorable than expected. The two major advantages of test-markets discussed in the chapter are the real-world setting and the ease in interpretation and communication of results. These advantages have to be weighed against several key disadvantages. These include the great amount of money that it costs to conduct a test-market, the length of time it takes to design, implement, and analyze a test-market, and the loss of secrecy that comes when the product is marketed publicly.

Key Terms and Concepts

between-subjects design, *222*
blocking variables, *210*
cell, *214*
cohort effect, *223*
confound, *216*
constancy of conditions, *220*
control group, *213*
counterbalancing, *220*
covariate, *210*
demand characteristic, *217*
demand effect, *218*
experimental condition, *210*

experimental group, *213*
experimental treatment, *212*
external validity, *224*
field experiments, *221*
history effect, *223*
instrumentation effect, *223*
interaction effect, *211*
internal validity, *222*
laboratory experiment, *220*
main effect, *210*
manipulation check, *222*
maturation effect, *223*

mortality effect (sample attrition), *224*
placebo, *219*
placebo effect, *219*
randomization, *215*
repeated measures, *216*
subjects, *209*
systematic or nonsampling error, *215*
tachistoscope, *221*
test-market sabotage, *228*
test units, *214*
testing effects, *223*
within-subjects design, *222*

Questions for Review and Critical Thinking

1. Define *experimental condition, experimental treatment,* and *experimental group.* How are these related to the implementation of a valid manipulation?

2. A tissue manufacturer that has the fourth-largest market share plans to experiment with a 50¢ off coupon during November and a buy one, get one free coupon during December. The experiment will take place at Target stores in St. Louis and Kansas City. Sales will be recorded by scanners from which mean tissue sales for each store for each month can be computed and interpreted.
   a. What are the experimental variable and the dependent variable?
   b. Prepare a mock experimental graph that shows hypothetical results (simply guess at what the mean values for each experimental condition would be).

3. What is the difference between a *main effect* and an *interaction* in an experiment? In question 2, what will create a main effect? Is an interaction possible?

4. In what ways might the design in question 2 yield systematic or nonsampling error?

5. How can experimental graphs be used to show main effects and interactions?

6. What purpose does the random assignment of subjects serve?

7. Why is an experimental confound so damaging to the conclusions drawn from an experiment?

8. What are demand characteristics? How can they be minimized?

9. **ETHICS** Suppose researchers were experimenting with how much more satisfied consumers are with a "new and improved" version of some existing product. How might the researchers design a placebo within an experiment testing this research question? Is using such a placebo ethical or not?

10. If a company wanted to know whether to implement a new management training program based on how much it would improve ROI in its southwest division, would you recommend a field or lab experiment?

11. **'NET** Suppose you wanted to test the effect of three different e-mail requests inviting people to participate in a survey posted on the Internet. One simply contained a hyperlink with no explanation, the other said if someone participated $10 would be donated to charity, and the other said if someone participated he or she would have a chance to win $1,000. How would this experiment be conducted differently based on whether it was a between-subjects or within-subjects design? What are the advantages of a between-subjects design?

12. What is a manipulation check? How does it relate to internal validity?
13. **ETHICS** What role does debriefing play in ensuring that experimental procedures are consistent with good ethical practice?
14. Define internal validity and external validity. It's been said that external validity decreases when internal validity is high. Do you believe that is so? Explain your answer.

15. The idea of nonspurious association was introduced in Chapter 3. How does a confounding variable affect whether an association is spurious or nonspurious?
16. Why is a test-market usually considered an experiment?
17. When is test-marketing likely to be conducted? When is it not as appropriate? Which type of validity is most relevant to test-marketing?
18. What are the advantages and disadvantages of test-marketing?

Research Activities

1. Consider the situation of a researcher approached by Captain John's in the Research Snapshot on page 215.
   a. Provide a critique of the procedures used to support the claim that Sea Snapper's product is superior. Prepare it in a way that it could be presented as evidence in court.
   b. Design an experiment that would provide a more valid test of the research question, "Do consumers prefer Sea Snapper fish sticks compared to Captain John's fish sticks?"

2. Conduct a taste test involving some soft drinks with a group of friends. Pour them several ounces of three popular soft drinks and simply label the cups A, B, and C. Make sure they are blind to the actual brands. Then, let them drink as much as they want and record how much of each they drink. You may also ask them some questions about the drinks. Then, allow other subjects to participate in the same test, but this time, let them know what the three brands are. Record the same data and draw conclusions. Does brand knowledge affect behavior and attitudes about soft drinks?

Case 9.1 Examining Product Failure at No-Charge Electronics

No-Charge Electronics owner Buzz Auphf needs to know how much product failure affects customer loyalty. Buzz contacts David Handy, a local market researcher, and they ultimately decide on examining a research question asking, "How do current customers react to different levels of product failure?" David designs the following experiment to examine the causal effect of product failure on customer purchase intentions, satisfaction, and loyalty.

The experiment is implemented via e-mail using a sample of current and prospective customers. Three free MP3 movies are provided as an incentive to participate. Subjects are asked to click

through to an Internet site to download a product that will enhance their computer's graphics capability. In the low-failure condition, after the subjects click to the site, there is no change in the graphics of their computers. In the high-failure condition, once they click through to the site, the subjects' computers go into an infinite loop of obscene graphical images until a message arrives indicating that a severe virus has infected their computer and some files may be permanently damaged. This goes on for forty-five minutes with no remedy. At that time, a debriefing message pops up telling subjects that it was all part of an experiment and that their computer should now function properly. Prepare a position statement either agreeing or disagreeing that the experiment is consistent with good ethical practice.

Case 9.2 Tooheys

Sixty-six willing Australian drinkers helped a Federal Court judge decide that Tooheys didn't engage in misleading or deceptive advertising for its 2.2 beer. The beer contains 2.2 percent alcohol, compared to 6 percent for other beers leading to a claim that could be interpreted as implying it was non-alcoholic.

Volunteers were invited to a marathon drinking session after the Aboriginal Legal Service claimed Tooheys' advertising implied beer drinkers could imbibe as much 2.2 as desired without becoming legally intoxicated. Drunken driving laws prohibit anyone with a blood-alcohol level above 0.05 from getting behind the wheel in Australia.

So, an experiment was conducted to see what happens when a lot of 2.2 is consumed. But the task wasn't easy or that much fun. Some subjects couldn't manage to drink the required 10 "middies," an Aussie term for a beer glass of 10 fluid ounces, over the course of an hour.

Thirty-six participants could manage only nine glasses. Four threw up and were excluded. Two more couldn't manage the "minimum" nine glasses and had to be replaced.

Justice J. Beaumont observed that consuming enough 2.2 in an hour to reach the 0.05 level was "uncomfortable and therefore an unlikely process." Because none of the ads mentioned such extreme quantities, he ruled they couldn't be found misleading or deceptive.[24]

Questions
1. Would a lab experiment or a field experiment be more "valid" in determining whether Tooheys could cause a normal beer consumer to become intoxicated? Explain.
2. Describe an alternate research design that would have higher validity.
3. Is the experiment described in this story consistent with good ethical practice? Likewise, comment on how the design described in part 2 would be made consistent with good ethical practices.
4. Is validity or ethics more important?

© GETTY IMAGES/ PHOTODISC GREEN

Part 3
Measurement

© BRAND X PICTURES/JUPITER IMAGES

CHAPTER 10
Measurement and Attitude Scaling

CHAPTER 11
Questionnaire Design

CHAPTER 10
MEASUREMENT AND ATTITUDE SCALING

After studying this chapter, you should be able to

1. Determine what needs to be measured based on a research question or hypothesis
2. Distinguish levels of scale measurement
3. Know how to form an index or composite measure
4. Perform a basic assessment of scale reliability and validity
5. Define attitude and understand why it is so important in business research
6. Produce a scale that measures an attitudinal concept
7. Implement a multi-attribute model

Chapter Vignette: Do You Know How to Score?

What if you could predict a firm's profitability by asking consumers a single survey question? Obviously, such a breakthrough would be extremely beneficial in diagnosing problems with company performance and trying to take corrective action. This is the idea behind the net promoter score (NPS). It represents how favorable a customer is toward a business by asking them a single survey item scored on a 0 to 10 scale:

On the 0 to 10 point scale shown below, how likely is it that you would recommend Blackberry to a friend or colleague?										
0	1	2	3	4	5	6	7	8	9	10

Consumers are labeled based on their scale response. A score of 6 or below is associated with a label of detractor, a score of 7 or 8 is labeled passively satisfied, and a score of 9 or 10 signifies a promoter. Companies with a high proportion of promoters are said by some to significantly outperform competitors.

Obviously, the simplicity of this approach is attractive to many businesses. However, the method is not without controversy. Questions about the usefulness and the validity of this approach have surfaced. Some question exactly what this item measures. The content does not match well with satisfaction, nor does it perfectly match loyalty or patronage intention. Each is undoubtedly important. The NPS best represents an intent to spread positive word of mouth. Others question the one-size-fits-all approach or suggest that although the item may

© WORKBOOK STOCK/JUPITER IMAGES

predict, the prediction accuracy is far from perfect and leaves room for other concepts to explain variance in performance. Still others question just how well this single item predicts performance by conducting survey research and tying the result to firm performance.

Some question how valuable this single rating item really is. They claim that without controlling for other factors, any correlation that is found could be misleading. Alternatively, some firms have broken their organizations down into functions (service, sales, etc.) and developed an NPS for each area, claiming the information obtained is richer and more useful. However, despite the shortcomings, it is doubtful that competitive firms would trade even a single promoter for dozens of detractors or even a handful of passively satisfied customers. So, this single item certainly helps managers know the score![1]

Introduction

Anyone who has ever followed a recipe knows the importance of good measurement. Following a recipe may seem easy, but understanding the quantities represented and the units of measure can be critical. If a mistake is made in measuring something, the dish may be completely ruined. Just as in the culinary arts, business and marketing concepts can often be measured in more than one way. Also, researchers often may have to use imperfect measurement devices. When a concept is measured poorly, the "recipe" is a likely disaster. Only in this case, the "recipe" is usually an important business decision poorly made instead of a ruined dish.

What to Measure

What does it mean for a business to perform well? Managers can't know if their business is performing well without good measurement. However, researchers may not always know exactly what defines good performance.

measurement

The process of describing some property of a phenomenon of interest, usually by assigning numbers in a reliable and valid way.

The decision statement, corresponding research questions, and research hypotheses can be used to decide what concepts need to be measured in a given project. **Measurement** is the process of describing some property of a phenomenon, usually by assigning numbers, in a reliable and valid way. The numbers convey information about the property being measured. When numbers are used, the researcher must have a rule for assigning a number to an observation in a way that provides an accurate description.

Measurement can be illustrated by thinking about the way instructors assign students' grades. A grade represents a student's performance in a class. Students with higher performance should receive a different grade than do students with lower performance. Even the apparently simple concept of student performance is measured in many different ways. Consider the following options:

1. A student can be assigned a letter corresponding to his/her performance as is typical of U.S.-based grading systems.
   a. A — Represents excellent performance
   b. B — Represents good performance
   c. C — Represents average performance
   d. D — Represents poor performance
   e. F — Represents failing performance
2. A student can be assigned a number from 1 to 20, which is the system more typically used in France.
   a. 20 — Represents outstanding performance
   b. 11–20 — Represent differing degrees of passing performance
   c. Below 11 — Represent failing performance
3. A student can be assigned a number corresponding to a percentage performance scale.
   a. 100 percent — Represents a perfect score. All assignments are performed correctly.

Take a look at the section of the student survey shown in the screenshot. Suppose someone thought the items made a composite scale and you are asked to analyze its quality. Answer the following questions:

1. Is the level of measurement nominal, ordinal, interval, or ratio?
2. Assuming the scale items represent studying concentration, do you think any of the items need to be reverse-coded before a summated scale could be formed? If so, which ones?
3. Using the data for these items, compute the coefficient α and draw some conclusion about the scale's reliability.

4. At this point, how much can be said about the scale's validity? Are there any items that do not belong on the scale?

Please read the following statements. After reading click the square that best describes how much you agree with each statement.

	Strongly Agree	Agree	Neutral	Disagree	Strongly Disagree
I make time to study every day.	○	○	○	○	○
I know the material better after I study.	○	○	○	○	○
I can't study when it's quiet.	○	○	○	○	○
I prefer to not be around others when I study.	○	○	○	○	○
I can study the night before and be ready for a test.	○	○	○	○	○
I like to study with others.	○	○	○	○	○
I arrange time to study with others.	○	○	○	○	○

b. 60–99 percent — Represents differing degrees of passing performance, each number representing the proportion of correct work.
c. 0–59 percent — Represents failing performance but still captures proportion of correct work.

4. A student can be assigned one of two letters corresponding to performance.
a. P — Represents a passing mark
b. F — Represents a failing mark

Each scale also has the potential of producing error or some lack of validity. Exhibit 10.1 illustrates a common student performance measurement application.

Student	Percentage Grade	Difference from Next Highest Grade	Letter Grade
1	79.4%	0.5%	C
2	70.0%	9.4%	C
3	69.0%	1.0%	D
4	79.9%	NA	B

EXHIBIT 10.1
Are There Any Validity Issues with This Measurement?

Often, instructors may use a percentage scale all semester long and then at the end, have to assign a letter grade for a student's overall performance. Does this produce any measurement problems? Consider two students who have percentage scores of 79.4 and 70.0, respectively. The most likely outcome when these scores are translated into "letter grades" is that each receives a C (the common ten-point spread would yield a 70–80 percent range for a C). Consider a third student who finishes with a 69.0 percent average and a fourth student who finishes with a 79.9 percent average.

Which students are happiest with this arrangement? The first two students receive the same grade, even though their scores are 9.4 percent apart. The third student gets a grade lower (D) performance than the second student, even though their percentage scores are only 1.0 percentage point different. The fourth student, who has a score only 0.5 percent higher than the first student, would receive a B. Thus, the measuring system (final grade) suggests that the fourth student outperformed the first (assuming that 79.9 is rounded up to 80) student (B versus C), but the first student did not outperform the second (each gets a C), even though the first and second students have the greatest difference in percentage scores.

A strong case can be made that error exists in this measurement system. All measurement, particularly in the social sciences, contains error. Researchers, if we are to represent concepts truthfully, must make sure that the measures used, if not perfect, are accurate enough to yield correct conclusions. Making use of measures requires that the flaws in measures are at least somewhat understood. When this is the case, researchers can sometimes account for the error statistically. Ultimately, research would be impossible without measurement.

Concepts

concept

A generalized idea that represents something of meaning.

A researcher has to know what to measure before knowing how to measure something. The problem definition process should suggest the concepts that must be measured. A **concept** can be thought of as a generalized idea that represents something of meaning. Concepts such as *age, sex, education,* and *number of children* are relatively concrete having relatively unambiguous meanings. They present few problems in either definition or measurement. Other concepts are more abstract. Concepts such as *loyalty, personality, channel power, trust, corporate culture, customer satisfaction, value,* and so on are more difficult to both define and measure. For example, *loyalty* has been measured as a combination of customer share, the relative proportion of a person's purchases going to one competing brand/store and commitment, or the degree to which a customer will sacrifice to do business with a brand/store.[2] The first component is a behavioral measure and the second is attitudinal.

Operational Definitions

operationalization

The process of identifying scale devices that correspond to properties of a concept involved in a research process.

Researchers measure concepts through a process known as **operationalization**. This process involves identifying scales that correspond to properties of the concept. **Scales**, just as a scale you may use to check your weight, provide a range of values that correspond to different characteristics in the concept being measured. In other words, scales provide **correspondence rules** that indicate that a certain value on a scale corresponds to some true value of a concept. Hopefully, they do this in a truthful way.

scale

A device providing a range of values that correspond to different characteristics or amounts of a characteristic exhibited in observing a concept.

Here is an example of a correspondence rule: "Assign numerals 1 through 7 according to how much individual customers trust a sales representative. If a customer judges a sales representative as completely trustworthy, assign a 7. If the sales rep is perceived as completely untrustworthy, assign the numeral 1. Numbers in between represent varying degrees of trust." The opening vignette describes the concept of NPS and its correspondence rules.

correspondence rules

Indicate the way that a certain value on a scale corresponds to some true value of a concept.

■ VARIABLES

Researchers use the variance in concepts to make meaningful diagnoses. Therefore, when we defined *variables*, we really were suggesting that variables capture different values of a concept. Scales capture a concept's variance and, as such, the scales provide the researcher's variables. Thus, for practical purposes, once a research project is under way, a *concept* and a *variable* represent essentially the same thing. Consider the following hypothesis:

> *H1: Experience* is positively related to *job performance.*

The hypothesis implies a relationship between two variables, experience and job performance. The variables capture variance in the experience and performance concepts. One employee may have fifteen years of experience and be a top performer. A second may have ten years experience and be a good performer. The scale used to measure experience is quite simple in this case and would involve simply providing the number of years an employee has been with the company. Job performance is captured by a scale in which a supervisor places the employee into a category.

◼ CONSTRUCTS

Sometimes, a single variable cannot capture a concept alone. Using multiple variables to measure one concept can often provide a more complete account of some concept than could any single variable. Even in the physical sciences, multiple measurements are often used to make sure an accurate representation is obtained. In social science, many concepts are measured with multiple measurements.

A **construct** is a term used for concepts that are measured with multiple variables. For instance, when a marketing researcher wishes to measure a salesperson's customer orientation, several variables like these may be used, each captured on a 1–5 scale of some type:

1. I offer the product that is best suited to a customer's problem.
2. A good employee has to have the customer's best interests in mind.
3. I try to find out what kind of products will be most helpful to a customer.[3]

Operational definitions translate conceptual definitions into measurement scales. An operational definition is like a manual of instructions or a recipe: even the truth of a statement like "Gaston likes seafood gumbo" depends on the recipe and the ingredients. Different instructions lead to different results.[4]

Levels of Scale Measurement ⬅

Marketing researchers use many scales or numbering systems. Not all scales capture the same richness in a measure. Not all concepts require a rich measure. But, all measures can be classified based on the way they represent distinctions between observations of the variable being captured. The four levels or types of scale measurement are *nominal, ordinal, interval,* and *ratio level scales.* Traditionally, the level of scale measurement is seen as important because it determines the mathematical comparisons that are allowable. Each of the four scale levels offers the researcher progressively more power in analyzing and testing the validity of a scale.

Nominal Scale

Nominal scales represent the most elementary level of measurement. A nominal scale assigns a value to an object for identification or classification purposes. The value can be a number, but does not have to be a number, because no quantities are being represented. In this sense, a nominal scale is truly a qualitative scale. Nominal scales are extremely useful even though some may consider them elementary.

Marketing researchers use nominal scales quite often. For instance, suppose Barq's Root Beer was experimenting with three different types of sweeteners (cane sugar, corn syrup, or fruit extract) in an effort to see which created the best tasting soft drink. Basically, Barq's researchers designed a taste test experiment.

construct

A term used to refer to concepts measured with multiple variables.

nominal scales

Represent the most elementary level of measurement in which values are assigned to an object for identification or classification purposes only.

Athletes wear nominal numbers on their jerseys.

Experimental subjects taste one of the three recipes and then rate how much they like it and how likely they would be to buy that particular drink. The researchers would like the experiment to be blind so that subjects' perceptions are not biased by their beliefs about different sweeteners. Thus, when subjects are actually asked to taste one of the three root beers, the drinks are labeled A, B, or C, not cane sugar, corn syrup, or fruit extract. The A, B and C becomes the measuring system that represents the variance in sweeteners.

Nominal scaling is arbitrary in the sense that each label can be assigned to any of the categories without introducing error; for instance, in the root beer example above, the researcher can assign the letter C to any of the three options without damaging scale validity. Cane sugar could just as properly be labeled C as A, or B. The researcher might use numbers instead of letters without any change in the validity of the measuring system. If so, cane sugar, corn syrup, and fruit extract might be identified with the numbers 1, 2, and 3, respectively, or even 543, −26, and 8080, respectively. Either set of numbers is equally valid since the numbers are not representing different quantities. They are simply identifying the type of sweetener.

We encounter nominal numbering systems all the time. Uniform numbers are nominal numbers. Tom Brady is identified on the football field by his jersey number. What is his number? Airport terminals are identified with a nominal numbering system. In the Atlanta airport, a departing traveler has to go through terminals T, A, B, C, and D before reaching an international departure gate at terminal E. School bus numbers are nominal in that they simply identify a bus. Elementary school buses sometimes use both a number and an animal designation to help small children get on the right bus. So, bus number "8" may also be the "tiger" bus.

The first drawing in Exhibit 10.2 depicts the number 7 on a horse's colors. This is merely a label to allow bettors and racing enthusiasts to identify the horse. The assignment of a 7 to this horse does not mean that it is the seventh fastest horse or that it is the seventh biggest, or anything else meaningful. But, the 7 does let you know when you have won or lost your bet!

Exhibit 10.3 lists some nominal scales commonly used by marketing researchers. Nominal scale properties mean the numbering system simply identifies things.

ordinal scales

Ranking scales allowing things to be arranged based on how much of some concept they possess.

Ordinal Scale

Ordinal scales have nominal properties, but they also allow things to be arranged based on how much of some concept they possess. In other words, an ordinal scale is a ranking scale. When a professor assigns an A, B, C, D, or F to a student at the end of the semester, he or she is using an ordinal scale.

Research participants often are asked to *rank order* things based on preference. So, preference is the concept, and the ordinal scale lists the options from most to least preferred, or vice versa. In this sense, ordinal scales are somewhat arbitrary, but not nearly as arbitrary as a nominal scale. Five objects can be ranked from 1–5 (least preferred to most preferred) or 1–5 (most preferred to least preferred) with no loss of meaning.

When business professors take some time off and go to the race track, even they know that a horse finishing in the "show" position has finished after the "win" and "place" horses (see the second drawing in Exhibit 10.2).

Without nominal scales, how would you know which terminal to go to at this airport?

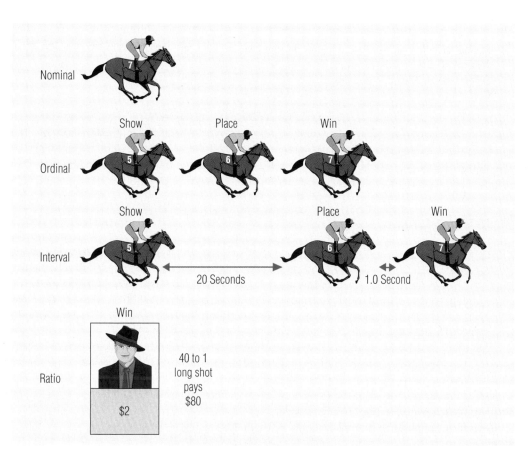

Nominal

Show   Place   Win

Ordinal

Show   Place   Win

Interval

20 Seconds   1.0 Second

Win

Ratio

40 to 1 long shot pays $80

$2

EXHIBIT 10.3

Facts About the Four Levels of Scales

Level	Examples	Numerical Operations	Descriptive Statistics
Nominal	Yes – No Female – Male Buy – Did Not Buy Postal Code: _____	Counting	• Frequencies • Mode
Ordinal	Rankings Choose from the Following: • Dissatisfied • Satisfied • Very Satisfied • Delighted Indicate Your Level of Education: • HS Diploma • Some College • Bachelor's Degree • Graduate Degree	Counting and Ordering	• Frequencies • Mode • Median • Range
Interval	100-Point Job Performance Ratings Assigned by Supervisors: 0% = Worst Performers 100% = Best Performers Temperature-Type Attitude Scales: Low Temperature = Bad Attitude High Temperature = Good Attitude	Common Arithmetic Operations	• Mean • Median • Variance • Standard Deviation
Ratio	Amount Purchased Salesperson Sales Volume Likelihood of performing some act: • 0%=No Likelihood to • 100%=Certainty Number of stores visited Time spent viewing a particular web page Number of web pages viewed	All Arithmetic Operations	• Mean • Median • Variance • Standard Deviation

The order of finish can be accurately represented by an ordinal scale using an ordered number rule:

- Assign 1 to the "win" position
- Assign 2 to the "place" position
- Assign 3 to the "show" position

Sometimes, the winning horse defeats the place horse by only a nose, but other times, the place horse defeats the show horse by 20 seconds or more. An ordinal scale does not tell by how much a horse won, but is good enough to separate winning bets from losing bets. Typical ordinal scales in marketing research ask respondents to rate brands, companies, and the like as excellent, good, fair, or poor. Researchers know excellent is higher than good, but they do not know by how much.

Interval Scale

interval scales

Scales that have both nominal and ordinal properties, but that also capture information about differences in quantities of a concept from one observation to the next.

Interval scales have both nominal and ordinal properties, but they also capture information about differences in quantities of a concept. So, not only would a sales manager know that a particular salesperson outperformed a colleague, but the manager would know by how much. If a professor assigns grades to term papers using a numbering system ranging from 1.0–20.0, not only does the scale represent the fact that a student with a 16.0 outperformed a student with a 12.0, but the scale would show by how much (4.0).

The third drawing in Exhibit 10.2 depicts a horse race in which the win horse is one second ahead of the place horse, which is 20 seconds ahead of the show horse. Not only are the horses identified by the order of finish, but the difference between each horse's performance is known. So, using an interval scale we know horse number 7 and horse number 6 performed similarly, but horse number 5 performed not nearly as well.

A classic example of an interval scale is a Fahrenheit temperature scale. Consider the following weather:

- June 6 was 80° F
- December 7 was 40° F

The interval Fahrenheit scale lets us know that December 7 was 40° F colder than June 6. But, we cannot conclude that December 7 was twice as cold as June 6. Although the actual numeral 80 is indeed twice as great as 40, remember that this is a scaling system. In this case, the scale is not iconic, meaning that it does not exactly represent some phenomenon. In fact, these temperatures can be converted to the more common Celsius scale. Then, the following would result:

- June 6 was 26.7° C
- December 7 was 4.4° C

Obviously, now we can see that December 7 was not twice as cold as June 6. December 7 was 40° F or 22.3° C cooler, depending upon your thermometer. Interval scales are very useful because they capture relative quantities in the form of distances between observations. No matter what thermometer is used, December 7 was colder than June 6.

Ratio Scale

ratio scales

Represent the highest form of measurement in that they have all the properties of interval scales with the additional attribute of representing absolute quantities; characterized by a meaningful absolute zero.

Ratio scales represent the highest form of measurement in that they have all the properties of interval scales with the additional attribute of representing absolute quantities. Interval scales represent only relative meaning whereas ratio scales represent absolute meaning. In other words, ratio scales provide iconic measurement. Zero, therefore, has meaning in that it represents an absence of some concept.

An absolute zero is a defining characteristic in determining between ratio and interval scales. For example, money is a way to measure economic value. Consider the following items offered for sale in an online auction:

- Antique railroad pocket watch circa 1910—sold for $50
- Authentic Black Forest cuckoo clock—sold for $75

- Antique gold-filled Elgin wristwatch circa 1950—sold for $100
- "Antique" 1970s digital watch—did not sell and there were no takers for free

We can make the ordinal conclusions that the cuckoo clock was worth more than the pocket watch and that the wristwatch was worth more than the cuckoo, all of which were worth more than the 1970s digital watch. We can make interval conclusions such as that the cuckoo was worth $25 more than the pocket watch. We can also conclude that the wristwatch was worth twice as much as the pocket watch and that the 1970s watch was worthless (selling price = $0.00). The latter two conclusions are possible because money price represents a ratio scale.

Temperature can also be captured by a ratio scale. The Kelvin scale begins at 0 K, corresponding to −273.2° on the Celsius scale (an interval scale). This temperature is known as absolute zero. Zero K is the point at which the kinetic energy of atoms in a water molecule approaches 0, meaning that they are moving as slowly as possible. This is as cold as water can get since there is no way of slowing the molecules further (they never completely stop). Thus, 0 K indeed has absolute meaning.

When a manager assigns a performance commission based directly on the amount of sales produced, the bonus is based on a ratio scale. Zero has an absolute meaning, particularly if you are the one without a bonus! Griff could decide to use a ratio sales measure to rank performance for the CRM division. This would be valid only if performance was truly equal to sales.

Mathematical and Statistical Analysis of Scales

While it is true that mathematical operations can be performed with numbers from nominal scales, the result may not have a great deal of meaning. For instance, a school district may perform mathematical operations on the nominal school bus numbers. With this, they may find that the average school bus number is 77.7 with a standard deviation of 20.5. Will this help them use the buses more efficiently or better assign bus routes? Probably not. Thus, although you can put numbers into formulas and perform calculations with almost any numbers, the researcher has to know the meaning behind the numbers before useful conclusions can be drawn.[5]

■ DISCRETE MEASURES

Discrete measures are those that take on only one of a finite number of values. A discrete scale is most often used to represent a classificatory variable. Therefore, discrete scales do not represent intensity of measures, only membership. Common discrete scales include any yes-or-no response, matching, color choices, or practically any scale that involves selecting from among a small number of categories. Thus, when someone is asked to choose from the following responses

- Disagree
- Neutral
- Agree

the result is a discrete value that can be coded 1, 2, or 3, respectively. This is also an ordinal scale to the extent that it represents an ordered arrangement of agreement. Nominal and ordinal scales are discrete measures.

Certain statistics are most appropriate for discrete measures. Exhibit 10.3 shows statistics for each scale level. The largest distinction is between statistics used for discrete versus continuous measures. For instance, the central tendency of discrete measures is best captured by the mode. When a student wants to know what the most likely grade is for MKTG4311, the mode will be very useful. Observe the results below from the previous semester:

A	5 Students	D	6 Students
B	20 Students	F	6 Students
C	12 Students		

discrete measures

Measures that take on only one of a finite number of values.

The mode is a "B" since more students obtained that value than any other value. Therefore, the "average" student would expect a B in MKTG4311.

■ CONTINUOUS MEASURES

continuous measures

Measures that reflect the intensity of a concept by assigning values that can take on any value along some scale range.

Continuous measures are those assigning values anywhere along some scale range in a place that corresponds to the intensity of some concept. Ratio measures are continuous measures. Thus, when we measure sales for each salesperson using the dollar amount sold, we are assigning continuous measures. A number line could be constructed ranging from the least amount sold to the most and a spot on the line would correspond exactly to a salesperson's performance.

Strictly speaking, interval scales are not necessarily continuous. Consider the following common type of survey question:

	Strongly Disagree	Disagree	Neutral	Agree	Strongly Agree
I enjoy participating in online auctions	1	2	3	4	5

This is a discrete scale because only the values 1, 2, 3, 4, or 5 can be assigned. Furthermore, it is an ordinal scale because it only orders based on agreement. We really have no way of knowing that the difference in agreement somebody marking a 5 and somebody marking a 4 is the same as the difference in agreement between somebody marking a 2 and somebody marking 1. The scale difference is 1 in either case but is the difference in true agreement the same? There is no way to know. Therefore, the mean is not an appropriate way of stating central tendency, and we really shouldn't use many common statistics on these responses.

However, as a scaled response of this type takes on more values, the error introduced by assuming that the differences between the discrete points are equal becomes smaller. This may be seen by imagining a *Likert scale* with a thousand levels of agreement rather than three or four. The differences between the different levels become so small with a thousand levels that only tiny errors could be introduced by assuming each interval is the same. Therefore, marketing researchers generally treat interval scales containing five or more categories of response as interval. When fewer than five categories are used, this assumption is inappropriate. So, interval scales are treated as continuous when five or more categories are used.

The researcher should keep in mind, however, the distinction between ratio and interval measures. Errors in judgment can be made when interval measures are treated as ratio. For example, attitude is usually measured with an interval scale. An attitude of zero means nothing. In fact, attitude would only have meaning in a relative sense. Therefore, attitude takes on meaning when one person's response is compared to another or through some other comparison.

The mean and standard deviation may be calculated from continuous data. Using the actual quantities for arithmetic operations is permissible with ratio scales. Thus, the ratios of scale values are meaningful. A ratio scale has all the properties of nominal, ordinal, and interval scales. However, the same cannot be said in reverse. An ordinal scale, for example, has nominal properties, but it does not have interval or ratio properties.

Reliable and Valid Index Measures

attribute

A single characteristic or fundamental feature of an object, person, situation, or issue.

Earlier, we distinguished constructs as concepts that require multiple variables to measure them adequately. Looking back to the chapter vignette, could it be that multiple items will be required to adequately represent customer promotion? Likewise, a consumer's commitment toward some brand or store is usually represented by multiple items. An **attribute** is a single characteristic or fundamental feature of an object, person, situation, or issue.

Indexes and Composites

Multi-item instruments for measuring a construct are either called *index measures* or *composite measures*. An **index measure** assigns a value based on how characteristic an observation is of the thing being measured. Indexes often are formed by putting several variables together. For example, a social class index is based on three weighted variables: income, occupation, and education. Usually, occupation is seen as the single best indicator and would be weighted highest. Someone with a highly prestigious occupation and a graduate degree but without a great income would be more characteristic of high social class than someone with a high income but lacking formal education and a prestigious occupation.

With an index, the different attributes may not be strongly correlated with each other. A person's income does not always relate strongly to their education. The American Consumer Satisfaction Index shows how satisfied American consumers are based on an index of satisfaction scores. Readers are likely not surprised to know that Americans appear more satisfied with soft drinks than they are with cable TV companies based on this index.[6]

Composite measures also assign a value based on a mathematical derivation of multiple variables. For example, restaurant satisfaction may be measured by combining questions such as "How satisfied are you with your restaurant experience today? How pleased are you with your visit to our restaurant? How satisfied are you with the overall service quality provided today?" For most practical applications, composite measures and indexes are computed in the same way.[7] However, composite measures are distinguished from index measures in that the composite's indicators should be both theoretically and statistically related to each other. In the customer satisfaction items listed above, one can hardly imagine that respondents would say they were highly satisfied and then provide a low score for how pleased they felt. That simply wouldn't make a lot of sense. Likewise, they should show correlation.

index measure

An index assigns a value based on how much of the concept being measured is associated with an observation. Indexes often are formed by putting several variables together.

composite measures

Assign a value to an observation based on a mathematical derivation of multiple variables.

Computing Scale Values

Exhibit 10.4 demonstrates how a composite measure can be created from common rating scales. This particular scale can be used to assess how much a consumer trusts a Web site.[8] This particular composite represents a **summated scale**. A summated scale is created by simply summing the response to each item making up the composite measure. In this case, the consumer would have a trust score of 13 based on responses to five items. A researcher may sometimes choose to average the scores rather than summing them. The advantage to this is that the composite measure is expressed on the same scale as are the items that make it up. So, instead of a 13, the consumer would have a score of 2.6. The information content is the same.

summated scale

A scale created by simply summing (adding together) the response to each item making up the composite measure. The scores can be but do not have to be averaged by the number of items making up the composite scale.

EXHIBIT 10.4
Computing a Composite Scale

Item	Strongly Disagree (SD) → Strongly Agree (SA)				
This site appears to be more trustworthy than other sites I have visited.	SD	(D)	N	A	SA
My overall trust in this site is very high.	SD	D	(N)	A	SA
My overall impression of the believability of the information on this site is very high.	SD	(D)	N	A	SA
My overall confidence in the recommendations on this site is very high.	SD	(D)	N	A	SA
The company represented in this site delivers on its promises.	SD	D	N	(A)	SA

Computation:
Scale Values: SD = 1, D = 2, N = 3, A = 4, SA = 5

Thus, the Trust score for this consumer is
$$2 + 3 + 2 + 2 + 4 = 13$$

Recoding Made Easy

Most computer statistical software makes scale recoding easy. The screenshot shown here is from SPSS, perhaps the most widely used statistical software in business-related research. All that needs to be done to reverse-code a scale is to go through the right click-through sequence. In this case, the following steps would be followed:

1. Click on transform.
2. Click on recode.
3. Choose to recode into the same variable.
4. Select the variable(s) to be recoded.
5. Click on old and new values.
6. Use the menu that appears to enter the old values and the matching new values. Click add after entering each pair.
7. Click continue.

This would successfully recode variable X13 in this case.

Sometimes, a response may need to be reverse–coded before computing a summated or averaged scale value. **Reverse coding** means that the value assigned for a response is treated oppositely from the other items. If a sixth item was included on the trust scale that said, "I do not trust this Web site," reverse coding would be necessary to make sure the composite made sense. The content of this item is the reverse of trust (distrust), so the scale itself should be reversed. Thus, on a 5-point scale, the values are reversed as follows:

reverse coding

Means that the value assigned for a response is treated oppositely from the other items.

- 5 becomes 1
- 4 becomes 2
- 3 stays 3
- 2 becomes 4
- 1 becomes 5

The Research Snapshot above shows how a recode can be carried out using SPSS.

Reliability

reliability

An indicator of a measure's internal consistency.

Reliability is an indicator of a measure's internal consistency. Consistency is the key to understanding reliability. A measure is reliable when different attempts at measuring something converge on the same result. If a professor's marketing research tests are reliable, a student should tend toward consistent scores on all tests. In other words, a student that makes an 80 on the first test should make scores close to 80 on all subsequent tests. If it is difficult to predict what students would make on a test by examining their previous test scores, the tests probably lack reliability.

internal consistency

Represents a measure's homogeneity or the extent to which each indicator of a concept converges on some common meaning.

■ INTERNAL CONSISTENCY

Internal consistency is a term used by researchers to represent a measure's homogeneity. An attempt to measure trust may require asking several similar but not identical questions. The set of items that make up a measure are referred to as a *battery* of scale items. *Internal consistency* of a multiple-item measure can be measured by correlating scores on subsets of items making up a scale.

The **split-half method** of checking reliability is performed by taking half the items from a scale (for example, odd-numbered items) and checking them against the results from the other half (even-numbered items). The two scale *halves* should correlate highly. They should also produce similar scores. However, multiple techniques exist for estimating scale reliability.

Coefficient alpha (α) is the most commonly applied estimate of a composite scale's reliability.[9] Coefficient α estimates internal consistency by computing the average of all possible split-half reliabilities for a multiple-item scale. The coefficient demonstrates whether or not the different items converge. Although coefficient α does not address validity, many researchers use α as the sole indicator of a scale's quality largely because it is simply and readily computed by statistical programs like SPSS. Coefficient α can only take on values ranging from 0, meaning no consistency among items (they are all statistically independent), to 1, meaning complete consistency (all items yield perfect correlation with each other).

Generally speaking, scales exhibiting a coefficient α between 0.80 and 0.96 are considered to have very good reliability. Scales with a coefficient α between 0.70 and 0.80 are considered to have good reliability, and an α value between 0.60 and 0.70 indicates fair reliability. When the coefficient α is below 0.60, the scale has poor reliability.[10] Researchers generally report coefficient α for each composite measure involved in a study.

■ TEST-RETEST RELIABILITY

The **test-retest method** of determining reliability involves administering the same scale or measure to the same respondents at two separate times to test for stability. If the measure is stable over time, the test, administered under the same conditions each time, should obtain similar results. Test-retest reliability represents a measure's repeatability.

Suppose a researcher at one time attempts to measure buying intentions and finds that 12 percent of the population is willing to purchase a product. If the study is repeated a few weeks later under similar conditions, and the researcher again finds that 12 percent of the population is willing to purchase the product, the measure appears to be reliable. High stability correlation or consistency between two measures at time 1 and time 2 indicates high reliability.

Assume that a person does not change his or her attitude about dark beer. Attitude might be measured with an item like the one shown below:

I prefer dark beer to all other types of beer.

If repeated measurements of that individual's attitude toward dark beer are taken with the same scale, a reliable instrument will produce the same results each time the scale is measured. Thus one's attitude in March 2009 should tend to be the same as one's attitude in October 2009 or May 2010. When a measuring instrument produces unpredictable results from one testing to the next, the results are said to be unreliable because of error in measurement.

Reliability is a necessary but not sufficient condition for validity. A reliable scale may not be valid. For example, a purchase intention measurement technique may consistently indicate that 20 percent of those sampled are willing to purchase a new product. Whether the measure is valid depends on whether 20 percent of the population indeed purchases the product. A reliable but invalid instrument will yield consistently inaccurate results. Perhaps you've come across results from polls or other research in the media that appear reliable but inaccurate in this manner?

split-half method

A method for assessing internal consistency by checking the results of one-half of a set of scaled items against the results from the other half.

coefficient alpha (α)

The most commonly applied estimate of a multiple item scale's reliability. It represents the average of all possible split-half reliabilities for a construct.

test-retest method

Administering the same scale or measure to the same respondents at two separate points in time to test for stability.

Here are some results from using a software package to estimate coefficient α for a 5-item scale measuring the positive feelings shoppers had during a shopping trip. The results show a value of 0.96 for the scale. Also, the item-total statistics indicate that all the items correlate highly with the scale. Overall, these are positive results.

Reliability

Scale: Positive Feelings

Case Processing Summary

		N	%
Cases	Valid	457	100.0
	Excluded[a]	0	.0
	Total	457	100.0

a. Listwise deletion based on all variables in the procedure.

Reliability Statistics

Cronbach's Alpha	N of Items
.960	5

Item-Total Statistics

	Scale Mean if Item Deleted	Scale Variance if Item Deleted	Corrected Item-Total Correlation	Cronbach's Alpha if Item Deleted
Excited...	14.58	51.459	.859	.955
Happy	14.16	51.611	.886	.950
Interested	14.04	50.138	.891	.949
Pleased	14.29	51.352	.910	.946
Satisfied	14.30	51.603	.886	.950

Validity

validity

The accuracy of a measure or the extent to which a score truthfully represents a concept.

Good measures should be both precise and accurate. Reliability represents how precise a measure is in that the different attempts at measuring the same thing converge on the same point. Accuracy deals more with how a measure assesses the intended concept. **Validity** is the accuracy of a measure or the extent to which a score truthfully represents a concept.

Achieving validity is not a simple matter. Researchers who study job performance often result to asking employees to self-rate their own performance. A multiple item self-rated performance scale is usually reliable, but does one's opinion about him/her self really reflect performance? Perhaps some bias may creep in causing the scale to represent something besides true job performance.

face (content) validity

A scale's content logically appears to reflect what was intended to be measured.

Researchers need to know if their measures are valid. The question of validity expresses the researcher's concern with accurate measurement. Validity addresses the problem of whether a measure (for example, an attitude measure used in marketing) indeed measures what it is supposed to measure. When a measure lacks validity, any conclusions based on that measure are also likely to be faulty.

criterion validity

The ability of a measure to correlate with other standard measures of similar constructs or established criteria.

Students should be able to empathize with the following validity problem. Consider the controversy about highway patrol officers using radar guns to clock speeders. A driver is clocked at 75 mph in a 55 mph zone, but the same radar gun aimed at a house registers 28 mph. The error occurred because the radar gun had picked up impulses from the electrical system of the squad car's idling engine. The house was probably not speeding—and the radar gun was probably not completely valid.

Establishing Validity

Researchers have attempted to assess validity in many ways. They attempt to provide some evidence of a measure's degree of validity by answering a variety of questions. Is there a consensus among my colleagues that my attitude scale measures what it is supposed to measure? Does my measure correlate with other measures of the same concept? Does the behavior expected from my measure predict actual observed behavior? The three basic aspects of validity are *face* or *content validity*, *criterion validity,* and *construct validity*.

Face (content) validity refers to the subjective agreement among professionals that a scale logically reflects the concept being measured. Simply, do the test items make sense given a concept's definition? When an inspection of the test items convinces experts that the items match the definition, the scale is said to have face validity.

Criterion validity addresses the question, "Does my measure correlate with measures of the similar concepts or known quantities?" Criterion validity may be classified as either *concurrent validity* or *predictive validity* depending on the time sequence in which the new measurement scale and the criterion measure

A golfer may hit reliable but not valid putts and thus tend to miss them in some repeated fashion. This golfer's putts tend to converge to the left of—rather than in—the hole!

are correlated. If the new measure is taken at the same time as the criterion measure and is shown to be valid, then it has concurrent validity. Predictive validity is established when a new measure predicts a future event. The two measures differ only on the basis of a time dimension—that is, the criterion measure is separated in time from the predictor measure.

A practical example of predictive validity is illustrated by a commercial research firm's test of the relationship between a rough commercial's effectiveness (as determined, for example, by recall scores) and a finished commercial's effectiveness (also by recall scores). Ad agencies often test animatic rough, photomatic rough, or live-action rough commercials before developing actual finished commercials. One marketing research consulting firm suggests that this testing has high predictive validity. Rough commercial recall scores provide correct estimates of the final finished commercial recall scores more than 80 percent of the time.[11] While face (content) validity is a subjective evaluation, criterion validity provides a more rigorous empirical test.

Construct validity exists when a measure reliably measures and truthfully represents a unique concept. Construct validity consists of several components, including:

- Face or content validity
- Convergent validity
- Criterion or validity
- Discriminant validity

Convergent validity is another way of expressing internal consistency. Highly reliable scales contain convergent validity. Criterion validity and face validity were discussed in the preceding paragraphs. **Discriminant validity** represents how unique or distinct is a measure. A scale should not correlate too highly with a measure of a different construct. For example, a customer satisfaction measure should not correlate too highly with a cognitive dissonance scale if the two concepts are truly different. As a rough rule of thumb, when two scales are correlated above 0.75, discriminant validity may be an issue. Multivariate procedures like factor analysis can be useful in establishing construct validity. The reader is referred to other sources for a more detailed discussion.[12]

construct validity

Exists when a measure reliably measures and truthfully represents a unique concept; consists of several components including face validity, convergent validity, criterion validity, and discriminant validity.

convergent validity

Another way of expressing internal consistency; highly reliable scales contain convergent validity.

discriminant validity

Represents how unique or distinct is a measure; a scale should not correlate too highly with a measure of a different construct.

Reliability versus Validity

The differences between reliability and validity can be illustrated by the rifle targets in Exhibit 10.5. Suppose someone fires an equal number of rounds with a century-old rifle and a modern rifle.[13] The shots from the older gun are considerably scattered, but those from the newer gun are closely clustered. The variability of the old rifle compared with that of the new one indicates it is less reliable. The target on the right illustrates the concept of a systematic bias influencing validity. The shots fired with the new rifle are reliable because they show little variance. However, because the person firing the gun is not very good at it, they all miss the target in much the same way. The shots are reliable, but not valid. Only if they were reliable and valid would it be a good idea to test by having him shoot an apple off your head!

EXHIBIT 10.5
Reliability and Validity on Target

Old Rifle
Low Reliability
(Target A)

New Rifle
High Reliability
(Target B)

New Rifle—Bad Shot
Reliable but not Valid
(Target C)

What Is an Attitude?

attitude

An enduring disposition to consistently respond in a given manner to various aspects of the world; composed of affective, cognitive, and behavioral components.

"You've got a bad attitude!" Perhaps many of us have heard this phrase before. The idea is that one's disposition about the relevant matter is not positive and the result is less than productive behavior. Formally, an **attitude** is a social-psychological concept that can be defined as a relatively enduring predisposition to respond consistently to various things including people, activities, events, and objects. Attitudes are predispositions toward behavior and as such represent rules that inform a person of the appropriate reaction in a given situation. If someone's attitude toward broccoli is best described as a dislike, then that person is likely to avoid eating, smelling or even approaching any dish with the obvious presence of broccoli. If a fan "loves the Bulldogs," he or she is more likely to buy tickets to their games and to attend them. Additionally, attitudes are latent constructs and because of this, they are not directly observable.

Attitudes are thought to have three components:

- An affective component that expresses how much affinity someone has toward the relevant matter. More simply, this is the feeling of liking or not liking something. For example, a consumer might say "I love Wendy's." This would express very high liking.
- A cognitive component that represents a person's awareness and knowledge of the relevant matter. In other words, what a person believes about the subject matter. When someone says, "Wendy's has a wide selection," they are expressing knowledge or a belief about this particular consumer alternative.
- A behavioral component that represents the action that corresponds to a certain type of attitude. If the attitude is positive, the person will display approach responses. If the attitude is negative, the person will display avoidance reactions. "I'll never eat at Wendy's again" expresses a behavioral component of a negative attitude. Often, the behavioral component is expressed as intentions of future behavior.

Sometimes researchers need to study overall attitude. Other times, they may focus on one of these components more than others. Whenever overall attitude or any of these components are measured through survey research, the researcher is conducting attitudinal research.

Marketing managers place a great deal of importance on attitudes because they have been shown to predict behavior with some accuracy. If consumers' aggregate attitude about some product can be changed, sales volume will increase accordingly. If employees' aggregate attitude about their job improves, their work output is likely to increase in proportion. Further, if the knowledge about a product can be changed, the product can be repositioned to capture some new market. For example, Lucozade was transformed from a liquid nutritional supplement for pediatric digestive illness patients into a sports and fitness drink for adults.[14]

This brand transformation required careful coordination of communications with consumers that involved advertising and merchandising. Additionally, a great deal of survey research tracked consumers' attitudes along the way.

Lucozade was transformed from a product for children with stomach problems into a sports, fitness, and energy product for adults. Attitudinal research helped track this brand transformation.

PHOTO COURTESY OF VICKI BEAVER.

Attitudinal Rating Scales

Researchers face a wide variety of choices in measuring attitudinal concepts. One reason for the variety is that no complete consensus exists over just what constitutes an attitude or an attitudinal variable. Researchers generally argue that the affective, cognitive, and behavioral components of an attitude can be measured by different means. For example, sympathetic nervous system responses may be recorded using physiological measures to quantify affect, but they are not good measures of behavioral intentions. Direct verbal statements concerning affect, belief, or behavior are used to measure behavioral intent. However, attitudes may also be interpreted using qualitative techniques like those discussed in Chapter 5.

Research may assess the affective (emotional) components of attitudes through physiological measures like galvanic skin response (GSR), blood pressure, and pupil dilation. These measures provide a means of assessing attitudes without verbally questioning the respondent. In general, they can provide a gross measure of likes or dislikes, but they are not extremely sensitive to the different gradients of an attitude.

Obtaining verbal statements from respondents generally requires that the respondents perform a task such as ranking, rating, sorting, or making choices. A **ranking** task requires the respondent to rank order a small number of stores, brands, feelings, or objects on the basis of overall preference or some characteristic of the stimulus. **Rating** asks the respondent to estimate the magnitude or the extent to which some characteristic exists. A quantitative score results. The rating task involves marking a response indicating one's position using one or more attitudinal or cognitive scales. A **sorting** task might present the respondent with several product concepts printed on cards and require the respondent to classify the concepts by placing the cards into groups (stacks of cards). Another type of attitude measurement is **choice** between two or more alternatives. If a respondent chooses one object over another, the researcher assumes that the respondent prefers the chosen object, at least in this setting.

Marketing researchers commonly use rating scales to measure attitudes. This section discusses many rating scales designed to enable respondents to report the intensity of their attitudes. In its most basic form, attitude scaling requires that an individual agree or disagree with a statement or indicate how much some term describes his or her feeling. For example, respondents in a political poll may be asked whether they agree or disagree with a statement like, "Politicians are likable." Or, an individual might indicate whether he or she likes or dislikes jalapeño bean dip. This type of self-rating scale merely classifies respondents into one of two categories, thus having only the properties of a nominal scale, and the types of mathematical analysis that may be used with this basic scale are limited.

Simple attitude scaling can be a practical way of implementing a survey when questionnaires are extremely long, when respondents have little education, or for other specific reasons. In fact, a number of simplified scales are merely checklists where a respondent indicates past experience, preference or likes and dislikes simply by checking an item. A recent checklist survey showed that 77 percent of small business owners believe small and medium size businesses "have less bureaucracy," 76 percent said smaller companies "have more flexibility" than large ones, and 73 percent were optimistic heading into 2008 as opposed to 75 percent indicating optimism at the end of 2006.[15] Answers like these can be obtained very quickly through simple questioning techniques.

Most attitude theorists believe that attitudes vary along a continuum. Thus, the purpose of an attitude scale is to find an individual's position on the continuum. However, simple nominal scales do not allow for fine distinctions between attitudes. Several other scales have been developed for making more precise measurements. The following sections describe the most popular techniques for measuring attitudes.

Category Scales

The simplest rating scale contains only two response categories: agree/disagree. For instance, a researcher might include a simple question like this:

I like the idea of attending Southpaw State University.

☐ *Yes*   ☐ *No*

ranking

A measurement task that requires respondents to rank order a small number of stores, brands, or objects on the basis of overall preference or some characteristic of the stimulus.

rating

A measurement task that requires respondents to estimate the magnitude of a characteristic or quality that a brand, store, or object possesses.

sorting

A measurement task that presents a respondent with several objects or product concepts and requires the respondent to arrange the objects into piles or classify the product concepts.

choice

A measurement task that identifies preferences by requiring respondents to choose between two or more alternatives

Generally, consumers act in a way consistent with their attitudes. Therefore, attitudes are a popular marketing research topic.

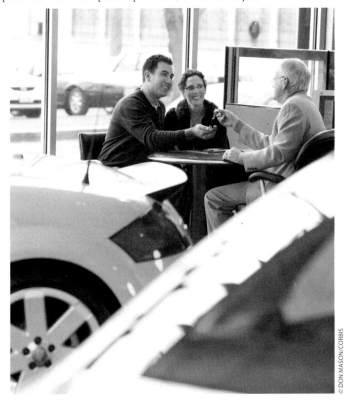

Expanding the response categories provides the respondent with more flexibility in the rating task. Even more information is provided if the categories are ordered according to a particular descriptive or evaluative dimension. Consider the following question:

How often do you think favorably about attending Southpaw State University?

☐ *Never*   ☐ *Rarely*   ☐ *Sometimes*   ☐ *Often*   ☐ *Very often*

category scale

A rating scale that consists of several response categories, often providing respondents with alternatives to indicate positions on a continuum.

This **category scale** measures attitude with greater sensitivity than a two-point response scale. By having more choices, the potential exists to provide more information. However, a researcher will create measurement error if he/she uses a category scale for something that is truly bipolar (yes/no, female/male, member/non-member, and so on).

Response category wording is an extremely important factor. Exhibit 10.6 shows some common wordings used in category scales measuring common marketing research variables. As you can see, the more categories, the more difficulty a researcher has in coming up with precise and readily understandable category labels.

EXHIBIT 10.6 **Selected Category Scales**

Quality				
Excellent	Good	Fair	Poor	
Very good	Fairly good	Neither good nor bad	Not very good	Not good at all
Well above average	Above average	Average	Below average	Well below average

Importance				
Very important	Fairly important	Neutral	Not so important	Not at all important

Interest				
Very interested		Somewhat interested		Not very interested

Satisfaction				
Completely satisfied	Somewhat satisfied	Neither satisfied nor dissatisfied	Somewhat dissatisfied	Completely dissatisfied
Very satisfied	Quite satisfied	Somewhat satisfied	Not at all satisfied	

Frequency				
All of the time	Very often	Often	Sometimes	Hardly ever
Very often	Often	Sometimes	Rarely	Never
All of the time	Most of the time	Some of the time	Just now and then	

Truth				
Very true	Somewhat true	Not very true	Not at all true	
Definitely yes	Probably yes	Probably no	Definitely no	

Uniqueness				
Very different	Somewhat different	Slightly different	Not at all different	
Extremely unique	Very unique	Somewhat unique	Slightly unique	Not at all unique

The Likert Scale

The Likert scale may well be the most commonly applied scale format in marketing research. Likert scales are simple to administer and understand. Likert scales were developed by and named after Rensis Likert, a 20th century social scientist. With a **Likert scale**, respondents indicate their attitudes by checking how strongly they agree or disagree with carefully constructed statements. The scale results reveal the respondent's attitude ranging from very positive to very negative. Individuals generally choose from multiple response alternatives such as, strongly agree, agree, neutral, disagree, and strongly disagree. Researchers commonly employ five choices although they also often use six, seven or even more response points. In the following example, from a study of food-shopping behavior, there are five alternatives:

Likert scale

A measure of attitudes designed to allow respondents to rate how strongly they agree or disagree with carefully constructed statements, ranging from very positive to very negative attitudes toward some object.

I like to go to Wal-Mart when buying food for my family.				
Strongly disagree	Disagree	Neutral	Agree	Strongly agree
☐	☐	☐	☐	☐
(1)	(2)	(3)	(4)	(5)

Researchers assign scores to each possible response. In this example, numerical scores of 1, 2, 3, 4, and 5 are assigned to each level of agreement, respectively. The numerical scores, shown in parentheses, may not be printed on the questionnaire. Typically, with paper and pencil questionnaires, the numbers are displayed primarily because they facilitate data coding. The numbers are much less likely to be displayed as researchers increasingly adopt electronic questionnaires. Here, strong agreement indicates the most favorable attitude on the statement, and a numerical score of 5 is assigned to this response.

Realize that if the statement were worded in a way that indicated dislike for shopping for food at Wal-Mart, a 5 would mean a less favorable attitude about this activity. For example, responses to the item above could even be combined with those from an item like this:

Wal-Mart is a bad place to shop for fresh foods.				
Strongly disagree	Disagree	Neutral	Agree	Strongly agree
☐	☐	☐	☐	☐
(1)	(2)	(3)	(4)	(5)

However, before a composite scale could be created, the responses to this item would have to be reverse coded as shown previously. An attitude score is arbitrary and has little cardinal meaning—in other words, attitude scores are at best interval and not ratio. They could also just as easily be scored so that a higher score indicated less favorable attitudes. However, the convention is to score attitude scales so that a higher score means a more favorable attitude.

■ SELECTING ITEMS FOR A LIKERT SCALE

Typically, a researcher will use multiple items to represent a single attitudinal concept. The researcher may generate a large number of statements before putting together the final questionnaire. A pretest may be conducted using these items allowing for an *item analysis* to be performed. The item analysis helps select items that evoke a wide response (meaning all respondents are not selecting the same response point such as all strongly agree) allowing the item to discriminate among those with positive and negative attitudes. Items are also analyzed for clarity or unusual response patterns. Thus, the final Likert items should be clearly understood and elicit an accurate range of responses corresponding to respondents' true attitudes.

Assessing Item and Scale Quality

Another big advantage of using multiple items is that reliability and validity can be estimated using a wide range of statistical approaches. For instance, coefficient α for reliability can only be assessed with multiple items. Later chapters will discuss multivariate procedures for assessing validity in more detail. These are also facilitated by using multiple items. In the end, only a set of items that show acceptable reliability and validity should be summed or averaged for scores representing hypothetical constructs. Unfortunately, not all researchers are willing or able to thoroughly assess reliability and validity. Without this assessment, the researcher has no way of knowing exactly what the items represent or how well they represent anything of interest.

Semantic Differential

semantic differential

A measure of attitudes that consists of a series of seven-point rating scales that use bipolar adjectives to anchor the beginning and end of each scale.

A **semantic differential** is a scale type that has respondents describe their attitude using a series of bipolar rating scales. Bipolar rating scales involve respondents choosing between opposing adjectives—such as "good" and "bad," "modern" and "old-fashioned," or "clean" and "dirty." One adjective anchors the beginning and the other the end (or poles) of the scale. The subject makes repeated judgments about the concept under investigation on each of the scales. Exhibit 10.7 shows an example semantic differential approach for assessing consumer attitudes toward hypermarts.

EXHIBIT 10.7
An Example Semantic Differential Scale

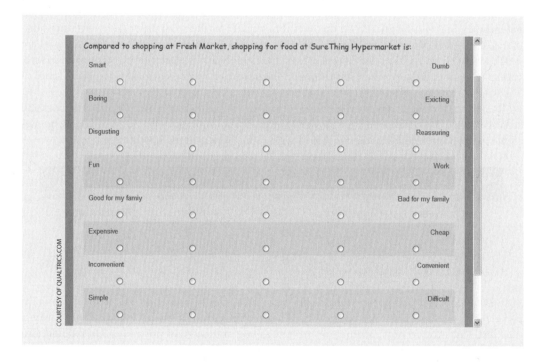

COURTESY OF QUALTRICS.COM

The scoring of the semantic differential can be illustrated using the scale bounded by the anchors "modern" and "old-fashioned." Respondents are instructed to check the place that indicates the nearest appropriate adjective. From left to right, the scale intervals are interpreted as "extremely modern," "very modern," "slightly modern," "neither modern nor old-fashioned," "slightly old-fashioned," "very old-fashioned," and "extremely old-fashioned":

Extremely modern	Very modern	Slightly modern	Neither modern nor old-fashioned	Slightly old-fashioned	Very old-fashioned	Extremely old-fashioned
☐	☐	☐	☐	☐	☐	☐

■ SEMANTIC DIFFERENTIALS AND MEANING

The semantic differential technique originally was developed as a method for measuring the meanings of objects or the "semantic space" of interpersonal experience.[16] Researchers see the semantic differential as versatile and useful in a wide variety of business situations.

When opposites are available, the semantic differential is a good scale choice. In typical attitude or image studies, simple anchors such as very unfavorable and very favorable work well. However, the validity of the semantic differential depends on finding scale anchors that are semantic opposites and this can sometimes prove difficult. For example, consider the following scale in which the respondent is asked to place a check on the line closest to the way they feel about the phrase:

Shopping at Bebe makes me:

Happy __ __ __ __ __ __ __ **Sad**

Few would question that sad is the opposite of happy. However, what if this were to be combined with an item capturing how angry shopping at Bebe makes a respondent feel? Then, what would the opposite of angry be? Clearly, using happy as the opposite of angry would present a problem because the items above suggests happy is the opposite of sad. Thus, a semantic differential may not be best for capturing anger unless some distinctive and unambiguous opposite can be found.

■ SCORING SEMANTIC DIFFERENTIALS

Like Likert scales, a numerical score can be assigned to each position on a semantic differential scale. For a seven-point semantic differential the scores could be 1, 2, 3, 4, 5, 6, 7 or −3, −2, −1, 0, +1, +2, +3. Marketing researchers generally assume that the semantic differential provides interval data. This assumption does have critics who argue that the data have only ordinal properties because the numerical scores are arbitrary and there is no way of knowing that the differences between choices are equal. Practically, the vast majority of social science researchers treat semantic differential scales as metric (at least interval). This is justified because the amount of error introduced by assuming the intervals between choices are equal (even though this is uncertain at best) is fairly small.

Constant-Sum Scale

A **constant-sum scale** demands that respondents divide points among several attributes to indicate their relative importance. Suppose United Parcel Service (UPS) wishes to determine the importance of delivery attributes such as accurate invoicing, delivery as promised, and price to organizations that use its service in business-to-business marketing. Respondents might be asked to divide a constant sum of 100 points to indicate the relative importance of those attributes:

> *Divide 100 points among the following characteristics of a delivery service according to how important each characteristic is to you when selecting a delivery company.*
> _____ *Accurate invoicing*
> _____ *Delivery as promised*
> _____ *Lower price*

The constant-sum scale requires respondents to understand that their responses should total to the number of points being allocated. In the case above, that number is 100. As the number of stimuli increases, this technique becomes increasingly complex. Fortunately, with electronic questionnaires math errors can be eliminated by having the software trigger an error notice whenever the responses provided do not match the total. The respondent could adjust the responses until the sums do indeed match the total. If respondents follow the instructions correctly, the results will approximate interval measures.

This technique may be used for measuring brand preference. The approach, which is similar to the paired-comparison method, is as follows:

> *Divide 100 points among the following brands according to your preference for each brand:*
> _____ *Brand A*
> _____ *Brand B*
> _____ *Brand C*

constant-sum scale

A measure of attitudes in which respondents are asked to divide a constant sum to indicate the relative importance of attributes; respondents often sort cards, but the task may also be a rating task.

Although the constant sum scale is widely used, strictly speaking, the scale is flawed because the last response is completely determined by the way the respondent has scored the other choices. Although this is probably somewhat complex to understand, the fact is that practical reasons often outweigh this concern.

Graphic Rating Scales

graphic rating scale

A measure of attitude that allows respondents to rate an object by choosing any point along a graphic continuum.

A **graphic rating scale** presents respondents with a graphic continuum. The respondents are allowed to choose any point on the continuum to indicate their attitude. Exhibit 10.8 shows a traditional graphic scale, ranging from one extreme position to the opposite position. Typically a respondent's score is determined by measuring the length (in millimeters) from one end of the graphic continuum to the point marked by the respondent. Many researchers believe that scoring in this manner strengthens the assumption that graphic rating scales of this type are interval scales. Alternatively, the researcher may divide the line into predetermined scoring categories (lengths) and record respondents' marks accordingly. In other words, the graphic rating scale has the advantage of allowing the researcher to choose any interval desired for scoring purposes. The disadvantage of the graphic rating scale is that there are no standard answers.

EXHIBIT 10.8
Graphic Rating Scale

Please evaluate each attribute in terms of how important it is to you by placing an X at the position on the horizontal line that most reflects your feelings.

Seating comfort   Not important _____ Very important

In-flight meals   Not important _____ Very important

Airfare   Not important _____ Very important

Graphic rating scales are not limited to straight lines as sources of visual communication. Picture response options or another type of graphic continuum may be used to enhance communication with respondents.

Research to investigate children's attitudes has used happy-sad face scales. Exhibit 10.9 illustrates one such approach. Here, the respondent chooses an attitude by sliding the scale up and down using the tab to the right of the face. As the respondent moves the tab up or down, the face smiles or frowns, correspondingly. The first respondent is fairly pleased with the idea of

EXHIBIT 10.9

Choose the Face that Matches Your Attitude: A Happy/Sad Face Scale

Respondent 1:

Please use the sliding scale to choose the face that best describes your attitude toward purchasing hot breakfast items sold at Starbucks.

Respondent 2:

Please use the sliding scale to choose the face that best describes your attitude toward purchasing hot breakfast items sold at Starbucks.

hot breakfast items at Starbucks. However, the second respondent has a very negative attitude toward the idea. Notice the position of the tab corresponding to each face.

Among the attitude rating approaches discussed in this chapter, Likert scales and semantic differentials account for the majority of applications. The Research Snapshot above suggests that attitudes can help make a story complete.

Ranking

A ranking is different than a rating scale in that respondents simply order alternatives on some characteristic. Consumers often *rank order* their preferences so, in this sense, ranking scales have considerable validity. An ordinal scale may be developed by asking respondents to rank order (from most preferred to least preferred) a set of objects or attributes. Respondents easily understand the task of rank ordering product attributes or arranging a set of brand names according to preference. Like the constant-sum scale however, the ranking scale suffers from inflexibility in that if we know how someone ranked five out of six alternatives, we know the answer to the sixth. Thus, the characteristics are not independently rated as in most types of ratings scales. Additionally, ordinal scaling only allows us to know that one option is preferred over another—not how much one option is preferred over another.

Paired Comparisons

Consider a situation in which a chain saw manufacturer learned that a competitor had introduced a new lightweight (6-pound) chain saw. The manufacturer's lightest chain saw weighed 9 pounds. Executives wondered if they needed to introduce a 6-pound chain saw into the product line. The research design chosen was a **paired comparison**. A 6-pound chain saw was designed, and a prototype built. To control for color preferences, the competitor's chain saw was painted the same color as the 9- and 6-pound chain saws. Respondents were presented with two chain saws at a time and asked to pick which of the two they preferred. Three pairs of comparisons were required to determine the most preferred chain saw.

paired comparison

A measurement technique that involves presenting the respondent with two objects and asking the respondent to pick the preferred object; more than two objects may be presented, but comparisons are made in pairs.

The following question illustrates the typical format for asking about paired comparisons.

I would like to know your overall opinion of two brands of adhesive bandages. They are Curad and Band-Aid. Overall, which of these two brands—Curad or Band-Aid—do you think is the better one? Or are both the same?

Curad is better. _____
Band-Aid is better. _____
They are the same. _____

If researchers wish to compare four brands of pens on the basis of attractiveness or writing quality, six comparisons $[(n)(n-1)/2]$ will be necessary. Paired comparisons are sometimes used to assess similarity instead of preference by asking which of the two choices is more similar to some third choice.

When comparing only a few items, such as products or advertisements, ranking objects with respect to one attribute is not difficult. As the number of items increases, the number of comparisons increases geometrically. If the number of comparisons is too large, respondents may become fatigued and no longer carefully discriminate among them.

Direct Assessment of Consumer Attitudes

Attitudes, as hypothetical constructs, cannot be observed directly. We can, however, infer one's attitude by the way he or she responds to multiple attitude indicators. A summated rating scale can be made up of three indicators of attitude. Consider the following three semantic differential items that may capture a consumer's attitude toward Microsoft Word:

very good ___ ___ ___ ___ ___ ___ ___ *very bad*

very unfavorable ___ ___ ___ ___ ___ ___ ___ *very favorable*

very positive ___ ___ ___ ___ ___ ___ ___ *very negative*

The terminology is such that now attitude would be represented as a latent (unobservable) construct indicated by a consumer's response to these items. How do you feel about Microsoft Word?

Ranking, Sorting, Rating, or Choice Technique?

The decision whether to use ranking, sorting, rating, or a choice technique is determined largely by the problem definition and especially by the type of statistical analysis desired. For example, ranking provides only ordinal data, limiting the statistical techniques that may be used.

Monadic or Comparative Scale?

If the scale to be used is not a ratio scale, the researcher must decide whether to include a standard of comparison in the verbal portion of the scale. Consider the following rating scale:

Now that you've had your automobile for about one year, please tell us how satisfied you are with its engine power and pickup.

Completely Dissatisfied	Dissatisfied	Somewhat Satisfied	Satisfied	Completely Satisfied
☐	☐	☐	☐	☐

monadic rating scale

Any measure of attitudes that asks respondents about a single concept in isolation.

comparative rating scale

Any measure of attitudes that asks respondents to rate a concept in comparison with a benchmark explicitly used as a frame of reference.

This is a **monadic rating scale**, because it asks about a single concept (the brand of automobile the individual actually purchased) in isolation. The respondent is not given a specific frame of reference. A **comparative rating scale** asks a respondent to rate a concept, such as a specific brand, in comparison with a benchmark—perhaps another similar concept, such as a competing brand—explicitly used as a frame of reference. In many cases, the comparative rating scale presents an ideal situation as a reference point for comparison with the actual situation.

Please indicate how the amount of authority in your present position compares with the amount of authority that would be ideal for this position.

Too much □   About right □   Too little □

What Type of Category Labels, If Any?

We have discussed verbal labels, numerical labels, and unlisted choices. Many rating scales have verbal labels for response categories because researchers believe they help respondents better understand the response positions. The maturity and educational levels of the respondents will influence this decision. The semantic differential, with unlabeled response categories between two bipolar adjectives, and the numerical scale, with numbers to indicate scale positions, often are selected because the researcher wishes to assume interval-scale data.

How Many Scale Categories or Response Positions?

Should a category scale have four, five, or seven response positions or categories? Or should the researcher use a graphic scale with an infinite number of positions? The original developmental research on the semantic differential indicated that five to eight points is optimal. However, the researcher must determine the number of meaningful positions that is best for the specific project. This issue of identifying how many meaningful distinctions respondents can practically make is basically a matter of sensitivity. For example, how sensitively can students discriminate the difficulty of college courses? The answer to the question may help determine the number of response categories.

The number of response categories can influence research conclusions. Think about a service employee asked to respond to an item asking about job satisfaction using a two-point response scale of either "no" or "yes." Can the two-point scale adequately capture the range of responses that employees might actually feel? Would we really expect that all people who respond "yes" have the same amount of satisfaction? Typically, a yes or no satisfaction question will yield about 80 percent yes responses. In other words, the data are typically skewed with a small number of scale points. If the scale is expanded to the typical five-point Likert format, the "yes" responses are likely to be spread across multiple categories. Similarly, a scale with too few points may suppress variance that truly exists. Thus, a scale should be adequately sensitive to actually capture a respondent's opinion or feelings.

What happens if the same question is asked with scales of varying numbers of response categories? Some research suggests that skewness is reduced by including more scale points, particularly for attitudinal and satisfaction type items. Additionally, including more scale points produces less extreme patterns of results with typical responses closer to the midpoint of the scale. Thus, as long as adding category responses does not become taxing to respondents, more categories are better than fewer. However, scales with five to ten scale points typically display results suggesting they are appropriate for use in statistical procedures like regression.[17]

Balanced or Unbalanced Rating Scale?

The fixed-alternative format may be balanced or unbalanced. For example, the following question, which asks about parent-child decisions relating to television program watching, is a **balanced rating scale**:

Who decides which television programs your children watch?

_____ *Child decides all of the time.*
_____ *Child decides most of the time.*
_____ *Child and parent decide together.*
_____ *Parent decides most of the time.*
_____ *Parent decides all of the time.*

This scale is balanced because a neutral point, or point of indifference, is at the center of the scale.

balanced rating scale

A fixed-alternative rating scale with an equal number of positive and negative categories; a neutral point or point of indifference is at the center of the scale.

unbalanced rating scale

A fixed-alternative rating scale that has more response categories at one end than the other resulting in an unequal number of positive and negative categories.

Unbalanced rating scales may be used when responses are expected to be distributed at one end of the scale, producing a skewed distribution. The skewed distribution may indicate error and can also interfere with the ability to draw meaningful statistical inferences. Marketing researchers often face situations where "end-piling" will occur. One reason for this is that researchers often ask questions for which respondents are fully expected to give more positive than negative responses. For instance, satisfaction scales (job or customer) generally show this pattern. After all, if an employee has stayed in one job for some years or a customer has already selected a place to do business, we should expect that they would provide a positive response. Unbalanced scales, such as the following one, may mitigate this type of "end piling":

Completely Dissatisfied	Dissatisfied	Somewhat Satisfied	Satisfied	Completely Satisfied
☐	☐	☐	☐	☐

Notice that there are three "satisfied" responses and only two "dissatisfied" responses above. The choice of a balanced or unbalanced scale generally depends on the nature of the concept or the researcher's knowledge about attitudes toward the stimulus to be measured. When respondents are expected to be predisposed toward one end of a concept or the other, unbalanced scales are appropriate. Otherwise, researchers are better off with balanced scales.

Forced-Choice Scales?

forced-choice rating scale

A fixed-alternative rating scale that requires respondents to choose one of the fixed alternatives.

non-forced-choice scale

A fixed-alternative rating scale that provides a "no opinion" category or that allows respondents to indicate that they cannot say which alternative is their choice.

In many situations, a respondent has not formed an attitude toward the concept being studied and simply cannot provide an answer. If a **forced-choice rating scale** compels the respondent to answer, the response is merely a function of the question. If answers are not forced, the midpoint of the scale may be used by the respondent to indicate unawareness as well as indifference. If many respondents in the sample are expected to be unaware of the attitudinal object under investigation, this problem may be eliminated by using a **non-forced-choice scale** that provides a "no opinion" category, as in the following example:

How does the Bank of Commerce compare with the First National Bank?

☐ *Bank of Commerce is better than First National Bank.*

☐ *Bank of Commerce is about the same as First National Bank.*

☐ *Bank of Commerce is worse than First National Bank.*

☐ *Can't say.*

Asking this type of question allows the investigator to separate respondents who cannot make an honest comparison from respondents who have had experience with both banks. The argument for forced choice is that people really do have attitudes, even if they are unfamiliar with the banks, and should be able to answer the question. Respondents are not provided with an easy out by simply selecting "neutral." The use of forced-choice questions is associated with higher incidences of "no answer." Perhaps when respondents really can't make up their mind, they will leave an item blank if they are given that choice. Internet surveys make forced-choice questions easy to implement because the delivery can be set up so that a respondent cannot go to the next question until the previous question is answered. Realize, however, if a respondent truly has no opinion, and the no opinion option is not included, he or she may give a bogus response or simply quit responding to the questionnaire. Thus, if the researcher believes the respondent may have trouble making up his or her mind, a "no answer" option may be provided for respondents. This is usually done out to the side of the valid scale items.

TO THE POINT

Refusing to have an opinion is a way of having one, isn't it?

—Luigi Pirandello

Single or Multiple Items?

Whether to use a single measure or an index measure depends on the complexity of the issue to be investigated, the number of dimensions the issue contains, and whether individual attributes of the stimulus are part of a holistic attitude or are seen as separate items. The researcher's conceptual definition will be helpful in making this choice. Some very simple or concrete concepts can be assessed with a single item. "Did you visit the dealership?" "Do you like pistachio ice cream?" Other indices such as social class require multiple items. Latent constructs also generally require multiple items.

Attitudes and Intentions

Behavioral researchers often model behavior as a function of intention, which in turn, is considered a function of attitudes. Attitudes are considered a function of a person's beliefs about some activity weighted by their evaluations of those characteristics. This type of research is sometimes referred to as a **multi-attribute model** or reasoned action approach. For example, a consumer's attitude to opt in to SMS advertising can be modeled by their intention to do so, which in turn, is a function of their attitude.[18] Likewise, a researcher may first measure attitude as a way of knowing how likely a consumer would be to purchase apparel made of American alligator skin.

multi-attribute model

A model that constructs an attitude score based on the multiplicative sum of beliefs about an option times the evaluation of those belief characteristics

Multi-attribute Attitude Score

Attitudes are modeled with a multi-attribute approach by taking belief scores assessed with some type of rating scale like those described and multiplying each belief score by an evaluation also supplied using some type of rating scale, and then summing each resulting product. For instance, a series of Likert statements might assess a respondent's beliefs about the reliability, price, service, and styling of a Honda Fit.

The Honda Fit is the most reliable car in its class.	*SD*	*D*	*N*	*A*	*SA*
The Honda Fit has a low price for a car of its type.	*SD*	*D*	*N*	*A*	*SA*
I know that my Honda dealer will provide great service if I buy a Honda Fit.	*SD*	*D*	*N*	*A*	*SA*
The Honda Fit is one of the most stylish cars you can buy.	*SD*	*D*	*N*	*A*	*SA*

Then, respondents may use a simple rating scale to assess how good or bad each charcteristic is. For example, the scale may appear something like this with instructions for the respondent to indicate the relative evaluation of each characteristic.

All things considered …

Buying a car that is reliable is

Very bad ☐ ☐ ☐ ☐ ☐ ☐ Very good

Buying a car with a low price is

Very bad ☐ ☐ ☐ ☐ ☐ ☐ Very good

Buying a car from a dealer with excellent service is

Very bad ☐ ☐ ☐ ☐ ☐ ☐ Very good

Buying a car with the latest styling is

Very bad ☐ ☐ ☐ ☐ ☐ ☐ Very good

The respondent's attitude toward buying a Honda Fit would be found by multiplying beliefs by evaluations. If a respondent provided the following belief scores using Likert scales for each belief item

Honda Fit reliability	*5*
Honda Fit pricing	*3*
Honda Fit dealer service	*2*
Honda Fit styling	*1*

and the following evaluation scores using the rating scale shown in the preceding

Reliability	*6*
Low pricing	*3*
Dealer service	*4*
Styling	*2*

then her attitude score could be computed as

Beliefs	×	Evaluations	=	(B)(E)
5		6		30
3		3		9
2		4		8
1		2		2
	Total			49

The multi-attribute attitude score for this consumer would be 49. A researcher may also ask respondents to rate a competitor's product. In this case, the product might be a Ford Focus. Using the same four characteristics, a score for the competitor can be obtained. The scores can then be compared to see which brand has a competitive advantage in terms of consumer attitudes.

This type of approach is frequently employed. The key advantages lie in how diagnostic the results can be. Not only can a researcher provide management with feedback on the relative attitude scores, but he or she can also identify characteristics that are most in need of being improved. In particular, poor belief scores on characteristics that respondents rate very favorably (or as highly important) indicate the characteristics that most need to be changed to improve competitive positioning. In this case, the Fit does well on reliability, and the strong belief score on this characteristic is largely responsible for shaping this consumer's attitude. If the Ford Focus scored only a 2 on reliability, the result would diagnose a problem that should be addressed. The focus has a relatively low score on a very meaningful characteristic.

Behavioral Intention

According to reasoned action theory, people form intentions consistent with the multi-attribute attitude score. Intentions represent the behavioral expectations of an individual toward an attitudinal object. Typically, the component of interest to marketers is a buying intention, a tendency to seek additional information, or plans to visit a showroom. Category scales for measuring the behavioral component of an attitude ask about a respondent's likelihood of purchase or intention to perform some future action, using questions such as the following:

How likely is it that you will purchase a Honda Fit?

- *I definitely will buy.*
- *I probably will buy.*
- *I might buy.*
- *I probably will not buy.*
- *I definitely will not buy.*

The attitude scores obtained above should correlate positively with the behavioral intent scores.

- Well-stated hypotheses are extremely useful in designing a research project. Each hypothesis reveals the concepts that have to be measured during the research project.
- Coefficient α provides an estimate of scale reliability. It is only applicable to multiple item scales—particularly those with three or more items to be formed into a composite. The following guide can be used in judging the results from estimating coefficient α.
  - Above 0.8, very good reliability
    - Scale can be used as is from a reliability standpoint.
  - From 0.7 to 0.79, good reliability
    - Scale can be used as is from a reliability standpoint.
- From 0.6 to 0.69, fair reliability
  - Scale can be used as is with caution.
  - Below 0.6, further refinement or modifications to the scale must be made before using.
- Attitudinal research can involve numerous types of ranking or rating scales such as a Likert or semantic differential.
  - Whenever there is a question about the number of scale points to use, it is better to use more rather than fewer scale points
  - When using an even number of scale points, researchers should consider providing an option outside of the scale for respondents who simply cannot reach a decision.
- Attitude scores have no absolute meaning so results for more than one company are needed to provide reference.

Summary

1. Determine what needs to be measured based on a research question or hypothesis. Researchers can determine what concepts must be measured by examining research questions and hypotheses. A hypothesis often states that one concept is related to another or that differences in some outcome concept will be observed across different groups. Therefore, the concepts listed in the hypotheses must have operational measures if the research testing them is to be performed.

2. Distinguish levels of scale measurement. Four levels of scale measurement can be identified. Each level is associated with increasingly more complex properties. Nominal scales assign numbers or letters to objects for identification or classification. Ordinal scales arrange objects based on relative magnitude of a concept. Thus, ordinal scales represent rankings. Interval scales also represent an ordering based on relative amounts of a concept, but they also capture the differences between scale values. Thus, interval scales allow stimuli to be compared to each other based on the difference in their scale scores. Ratio scales are absolute scales, starting with absolute zeros at which there is a total absence of the attribute. Nominal and ordinal scales are discrete. The mode is the best way to represent central tendency for discrete measures. Ratio measures are continuous and interval scales are generally treated as continuous. For continuous measures, the mean represents a valid representation of central tendency.

3. Know how to form an index or composite measure. Indexes and composite measures are formed by combining scores from multiple items. For instance, a composite score can be formed by adding the scores to multiple scale items, each intended to represent the same concept. Index scores and composite measures scores are often obtained in much the same way. However, they differ theoretically in that index scores do not have to be theoretically or statistically related to one another. Thus, reliability, validity, and sensitivity are characteristics of good measurement. Reliability represents the consistency and repeatability of a measure. Validity refers to the degree to which the instrument measures the concept the researcher wants to measure.

4. Perform a basic assessment of scale reliability and validity. Reliability is most often assessed using coefficient α. Coefficient α should be at least above 0.6 for a scale to be considered as acceptably reliable. Validity is assessed in components. A measure that has adequate construct validity is one that is likely to be well measured. Construct validity consists of face or content validity, convergent validity (internal consistency), discriminant validity, and criterion validity. Statistical procedures like factor analysis can be helpful in providing evidence of construct validity.

5. Define attitude and understand why it is so important in business research. Attitudes are a relatively enduring predisposition to respond consistently to various things including people, activities, events and objects. Attitudes are predispositions toward behavior and as such represent rules that inform a person as to the appropriate reaction in a given situation. Attitudes consist of three components: the affective, or the emotions or feelings involved; the cognitive, or awareness or knowledge; and the behavioral, or the predisposition to action. Attitudes are so important because when an attitude is known, behavior can be predicted with some degree of confidence.

6. **Produce a scale that measures an attitudinal concept.** With a Likert scale, respondents indicate their attitudes by checking how strongly they agree or disagree with carefully constructed statements. An attitude can be represented with a series of Likert scale items. Typically, Likert scales contain between five and seven response points. A five-item Likert scale states a phrase with which a respondent expresses agreement. The response points would be "strongly disagree," "disagree," "neutral," "agree," "strongly agree." A semantic differential uses a series of attitude scales anchored by bipolar adjectives. The respondent indicates where his or her attitude falls between the polar attitudes. Constant-sum scales require the respondent to divide a constant sum into parts, indicating the weights to be given to various attributes of the item being studied.

7. **Implement a multi-attribute model.** A multiattribute model represents a respondent's attitude about some activity, object, event, or idea by taking belief scores assessed with some type of rating scale and multiplying each belief score by an evaluation of the matching characteristic, also supplied using some type of rating scale, and then summing those products together. These attitude scores are expected to predict behavioral intentions with some degree of confidence. Multi-attribute models provide highly diagnostic information to competitive businesses and thus, they are widely applied.

Key Terms and Concepts

attribute, *246*
attitude, *252*
balanced rating scale, *261*
category scale, *254*
choice, *253*
coefficient alpha (α), *249*
comparative rating scale, *260*
composite measures, *247*
concept, *240*
constant-sum scale, *257*
construct, *241*
construct validity, *251*
continuous measures, *246*
convergent validity, *251*
correspondence rules, *240*
criterion validity, *250*

discrete measures, *245*
discriminant validity, *251*
face (content) validity, *250*
forced-choice rating scale, *262*
graphic rating scale, *258*
index measure, *247*
internal consistency, *248*
interval scales, *244*
Likert scale, *255*
measurement, *238*
monadic rating scale, *260*
multi-attribute model, *263*
non-forced-choice scale, *262*
nominal scales, *241*
operationalization, *240*
ordinal scales, *242*

paired comparison, *259*
ranking, *253*
rating, *253*
reliability, *248*
reverse coding, *248*
ratio scales, *244*
scale, *240*
semantic differential, *256*
sorting, *253*
split-half method, *249*
summated scale, *247*
test-retest method, *249*
unbalanced rating scale, *262*
validity, *250*

Questions for Review and Critical Thinking

1. Define *measurement*. How is your performance in a marketing research class being measured?
2. What is the difference between a *concept* and a *construct*? In what ways is the definition of the term *variable* similar or different?
3. Consider the following research questions or hypotheses. What variables need to be measured in each?
   a. What are the characteristics of consumers who belong to the frequent shopper segment of GameStop (video games and accessories) stores?
   b. The temperature inside the market will determine how much time that shoppers spend in the store such that when the store is cold they will spend less time shopping than when the store is warm.
   c. The more times a consumer is exposed to an advertisement the more product features they will be able to recall.
   d. Product price is positively related to product quality.
4. An official in the financial office is considering an applicant for financial aid. The officer uses the following process. If the student has a GPA in the 90th percentile among the admission group, 5 points are added. If the student has an ACT or SAT score in the 90th percentile among the admission group, 5 points are added. If the student comes from a family whose cumulative household income was less than $70,000/year for the last 3 years, 8 points are added. If the student is from out of state, 5 points are added. What variables are being used to determine eligibility for this financial aid? What would your approximate score be on this scale? Is it best described as an index or a composite scale? Explain your response.
5. Describe the four different levels of scale measurement.
6. Consider the different grading measuring scales described at the beginning of the chapter. Describe what level of measurement is represented by each. Which method do you think contains the least opportunity for error?
7. Look at the responses to the following survey items that describe how stressful consumers believed a Christmas shopping trip was

using a ten-point scale ranging from 1 (= no stress at all) to 10 (= extremely stressful):

a. How stressful was finding a place to park? _9_
b. How stressful was the checkout procedure? _5_
c. How stressful was trying to find exactly the right product? _4_
d. How stressful was finding a store employee? _6_
   i. What would be the stress score for this respondent based on a summated scale score?
   ii. What would be the stress score for this respondent based on an average composite scale score?
   iii. Do any items need to be reverse-coded? Why or why not?
   iv. How could the concept of split-half reliability be applied using a sample of 100 respondents who gave answers to these four questions?

8. How is it that marketing researchers can justify treating a seven-point Likert scale as interval?

9. What are the components of construct validity? Describe each.

10. Why might a researcher wish to use more than one question to measure satisfaction with a particular aspect of retail shopping?

11. How can a researcher assess the reliability and validity of a multi-item composite scale?

12. Indicate whether the following measures use a nominal, ordinal, interval, or ratio scale:
   a. Prices on the stock market
   b. Marital status, classified as "married" or "never married"
   c. Whether a respondent has ever been unemployed
   d. Professorial rank: assistant professor, associate professor, or professor
   e. Course grades: A, B, C, D, or F
   f. Blood-alcohol content
   g. The color of one's eyes
   h. The size of one's pupils

13. What is an *attitude*? Why do businesses place so much emphasis on measuring attitudinal concepts?

14. Attitudes are sometimes called tri-partite, meaning they have three components. What are the three components of an attitude?

15. Distinguish between *rating* and *ranking*. Which is a better attitude measurement technique? Why?

16. Construct a Likert scale that would measure student attitudes toward constructing a new business building on campus.

17. What is the difference between a five-item and a six-item Likert scale?

18. Describe the way a semantic differential scale could be constructed to measure the behavioral component of attitudes.

19. What is a fundamental weakness of a constant sum or ranking scale?

20. In each of the following, identify the type of scale and evaluate it:
   a. A U.S. representative's questionnaire sent to constituents:

   Do you favor or oppose the Fair Tax Proposal?

In Favor	Opposed	No Opinion
☐	☐	☐

   b. How favorable are you toward the Fair Tax Proposal?

   Very unfavorable ☐ ☐ ☐ ☐ ☐ *Very favorable*

   c. A psychographic statement asking the respondent to circle the appropriate response:

   I shop a lot for specials.

Strongly disagree	Disagree	Neutral	Agree	Strongly agree
1	2	3	4	5

21. What is a multi-attribute model of consumer attitudes?

22. Look at the table. The b columns represent belief scores for two competing products. The e column represents the evaluations of those characteristics. Compute the attitude score for each competitor and comment on the competitive positioning of each.

Characteristic	b—Brand A	b—Brand B	e
Price	5	3	6
Quality	6	2	3
Convenience	1	2	4
Ease of use	3	5	1
Looks	1	7	5

23. If a Likert summated scale has 10 scale items, do all 10 items have to be phrased as either positive or negative statements, or can the scale contain a mix of positive and negative statements? Explain.

24. **ETHICS** A researcher thinks many respondents will answer "don't know" or "can't say" if these options are printed on an attitude scale along with categories indicating level of agreement. The researcher does not print either "don't know" or "can't say" on the questionnaire because the resulting data would be more complicated to analyze and report. Is this proper?

25. **'NET** SRI International investigates U.S. consumers by asking questions about their attitudes and values. It has a Web site so people can VALS-type themselves. To find out your VALS type, go to http://www.sric-bi.com/VALS/presurvey.shtml.

Research Activities

1. **'NET** As well as possible, find out and describe how *Sales and Marketing Management* magazine constructs its buying-power index.

2. Define each of the following concepts, and then operationally define each one by providing correspondence rules between the definition and the scale:
   a. A good bowler
   b. The television audience for *The Tonight Show*
   c. Purchasing intention for a palm-sized computer
   d. Consumer involvement with cars
   e. A workaholic
   f. Fast-food restaurant
   g. The American Dream

3. **'NET** Use the ACSI scores found at http://www.theacsi.org to respond to this question. Using the most recent two years of data, test the following two hypotheses:
   a. American consumers are more satisfied with breweries than they are with wireless telephone services.
   b. **'NET** American consumers are more satisfied with discount and department stores than they are with automobile companies.

4. **'NET/ETHICS** Go to http://www.queendom.com/tests. Click on the lists of personality tests. Take the hostility test. Do you think this is a reliable and valid measure of how prone someone is to generally act in a hostile manner? Would it be ethical to assign prospective employees a hostility score to be used in a hiring index based on results from this or a similar test?

Case 10.1 Attitudes toward Technology and Lifestyle

© GETTYIMAGES/ PHOTODISC GREEN

A marketing research company sent the attitude scales in Case Exhibit 10.1–1 to members of its consumer panel. Other questions on the questionnaire were about ownership and/or use of computers, consumer electronic devices, satellite TV ownership, cellular phones, and Internet activity.

Questions
1. What type of attitude scale appears in the case study?
2. Evaluate the list of statements. Do the statements appear to measure a single concept?
3. What do they appear to be measuring?

CASE EXHIBIT 10.1–1 **Attitude Scale**

Below is a list of statements that may or may not be used to describe your attitudes toward technology and your lifestyle. Please indicate to what extent each statement describes your attitudes by placing an X in a box from 1 to 10, where 10 means that statement "Describes your attitudes completely" and a 1 means that statement "Does not describe your attitudes at all." (X ONE BOX ACROSS FOR EACH STATEMENT.)

	Does Not Describe Your Attitudes At All									Describes Your Attitudes Completely
	1	2	3	4	5	6	7	8	9	10
I like to impress people with my lifestyle.	☐	☐	☐	☐	☐	☐	☐	☐	☐	☐
Technology is important to me.	☐	☐	☐	☐	☐	☐	☐	☐	☐	☐
I am very competitive when it comes to my career.	☐	☐	☐	☐	☐	☐	☐	☐	☐	☐
Having fun is the whole point of life.	☐	☐	☐	☐	☐	☐	☐	☐	☐	☐
Family is important, but I have other interests that are just as important to me.	☐	☐	☐	☐	☐	☐	☐	☐	☐	☐
I am constantly looking for new ways to entertain myself.	☐	☐	☐	☐	☐	☐	☐	☐	☐	☐
Making a lot of money is important to me.	☐	☐	☐	☐	☐	☐	☐	☐	☐	☐
I spend most of my free time doing fun stuff with my friends.	☐	☐	☐	☐	☐	☐	☐	☐	☐	☐
I like to spend time learning about new technology products.	☐	☐	☐	☐	☐	☐	☐	☐	☐	☐
I like to show off my taste and style.	☐	☐	☐	☐	☐	☐	☐	☐	☐	☐
I like technology.	☐	☐	☐	☐	☐	☐	☐	☐	☐	☐
My family is by far the most important thing in my life.	☐	☐	☐	☐	☐	☐	☐	☐	☐	☐
I put a lot of time and energy into my career.	☐	☐	☐	☐	☐	☐	☐	☐	☐	☐
I am very likely to purchase new technology products or services.	☐	☐	☐	☐	☐	☐	☐	☐	☐	☐
I spend most of my free time working on improving myself.	☐	☐	☐	☐	☐	☐	☐	☐	☐	☐

After studying this chapter, you should be able to

1. Know the key decisions in questionnaire design
2. Choose between open-ended and fixed-alternative questions
3. Summarize guidelines for avoiding mistakes in questionnaire design
4. Describe how the proper sequence of questions may improve a questionnaire
5. Discuss how to design a questionnaire layout
6. Describe criteria for pretesting and revising a questionnaire and for adapting it to global markets

Chapter Vignette: J.D. Power Asks Consumers to Get Real

Are you driving your dream car? Most of us can't, because we bump up against the practical reality that we can't pay for every great new feature. As carmakers consider adding new features, they have to evaluate not only which ones appeal to consumers but also which ones will actually sell, considering their likely cost. J.D. Power and Associates recently addressed this issue in a survey of about seventeen thousand consumers.[1]

In the J.D. Power survey, consumers were asked whether they were familiar with 22 different emerging technologies. Then they were asked about their interest in each technology, rating their interest using a scale ("definitely interested," "probably interested," and so on). Next, the study indicated the likely price of each technology, and consumers were asked their interest, given the price. The results ranked the features according to interest level, based on the percentage who indicated they were either definitely or probably interested in the feature.

Learning price information often changed consumers' interest levels. Night vision systems appealed to 72 percent of consumers, placing it in second place in the rankings. But when consumers learned the systems would likely add $1,500 to the price of a car, this technology dropped to a rank of 17, near the bottom. In contrast, HD radio ranked in sixteenth place until consumers saw a price tag of just $150. That price pushed the feature up to third place. Still, two features remained in the top five even with pricing information: run-flat tires and stability control. And three of the bottom-five features—a reconfigurable cabin, lane departure warning system, and smart sensing power-swing front doors—stayed in the bottom rankings. Automakers can use findings such as these to determine which features are price-sensitive and which might be appealing even at a higher price.

In the J.D. Power survey, answers changed when respondents were given more information. This chapter outlines a procedure for questionnaire design, which addresses concerns such as the wording and order of questions and the layout of the questionnaire.

By now, you are probably quite familiar with the online course questionnaire. As you went through the questionnaire, did you spot any problem questions? You should be able to describe the problems better after finishing this chapter. Here are some questions to consider:

- What are problem items, if any?
- Are there any topics covered in the survey that would result in more valid responses through a) a phone interview or b) a personal interview?
- Look at the section of the questionnaire shown. Describe any potential problems with these particular items using terminology from the chapter. In other words, do the items display characteristics that should be avoided?

Please read the following statements. After reading click the square that best describes whether you agree or disagree with the statement.					
	Strongly Agree	Agree	Neutral	Disagree	Strongly Disagree
I visit a website from another country at least once a week.	○	○	○	○	○
I feel that keeping up with the opinions of other nations is important.	○	○	○	○	○
I think it's important to go to the library and read a newspaper every week.	○	○	○	○	○
It is important to understand the opinions of other countries.	○	○	○	○	○
I think it's important to engage my friends from other countries as to what it's like where they are from.	○	○	○	○	○
I don't have enough time to read a newspaper.	○	○	○	○	○
I get my opinions on other countries from television.	○	○	○	○	○

COURTESY OF QUALTRICS.COM

© GEORGE DOYLE

Introduction

Survey researchers use a questionnaire like a carpenter uses a hammer. The questionnaire is the primary tool for building responses to research questions. Many people may believe asking a question is really very simple. But, the quality of response can't be expected to be good when the question itself was bad.

The importance of question wording is easily overlooked, but questionnaire design is one of the most critical stages in the survey research process. Businesspeople and managers who are inexperienced at marketing research frequently believe that constructing a questionnaire is a simple task that they can do without the assistance of a professional researcher. Amateur researchers like these think a short questionnaire can be written in minutes. Unfortunately, newcomers who naively believe a good printer is all a person needs to construct a questionnaire generally end up with useless results. Ask a bad question, get bad results.

Basic Considerations in Questionnaire Design

Good questionnaire design requires far more than correct grammar. People don't understand questions just because they are grammatically correct. Respondents simply may not know what is being asked. They may be unaware of the product or topic of interest. They may confuse the subject with something else. The question may not mean the same thing to everyone interviewed. Finally, people may refuse to answer personal questions. Most of these problems can be minimized, however, if a skilled researcher composes the questionnaire.

Even though we discuss questionnaire items as questions, often they are not questions at all but simply words, statements, phrases, or images that are used to evoke a response. We saw examples of different approaches in the previous chapter.

For a questionnaire to fulfill a researcher's purposes, the questions must meet the basic criteria of *relevance* and *accuracy*. To achieve these ends, a researcher who is systematically planning a questionnaire's design must make several decisions—typically, but not always, the decisions take place in the following sequence:

1. What should be asked?
2. How should questions be phrased?

3. In what sequence should the questions be arranged?
4. What questionnaire layout will best serve the research objectives?
5. How should the questionnaire be pretested? Does the questionnaire need to be revised?

What Should Be Asked?

Certain decisions made during the early stages of the research process will influence the questionnaire design. The preceding chapters stressed good problem definition and clear research questions. This leads to specific research hypotheses that in turn, clearly indicate what must be measured. Different types of questions may be better at measuring certain things than are others. In addition, the communication medium used for data collection—that is, telephone interview, personal interview, snail mail, or Web-based questionnaire—must be determined. This decision is another forward linkage that influences the structure and content of the questionnaire. The specific questions to be asked will be a function of the previous decisions.

The latter stages of the research process will have an important impact on questionnaire wording. The questions that should be asked will, of course, take the form of data analysis into account. When designing the questionnaire, the researcher should consider the types of statistical analysis that will be conducted.

Questionnaire Relevancy

A questionnaire is *relevant* to the extent that all information collected addresses a research question that will help the decision maker address the current marketing problem. Asking a wrong question or an irrelevant question is a common pitfall. If the marketing task is to pinpoint store image problems, questions asking for political opinions may be irrelevant. The researcher should be specific about data needs and have a rationale for each item requesting information. Irrelevant questions are more than a nuisance because they make the survey needlessly long. In a study where two samples of the same group of businesses received either a one-page or a three-page questionnaire, the response rate was nearly twice as high for the one-page survey.[2]

Conversely, many researchers, after conducting surveys, find that they omitted some important questions. Therefore, when planning the questionnaire design, researchers must think about possible omissions. Is information on the relevant demographic and psychographic variables being collected? Would certain questions help clarify the answers to other questions? Will the results of the study provide the answer to the marketing manager's problem?

Questionnaire Accuracy

Once a researcher decides what should be asked, the criterion of accuracy becomes the primary concern. *Accuracy* means that the information is valid. While experienced researchers generally believe that questionnaires should use simple, understandable, unbiased, unambiguous, and non-irritating words, no step-by-step procedure for ensuring accuracy in question writing can be generalized across projects. Obtaining accurate answers from respondents depends strongly on the researcher's ability to design a questionnaire that will facilitate recall and motivate respondents to cooperate. Respondents tend to be more cooperative when the subject of the research interests them. When questions are not lengthy, difficult to answer, or ego threatening, there is a higher probability of obtaining unbiased answers.

Question wording and sequence also substantially influence accuracy, which can be particularly challenging when designing a survey for technical audiences. The Department of Treasury commissioned a survey of insurance companies to evaluate their offering of terrorism insurance as required by the government's terrorism reinsurance program. But industry members complained that the survey misused terms such as "contract" and "high risk," which have precise meanings for insurers, and asked for policy information "to date," without specifying which date. These questions caused confusion and left room for interpretation, calling the survey results into question.[3]

Question Phrasing: Open- or Close-Ended Statements?

Questions can be phrased in any one of many ways. The research may choose from many standard question formats developed over time in previous research studies. This section presents a classification of question types and provides some helpful guidelines for writing questions.

Open-Ended Response versus Fixed-Alternative Questions

Two basic types of questions can be identified based on the amount of freedom respondents have in answering. Thus, they call for responses that are either open-ended or closed (from a fixed set of choices).

open-ended response questions

Questions that pose some problem and ask respondents to answer in their own words.

Open-ended response questions pose some problem or topic and ask respondents to answer in their own words. If the question is asked in a personal interview, the interviewer may probe for more information, as in the following examples:

- *What names of local banks can you think of offhand?*
- *What comes to mind when you look at this advertisement?*
- *In what way, if any, could this product be changed or improved? I'd like you to tell me anything you can think of, no matter how minor it seems.*
- *What things do you like most about Federal Express's service?*
- *Why do you buy more of your clothing in Nordstrom than in other stores?*
- *How can our stores better serve your needs?*
- *Please tell me anything at all that you remember about the BMW commercial you saw last night.*

Open-ended response questions are free-answer questions. They may be contrasted with **fixed-alternative questions**—sometimes called *closed questions*—which give respondents specific limited-alternative responses and ask them to choose the one closest to their own viewpoints. For example:

fixed-alternative questions

Questions in which respondents are given specific, limited-alternative responses and asked to choose the one closest to their own viewpoint.

Did you use any commercial feed or supplement for livestock or poultry in 2006?

☐ *Yes*   ☐ *No*

Compared with ten years ago, would you say that the quality of most products made in Japan today is higher, about the same, or not as good?

☐ *Higher*
☐ *About the same*
☐ *Not as good*

Do you think the Renewable Energy Partnership Program has affected your business?

☐ *Yes, for the better*
☐ *Yes, for the worse*
☐ *Not especially*

In which type of bookstore is it easier for you to shop—a regular bookstore or a Web-based bookstore?

☐ *Regular "brick and mortar" bookstore*
☐ *Web bookstore*

How much of your shopping for clothes and household items do you do in wholesale club stores?

☐ *All of it*
☐ *Most of it*
☐ *About one-half of it*
☐ *About one-quarter of it*
☐ *Less than one-quarter of it*

■ USING OPEN-ENDED RESPONSE QUESTIONS

Open-ended response questions are most beneficial when the researcher is conducting exploratory research, especially when the range of responses is not known. Such questions can be used to learn which words and phrases people spontaneously give to the free-response question. Respondents are free to answer with whatever is uppermost in their minds. By obtaining free and uninhibited responses, the researcher may find some unanticipated reaction toward the product. Such responses will reflect the flavor of the language that people use in talking about goods or services and thus may provide a source of new ideas for advertising copywriting or a good way of wording structured scale items. Also, open-ended response questions are valuable at the beginning of an interview. They are good first questions because they allow respondents to warm up to the questioning process.

The cost of administering open-ended response questions is substantially higher than that of administering fixed-alternative questions because the job of editing, coding, and analyzing the data is quite extensive. As each respondent's answer is somewhat unique, there is some difficulty in categorizing and summarizing the answers. The process requires that an editor go over a sample of questions to develop a classification scheme. This scheme is then used to code all answers according to the classification scheme.

Another potential disadvantage of the open-ended response question is the possibility that interviewer bias will influence the answer. While most interviewer instructions state that answers are to be recorded verbatim, rarely does even the best interviewer get every word spoken by the respondent. Interviewers have a tendency to take shortcuts. When this occurs, the interviewer may well introduce error because the final answer may reflect a combination of the respondent's and interviewer's ideas.

Also, articulate individuals tend to give longer answers to open-ended response questions. Such respondents often are better educated and from higher income groups and therefore may not be representative of the entire population, and yet they may give a large share of the responses.

■ USING FIXED-ALTERNATIVE QUESTIONS

In contrast, fixed-alternative questions require less interviewer skill, take less time, and are easier for the respondent to answer. This is because answers to closed questions are classified into standardized groupings prior to data collection. Standardizing alternative responses to a question provides comparability of answers, which facilitates coding, tabulating, and ultimately interpreting the data.

However, when a researcher is unaware of the potential responses to a question, fixed-alternative questions obviously cannot be used. If the researcher assumes what the responses will be but is in fact wrong, he or she will have no way of knowing the extent to which the assumption was incorrect. Sometimes this type of error comes to light after the questionnaire has been used. Researchers found cross-cultural misunderstandings in a survey of mothers called the Preschooler Feeding Questionnaire. By talking to a group of African-American mothers, a researcher at the University of Chicago determined that they had experiences with encouraging children to eat more and using food to calm children, but they used different language for these situations than the questionnaire used, so they misinterpreted some questions.[4]

Unanticipated alternatives emerge when respondents believe that closed answers do not adequately reflect their feelings. They may make comments to the interviewer or write additional answers on the questionnaire indicating that the exploratory research did not yield a complete array of responses. After the fact, little can be done to correct a closed question that does not provide enough alternatives. Therefore, a researcher may find exploratory research with open-ended responses valuable before writing a descriptive questionnaire. The researcher should strive to ensure that there are sufficient response choices to include almost all possible answers.

Respondents may check off obvious alternatives, such as price or durability, if they do not see the choice they would prefer. Also, a fixed-alternative question may tempt respondents to check an answer that is more prestigious or socially acceptable than the true answer. Rather than stating that they do not know why they chose a given product, they may select an alternative among those presented, or as a matter of convenience, they may select a given alternative rather than think of the most correct response.

Most questionnaires mix open-ended and closed questions. As we have discussed, each form has unique benefits. In addition, a change of pace can eliminate respondent boredom and fatigue.

Types of Fixed-Alternative Questions

Earlier in the chapter a variety of fixed-alternative questions were presented. We will now identify and categorize the various types.

The **simple-dichotomy (dichotomous-alternative) question** requires the respondent to choose one of two alternatives. The answer can be a simple "yes" or "no" or a choice between "this" and "that." For example:

Did you make any long-distance calls last week?

☐   *Yes*   ☐   *No*

Several types of questions provide the respondent with *multiple-choice alternatives*. The **determinant-choice question** requires the respondent to choose one—and only one—response from among several possible alternatives. For example:

Please give us some information about your flight. In which section of the aircraft did you sit?

☐   *First class*
☐   *Business class*
☐   *Coach class*

The **frequency-determination question** is a determinant-choice question that asks for an answer about the general frequency of occurrence. For example:

How frequently do you watch the MTV television channel?

☐   *Every day*
☐   *5–6 times a week*
☐   *2–4 times a week*
☐   *Once a week*
☐   *Less than once a week*
☐   *Never*

Attitude rating scales, such as the Likert scale, semantic differential, Stapel scale, and so on, are fixed-alternative questions too. These scales were discussed in Chapter 10.

The **checklist question** allows the respondent to provide multiple answers to a single question. The respondent indicates past experience, preference, and the like merely by checking off items. In many cases the choices are adjectives that describe a particular object. A typical checklist question might ask the following:

Please check which of the following sources of information about investments you regularly use, if any.

☐   *Personal advice of your broker(s)*
☐   *Brokerage newsletters*
☐   *Brokerage research reports*
☐   *Investment advisory service(s)*
☐   *Conversations with other investors*
☐   *Web page(s)*
☐   *None of these*
☐   *Other (please specify) _____*

A major problem in developing dichotomous or multiple-choice alternatives is the framing of the response alternatives. There should be no overlap among categories. Alternatives should be *mutually exclusive,* meaning only one dimension of an issue should be related to each alternative. The following listing of income groups illustrates a common error:

- *Under $15,000*
- *$15,000–$30,000*
- *$30,000–$55,000*
- *$55,000–$70,000*
- *Over $70,000*

---

simple-dichotomy (dichotomous-alternative) question

A fixed-alternative question that requires the respondent to choose one of two alternatives.

determinant-choice question

A fixed-alternative question that requires the respondent to choose one response from among multiple alternatives.

frequency-determination question

A fixed-alternative question that asks for an answer about general frequency of occurrence.

checklist question

A fixed-alternative question that allows the respondent to provide multiple answers to a single question by checking off items.

How many people with incomes of $30,000 will be in the second group, and how many will be in the third group? A respondent who actually had a $30,000 income could equally as likely choose either. Researchers have no way of knowing how a true $30,000–per-year respondent responded. Grouping alternatives without forethought about analysis is likely to diminish accuracy.

Also, few people relish being in the lowest category. To negate the potential bias caused by respondents' tendency to avoid an extreme category, researchers often include a category lower than the lowest expected answers.

Phrasing Questions for Self-Administered, Telephone, and Personal Interview Surveys

The means of data collection—telephone interview, personal interview, self-administered questionnaire—will influence the question format and question phrasing. In general, questions for mail, Internet, and telephone surveys must be less complex than those used in personal interviews. Questionnaires for telephone and personal interviews should be written in a conversational style. Exhibit 11.1 illustrates how a question may be revised for a different medium.

EXHIBIT 11.1

Reducing Question Complexity by Providing Fewer Responses for Telephone Interviews

Mail Form:

How satisfied are you with your community?

1 Very satisfied
2 Quite satisfied
3 Somewhat satisfied
4 Slightly satisfied
5 Neither satisfied nor dissatisfied
6 Slightly dissatisfied
7 Somewhat dissatisfied
8 Quite dissatisfied
9 Very dissatisfied

Revised for Telephone:

How satisfied are you with your community? Would you say you are very satisfied, somewhat satisfied, neither satisfied nor dissatisfied, somewhat dissatisfied, or very dissatisfied?

Very satisfied	1
Somewhat satisfied	2
Neither satisfied nor dissatisfied	3
Somewhat dissatisfied	4
Very dissatisfied	5

Source: Don A. Dillman, *Mail and Telephone Surveys: The Total Design Method* (New York: John Wiley & Sons, 1978), p. 209. Reprinted with permission of John Wiley & Sons, Inc.

In a telephone survey about attitudes toward police services, the questionnaire not only asked about general attitudes such as how much respondents trust their local police officers and whether the police are "approachable," "dedicated," and so on, but also provided basic scenarios to help respondents put their expectations into words. For example, the interviewer asked respondents to imagine that someone had broken into their home and stolen items, and that the respondent called the police to report the crime. The interviewer asked how quickly or slowly the respondent expected the police to arrive.[5]

When a question is read aloud, remembering the alternative choices can be difficult. Consider the following question from a personal interview:

There has been a lot of discussion about the potential health risks to nonsmokers from tobacco smoke in public buildings, restaurants, and business offices. How serious a health threat to you personally is the inhaling of this secondhand smoke, often called passive smoking: Is it a very serious health threat, somewhat serious, not too serious, or not serious at all?

1. Very serious
2. Somewhat serious

3. *Not too serious*
4. *Not serious at all*
5. *(Don't know)*

The last portion of the question was a listing of the four alternatives that serve as answers. This listing at the end is often used in interviews to remind the respondent of the alternatives, since they are not presented visually. The fifth alternative, "Don't know," is in parentheses because, although the interviewer knows it is an acceptable answer, it is not read. The researcher only uses this response when the respondent truly cannot provide an answer.

The data collection technique also influences the layout of the questionnaire. Layout will be discussed later in the chapter.

Avoiding Mistakes

No hard-and-fast rules determine how to develop a questionnaire. Fortunately, research experience has yielded some guidelines that help prevent the most common mistakes.

TO THE POINT

I don't know the rules of grammar. . . . If you're trying to persuade people to do something, or buy something, it seems to me you should use their language, the language they use every day, the language in which they think. We try to write in the vernacular.

—David Ogilvy

Avoid Complexity: Simpler Language is Better

Words used in questionnaires should be readily understandable to all respondents. The researcher usually has the difficult task of adopting the conversational language of people at the lower education levels without talking down to better-educated respondents. Remember, not all people have the vocabulary of a college graduate. Many consumers, for instance, have never gone beyond a high school education.

Respondents can probably tell an interviewer whether they are married, single, divorced, separated, or widowed, but providing their *marital status* may present a problem. The technical jargon of top corporate executives should be avoided when surveying retailers or industrial users. "Brand image," "positioning," "marginal analysis," and other corporate language may not have the same meaning for or even be understood by a store owner-operator in a retail survey. The vocabulary used in the following question from an attitude survey on social problems probably would confuse many respondents:

> *When effluents from a paper mill can be drunk and exhaust from factory smokestacks can be breathed, then humankind will have done a good job in saving the environment. . . . Don't you agree that what we want is zero toxicity: no effluents?*

Besides being too long and confusing, this question is leading.

Avoid Leading and Loaded Questions

leading question

A question that suggests or implies certain answers.

Leading and loaded questions are a major source of bias in question wording. A **leading question** suggests or implies certain answers. A media study of environmental consciousness asked consumers this question:

> *Many people are washing their clothes less often because of concerns for the environment. How has your concern for the environment affected the way you wash and wear clothes?*

> ☐ *Wash less*   ☐ *No change*   ☐ *Wash more*

The potential "bandwagon effect" implied in this question threatens the study's validity. *Partial mention of alternatives* is a variation of this phenomenon:

> *Do small imported cars, such as a Smart Car, get better gas mileage than small U.S. made cars? How do you generally spend your free time, watching television or what?*

loaded question

A question that suggests a socially desirable answer or is emotionally charged.

A **loaded question** suggests a socially desirable answer or is emotionally charged. Consider the following question from a survey about media influence on cooking and home-decorating behavior:[6]

What most influences you to buy food equipment?

- [ ] *My own need for equipment at the time*
- [ ] *Salesperson at store*
- [ ] *Food magazines*
- [ ] *Food shows on TV*
- [ ] *Internet food sites*
- [ ] *Family or friends*
- [ ] *Food/dining section of newspaper*
- [ ] *Other*
- [ ] *I rarely/never buy food preparation equipment*

Over half the respondents chose the first alternative. Although this question is not emotionally loaded, many people could be reluctant to say they are swayed by the media rather than making purchases out of their own, independently experienced need.

A television station produced the following 10-second spot asking for viewer feedback:

We are happy when you like programs on Channel 7. We are sad when you dislike programs on Channel 7. Write us and let us know what you think of our programming.

Few people wish to make others sad. This question may elicit positive comments disproportionate to negative comments.

Certain answers to questions are more socially desirable than others. For example, a truthful answer to the following classification question might be painful:

Where did you rank academically in your high school graduating class?

- [ ] *Top quarter*
- [ ] *2nd quarter*
- [ ] *3rd quarter*
- [ ] *4th quarter*

When taking personality or psychographic tests, respondents frequently can interpret which answers are most socially acceptable even if those answers do not portray their true feelings. For example, which are the socially desirable answers to the following questions on a self-confidence scale?

I feel capable of handling myself in most social situations.

- [ ] *Agree*   [ ] *Disagree*

I seldom fear my actions will cause others to have low opinions of me.

- [ ] *Agree*   [ ] *Disagree*

An experiment conducted in the early days of polling illustrates the unpopularity of change.[7] Comparable samples of respondents were simultaneously asked two questions about the presidential succession. One sample was asked, **"Would you favor or oppose adding a law to the Constitution preventing a president from succeeding himself more than once?"** The other sample was asked, **"Would you favor or oppose changing the Constitution in order to prevent a president from succeeding himself more than once?"** Fifty percent of respondents answered negatively to the first question. For the second question, 65 percent of respondents answered negatively. Thus, the public would rather add to than change the Constitution.

Asking respondents "how often" they use a product or visit a store leads them to generalize about their habits, because there usually is some variance in their behavior. In generalizing, a person is likely to portray an *ideal* behavior rather than an *average* behavior. For instance, brushing your teeth after each meal may be ideal, but busy people may skip a brushing or two. An introductory **counterbiasing statement** or preamble to a question that reassures respondents that their "embarrassing" behavior is not abnormal may yield truthful responses:

Some people have the time to brush three times daily but others do not. How often did you brush your teeth yesterday?

counterbiasing statement

An introductory statement or preamble to a potentially embarrassing question that reduces a respondent's reluctance to answer by suggesting that certain behavior is not unusual.

If a question embarrasses the respondent, it may elicit no answer or a biased response. This is particularly true with respect to personal or classification data such as income or education. The problem may be mitigated by introducing the section of the questionnaire with a statement such as this:

To help classify your answers, we'd like to ask you a few questions. Again, your answers will be kept in strict confidence.

A question statement may be leading because it is phrased to reflect either the negative or the positive aspects of an issue. To control for this bias, the wording of attitudinal questions may be reversed for 50 percent of the sample. This **split-ballot technique** is used with the expectation that two alternative phrasings of the same question will yield a more accurate total response than will a single phrasing. For example, in a study on small-car buying behavior, one-half of a sample of imported-car purchasers received a questionnaire in which they were asked to agree or disagree with the statement **"Small U.S. cars are cheaper to maintain than small imported cars."** The other half of the import-car owners received a questionnaire in which the statement read **"Small imported cars are cheaper to maintain than small U.S. cars."**

split-ballot technique

Using two alternative phrasings of the same question for respective halves of a sample to elicit a more accurate total response than would a single phrasing.

Avoid Ambiguity: Be as Specific as Possible

Items on questionnaires often are ambiguous because they are too general. Consider such indefinite words as *often, occasionally, regularly, frequently, many, good,* and *poor.* Each of these words has many different meanings. For one consumer *frequent* reading of *Fortune* magazine may be reading six or seven issues a year. Another consumer may think reading two issues a year is frequent.

Questions such as the following one, used in a study measuring the reactions of consumers to a television boycott, should be interpreted with care:

Please indicate the statement that best describes your family's television viewing during the boycott of Channel 7.

☐ *We did not watch any television programs on Channel 7.*
☐ *We watched hardly any television programs on Channel 7.*
☐ *We occasionally watched television programs on Channel 7.*
☐ *We frequently watched television programs on Channel 7.*

Some marketing scholars have suggested that the rate of diffusion of an innovation is related to the perception of product attributes such as *divisibility,* which refers to the extent to which the innovation may be tried or tested on a limited scale.[8] An empirical attempt to test this theory using semantic differentials was a disaster. Pretesting found that the bipolar adjectives *divisible–not divisible* were impossible for consumers to understand because they did not have the theory in mind as a frame of reference. A revision of the scale used these bipolar adjectives:

Testable ____ ____ ____ ____ ____ ____ *Not testable*
(sample use possible)   *(sample use not possible)*

However, the question remained ambiguous because the meaning was still unclear.

A brewing industry study on point-of-purchase advertising (store displays) asked:

What degree of durability do you prefer in your point-of-purchase advertising?

☐ *Permanent (lasting more than 6 months)*
☐ *Semipermanent (lasting from 1 to 6 months)*
☐ *Temporary (lasting less than 1 month)*

Here the researchers clarified the terms *permanent, semipermanent,* and *temporary* by defining them for the respondent. However, the question remained somewhat ambiguous. Beer marketers often use a variety of point-of-purchase devices to serve different purposes—in this case, what is the purpose? In addition, analysis was difficult because respondents were merely asked to indicate a preference rather than a *degree* of preference. Thus, the meaning of a question may not be clear because the frame of reference is inadequate for interpreting the context of the question.

A student research group asked this question:

What media do you rely on most?

☐ *Television*
☐ *Radio*
☐ *Internet*
☐ *Newspapers*

This question is ambiguous because it does not ask about the content of the media. "Rely on most" for what—news, sports, entertainment?

Avoid Double-Barreled Items

A question covering several issues at once is referred to as a **double-barreled question** and should always be avoided. Making the mistake of asking two questions rather than one is easy—for example, **"Please indicate how much you agree with the following statement: 'Labor unions and management are responsible for the auto crisis.'"** Which intermediaries are responsible, the wholesalers or the retailers?

double-barreled question

A question that may induce bias because it covers two issues at once.

When multiple questions are asked in one question, the results may be exceedingly difficult to interpret. Consider the following question from a magazine's survey entitled "How Do You Feel about Being a Woman?":

Between you and your husband, who does the housework (cleaning, cooking, dishwashing, laundry) over and above that done by any hired help?

☐ *I do all of it.*
☐ *I do almost all of it.*
☐ *I do over half of it.*
☐ *We split the work fifty-fifty.*
☐ *My husband does over half of it.*

The answers to this question do not tell us if the wife cooks and the husband washes the dishes. The Research Snapshot on the next page provides additional insight into this question.

A survey by a consumer-oriented library asked,

Are you satisfied with the present system of handling "closed-reserve" and "open-reserve" readings? (Are enough copies available? Are the required materials ordered promptly? Are the borrowing regulations adequate for students' use of materials?)

☐ *Yes*   ☐ *No*

A respondent may feel torn between a "yes" to one part of the question and a "no" to another part. The answer to this question does not tell the researcher which problem or combination of problems concerns the library user. Further, a Likert statement from a study dealing with student perceptions of managerial ethics:

National Sales Managers buy liquor and prostitutes for   SD   D   N   A   SA
important customers

The item intends to discover students' attitudes about selling as a career.[9] However, perhaps this would be better as two separate questions rather than one to learn respondents' specific beliefs. Then no ambiguity would exist about what sales managers might buy for customers. A sales manager who takes a customer out for dinner may buy drinks but might never think of buying prostitutes. So, as is, what would a strongly agree or strongly disagree response really mean?

The following comment offers good advice regarding double-barreled questions:

Generally speaking, it is hard enough to get answers to one idea at a time without complicating the problem by asking what amounts to two questions at once. If two ideas are to be explored, they deserve at least two questions. Since question marks are not rationed, there is little excuse for the needless confusion that results [from] the double-barreled question.[10]

Who's *Really* Doing the Housework?

Married women have been a large part of the workforce for decades, but wives continue to complain that when both spouses hold jobs, women bear the heavier responsibility for housework. Researchers have recently considered whether the problem is one of fairness or misperception.

Some evidence suggests that the difference in estimates depends partly on data gathering. First, it matters whom the researchers question and when they ask. If the study asks men and women to recall how they used their time at home, both groups tend to overestimate the time they devote to housework. Also, defining time spent on housework turns out to be more complex than you might guess. Why? People often combine activities. For example, someone might grab an armload of dirty clothes to shove into the washing machine on the way to the den to use the computer. Is that housework?

Detailed data from the long-term Sloan 500 Family Study provide some insights. This study used the Experience Sampling Method (ESM) to overcome problems associated with asking people to remember how they used their time. With ESM, participants wear programmed wristwatches that beep at randomly chosen times. Whenever the watch beeps, participants are supposed to answer a short questionnaire indicating what their primary and secondary activities are and what they are thinking about at that time. With regard to housework, researchers found that if they count time spent on housework as either a primary or secondary activity, the overreporting of housework time shrinks. If the definition of housework is further expanded to include time spent thinking about it—not necessarily procrastinating, but maybe planning or managing household tasks—the overreporting shrinks again. The way housework is defined also affects the size of the gap between husbands' and wives' contributions.

Source: Based on Yun-Suk Lee and Linda J. Waite, "Husbands' and Wives' Time Spent on Housework: A Comparison of Measures," *Journal of Marriage and Family* 67, no. 2 (2005): 328–36, abstract downloaded from OCLC First Search, http://firstsearch.oclc.org; Barbara Schneider and Linda Waite, "Timely and Timeless: Working Parents and Their Children," Conference on Work, Family, Health and Well-Being, Washington, DC (June 16–18, 2003), downloaded from Maryland Population Research Center Web site, http://www.popcenter.umd.edu; Alfred P. Sloan Center on Parents, Children and Work, "Overview of Center Research," http://www.sloanworkingfamilies.org, accessed March 8, 2006.

© RF CORBIS

© GEORGE DOYLE & CIARAN GRIFFIN

Avoid Making Assumptions

Consider the following question:

Should Macy's continue its excellent gift-wrapping program?

☐ *Yes*   ☐ *No*

This question has a built-in assumption: that people believe the gift-wrapping program is excellent. By answering "yes," the respondent implies that the program is, in fact, excellent and that things are fine just as they are. When a respondent answers "no," the opinion is to discontinue the program implying that it isn't excellent. But, perhaps the respondent simply doesn't think gift wrapping offers any value whether the service is excellent or not.

Another frequent mistake is assuming that the respondent had previously thought about an issue. For example, the following question appeared in a survey concerning Jack-in-the-Box: **"Do you think Jack-in-the-Box restaurants should consider changing their name?"** Respondents have not likely thought about this question beforehand. Most respondents answered the question even though they had no prior opinion concerning the name change. Researchers that desire an informed opinion will end up with responses based on too low a level of involvement in a case like this.

Avoid Burdensome Questions That May Tax the Respondent's Memory

A simple fact of human life is that people forget. Researchers writing questions about past behavior or events should recognize that certain questions may make serious demands on the respondent's memory. Writing questions about prior events requires a conscientious attempt to minimize the problems associated with forgetting.

In many situations, respondents cannot recall answers. For example, a telephone survey conducted during the 24-hour period following the airing of the Super Bowl might establish whether the respondent watched the Super Bowl and then ask, "Do you recall any commercials on that program?" If the answer is positive, the interviewer might ask, "What brands were advertised?" These two questions measure **unaided recall**, because they give the respondent no clue as to the brand of interest.

If the researcher suspects that the respondent may have forgotten the answer to a question, he or she may rewrite the question in an **aided-recall** format—that is, in a format that provides a clue to help jog the respondent's memory. For instance, the question about an advertised beer in an aided-recall format might be "Do you recall whether there was a brand of beer advertised on that program?" or "I am going to read you a list of beer brand names. Can you pick out the name of the beer that was advertised on the program?" While aided recall is not as strong a test of attention or memory as unaided recall, it is less taxing to the respondent's memory.

Telescoping and squishing are two additional consequences of respondents' forgetting the exact details of their behavior. *Telescoping* occurs when respondents believe that past events happened more recently than they actually did. The opposite effect, *squishing,* occurs when respondents think that recent events took place longer ago than they really did. A solution to this problem may be to refer to a specific event that is memorable—for example, "How often have you gone to a sporting event since the World Series?" Because forgetting tends to increase over time, the question may concern a recent period: "How often did you watch HBO on cable television last week?" (During the editing stage, the results can be transposed to the appropriate time period.)

In situations in which "I don't know" or "I can't recall" is a meaningful answer, simply including a "don't know" response category may solve the question writer's problem.

Order Bias

The order of questions, or the question sequence, may serve several functions for the researcher. If the opening questions are interesting, simple to comprehend, and easy to answer, respondents' cooperation and involvement can be maintained throughout the questionnaire. Asking easy-to-answer questions teaches respondents their role and builds their confidence.

A mail survey among department store buyers drew an extremely poor return rate. A substantial improvement in response rate occurred, however, when researchers added some introductory questions seeking opinions on pending legislation of great importance to these buyers. Respondents completed all the questions, not only those in the opening section.

In their attempt to "warm up" respondents toward the questionnaire, student researchers frequently ask demographic or classificatory questions at the beginning. This generally is not advisable, because asking for personal information such as income level or education may embarrass or threaten respondents. Asking potentially embarrassing questions at the middle or end of the questionnaire usually is better, after rapport has been established between respondent and interviewer.

Order bias can result from a particular answer's position in a set of answers or from the sequencing of questions. In political elections in which candidates lack high visibility, such as elections for county commissioners and judges, the first name listed on the ballot often receives the highest percentage of votes. For this reason, many election boards print several ballots so that each candidate's name appears in every possible position on the ballot.

Order bias can also distort survey results. For example, suppose a questionnaire's purpose is to measure levels of awareness of several charitable organizations. If Big Brothers and Big Sisters is always mentioned first, the American Red Cross second, and the American Cancer Society third, Big Brothers and Big Sisters may receive an artificially high awareness rating because respondents are prone to yea-saying (by indicating awareness of the first item in the list).

Asking specific questions before asking about broader issues is a common cause of order bias. For example, bias may arise if questions about a specific clothing store are asked prior to those concerning the general criteria for selecting a clothing store. Suppose a respondent indicates in the first

---

unaided recall

Asking respondents to remember something without providing any clue.

aided-recall

Asking the respondent to remember something and giving them a clue to help.

order bias

Bias caused by the influence of earlier questions in a questionnaire or by an answer's position in a set of answers.

portion of a questionnaire that she shops at a store where parking needs to be improved. Later in the questionnaire, to avoid appearing inconsistent, she may state that parking is less important than she really believes it is. Specific questions may thus influence the more general ones. As a result, it is advisable to ask general questions before specific questions to obtain the freest of open-ended responses. This procedure, known as the **funnel technique**, allows the researcher to understand the respondent's frame of reference before asking more specific questions about the level of the respondent's information and the intensity of his or her opinions.

funnel technique

Asking general questions before specific questions in order to obtain unbiased responses.

Consider how later answers might be biased by previous questions in this questionnaire on environmental pollution:

Circle the number on the following table that best expresses your feelings about the severity of each environmental problem:

Problem	Not Severe				Extremely Severe
Air pollution from automobile exhausts	1	2	3	4	5
Air pollution from open burning	1	2	3	4	5
Air pollution from industrial smoke	1	2	3	4	5
Air pollution from foul odors	1	2	3	4	5
Noise pollution from airplanes	1	2	3	4	5
Noise pollution from cars, trucks, motorcycles	1	2	3	4	5
Noise pollution from industry	1	2	3	4	5

Not surprisingly, researchers found that the responses to the air pollution questions were highly correlated—in fact, almost identical.

With attitude scales, there also may be an *anchoring effect*. The first concept measured tends to become a comparison point from which subsequent evaluations are made. Randomization of items on a questionnaire susceptible to the anchoring effect helps minimize order bias.

A related problem is bias caused by the order of alternatives on closed questions. To avoid this problem, the order of these choices should be rotated if producing alternative forms of the questionnaire is possible. However, marketing researchers rarely print alternative questionnaires to eliminate problems resulting from order bias. A more common practice is to pencil in *X*s or check marks on printed questionnaires to indicate where the interviewer should start a series of repetitive questions. For example, the capitalized phrases in the following question provide instructions to the interviewer to "rotate" brands, starting with the one checked:

I would like to determine how likely you would be to buy certain brands of candy in the future. Let's start with (X'ED BRAND). (RECORD BELOW UNDER APPROPRIATE BRAND. REPEAT QUESTIONS FOR ALL REMAINING BRANDS.)

Start Here:	( ) Mounds	(X) Almond Joy	( ) Snickers
Definitely would buy	−1	−1	−1
Probably would buy	−2	−2	−2
Might or might not buy	−3	−3	−3
Probably would not buy	−4	−4	−4
Definitely would not buy	−5	−5	−5

One advantage of Internet surveys is the ability to reduce order bias by having the computer randomly order questions and/or response alternatives. With complete randomization, question order is random and respondents see response alternatives in different random positions.

Asking a question that does not apply to the respondent or that the respondent is not qualified to answer may be irritating or cause a biased response because the respondent wishes to please the interviewer or to avoid embarrassment. Including a **filter question** minimizes the chance of asking questions that are inapplicable. Asking **"Where do you generally have check-cashing problems in Springfield?"** may elicit a response even though the respondent has had no check-cashing problems. He or she may wish to please the interviewer with an answer. A filter question such as **"Do you ever have a problem cashing a check in Springfield? — Yes — No"** would screen out the people who are not qualified to answer.

filter question

A question that screens out respondents who are not qualified to answer a second question.

Another form of filter question, the **pivot question,** can be used to obtain income information and other data that respondents may be reluctant to provide. For example,

pivot question

A filter question used to determine which version of a second question will be asked.

"Is your total family income over or under $50,000?" IF UNDER, ASK, "Is it over or under $25,000?" IF OVER, ASK, "Is it over or under $75,000?"

Under $25,000   *$50,001–$75,000*
$25,001–$50,000   *Over $75,000*

Exhibit 11.2 gives an example of a flowchart plan for a questionnaire. Structuring the order of the questions so that they are logical will help to ensure the respondent's cooperation and eliminate confusion or indecision. The researcher maintains legitimacy by making sure that the respondent can comprehend the relationship between a given question (or section of the questionnaire) and

EXHIBIT 11.2 **Flow of Questions to Determine the Level of Prompting Required to Stimulate Recall**

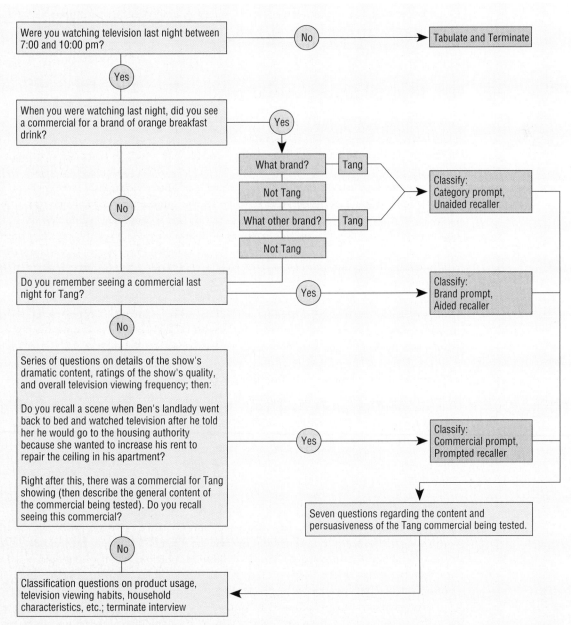

Source: "General Foods Corporation: Tang Instant Breakfast Drink (B)," © 1978 F. Stewart DeBruicker and Harvey N. Singer, The Wharton School, University of Pennsylvania. Reprinted with permission.

the overall purpose of the study. Furthermore, a logical order may aid the individual's memory. Transitional comments explaining the logic of the questionnaire may ensure that the respondent continues. Here are two examples:

> *We have been talking so far about general shopping habits in this city. Now I'd like you to compare two types of grocery stores—regular supermarkets and grocery departments in wholesale club stores.*
>
> *So that I can combine your answers with those of other farmers who are similar to you, I need some personal information about you. Your answers to these questions—as to all of the others you've answered—are confidential, and you will never be identified to anyone without your permission. Thanks for your help so far. If you'll answer the remaining questions, it will help me analyze all your answers.*

What Is the Best Layout?

Good layout and physical attractiveness are crucial in mail, Internet, and other self-administered questionnaires. For different reasons, a good layout in questionnaires designed for personal and telephone interviews is also important.

Traditional Questionnaires

A good layout is neat and attractive, and the instructions for the interviewer should be easy to follow. The responses "It Depends," "Refused," and "Don't Know" enclosed in a box to the side indicate that these answers are acceptable but responses from the five-point scale are preferred.

Often rate of return can be increased by using money that might have been spent on an incentive to improve the attractiveness and quality of the questionnaire. Mail questionnaires should never be overcrowded. Margins should be of decent size, white space should be used to separate blocks of print, and the unavoidable columns of multiple boxes should be kept to a minimum. A question should not begin on one page and end on another page. Splitting questions may cause a respondent to read only part of a question, to pay less attention to answers on one of the pages, or to become confused.

Questionnaires should be designed to appear as short as possible. A booklet form of questionnaire is preferable to stapling a large number of pages together. Also, do not try to put too many questions on a page or on a single computer screen. In situations in which it is necessary to conserve space on the questionnaire or to facilitate data entry or tabulation of the data, a multiple-grid layout may be used. The **multiple-grid question** presents several similar questions and corresponding response alternatives arranged in a grid format. For example:

multiple-grid question
Several similar questions arranged in a grid format.

> *Airlines often offer special fare promotions. On a vacation trip would you take a connecting flight instead of a nonstop flight if the connecting flight were longer?*

	Yes	No	Not sure
One hour longer?	☐	☐	☐
Two hours longer?	☐	☐	☐
Three hours longer?	☐	☐	☐

By using several forms, special instructions, and other tricks of the trade, the researcher can design the questionnaire to facilitate the interviewer's job of following interconnected questions. Exhibits 11.3 and 11.4 (on pages 286–287) illustrate portions of telephone and personal interview questionnaires. Note how the layout and easy-to-follow instructions for interviewers in Questions 1, 2, and 3 of Exhibit 11.3 help the interviewer follow the question sequence.

Instructions are often capitalized or printed in bold to alert the interviewer that it may be necessary to proceed in a certain way. For example, if a particular answer is given, the interviewer or respondent may be instructed to skip certain questions or go to a special sequence of questions. To facilitate coding, question responses can be precoded when possible, as in Exhibit 11.3.

EXHIBIT 11.3 **Telephone Questionnaire with Skip Questions**

1. Did you take the car you had checked to the Standard Auto Repair Center for repairs?

   —1 Yes   **(SKIP TO Q. 3)**   —2 No

2. **(IF NO, ASK:)** Did you have the repair work done?

   —1 Yes   —2 No

   ↓   ↓

1. Where was the repair work done? _____   1. Why didn't you have the car repaired?
   _____   _____
                                                      _____
2. Why didn't you have the repair work done   _____
   at the Standard Auto Repair Center? _____
   _____
   _____

3. **(IF YES TO Q. 1, ASK:)** How satisfied were you with the repair work? Were you . . .

   —1 Very satisfied

   —2 Somewhat satisfied

   —3 Somewhat dissatisfied

   —4 Very dissatisfied

   (IF SOMEWHAT OR VERY DISSATISFIED:) In what way were you dissatisfied?
   _____
   _____

4. **(ASK EVERYONE:)** Do you ever buy gas at the 95th Street Standard Center?

   —1 Yes   —2 No   **(SKIP TO Q. 6)**

5. **(IF YES, ASK:)** How often do you buy gas there?

   —1 Always

   —2 Almost always

   —3 Most of the time

   —4 Part of the time

   —5 Hardly ever

6. Have you ever had your car washed there?

   —1 Yes   —2 No

7. Have you ever had an oil change or lubrication done there?

   —1 Yes   —2 No

Exhibit 11.4 illustrates some other useful techniques that are possible with personal interviews. Questions 3 and 6 instruct the interviewer to hand the respondent a card bearing a list of alternatives. Cards may help respondents grasp the intended meaning of the question and remember all the brand name or other items they are being asked about. Also, Questions 2, 3, and 6 instruct the interviewer that rating of the banks will start with the bank that has been checked in red pencil on the printed questionnaire. The name of the red-checked bank is not the same on every questionnaire. By rotating the order of the check marks, the researchers attempted to reduce order bias caused by respondents' tendency to react more favorably to the first set of questions.

It's Not Always What You Ask, but How You Ask It!

Are there certain types of things that are best discussed face to face? Or, are there some things you'd rather ask a friend by email? Just as in everyday life, survey responses can vary based on the medium used. For instance, can you expect people to be 100 percent honest when you ask them sensitive questions that may even sometimes have moral content? Or, if you are phoned and asked to list your favorite brand, would you give the same response as if you were asked that question on a comprehensive Web survey? Well, the evidence suggests that in either case differences in responses should be expected based on the question medium.

- "Do you give financial support to charitable causes on a regular basis?"
- "Do you go to church on a regular basis?"
- "Have you had an alcoholic drink in the last week?"

Are these sensitive questions? Results of asking people these questions varies based on how they are asked. Specifi-

cally, people who are asked these questions on the telephone give responses that are more protective of their image than do people asked the very same questions via a typical Internet-type questionnaire. Phone survey results suggest a 10 percent difference in the response to the charitable giving question with phone respondents displaying a greater inclination to give to charities than people answering the question via the electronic questionnaire. On the phone, almost 6 in 10 respondents report going to church almost weekly but via the computer, that number drops to 1 in 4. Less than half of all phone respondents had a drink in one week but over half of the computer questionnaire respondents reported that they had a drink.

Brand ratings also vary based on the way questions are asked. That's partly why in the same period you might see a poll showing T.J. Maxx as the leading brand and another may have Google. Some of the companies that conduct these polls rely on telephone interviews and others rely on comprehensive questionnaires delivered by mail or on the Internet. In any case, these results make the case that the way a question is asked is equally as important as how the question is asked!

Sources: Boyle, M., "Microsoft and GE: Not Old and In the Way," *Fortune* (October 31, 2007), http://money.cnn.com/2007/10/31/magazines/fortune/microsoft_ge.fortune/index.htm, accessed September 12, 2008; Gamerman, E., "When Voters Lie," *Wall Street Journal* (August 2, 2008), W1; Seattle Times, "Microsoft Brand Sinks in this Survey," (March 23, 2008), http://seattletimes.nwsource.com/html/microsoft/2004301551_btdownload24.html, accessed September 12, 2008.

For a questionnaire investigating teaching students' experience with Web-based instruction, the researcher had the questionnaire reviewed first by university faculty members to ensure the questions were valid, then asked 20 teaching students to try answering the questions and indicate any ambiguities they noticed. Their feedback prompted changes in the format and wording. Pretesting was especially helpful because the English-language questionnaire was used in a school in the United Arab Emirates, where English is spoken but is not the primary language.[14]

Tabulating the results of a pretest helps determine whether the questionnaire will meet the objectives of the research. A **preliminary tabulation** often illustrates that, although respondents can easily comprehend and answer a given question, that question is inappropriate because it does not provide relevant information to help solve the marketing problem. Consider the following example from a survey among distributors of power-actuated tools such as stud drivers concerning the percentage of sales to given industries:

preliminary tabulation

A tabulation of the results of a pretest to help determine whether the questionnaire will meet the objectives of the research.

Please estimate what percentage of your fastener and load sales go to the following industries:

_____ *% heating, plumbing, and air conditioning*

_____ *% carpentry*

_____ *% electrical*

_____ *% maintenance*

_____ *% other (please specify)*

The researchers were fortunate to learn that asking the question in this manner made it virtually impossible to obtain the information actually desired. Most respondents' answers did not total 100 percent, and the question had to be revised. In general, getting respondents to add everything correctly is a problem. Pretesting difficult questions such as these is essential.

What administrative procedures should be implemented to maximize the value of a pretest? Administering a questionnaire exactly as planned in the actual study often is not possible. For example, mailing out a questionnaire might require several weeks that simply cannot be spared. Pretesting a questionnaire in this manner would provide important information on response rate but may not point out why questions were skipped or what questions are ambiguous or confusing. Personal interviewers can record requests for additional explanation or comments that indicate respondents' difficulty with question sequence or other factors. This is the primary reason why interviewers are often used for pretest work. Self-administered questionnaires are not reworded to be personal interviews, but interviewers are instructed to observe respondents and ask for their comments after they complete the questionnaire. When pretesting personal or telephone interviews, interviewers may test alternative wordings and question sequences to determine which format best suits the intended respondents.

No matter how the pretest is conducted, the researcher should remember that its purpose is to uncover any problems that the questionnaire may cause. Thus, pretests typically are conducted to answer questions about the questionnaire such as the following:

- Can the questionnaire format be followed by the interviewer?
- Does the questionnaire flow naturally and conversationally?
- Are the questions clear and easy to understand?
- Can respondents answer the questions easily?
- Which alternative forms of questions work best?

Pretests also provide means for testing the sampling procedure—to determine, for example, whether interviewers are following the sampling instructions properly and whether the procedure is efficient. Pretests also provide estimates of the response rates for mail surveys and the completion rates for telephone surveys.

Usually a questionnaire goes through several revisions. The exact number of revisions depends on the researcher's and client's judgment. The revision process usually ends when both agree that the desired information is being collected in an unbiased manner.

Designing Questionnaires for Global Markets

Now that marketing research is being conducted around the globe, researchers must take cultural factors into account when designing questionnaires. The most common problem involves translating a questionnaire into other languages. A questionnaire developed in one country may be difficult to translate because equivalent language concepts do not exist or because of differences in idiom and vernacular. Although Spanish is spoken in both Mexico and Venezuela, one researcher found out that the Spanish translation of the English term *retail outlet* works in Mexico but not in Venezuela. Venezuelans interpreted the translation to refer to an electrical outlet, an outlet of a river into an ocean, or the passageway onto a patio.

Counting on an international audience to speak a common language such as English does not necessarily bridge these gaps, even when the respondents actually do speak more than one language. Cultural differences incorporate many shades of meaning that may not be captured by a survey delivered in a language used primarily for, say, business transactions. In a test of this idea, undergraduate students in 24 countries completed questionnaires about attitudes toward school and career. Half received the questionnaire in English, and half in their native language. The results varied, with country-to-country differences being smaller when students completed the questionnaire in English.[15]

International marketing researchers often have questionnaires back translated. **Back translation** is the process of taking a questionnaire that has previously been translated from one language to another and having it translated back again by a second, independent translator. The back translator is often a person whose native tongue is the language that will be used for the questionnaire. This process can reveal inconsistencies between the English version and the translation. For example, when a soft-drink company translated its slogan "Baby, it's cold inside" into Cantonese for research in Hong Kong, the result read "Small Mosquito, on the inside, it is very cold." In Hong Kong, *small mosquito* is a colloquial expression for a small child. Obviously the intended meaning of the advertising message had been lost in the translated questionnaire.[16]

back translation

Taking a questionnaire that has previously been translated into another language and having a second, independent translator translate it back to the original language.

- When designing items to go onto a questionnaire:
  - Simpler wording is better than complex wording.
    - Phrase items as if they were being asked to the person in the sample that will have the most difficulty understanding them.
    - Break complicated ideas into multiple questions.
- A researcher with a strong opinion toward the decision issues is prone to construct leading and loaded questions. Often, this is unintentional.
  - When possible, have an objective person involved in wording questionnaire items.
- Questionnaires should be short. But, for any length questionnaire, the respondent should know about how long it will take to complete at the beginning.
  - Include a status bar whenever possible.
  - Expect response quality to drop as questionnaires take five minutes or longer.

- Long questionnaires should include some check questions to make sure respondents are still paying attention. These should be questions such as an instruction to mark 4 for an item or sequential questions that contain opposite responses.
- Dependent variables should usually be measured before independent variables.
- Sensitive items are generally best collected through impersonal media like mail or Internet questionnaires.
  - But, when asking questions that a respondent believes can be verified easily (i.e., a bank asking typical credit card balance), more accurate answers result when respondents are not anonymous.

© GEORGE DOYLE & CIARAN GRIFFIN

Summary

1. Know the key decisions in questionnaire design. The data gathered via a questionnaire must be both relevant and accurate to be of value. A researcher who is systematically planning a questionnaire's design must face several decisions that will shape the value of the questionnaire. What should be asked? How should questions be phrased? In what sequence should the questions be arranged? What questionnaire layout will best serve the research objectives? How should the questionnaire be pretested? Does the questionnaire need to be revised?

2. Choose between open-ended and fixed-alternative questions. Knowing how each question should be phrased requires some knowledge of the different types of questions possible. Open-ended response questions pose some problem or question and ask the respondent to answer in his or her own words. Fixed-alternative questions require less interviewer skill, take less time, and are easier to answer. In fixed-alternative questions the respondent is given specific limited alternative responses and asked to choose the one closest to his or her own viewpoint. Standardized responses are easier to code, tabulate, and interpret. Care must be taken to formulate the responses so that they do not overlap. Respondents whose answers do not fit any of the fixed alternatives may be forced to select alternatives that do not communicate what they really mean. Open-ended response questions are especially useful in exploratory research or at the beginning of a questionnaire. They make a questionnaire more expensive to analyze because of the uniqueness of the answers. Also, interviewer bias can influence the responses to such questions.

3. Summarize guidelines for avoiding mistakes in questionnaire design. Some guidelines for questionnaire construction have emerged from research experience. The language should be simple to allow for variations in educational level. Researchers should avoid leading or loaded questions, which suggest answers to the respondents, as well as questions that induce them to give socially desirable answers. Respondents have a bias against questions that suggest changes in the status quo. Their reluctance to answer personal questions can be reduced by explaining the need for the questions and by assuring respondents of the confidentiality of their replies. The researcher should carefully avoid ambiguity in questions. Another common problem is the double-barreled question, which asks two questions at once.

4. Describe how the proper sequence of questions may improve a questionnaire. Question sequence can be very important to the success of a survey. The opening questions should be designed to capture respondents' interest and keep them involved. Personal questions should be postponed to the middle or end of the questionnaire. General questions should precede specific ones. In a series of attitude scales the first response may be used as an anchor for comparison with the other responses. The order of alternatives on closed questions can affect the results. Filter questions are useful for avoiding unnecessary questions that do not apply to a particular respondent. Such questions may be put into a flowchart for personal or telephone interviewing.

5. Discuss how to design a questionnaire layout. The layout of a mail or other self-administered questionnaire can affect its response rate. An attractive questionnaire encourages a response, as does a carefully phrased title. Internet questionnaires present unique design issues. Decisions must be made about the use of color, graphics, animation, sound, and other special layout effects that the Internet makes possible.

6. Describe criteria for pretesting and revising a questionnaire and for adapting it to global markets. Pretesting helps reveal errors while they can still be corrected easily. A preliminary tabulation may show that, even if respondents understand questions, the responses are not relevant to the marketing problem. Often, the most efficient way to conduct a pretest is with interviewers to generate quick feedback. International marketing researchers must take cultural factors into account when designing questionnaires. The most widespread problem involves translation into another language. International questionnaires are often back translated.

Key Terms and Concepts

aided-recall, *281*
back translation, *293*
check boxes, *289*
checklist question, *274*
counterbiasing statement, *277*
determinant-choice question, *274*
double-barreled question, *279*
drop-down box, *289*
error trapping, *291*
filter question, *282*
fixed-alternative questions, *272*

forced answering software, *291*
frequency-determination question, *274*
funnel technique, *282*
interactive help desk, *291*
leading question, *276*
loaded question, *276*
multiple-grid question, *284*
open-ended boxes, *289*
open-ended response questions, *272*
order bias, *281*
pivot question, *283*

preliminary tabulation, *292*
push button, *288*
radio button, *289*
simple-dichotomy (dichotomous-alternative) question, *274*
split-ballot technique, *278*
status bar, *288*
unaided recall, *281*
variable piping software, *291*

Questions for Review and Critical Thinking

1. Evaluate and comment on the following questions, taken from several questionnaires:

   a. A university computer center survey on SPSS usage:

   How often do you use SPSS statistical software? Please check one.

   - *Infrequently (once a semester)*
   - *Occasionally (once a month)*
   - *Frequently (once a week)*
   - *All the time (daily)*

   b. A survey of advertising agencies:

   Do you understand and like the Federal Trade Commission's new corrective advertising policy?

   ——*Yes*　——*No*

   c. A survey on a new, small electric car:

   Assuming 90 percent of your driving is in town, would you buy this type of car?

   ——*Yes*　——*No*
   If this type of electric car had the same initial cost as a current "Big 3" full-size, fully equipped car, but operated at one-half the cost over a five-year period, would you buy one?

   ——*Yes*　——*No*

   d. A student survey:

   Since the beginning of this semester, approximately what percentage of the time do you get to campus using each of the forms of transportation available to you per week?

Walk —— Bicycle ——
Public transportation —— Motor vehicle ——

e.   A survey of motorcycle dealers:

Should the company continue its generous cooperative advertising program?

f.   A survey of media use by farmers:

Thinking about yesterday, put an X in the box below for each quarter-hour time period during which, so far as you can recall, you personally listened to radio. Do the same for television.

If you did not watch TV any time yesterday, X here ☐
If you did not listen to radio any time yesterday, X here ☐

g.   A government survey of gasoline retailers:

Suppose the full-service pump selling price for regular gasoline is 232.8 cents per gallon on the first day of the month. Suppose on the 10th of the month the price is raised to 234.9 cents per gallon, and on the 25th of the month it is reduced to 230.9 cents per gallon. In order to provide the required data you should list the accumulator reading on the full-service regular gasoline pump when the station opens on the 1st day, the 10th day, and the 25th day of the month and when the station closes on the last day of the month.

h.   An anti-gun-control group's survey:

Do you believe that private citizens have the right to own firearms to defend themselves, their families, and their property from violent criminal attack?

——Yes   ——No

i.   A survey of the general public:

In the next year, after accounting for inflation, do you think your real personal income will go up or down?

1. *Up*
2. *(Stay the same)*
3. *Down*
4. *(Don't know)*

j.   **ETHICS** A survey of the general public:

Some people say that companies should be required by law to label all chemicals and substances that the government states are potentially harmful. The label would tell what the chemical or substance is, what dangers it might pose, and what safety procedures should be used in handling the substance. Other people say that such laws would be too strict. They say the law should require labels on only those chemicals and substances that the companies themselves decide are potentially

harmful. Such a law, they say, would be less costly for the companies and would permit them to exclude those chemicals and substances they consider to be trade secrets. Which of these views is closest to your own?

1. *Require labels on all chemicals and substances that the government states are potentially harmful.*
2. *(Don't know)*
3. *Require labels on only those chemicals and substances that companies decide are potentially harmful.*

k.   A survey of voters:

Since agriculture is vital to our state's economy, how do you feel about the administration's farm policies?

Strongly favor
Somewhat favor
Somewhat oppose
Strongly oppose
Unsure

2.   The following question was asked of a sample of television viewers:

We are going to ask you to classify the type of fan you consider yourself to be for different sports and sports programs.

- **Diehard Fan: Watch games, follow up on scores and sports news multiple times a day**
- **Avid Fan: Watch games, follow up on scores and sports news once a day**
- **Casual Fan: Watch games, follow up on scores and sports news occasionally**
- **Championship Fan: Watch games, follow up on scores and sports news only during championships or playoffs**
- **Non-Fan: Never watch games or follow up on scores**
- **Anti-Fan: Dislike, oppose, or object to a certain sport**

Does this question do a good job of avoiding ambiguity?

3.   How might the wording of a question about income influence respondents' answers?

4.   What is the difference between a *leading question* and a *loaded question*?

5.   Design one or more open-ended response questions to measure reactions to a magazine ad for a Xerox photocopier.

6.   Design one or more questions to measure how a person who has just been shown a television commercial might describe the commercial.

7.   Evaluate the layout of the filter question that follows:

8.   It has been said that surveys show that consumers hate advertising, but like specific ads. Comment.

9.   Design a complete questionnaire to evaluate a new fast-food fried chicken restaurant.

10. Design a short but complete questionnaire to measure consumer satisfaction with an airline.

11. Develop a checklist of things to consider in questionnaire construction.

12. Design a complete personal interview questionnaire for a zoo that wishes to determine who visits the zoo and how they evaluate it.

13. Design a complete self-administered questionnaire for a bank to give to customers immediately after they open new accounts.

14. Design a questionnaire for your local Big Brothers and Big Sisters organization to investigate awareness of and willingness to volunteer time to this organization.

15. Design a questionnaire for a bank located in a college town to investigate the potential for attracting college students as checking account customers.

16. The Apple Assistance Center is a hotline to solve problems for users of Macintosh computers and other Apple products. Design a short (postcard-size) consumer satisfaction/service quality questionnaire for the Apple Assistance Center.

17. 'NET Visit the following Web site: http://www.history.org. What type of questions might be asked in a survey to evaluate the effectiveness of this Web site in terms of being informative and in terms of being an effective sales medium?

18. A client tells a researcher that she wants a questionnaire that evaluates the importance of 30 product characteristics and rates her brand and 10 competing brands on these characteristics. The researcher believes that this questionnaire will induce respondent fatigue because it will be far too long. Should the researcher do exactly what the client says or risk losing the business by suggesting a different approach?

19. ETHICS A lobbying organization designs a short questionnaire about its political position. It also includes a membership solicitation with the questionnaire. Is this approach ethical?

20. 'NET Visit Mister Poll at http://www.misterpoll.com, where you will find thousands of user-contributed polls on every imaginable topic from the controversial to the downright zany. What you find will depend on when you visit the site. However, you might find something such as a Movie Poll, where you pick your favorite film of the season. Evaluate the questions in the poll.

21. 'NET Try to find two friends that know the same foreign language. Write 10 Likert questions that measure how exciting a retail store environment is to shop in. Have one of your friends interpret the question into the foreign language. Have the other take the translation and state each question in English. How similar is the translated English to the original English? Comment.

22. List the decisions that researchers face in trying to construct a valid and reliable questionnaire. At what stage do you think most questionnaires directed at students are most likely to go wrong?

Research Activity

1. Design eight questions that assess how effective an undergraduate college business course has been.

Case 11.1 Frontier Golf Simulators

© GETTY IMAGES/
PHOTODISC GREEN

It's "Virtually" the Same Game?!

Prepared by Kevin James, Louisiana Tech University

The business of sports is growing tremendously and it is fueled in part by athletes that take on celebrity status. None typifies this better than Tiger Woods. Tiger is a brand representing a multimillion dollar entity unto itself. Traditionally, golf had a stigma of being for wealthy, stodgy, old businessmen who hardly knew how to have a good time. That image is common in many countries outside of the United States to this day. Companies like Nike and Callaway have invested large sums of money and effort to draw a different and more diverse demographic to the game of golf.

With the changing demographic of the actual players comes a marketing challenge of just how to best meet the needs of these segments that are quite new to the game. For instance, indoor golf simulators have started to increase in popularity and offer a chance to play some golf even in an urban setting. These simulators have the distinct advantage of being able to accurately show the player's ball flight and ball spin, as well as the actual yardage the ball travels. A further advantage is that with these simulators, a foursome can finish an entire round of golf in just under an hour instead of four hours or more! Additionally, this round of golf can be played at St. Andrews or Pebble Beach without the expense and hassle of traveling to these mystical sites.

Brian Scheffler is the Director of Marketing for Frontier Golf Simulators, a San Antonio, Texas-based company which operates five state-of-the-art golf simulators. The pricing structure is either $30 per hour for "walk-ins" or a player can take a membership much like he or she might at a real golf club. In addition to the simulators, the facility has a restaurant and bar so that patrons can eat and drink while they tee it up. Brian has the unique challenge of marketing and ultimately selling time on these simulators. Unfortunately, Mr. Scheffler is unsure how to best spend his very limited marketing budget. Mr. Scheffler understands that the traditional golfer has different wants and needs than does the entertainment-seeking golfer. Does virtual golf offer value in the same way as real golf? If not, the simulators may not appeal to real or traditional golfers at all.

Faced with not knowing exactly what people like most about the simulators, Brian decides to create a survey to determine what people like most about their simulator experience and how to most effectively market his product to maximize the customer's experience and ultimately create returning customers.

1. What are some of the issues Brian should consider when designing the survey?
2. What types of issues can be addressed with open-ended questions and what type of issues can be addressed with fixed-alternative questions?
3. How would the structure of the survey change if Brian decides to administer the survey via the telephone versus face-to-face mall intercept interviews?
4. Develop a survey that will address Brian's need to better understand his customers.

Case 11.2 McDonald's Spanish Language Questionnaire

The questions in Case Exhibit 11.2–1, about a visit to McDonald's, originally appeared in Spanish and were translated into English.

Questions

1. What is the typical process for developing questionnaires for markets where consumers speak a language other than English?
2. Find someone who speaks Spanish and have him or her back translate the questions that appear in Case Exhibit 11.2–1. Are these Spanish-language questions adequate?

CASE EXHIBIT 11.2–1 **McDonald's Questionnaire**

AQUI ➡ SE EMPIEZA	1. En general, ¿qué tan satisfecho/a quedó con su visita a este McDonald's hoy?	😞 NADA SATISFECHO/A .... [1] [2] [3] [4] [5]	MUY SATISFECHO/A 😊
	2. Su visita fue....... Adentro (A) o en el Drive-thru (DT)	[A] Adentro	[DT] Drive-thru
	3. Su visita fue....... Durante el Desayuno (D), Almuerzo (A), Cena (C)	[D] Desayuno	[A] Almuerzo [A] Cena
	4. Su visita fue....... Entre semana (E) o Fin de semana (F)	[E] Entre semana	[F] Fin de semana
COMIDA	5. ¿Quedó satisfecho/a con la comida que recibió hoy? Si NO, ¿cuál fue el problema? Favor de rellenar el(los) círculo(s) apropiado(s).	[S] Sí Sandwich / platillo frío Apariencia desagradable Mal sabor de la comida Pocas papas en la bolsa / caja Papas / tortitas de papa frías Papas no bien saladas Bebida aguada / de mal sabor	[N] No ◀ ▢ ▢ ▢ ▢ ▢ ▢

Part 4
Sampling and Statistical Theory

© MATTHIAS CLAMER/STONE+/GETTY IMAGES

CHAPTER 12
Sampling Designs and
Sampling Procedures

CHAPTER 13
Determination of Sample Size:
A Review of Statistical Theory

CHAPTER 12
SAMPLING DESIGNS AND SAMPLING PROCEDURES

After studying this chapter, you should be able to

1. Explain reasons for taking a sample rather than a complete census
2. Describe the process of identifying a target population and selecting a sampling frame
3. Compare random sampling and systematic (nonsampling) errors with an emphasis on how the Internet is intertwined with this issue
4. Identify the types of nonprobability sampling, including their advantages and disadvantages
5. Summarize various types of probability samples
6. Discuss how to choose an appropriate sample design

Chapter Vignette: At Cadbury, Gum Chewing Takes Expertise

After Cadbury Schweppes acquired Pfizer's candy brands, including Bubbaloo, Dentyne, and Trident, new technology and marketing research pointed the company to a new product idea.[1] From a consumer survey, Cadbury knew that most Americans chew gum, and more than two-thirds of those gum chewers said one reason was to avoid snacking. Looking for a product that would serve as a junk-food alternative, company researchers identified gum pellets with liquid centers as a possible new product. Pfizer's sale to Cadbury had included a manufacturing technology that used different flavors for the candy coating and liquid filling. By delivering two flavors and three textures (crunchy, chewy, and liquid), Cadbury hoped the new gum would satisfy customers' cravings for more substantial snacks. And the small pellets of gum seemed more adult-friendly than other liquid-center gums, which were sold under the Freshen Up and Bubbaloo brands.

The developers' next step was to come up with appealing flavor combinations. Peppermint was one obvious choice since most gum has a mint flavor, which tends to maintain a good taste in the chewer's mouth. Another idea came from consumer testing showing that the most popular fruit flavor is strawberry. Cadbury worked with food scientists to select a strawberry flavoring that was less like the jam-sweet flavor popular with children and more like the taste of a fresh strawberry. Then company marketers selected vanilla centers for the mint gum and lime centers for the strawberry gum.

Finally, the new products were ready for consumer testing. Here, Cadbury faced a problem typically associated with testing foods: Most consumers don't pay enough attention to tastes and smells to give helpful feedback. Their comments are vague, so a truly random sample of the consumer population would not give the company the information it needed. Instead, Cadbury recruited a sample from a sensory panel. Panel members passed tests rating their sense of smell and even the rate at which they salivate. Cadbury trained the panelists for the gum-chewing job, teaching them to chew steadily along with the beats of a metronome.

Testers chewed samples of the gum for precisely three minutes, timing themselves with electronic clocks. At the end of each chewing period, a panel leader asked for comments. Panelists cleared their palates with crackers and water before trying the next sample. Eventually, the panelists provided enough feedback for the company to pinpoint winning flavor combinations and move on to engineering the production process.

Just as Cadbury needed a sample of gum chewers to make judgments about its products, sampling is a familiar part of daily life. A customer in a bookstore picks up a book, looks at the cover, and skims a few pages to get a sense of the writing style and content before deciding whether to buy. A high school student visits a college Web site to listen to a classroom lecture and view the notes. Selecting a university on the basis of one Web site visit may not be scientific sampling, but in a personal situation, it may be a meaningful and practical sampling experience. When measuring every item in a population is impossible, inconvenient, or too expensive, we intuitively take a sample.

Although sampling is commonplace in daily activities, these familiar samples are seldom scientific. For researchers, the process of sampling can be quite complex. Sampling is a central aspect of marketing research, requiring in-depth examination. Sampling does much to determine how realistic marketing results will be. This chapter explains the nature of sampling and ways to determine the appropriate sample design.

Introduction

The sampling process involves drawing conclusions about an entire population by taking measurements from only a portion of all population elements. Sampling makes research possible in cases where taking measurements from everyone or on everything is impossible. A **sample** can be defined as a subset, or some part, of a larger population, from which population characteristics are estimated.

Sampling is defined in terms of the population being studied. A **population (universe)** is any complete group—for example, of people, sales territories, stores, products, or college students—whose members share some common set of characteristics. Each individual member is referred to as a **population element**.

Researchers could study every element of a population to draw some conclusion. A **census** is an investigation of all the individual elements that make up the population—a total enumeration rather than a sample. Thus, if we wished to know whether more adult Texans drive pickup trucks than sedans, we could contact every adult Texan and find out whether or not they drive a pickup truck or a sedan. We would then know the answer to this question definitively.

sample
A subset, or some part, of a larger population.

population (universe)
Any complete group of entities that share some common set of characteristics.

population element
An individual member of a population.

census
An investigation of all the individual elements that make up a population.

Why Sample?

At a wine-tasting, guests sample wine by having a small taste from multiple bottles of wine. From this, the consumer decides if he or she likes a particular wine. If each guest consumed the entire bottle before making a decision, he or she would be far too inebriated to have any idea about the other bottles. In addition, if the goal is to decide whether or not the wines taste good, giving each person a bottle of wine would soon get very expensive. Similarly, and for some of the same reasons, scientific studies try to draw conclusions about populations by measuring a small portion (sample) rather than taking a census.

Pragmatic Reasons

Applied marketing research projects usually have budget and time constraints. If Ford Motor Corporation wished to take a census of past purchasers' reactions to the company's recalls of defective models, the researchers would have to contact millions of automobile buyers. Some of them

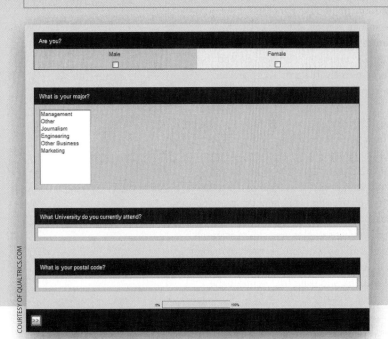

This survey asks a variety of questions of college students. Suppose you were an online university interested in studying the habits of college students in general. Consider the following questions:

1. How well do the results collected from this survey represent the market for undergraduate college students?
2. How well do the results represent American undergraduate college students? [Hint: Compare the profile on the questions shown below with data showing typical characteristics of American undergraduate students.]
3. How well do the results represent American business students?
4. Can the data be stratified in a way that would allow it to represent more specific populations? Explain your answer.

would be inaccessible (for example, out of the country), and it would be impossible to contact all these people within a short time period.

A researcher who wants to investigate a population with an extremely small number of population elements may elect to conduct a census rather than a sample because the cost, labor, and time drawbacks would be relatively insignificant. For a company that wants to assess salespersons' satisfaction with its computer networking system, circulating a questionnaire to all 25 of its employees is practical. In most situations, however, many practical reasons favor sampling. Sampling cuts costs, reduces labor requirements, and gathers vital information quickly. These advantages may be sufficient in themselves for using a sample rather than a census, but there are other reasons. The Research Snapshot on page 306 describing the origins of the Gallup poll describe its very practical origins. Ultimately, sampling is a practical matter.

Accurate and Reliable Results

Another major reason for sampling is that most properly selected samples give results that are reasonably accurate. If the elements of a population are quite similar, only a small sample is necessary to accurately portray the characteristic of interest. Thus, a population consisting of 10,000 eleventh grade students in all-boys Catholic high schools will require a smaller sample than a broader population consisting of 10,000 high school students from coeducational, public, secondary schools.

A visual example of how different-sized samples allow one to draw conclusions is provided in Exhibit 12.1. A sample is similar to a jigsaw puzzle that isn't solved yet. Even without looking at the box cover, the puzzler probably doesn't have to wait until every piece is in place to draw a conclusion of what the picture will be. However, as more pieces are put in place, which is analogous to more units being sampled, conclusions can be made with greater confidence. Thus, larger samples allow conclusions to be drawn with more confidence that they truly represent the population.

A sample may even on occasion be more accurate than a census. Interviewer mistakes, tabulation errors, and other nonsampling errors may increase during a census as workers suffer from burnout, fatigue, incompetence, or dishonesty. In a sample, increased accuracy may sometimes be possible because the fieldwork and tabulation of data can be more closely supervised. In a field survey, a small, well-trained, closely supervised group may do a more careful and accurate

EXHIBIT 12.1

A Puzzle Is a Sample Until It Is Done! The Sample Allows One to Guess at the Picture.

job of collecting information than a large group of nonprofessional interviewers who try to contact everyone. The U.S. Census Bureau conducts surveys on samples of populations as a way of checking the accuracy of the actual census of those populations. If the conclusions drawn from the sample disagree with the census results, the census is deemed inaccurate and becomes a candidate to be redone because an accurate census is required by law every 10 years.

Destruction of Test Units

Many research projects, especially those in quality-control testing, require the destruction of the items being tested. If a manufacturer of firecrackers wished to find out whether each unit met a specific production standard, no product would be left after the testing. This is the exact situation in many marketing strategy experiments. For example, if an experimental sales presentation were presented to every potential customer, no prospects would remain to be contacted after the experiment. In other words, if there is a finite population and everyone in the population participates in the research and cannot be replaced, no population elements remain to be selected as sampling units. The test units have been destroyed or ruined for the purpose of the research project. Obviously, taking a census in these cases would not be too wise!

5. Summarize various types of probability samples. Probability samples are based on chance selection procedures. These include simple random sampling, systematic sampling, stratified sampling, and cluster sampling. With these techniques, random sampling error can be accurately predicted. The process for selecting sample units from a population is described in the chapter. A true probability sample can be costly both in terms of money and time.

6. Discuss how to choose an appropriate sample design. A researcher who must determine the most appropriate sampling design for a specific project will identify a number of sampling criteria and evaluate the relative importance of each criterion before selecting a design. The most common criteria concern accuracy requirements, available resources, time constraints, knowledge availability, and analytical requirements. Internet sampling presents some unique issues. Researchers must be aware that samples may be unrepresentative because not everyone has a computer or access to the Internet. Convenience samples drawn from Web site visitors can create problems. Drawing a probability sample from an established consumer panel whose members opt in can be effective.

Key Terms and Concepts

census, *301*
cluster sampling, *318*
convenience sampling, *312*
disproportional stratified sample, *317*
judgment (purposive) sampling, *312*
multistage area sampling, *319*
nonprobability sampling, *311*
online panels, *307*
opt in, *310*

population (universe), *301*
population element, *301*
primary sampling unit (PSU), *307*
probability sampling, *311*
proportional stratified sample, *317*
quota sampling, *313*
random sampling error, *308*
reverse directory, *307*
sample, *301*

sampling frame, *306*
sampling frame error, *306*
sampling unit, *307*
secondary sampling unit, *307*
simple random sampling, *314*
snowball sampling, *313*
stratified sampling, *315*
systematic sampling, *315*
tertiary sampling unit, *307*

Questions for Review and Critical Thinking

1. If you decide whether you want to see a new movie or television program on the basis of the "coming attractions" or television commercial previews, are you using a sampling technique? Could this be described as a scientific sampling technique?
2. What is the difference between a population and a sample? What are the reasons why a sampling process is so often used in place of a census? Why is it that a population can sometimes be as accurate as, or more accurate than, a census?
3. How can a market researcher try to be confident that the target population involved in some research situation is defined properly?
4. How might the target population differ for a researcher doing separate projects for two retailing companies—one for A&F and one for Nordstrom?
5. Name some possible sampling frames for the following:
   a. An online travel agency like Orbitz.com
   b. Golf course greenskeepers (responsible for the condition of the golf course)
   c. Dog owners
   d. Harley Davidson owners
   e. Tattoo wearers
   f. Minority-owned businesses
   g. Women over six feet tall
   h. Children who may consider engineering as a career
   i. Fast-food consumers in California
6. Describe the difference between a random and systematic sampling error.
7. What is a nonprobability sample? What are some examples?
8. Is a convenience sample ever appropriate? Explain.

9. When would a researcher use a judgment, or purposive, sample?
10. A telephone interviewer asks, "I would like to ask you about race. Are you Native American, Hispanic, African-American, Asian, or white?" After the respondent replies, the interviewer says, "We have conducted a large number of surveys with people of your background, and we do not need to question you further. Thank you for your cooperation." What type of sampling is likely being used?
11. What role can screening questions play in trying to understand and control systematic variance from sources such as Internet surveys, online panels or other types of directories?
12. What are the benefits of stratified sampling?
13. What geographic units within a metropolitan area are useful for sampling?
14. Outline the step-by-step procedure you would use to select the following:
   a. A simple random sample of 150 students from the student list at your university
   b. A quota sample of 50 light users and 50 heavy users of beer in a shopping mall intercept study
   c. A stratified sample of 50 mechanical engineers, 40 electrical engineers, and 40 civil engineers from the subscriber list of an engineering journal
15. Selection for jury duty is supposed to be a totally random process. Comment on the following computer selection procedures, and determine if they are indeed random:
   a. A program instructs the computer to scan the list of names and pick names that were next to those from the last scan.

b. Three-digit numbers are randomly generated to select jurors from a list of licensed drivers. If the weight information listed on the license matches the random number, the person is selected.

c. The juror source list is obtained by merging a list of registered voters with a list of licensed drivers.

16. Provide an example of marketing research in which a sample that is truly representative of all of North America is needed. When would the relevant target population for marketing research be all U.S. consumers? How often would such a target population be needed?

17. ETHICS To ensure a good session, a company selects focus group members from a list of articulate participants instead of conducting random sampling. The client did not inquire about sample selection when it accepted the proposal. Is this ethical?

18. 'NET Go to http://www.reversephonedirectory.com and put in your phone number. How accurate is this database?

19. 'NET Go to the U.S. Census Bureau's home page at http://www.census.gov, click on M in Subjects A to Z, and then click on Metropolitan Area and State Data Book. You can find profiles of every state from this Web site. Suppose a representative sample of the state of Louisiana is used to represent the current U.S. population. How well does Louisiana represent the United States overall? How well does Louisiana represent California or Maine? Use the profiles of the states and of the country to form your opinion.

Research Activity

1. Develop a sampling plan to study the lunch habits of undergraduate and graduate students of your university. Research questions involve who has the most market share and what are the preferred food types and price points for this particular school. Explain your choices.

Case 12.1 Who's Fishing?

© GETTY IMAGES/ PHOTODISC GREEN

Washington Times columnist Gene Mueller writes about fishing and other outdoor sporting activities.[14] Mueller commented recently that although interest groups express concerns about the impact of saltwater fishers on the fish population, no one really knows how many people fish for recreation or how many fish they catch. This situation would challenge marketers interested in the population of anglers.

How could a marketer get an accurate sample? One idea would be to contact residents of coastal counties using random-digit dialing. This sampling frame would include many, if not all, of the people who fish in the ocean, but it would also include many people who do not fish—or who fish for business rather than recreation. A regional agency seeking to gather statistics on anglers, the Atlantic Coastal Cooperative Statistics Program, prefers to develop a sampling frame more related to people who fish.

Another idea would be to use state fishing license records. Privacy would be a drawback, however. Some people might not want their records shared, and they might withhold phone numbers. Further complicating this issue for Atlantic fishing is that most states in the Northeast do not require a license for saltwater fishing. Also exempt in some states are people who fish from the shore and from piers.

A political action group called the Recreational Fishing Alliance suggests that charter fishing businesses collect data.

Questions

1. Imagine that an agency or business has asked for help in gathering data about the number of sports anglers who fish off the coast of Georgia. What advice would you give about sampling? What method or combination of methods would generate the best results?

2. What other criteria besides accuracy would you expect to consider? What sampling methods could help you meet those criteria?

CHAPTER 13
DETERMINATION OF SAMPLE SIZE:
A REVIEW OF STATISTICAL THEORY

LEARNING OUTCOMES

After studying this chapter, you should be able to

1. Use descriptive statistics indicating central tendency and dispersion to make inferences about a population
2. Distinguish among population, sample, and sampling distributions
3. Explain the central-limit theorem
4. Use confidence intervals to express population estimates
5. Understand the major issues in specifying sample size

Chapter Vignette: Bigger Is Better—Right?

© PYMCA/JUPITER IMAGES

Product innovation is always a risky business. Marketing efforts for technologically oriented products like video game consoles and games have to be highly innovative. What kinds of games *should* be created? How racy should they be, particularly when aimed for a less-than-mature audience? One study indicates that 60 percent of American consumers believe that there is too much violence in video games. In fact, the same study reports that 55 percent of gamers believe more regulation is needed to curb violence in new video games. Another study conducted by a gaming company provides different data. It suggests that 75 percent of parents with adolescent children do not believe that violence in video games harms their children. Still another provides *top-box* statistics showing that 40 percent of Nintendo GameCube owners are highly likely to buy a new game that has been concept tested. Several decisions have to be made:

- Should the federal government implement law that further restricts the amount of violence and material with adult content in video games?
- Should gaming companies continue to push the envelope on gratuitous violence and sex in video games?
- Should a video game be developed and marketed based on a 40 percent top-box result?

How good are the descriptive statistics discussed previously in helping make decisions like these? Before jumping to conclusions, consider some details seldom reported in media accounts of opinion results. The 60 and 55 percent figures come from a national consumer panel of 1,100 consumers. The 75 percent figure from parents is taken from a focus group of

12 consumers. The 40 percent top-box result is based on input from 150 GameCube owners in Texas aged 12 to 17 years old.

Knowing the size of the sample certainly helps us know how valuable the information is. In the first case, a sample of 1,100 means that sample result is likely within 2 to 3 percent of the actual population values. Thus, a majority of consumers and even gamers appear concerned. In the second case, a sample of 12 means that the true population value could actually be 100 percent, meaning all parents are not concerned about the effect of violence on their own children, or it could be practically 0 per cent! Finally, in the third case, the sample of 150 consumers means the actual population value can be confidently projected to be between 32 and 48 percent.

Is there enough confidence to act? Not all decisions are the same. Enacting federal legislation is no small matter and steps that restrict market freedom should be considered only with very solid data. Thus, the sample of 1,100 provides a relatively high degree of confidence, but perhaps this alone isn't quite enough. The political and financial risks associated with a bad regulatory decision require very great precision. On the other hand, introducing a new video game, particularly if it is a variant of one that already exists, is not so risky and less precision is needed. If 40 percent is the benchmark upon which to make the go—no go decision for the firm, the 32 to 48 percent range may provide enough confidence to move forward. While the firm might like more specific evidence, a larger sample will be costly in both money and time. Further, the longer the introduction is put off, the greater the risk that a competitor will be able to upstage the new introduction. So, at least in this case, bigger may not be better![1]

Introduction

The first portion of the chapter summarizes key statistical concepts necessary for understanding the theory that underlies the derivation of sample size. Students who need to review the basic aspects of statistics theory should pay particular attention to this material. Even those students who received good grades in elementary statistics classes probably will benefit from a quick review of these basic statistical concepts. The chapter then turns to issues related to sample size and the degree with which this affects the confidence with which population estimates can be made.

Raw data alone are seldom useful. They have to be organized and summarized to become useful and have the possibility of becoming actual market intelligence. The most basic ways for doing this include frequency distributions, proportions, and measures of central tendency and dispersion. Beyond these results, information about the sample helps decision makers know how much confidence can be placed in a given number.

Basic Descriptive and Inferential Statistics

The *Statistical Abstract of the United States* presents table after table of figures associated with numbers of births, number of employees in each county of the United States, and other data that the average person calls "statistics." They are descriptive statistics. Another type of statistics, inferential statistics, is used to make inferences about a whole population from a sample. For example, when a firm test-markets a new product in Sacramento and Birmingham, it wishes to make an inference from these sample markets to predict what will happen throughout the United States. So, two applications of statistics exist: (1) to describe characteristics of the population or sample and (2) to generalize from a sample to a population.

What Are Sample Statistics and Population Parameters?

The primary purpose of inferential statistics is to make a judgment about a population, or the total collection of all elements about which a researcher seeks information. A sample is a subset or relatively small portion of the total number of elements in a given population. Data from a sample are always uncertain but when data come from all elements of a population, certainty is possible.

You probably recall responding to the part of the student survey shown in the screenshot. Using data obtained from the students responding to this survey and the assumptions provided, reply to the questions that follow.

1. Suppose a marketing manager was trying to determine how many students had only one e-mail account that they used

regularly. Their intention is to market additional Internet services to students who have only one or no e-mail account.

   a. What is the proportion of students in the sample that have more than one e-mail account?

   b. What is the 95% confidence interval for this proportion?

   c. What is the 99% confidence interval for this proportion?

   d. If the student population is several million students, what sample size is needed to estimate the actual proportion of students with less than 2 e-mail accounts within $+/-1\%$?

   e. What sample size is needed to estimate the actual proportion of students with less than 2 e-mail accounts within $+/-5\%$?

   f. If the decision to launch this marketing activity involves an investment of approximately $75,000 for this company (with median annual revenues of $3M), what level of precision would you recommend?

   g. Approximately what level of precision exists given the total sample size available to you to make the computation in part a?

© GEORGE DOYLE

COURTESY OF QUALTRICS.COM

sample statistics

Variables in a sample or measures computed from sample data.

population parameters

Variables in a population or measured characteristics of the population.

frequency distribution

A set of data organized by summarizing the number of times a particular value of a variable occurs.

Sample statistics are measures computed from sample data. **Population parameters** are measured characteristics of a specific population. Sample statistics are used to make inferences (guesses) about population parameters.[2] In our notation, we will generally represent population parameters with Greek lowercase letters—for example, μ or α—and sample statistics with English letters, such as X or S.

■ FREQUENCY DISTRIBUTIONS

One of the most common ways to summarize a set of data is to construct a *frequency table*, or **frequency distribution**. The process begins with recording the number of times a particular value of a variable occurs. This is the frequency of that value. Continuing the example of a telephone survey for a savings and loan association, Exhibit 13.1 represents a frequency distribution of respondents' answers to a question that asked how much money customers had in their bank account.

EXHIBIT 13.1

Frequency Distribution of Deposits

Amount	Frequency (Number of People Who Hold Deposits in Each Range)
Under $3,000	499
$3,000 — $4,999	530
$5,000 — $9,999	562
$10,000 — $14,999	718
$15,000 or more	811
	3,120

A similar method is a distribution of relative frequency, or a **percentage distribution**. To develop a frequency distribution of percentages, divide the frequency of each value by the total number of observations, and multiply the result by 100. Based on the data in Exhibit 13.1, Exhibit 13.2 shows the percentage distribution of deposits; that is, the percentage of people holding deposits within each range of values.

percentage distribution

A frequency distribution organized into a table (or graph) that summarizes percentage values associated with particular values of a variable.

EXHIBIT 13.2
Percentage Distribution of Deposits

Amount	Percent (Percentage of People Who Hold Deposits in Each Range)
Under $3,000	16
$3,000 — $4,999	17
$5,000 — $9,999	18
$10,000 — $14,999	23
$15,000 or more	26
	100

Probability is the long-run relative frequency with which an event will occur. Inferential statistics uses the concept of a probability distribution, which is conceptually the same as a percentage distribution except that the data are converted into probabilities. Exhibit 13.3 shows the probability distribution of the savings and loan deposits.

probability

The long-run relative frequency with which an event will occur.

EXHIBIT 13.3
Probability Distribution of Deposits

Amount	Probability
Under $3,000	.16
$3,000 — $4,999	.17
$5,000 — $9,999	.18
$10,000 — $14,999	.23
$15,000 or more	.26
	1.00

■ PROPORTIONS

Frequencies can also be expressed in terms of percentages. When a frequency distribution portrays only a single characteristic in terms of a percentage of the total, it defines the **proportion** of occurrence. A proportion, such as the proportion of tenured professors at a university, indicates the percentage of population elements that successfully meet some standard concerning the particular characteristic. A proportion may be expressed as a percentage, a fraction, or a decimal value. In the example used here and illustrated in Exhibit 13.3, the probabilities are equal to the proportion of consumers in each deposit category. For example, 23 percent have a bank balance between $10,000 and $14,999.

proportion

The percentage of elements that meet some criterion.

■ TOP-BOX SCORES

Managers are often very interested in the proportion of consumers choosing extreme responses. A **top-box score** generally refers to the portion of respondents who choose the most favorable response toward a company. Typically, this means the portion that would highly recommend a business to a friend or, if the scale item simply addresses buying intentions, the portion expressing the highest likelihood of doing business again. The logic is that respondents who choose the most extreme response are really quite unique compared to the others. Managers are often asking what the top-box score or number is.[3]

top-box score

Proportion of respondents who chose the most positive choice in a multiple choice question.

Measures of Central Tendency

On a typical day, a sales manager counts the number of sales calls each sales representative makes. He or she wishes to inspect the data to find the center, or middle area, of the frequency distribution. Put another way, what is the most typical number of sales calls? Central tendency can be measured with the mean, median, or mode. Each is determined in a slightly different way.

■ THE MEAN

mean

A measure of central tendency; the arithmetic average.

We all have been exposed to the average known as the **mean**. The mean is simply the arithmetic average, and it is a common measure of central tendency. To express this mathematically, we use the summation symbol, the capital Greek letter *sigma* (Σ). A typical use might look like this:

$$\sum_{i=1}^{n} X_i$$

which is a shorthand way to write the sum

$$X_1 + X_2 + X_3 + X_4 + X_5 + \cdots + X_n$$

Below the Σ is the initial value of an index, usually, i, j, or k, and above it is the final value, in this case n, the number of observations. The shorthand expression says to replace i in the formula with the values from 1 to 8 and total the observations obtained. Without changing the basic formula, the initial and final index values may be replaced by other values to indicate different starting and stopping points.

Suppose a sales manager supervises the eight salespeople listed in Exhibit 13.4. To express the sum of the salespeople's calls in Σ notation, we just number the salespeople (this number becomes the index number) and associate subscripted variables with their numbers of calls:

EXHIBIT 13.4
Number of Sales Calls per Day by Salesperson

Index		Salesperson	Variable		Number of Calls
1	=	Mike	X_1	=	4
2	=	Patty	X_2	=	3
3	=	Billie	X_3	=	2
4	=	Bob	X_4	=	5
5	=	John	X_5	=	3
6	=	Frank	X_6	=	3
7	=	Chuck	X_7	=	1
8	=	Samantha	X_8	=	5
		Total			26

We then write an appropriate Σ formula and evaluate it:

$$\sum_{i=1}^{8} X_i = X_1 + X_2 + X_3 + X_4 + X_5 + X_6 + X_7 + X_8$$
$$= 4 + 3 + 2 + 5 + 3 + 3 + 1 + 5$$
$$= 26$$

This notation is the numerator in the formula for the arithmetic mean:

$$\text{Mean} = \frac{\sum_{i=1}^{n} X_i}{n} = \frac{26}{8} = 3.25$$

The notation $\sum_{i=1}^{n} X_i$ means add together all the Xs whose subscripts are between 1 and n inclusive, where n equals the number of observations. Here there are eight observations so i varies between 1 and 8. The formula shows that the mean number of sales calls in this example is 3.25.

Researchers generally wish to know the population mean, μ (lowercase Greek letter *mu*), which is calculated as follows:

$$\mu = \frac{\sum_{i=1}^{N} X_i}{N}$$

where

N = number of members in the population

Often we will not have enough data to calculate the population mean, μ, so we will calculate a sample mean, $\overline{X}$ (read "X bar"), with the following formula:

$$\overline{X} = \frac{\sum_{i=1}^{n} X_i}{n}$$

where

n = number of observations made in the sample

More likely than not, you already know how to calculate a mean. However, knowing how to distinguish among the symbols Σ, μ, and X is helpful to understand statistics.

In this introductory discussion of the summation sign (Σ), we have used very detailed notation that includes the subscript for the initial index value (i) and the final index value (n). However, from this point on, references to Σ will sometimes omit the subscript for the initial index value (i) and the final index value (n). The mean is the most widely applied measure of central tendency. However, the mean can sometimes be misleading, particularly when extreme values or outliers are present.

■ THE MEDIAN

The next measure of central tendency, the **median**, is the midpoint of the distribution, or the 50th percentile. In other words, the median is the value below which half the values in the sample fall. In the sales manager example, 3 is the median because half the observations are greater than 3 and half are less than 3. The median is a better indicator of central tendency in the presence of extreme values or outliers. For instance, a professor gives a marketing research test and one student makes a 99, another makes a 98, but the next highest grade is 51 with the remaining 17 grades ranging from 30 to 50. In this case, if the professor curves the grades so that everyone who scores "above average" will pass, the result could be only 5 or 6 students passing as the mean would be on the order of 46. Perhaps the students would prefer a curve based around the median which would mean that half of the students would pass by definition.

median

A measure of central tendency that is the midpoint; the value below which half the values in a distribution fall.

■ THE MODE

In the apparel industry, *mode* refers to the most popular fashion. In statistics the **mode** is the measure of central tendency that identifies the value that occurs most often. In our example of sales calls, Patty, John, and Frank each made three sales calls. The value 3 occurs most often, so 3 is the mode. The mode is determined by listing each possible value and noting the number of times each value occurs. The mode is the best measure of central tendency for data that is less than interval and for data that are distributed unimodally with one large peak (many observations have the same response).

mode

A measure of central tendency; the value that occurs most often.

Measures of Dispersion

The mean, median, and mode summarize the central tendency of frequency distributions. Accurate analysis of data also requires knowing the tendency of observations to depart from the central tendency. Thus, another way to summarize the data is to calculate the dispersion of the data, or how the observations vary from the mean. Consider, for instance, the twelve-month sales patterns of the two products shown in Exhibit 13.5. Both have a mean monthly sales volume of 200 units, but the dispersion of observations for product B is much greater than that for product A. There are several measures of dispersion.

EXHIBIT 13.5
Sales Levels for Two Products with Identical Average Sales

	Units Product A	Units Product B
January	196	150
February	198	160
March	199	176
April	200	181
May	200	192
June	200	200
July	200	201
August	201	202
September	201	213
October	201	224
November	202	240
December	202	261
Average	**200**	**200**

■ THE RANGE

The simplest measure of dispersion is the range. It is the distance between the smallest and the largest values of a frequency distribution. In Exhibit 13.5, the range for product A is between 196 units and 202 units (6 units), whereas for product B the range is between 150 units and 261 units (111 units). The range does not take into account all the observations; it merely tells us about the extreme values of the distribution.

Just as people may be fat or skinny, distributions may be fat or skinny. While we do not expect all observations to be exactly like the mean, in a skinny distribution they will lie a short distance from the mean. Product A is an example; the observations are close together and reasonably close to the mean. In a fat distribution, such as the one for Product B, they will be spread out. Exhibit 13.6 illustrates this concept graphically with two frequency distributions that have identical modes, medians, and means but different degrees of dispersion.

EXHIBIT 13.6
Low Dispersion versus High Dispersion

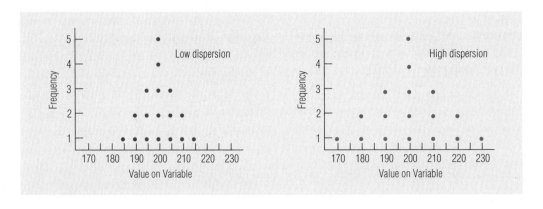

The interquartile range is the range that encompasses the middle 50 percent of the observations—in other words, the range between the bottom quartile (lowest 25 percent) and the top quartile (highest 25 percent).

■ DEVIATION SCORES

A method of calculating how far any observation is from the mean is to calculate individual deviation scores. To calculate a deviation from the mean, use the following formula:

$$d_{i_i} = X_i - \overline{X}$$

For the value of 150 units for product B for the month of January, the deviation score is -50; that is, $150 - 200 = -50$. If the deviation scores are large, we will have a fat distribution because the distribution exhibits a broad spread.

■ WHY USE THE STANDARD DEVIATION?

Statisticians have derived several quantitative indexes to reflect a distribution's spread, or variability. The *standard deviation* is perhaps the most valuable index of spread, or dispersion. Students often have difficulty understanding it. Learning about the standard deviation will be easier if we first look at several other measures of dispersion that may be used. Each of these has certain limitations that the standard deviation does not.

First is the average deviation. We compute the average deviation by calculating the deviation score of each observation value (that is, its difference from the mean), summing these scores, and then dividing by the sample size (n):

$$\text{Average deviation} = \frac{\Sigma\,(X_i - \overline{X})}{n}$$

While this measure of spread seems interesting, it is never used. Positive deviation scores are canceled out by negative scores with this formula, leaving an average deviation value of zero no matter how wide the spread may be. Hence, the average deviation is a useless spread measure.

One might correct for the disadvantage of the average deviation by computing the absolute values of the deviations. In other words, we ignore all the positive and negative signs and use only the absolute value of each deviation. The formula for the mean absolute deviation is

$$\text{Mean absolute deviation} = \frac{\Sigma\,|X_i - \overline{X}|}{n}$$

While this procedure eliminates the problem of always having a zero score for the deviation measure, it becomes even more useful to express deviations in terms of variance.

Variance

Another means of eliminating the sign problem caused by the negative deviations canceling out the positive deviations is to square the deviation scores. The following formula gives the mean squared deviation:

$$\text{Mean squared deviation} = \frac{\Sigma\,(X_i - \overline{X})^2}{n}$$

This measure is useful for describing the sample variability. However, we typically wish to make an inference about a population from a sample, and so the divisor $n - 1$ is used rather than n in most pragmatic marketing research problems.[4] The divisor changes from n to $n - 1$ to provide an unbiased estimator. This new measure of spread, called **variance**, has the following formula:

$$\text{Variance} = S^2 = \frac{\Sigma\,(X_i - \overline{X})^2}{n - 1}$$

variance

A measure of variability or dispersion. Its square root is the standard deviation.

Variance is a very good index of dispersion. The variance, S^2, will equal zero if and only if each and every observation in the distribution is the same as the mean. The variance will grow larger as the observations tend to differ increasingly from one another and from the mean.

Standard Deviation

While the variance is frequently used in statistics, it has one major drawback. The variance reflects a unit of measurement that has been squared. For instance, if measures of sales in a territory are made in dollars, the mean number will be reflected in dollars, but the variance will be in squared dollars. Because of this, statisticians often take the square root of the variance. Using the square root of the variance for a distribution, called the **standard deviation**, eliminates the drawback of having the measure of dispersion in squared units rather than in the original measurement units. The formula for the standard deviation is

$$S = \sqrt{S^2} = \sqrt{\frac{\sum (X_i - \overline{X})^2}{n - 1}}$$

Exhibit 13.7 illustrates that the calculation of a standard deviation requires the researcher to first calculate the sample mean. In the example with eight salespeople's sales calls (Exhibit 13.4), we calculated the sample mean as 3.25. Exhibit 13.7 illustrates how to calculate the standard deviation for these data.

EXHIBIT 13.7

Calculating a Standard Deviation: Number of Sales Calls per Day for Eight Salespeople

X	$(X - \overline{X})$	$(X - \overline{X})^2$
4	$(4 - 3.25) = .75$	.5625
3	$(3 - 3.25) = -.25$	.0625
2	$(2 - 3.25) = -1.25$	1.5625
5	$(5 - 3.25) = 1.75$	3.0625
3	$(3 - 3.25) = -.25$	.0625
3	$(3 - 3.25) = -.25$	.0625
1	$(1 - 3.25) = -2.25$	5.0625
5	$(5 - 3.25) = 1.75$	3.0625
$\sum^a$	a^0	13.5000

$$n = 8 \qquad \overline{X} = 3.25$$

$$S = \sqrt{\frac{\sum (X - \overline{X})^2}{n - 1}} = \sqrt{\frac{13.5}{8 - 1}} = \sqrt{\frac{13.5}{7}} = \sqrt{1.9286} = 1.3887$$

[a]The summation of this column is not used in the calculation of the standard deviation.

At this point we can return to thinking about the original purpose for measures of dispersion. We want to summarize the data from survey research and other forms of marketing research. Indexes of central tendency, such as the mean, help us interpret the data. In addition, we wish to calculate a measure of variability that will give us a quantitative index of the dispersion of the distribution. We have looked at several measures of dispersion to arrive at two very adequate means of measuring dispersion: the variance and the standard deviation. The formula given is for the sample standard deviation, S.

The formula for the population standard deviation, σ, which is conceptually very similar, has not been given. Nevertheless, you should understand that σ measures the dispersion in the population and S measures the dispersion in the sample. These concepts are crucial to understanding statistics. Remember, the student must learn the language of statistics to use it in a research project. If you do not understand the language at this point, review this material now.

Distinguish Between Sample and Sample Distribution

Roulette is a common casino game and a casino may contain many roulette wheels. If someone wanted to know whether the roulette wheels were fair, they may make many observations of which number the ball lands on as the result of a spin. The results would follow some pattern. While it might not be possible to record the results of all spins of the roulette wheel, someone could probably record results over a several-hour period on one or more wheels. This basic image provides the idea behind statistical distributions.

By recording the results of spins of the roulette wheel, one could find a pattern or distribution of the results.

The Normal Distribution

One of the most common probability distributions in statistics is the **normal distribution**, commonly represented by the *normal curve*. This mathematical and theoretical distribution describes the expected distribution of sample means and many other chance occurrences. The normal curve is bell shaped, and almost all (99.7 percent) of its values are within ±3 standard deviations from its mean. An example of a normal curve, the distribution of IQ scores, appears in Exhibit 13.8. The IQ score is normed to 100 meaning that 100 is an average IQ score. In this example, 1 standard deviation for IQ equals 15. Someone with an IQ score of 70 is 2 standard deviations below average and scores better than 2.14 percent of others. A person scoring 145 is 3 standard deviations above average and better than 99.8 percent of others.

normal distribution

A symmetrical, bell-shaped distribution that describes the expected probability distribution of many chance occurrences.

EXHIBIT 13.8
Normal Distribution: Distribution of Intelligence Quotient (IQ) Scores

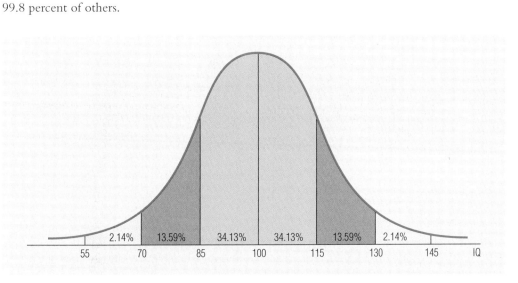

| 2.14% | 13.59% | 34.13% | 34.13% | 13.59% | 2.14% | |
| 55 | 70 | 85 | 100 | 115 | 130 | 145 | IQ |

The **standardized normal distribution** is a specific normal curve that has several characteristics:

1. It is symmetrical about its mean.
2. The mean identifies the normal curve's highest point (the mode) and the vertical line about which this normal curve is symmetrical.

standardized normal distribution

A purely theoretical probability distribution that reflects a specific normal curve for the standardized value, *z*.

© NIJK NENZIC/SHUTTERSTOCK

3. The normal curve has an infinite number of cases (it is a continuous distribution), and the area under the curve has a probability density equal to 1.0.
4. The standardized normal distribution has a mean of 0 and a standard deviation of 1.

Exhibit 13.9 illustrates these properties. Exhibit 13.10 is a summary version of the typical standardized normal table found at the end of most statistics textbooks. A more complex table of areas under the standardized normal distribution can be found on the Internet at http://davidmlane.com/hyperstat/z_table.html or in the statistical appendix on the www.cengage.com/marketing/zikmund.

EXHIBIT 13.9
Standardized Normal Distribution

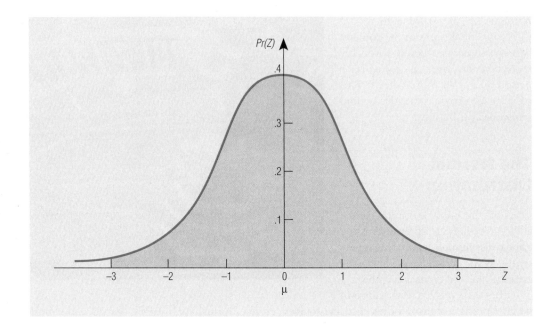

EXHIBIT 13.10 **Standardized Normal Table: Area Under Half of the Normal Curve**[a]

Z Standard Deviations from the Mean (Units)	Z Standard Deviations from the Mean (Tenths of Units)[a]									
	.0	.1	.2	.3	.4	.5	.6	.7	.8	.9
0.0	.000	.040	.080	.118	.155	.192	.226	.258	.288	.315
1.0	.341	.364	.385	.403	.419	.433	.445	.455	.464	.471
2.0	.477	.482	.486	.489	.492	.494	.495	.496	.497	.498
3.0	.499	.499	.499	.499	.499	.499	.499	.499	.499	.499

[a]Area under the segment of the normal curve extending (in one direction) from the mean to the point indicated by each row-column combination. For example, about 68 percent of normally distributed events can be expected to fall within 1.0 standard deviation on either side of the mean (0.341 × 2). An interval of almost 2.0 standard deviations around the mean will include 95 percent of all cases (.477 + .477).

The standardized normal distribution is a purely theoretical probability distribution, but it is a most useful distribution in inferential statistics. Statisticians have spent a great deal of time and effort making it convenient for researchers to find the probability of any portion of the area under the standardized normal distribution. All we have to do is transform, or convert, the data from other observed normal distributions to the standardized normal curve. In other words, the standardized normal distribution is extremely valuable because we can translate, or transform, any normal variable, X, into the standardized value, Z. Exhibit 13.11 illustrates how either a skinny distribution or a fat distribution can be converted into the standardized normal distribution. This ability to transform normal variables has many pragmatic implications for the marketing researcher.

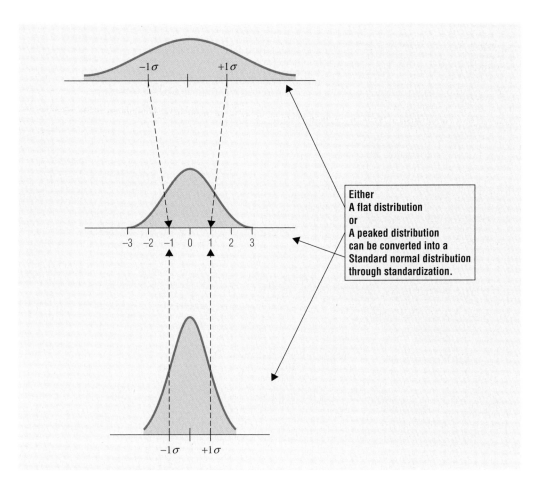

Either
A flat distribution
or
A peaked distribution
can be converted into a
Standard normal distribution
through standardization.

The standardized normal table and other probability distributions used to be printed at the back of most statistics and research books. However, today they are easy to find and use via the Web. The companion Web site for this text also includes these distributions in an appendix.

Computing the standardized value, Z, of any measurement expressed in original units is simple: Subtract the mean from the value to be transformed, and divide by the standard deviation (all expressed in original units). The formula for this procedure and its verbal statement follow. In the formula, note that σ, the population standard deviation, is used for calculation.[5]

$$\text{Standardized value} = \frac{\text{Value to be transformed} - \text{Mean}}{\text{Standard deviation}}$$

$$Z = \frac{X - \mu}{\sigma}$$

where

μ = hypothesized or expected value of the mean

Suppose that in the past a toy manufacturer has experienced mean sales, μ, of 9,000 units and a standard deviation, σ, of 500 units during September. The production manager wishes to know whether wholesalers will demand between 7,500 and 9,625 units during September of the upcoming year. Because no tables are available showing the distribution for a mean of 9,000 and a standard deviation of 500, we must transform our distribution of toy sales, X, into the standardized form using our simple formula. The following computation shows that the probability (Pr) of obtaining sales in this range is equal to .893:

$$Z = \frac{X - \mu}{\sigma} = \frac{7,500 - 9,000}{500} = -3.00$$

$$Z = \frac{X - \mu}{\sigma} = \frac{9,625 - 9,000}{500} = 1.25$$

Using Exhibit 13.10, we find that

When $Z = -3.00$, the area under the curve (probability) equals 0.499.

When $Z = 1.25$, the area under the curve (probability) equals 0.394.

Thus, the total area under the curve is .499 + .394 = .893. (The area under the curve corresponding to this computation is the shaded areas in Exhibit 13.12.) The sales manager, therefore, knows there is a .893 probability that sales will be between 7,500 and 9,625.

EXHIBIT 13.12

Standardized Distribution Curve

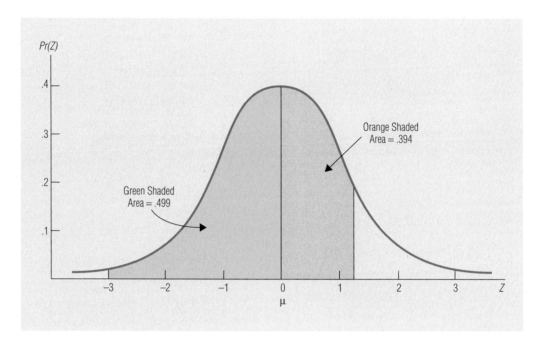

Population Distribution and Sample Distribution

Before we outline the technique of statistical inference, three additional types of distributions must be defined: population distribution, sample distribution, and sampling distribution. When conducting a research project or survey, the researcher's purpose is not to describe the sample of respondents, but to make an inference about the population. As defined previously, a population, or universe, is the total set, or collection, of potential units for observation. The sample is a smaller subset of this population.

population distribution

A frequency distribution of the elements of a population.

sample distribution

A frequency distribution of a sample.

A frequency distribution of the population elements is called a **population distribution**. The mean and standard deviation of the population distribution are represented by the Greek letters μ and σ. A frequency distribution of a sample is called a **sample distribution**. The sample mean is designated $\overline{X}$, and the sample standard deviation is designated S.

Sampling Distribution

The concepts of population distribution and sample distribution are relatively simple. However, we must now introduce another distribution, which is the crux of understanding statistics: the *sampling distribution of the sample mean*. The sampling distribution is a theoretical probability distribution that in actual practice would never be calculated. Hence, practical, business-oriented students have difficulty understanding why the notion of the sampling distribution is important. Statisticians, with their mathematical curiosity, have asked themselves, "What would happen if we were to draw a large number of samples (say, 50,000), each having n elements, from a specified population?" Assuming that the samples were randomly selected, the sample means, $\overline{X}$s, could be arranged in a frequency distribution. Because different people or sample units would be selected in the different samples, the sample means would not be exactly equal. The shape of the sampling distribution is of considerable importance to statisticians. If the sample size is sufficiently large and if the samples are randomly drawn, we know from the central-limit theorem that the sampling distribution of the mean will be approximately normally distributed.

A formal definition of the sampling distribution is as follows:

*A **sampling distribution** is a theoretical probability distribution that shows the functional relation between the possible values of some summary characteristic of n cases drawn at random and the probability (density) associated with each value over all possible samples of size n from a particular population.*[6]

The sampling distribution's mean is called the *expected value* of the statistic. The expected value of the mean of the sampling distribution is equal to μ. The standard deviation of a sampling distribution of $\overline{X}$ is called **standard error of the mean** ($S_{\overline{X}}$) and is approximately equal to

$$S_{\overline{X}} = \frac{\sigma}{\sqrt{n}}$$

To review, for us to make an inference about a population from a sample, we must know about three important distributions: the population distribution, the sample distribution, and the sampling distribution. They have the following characteristics:

	Mean	Standard Deviation
Population distribution	μ	σ
Sample distribution	X	S
Sampling distribution	$\mu_X = \mu$	$S_{\overline{X}}$

sampling distribution

A theoretical probability distribution of sample means for all possible samples of a certain size drawn from a particular population.

standard error of the mean

The standard deviation of the sampling distribution.

We now have much of the information we need to understand the concept of statistical inference. To clarify why the sampling distribution has the characteristic just described, we will elaborate on two concepts: the standard error of the mean and the central-limit theorem. You may be wondering why the standard error of the mean, $S_{\overline{X}}$, is defined as $S_{\overline{X}} = \sigma/\sqrt{n}$. The reason is based on the notion that the variance within the sampling distribution of the mean will be less if we have a larger sample size for independent samples. We can see intuitively that a larger sample size allows the researcher to be more confident that the sample mean is closer to the population mean. In actual practice, the standard error of the mean is estimated using the sample's standard deviation. Thus, $S_{\overline{X}}$ is estimated using $S/\sqrt{n}$.

Note that as sample size increases, the spread of the sample means around μ decreases. Thus, with a larger sample size we will have a skinnier sampling distribution.

Central-Limit Theorem

Finding that the means of random samples of a sufficiently large size will be approximately normal in form and that the mean of the sampling distribution will approach the population mean is very useful. Mathematically, this is the assertion of the **central-limit theorem**, which states, as the sample size, *n*, increases, the distribution of the mean, $\overline{X}$, of a random sample taken from practically any population approaches a normal distribution (with a mean μ and a standard deviation $\sigma/\sqrt{n}$).[7] The central-limit theorem works regardless of the shape of the original population distribution. In other words, the distribution of averages quickly approaches normal as sample size increases. Exhibit 13.13 on the next page illustrates how the distribution of means of bimodal observations will increasingly approach normal.

A simple example will demonstrate the central-limit theorem. Assume that a consumer researcher is interested in the number of dollars children spend on toys each month. Assume further that the population the consumer researcher is investigating consists of eight-year-old children in a certain school. In this elementary example, the population consists of only six

central-limit theorem

The theory that, as sample size increases, the distribution of sample means of size *n*, randomly selected, approaches a normal distribution.

EXHIBIT 13.13
The Mean Distribution of Any Distribution Approaches Normal as _n_ Increases

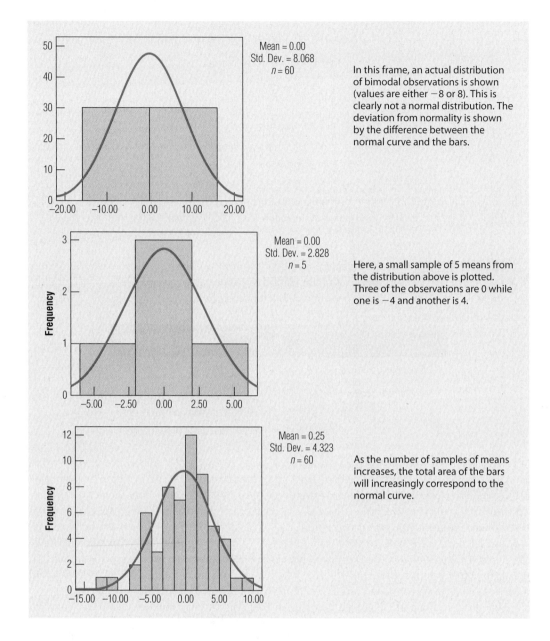

Mean = 0.00
Std. Dev. = 8.068
_n_ = 60

In this frame, an actual distribution of bimodal observations is shown (values are either −8 or 8). This is clearly not a normal distribution. The deviation from normality is shown by the difference between the normal curve and the bars.

Mean = 0.00
Std. Dev. = 2.828
_n_ = 5

Here, a small sample of 5 means from the distribution above is plotted. Three of the observations are 0 while one is −4 and another is 4.

Mean = 0.25
Std. Dev. = 4.323
_n_ = 60

As the number of samples of means increases, the total area of the bars will increasingly correspond to the normal curve.

individuals. Exhibit 13.14 shows the population distribution of toy expenditures. Alice, a relatively deprived child, has only $1 per month, whereas Freddy, the rich kid, has $6 to spend. The average expenditure on toys each month is $3.50, so the population mean, μ, equals 3.5 (see Exhibit 13.15).

EXHIBIT 13.14
Population Distribution: Hypothetical Toy Expenditures

Child	Toy Expenditures
Alice	$1.00
Becky	2.00
Noah	3.00
Tobin	4.00
George	5.00
Freddy	6.00

X
$1.00
2.00
3.00
4.00
5.00
6.00
Σ $21.00

Calculations: $\mu = \dfrac{\Sigma X}{n} = \dfrac{21}{6} = 3.5 = \mu_{\bar{x}}$

EXHIBIT 13.15
Calculation of Population Mean

Now assume that we do not know everything about the population, and we wish to take a sample size of two, to be drawn randomly from the population of the six individuals. How many possible samples are there?

The answer is 15, as follows (these are the possible combinations):

1, 2
1, 3 *2, 3*
1, 4 *2, 4* *3, 4*
1, 5 *2, 5* *3, 5* *4, 5*
1, 6 *2, 6* *3, 6* *4, 6* *5, 6*

A skeptic about the central limit theorem can compute each of these 15 sample means easily and then plot a frequency distribution of each of these means to see that indeed the distribution is approximately normal. If we increased the sample size to three, four, or more, the distribution of sample means would more closely approximate a normal distribution. While this simple example is not a proof of the central-limit theorem, it should give you a better understanding of the nature of the sampling distribution of the mean.

This theoretical knowledge about distributions can be used to solve two practical marketing research problems: estimating parameters and determining sample size.

Estimation of Parameters and Confidence Intervals

A catalog retailer, such as Land's End, may rely on sampling and statistical estimation to prepare for Christmas orders. The company can expect that 28 days after mailing a catalog, it will have received *X* percent of the orders it will get. With this information, the company can tell within 5 percent how many ties it will sell by Christmas. Making a proper inference about population parameters is highly practical for a marketer that must have the inventory appropriate for a short selling season.

Suppose you are a product manager for Beatrice Foods and you recently conducted a taste test to measure intention to buy a reformulated Swiss Miss Lite Cocoa Mix. The results of the research indicate that when the product was placed in eight hundred homes and a callback was made two weeks later, 80 percent of the respondents said they would buy it: 76 percent of those who had not previously used low-calorie cocoa and 84 percent of those who had. How can you be sure there were no statistical errors in this estimate? How confident can you be of these figures?

Students often wonder whether statistics are really used in the business world. The two situations just described provide examples of the need for statistical estimation of parameters and the value of statistical techniques as managerial tools.

RESEARCH SNAPSHOT

Measuring Viewership . . . with Confidence

Media research firms like Arbitron and Nielsen provide data on audience sizes after programs have aired, but can advertisers predict audiences ahead of time? One way to get an estimate is to ask people about their intended media behavior. For example, Harris Interactive used an online poll to ask people whether they intended to watch the Winter Olympics held in Turin, Italy, and if so, which events they planned to watch.

The Harris poll obtained responses from 1,002 adults. The data represented percentages who planned to watch any of the television coverage of the Olympics and percentages who planned to watch specific events. Results were segmented by age, sex, and other demographics. According to the researchers, the confidence level was 95 percent that the sampling error was not greater than ±3 percentage points.

The poll found that 61 percent of men and 69 percent of women planned to watch the Winter Olympics. Given the confidence interval, we can say with 95 percent confidence that more women than men planned to watch, because the true value for men would be within the range of 58 percent to 64 percent and the true value for women would be between 66 percent and 72 percent. However, we cannot say from this poll whether more men or women actually watched the games. For that, advertisers had to wait for the after-the-fact data from the media researchers. Finding data on actual ratings can be difficult because selling this data is a large part of Nielsen's business. However, in 2008, just over 20 million Americans tuned in to the Olympics on one of the first two nights. Thus, over the entire two-week period, chances are that the 2006 confidence interval expectations were exceeded.

Source: Based on "Two-Thirds of U.S. Adults Plan to Watch the Winter Olympics," *Wall Street Journal* (February 10, 2006), http://online.wsj.com; Liz Clarke, "2006 Winter Olympic Games," *Washington Post* (February 21, 2006), http://www.washingtonpost.com; Futterman, M. and S. Schechner, "NBC's Olympic Ratings Get a Web-Based Boost," *Wall Street Journal* 252 (August 11, 2008), B7.

Point Estimates

Our goal in using statistics is to make an estimate about population parameters. A population mean, μ, and standard deviation, σ, are constants, but in most instances of marketing research, they are unknown. To estimate population values, we are required to sample. As we have discussed, $\overline{X}$ and S are random variables that will vary from sample to sample with a certain probability (sampling) distribution. The Research Snapshot above discusses estimates of Olympic game viewership.

Consider a practical example of a prospective racquetball entrepreneur who wishes to estimate the average number of days players participate in this sport each week. When statistical inference is needed, the population mean, μ, is a constant but unknown parameter. To estimate the average number of playing days, we could take a sample of three hundred racquetball players throughout the area where our entrepreneur is thinking of building club facilities. If the sample mean, $\overline{X}$, equals 2.6 days per week, we might use this figure as a **point estimate**. This single value, 2.6, would be the best estimate of the population mean. However, we would be extremely lucky if the sample estimate were exactly the same as the population value. A less risky alternative would be to calculate a confidence interval.

point estimate

An estimate of the population mean in the form of a single value, usually the sample mean.

Confidence Intervals

If we specify a range of numbers, or interval, within which the population mean should lie, we can be more confident that our inference is correct. A **confidence interval estimate** is based on the knowledge that $\mu = \overline{X} \pm$ a small sampling error. After calculating an interval estimate, we can determine how probable it is that the population mean will fall within this range of statistical values. In the racquetball project, the researcher, after setting up a confidence interval, would be able to make a statement such as "With 95 percent confidence, I think that the average number of days played per week is between 2.3 and 2.9." This information can be used to estimate market demand because the researcher has a certain confidence that the interval contains the value of the true population mean.

The crux of the problem for a researcher is to determine how much random sampling error to tolerate. In other words, what should the confidence interval be? How much of a gamble should be taken that μ will be included in the range? Do we need to be 80 percent, 90 percent,

confidence interval estimate

A specified range of numbers within which a population mean is expected to lie; an estimate of the population mean based on the knowledge that it will be equal to the sample mean plus or minus a small sampling error.

or 99 percent sure? The **confidence level** is a percentage or decimal that indicates the long-run probability that the results will be correct. Traditionally, researchers have used the 95 percent confidence level. While there is nothing magical about the 95 percent confidence level, it is conventional to select this confidence level in our examples.

As mentioned, the point estimate gives no information about the possible magnitude of random sampling error. The confidence interval gives the estimated value of the population parameter, plus or minus an estimate of the error. We can express the idea of the confidence interval as follows:

$$\mu = \overline{X} \pm \text{a small sampling error}$$

More formally, assuming that the researchers select a large sample (more than thirty observations), the small sampling error is given by

$$\text{Small sampling error} = Z_{c.l.} S_{\overline{X}}$$

where

$Z_{c.l.}$ = value of Z, or standardized normal variable, at a specified confidence level (c.l.)

$S_{\overline{X}}$ = standard error of the mean

The precision of our estimate is indicated by the value of $Z_{c.l.} S_{\overline{X}}$. It is useful to define the range of possible error, E, as follows:

$$E = Z_{c.l.} S_{\overline{X}}$$

Thus,

$$\mu = \overline{X} \pm E$$

where

$\overline{X}$ = sample mean (commonly pronounced X-bar)

E = range of sampling error

or

$$\mu = \overline{X} \pm Z_{c.l.} S_{\overline{X}}$$

The expression of "confidence" using $\pm E$ is stated as one-half of the total confidence interval. One half of the interval is less than the mean and the other half is greater than the mean.

The following step-by-step procedure can be used to calculate confidence intervals:

1. Calculate $\overline{X}$ from the sample.
2. Assuming σ is unknown, estimate the population standard deviation by finding S, the sample standard deviation.
3. Estimate the standard error of the mean, using the following formula:

$$S_{\overline{X}} = \frac{S}{\sqrt{n}}$$

4. Determine the Z-value associated with the desired confidence level. The confidence level should be divided by 2 to determine what percentage of the area under the curve to include on each side of the mean.
5. Calculate the confidence interval.

The following example shows how calculation of a confidence interval can be used in preparing a demographic profile, a useful tool for market segmentation. Suppose you plan to open a sporting goods store to cater to working women who play golf. In a survey of 100 women in your market area, you find that the mean age ($\overline{X}$) is 37.5 years, with a standard deviation (S) of 12.0 years. Even though 37.5 years is the "expected value" and the best guess for the true mean age in the population (μ), the likelihood is that the mean is not exactly 37.5. Thus, a confidence interval around the sample mean computed using the steps just given will be useful:

1. $\overline{X} = 37.5$ years
2. $S = 12.0$ years

confidence level

A percentage or decimal value that tells how confident a researcher can be about being correct; it states the long-run percentage of confidence intervals that will include the true population mean.

3. $S_{\bar{X}} = \dfrac{12.0}{\sqrt{100}} = 1.2$

4. Suppose you wish to be 95 percent confident—that is, assured that 95 times out of 100, the estimates from your sample will include the population parameter. Including 95 percent of the area requires that 47.5 percent (one-half of 95 percent) of the distribution on each side be included. From a Z-table (see Exhibit 13.10 or the full table available on the companion web site), you find that 0.475 corresponds to the Z-value 1.96.

5. Substitute the values for $Z_{c.l.}$ and $S_{\bar{X}}$ into the confidence interval formula:

$$\mu = 37.5 \pm (1.96)(1.2)$$
$$= 37.5 \pm 2.352$$

You can thus expect that μ is contained in the range from 35.15 to 39.85 years. Intervals constructed in this manner will contain the true value of μ 95 percent of the time.

Step 3 can be eliminated by entering S and n directly in the confidence interval formula:

$$\mu = \bar{X} \pm Z_{c.l.} \frac{S}{\sqrt{n}}$$

Remember that $S/\sqrt{n}$ represents the standard error of the mean, $S_{\bar{X}}$. Its use is based on the central-limit theorem.

If you wanted to increase the probability that the population mean will lie within the confidence interval, you could use the 99 percent confidence level, with a Z-value of 2.57. You may want to calculate the 99 percent confidence interval for the preceding example; you can expect that μ will be in the range between 34.416 and 40.584 years.

We have now examined the basic concepts of inferential statistics. You should understand that sample statistics such as the sample means, $\bar{X}$s, can provide good estimates of population parameters such as μ. You should also realize that there is a certain probability of being in error when you estimate a population parameter from sample statistics. In other words, there will be a random sampling error, which is the difference between the survey results and the results of surveying the entire population. If you have a firm understanding of these basic terms and ideas, which are the essence of statistics, the remaining statistics concepts will be relatively simple for you. The Research Snapshot on the next page shows how simple descriptive statistics can be used to contrast Wal-Mart and Target shoppers.

Sample Size

Random Error and Sample Size

When asked to evaluate a marketing research project, most people, even those with little marketing research training, begin by asking, "How big was the sample?" Intuitively we know that the larger the sample, the more accurate the research. This is in fact a statistical truth; random sampling error varies with samples of different sizes. In statistical terms, increasing the sample size decreases the width of the confidence interval at a given confidence level. When the standard deviation of the population is unknown, a confidence interval is calculated using the following formula:

$$\text{Confidence interval} = \bar{X} \pm Z\frac{S}{\sqrt{n}}$$

Observe that the equation for the plus or minus error factor in the confidence interval includes n, the sample size:

$$E = Z\frac{S}{\sqrt{n}}$$

If n increases, E is reduced.

We already noted that it is not necessary to take a census of all elements of the population to conduct an accurate study. The laws of probability give investigators sufficient confidence

Target and Wal-Mart Shoppers Really Are Different

Scarborough Research conducts ongoing consumer research that combines a telephone interview on media behavior with mail and Internet surveys about shopping habits and lifestyle to provide detailed data about television viewing and other consumer habits. They measure continuously and present reports periodically. Scarborough recognizes the importance of sample size for minimizing errors. The result is a sample including over 220,000 adults in 81 designated market areas used to estimate characteristics of the U.S. population.

An example is a comparison of consumers who shop exclusively at either Target or Wal-Mart. When respondents were asked to identify the stores at which they had shopped during the preceding three months, the largest share (40 percent) named both Target and Wal-Mart. However, 31 percent shopped at Wal-Mart but not Target, and 12 percent shopped at Target but not Wal-Mart. Scarborough compared the consumer behavior of the latter two groups.

Target shoppers who shunned Wal-Mart were more likely to shop at more upscale stores, including Macy's and Nordstrom. They also were more likely than the average shopper to visit many different stores. To a Target-only shopper, value is defined by quality and choice. Wal-Mart shoppers who stayed away from Target were more likely to shop at discounters such as Dollar General and Kmart, and they were more likely to be at least 50 years old. Wal-Mart shoppers define value in a utilitarian way by emphasizing price and convenience. Target-only shoppers tended to be younger and were more likely to have a high household income.

Given a U.S. adult population of approximately 240 million, do you think the sample size is adequate to make these comparisons?

Source: Based on Scarborough Research, "In the Battle for Discount Shoppers, Target and Wal-Mart Find Brand Loyalty in Different Customer Groups," news release (September 19, 2005), http://www.scarborough.com, accessed September 24, 2008; Scarborough Research, "About Scarborough: Methodology," http://www.scarborough.com, accessed September 24, 2008.

This Web page from Scarborough defines its survey methodology in some detail. Information about the sample size is included.

regarding the accuracy of data collected from a sample. Knowledge of the characteristics of the sampling distribution helps researchers make reasonably precise estimates.

Students familiar with the law of diminishing returns in economics will easily grasp the concept that increases in sample size reduce sampling error at a *decreasing rate*. For example, doubling a sample of 1,000 will reduce random sampling error by 1 percentage point, but doubling the sample from 2,000 to 4,000 will reduce random sampling error by only another half percentage point. More technically, random sampling error is inversely proportional to the square root of n. Thus, the main issue becomes one of determining the optimal sample size.

Factors in Determining Sample Size for Questions Involving Means

Three factors are required to specify sample size: (1) the variance, or heterogeneity, of the population; (2) the magnitude of acceptable error; and (3) the confidence level. Suppose a researcher wishes to find out whether nine-year-old boys are taller than four-year-old boys. Intuitively we know that even with a very small sample size, the correct information probably will be obtained. This is based on the fact that the determination of sample size depends on the research question and the variability within the sample.

The *variance*, or *heterogeneity*, of the population is the first necessary bit of information. In statistical terms, this refers to the *standard deviation* of the population. Only a small sample is required if the population is homogeneous. For example, predicting the average age of graduate students requires a smaller sample than predicting the average age of people who visit the zoo. As *heterogeneity* increases, so must sample size. A pharmaceutical company testing the effectiveness of an acne medicine, for instance, should require a sample large enough to account for the varying range of skin types.

The *magnitude of error,* or the confidence interval, is the second necessary bit of information. Defined in statistical terms as *E,* the magnitude of error indicates how precise the estimate must be. It indicates a certain precision level. From a managerial perspective, the importance of the decision in terms of profitability will influence the researcher's specifications of the range of error. If, for example, favorable results from a test-market sample will result in the construction of a new plant and unfavorable results will dictate not marketing the product, the acceptable range of error probably will be small; the cost of an error would be too great to allow much room for random sampling errors. In other cases, the estimate need not be extremely precise. Allowing an error of $\pm\$1,000$ in total family income instead of $E = \pm 50$ may be acceptable in most market segmentation studies.

The third factor of concern is the *confidence level.* In our examples, we will typically use the 95 percent confidence level. This, however, is an arbitrary decision based on convention; there is nothing sacred about the 0.05 chance level (that is, the probability of 0.05 of the true population parameter being incorrectly estimated). Exhibit 13.16 summarizes the information required to determine sample size.

EXHIBIT 13.16

Statistical Information Needed to Determine Sample Size for Questions Involving Means

Variable	Symbol	Typical Source of Information
Standard deviation	S	Pilot study or rule of thumb
Magnitude of error	E	Managerial judgment or calculation ($ZS_{\bar{x}}$)
Confidence level	$Z_{c.l.}$	Managerial judgment

Estimating Sample Size for Questions Involving Means

Once the preceding concepts are understood, determining the actual size for a simple random sample is quite easy. The researcher must follow three steps:

1. Estimate the standard deviation of the population.
2. Make a judgment about the allowable magnitude of error.
3. Determine a confidence level.

The only problem is estimating the standard deviation of the population. Ideally, similar studies conducted in the past will give a basis for judging the standard deviation. In practice, researchers who lack prior information conduct a pilot study to estimate the population parameters so that another, larger sample of the appropriate sample size may be drawn. This procedure is called *sequential sampling* because researchers take an initial look at the pilot study results before deciding on a larger sample to provide more precise information.

A rule of thumb for estimating the value of the standard deviation is to expect it to be one-sixth of the range. If researchers conducting a study on television purchases expected the price paid to range from $100 to $700, a rule-of-thumb estimate for the standard deviation would be $100.

For the moment, assume that the standard deviation has been estimated in some preliminary work. If our concern is to estimate the mean of a particular population, the formula for sample size is

$$n = \left(\frac{ZS}{E}\right)^2$$

where

Z = standardized value that corresponds to the confidence level

S = sample standard deviation or estimate of the population standard deviation

E = acceptable error amount, plus or minus error factor (recall the range is one-half of the total confidence interval)[8]

Suppose a survey researcher studying annual expenditures on lipstick wishes to have a 95 percent confidence level ($Z = 1.96$) and a range of error (E) of less than \$2. If the estimate of the standard deviation is \$29, the sample size can be calculated as follows:

$$n = \left(\frac{ZS}{E}\right)^2 = \left(\frac{(1.96)(29)}{2}\right)^2 = \left(\frac{56.84}{2}\right)^2 = 28.42^2 = 808$$

If a range of error (E) of \$4 is acceptable, sample size can be reduced:

$$n = \left(\frac{ZS}{E}\right)^2 = \left(\frac{(1.96)(29)}{4}\right)^2 = \left(\frac{56.84}{4}\right)^2 = 14.21^2 = 202$$

Thus, doubling the range of acceptable error reduces sample size requirements dramatically. Stated conversely in a general sense, doubling sample size will reduce error by only approximately one-quarter. Thus, the added precision may often not be worth the added costs.

Population Size and Sample Size

The ACNielsen Company estimates television ratings. Throughout the years, it has been plagued with questions about how it is possible to rate 100 million plus television homes with a sample of approximately 5,000 households. The answer to that question is that in most cases the size of the population does not have a major effect on the sample size. As we have indicated, the variance of the population has the largest effect on sample size. However, a finite correction factor may be needed to adjust a sample size that is more than 5 percent of a finite population. If the sample is large relative to the population, the foregoing procedures may overestimate sample size, and the researcher may need to adjust sample size. The finite correction factor is:

$$\sqrt{\frac{(N-n)}{(N-1)}}$$

where

$N =$ population size

$n =$ sample size.

Determining Sample Size for Proportions

Researchers frequently are concerned with determining sample size for problems that involve estimating population proportions or percentages. When the question involves the estimation of a proportion, the researcher requires some knowledge of the logic for determining a confidence interval around a sample proportion estimation (p) of the population proportion (π). For a confidence interval to be constructed around the sample proportion (p), an estimate of the standard error of the proportion (S_p) must be calculated and a confidence level specified.

The precision of the estimate is indicated by the value $Z_{c.l.}S_p$. Thus, the plus-or-minus estimate of the population proportion is

$$\text{Confidence interval} = p \pm Z_{c.l.}S_p$$

If the researcher selects a 95 percent probability for the confidence interval, $Z_{c.l.}$ will equal 1.96 (from Z-table). The formula for S_p is

$$S_p = \sqrt{\frac{pq}{n}} \text{ or } S_p = \sqrt{\frac{p(1-p)}{n}}$$

where

$S_p =$ estimate of the standard error of the proportion

$p =$ proportion of successes

$q = 1 - p$, or proportion of failures

Suppose that 20 percent of a sample of 1,200 television viewers recall seeing an advertisement. The proportion of successes (p) equals 0.2, and the proportion of failures (q) equals 0.8. We estimate the 95 percent confidence interval as follows:

$$\text{Confidence Interval} = p \pm Z_{c.l.}S_p$$

$$= 0.2 \pm 1.96S_p$$

$$= 0.2 \pm 1.96\sqrt{\frac{p(1-p)}{n}}$$

$$= 0.2 \pm 1.96\sqrt{\frac{0.2(1-0.2)}{1,200}}$$

$$= 0.2 \pm 1.96\sqrt{\frac{0.16}{1,200}}$$

$$= 0.2 \pm 1.96(0.0115)$$

$$= 0.2 \pm 0.023$$

Thus, the population proportion who see an advertisement is estimated to be included in the interval between 0.177 (0.2 − 0.023) and 0.223 (0.2 + 0.023), or roughly between 18 and 22 percent, with 95 percent confidence (95 out of 100 times).

Sample size for a proportion requires the researcher to make a judgment about confidence level and the maximum allowance for random sampling error. Furthermore, the size of the proportion influences random sampling error, so an estimate of the expected proportion of successes must be made, based on intuition or prior information. The formula is

$$n = \frac{Z_{c.l.}^2\, pq}{E^2}$$

where

n = number of items in sample

$Z_c^2 l.$ = square of the confidence level in standard error units

p = estimated proportion of successes

$q = 1 - p$, or estimated proportion of failures

E^2 = square of the maximum allowance for error between the true proportion and the sample proportion, or $Z_{c.l.}S_p$ squared

Suppose a researcher believes that a simple random sample will show that 60 percent of the population (p) recognizes the name of an automobile dealership. The researcher wishes to estimate with 95 percent confidence ($Z_{c.l.} = 1.96$) that the allowance for sampling error is not greater than 3.5 percentage points (E). Substituting these values into the formula gives

$$n = \frac{(1.96)^2(0.6)(0.4)}{0.035^2}$$

$$= \frac{(3.8416)(0.24)}{0.001225}$$

$$= \frac{0.922}{0.001225}$$

$$= 753$$

Determining Sample Size on the Basis of Judgment

Just as sample units may be selected to suit the convenience or judgment of the researcher, sample size may also be determined on the basis of managerial judgments. Using a sample size similar to

© GEORGE DOYLE & CIARAN GRIFFIN

- Measures of central tendency are often used.
  - The mean is the most commonly used measure of central tendency.
  - The median is more appropriate than the mean as a measure of central tendency when the data display extreme values or outliers.
  - The mode is most appropriate as a measure of central tendency when the data are less than interval.
- Sample size estimates often require some estimate of the standard deviation that will exist in the sample.
  - A rule of thumb for estimating the standard deviation is that it will be about one-sixth of the expected range.

- Larger samples allow predictions with greater precision that can be expressed over a smaller range.
  - Increases in precision usually require disproportionately large increases in sample size.
  - Larger samples require more resources.
- The amount of risk involved in a decision should be strongly considered in making decisions about the sample.
  - Only the riskiest of decisions require very large samples (i.e., thousands of respondents).
  - Samples of 300−500 respondents can provide adequate results for many marketing decisions that do not involve extremely high risk.

those used in previous studies provides the inexperienced researcher with a comparison with other researchers' judgments.

Another judgmental factor that affects the determination of sample size is the selection of the appropriate item, question, or characteristic to be used for the sample size calculations. Several different characteristics affect most studies, and the desired degree of precision may vary for these items. The researcher must exercise some judgment to determine which item will be used. Often the item that will produce the largest sample size will be used to determine the ultimate sample size. However, the cost of data collection becomes a major consideration, and judgment must be exercised regarding the importance of such information.

Another consideration stems from most researchers' need to analyze various subgroups within the sample. For example, suppose an analyst wishes to look at differences in retailers' attitudes by geographic region. The analyst will want to make sure to sample an adequate number of retailers in the New England, Mid-Atlantic, and South Atlantic regions to ensure that subgroup comparisons are reliable. There is a judgmental rule of thumb for selecting minimum subgroup sample size: Each subgroup to be separately analyzed should have a minimum of 100 units in each category of the major breakdowns. The total sample size is computed by totaling the sample sizes necessary for these subgroups.

Summary

1. Use descriptive statistics indicating central tendency and dispersion to make inferences about a population. Calculating a mean and a standard deviation to "describe" or profile a sample is a commonly applied descriptive statistical approach. Inferential statistics investigate samples to draw conclusions about entire populations. If a mean is computed and then compared to some preconceived standard, then inferential statistics are being implemented. A frequency distribution shows how frequently each response or classification occurs. A simple tally count illustrates a frequency distribution. A proportion indicates the percentage of group members that have a particular characteristic. Three measures of central tendency are commonly used: the mean, the median, and the mode. These three values may differ, and care must be taken to understand distortions that may arise from using the wrong measure of central tendency. Measures of dispersion further describe a distribution. The range is the difference between the largest and smallest values observed. The most useful measures of dispersion are the variance and standard deviation.

2. Distinguish among population, sample, and sampling distributions. The techniques of statistical inference are based on the relationship among the population distribution, the sample distribution, and the sampling distribution. The population distribution is a frequency distribution of the elements of a population. The sample distribution is a frequency distribution of a sample.

A sampling distribution is a theoretical probability distribution of sample means for all possible samples of a certain size drawn from a particular population. The sampling distribution's mean is the expected value of the mean, which equals the population's mean. The standard deviation of the sampling distribution is the standard error of the mean, approximately equal to the standard deviation of the population, divided by the square root of the sample size.

3. Explain the central-limit theorem. The central-limit theorem states that as sample size increases, the distribution of sample means of size *n*, randomly selected, approaches a normal distribution. This means that even if some distribution has some non-normal distribution, the distribution of averages taken from samples of these numbers is normally distributed. This allows inferential statistics to be used. This theoretical knowledge can be used to estimate parameters and determine sample size.

4. Use confidence intervals to express population estimates. Estimating a population mean with a single value gives a point estimate. The confidence interval estimate is a range of numbers within which the researcher is confident that the population mean will lie. The confidence level is a percentage that indicates the long-run probability that the confidence interval estimate will be correct. Many research problems involve the estimation of proportions. Statistical techniques may be used to determine a confidence interval around a sample proportion.

5. Understand the major issues in specifying sample size. The statistical determination of sample size requires knowledge of (1) the variance of the population, (2) the magnitude of acceptable error, and (3) the confidence level. Several computational formulas are available for determining sample size. Furthermore, a number of easy-to-use tables have been compiled to help researchers calculate sample size. The main reason a large sample size is desirable is that sample size is related to random sampling error. A smaller sample makes a larger error in estimates more likely.

Key Terms and Concepts

central-limit theorem, *337*
confidence interval estimate, *340*
confidence level, *341*
frequency distribution, *326*
mean, *328*
median, *329*
mode, *329*
normal distribution, *333*

percentage distribution, *327*
point estimate, *340*
population distribution, *336*
population parameters, *326*
probability, *327*
proportion, *327*
sample distribution, *336*
sample statistics, *326*

sampling distribution, *337*
standard deviation, *332*
standard error of the mean, *337*
standardized normal distribution, *333*
top-box score, *327*
variance, *331*

Questions for Review and Critical Thinking

1. What is the difference between descriptive and inferential statistics?
2. Suppose the speed limits in thirteen countries in miles per hour are as follows:

Country	Highway Miles per Hour
Italy	87
France	82
Hungary	75
Belgium	75
Portugal	75
Great Britain	70
Spain	62
Denmark	62
Netherlands	62
Greece	62
Japan	62
Norway	56
Turkey	56

What is the mean, median, and mode for these data? Feel free to use your computer (statistical software or spreadsheet) to get the answer. Which is the best measure of central tendency for this data?

3. Prepare a frequency distribution for the data in question 2.
4. Why is the standard deviation rather than the average deviation typically used?
5. Calculate the standard deviation for the data in question 2.
6. Draw three distributions that have the same mean value but different standard deviation values. Draw three distributions that have the same standard deviation value but different mean values.
7. A manufacturer of MP3 players surveyed one hundred retail stores in each of the firm's sales regions. An analyst noticed that in the South Atlantic region the average retail price was $165 (mean) and the standard deviation was $30. However, in the Mid-Atlantic region the mean price was $170, with a standard deviation of $15. What do these statistics tell us about these two sales regions?

8. What is the sampling distribution? How does it differ from the sample distribution?
9. What would happen to the sampling distribution of the mean if we increased sample size from 5 to 25?
10. Suppose a fast-food restaurant wishes to estimate average sales volume for a new menu item. The restaurant has analyzed the sales of the item at a similar outlet and observed the following results:

$$\overline{X} = 500 \text{ (mean daily sales)}$$
$$S = 100 \text{ (standard deviation of sample)}$$
$$n = 25 \text{ (sample size)}$$

The restaurant manager wants to know into what range the mean daily sales should fall 95 percent of the time. Perform this calculation.
11. In the example on page 345 of research on lipstick, where $E = \$2$ and $S = \$29$, what sample size would we require if we desired a 99 percent confidence level?
12. Suppose you are planning to sample cat owners to determine the average number of cans of cat food they purchase monthly. The following standards have been set: a confidence level of 99 percent and an error of less than 5 units. Past research has indicated that the standard deviation should be 6 units. What is the required sample size?
13. What is a standardized normal curve?
14. **ETHICS** Using the formula in this chapter, a researcher determines that at the 95 percent confidence level, a sample of 2,500

is required to satisfy a client's requirements. The researcher actually uses a sample of 1,200, however, because the client has specified a budget cap for the survey. What are the ethical considerations in this situation?
15. **'NET** Go to http://www.dartmouth.edu/~chance/ to visit the Chance course. The Chance course is an innovative program to creatively teach introductory materials about probability and statistics. The Chance course is designed to enhance quantitative literacy. Numerous videos can be played online.
16. **'NET** Go to http://www.researchinfo.com. Click on "Market Research Calculators." Which of the calculators can be used to help find the sample size required? How big of a sample is needed to make an inference about the U.S. population $+/-5$ percent? How large a sample is needed to make an inference about the population of Norway $+/-5$ percent? Remember, population statistics can be found in the *CIA World Factbook* online. Comment.
17. **'NET** A random number generator and other statistical information can be found at http://www.random.org. Flip some virtual coins. Perform 20 flips with an Aurelian coin. Perform 20 flips with a Constatius coin. Perform frequency tables for each result. What conclusion might you draw? Would the result change if you flipped the coins 200 times or 2,000 times?

Research Activities

1. **'NET** Go to http://www.surveypro.com. Click on pricing. Write a brief report that describes how prices are charged to someone wishing to use this service to host a survey. What happens as the desired sample size increases? Why is this?
2. **'NET** Use an online library service to find basic business research studies that report a "response rate" or number of respondents compared to number of contacts. You may wish to consult

journals such as the *Journal of Business Research,* the *Journal of Marketing,* the *Journal of the Academy of Marketing Science* or the *Journal of Personal Selling and Sales Management.* Find at least 25 such studies. What is the average response rate across all of these studies? Do there appear to be any trends or factors that are associated with lower response rates? Write a brief report on your findings.

Case 13.1 Coastal Star Sales Corporation

Download the data sets for this case from www .cengage.com/marketing/zikmund *or request them from your instructor.*

Coastal Star Sales Corporation is a West Coast wholesaler that markets leisure products from several manufacturers. Coastal Star has an 80-person sales force that sells to wholesalers in a six-state area, which is divided into two sales regions. Case Exhibit 13.1–1 shows the names of a sample of eleven salespeople, some descriptive information about each person, and sales performance for each of the last two years.

Questions
1. Calculate a mean and a standard deviation for each variable.

2. Set a 95 percent confidence interval around the mean for each variable.
3. Calculate the median, mode, and range for each variable.
4. Organize the data for current sales into a frequency distribution with three classes: (a) under $500,000, (b) $500,000 to $999,999, and (c) $1,000,000 and over.
5. Organize the data for years of selling experience into a frequency distribution with two classes: (a) less than five years and (b) five or more years.
6. Convert the frequency distributions from question 5 to percentage distributions.

CASE EXHIBIT 13.1–1   **Salesperson Data: Coastal Star Sales Corporation**

				Sales	
Region	Salesperson	Age	Years of Experience	Previous Year	Current Year
Northern	Jackson	40	7	$ 412,744	$ 411,007
Northern	Gentry	60	12	1,491,024	1,726,630
Northern	La Forge	26	2	301,421	700,112
Northern	Miller	39	1	401,241	471,001
Northern	Mowen	64	5	448,160	449,261
Southern	Young	51	2	518,897	519,412
Southern	Fisk	34	1	846,222	713,333
Southern	Kincaid	62	10	1,527,124	2,009,041
Southern	Krieger	42	3	921,174	1,030,000
Southern	Manzer	64	5	463,399	422,798
Southern	Weiner	27	2	548,011	422,001

Part 5
Analysis and Reporting

© NONSTOCK/JUPITER IMAGES

CHAPTER 14
Basic Data Analysis

CHAPTER 15
Testing for Differences Between
Groups and for Relationships
Among Variables

CHAPTER 16
Communicating Research Results

CHAPTER 14
BASIC DATA ANALYSIS

LEARNING OUTCOMES

After studying this chapter, you should be able to

1. Prepare qualitative data for interpretation or data analysis
2. Know what descriptive statistics are and why they are used
3. Create and interpret tabulation tables
4. Use cross-tabulations to display relationships
5. Perform basic data transformations
6. List different computer software products designed for descriptive statistical analysis
7. Understand the basics of testing hypotheses using inferential statistics.

Chapter Vignette: Pizza Targets

We all sometimes have trouble deciding where to eat or shop. Consumers have some idea in mind about the type of food they wish to eat, the atmosphere they want to experience, and the price they wish to pay. They use these *benchmarks* in the decision-making process.

Consider the other side of the coin. Companies like Domino's, Papa John's, and Pizza Hut each operate thousands of stores and have to decide which locations will remain open and where new locations are needed. Domino's operates over 8,300 stores across the United States and in over 55 countries internationally.[1] However, recent trends show approximately a 6 percent drop in same-store U.S. sales while international same-store sales have increased by over 5 percent. In recent years, Domino's has closed over 400 stores and is considering closing more stores around the United States in a reponse to poor store-unit sales.[2]

© VICKI BEAVER

Location decisions are very important in retailing, and an important part of the marketing strategy for firms like Domino's involves rules that help make these decisions. Restaurants and retailers with thousands of locations can establish benchmarks based on historical performance trends. Pizza Hut, Domino's, and their major competitors can use demographic data to help identify potentially good restaurant locations, and they can use demographics along with profitability and sales growth statistics to help make store closure decisions.

Fortunately for Domino's, families and college students eat a lot of pizza. Researchers may be asked to perform research to determine if enough families live within a 10-minute drive to support a restaurant. Location rules may involve comparing a sample's demographic characteristics to demographic benchmarks. For instance, if historical data indicated that a successful restaurant generally was surrounded by families with an average of 1.5 children or more, the research may sample prospective locations and compare the observed average family size to this benchmark. Similarly, the company may have benchmarks for household income or the proportion of specific ethnic groups within a market. Benchmarks like these can help make difficult decisions like these manageable.

Introduction

We now turn to research tools that allow inferences to be made. These inferences often involve testing some hypothesis that states a condition thought to exist in a population. As researchers, we infer whether or not that condition exists based on what we observe in a sample. Alternatively, the research could be more exploratory and the statistics could be directed simply at a search for some pattern within the data. On rare occasions, the data may represent a census of a population, in which case no statistical inferences are necessary because parameters are known. Descriptive statistical tools like these provide a straightforward way of succinctly describing the information content within a data set.

Coding Qualitative Responses

Researchers often summarize and bring meaning to qualitative data by developing some type of logical coding scheme. The interpretation of these responses may be aided by some type of computer analysis. A researcher will even combine an interpretive approach with basic quantitative analyses to address a research question. Either way, some coding is necessary. Any mistakes in coding can dramatically change the conclusions. **Coding** represents the way a specific meaning is assigned to a response within previously edited data. Codes represent the meaning in data by assigning some measurement symbol to different categories of responses. This may be a number, letter, or word. The proper form of coding can be tied back to the level of measurement present. Nominal measurement can be represented by a word, letter, or any identifying mark. On the other hand, numbers typically are most appropriate for ordinal, interval, or ratio measures.

Thus, **codes** often, but not always, are numerical symbols. However, they are more broadly defined as rules for interpreting, classifying, and recording data. In interpretive research, numbers are seldom used for codes. In qualitative research, the codes are usually words or phrases that represent themes. For example, a qualitative researcher may apply a code to a hermeneutic unit describing in detail a respondent's reactions to several different glasses of wine. After reading through the text several times, and applying a word-counting routine, the researcher realizes that appearance, the nose (aroma), and guessing (trying to guess what the wine will be like or what type of wine is in the glass) are important themes. A code is assigned to these categories. After considerable thought and questioning of the experience, the researcher builds a network, or grounded theory, that suggests how a wine may come to be associated with feelings of romance.

coding

The process of assigning a numerical score or other character symbol to previously edited data.

codes

Rules for interpreting, classifying, and recording data in the coding process; also, the actual numerical or other character symbols assigned to raw data.

Structured Qualitative Responses and Dummy Variables

Qualitative responses to structured questions such as "yes" or "no" can be stored in a data file with letters such as "Y" or "N." Alternatively, they can be represented with numbers, one each to represent the respective category. So, the number 1 can be used to represent "yes" and 2 can be used to represent "no." Since this represents a nominal numbering system, the actual numbers used are arbitrary.

Even though the codes are numeric, the variable is classificatory, simply separating the positive from the negative responses. For statistical purposes the research may consider adopting **dummy coding** for dichotomous responses like yes or no. Dummy coding assigns a 0 to one category and a 1 to the other. So, for yes/no responses, a 0 could be "no" and a 1 would be "yes." Similarly, a "1" could represent a female respondent and a "0" would be a male respondent. Dummy coding provides the researcher with more flexibility in how structured, qualitative responses are analyzed statistically. Dummy coding can be used when more than two categories exist, but because a dummy variable can only represent two categories, multiple dummy variables are needed to represent a single qualitative response that can take on more than two categories. In fact, the rule is that if k is the number of categories for a qualitative variable, $k - 1$ dummy variables are needed to represent the variable.

An alternative to dummy coding is **effects coding**. Effects coding is performed by assigning a $+1$ to one value of a dichotomous variable and a -1 to the other. Dummy coding is more widely used in general, although effects coding has some advantages in the way experimental results are

dummy coding

Numeric "1" or "0" coding where each number represents an alternate response such as "female" or "male."

effects coding

An alternative to dummy coding using the values of -1 and 1 to represent two categories of responses.

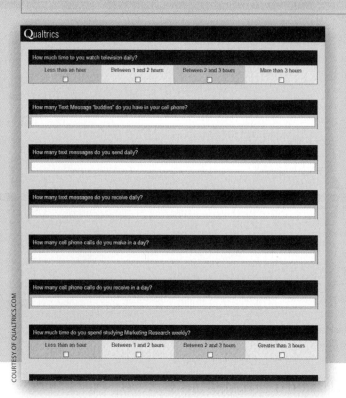

Take a look at the section of the student survey shown.

Compute the appropriate descriptive statistic for each question using the data from the results for your class or school (across all sections of marketing research classes taking the survey). What conclusions would you draw from these results?

presented. Either way is an acceptable technique for coding structured qualitative data. Either way, the qualitative data is now represented in a way that facilitates basic data analysis.

The Nature of Descriptive Analysis

descriptive analysis

The elementary transformation of raw data in a way that describes the basic characteristics such as central tendency, distribution, and variability.

Perhaps the most basic statistical analysis is descriptive analysis. **Descriptive analysis** is the elementary transformation of data in a way that describes the basic characteristics such as central tendency, distribution, and variability. A researcher takes responses from 1,000 American consumers and tabulates their favorite soft drink brand and the price they expect to pay for a six-pack of that product. The mode for favorite soft drink and the average price across all 1,000 consumers would be descriptive statistics that describe central tendency in two different ways. Averages, medians, modes, variance, range, and standard deviation typify widely applied descriptive statistics.

Descriptive statistics can summarize responses from large numbers of respondents in a few simple statistics. When a sample is used, the sample descriptive statistics are used to make inferences about characteristics of the entire population of interest. The researcher examining descriptive statistics for any particular variable is using univariate statistics. Descriptive statistics are simple but powerful. Because they are so simple, descriptive statistics are used very widely.

In an earlier chapter, we learned that the level of scale measurement can help the researcher choose the most appropriate statistical tool. Exhibit 14.1 shows the specific descriptive statistic appropriate for each level of measurement. Also, remember that all statistics appropriate for lower-order scales (nominal is the lowest) are suitable for higher-order scales (ratio is the highest). So, a frequency table could also be used for interval or ratio data. Frequencies can be represented graphically as shown and are a good way of visually depicting typical survey results.

Consider the following data. Sample consumers were asked where they most often purchased beer. The result is a nominal variable which can be described with a frequency distribution (see the bar chart in Exhibit 14.1). Ten percent indicated they most often purchased beer in a drug store, 45 percent indicated a convenience store, 35 percent indicated a grocery store, and 7 percent indicated a specialty store. Three percent listed "other" (not shown in the bar chart). The mode is convenience store since more respondents chose this than any other category. A similar distribution

EXHIBIT 14.1
Levels of Scale Measurement and Suggested Descriptive Statistics

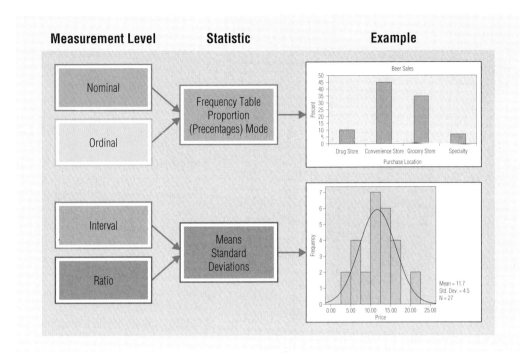

may have been obtained if the chart plotted the number of respondents ranking each store as their favorite type of place to purchase beer.

The bottom part of Exhibit 14.1 displays example descriptive statistics for interval and ratio variables. In this case, the chart displays results of a question asking respondents how much they typically spend on a bottle of wine purchased in a store. The mean and standard deviation are displayed beside the chart as 11.7 and 4.5, respectively. Additionally, the frequency distribution is shown with a histogram. A **histogram** is a graphical way of showing the frequency distribution in which the height of a bar corresponds to the frequency of a category. Histograms are useful for any type of data, but with continuous variables (interval or ratio) the histogram is useful for providing a quick assessment of the distribution of the data. A normal distribution line is superimposed over the histogram providing an easy comparison to see if the data are skewed or multi-modal.

histogram

A graphical way of showing a frequency distribution in which the height of a bar corresponds to the observed frequency of the category.

Creating and Interpreting Tabulation

Tabulation refers to the orderly arrangement of data in a table or other summary format. When this tabulation process is done by hand the term *tallying* is used. Counting the different ways respondents answered a question and arranging them in a simple tabular form yields a **frequency table**. The actual number of responses to each category is a variable's frequency distribution. A simple tabulation of this type is sometimes called a *marginal tabulation*.

Simple tabulation tells the researcher how frequently each response occurs. This starting point for analysis requires the researcher to count responses or observations for each category or code assigned to a variable. A frequency table showing where consumers generally purchase beer can be computed easily. The tabular results that correspond to the chart would appear as follows:

tabulation

The orderly arrangement of data in a table or other summary format showing the number of responses to each response category; tallying.

frequency table

A table showing the different ways respondents answered a question.

Response	Frequency	Percent	Cumulative Percentage
Drug store	50	10	10
Convenience store	225	45	55
Grocery store	175	35	90
Specialty	35	7	97
Other	15	3	100

Web sites like this one provide a secondary data source in the form of descriptive statistics or details that can easily be used to compute tabulations, means, cross-tabulations, and so on.

The frequency column shows the tally result or the number of respondents listing each store, respectively. The percent column shows the total percentage in each category. The cumulative percentage shows the percentage indicating either a particular category or any preceding category as their preferred place to purchase beer. From this chart, the mode indicates that the typical consumer buys beer at the convenience store since more people indicated this as their top response.

Similarly, a recent tabulation of Americans' responses to the simple question of "Who is your favorite TV personality?" revealed the response varied by generation. For respondents aged 18–30 (Echo Boomers), Stephen Colbert was listed first. For respondents aged 31–42 (Gen X), Jay Leno and Jon Stewart tied as the preferred TV personalities, Oprah Winfrey was the top TV celebrity for Boomers (43–61), and she is tied with Bill O'Reilly among Matures (62+).[3] The idea that generation may influence choice of favorite celebrity brings us to cross-tabulation.

Cross-Tabulation

A frequency distribution or tabulation can address many research questions. As long as a question deals with only one categorical variable, tabulation is probably the best approach. Although frequency counts, percentage distributions, and averages summarize considerable information, simple tabulation may not yield the full value of the research. **Cross-tabulation** is the appropriate technique for addressing research questions involving relationships among multiple less-than interval variables. A cross-tabulation is a combined frequency table. Cross-tabulation allows the inspection and comparison of differences among groups based on nominal or ordinal categories. One key to interpreting a cross-tabulation table is comparing the observed table values with hypothetical values that would result from pure chance.

Exhibit 14.2 summarizes several cross-tabulations from consumers' responses to a questionnaire on ethical behavior in the United States.[4] Panel A suggests how two questionable behaviors (variables—taking home supplies, calling in sick) may vary with basic demographic variables. A researcher interested in the relative ethical perspectives of business executives and the general public can inspect panel B and compare the two groups. If business executives and the general public have the same ethical attitudes, the observed percentages should be equal for each question. This does not appear to be the case. The data lead to the conclusion that business executives participate in these behaviors more than the general public. However, before reaching the conclusion that business executives are less ethical than the general public, one must carefully scrutinize this finding for possible extraneous variables.

cross-tabulation

The appropriate technique for addressing research questions involving relationships among multiple less-than interval variables; results in a combined frequency table displaying one variable in rows and another in columns.

Contingency Tables

contingency table

A data matrix that displays the frequency of some combination of possible responses to multiple variables; cross-tabulation results.

Exhibit 14.3 shows example cross-tabulation results using contingency tables. A **contingency table** is a data matrix that displays the frequency of some combination of possible responses to multiple variables. Two-way contingency tables, meaning they involve two less-than interval variables, are used most often. A three-way contingency table involves three less-than interval variables. Beyond three variables, contingency tables become difficult to analyze and explain easily.

EXHIBIT 14.2 **Cross-Tabulation Tables from a Survey on Ethics in America**

(A) Reported Behavior (Percentage of General Public Who Have Ever Done Each Activity)						
	Age		Gender		Education	
Activity	Under 50 Years Old	Over 50 Years Old	Men	Women	College Graduate	High School Graduate
Taken home work supplies	50	20	47	33	58	21
Called in sick to work when not ill	40	18	Not reported		36	21

(B) Reported Behavior (Percentage Who Have Ever Done Each Activity)		
Activity	Business Executives	General Public
Taken home work supplies	74	40
Called in sick to work when not ill	14	31
Used company telephone for personal long-distance calls	78	15
Overstated deductions somewhat on tax forms	35	13
Driven while drunk	80	33
Saw a fellow employee steal something at work and did not report it	7	26

From Roger Ricklefs, "Ethics in America," *The Wall Street Journal*, October 31, 1983, pp. 33, 42; November 1, 1983, p. 33; November 2, 1983, p. 33; and November 3, 1983, pp. 33, 37.

EXHIBIT 14.3

Different Ways of Depicting the Cross-Tabulation of Biological Sex and Target Patronage

(A) Cross-Tabulation of Question "Do you shop at Target?" by Sex of Respondent			
	Yes	No	Total
Men	150	75	225
Women	180	45	225
Total	330	120	450

(B) Percentage Cross-Tabulation of Question "Do you shop at Target?" by Sex of Respondent, Row Percentage			
	Yes	No	Total (Base)
Men	66.7%	33.3%	100% (225)
Women	80.0%	20.0%	100% (225)

(C) Percentage Cross-Tabulation of Question "Do you shop at Target?" by Sex of Respondent, Column Percentage		
	Yes	No
Men	45.5%	62.5%
Women	54.5%	37.5%
Total	100%	100%
(Base)	(330)	(120)

Two variables are depicted in the contingency table shown in panel A:

- Row Variable: Biological Sex _____M _____F
- Column Variable: "Do you shop at Target? YES or NO"

Several conclusions can be drawn initially by examining the row and column totals:

1. 225 men and 225 women responded as can be seen in the row totals column. This means that altogether 450 consumers responded.
2. Out of this 450 total consumers, 330 consumers indicated that "yes" they do shop at Target and 120 indicated "no," they do not shop at Target. This can be observed in the column totals at the bottom of the table. These row and column totals often are called **marginals** because they appear in the table's margins.

Researchers usually are more interested in the inner cells of a contingency table. The inner cells display conditional frequencies (combinations). Using these values, we can draw some more specific conclusions:

3. Out of 330 consumers who shop at Target, 150 are male and 180 are female.
4. Alternatively, out of the 120 respondents not shopping at Target, 75 are male and 45 are female.

This finding helps us know whether the two variables are related. If men and women equally patronize Target, we would expect that hypothetically 165 of the 330 shoppers would be male and 165 would be female. Clearly, these hypothetical expectations (165m/165f) are not observed. What is the implication? A relationship exists between respondent sex and shopping choice. Specifically, Target shoppers are more likely to be female than male. Notice that the same meaning could be drawn by analyzing non-Target shoppers.

A two-way contingency table like the one shown in part A is referred to as a *2 × 2 table* because it has two rows (Men and Women) and two columns (Yes and No). Each variable has two levels. A two-way contingency table displaying two variables one (the row variable) with three levels and the other with four levels would be referred to as a *3 × 4 table*. Any cross-tabulation table may be classified according to the number of rows by the number of columns (*R* by *C*).

marginals
Row and column totals in a contingency table, which are shown in its margins.

Percentage Cross-Tabulations

When data from a survey are cross-tabulated, percentages help the researcher understand the nature of the relationship by making relative comparisons simpler. The total number of respondents or observations may be used as a **statistical base** for computing the percentage in each cell. When the objective of the research is to identify a relationship between answers to two questions (or two variables), one of the questions is commonly chosen to be the source of the base for determining percentages. For example, look at the data in parts A, B, and C of Exhibit 14.3. Compare part B with part C. Selecting either the row percentages or the column percentages will emphasize a particular comparison or distribution. The nature of the problem the researcher wishes to answer will determine which marginal total will serve as a base for computing percentages.

Fortunately, a conventional rule determines the direction of percentages. The rule depends on which variable is identified as an independent variable and which is a dependent variable. Simply put, independent variables should form the rows in a contingency table. The marginal total of the independent variable should be used as the base for computing the percentages. Although survey research does not establish cause-and-effect evidence, one might argue that it would be logical to assume that a variable such as biological sex might predict beverage preference. This makes more sense than thinking that beverage preference would determine biological sex.

statistical base
The number of respondents or observations (in a row or column) used as a basis for computing percentages.

Elaboration and Refinement

The *Oxford Universal Dictionary* defines *analysis* as "the resolution of anything complex into its simplest elements." Once a researcher has examined the basic relationship between two variables, he or she may wish to investigate this relationship under a variety of different conditions. Typically, a third variable is introduced into the analysis to elaborate and refine the researcher's understanding by specifying the conditions under which the relationship between the first two variables is strongest and weakest. In other words, a more elaborate analysis asks, "Will interpretation of the relationship be modified if other variables are simultaneously considered?"

Elaboration analysis involves the basic cross-tabulation within various subgroups of the sample. The researcher breaks down the analysis for each level of another variable. If the researcher has cross-tabulated shopping preference by sex (see Exhibit 14.3) and wishes to investigate another variable (say, marital status), a more elaborate analysis may be conducted. Exhibit 14.4 breaks down the responses to the question "Do you shop at Target?" by sex and marital status. The data show women display the same preference whether married or single. However, married men are much more likely to shop at Target than are single men. The analysis suggests that the original conclusion about the relationship between sex and shopping behavior for women be retained. However, a relationship that was not discernible in the two-variable case is evident. Married men more frequently shop at Target than do single men.

	Single		Married	
	Men	Women	Men	Women
"Do you shop at Target?"				
Yes	55%	80%	86%	80%
No	45%	20%	14%	20%

elaboration analysis

An analysis of the basic cross-tabulation for each level of a variable not previously considered, such as subgroups of the sample.

EXHIBIT 14.4

Cross-Tabulation of Marital Status, Sex, and Responses to the Question "Do You Shop at Target?"

moderator variable

A third variable that changes the nature of a relationship between the original independent and dependent variables.

data transformation

Process of changing the data from their original form to a format suitable for performing a data analysis addressing research objectives.

The finding is consistent with an interaction effect. The combination of the two variables, sex and marital status, is associated with differences in the dependent variable. Interactions between variables examine moderating variables. A **moderator variable** is a third variable that changes the nature of a relationship between the original independent and dependent variables. Marital status is a moderator variable in this case. The interaction effect suggests that marriage changes the relationship between sex and shopping preference.

In other situations the addition of a third variable to the analysis may lead us to reject the original conclusion about the relationship. When this occurs, the elaboration analysis suggests the relationship between the original variables is spurious.

How Many Cross-Tabulations?

Surveys may ask dozens of questions and hundreds of categorical variables can be stored in a data warehouse. Computer-assisted marketing researchers can "fish" for relationships by cross-tabulating every categorical variable with every other categorical variable. Thus, every possible response becomes a possible explanatory variable. A researcher addressing an exploratory research question may find some benefit in such a fishing expedition. Software exists that can automatically search through volumes of cross-tabulations. These may even provide some insight into the market segment structure for some product. Alternatively, the program may flag the cross-tabulations suggesting the strongest relationship. CHAID (chi-square automatic interaction detection) software exemplifies software that makes searches through large numbers of variables possible.[5] Data-mining can be conducted in a similar fashion and may suggest relationships that are worth considering further.

Outside of exploratory research, researchers should conduct cross-tabulations that address specific research questions or hypotheses. When hypotheses involve relationships among two categorical variables, cross-tabulations are the right tool for the job.

Data Transformation

Simple Transformations

Data transformation (also called *data conversion*) is the process of changing the data from their original form to a format suitable for performing a data analysis that will achieve research objectives. Researchers often modify the values of scalar data or create new variables. For example, many researchers believe that less response bias will result if interviewers ask respondents for their year of birth rather than their age. This presents no problem for the research analyst, because a simple data transformation is possible. The raw data coded as birth year can easily be transformed to age by subtracting the birth year from the current year.

In earlier chapters, we discussed recoding and creating summated scales. These also are common data transformations.

Collapsing or combining adjacent categories of a variable is a common form of data transformation used to reduce the number of categories. A Likert scale may sometimes be collapsed into a smaller number of categories. For instance, consider the following Likert item administered to a sample of state university seniors:

	Strongly Disagree	Disagree	Neutral	Agree	Strongly Agree
I am satisfied with my college experience at this university	☐	☐	☐	☐	☐

The following frequency table describes results for this survey item:

Strongly Disagree	Disagree	Neutral	Agree	Strongly Agree
110	30	15	35	210

The distribution is bimodal because two peaks exist in the distribution, one at either end of the scale. Since the vast majority of respondents (80 percent = (110 + 210)/400) indicated either strongly disagree or strongly agree, the variable closely resembles a categorical variable. Customers either strongly disagreed or agreed with the statement. So, the research may wish to collapse the responses into two categories. While multiple ways exist to accomplish this, the researcher may assign the value zero to all respondents who either strongly disagreed or disagreed and the value one to all respondents who either agreed or strongly agreed. Respondents marking neutral would be excluded from analysis.

Perhaps the 110 dissatisfied students differ in some important way from the 210. Perhaps their exam scores are also bimodal. Exhibit 14.5 shows an example of a bimodal distribution.

EXHIBIT 14.5
Bimodal Distributions Are Consistent with Transformations into Categorical Values

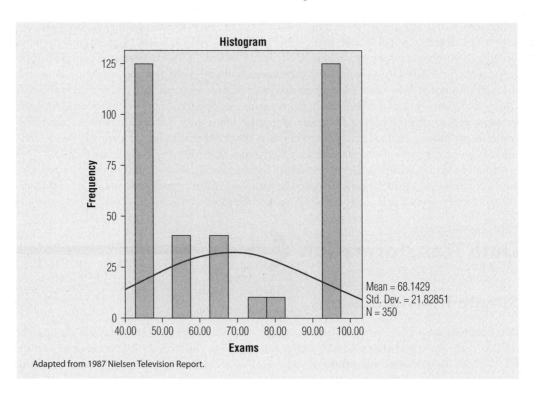

Adapted from 1987 Nielsen Television Report.

Problems with Data Transformations

Researchers often perform a median split to collapse a scale with multiple response points into two categories. The **median split** means respondents below the observed median go into one category and respondents above the median go into another. Although this is common, the approach is best applied only when the data do indeed exhibit bimodal characteristics. When the data are unimodal, such as would be the case with normally distributed data, a median split will lead to error.

Exhibit 14.6 illustrates this problem. Clearly, most respondents either slightly agree or slightly disagree with this statement. The central tendency could be represented by the median of 3.5, a mean of 3.5, or the mode of 3.5 (3 and 4 each have the same number of responses so the mode is set between the two). The "outliers," if any, appear to be those not indicating something other than slight agreement or slight disagreement. In all likelihood, the respondents indicating slight disagreement are more similar to those indicating slight agreement than they are to those respondents indicating strong disagreement. Yet, the recode places values 1 and 3 in the same new category, but places values 3 and 4 in a different category (see the recoding scheme in Exhibit 14.6). The distribution does not support a median split into two categories and so a transformation collapsing these values into agreement and disagreement is inappropriate.

median split

Dividing a data set into two categories by placing respondents below the median in one category and respondents above the median in another.

EXHIBIT 14.6 **The Problem with Median Splits with Unimodal Data**

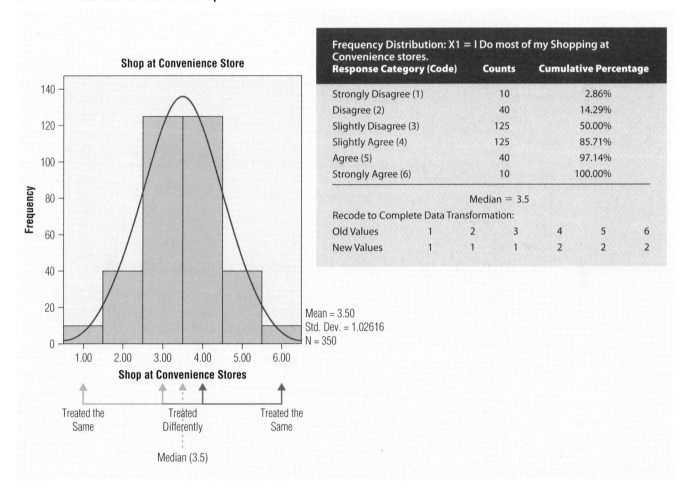

When a sufficient number of responses exist and a variable is ratio, the researcher may choose to delete one-fourth to one-third of the responses around the median to effectively ensure a bimodal distribution. This helps to mitigate the logical inconsistency illustrated in Exhibit 14.6. Median splits should always be performed only with great care and with adequate justification, though, as the inappropriate

Wine Index Can Help Retailers

Indexes can be very useful, and researchers are sometimes asked to create index values from secondary data.

Using 1968 U.S. wine consumption as a base, the current wine consumption index for the United Kingdom is 4.7, South Africa's index value is 2.2, Israel's index is 0.3, Luxembourg's wine index is 13.0 (52.7 liters/person/year) but the top of the list is Vatican City where the just under 1,000 residents have a wine index of 15.3! This information would be helpful in making decisions about the amount of space and attention given to wine in different countries. Similarly, U.S. retailers could compute wine or beer indices by state. Policy agencies could also chart indices on alcohol consumption that may be helpful in regulating underage consumption.

Sources: Per capita consumption figures derived from The Wine Institute, http://www.wineinstitute.org/ as accessed October 7, 2008.

collapsing of continuous variables into categorical variables ignores the information contained within the untransformed values. Justification for a median slit commonly is found in the ability to apply a more parsimonious statistical approach than would be possible using the raw data values.

Index Numbers

index numbers

Scores or observations recalibrated to indicate how they relate to a base number.

The consumer price index and wholesale price index are secondary data sources that are frequently used by marketing researchers. Price indexes, like other **index numbers**, represent simple data transformations that allow researchers to track a variable's value over time and compare a variable(s) with other variables. Recalibration allows scores or observations to be related to a certain base period or base number.

For instance, if the data are time-related, a base year is chosen. The index numbers are then computed by dividing each year's activity by the base-year activity and multiplying by 100. Index numbers require ratio measurement scales. Marketing managers may often chart consumption in some category over time. Grocers may wish to chart the U.S. wine consumption index. Using 1968 as a base year (4.05 liters per year), the 2007 U.S. wine consumption index is just over 2.3, meaning that the typical American consumer drinks 9.35 liters of wine per year (see the Research Snapshot above).[6]

Tabular and Graphic Methods of Displaying Data

Tables, graphs, and charts may simplify and clarify data. Graphical representations of data may take a number of forms, ranging from a computer printout to an elaborate pictograph. Tables, graphs, and charts, however, all facilitate summarization and communication. For example, see how the simple frequency table and histogram shown in Exhibit 14.6 provide a summary that quickly and easily communicates meaning that would be more difficult to see if all 350 responses were viewed separately.

Today's researcher has many convenient tools to quickly produce charts, graphs, or tables. Even basic word processing programs like Word include chart functions that can construct the chart within the text document. Bar charts (histograms), pie charts, curve/line diagrams, and scatter plots are among the most widely used tools. Some choices match well with certain types of data and analyses.

Computer Programs for Analysis

Statistical Packages

Just about 50 years ago, the thought of a typical U.S. company performing even basic statistical analyses like cross-tabulations on a thousand or more observations was unrealistic. The personal computer brought this capability not just to average companies, but even to small companies with limited resources. Today, computing power is seldom a barrier to completing a research project.

In the 1980s and early 1990s, when the PC was still a relatively novel innovation, specialized statistical software formerly used on mainframe computers made its way into the personal computing market. Today, most spreadsheet packages can perform a wide variety of basic statistical options. Excel's basic data analysis tool will allow descriptive statistics including frequencies and measures of central tendency to be easily computed.[7] Most of the basic statistical features are now menu driven, reducing the need to memorize function labels. Spreadsheet packages like Excel continue to evolve and become more viable for performing many basic statistical analyses (see Exhibit 14.7).

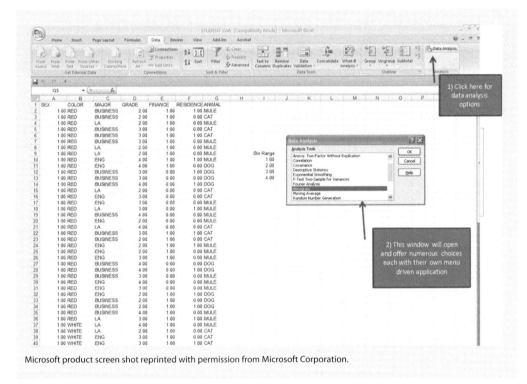

EXHIBIT 14.7

Using Excel for Basic Data Analysis

Despite the advances in spreadsheet applications, commercialized statistical software packages remain extremely popular among researchers. They continue to become easier to use and more compatible with other data interface tools including spreadsheets and word processors. Like any specialized tool, statistical packages are more tailored to the types of analyses performed by statistical analysts, including marketing researchers. Thus, any serious business or social science researcher should still become familiar with at least one general computer software package.

Two of the most popular general statistical packages are SAS (http://www.sas.com) and SPSS (http://www.spss.com). SAS revenues exceed $1.5 billion and its software can be found on computers worldwide. SAS was founded in 1976, and its statistical software historically has been widely used in engineering and other technical fields. SPSS was founded in 1968 and its sales exceed $224 million. SPSS stands for *Statistical Package for the Social Sciences*. SPSS is commonly used by university business and social science students. Marketing researchers have traditionally used SPSS more than any other statistical software tool. SPSS has been viewed as more user-friendly in the past. However, today's versions of both SPSS and SAS are very user friendly and give the user the option of using drop-down menus to conduct analysis rather than writing computer code.

Excel, SAS, and SPSS account for most of the statistical analysis conducted in marketing research. University students are sometimes exposed to MINITAB. MINITAB's revenues are approximately $10 million per year. Economists sometimes favor MINITAB; however, it has traditionally been viewed as less user-friendly than other choices such as SPSS.

In the past, data entry was an issue as specific software required different types of data input. Today, however, all the major software packages including SAS and SPSS can work from data entered into a spreadsheet. The spreadsheets can be imported into the data windows or simply read by the program. Most conventional online survey tools will return data to the user in the form of either an SPSS data file, an Excel spreadsheet, or a plain text document.

Exhibit 14.8 shows a printout of descriptive statistics generated by SAS for two variables: EMP (number of employees working in an MSA, or Metropolitan Statistical Area) and SALES (sales volume in dollars in an MSA) for 10 MSAs. The number of data elements (N), mean, standard deviation, and other descriptive statistics are displayed. SAS output is generally simple and easy to read.

EXHIBIT 14.8 SAS Computer Output of Descriptive Statistics

State = NY Variable	N	Mean	Standard Deviation	Minimum Value	Maximum Value	Std Error of Mean	Sum	Variance	C.V.
EMP	10	142.930	232.665	12.800	788.800	73.575	1429.300	54133.0	162.782
SALES	10	5807.800	11905.127	307.000	39401.000	3764.732	58078.000	141732049.1	204.985

Key: EMP = number of employees (000)   SALES = Sales (000)

As an example of SPSS output, each histogram shown in the exhibits on pages 360–361 was created by SPSS. By clicking on "charts" in the SPSS tool menu, one can see the variety of charts that can be created. The key place to click to generate statistical results in tabular form is "analyze." Here, one can see the many types of analysis that can be created. In this chapter, the choices found by clicking on "analyze" and then "descriptive statistics" are particularly relevant.

Exhibit 14.9 shows an SPSS cross-tabulation of two variables, class status and smoking behavior. The data come from a sample intercepted on an urban university campus. It addresses the research question, "Does smoking on campus vary across groups?" More non-smokers than smokers are found. However, the results show that graduate students, and to a lesser extent instructors, smoke more than the norm. The SPSS user can ask for any number of statistics and percentages to be included with this output by clicking on the corresponding options.

EXHIBIT 14.9
Examples of SPSS Output for Cross-Tabulation

CLASS * SMOKING Cross-Tabulation				
		Smoking		
Count		Smoker	Non-smoker	Total
Class	instructors	7	9	16
	undergraduate	9	22	31
	graduate	15	10	25
	career	6	6	12
Total		37	47	84

Interpretation

An interpreter at the United Nations translates a foreign language into another language to explain the meaning of a foreign diplomat's speech. In marketing research, the interpretation process explains the meaning of the data. After the statistical analysis of the data, inferences and conclusions about their meaning are developed.

A distinction can be made between *analysis* and *interpretation*. **Interpretation** is drawing inferences from the analysis results. Inferences drawn from interpretations lead to managerial implications. In other words, each statistical analysis produces results that are interpreted with respect to insight into a particular decision. The logical interpretation of the data and statistical analysis are

interpretation

The process of drawing inferences from the analysis results.

closely intertwined. When a researcher calculates a cross-tabulation of a demographic variable with brand choice, an interpretation is drawn suggesting that one segment may be more or less likely to choose a given brand. This interpretation of the statistical analysis may lead to a suggestion that a brand be withdrawn from certain demographic markets.

From a management perspective, however, the qualitative meaning of the data and their managerial implications are an important aspect of the interpretation. Consider the crucial role played by interpretation of research results in investigating one new product, a lip stain that could color the lips a desired shade semi-permanently and last for about a month at a time:

> *The lip stain idea, among lipstick wearers, received very high scores on a rating scale ranging from "excellent" to "poor," presumably because it would not wear off. However, it appeared that even among routine wearers of lipstick the idea was being rated highly more for its interesting, even ingenious, nature than for its practical appeal to the consumer's personality. They liked the idea, but for someone else, not themselves. . . . [Careful interpretation of the data] revealed that not being able to remove the stain for that length of time caused most women to consider the idea irrelevant in relation to their own personal needs and desires. Use of the product seems to represent more of a "permanent commitment" than is usually associated with the use of a particular cosmetic. In fact, women attached overtly negative meaning to the product concept, often comparing it with hair dyes instead of a long-lasting lipstick.*[8]

This example shows that interpretation is crucial. However, the process is difficult to explain in a textbook because there is no one best way to interpret data. Many possible interpretations of data may be derived from a number of thought processes. Experience with selected cases will help you develop your own interpretative ability.

Data are sometimes merely reported and not interpreted. Research firms may provide reams of computer output that do not state what the data mean. At the other extreme, some researchers tend to analyze every possible relationship between each and every variable in the study. Such an approach is a sign that the research problem was not adequately defined prior to beginning the research and the researcher really doesn't know what business decision the research is addressing. Researchers who have a clear sense of the purpose of the research do not request statistical analysis of data that have little or nothing to do with the primary purpose of the research.

> **TO THE POINT**
>
> *The thing to do is to supply light.*
>
> —Woodrow Wilson

Hypothesis Testing Using Basic Statistics

Descriptive research and causal research designs often climax with hypotheses tests. Generally, hypotheses should be stated in concrete fashion so that the method of empirical testing seems almost obvious.

Empirical testing typically involves inferential statistics. This means that an inference can be made about some population based on observations of a sample representing that population. Statistical analysis can be divided into several groups based on how many variables are involved:

- **Univariate statistical analysis** tests hypotheses involving only one variable.
- **Bivariate statistical analysis** tests hypotheses involving two variables.
- **Multivariate statistical analysis** tests hypotheses and models involving multiple (three or more) variables or sets of variables.

For now, the focus is on univariate statistics. Thus, we examine statistical tests appropriate for drawing inferences about a single variable.

Hypothesis Testing Procedure

Hypotheses are tested by comparing an educated guess with empirical reality. The process can be described as follows:

- First, the hypothesis is derived from the research objectives. The hypothesis should be stated as specifically as possible and should be theoretically sound.
- Next, a sample is obtained and the relevant variables are measured. In univariate tests, only one variable is of interest.

univariate statistical analysis

Tests of hypotheses involving only one variable.

bivariate statistical analysis

Tests of hypotheses involving two variables.

multivariate statistical analysis

Statistical analysis involving three or more variables or sets of variables.

- The measured value obtained in the sample is compared to the value either stated explicitly or implied in the hypothesis. If the value is consistent with the hypothesis, the hypothesis is supported. If the value is not consistent with the hypothesis, the hypothesis is not supported.

A univariate hypothesis consistent with the chapter vignette would be:

H1: The average number of children per family in zip code 70360 is greater than 1.5.

If a sample is drawn from this zip code and the average number of children per family is 0.075, the hypothesis is not supported. If the average number of children is 3.3, the hypothesis is supported. As the mean becomes smaller and approaches the theoretical expected value of 1.5, the chance becomes smaller that the hypothesis can indeed be supported. The exact point where the hypothesis changes from not being supported to being supported depends on how much risk the researcher is willing to accept and on the variability of the measure.

Univariate hypotheses are typified by tests comparing some observed sample mean against a benchmark value. The test addresses the question, is the sample mean truly different from the benchmark? But, how different is really different? If the observed sample mean is 1.55 and the benchmark is 1.50, would the hypothesis still be supported? Probably not! When the observed mean is so close to the benchmark, we do not have sufficient confidence that a second set of data using a new sample taken from the same population might not produce a finding conflicting with the benchmark. In contrast, when the mean turns out well above 1.50, perhaps 3.3, then we could more easily trust that another sample would not produce a mean equal to or less than 1.50.

While the terminology of null and alternative hypotheses is common in statistical theory, it is also commonly confusing. Therefore, we'll avoid using the term *null hypothesis* when at all possible. Students usually understand hypothesis testing more easily by focusing on what the findings should look like if the proposed hypothesis is true. If the hypothesis above is true, an observed sample's mean should be noticeably greater than 1.50. We test to see if this idea can be supported by the empirical evidence. A statistical test's significance level or p-value becomes a key indicator of whether or not a hypothesis can be supported.

Significance Levels and p-values

significance level

A critical probability associated with a statistical hypothesis test that indicates how likely an inference supporting a difference between an observed value and some statistical expectation is true. The acceptable level of Type I error.

A **significance level** is a critical probability associated with a statistical hypothesis test that indicates how likely it is that an inference supporting a difference between an observed value and some statistical expectation is true. The term **p-value** stands for probability-value and is essentially another name for an *observed* or *computed* significance level. Exhibit 14.10 discusses interpretations of p-values for different kinds of statistical tests. The probability in a p-value is that the statistical expectation (null) for a given test is true. So, low p-values mean there is little likelihood that the statistical expectation is true. This means the researcher's hypothesis positing (suggesting) a difference between an observed mean and a population mean, or between an observed frequency and a population frequency, or for a relationship between two variables, is likely supported.

p-value

Probability value, or the observed or computed significance level; p-values are compared to significance levels to test hypotheses.

Traditionally, researchers have specified an acceptable significance level for a test prior to the analysis. Later, we will discuss this as an acceptable amount of Type I error. For most applications, the acceptable amount of error, and therefore the acceptable significance level, is 0.1, 0.05, or 0.01. If the p-value resulting from a statistical test is less than the pre-specified significance level, then a hypothesis implying differences is supported.

Type I and Type II Errors

Hypothesis testing using sample observations is based on probability theory. We make an observation of a sample and use it to infer the probability that some observation is true within the population the sample represents. Because we cannot make any statement about a sample with complete certainty, there is always the chance that an error will be made. When a researcher makes the observation using a census, meaning that every unit (person or object) in a population is measured, then conclusions are certain. Researchers very rarely use a census though and thus, they are susceptible to two types of inferential errors (see Research Snapshot on the next page).

The Law and Type I and Type II Errors

Although most attorneys and judges do not concern themselves with the statistical terminology of Type I and Type II errors, they do follow this logic. For example, our legal system is based on the concept that a person is innocent until proven guilty. Assume that the null hypothesis is that the individual is innocent. If we make a Type I error, we will send an innocent person to prison. Our legal system takes many precautions to avoid Type I errors. A Type II error would occur if a guilty party were set free (the null hypothesis would have been accepted). Our society places such a high value on avoiding Type I errors that Type II errors are more likely to occur.

© CORBIS RF

© GEORGE DOYLE & CIARAN GRIFFIN

EXHIBIT 14.10
p-Values and Statistical Tests

Test Description	Test Statistic	
Compare an Observed Mean with Some Predetermined Value	Z or t-test—Low p-values Indicate the Observed Mean Is Different than Some Predetermined Value (Often 0)	$\alpha = .025$ $\alpha = .025$ $m = 3.0$ $\overline{X}$
Compare an Observed Frequency with a Predetermined Value	X^2—Low p-values Indicate that Observed Frequency Is Different than Predetermined Value	df = 1 1
Compare an Observed Proportion with Some Predetermined Value	Z or t-test for Proportions—Low p-values Indicate that the Observed Proportion Is Different than the Predetermined Value	50%
Bivariate Tests:		
Compare Whether Two Observed Means Are Different from One Another.	Z or t-test—Low p-values Indicate the Means Are Different	$\mu = 0$
Compare Whether Two Less-than Interval Variables Are Related Using Cross-tabs	X^2—Low p-values Indicate the Variables Are Related to One Another	df = 3 3
Compare Whether Two Interval or Ratio Variables Are Correlated to One Another	t-test for Correlation— Low p-values Indicate the Variables Are Related to One Another	r = 0

Type I Error

Suppose the observed sample mean described above leads to the conclusion that the mean is greater than 1.5 when in fact the true population mean is equal to 1.5. A **Type I error** has occurred. A Type I error occurs when a condition that is true in the population is rejected based on statistical observations. When a researcher sets an acceptable significance level a priori (α), he or she is determining how much tolerance he or she has for a Type I error. Simply put, a Type I error occurs

Type I error

An error caused by rejecting the null hypothesis when it is true; has a probability of alpha. Practically, a Type I error occurs when the researcher concludes that a relationship or difference exits in the population when in reality it does not exist.

- A frequency table can be a very useful way to depict basic tabulations.
- Cross-tabulation and contingency tables are a simple and effective way to examine relationships among less than interval variables.
  - When a distinction can be made between independent and dependent variables (that are nominal or ordinal), the convention is that rows are independent variables and columns are dependent variables.
- A continuous variable that displays a bimodal distribution is appropriate for a median split.

- Median splits should be performed on variables that display a normal distribution only with caution.
- Importantly, median splits on continuous variables should be performed only after deleting one-fourth to one-third of the responses around the median to help prevent logically inconsistent classifications.

© GEORGE DOYLE & CIARAN GRIFFIN

when the researcher concludes that there is a statistical difference based on a sample result when in reality one does not exist. When testing for relationships, a Type I error occurs when the researcher concludes a relationship exists when in fact one does not exist.

Type II Error

Type II error

An error caused by failing to reject the null hypothesis when the alternative hypothesis is true; has a probability of beta. Practically, a Type II error occurs when a researcher concludes that no relationship or difference exists when in fact one does exist.

If the alternative condition is in fact true (in this case the mean is not equal to 1.5) but we conclude that we should not reject the belief that the mean equals 1.5, we make what is called a **Type II error**. A type II error is the probability of failing to reject a false null hypothesis. Alternatively, one can think of this as failing to identify a hypothesized difference using a sample result when one really does exist in the population. This incorrect decision is called beta (β). In practical terms, a Type II error means that we fail to reach the conclusion that some difference between an observed mean and a benchmark exists when in fact the difference is very real. In terms of a bivarate correlation, a Type II error would mean the idea that a relationship exists between two variables is rejected when in fact the relationship does indeed exist.

Unfortunately, without increasing sample size the researcher cannot simultaneously reduce Type I and Type II errors. They are inversely related. Thus, reducing the probability of a Type II error increases the probability of a Type I error. In marketing problems, Type I errors generally are considered more serious than Type II errors. Thus more emphasis is placed on determining the significance level, α, than in determining β.[9]

Summary

1. Prepare qualitative data for interpretation or data analysis. Qualitative data interpretation benefits from coding. Coding involves assigning some representative value to units of data having similar meaning. One of the most basic forms of coding is dummy coding. Dummy coding involves representing dichotomies with values of 0 and 1.

2. Know what descriptive statistics are and why they are used. Descriptive analyses provide descriptive statistics. These include measures of central tendency and variation. Statistics such as the mean, mode, median, range, variance, and standard deviation are all descriptive statistics. These statistics provide a basic summary describing the basic properties of a variable.

3. Create and interpret tabulation tables. Statistical tabulation is another way of saying that we count the number of observations in each possible response category. In other words, tabulation is the same as tallying. Tabulation is an appropriate descriptive analysis for less-than interval variables. Frequency tables and histograms are used to display tabulation results.

4. Use cross-tabulations to display relationships. Cross-tabulation is the appropriate technique for assessing relationships among multiple less-than interval variables. The key to interpreting a cross-tabulation result is to compare actual observed values with hypothetical values that would result from pure chance. When observed results vary from these values, a relationship is indicated.

5. Perform basic data transformations. Data transformations are often needed to assist in data analysis and involve changing the mathematical form of data in some systematic way. Basic data transformations include reverse coding, summating scales, creating index numbers, and collapsing a variable based on a median split.

6. List different computer software products designed for descriptive statistical analysis. While spreadsheets like Excel have improved with respect to their ability to conduct basic statistical analyses, marketing researchers still rely heavily on specialized statistical software. SAS and SPSS are two of the best-known statistical packages. Each is available for even the most basic modern PC and can be used with a drop-down window interface, practically eliminating the need for writing computer code.

7. Understand the basics of testing hypotheses using inferential statistics. Hypothesis testing can involve univariate, bivariate, or multivariate statistics. A p-value is the probability value associated with a statistical test. The probability in a p-value is the probability that the expected value for some test distribution is true. In other words, for a *t*-test, the expected value of the *t*-distribution is 0. If a researcher is testing whether or not a variable is significantly different from 0, then the p-value that results from the corresponding computed *t*-value represents the probability that the true population mean is actually 0. For most marketing research hypotheses, a low p-value supports the hypothesis. If a p-value is lower than the researcher's acceptable significance level (i.e., .05), then the hypothesis is usually supported.

Key Terms and Concepts

bivariate statistical analysis, *365*	elaboration analysis, *359*	p-value, *366*
coding, *353*	frequency table, *355*	significance level, *366*
codes, *353*	histogram, *355*	statistical base, *358*
contingency table, *356*	index numbers, *362*	tabulation, *355*
cross-tabulation, *356*	interpretation, *364*	Type I error, *367*
data transformation, *359*	marginals, *358*	Type II error, *368*
descriptive analysis, *354*	median split, *361*	univariate statistical analysis, *365*
dummy coding, *353*	moderator variable, *359*	
effects coding, *353*	multivariate statistical analysis, *365*	

Questions for Review and Critical Thinking

1. How does coding allow qualitative data to become useful to a researcher?

2. What are five descriptive statistics used to describe the basic properties of variables?

3. What is a *histogram?* What is the advantage of overlaying a normal distribution over a histogram?

4. A survey asks respondents to respond to the statement "My work is interesting." Interpret the frequency distribution shown here (taken from an SPSS output):

Category Label	Code	Abs. Freq.	Rel. Freq. (Pct.)	Adj. Freq. (Pct.)	Cum. Freq. (Pct.)
Very true	1	650	23.9	62.4	62.4
Somewhat true	2	303	11.2	29.1	91.5
Not very true	3	61	2.2	5.9	97.3
Not at all true	4	28	1.0	2.7	100.0
	•	1,673	61.6	Missing	
	Total	2,715	100.0	100.0	
Valid cases	1,042		Missing cases	1,673	

5. Use the data in the following table to
   a. prepare a frequency distribution of the respondents' ages

   b. cross-tabulate the respondents' genders with cola preference
   c. identify any outliers

Individual	Gender	Age	Cola Preference	Weekly Unit Purchases
John	M	19	Coke	2
Al	M	17	Pepsi	5
Bill	M	20	Pepsi	7
Mary	F	20	Coke	2
Jim	M	18	Coke	4
Karen	F	16	Coke	4
Tom	M	17	Pepsi	12
Sassi	F	22	Pepsi	6
Amie	F	20	Pepsi	2
Dawn	F	19	Pepsi	3

6. Data on the average size of a soda (in ounces) at all thirty major league baseball parks are as follows: 14, 18, 20, 16, 16, 12, 14, 16, 14, 16, 16, 16, 14, 32, 16, 20, 12, 16, 20, 12, 16, 16, 24, 16, 16, 14, 14, 12, 14, 20. Compute descriptive statistics for this variable including a box and whisker plot. Comment on the results.

7. The following computer output shows a cross-tabulation of frequencies and provides frequency number (N) and row (R) percentages.
   a. Interpret this output including an impression about whether or not the row and column variables are related.
   b. Critique the way the analysis is presented.

Have You Read a Book in Past 3 Months?	Have High School Diploma?		Total
	Yes	No	
Yes	489 73.8	174 26.2	663
No	473 55.6	378 44.4	851
	......	......	......
TOTAL	962	552	1514

8. List and describe at least three basic data transformations.

9. What conditions suggest that a ratio variable should be transformed into a dichotomous (two group) variable represented with dummy coding?

10. ETHICS A data processing analyst for a research supplier finds that preliminary computer runs of survey results show that consumers love a client's new product. The employee buys a large block of the client's stock. Is this ethical?`

11. 'NET Use a Web site such as http://www.styledrops.com to find some prices for 4 Prada handbags, 4 Gucci handbags, 4 Yves Saint Laurent handbags, 4 Burberry handbags, and 4 Ferragamo handbags. Enter these into a spreadsheet. Using the lowest priced Prada handbag as a base, compute an index displaying the price of all other handbags. Which brand offers the best value in your opinion? Compute the appropriate statistic for central tendency using the spreadsheet and one other method (which could be SPSS or SAS). Use the chart feature (in Excel or another package) to depict the prices as a frequency distribution.

12. Investigate to see which of the software packages discussed in the chapter are available to you either through your university or via the use of this book. Explore the programs. Which seems most user friendly at this point?

13. Describe the basic hypothesis testing procedure.

14. What is a p-value and how is it used?

Research Activities

1. 'NET Go the Web site for the Chicago Cubs baseball team (http://chicago.cubs.mlb.com). Use either the schedule listing or the stats information to find their record in the most recent season. Create a data file with a variable indicating whether each game was won or lost and a variable indicating whether the game was played at home in Wrigley Field or away from home. Using computerized software like SPSS or SAS,
   a. Compute a frequency table and histogram for each variable.

   b. Use cross-tabulations to examine whether a relationship exists between where the game is played (home or away) and winning.
   c. Extra Analysis: Repeat the analyses for the Houston Astros baseball team (http://www.astros.com). What does this suggest for the relationship between playing at home and winning?

2. 'NET Go to http://www.spss.com and click on a few tabs such as "Solutions," "Software," and "Customers." What kinds of business problems can SPSS products help address?

Case 14.1 Body on Tap

© GETTY IMAGES/ PHOTODISC GREEN

A few years ago Vidal Sassoon, Inc., took legal action against Bristol–Myers over a series of TV commercials and print ads for a shampoo that had been named Body on Tap because of its beer content.[10] The prototype commercial featured a well-known high fashion model saying, "In shampoo tests with over 900 women like me, Body on Tap got higher ratings than Prell for body. Higher than Flex for conditioning. Higher than Sassoon for strong, healthy-looking hair."

The evidence showed that several groups of approximately 200 women each tested just one shampoo. They rated it on a six-step qualitative scale, from "outstanding" to "poor," for 27 separate attributes, such as body and conditioning. It became clear that 900 women did not, after trying both shampoos, make product-to-product comparisons between Body on Tap and Sassoon or between Body on Tap and any of the other brands mentioned. In fact, no woman in the tests tried more than one shampoo.

The claim that the women preferred Body on Tap to Sassoon for "strong, healthy-looking hair" was based on combining the data for the "outstanding" and "excellent" ratings and discarding the lower four ratings on the scale. The figures then were 36 percent for Body on Tap and 24 percent (of a separate group of women) for Sassoon. When the "very good" and "good" ratings were combined with the "outstanding" and "excellent" ratings, however, there was only a difference of 1 percent between the two products in the category of "strong, healthy-looking hair."

The research was conducted for Bristol–Myers by Marketing Information Systems, Inc. (MISI), using a technique known as blind monadic testing. The president of MISI testified that this method typically is employed when what is wanted is an absolute response to a product "without reference to another specific product." Although he testified that blind monadic testing was used in connection with comparative advertising, that was not the purpose for which Bristol–Myers retained MISI. Rather, Bristol–Myers wished to determine consumer reaction to the introduction of Body on Tap. And Sassoon's in-house research expert stated flatly that blind monadic testing cannot support comparative advertising claims.

Question

Comment on the professionalism of the procedures used to make the advertising claim. Why do you believe the researchers performed the data transformations described?

CHAPTER 15
TESTING FOR DIFFERENCES BETWEEN GROUPS AND FOR RELATIONSHIPS AMONG VARIABLES

After studying this chapter, you should be able to

1. Choose the appropriate statistic.
2. Construct a cross-tabulation table and the corresponding χ^2 statistic.
3. Use a *t*-test to compare a difference between two means.
4. Conduct a one-way analysis of variance test (ANOVA).
5. Appreciate the practicality of modern statistical software packages.
6. Use the GLM to represent a generalized statistical model.

Chapter Vignette: Is the Price Right?

The objective in most of the pricing games on *The Price is Right* is knowing the right price. When consumers know the right price, they save money, and saving money can be very exciting. Perhaps *The Price is Right* is ready for a new pricing game called "Bricks or Clicks"? The game would involve examining several products and then letting the host know whether or not a specific product is priced lower on the Internet (clicks) or at a traditional retailer (bricks).

Are prices lower on the Internet? This has been a subject of much debate over the last decade. In the early days of Internet retailing, so-called experts made many grand predictions about how e-tailing would evolve. A few predictions may have been correct, but most have proved wrong. For instance, some predicted that e-tailing would make traditional retailers obsolete. Almost all predictions involving price forecasted that the wide availability of price information on the Internet would force prices to their lowest level. Smart software systems called *bots* would quickly search the Internet and inform the consumer where an item could be purchased at the lowest price. However, consumers who think the Internet is always the avenue to the lowest price may not be right.[1]

Are prices offered by e-tailers really lower? Are the price discounts greater on the Internet? The answers depend on what a consumer is trying to buy. A 2001 study of the prices of DVDs showed the following average prices:[2]

Retail Type	DVD Average Price	DVD Percentage-Price
E-tailers	$19.92	72.0%
Traditional (multi-channel retailers)	$23.19	83.9%

A comparison of the prices suggests that dot-com retailers offer better prices.

Case closed? Not so fast! If consumers need a DVD player instead of a DVD, they may have better luck with a more traditional retailer, or at least one that offers both real and virtual retail shopping opportunities (multi-channel). In consumer electronics, the following results are seen:

Retail Type	DVD Player Average Price	Percentage-Price
E-tailers	$371.95	75.6%
Multi-channel retailers	$360.30	74.8%

© AP PHOTO/DEVORK DJANSEZIAN

A comparison of these prices suggests that the multi-channel retailers offer better prices. Even though they may never appear on a television game show, consumers and businesses alike find many occasions to compare prices.

Introduction

The vignette describes some comparisons involving prices over two groups. The groups represent the type of retailer. If we look at the type of retailer as a categorical variable and prices as an interval variable, these comparisons really involve drawing inferences about how one variable, type of retailer, influences another, prices. A surprising number of inferences involve two variables. In fact, sometimes even a more complex analysis may be reduced to a two-variable comparison because presenting the results becomes very simple. This chapter illustrates some common ways that such statistical tests can be performed.

What Is the Appropriate Test Statistic?

In marketing research, differences in behavior, characteristics, beliefs, opinions, emotions, or attitudes are commonly examined. For example, in the most basic experimental design, the researcher tests differences between subjects assigned to an experimental group and subjects assigned to the control group. A survey researcher may be interested in whether male and female consumers purchase a product in the same amount. Business researchers may also test whether or not business units in Europe are as profitable as business units in the United States. Such tests are bivariate **tests of differences** when they involve only two variables: a variable that acts like a dependent variable and a variable that acts as a classification variable.

test of differences

An investigation of a hypothesis stating that two (or more) groups differ with respect to measures on a variable.

Exhibit 15.1 on the next page illustrates that the type of measurement, the nature of the comparison, and the number of groups to be compared influence the statistical choice. Often researchers are interested in testing differences in mean scores between groups or in comparing how two groups' scores are distributed across possible response categories. We will focus our attention on these issues.[3] The rest of the chapter focuses on how to choose the right statistic for two-group comparisons and perform the corresponding test. Exhibit 15.1 on the next page provides a frame of reference for the rest of the chapter by illustrating various possible comparisons involving a few golfers.

More generally, choosing the right statistic boils down to what type and how many variables are involved in the research question being examined. In this text, practically all the hypotheses can be expressed either as tests of differences between groups or as relationships among variables. Generally, we can group variables based on whether they are dependent or independent. Dependent variables respond to independent variables.

By answering the question of how many independent variables (IV) and what is the scale level of the variables, finding an appropriate statistic is easy. Exhibit 15.2 on page 375 provides a useful guide in choosing a test statistic under these circumstances. Notice that in several cases the appropriate statistic would be a statistic that is beyond the scope of this text. Fortunately, the tests that are described here are very commonly used in marketing research and account for a large bulk of inferential tests. Users may find it useful to refer back to this particular exhibit when trying to decide which statistical tool fits a given research question or hypothesis.

Market research reports very often involve cross-tabulation tables. For instance, if a researcher is interested in testing whether male golfers will select a domestic or imported name brand, the research question involves a categorical (nominal) independent variable, a consumer's sex, and a categorical (nominal) dependent variable, brand type. Thus, the test would involve a single less than interval dependent variable and a single less than interval independent variable. The appropriate tool therefore is a χ^2 test computed from the corresponding 2 (Male/Female) $\times$ 2 (Domestic/Imported) cross-tabulation table.

How many hours do you spend online Daily?

Do you have more than one email address that you use regularly?

| Yes | No |
| ☐ | ☐ |

How often do you check your email?

| 1-3 times a week | 4-6 times a week | 1-2 times a day | 3-4 times a day | > 4 times a day |
| ☐ | ☐ | ☐ | ☐ | ☐ |

Do you Instant Message?

| Yes | No |
| ☐ | ☐ |

0% 100%

Are men or women more preoccupied with their mobile phones and Internet networking opportunities? You may be able to answer this question by looking at the data from the student survey. Test the following hypotheses using data obtained from the survey either from your class only or using data obtained from all users (either from the Web site or from your instructor):

H_1: Women are more likely to instant message than men.

H_2: Men are more likely to have more than one e-mail address.

H_3: Women check their e-mail more often than do men.

H_4: Men spend more time online daily than do women.

EXHIBIT 15.1 **Some Bivariate Hypotheses**

| Information | Golfer | | | Hypothesis or Research Question | Level of Measurement Involved | Statistic Used | Comment | Result |
	Dolly	Lori	Mel					
Average Driver Distance (meters)	135	150	185	Lori hits her drives further than Dolly	Golfer = Nominal; Drive Distance = Ratio	Independent Samples t-test to compare mean distance	The data for Lori and Dolly are used.	Supported ($t = 2.07$, df = 56, p < .05)
σ		30	25	30					
Average 7-Wood Distance (meters)	140	145	150	Mel hits her driver further than her 7-wood	Club = Nominal (7-wood or driver); 7-Wood Distance = Ratio	Paired-Samples t-test to compare mean distances for Mel	Only the data for Mel are used (std of diff = 30)	Supported ($t = 6.39$, df = 29, p < .05)
σ		30	30	30					
Sample size (number of balls hit)	28 drives 28 7-woods	30 drives 28 7-woods	29 drives 28 7-woods	A relationship exists between golfers and 7-wood distance	Golfer = Nominal; Distance = Ratio	One-Way ANOVA to compare means for the three groups	All data for 7-wood distance are used (MSE = 30)	Not supported (F = 0.83, ns)
Number of Drives in Fairway	4	22	11	Mel drives the ball more accurately than Dolly	Golfer = Nominal; Accuracy = Nominal (Right, Fairway, Left)	Cross-Tabulation with χ^2 Statistic	Resulting cross tabulation table is 2 rows × 3 columns (rows = golfer and columns = accuracy (fairway, right left)	Supported ($\chi^2 = 10.3$, df = 3, p < .05)
Drives missing right of fairway	16	7	9	A relationship exist between golfers and accuracy	Golfer = Nominal; Accuracy = Nominal (Right, Fairway, Left)	Cross-Tabulation with χ^2 Statistic	Cross-tabulation is now 3 rows × 3 columns	Supported ($\chi^2 = 23.7$, df = 4, p < .05)
Drives missing left of fairway	8	1	9					

EXHIBIT 15.2 Choosing the Right Statistic

Independent Variables:	Dependent Variables		
	1 Nominal / Ordinal DV	1 at Least Interval DV	More than 1 DV
1 Nominal/Ordinal IV	Cross-Tabulation with χ^2 Test	t-test or One-Way ANOVA	Multivariate Analysis
2 or More Nominal/ Ordinal IVs	Cross-Tabulation with χ^2 Test	n-Way ANOVA	Multivariate ANOVA
At Least 1 Nominal/ Ordinal IV and at Least 1 Interval or Ratio IV	Multivariate Analyses— (Logistic Regression)	Full-Factorial ANCOVA	Multivariate MANCOVA
1 Interval/Ratio IV	t-test	Simple Regression	Multivariate Regression
1 or More Interval/ Ratio IVs	Multivariate Analyses— (Logistic Regression)	Multiple Regression	Multivariate Analyses such as Path Model

Color Code:

Beyond the Scope of this Text

Variations of the GLM illustrated in Chapter

Independent Variable Condition

Dependent Variable Condition

Bivariate test illustrated in Chapter

Cross-Tabulation Tables:
The χ^2 Test for Goodness-of-Fit

Cross-tabulation was introduced in the previous chapter as a way of representing relationships between variables. Cross-tabulations are intuitive and easily understood. They also lend themselves well to graphical analysis using tools like bar charts.

Researchers use two-variable cross-tabulations the most because the results can be very easily communicated. Cross-tabulations are much like tallying. When two variables exist, each with two categories, four cells result. Each cell contains the count of observations matching a particular combination of characteristics. The χ^2 distribution provides a means for testing the statistical significance of a contingency table. In other words, the bivariate χ^2 test examines the statistical significance of relationships among two less-than interval variables.

The χ^2 test for a contingency table involves comparing the observed frequencies (O_i) with the expected frequencies (E_i) in each cell of the table. The goodness- (or closeness-) of-fit of the observed distribution with the expected distribution is captured by this statistic. Remember that the convention is that the row variable is considered the independent variable and the column variable is considered the dependent variable. Cross-tabulation is appropriate when both variables are nominal or ordinal; however, interval variables are sometimes used in a cross-tabulation if the range is very small—meaning the variable only takes on values of 1, 2, or 3, for example. Once a variable has more than four categories, a cross-tabulation table can be difficult to interpret.

We could use a χ^2 test to examine a research question asking whether or not Papa John's restaurants were more likely to be located in a stand-alone location or in a shopping center. The

TO THE POINT

You got to be careful if you don't know where you're going, because you might not get there.

—Yogi Berra

univariate (one-dimensional) analysis suggests that the majority of the locations (60 percent) are stand-alone units:

Location	One-Way Frequency Table
Stand-alone	60 stores
Shopping Center	40 stores
Total	100 stores

Is there any effect of location on Papa John's restaurants? Suppose the researcher analyzes the situation further by examining the following bivariate hypothesis:

Stand-alone locations are more likely to be profitable than are shopping center locations.

While the researcher is unable to obtain the dollar figures for profitability of each unit, a press release indicates which Papa John's units were profitable and which were not. Cross-tabulation using a χ^2 test is appropriate because

- The independent variable (location) is less–than interval.
- The dependent variable (profitable/not profitable) is less–than interval.

The data can be recorded in the following 2×2 contingency table:

Location	Profitable	Not Profitable	Total
Stand-alone	50	10	60
Shopping Center	15	25	40
Totals	65	35	100

Several conclusions appear evident. One, it seems that more stores are profitable than not profitable (65 versus 35, respectively). Secondly, more of the profitable restaurants seem to be in stand-alone locations (50 out of 65). However, is the difference strong enough to be statistically significant?

Is the observed difference between stand-alone and shopping center locations the result of chance variation due to random sampling? Is the discrepancy more than sampling variation? The χ^2 test allows us to conduct tests for significance in the analysis of the $R \times C$ contingency table (where $R =$ row and $C =$ column). The formula for the χ^2 statistic is the same as that for one-way frequency tables:

$$\chi^2 = \sum \frac{(O_i - E_i)^2}{E_i}$$

where

$\chi^2 =$ chi-square statistic

$O_i =$ observed frequency in the ith cell

$E_i =$ expected frequency in the ith cell

Again, as in a univariate χ^2 test, a frequency count of data that nominally identify or categorically rank groups is acceptable.

If the researcher's hypothesis is true, the frequencies shown in the contingency table should not resemble a random distribution. In other words, if location has no effect on profitability, the profitable and unprofitable stores would be spread evenly across the two location categories. This is really the logic of the test in that it compares the observed frequencies with the theoretical expected values for each cell.

After obtaining the observations for each cell, the expected values for each cell must be obtained. The expected values for each cell can be computed easily using this formula:

$$E_{ij} = \frac{R_i C_j}{n}$$

where

R_i = total observed frequency count in the ith row

C_j = total observed frequency count in the jth column

n = sample size

Only the total column and total row values are needed for this calculation. Thus, the calculation could be performed before the data are even tabulated. The following values represent the expected values for each cell:

Location	Profitable	Not Profitable	Total
Stand-alone	(60 × 65)/100 = 39	(60 × 35)/100 = 21	60
Shopping Center	(40 × 65)/100 = 26	(40 × 35)/100 = 14	40
Totals	65	35	100

Notice that the row and column totals are the same for both the observed and expected contingency matrices. These values also become useful in providing the substantive interpretation of the relationship. Variance from the expected value indicates a relationship.

The actual bivariate χ^2 test value can be calculated in a same manner as for a univariate test. The one difference is that the degrees of freedom are obtained by multiplying the number of rows minus one $(R - 1)$ times the number of columns minus one $(C - 1)$ rather than simply the number of cells minus one:

$$\chi^2 = \sum \frac{(O_i - E_i)^2}{E_i}$$

with $(R - 1)(C - 1)$ degrees of freedom. The observed and expected values can be plugged into the formula as follows:

$$\chi^2 = \frac{(50 - 39)^2}{39} + \frac{(10 - 21)^2}{21} + \frac{(15 - 26)^2}{26} + \frac{(25 - 14)^2}{14}$$

$$= 3.102 + 5.762 + 4.654 + 8.643$$

$$= 22.16$$

The number of degrees of freedom equals 1:

$$(R - 1)(C - 1) = (2 - 1)(2 - 1) = 1$$

From an Internet chi-square calculator (such as www.danielsoper.com/statcalc/calc11.aspx) or the chi-square distribution table on the companion web site (www.cengage.com/marketing/zikmund), we see that the critical value at the 0.05 probability level with 1 d.f. is 3.84. Thus, we are 95 percent confident that the observed values do not equal the expected values. Before the hypothesis can be supported, however, the researcher must check and see that the deviations from the expected values are in the hypothesized direction. Since the difference between the stand-alone locations' observed profitability and the expected values for that cell are positive, the hypothesis is supported. Location is associated with profitability. Thus, testing the hypothesis involves two key steps:

1. Examine the statistical significance of the observed contingency table.

The cross-tab window in SPSS. In this case, a cross-tab between the variables salespeople and store would be conducted.

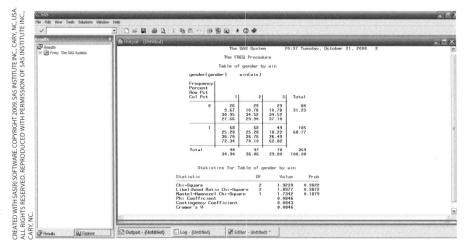

A cross-tabulation result from SAS showing an insignificant difference between men and women on a dependent variable "win."

2. Examine whether the differences between the observed and expected values are consistent with the hypothesized prediction.

Proper use of the χ^2 test requires that each expected cell frequency (E) have a value of at least 5. If this sample size requirement is not met, the researcher should take a larger sample as a way of increasing the frequency.

The SAS screenshot shown on this page shows a cross-tabulation result depicting whether or not men or women are more successful at winning a hand of blackjack (a card game). Each person played three games and the "win" variable indicates whether they won 1, 2, or 3 of the games. The results show no difference between men and women as the chi-square test is not significant ($p = .38$). Thus, the cell values show approximately the same proportion of people in each cell although more women than men took part in the contest (84 men and 185 women).

The *t*-Test for Comparing Two Means

Independent Samples *t*-Test

When a researcher needs to compare means for a variable grouped into two categories based on some less–than interval variable, a *t*-test is appropriate. One way to think about this is as testing the way a dichotomous (two-level) independent variable is associated with changes in a continuous dependent variable. Several variations of the *t*-test exist.

independent samples *t*-test

A test for hypotheses stating that the mean scores for some interval- or ratio-scaled variable grouped based on some less-than interval classificatory variable are not the same.

Most typically, the researcher will apply the **independent samples *t*-test**, which tests the differences between means taken from two independent samples or groups. So, for example, if we measure the price for some designer jeans at 30 different retail stores, of which 15 are Internet-only stores (pure clicks) and 15 are traditional stores, we can test whether or not prices are different based on store type with an independent samples *t*-test. The *t*-test for difference of means assumes the two samples (one Internet and one traditional store) are drawn from normal distributions and that the variances of the two populations are approximately equal (homoscedasticity).

Independent Samples *t*-test Calculation

The *t*-test actually tests whether or not the differences between two means is zero. Not surprisingly, this idea can be expressed as the difference between two population means:

$$\mu_1 = \mu_2, \text{ which is equivalent to, } \mu_1 - \mu_2 = 0$$

However, since this is inferential statistics, we test the idea by comparing two sample means ($\overline{X}_1 - \overline{X}_2$).

A verbal expression of the formula for *t* is

$$t = \frac{\text{Sample Mean 1} - \text{Sample Mean 2}}{\text{Variability of random means}}$$

Thus, the *t*-value is a ratio with information about the difference between means (provided by the sample) in the numerator and the standard error in the denominator. The question is whether the observed differences have occurred by chance alone. To calculate t, we use the following formula:

$$t = \frac{\overline{X}_1 - \overline{X}_2}{S_{\overline{X}_1 - \overline{X}_2}}$$

where

$\overline{X}_1$ = mean for group 1

$\overline{X}_2$ = mean for group 2

$S_{\overline{X}_1 - \overline{X}_2}$ = pooled, or combined, standard error of difference between means

A **pooled estimate of the standard error** is a better estimate of the standard error than one based on the variance from either sample. The pooled standard error of the difference between means of independent samples can be calculated using the following formula:

$$S_{\overline{X}_1 - \overline{X}_2} = \sqrt{\left(\frac{(n_1 - 1)S_1^2 + (n_2 - 1)S_2^2}{n_1 + n_2 - 2}\right)\left(\frac{1}{n_1} + \frac{1}{n_2}\right)}$$

where

S_1^2 = variance of group 1

S_2^2 = variance of group 2

n_1 = sample size of group 1

n_2 = sample size of group 2

pooled estimate of the standard error

An estimate of the standard error for a t-test of independent means that assumes the variances of both groups are equal.

Are business majors or sociology majors more positive about a career in business? A t-test can be used to test the difference between sociology majors and business majors on scores on a scale measuring attitudes toward business. We will assume that the attitude scale is an interval scale. The result of the simple random sample of these two groups of college students is shown below:

Business Students	Sociology Students
$\overline{X}_1 = 16.5$	$\overline{X}_2 = 12.2$
$S_1 = 2.1$	$S_2 = 2.6$
$n_1 = 21$	$n_2 = 14$

A high score indicates a favorable attitude toward business. This particular t-test tests whether the difference in attitudes between sociology and business students is significant. A higher t-value is associated with a lower p-value. As the t gets higher and the p-value gets lower, the researcher has more confidence that the means are truly different. The relevant data computation is

$$S_{\overline{X}_1 - \overline{X}_2} = \sqrt{\left(\frac{(n_1 - 1)S_1^2 + (n_2 - 1)S_2^2}{n_1 + n_2 - 2}\right)\left(\frac{1}{n_1} + \frac{1}{n_2}\right)}$$

$$= \sqrt{\left(\frac{(20)(2.1)^2 + (13)(2.6)^2}{33}\right)\left(\frac{1}{21} + \frac{1}{14}\right)}$$

$$= 0.797$$

The calculation of the t-statistic is:

$$t = \frac{\overline{X}_1 - \overline{X}_2}{S_{\overline{X}_1 - \overline{X}_2}}$$

$$t = \frac{16.5 - 12.2}{0.797}$$

$$= \frac{4.3}{0.797}$$

$$= 5.395$$

In a test of two means, degrees of freedom are calculated as follows:

$$d.f. = n - k$$

where

$$n = n_1 + n_2$$

$k =$ number of groups

In our example d.f. equals 33 (21 + 14 − 2). If the 0.01 level of significance is selected, reference to the tabled values of the *t*-distribution (see www.cengage.com/marketing/zikmund or a web based p-value calculator) yields the critical *t*-value. The critical *t*-value of 2.75 must be surpassed by the observed *t*-value if the hypothesis test is to be statistically significant at the 0.01 level. The calculated value of *t*, 5.39, far exceeds the critical value of *t* for statistical significance, so it is significant at $\alpha = 0.01$. The p-value is less than 0.01. In other words, this research shows that business students have significantly more positive attitudes toward business than do sociology students. The Research Snapshot on the next page provides an overview of situations calling for an independent samples *t*-test.

Practically Speaking

In practice, computer software is used to compute the *t*-test results. Exhibit 15.3 displays a typical *t*-test printout. These particular results examine the following research question:

RQ: Does religion relate to price sensitivity?

This question was addressed in the context of restaurant and wine consumption by allowing 100 consumers to sample a specific wine and then tell the researcher how much they would be willing to pay for a bottle of the wine. The sample included 57 Catholics and 43 Protestants. Because no direction of the relationship is stated (no hypothesis is offered), a two-tailed test is appropriate.

EXHIBIT 15.3 Independent Samples *t*-Test Results

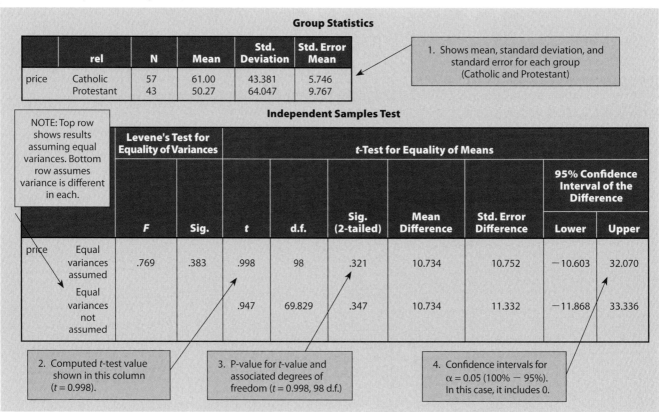

Group Statistics

	rel	N	Mean	Std. Deviation	Std. Error Mean	
price	Catholic	57	61.00	43.381	5.746	1. Shows mean, standard deviation, and standard error for each group (Catholic and Protestant)
	Protestant	43	50.27	64.047	9.767	

Independent Samples Test

NOTE: Top row shows results assuming equal variances. Bottom row assumes variance is different in each.

		Levene's Test for Equality of Variances		t-Test for Equality of Means					95% Confidence Interval of the Difference	
		F	Sig.	t	d.f.	Sig. (2-tailed)	Mean Difference	Std. Error Difference	Lower	Upper
price	Equal variances assumed	.769	.383	.998	98	.321	10.734	10.752	−10.603	32.070
	Equal variances not assumed			.947	69.829	.347	10.734	11.332	−11.868	33.336

2. Computed *t*-test value shown in this column (*t* = 0.998).

3. P-value for *t*-value and associated degrees of freedom (*t* = 0.998, 98 d.f.)

4. Confidence intervals for $\alpha = 0.05$ (100% − 95%). In this case, it includes 0.

Expert "T-eeze"

When is an independent samples *t*-test appropriate? Once again, we can find out by answering some simple questions:

- Is the dependent variable interval or ratio?
- Can the dependent variable scores be grouped based upon some categorical variable?
- Does the grouping result in scores drawn from independent samples?

- Are two groups involved in the research question?

When the answer to all questions is yes, an independent samples *t*-test is appropriate. Often, business researchers may wish to examine how some process varies between novices and experts. Consider the following example.

Researchers looked at the difference in decision speed for expert and novice salespeople faced with the same situation. Decision speed is a ratio dependent variable and the scores are grouped based on whether or not the salesperson is an expert or a novice. Thus, this categorical variable produces two groups. The results across 40 respondents, 20 experts and 20 novices, are shown at the bottom left.

The average difference in decision time is 38 seconds. Is this significantly different from 0? The calculated *t*-test is 2.76 with 38 d.f. The one-tailed p-value is 0.0045; thus the conclusion is reached that experts do take less time to make a decision than do novices.

Decision Time (seconds)

Series 1

Novices   Experts

Source: Shepherd, D. G., S. F. Gardial, M. G. Johnson and J. O. Rentz, "Cognitive Insights into the Highly Skilled or Expert Salesperson," *Psychology and Marketing* 23 (February 2006), 115–138. Reprinted with permission of John Wiley & Sons, Inc.

Although instructors still find some value in having students learn to perform the *t*-test calculations, computer generated *t*-test results are almost always generated and interpreted in practice today.

The interpretation of the *t*-test is made simple by focusing on either the p-value or the confidence interval and the group means. Here are the basic steps:

1. Examine the difference in means to find the "direction" of any difference. In this case, Catholics are willing to pay nearly $11 more than Protestants.
2. Compute or locate the computed *t*-test value. In this case, $t = 0.998$.
3. Find the p-value associated with this *t* and the corresponding degrees of freedom. Here, the p-value (two-tailed significance level) is 0.321. This suggests a 32 percent chance that the means are actually equal given the observed sample means. Assuming a 0.05 acceptable Type I error rate (α), the appropriate conclusion is that the means are not significantly different.
4. The difference can also be examined using the 95 percent confidence interval ($-10.603 < \bar{X}_1 - \bar{X}_2 < 32.070$). Since the confidence interval includes 0, we lack sufficient confidence that the true difference between the population means is not really 0. The result suggests that it may well be 0.

A few points are worth noting about this particular result. First, strictly speaking, the *t*-test assumes that the two population variances are equal. A slightly more complicated formula exists which will compute the *t*-statistic assuming the variances are not equal.[4] SPSS provides both results when an independent samples *t*-test is performed. The sample variances appear considerably different in this case as evidenced by the standard deviations for each group (43.4, 64.0). Nonetheless, the conclusions are the same using either assumption. In marketing research, we often deal with values that have variances close enough to assume equal variance. This isn't always the case in the physical sciences where variables may take on values of drastically different magnitude. Thus, the rule of thumb in marketing research is to use the equal variance assumption. In the vast majority of cases, the same conclusion will be drawn using either assumption.

Second, notice that even though the means appear to be not so close to each other, the statistical conclusion is that they are the same. The substantive conclusion is that Catholics and

Protestants would not be expected to pay different prices. Why is it that means do not appear to be similar, yet that is the conclusion? The answer lies in the variance. Respondents tended to provide very wide ranges of acceptable prices. Notice how large the standard deviations are compared to the mean for each group. Since the *t*-statistic is a function of the standard error, which is a function of the standard deviation, a lot of variance means a smaller *t*-value for any given observed difference. When this occurs, the researcher may wish to double-check for outliers. A small number of wild price estimates could be inflating the variance for one or both groups. An additional consideration would be to increase the sample size and test again.

Third, a *t*-test is used even though the sample size is greater than 30. Strictly speaking, a *Z*-test could be used to test this difference. Researchers often employ a *t*-test even with large samples. As samples get larger, the *t*-test and *Z*-test will tend to yield the same result. Although a *t*-test can be used with large samples, a *Z*-test should not be used with small samples. Also, a *Z*-test can be used in instances where the population variance is known ahead of time.

Paired-Samples *t*-Test

What happens when means need to be compared that are not from independent samples? Such might be the case when the same respondent is measured twice; for instance, when the respondent is asked to rate both how much he or she likes shopping on the Internet and how much he or she likes shopping in traditional stores. Since the liking scores are both provided by the same person, the assumption that they are independent is not realistic. Additionally, if one compares the prices the same retailers charge in their stores with the prices they charge on their Web sites, the samples cannot be considered independent because each pair of observations is from the same sampling unit.

> **paired-samples *t*-test**
>
> An appropriate test for comparing the scores of two interval variables drawn from related populations.

A **paired-samples *t*-test** is appropriate in this situation. The idea behind the paired-samples *t*-test can be seen in the following computation:

$$t = \frac{\bar{d}}{s_d / \sqrt{n}}$$

where $\bar{d}$ is the average difference between means, s_d is the standard deviation of the observed differences between means, and n is the number of observed differences between means. The test has degrees of freedom equal to one minus the total number of paired differences. Researchers also can compute the paired-samples *t*-test using statistical software. For example, using SPSS, the click-through sequence would be:

Analyze → *Compare Means* → *Paired-Samples* t-test

A dialog box then appears in which the "paired variables" should be entered. When a paired-samples *t*-test is appropriate, the two numbers being compared are usually scored as separate variables.

Exhibit 15.4 displays a paired samples *t*-test result. A sample of 143 young adult consumers was asked to rate how likely they would be to consider purchasing an engagement ring (or want their ring purchased) via (a) an Internet retailer and (b) a well-known jewelry store. Each respondent provided two responses much as in a within-subjects experimental design. The bar chart depicts the means for each variable (Internet purchase likelihood and store purchase likelihood). The *t*-test results suggest that average difference of -42.4 is associated with a *t*-value of -16.0. As can be seen using either the p-value (0.000 rounded to 3 decimals) or the confidence interval ($-47.6 < \bar{d} < -37.1$), which does not include 0, the difference is significantly different from 0. Therefore, the results suggest a higher likelihood to buy a wedding ring in a well-known real retail store than via an Internet merchant. Maybe that is a good idea!

Management researchers have used paired-samples *t*-tests to examine the effect of downsizing on employee morale. For instance, job satisfaction for a sample of employees can be measured immediately after the downsizing. Some months later, employee satisfaction can be measured again. The difference between the satisfaction scores can be compared using a paired-samples *t*-test. Results suggest that the employee satisfaction scores increase within a few months of the downsizing as evidenced by statistically significant paired-samples *t*-values.[5]

EXHIBIT 15.4 Example Results for a Paired-Samples *t*-Test

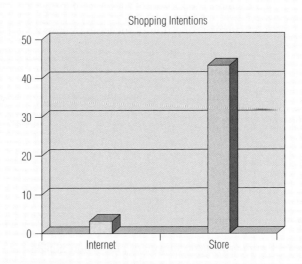

Paired-Samples Test

		Paired Differences							
					95% Confidence Interval of the Difference				
		Mean	Std. Deviation	Std. Error Mean	Lower	Upper	*t*	d.f.	Sig. (2-tailed)
Pair 1	int1 − int2	−42.388	31.660	2.648	−47.622	−37.154	−16.011	142	0.000

1. The average difference between observations is shown here.

3. 95% confidence interval shown here.

2. The computed *t*-value, d.f., and p-value are shown here.

The *Z*-Test for Comparing Two Proportions

What type of statistical comparison can be made when the observed statistics are proportions? Suppose a researcher wishes to test the hypothesis that wholesalers in the northern and southern United States differ in the proportion of sales they make to discount retailers. Testing whether the population proportion for group 1 (p_1) equals the population proportion for group 2 (p_2) is conceptually the same as the *t*-test of two means. This section briefly describes **Z-test for differences of proportions**, which requires a sample size greater than 30.

The test is appropriate for a hypothesis of this form:

$$H_0: \pi_1 = \pi_2$$

which may be restated as

$$H_0: \pi_1 - \pi_2 = 0$$

Comparison of the observed sample proportions p_1 and p_2 allows the researcher to ask whether the difference between two *large* random samples occurred due to chance alone. The *Z*-test statistic can be computed using the following formula:

$$Z = \frac{(p_1 - p_2) - (\pi_1 - \pi_2)}{S_{p_1 - p_2}}$$

Z-test for differences of proportions

A technique used to test the hypothesis that proportions are significantly different for two independent samples or groups.

SAS:

SPSS:

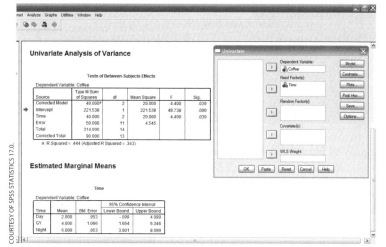

Two of the most popular software packages, SAS and SPSS, display ANOVA results for the coffee drinking problem.

■ USING VARIANCE COMPONENTS TO COMPUTE *F*-RATIOS

In ANOVA, the basic consideration for the *F*-test is identifying the relative size of variance components. The three forms of variation described briefly above are:

1. SSE—variation of scores due to random error or within-group variance due to individual differences from the group mean. This is the error of prediction.
2. SSB—systematic variation of scores between groups due to manipulation of an experimental variable or group classifications of a measured independent variable or between-group variance.
3. SST—the total observed variation across all groups and individual observations.

The Research Snapshot on the next page provides additional insight into the mechanics of ANOVA. In addition, the Web resources provided with the text provide some illustrations of how to perform an analysis like this using SPSS, SAS, or EXCEL.

Thus, we can partition total variability into *within-group variance* and *between-group variance*. The *F*-distribution is a function of the ratio of these two sources of variances:

$$F = f\left(\frac{SSB}{SSE}\right)$$

A larger ratio of variance between groups to variance within groups implies a greater value of *F*. If the *F*-value is large, the results are likely to be statistically significant.

■ A DIFFERENT BUT EQUIVALENT REPRESENTATION

F also can be thought of as a function of the between-group variance and total variance.

$$F = f\left(\frac{SSB}{SST - SSB}\right)$$

In this sense, the ratio of the thick black line to the blue line representing the total range of data presents the basic idea of the *F*-value.

Practically Speaking

Exhibit 15.6 displays the ANOVA result for the coffee-drinking example. Again, one advantage of living in modern times is that even a simple problem like this one need not be hand computed. Even though this example presents a small problem, one-way ANOVA models with more observations or levels would be interpreted similarly.

The first thing to check is whether or not the overall model *F* is significant. In this case, the computed *F* = 4.40 with 2 and 11 degrees of freedom. The p-value associated with this value is 0.039. Thus, we have high confidence in concluding that the group means are not all the same. Second, the researcher must remember to examine the actual means for each group to properly interpret the result. Doing so, the conclusion reached is that the night-shift people drink the most coffee, followed by the graveyard-shift workers, and then lastly, the day-shift workers.

More than One-Way

An independent samples *t*-test is a special case of one-way ANOVA. When the independent variable in ANOVA has only two groups, the results for an independent samples *t*-test and ANOVA will be the same.

The two sets of statistical results below demonstrate this fact. Both outputs are taken from the same data. The test considers whether men or women are more excited about a new Italian restaurant in their town. Sex2 is dummy coded so that 0 = men and 1 = women. Excitement was measured on a scale ranging from 0 to 6.

Independent Samples *t*-test Results:

Group Statistics

	Sex2	N	Mean	Std. Deviation	Std. Error Mean
Excitement	0.00	69	2.64	2.262	0.272
	1.00	73	2.32	2.140	0.250

Independent Samples Test

		Levene's Test for Equality of Variances		*t*-Test for Equality of Means					95% Confidence Interval of the Difference	
		F	Sig.	t	d.f.	Sig. (two-tailed)	Mean Difference	Std. Error Difference	Lower	Upper
Excitement	Equal variances assumed	1.768	.186	.873	140	.384	.323	.369	−.408	1.053
	Equal variances not assumed			.872	138.265	.385	.323	.370	−.409	1.054

In this case, we would conclude that men and women are equally excited—or unexcited as the case may be. The *t* of 0.873 with 140 d.f. is not significant (p = 0.384).

ANOVA Results:

Descriptives

		N	Mean	Std. Deviation	Std. Error	95% Confidence Interval for Mean		Minimum	Maximum
						Lower Bound	Upper Bound		
Excitement	0.00	69	2.64	2.262	0.272	2.09	3.18	0	7
	1.00	73	2.32	2.140	0.250	1.82	2.81	0	7
	Total	142	2.47	2.198	0.184	2.11	2.84	0	7

ANOVA

		Sum of Squares	d.f.	Mean Square	F	Sig.
Excitement	Between Groups	3.692	1	3.692	0.763	0.384
	Within Groups	677.695	140	4.841		
	Total	681.387	141			

Notice that the *F*-ratio shown in the ANOVA table is associated with the same p-value as is the *t*-value above. This is no accident since the *F* and *t* are mathematical functions of one another. So, when two groups are involved, the researcher can skin the cat either way!

General Linear Model

general linear model (GLM)

A way of explaining and predicting dependent variable based on fluctuations (variation) from its mean. The fluctuations are due to changes in independent variables.

Multivariate dependence techniques are variants of the **general linear model (GLM)**. Simply, the GLM is a way of modeling some process based on how different variables cause fluctuations from the average dependent variable. Fluctuations can come in the form of group means that differ from the overall mean as is in ANOVA or in the form of a significant slope coefficient as in regression.

GLM Equation

The basic idea can be thought of as follows:

$$\hat{Y}_i = \mu + \Delta X + \Delta F + \Delta XF$$

Here, μ represents a constant, which can be thought of as the overall mean of the dependent variable, ΔX and ΔF represent changes due to main effect independent variables (such as experimental variables) and blocking independent variables (such as covariates or grouping variables), respectively, and ΔXF represents the change due to the combination (interaction effect) of those variables. Realize that Y_i in this case could represent multiple dependent variables, just as X and F could represent multiple independent variables. Regression analysis and n-way ANOVA represent common forms that the GLM can take. SAS and SPSS both contained programs specifically referred to by GLM. They are particularly useful in analyzing data from experiments but GLM can also be used to produce regression results.

Regression Analysis

Simple regression investigates a *straight-line relationship* of the type:

$$Y = \alpha + \beta X,$$

where Y is a continuous dependent variable and X is an independent variable that is usually continuous, although a dichotomous nominal or ordinal variables can be included in the form of a dummy variable. Alpha (α) and beta (β) are two parameters that must be estimated so that the equation best represents a given set of data. These two parameters determine the height of the regression line and the angle of the line relative to horizontal. When these parameters change, the line changes. Regression techniques have the job of estimating values for these parameters that make the line *fit* the observations the best.

The result is simply a linear equation, or the equation for a line, just as in basic algebra! Parameter α represents the Y intercept (where the line crosses the y-axis) and β is the slope coefficient. The slope is the change in Y associated with a change of one unit in X. Slope may also be thought of as rise over run. That is, how much Y rises (or falls if negative) for every one unit change in the X-axis. A mathematical estimation of the line completes the regression progress by providing estimates for the intercept (b_0) and slope coefficient (b_1).

$$Y_i = b_1 + b_0 X_1 + e_i$$

■ INTERPRETING MULTIPLE REGRESSION ANALYSIS

multiple regression analysis

An analysis of association in which the effects of two or more independent variables on a single, interval-scaled dependent variable are investigated simultaneously.

Multiple regression analysis is an extension of simple regression analysis allowing a metric dependent variable to be predicted by multiple independent variables. Thus, one dependent variable is explained by more than one independent variable. When trying to explain sales, plausible independent variables include prices, economic factors, advertising intensity, and consumers' incomes in the area. A simple regression equation can be expanded to represent multiple regression analysis:

$$Y_i = b_0 + b_1 X_1 + b_2 X_2 + b_3 X_3 + \cdots + b_n X_n + e_i$$

■ PARAMETER ESTIMATE CHOICES

The estimates for α and β are the key to regression analysis. In most business research, the estimate of β is most important. The explanatory power of regression rests with β because this is where the direction and strength of the relationship between the independent and dependent variable is explained. A Y-intercept term is sometimes referred to as a constant because α represents a fixed point. An estimated slope coefficient is sometimes referred to as a regression weight, regression coefficient, parameter estimate, or sometimes even as a *path* estimate. The term path estimate is a descriptive term adapted because of the way hypothesized causal relationships are often represented in diagrams:

$$X \xrightarrow{\beta_1} Y$$

For all practical purposes, these terms are used interchangeably. Parameter estimates can be presented in either raw or standardized form. One potential problem with raw parameter estimates is due to the fact that, like covariance values, they reflect the measurement scale range. So, if a simple regression involved distance measured with miles, very small parameter estimates may indicate a strong relationship. In contrast, if the very same distance is measured with centimeters, a very large parameter estimate would be needed to indicate a strong relationship. Generally, the raw slope coefficient is abbreviated with a small letter **b**.

Researchers often explain regression results by referring to a **standardized regression coefficient (β)**. A standardized regression coefficient, like a correlation coefficient, provides a common metric allowing regression results to be compared to one another no matter what the original scale range may have been. Due to the mathematics involved in standardization, the standardized Y-intercept term is always 0.

Researchers use shorthand to label regression coefficients as either "raw" or "standardized." The most common shorthand is as follows:

- **B$_0$** or **b$_0$**—raw (unstandardized) Y-intercept term; an estimate of what was referred to as α above.
- **B$_1$** or **b$_1$**—raw regression coefficient or estimate.
- β_1—standardized regression coefficients.

The bottom line is that when the actual units of measurement are the focus of analysis, such as might be the case in trying to forecast sales during some period, raw (unstandardized) coefficients are most appropriate. When the goal is explanation of some outcome by examining a series of relationships, standardized regression coefficients are more appropriate because they allow for the size of the relationship for each independent variable can be compared directly. A β of .6 is a stronger relationship than a β of .2. With unstandardized coefficients, this comparison cannot be directly made.

standardized regression coefficient (β)

The estimated coefficient indicating the strength of relationship between an independent variable and dependent variable expressed on a standardized scale where higher absolute values indicate stronger relationships (range is from −1 to 1).

■ STEPS IN INTERPRETING A MULTIPLE REGRESSION MODEL

Multiple regression models often are used to test some proposed theoretical model. For instance, a researcher may be asked to develop and test a model explaining business unit performance. Why do some business units outperform others? Multiple regression models can be interpreted using these steps:

1. Examine the model F-test. If the test result is not significant, the model should be dismissed and there is no need to proceed to further steps.
2. Examine the individual statistical tests for each parameter estimate. Independent variables with significant results can be considered a significant explanatory variable.
3. Examine the model R^2. No cutoff values exist that can distinguish an acceptable amount of explained variation across all regression models. However, the absolute value of R^2 is more important when the researcher is more interested in prediction than explanation. In other words, the regression is run for pure forecasting purposes. When the model is more oriented toward explaining which variables are most important in explaining the dependent variable, cutoff values for the model R^2 are inappropriate.

4. A next step would be to diagnose multicollinearity. Simply put, this is the extent to which the independent variables are redundant. A detailed discussion of this topic is beyond the scope of this particular text. However, a simple check for problems can be obtained by taking a look at the Variance Inflation Factors (VIF). Most statistical packages allow these to be computed. VIFs of between 1 and 2 are generally not indicative of problems with multicollinearity. As they become larger, the results become more susceptible to interpretation problems because of overlap in the independent variables.

Exhibit 15.7 illustrates this step-by-step process using regression results from a SAS output. The regression model explains business unit profitability for a sample of 28 business units for a Fortune 500 company. The independent variables are hours (average hours spent in training for the workforce), budget (the percentage of the promotional budget used), and state (a dummy variable indicating whether the business unit is in Arizona and coded 0, or in Ohio and coded 1). In this case, the researcher is using a maximum acceptable Type I error rate of 0.05. The conclusion reached from this analysis is that hours spent in training seem to pay off in increased business unit profitability as evidenced by the significant, positive regression coefficient ($\beta = 0.55$, p < 0.05).

EXHIBIT 15.7 Interpreting Multiple Regression Results

```
                              The SAS System

                            The REG Procedure
                             Model: MODEL1
                          Dependent Variable:      Paid

                    Number of Observations Read      28
                    Number of Observations Used      28

                           Analysis of Variance

                                   Sum of        Mean
         Source            DF      Squares       Square      F Value      Pr > F

         Model              3      1770668       590223        19.38      <.0001
         Error             24       731035        30460
         Corrected Total   27      2501703

                 Root MSE              174.52738     R-Square      0.7078
                 Dependent Mean        654.03571     Adj R-Sq      0.6713
                 Coeff Var              26.68469

                          Parameter Estimates

                  Parameter     Standard                            Standardized
Variable    DF     Estimate       Error     t Value    Pr > |t|       Estimate      VIF

Intercept    1    -109.90538    217.46253     -0.51      0.6179              0
Hours        1       0.99438      0.27688      3.59      0.0015        0.55433      1.96
Budget       1       6.60121      3.54784      1.86      0.0751        0.28210      1.89
State        1     -66.36397     84.82434     -0.78      0.4416       -0.11073      1.65
```

1. Interpret model F-test. Test is significant (p < .05).

3. The model R^2 is interpreted. The IVs explain over 70% of variation in the dependent variable.

2. Interpret individual parameter estimates. In this case, only hours is significant based on a p-value below .05 (0.0015).

4. VIFs are checked for multicollinearity problems. None are indicated here.

- Cross-tabulations are widely applied in market research reports and presentations.
  - Take advantage of graphical tools like bar charts to present cross-tabulation results in presentations and reports.
  - Cross-tabulations are appropriate for research questions involving predictions of categorical dependent variables using categorical independent variables. These are usually nominal or ordinal.
    - When more than four categories exist, cross-tabulation tables can become difficult to present clearly.
    - Independent variables are placed in rows and dependent variables are placed in columns.
- A t-test is used to compare means between two groups.
  - An independent samples t-test predicts a continuous (interval or ratio) dependent variable with a categorical (nominal or ordinal) independent variable.

- A paired samples t-test compares means from two different responses from the same sampling unit. Therefore, the sampling is dependent.
- A one-way ANOVA extends the concept of an independent samples t-test to more than two groups.
  - Don't be fooled by the fact that it involves an F-test instead of a t-test. They are mathematically related and, in fact, an F-value is the square of a t-value that would result from the same analysis.
  - Stat packages usually have an ANOVA package or a one-way ANOVA package. However, general linear model procedures can also conduct these tests and offer more flexibility.
- Simple hand calculations can be useful in learning what statistical procedures actually do. However, in conducting actual tests, take advantage of computer software whenever permissible.

© GEORGE DOYLE & CIARAN GRIFFIN

Summary

1. Choose the appropriate statistic. A skilled researcher can quickly determine the appropriate statistic for a given research question. In this chapter, we learned that if the researcher can distinguish independent from dependent variables, know how many of each are involved in the analysis, and know the level of scale measurement for each, choosing the right statistic becomes easy.

2. Construct a cross-tabulation table and the corresponding χ^2 statistic. Bivariate statistical techniques analyze scores on two variables at a time. A cross-tabulation is a useful way of depicting and analyzing the way two categorical variables are related to one another. For instance, a nominal independent variable may be used to predict a nominal dependent variable. Cross-tabulations are very useful and lend themselves well to depicting results in charts. The χ^2 statistic is the test statistic appropriate for testing relationships among variables used in a cross-tabulation table. Higher χ^2 values are generally associated with lower p-values and therefore greater probability of a relationship between the row and column variable. The process of testing a hypothesis using a χ^2 statistic is similar in concept to practically all the hypotheses testing procedures that follow.

3. Use a t-test to compare a difference between two means. When a researcher needs to compare means for a variable grouped into two categories based on some less-than interval variable, a t-test is appropriate. An independent samples t-test examines whether a dependent variable like price differs based on a grouping variable like biological sex. Statistically, the test examines whether the difference between the mean for men and women is different from 0. Larger t-values are associated with smaller p-values and statistical significance. A paired-samples t-test examines whether or not the means from two variables that are not independent are different. A common situation calling for this test is when the two observations are from the same respondent. A simple before-and-after test calls for a paired-sample t-test so long as the dependent variable is continuous.

4. Conduct a one-way analysis of variance test (ANOVA). ANOVA is the appropriate statistical technique to examine the effect of a less-than interval independent variable on an at-least interval dependent variable. Conceptually, ANOVA partitions the total variability into three types: total variation, between-group variation, and within-group variation. As the explained variance represented by SSB becomes larger relative to SSE or SST, the ANOVA model is more likely to be significant, indicating that at least one group mean is different from another group mean.

5. Appreciate the practicality of modern statistical software packages. Hand calculations using a simple calculator can sometimes be a good way for getting the feel of exactly what some statistic is doing; however, even small applications are usually better performed with the help of some statistical software whether it be Excel, SPSS, SAS or some other package. This saves time and helps reduce mathematical errors.

6. Use the GLM to represent a generalized statistical model. The General Linear Model is a widely used way of representing statistical effects as systematic deviations from the population mean. ANOVA and Linear Regression are among the most common forms of the GLM.

Key Terms and Concepts

analysis of variance (ANOVA), *384*
between-groups variance, *386*
F-test, *387*
general linear model (GLM), *390*
grand mean, *386*

independent samples *t*-test, *378*
multiple regression analysis, *390*
paired-samples *t*-test, *382*
pooled estimate of the standard error, *379*
standardized regression coefficient (β), *391*

test of differences, *373*
within-group error or variance, *387*
Z-test for differences of proportions, *383*

Questions for Review and Critical Thinking

1. What statistical test of differences is appropriate in the following situations?
   a. Average campaign contributions (in $) of Democrats, Republicans, and Independents are to be compared.
   b. Advertising managers and brand managers have responded "yes," "no," or "not sure" to an attitude question. The advertising and brand managers' responses are to be compared.
   c. One-half of a sample received an incentive in a mail survey while the other half did not. A comparison of response rates is desired.
   d. A researcher believes that married men will push the grocery cart when grocery shopping with their wives. How would the hypothesis be tested?
   e. A manager wishes to compare the job performance of a salesperson before ethics training with the performance of that same salesperson after ethics training.

2. Perform a χ^2 test on the following data (hint: set up a spreadsheet to perform the calculations):
   a. Increased regulation is the best way to ensure safe products.

	Agree	Disagree	No Opinion
Managers	58	66	8
Line Employees	34	24	10
Totals	92	90	18

   b. Ownership of residence

	Yes	No
Male	25	20
Female	16	14

3. Interpret the following computer cross-tab output including a χ^2 test. Variable EDUCATION is a response to "What is your highest level of educational achievement?" HS means a high school diploma, SC means some college, BS means a bachelor's degree, and MBA means a master of business administration. Variable WIN is how well the respondent did on a set of casino games of chance. A 1 means they would have lost more than $100, a 2 means they approximately broke even, and a 3 means they won more than $100. What is the result of exploring a research question that education influences performance on casino gambling? Comment on your conclusion and any issues in interpreting the result.

The SAS System
The FREQ Procedure
Table of education by win

EDUCATION Frequency Percent Row Pct Col Pct	WIN			
	1	**2**	**3**	**Total**
MBA	3	10	4	17
	1.12	3.72	1.49	6.32
	17.65	58.82	23.53	
	3.19	10.31	5.13	
BS	11	19	12	42
	4.09	7.06	4.46	15.61
	26.19	45.24	28.57	
	11.70	19.59	15.38	
SC	33	30	27	90
	12.27	11.15	10.04	33.45
	35.67	33.33	30.00	
	35.11	30.93	34.62	
HS	47	38	35	120
	17.47	14.13	13.01	44.61
	29.17	31.67	29.17	
	50.00	39.18	44.57	
Total	94	97	78	269
	34.94	36.06	29.00	100.00

Statistics for Table of education by win

Statistic	DF	Value	Prob
Chi-Square	6	7.5275	0.2748

Sample Size = 269

Online Reports: Easy to Get, Easy to Ignore

A variety of commercially available computer programs provide detailed data on Web site usage. Among these titles are ClickTracks Analytics, Fireclick, Sane Solutions, Urchin, WebSideStore, WebtrafficIQ, and WebTrends. These programs can gather details and generate reports about the behavior of various customer segments who visit a Web site (for example, new visitors, returning visitors, and subscribers to the company's e-mail newsletter). Behaviors that can be tracked include the links that visitors click on, the purchases they make, the amount of time they spend at the Web site and the number of customers abandoning their electronic cart without making a purchase.

With reports so easy to obtain whenever they are needed or as frequently as every day, marketers can quickly accumulate mounds of data. But what do they do with the reports? Ideally, someone should be analyzing the reports and acting on the information. However, when reporters for *Network Computing* recently asked two hundred Web administrators about their use of Web analytics software, the responses indicated a widespread lack of follow-up. Almost all the administrators used the software, but not a single one could think of a change they had made to their Web sites in response to information they obtained from the resulting reports. Some of the lack of response is due to the fact that the results from these efforts are not reported effectively.

Source: Based on Jeffrey Rubin and Ravind Budhiraja, "Intelligence Services," *Network Computing* (July 7, 2005); Joshua Kaufman, "Practical Usability Testing," *Digital Web* (February 13, 2006), http://www.digital-web.com, accessed April 2, 2006.

oral presentation may be as simple as a short video conference with a manager at the client organization's location or as formal as a report to the company board of directors. One rule stands above all when preparing a presentation—be as simple as possible.

In either situation, the key to effective presentation is preparation. Communication specialists often suggest that a person preparing an oral presentation begin at the end.[6] In other words, while preparing a presentation, a researcher should think about what he or she wants the client to know when it has been completed. The researcher should select the three or four most important findings for emphasis and rely on the written report for a full summary. The researcher also needs to be ready to defend the results of the research. This is not the same as being defensive; instead, the researcher should be prepared to deal in a confident, competent manner with the questions that arise. Remember that even the most reliable and valid research project is worthless if the managers who must act on its results are not convinced of its importance.

As with written reports, a key to effective oral presentation is adapting to the audience. Delivering an hour-long formal speech when a 10-minute discussion is called for (or vice versa) will reflect poorly on both the presenter and the report.

Lecturing or reading to the audience is sure to impede communication at any level of formality. The presenter should refrain from reading prepared text word for word. By relying on brief notes, familiarity with the subject, and as much rehearsal as the occasion calls for, the presenter will foster better communication. He or she should avoid research jargon and use short, familiar words. The presenter should maintain eye contact with the audience and repeat the main points. Because the audience cannot go back and replay what the speaker has said, an oral presentation often is organized around a standard format: "Tell them what you are going to tell them, tell them, and tell them what you just told them."

Graphic and other visual aids can be as useful in an oral presentation as in a written one. Presenters can choose from a variety of media. Slides, overhead-projector acetates, and on-screen computer-generated graphics are useful for larger audiences. For smaller audiences, the researcher may put the visual aids on posters or flip charts. Another possibility is to make copies of the charts for each participant, possibly as a supplement to one of the other forms of presentation.

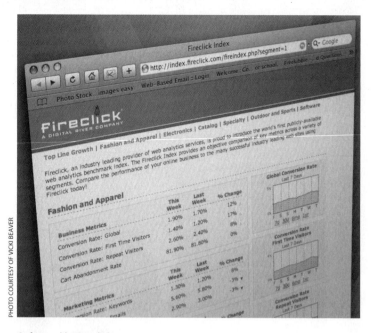

Software like Fireclicks can provide useful information to present in reports.

Whatever medium is chosen, each visual aid should be designed to convey a simple, attention-getting message that supports a point on which the audience should focus its thinking. As they do in written presentations, presenters should interpret graphics for the audience. The best slides are easy to read and interpret. Large typeface, multiple colors, bullets that highlight, and other artistic devices can enhance the readability of charts.

Using gestures during presentations also can help convey the message and make presentations more interesting. Also, invite participation from the audience. Here are some tips on actually making the presentation:[7]

- Generally, introduce yourself while displaying the title of the presentation. Acknowledge any others who materially assisted in the project.
- Open up your arms to embrace your audience. Keep your arms between your waist and shoulders.
- Drop your arms to your sides when not using them.

Some gestures are used to draw attention to points illustrated by visual aids. For these, gesturing with an open hand can seem more friendly and can even release tension related to nervousness. In contrast, a nervous speaker who uses a laser pointer may distract the audience as the pointer jumps around in the speaker's shaky hand.[8]

Reports on the Internet

Many clients want numerous employees to have access to research findings. One easy way to share data is to make executive summaries and reports available on a company intranet. In addition, a company can use information technology on the Internet to design questionnaires, administer surveys, analyze data, and share the results in a presentation-ready format. Real-time data capture allows for beginning-to-end reporting. A number of companies offer fully Web-based research management systems—for example, many companies also provide online research reports on key topics of interest. The Research Snapshot on page 411 discusses these in a little more detail.

The Research Follow-Up

research follow-up

Recontacting decision makers and/or clients after they have had a chance to read over a research report in order to determine whether additional information or clarification is necessary.

Research reports and oral presentations should communicate research findings so that managers can make business decisions. In many cases, the manager who receives the research report is unable to interpret the information and draw conclusions relevant to managerial decisions. For this reason, effective researchers do not treat the report as the end of the research process. They conduct a **research follow-up**, in which they recontact decision makers and/or clients after the latter have had a chance to read over the report. The purpose is to determine whether the researchers need to provide additional information or clarify issues of concern to management. Just as marketing research may help an organization learn about its customers' satisfaction, the research follow-up can help marketing research staffers ensure the satisfaction of their customers, marketing managers.

- Research reports, like all communications, are interpreted by the receiver. Try to be clear and unambiguous in preparing the research report.
  - Research reports should generally follow the principles of good technical writing.
  - Whenever possible, have someone else proof the report and slides before submitting them to the client or editor.
  - Whenever possible, stick to the standard outline for the paper.
- The executive summary is critically important because on occasion it is the only part read in detail by the client.
  - Keep it short—about 400 words maximum except for the longest reports.
  - Highlight the key findings with bullet points.
  - Write it last—after finishing the rest of the report and presentation.
- Consider the audience in preparing the report and presentation.
  - Make the communication understandable.
  - Avoid jargon and put any complex statistical output in a technical appendix.
- Use charts and tables to illustrate findings.
- Presentation slides should be clear and legible.
  - Err toward larger font, not smaller.
  - Err toward fewer words, not more.
- When slides are posted to be viewed via the Internet, annotate complex issues with pop-ups or balloon inserts.

© GEORGE DOYLE & CIARAN GRIFFIN

Summary

1. Define the parts of a research report following a standard format. A research report is an oral or written presentation of research findings directed to a specific audience to accomplish a particular purpose. Report preparation is the final stage of the research project. The consensus is that the format for a research report should include certain prefatory parts, the body of the report, and appended parts. The report format should be varied to suit the level of formality of the particular situation. The prefatory parts of a formal report include a title page, letters of transmittal and authorization, a table of contents, and a summary.

2. Explain how to use tables for presenting numerical information. Tables present large amounts of numerical information in a concise manner. They are especially useful for presenting several pieces of information about each item discussed. Short tables are helpful in the body of the report; long tables are better suited for an appendix. Each table should include a number, title, stubheads and bannerheads, footnotes for any explanations or qualifications of entries, and source notes for data from secondary sources.

3. Summarize how to select and use the types of research charts. Charts present numerical data in a way that highlights their relationships. Each chart should include a figure number, title, explanatory legends, and a source note for secondary sources. Pie charts show the composition of a total (the parts that make up a whole). Line graphs show the relationship of a dependent variable (on the vertical axis) to an independent variable (horizontal axis). Most commonly, the independent variable is time. Bar charts show changes in a dependent variable at discrete intervals of the independent variable—for example, comparing one year with another or one subset of the population with another. Researchers need to pay careful attention to avoid distorted interpretations of graphics based on manipulations of the scale values used on axes or some other intentional or careless inaccuracy.

4. Know how to give an effective oral presentation. Most research projects are reported on orally as well as in writing, so the researcher needs to prepare an oral presentation. The presentation should defend the results without being defensive. The presentation must be tailored to the situation and the audience. The presenter should practice delivering the presentation in a natural way, without reading to the audience. Graphic aids are useful supplements when they are simple and easy to read. Gestures also add interest and emphasis.

5. Discuss the importance of Internet reporting and research follow-up. Posting a summary of results online gives clients ready access to that information. Some online survey software processes the data and displays results in a presentation-ready format. In the follow-up stage of a research project, the researchers recontact decision makers after submitting the report. This helps the researchers determine whether they need to provide further information or clarify any issues of concern to management.

Key Terms and Concepts

conclusions and recommendations
    section, *404*
graphic aids, *405*
introduction section, *404*

oral presentation, *410*
report format, *400*
research follow-up, *412*
research methodology section, *404*

research report, *400*
results section, *404*

Questions for Review and Critical Thinking

1. What are the parts of a market research report?
2. How does an applied market research report differ from a basic or marketing research report?
3. What types of tables might be used to describe some of the various statistical tests discussed in previous chapters?
4. What is the difference between a *basic marketing research paper* and *an applied market research report*?
5. What is a *pie chart*? What is a *bar chart*? When might one be preferable over the other?
6. How might a marketing research unintentionally distort results of an independent t-test examining brand A's customer satisfaction against brand B's customer satisfaction where customer satisfaction is measured on a 0 to 100 point satisfaction scale (0 = no satisfaction to 100 = complete satisfaction)? How might the researcher intentionally distort the interpretation of these results?
7. What are some basic business research journals? Find some published research reports in these journals. How do they meet the standards set forth in this chapter?
8. What rules should be followed when preparing slides for computer-generated presentations?
9. **ETHICS** What ethical concerns arise when you prepare (or read) a report?
10. **ETHICS** A researcher working for Hi Time prepares a bar chart comparing the number of customers visiting two competing booths at a fashion trade show. One booth is the Hi Time booth, the other is for a competing company, So Cool. First, the chart is prepared as shown here:

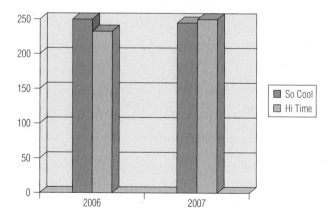

In preparing for a presentation to the Hi Time Board, the client tells the researcher that the chart doesn't seem to reflect the improvements made since 2008. Therefore, the researcher prepares the chart as shown here:

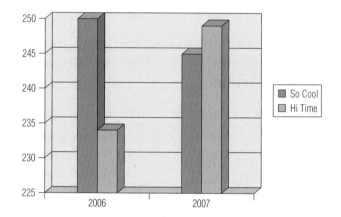

a. What has reformatting the bar chart accomplished?
b. Was it ethical for the client to ask for the bar chart to be redrawn?
c. Would it be ethical for the researcher to use the new chart in the presentation?

Research Activity

1. **'NET** Input "Starbucks" or "McDonald's" in an Internet search engine available through your library's reference service or even a general search engine such as Google News. Look at the articles for that company. Limit the search by using the word "report." Find one of the articles that actually presents some research reports, such as consumer reactions to a new product. Prepare PowerPoint slides that contain appropriate charts to present the results.

Case 16.1 Annenberg Public Policy Center

A recent study by the Annenberg Public Policy Center investigated one major area of marketing decisions: pricing practices.[9] Specifically, the study addressed consumer knowledge and attitudes about the practice of online retailers adjusting their prices according to customer characteristics, such as how frequently they buy from the retailer. For example, a Web site selling cameras charged different prices for the same model depending on whether the visitor to the site had previously visited sites that supply price comparisons. In general, charging different prices is called price discrimination and is legal unless it discriminates by race or sex or involves antitrust or price-fixing laws (such as two competitors agreeing to charge certain prices).

The Annenberg study consisted of telephone interviews conducted with a sample of 1,500 adults, screened to find persons who had used the Internet in the preceding 30 days. The questionnaire gathered demographic data and data about Internet usage. In addition, the interviewer read 17 statements about basic laws and practices related to price discrimination and the targeting of consumers according to their shopping behaviors. Respondents were asked whether each of these statements was true or false. Case Exhibits 16.1–1 through 16.1–4 summarize some of the results from this study.

Questions

1. The information provided here is not detailed enough for a formal report, but assume that you are making an informal report in a preliminary stage of the reporting process. Which of these findings do you want to emphasize as your main points? Why?

2. Prepare a written summary of the findings, using at least two tables or charts.

3. Prepare two tables or charts that would be suitable to accompany an oral presentation of these results. Are they different from the visual aids you prepared for question 2? Why or why not?

CASE EXHIBIT 16.1–1 **Selected Information about the Sample**

Sex	
Male	48%
Female	52%
Online Connection at Home	
Dial-up connection only	31%
Cable modem (with/without dial-up)	18%
DSL (with/without dial-up)	25%
Cable or DSL with another method	13%
Don't know	4%
No connection at home	9%
Self-Ranked Expertise Navigating the Internet	
Beginner	14%
Intermediate	40%
Advanced	34%
Expert	12%

Source: Joseph Turow, Lauren Feldman, and Kimberly Meltzer, "Open to Exploitation: American Shoppers Online and Offline," APPC report, June 2005, p. 15, downloaded at http://www.annenbergpublicpolicycenter.org.

CASE EXHIBIT 16.1–2 **Responses to Selected Knowledge Questions**

Statement	Response*		
	True	**False**	**Don't Know**
Companies today have the ability to follow my activity across many sites on the web.	**80%**	8%	12%
It is legal for an *online* store to charge different people different prices at the same time of day.	**38%**	29%	33%
By law, a site such as Expedia or Orbitz that compares prices on different airlines must include the lowest airline prices.	37%	**32%**	31%
It is legal for an *offline* store to charge different people different prices at the same time of day.	**29%**	42%	29%
When a website has a privacy policy, it means the site will not share my information with other websites or companies.	59%	**25%**	16%

*When the numbers do not add up to 100%, it is because of a rounding error. **Boldface** type indicates the correct answer.

Source: Joseph Turow, Lauren Feldman, and Kimberly Meltzer, "Open to Exploitation: American Shoppers Online and Offline," APPC report, June 2005, p. 20, downloaded at http://www.annenbergpublicpolicycenter.org. Accessed April 5, 2006.

CASE EXHIBIT 16.1–3 **Responses to Selected Attitude Questions**

Statement	Response*			
	Agree	Disagree	Neutral	Don't Know
It's okay if a store charges me a price based on what it knows about me.	8%	91%	—	1%
It's okay if an *online* store I use charges different people different prices for the same products during the same hour.	11%	87%	1%	1%
It would bother me to learn that other people pay less than I do for the same products.	76%	22%	1%	1%
It would bother me if websites I shop at keep detailed records of my buying behavior.	57%	41%	2%	1%
It's okay if a store I shop at frequently uses information it has about me to create a picture of me that improves the services it provides for me.	50%	47%	2%	1%

*When the numbers do not add up to 100%, it is because of a rounding error.

Source: Joseph Turow, Lauren Feldman, and Kimberly Meltzer, "Open to Exploitation: American Shoppers Online and Offline," APPC report, June 2005, p. 22, downloaded at http://www.annenbergpublicpolicycenter.org. Accessed April 7, 2006.

CASE EXHIBIT 16.1–4 **Predicting Knowledge Score from Selected Demographics**

	Unstandardized Regression Coefficient (B)	Standardized Regression Coefficient (β)
Education	0.630*	0.200
Income	0.383*	0.150
Self-perceived ability to navigate Internet	0.616*	0.149
Constant	2.687	
R^2	0.148	

*Significance <0.001 level.

Source: Joseph Turow, Lauren Feldman, and Kimberly Meltzer, "Open to Exploitation: American Shoppers Online and Offline," APPC report, June 2005, p. 29, downloaded at http://www.annenbergpublicpolicycenter.org. Accessed April 6, 2006.

A Final Note on Marketing Research

Hopefully, after reading and studying the material in this book, you can now understand and apply basic processes that help identify key information needs and turn raw data into intelligence. Thus, after sifting through a vast sea of information, this intelligence helps someone make a better decision, which, in turn, helps make someone's life better. The consumer who gets something of greater value is better off and the people who produced and marketed the product also are better off. Marketing research is a very important and useful area of knowledge that can lead to meaningful skills. The set of cases that follows provides the reader with one last chance to gain experience through real-world applications of marketing research. If you are still hungry for more about marketing research, there are many more advanced topics that can increase your skills in one of the specialized areas of research!

Part 6
Comprehensive Cases with Computerized Databases

© MARK HARWOOD/ICONICA/GETTY IMAGES

CASE 1
Attiring Situation

CASE 2
Say It Ain't So! Is This the Real Thing?

CASE 3
TABH, INC., Automotive Consulting

COMPREHENSIVE CASES

Case 1 Attiring Situation

RESERV is a national level placement firm specializing in putting retailers and service providers together with potential employees who fill positions at all levels of the organization. This includes entry-level positions and senior management positions. One international specialty clothing store chain has approached them with issues involving key characteristics of retail employees. The two key characteristics of primary interest involve the appearance of potential employees and problems with customer integrity.

Over the last five years, store management has adopted a very flexible dress code that allowed employees some flexibility in the way they dressed for work. Casual attire was permitted with the idea that younger customers could better identify with store employees, most of whom are younger than average. However, senior management had just become aware of how some very successful companies tightly control the appearance of their sales force. The Walt Disney Company, for example, has strict grooming policies for all employees, provides uniforms (or costumes) for most *cast members*, and does not permit any employee to work if they have a visible tattoo. Disney executives discuss many positive benefits from this policy and one is that customers are more responsive to the employees. Thus, it just may be that the appearance of employees can influence the behavior of customers. This influence can be from the greater identity that employees display—meaning, they stand out better and may encourage acquiescence through friendliness.

Senior research associate, Michael Neil, decides to conduct an experiment to examine relevant research questions including:

RQ1: How does employee appearance affect customer purchasing behavior?

RQ2: How does employee appearance affect customer ethics?

Mr. Neil decides the problem can best be attacked by conducting a laboratory experiment. In the experiment, two variables are manipulated in a between-subjects design. The experiment includes two experimental variables which are controlled by the researcher and subjects' biological sex which was recorded and included as a blocking variable. The experimental variables (and blocking variable) are:

Name	Description	Values
X_1	A manipulation of the attire of the service-providing employee	0 = Professional Attire (Neatly groomed w/ business attire) 1 = Unprofessional Attire (Unkempt hair w/ jeans and t-shirt)
X_2	The manner with which the service-providing employee tries to gain extra sales—or simply, the close approach	0 = Soft Close 1 = Hard Close
Gender	Subject's biological sex	0 = Male 1 = Female

The dependent variables include:

Name	Description	Range
Time	How much time the subject spent with the employee beyond what was necessary to choose the slacks and shirt.	0–10 minutes
Spend	How much of the $25 the subject spent on extra products offered for sale by the retail service provider	$0–$25
Keep	How much of the $25 the subject kept rather than returning to the researcher	$0–$25

Additionally, several variables were collected following the experiment that tried to capture how the subject felt during the exercise. All of these items were gathered using a 7-item semantic differential scale.

Name	Description
SD1	Low Quality–High Quality
SD2	Dislike–Like
SD3	Unfavorable–Favorable
SD4	Negative–Positive
SD5	Easy–Difficult
SD6	Restful–Tiring
SD7	Comfortable–Uncomfortable
SD8	Calm–Tense

The experiment was conducted in a university union. Subjects were recruited from the food court area. RESERV employees approached potential subjects and requested their participation in a study that examined how customers really bought things. Subjects would each receive vouchers that could be exchanged for merchandise in return for their participation. Each potential subject was informed that the participation could take between 20 and 40 minutes to complete. Upon agreeing to participate, subjects were escorted to a waiting area where they were provided with further instructions and mingled with other participants before entering a small room that was set up to resemble an actual retail clothing counter.

Each subject was told to play the role of a customer who had just purchased some dress slacks and a shirt. The employee was to complete the transaction. Once the subject entered the mock retail environment, a research assistant who was playing the role of the retail employee entered the room. As a retail sales associate, one important role was to suggest add-on sales. Several dozen accessory items ranging from socks and handkerchiefs to small jewelry items were displayed at the counter.

As a result of this experimental procedure, each subject was randomly assigned to one of four conditions, each corresponding to a unique combination of the experimental variables described above. In other words, the employee was either:

1. Dressed professionally and used a soft close (i.e., "Perhaps you would like to see some additional accessories") in trying to sell merchandise beyond the slacks and shirt.

2. Dressed unprofessionally and used a soft close.
3. Dressed professionally and used a hard close (i.e., "You really need to match this up with some coordinated accessories which happen to be on sale today only") in trying to sell merchandise beyond the slacks and shirt.
4. Dressed unprofessionally and used a hard close.

Thus, RESERV wishes to use this information to explain how employee appearance encourages shoppers to continue shopping (TIME) and spend money (SPEND). Rather than simply ask purchase intentions, each subject was given $25 (in one-dollar bills) which they were allowed to *spend* on accessories. This allowed each subject to participate in an actual transaction. In addition, the experiment did not provide explicit instructions on what was to be done with the money that was left over. Once the simulated shopping trip was complete, subjects were taken to another small room where they completed a questionnaire containing the semantic differential scales and demographic information alone and at their own pace. Because the instructions did not specifically tell subjects what to do with the money they possessed following the experiment, this allowed the researchers to operationalize a behavioral dependent variable (KEEP) that simulated questionable consumer behavior based on the implied assumption that the money was to be either handed to the research assistant when complete or turned in along with the questionnaire. In other words, subjects who kept money were considered as behaving less ethically than those who left the money behind or turned it in to a member of the research team.

Questions
1. Develop at least three hypotheses that correspond to the research questions.
2. Test the hypotheses using an appropriate statistical approach.
3. Suppose the researcher is curious about how the feelings captured with the semantic differentials influence the dependent variables SPEND and KEEP. Conduct an analysis to explore this possibility. Are any problems present in testing this?
4. Critique the experiment from an internal and external validity viewpoint.
5. What conclusions would be justified by management regarding their employee appearance policy?

Case 2 Say It Ain't So! Is This the Real Thing?

INTRODUCTION

David Ortega is the lead researcher for an upscale restaurant group hoping to add another chain that would compete directly with the upscale Smith and Wollensky restaurants (http://www.smithandwollensky .com). Smith and Wollensky is part of the Patina Restaurant Group. The average check for a customer at Smith and Wollensky is approximately $80 to $90.[1] Whenever a new venture of this type is planned, one has to wonder whether there are enough customers willing to pay premium prices given the large number of lesser priced alternatives. In fact, Smith and Wollensky is considering opening a lesser priced "Grill" that would be positioned so that the average customer check would be about half that of the original. What is it that people are willing to pay for and what sacrifices can be made to deliver a satisfying if not luxurious experience? How can he create a unique experience at a lower price? These are the questions facing David Ortega.

RESEARCH APPROACH

After considering how to study the issue, David decides a qualitative research approach will be useful. He hopes to develop a deep understanding of how the fine dining experience offers value—and perhaps some insights into what intangibles create value for consumers in general. After considering the different options, he decides on a phenomenological approach. The primary tool of investigation is conversational interviewing. David plans to enter into casual conversations with businesspeople in the lounge of the downtown Ritz Carlton. He begins the conversation by commenting on the wine he is sipping—something like, "It isn't bad, but it's hard to believe they get $15 for a glass of this stuff."

[1]MacNealy, Jeremy (2006), "Smith and Wollensky on the Grill," The Motley Fool, http://www.fool.com/News/mft/2006/mft06040425.htm, accessed November 6, 2008.

RESULTS

Two weeks later, David has completed "conversations" with five consumers. He found them very willing and free to talk about the things they indulge in. He develops a field log of notes from the consumers' comments. The notes are recorded verbatim.[2] The following field notes are highlighted:

Respondent	Date/Time	Text
Joe, wm, 55, attorney	12/5/08 – 10:15 PM	Well, wine doesn't have to be expensive to be good. Beyond some basic price point . . . maybe $14 a bottle . . . I find a lot of good wines. But, the wine has to fit the situation. It has to add something. A fake Rolex will tell time; but a real Rolex tells you about you. I don't mind paying for something that's unique—even though it might not be my cup of tea. Chateau Masur is like that. It's from Lebanon! It isn't always elegant or delicious, but it is always real. You always know it comes from some place very unique and is made under the most trying circumstances.
Sally, hf, 45, medical sales	12/7/08 – 5:45 PM	We pay too much for a lot of stuff though. I like things to be genuine. When you ask for crab you get crab—not Krab with a "K." It's made of fish you know!
		. . .
		I love old neighborhood Italian restaurants. They aren't always expensive. But, they have character. I think that it is very easy to spoil. I might not want a checkered red and white table cloth at home, but the Italian restaurant has to have one. I have to smell the garlic from the parking lot. And, that cheap Chianti, the kind with the basket cradle—it had better be from Italy—it tastes sooo good there. You know, you could pay more, but a nice dinner there with a couple of friends is worth a lot.
		You know, the people who make great wine or who have great restaurants kind of luck into it. I don't think they really ever sent out a survey asking what the restaurant or the wine should be like. I think they said "I am going to make this the way that I want it to be . . ." and it just happens to be right! They are so committed to the product that it works—no matter the price. But commitment like that costs a little more usually—although they aren't in it for the money.
Hebert, wm, 40, oil executive	12/8/08 – 11:00 PM	How old is it? The older it is, the more it is worth—yeah! I like this French wine that has "depuis 1574," maybe its name is Hugel (trying to recall). Imagine the same family running that company for hundreds of years. I like to think about the family in the vineyards—the old man on a tractor with his sons running around the sides. Their kids are hanging around the barn.
		. . .
		You know, you can buy cheap things and get cheated too. We are free to be cheated at any price point! (laughter) I remember bringing home a bottle of "Louisiana Hot Sauce." Man, that stuff didn't have any heat to it at all. When I looked at the bottle, do you know where it was from? . . . Man, it was from Tennessee . . . can you believe that, Louisiana Hot Sauce from Tennessee!! What a scam.
		. . . .
		When I buy something nice, I want it to be real. Burgundy should be from Burgundy. Bordeaux should be from Bordeaux. Champagne should be from Champagne—not Texas or California! (laughter) Because I know in Champagne, they know how to make Champagne—sparkling wine. They have perfected the methods over hundreds of years. A good glass of Champagne is worth what you pay!
Angela, bf, 60, insurance executive	12/9/08 – 6:45 PM	Look at this hotel . . . when you just look at the price you think 'this is crazy!' But, look at the attention to detail. Cleaning the floor is a production. Have you noticed the way they turn down your bed? Taking care of the plants is serious business to these people. I've stayed at a place like this in Florida—I loved it. At first, I couldn't put my finger on it. Then, it hit me. The place smelled like Florida. They have a way of giving everything the smell of sweet grass and citrus. It's terrific. Another one in California smelled of sandalwood and cypress. You have to be willing to pay more for people that care so much about what they do. Maybe that's your wine? Those smells make me think of those special places. When I drink a wine, I think about where it comes from too.
Burt, wm, 35, sales	12/9/08 – 9:30 PM	It's okay for something to be cheap . . . even fake! As long as I know it's fake. I've got three fake Rolexes. This one looks pretty good . . . looks genuine . . . but look at the way the second hand moves . . . it's jumping. A real one wouldn't do that!!
		I ate with this guy the other night who sent back a bottle of wine after ordering it. When the waiter pulled the cork, it didn't have Domaine Mas Blanc written on it—that's the name of the wine. He said, "How do I know it is real?" At first I thought he was crazy but after I looked at my fake Rolex . . . you know, I think he was right. When you spend $100 for a bottle, you want real stuff. But, if you spend $10 for a bottle of wine in a restaurant, who the hell cares? You didn't pay for it to be real . . . one day, when I pony up ten grand for a real Rolex, I'll send back the fakes!

Note: w = white; h = hispanic, f = female, m = male, etc.

[2]For more comments along this same line, see Beverland, M., "The Real Thing: Branding Authenticity in the Luxury Wine Trade," *Journal of Business Research* 59 (February 2006), 251–258; Beverland, M., "Crafting Brand Authenticity: The Case of Luxury Wines," *Journal of Management Studies* 42 (July 2005), 103–129; and Wolff, C., "Blending High Style and Authenticity," *Lodging Hospitality* 61 (November 1, 2005), 72–76.

RESULTS

David decides to use a word count to try to identify the main themes. Hopefully, these themes can help clarify the business problem. Perhaps if the information can't answer the questions above, it will point him in the right direction. Whatever the case, David feels the project has helped him better understand the total value proposition offered by restaurants, wines, hotels, and other products.

Questions

1. Comment on the research approach. Do you feel it was an appropriate choice?

2. ETHICS David did not inform these respondents that he was doing marketing research during these conversations. Why do you think he withheld this information and was it appropriate to do so?

3. 'NET Using the Internet, try to identify at least three restaurants that Smith and Wollensky competes with and three with whom the new S&W Grill may compete.

4. Try to interpret the discussions above. You may use one of the approaches discussed in the text. What themes should be coded? What themes occur most frequently? Can the different themes be linked together to form a unit of meaning?

5. What is the result of this research? What should David report back to the restaurant group?

Case 3 TABH, INC., Automotive Consulting

(Download the data sets for this case from www.cengage.com/marketing/zikmund or request them from your instructor.)
TABH consulting specializes in research for automobile dealers in the United States, Canada, Mexico, and Europe. Although much of their work is done on a pay-for fee basis with customers such as dealerships and dealership networks selling all major makes of automobiles, they also produce a monthly "white paper" that is sold via their Web site. This off-the-shelf research is purchased by other research firms and by companies within the auto industry itself. This month, they would like to produce a white paper analyzing the viability of college students attending schools located in small college towns as a potentially underserved market segment.

TABH management assigns a junior analyst named Michel Gonzalez to the project. Lacking time for a more comprehensive study, Michel decides to contact the traffic department at Cal Poly

University in Pomona, California, and at Central Missouri State University in Warrensburg, Missouri. Michel wishes to obtain data from the students' automobile parking registration records. Although both schools are willing to provide anonymous data records for a limited number of students, Cal Poly offers Michel a chance to visit during the registration period, which just happens to be next week. As a result, not only can Michel get data from students' registration forms, but a small amount of primary data can be obtained by intercepting students near the registration window. In return, Michel is asked to purchase a booth at the Cal Poly career fair.

As a result, Michel obtains some basic information from students. The information results in a small data set consisting of the follow observations for 100 undergraduate college students in Pomona, California:

Variable	Description
Sex	Student's sex dummy coded with 1 = female and 0 = male
Color	Color of a student's car as listed on his or her registration form
Major	Student's major field of study (Business, Liberal Arts (LA), or Engineering (ENG))
Grade	Student's grade record reported as the mode (A, B, or C)
Finance	Whether the student financed the car he or she is driving or paid for it with cash, coded 0 = cash payment and 1 = financed
Residence	Whether the student lives on campus or commutes to school, coded 0 = commute and 1 = on campus
Animal	Michel asks each student to quickly draw a cartoon about the type of car they would like to purchase. Students are told to depict the car as an animal in the cartoon. Although Michel expects to interpret these cartoons more deeply when time allows, the initial coding specifies what type of animal was drawn by each respondent. When Michel was unsure of what animal was drawn, a second researcher was conferred with to determine what animal was depicted. Some students depicted the car as a dog, some as a cat, and some as a mule.

The purpose of the white paper is to offer car dealers considering new locations a comparison of the profile of a small town university with the primary market segments for their particular automobile. For instance, a company specializing in small pickup trucks appeals to a different market segment than does a company specializing in two-door economy sedans. Many small towns currently do not have dealerships, particularly beyond the "Big 3." Although TABH cannot predict with certainty who may purchase the white paper, it particularly wants to appeal to companies with high sales growth in the United States, such as Kia (http://www.kia.com), Hyundai (http://www.hyundai-motor.com), and potentially European auto dealerships currently without significant U.S. distribution, such as Smart (http://www.smart.com), among others. TABH also

hopes the white paper may eventually lead to a customized project for one of these companies. Thus, the general research question is:

What are the automobile market segment characteristics of students attending U.S. universities in small towns?

This question can be broken down into a series of more specific questions:

- What segments can be identified based on identifiable characteristics of students?
- How do different segments view a car?
- What types of automobiles would be most in demand?

Questions

1. What types of tests can be performed using the data that may at least indirectly address the primary research question?

2. What do you think the primary conclusions of the white paper will be based on the data provided?

3. Assuming a small college town lacked an auto dealership (beyond Ford, GM, and Chrysler), what two companies should be most interested in this type of location? Use the Internet if necessary to perform some cursory research on different car companies.

4. What are the weaknesses in basing decisions on this type of research?

5. Are there key issues that may diminish the usefulness of this research?

6. What kinds of themes might emerge from the cartoon drawings?

7. Are there any ethical dilemmas presented in this case?

ENDNOTES

ENDNOTES

Chapter 1

1 Bennett, J., N. F. Boulette and N. Serena, "GM Slate Sweeping Rebates as Toyota Closes in on #1," *Wall Street Journal* – Eastern Edition, 251 (June 24, 2008), A1-A15; Traeger, C., "What are Automakers Doing for Women? Part I: GM Reaches Out," Edmunds.com (2008),www.edmunds.com/advice/womenfamilies/articles/105204/article.html, accessed June 16, 2008; Traeger, C., "What are Automakers Doing for Women? Part II: Toyota Taking an American Approach to Reaching Women," Edmunds.com (2008), www.edmunds.com/advice/specialreports/articles/106270/article.html, accessed June 12, 2008; *Automative News Europe*, "Industry Would Benefit from More Women Execs," 13 (May 12, 2008), 10.

2 Keyo, Michelle "Web Site of the Week: Jelly Belly: Using Sampling to Build a Customer Database," *Inc. Online* (1996), http://www.inc.com, December 9, 1996.

3 Penn, Catherine, "New Drinks Include a Health Benefit for 05," *Beverage Industry*, 96 (January 2005), 45–54.

4 Jelly Belly Candy Company (March 6, 2008). "April Fools' Day: Bamboozle Someone with New Jelly Belly BeanBoozled Jelly Beans: A Fools Errand and Silly Celebrations." Press release.

5 "U.S. Coffee Makers Perky as Consumption Increases," *Nations Restaurant Business*, 36 (April 22, 2002), 34; "U.S. Specialty Coffee Market in 30 Year Renaissance," http://www.cnn.com, December 15, 2000.

6 "Coffee: Demographics," in *The 2008 Beverage Market Research Handbook*, (Loganville, GA: Richard K. Miller & Associates, 2008), 98–100.

7 Kafka, Peter, "Bean-Counter," *Forbes*, 175 (February 28, 2005), 78–80. www.starbucks.com, accessed Oct. 30, 2008.

8 Garvin, Andrew P., "Evolve Approach to Serve Complex Market," *Marketing News* (September 15, 2005), 22.

9 Thomas, Jerry W., "Skipping MR a Major Error," *Marketing News* (March 4, 2002), 50.

10 Gibson, Lawrence D.,"Quo Vadis Marketing Research?" *Marketing Research*, 12 (Spring 2000), 36–41.

11 Matthew, Arnold,"FDA Delays DTC Draft Guidance to Study How Consumers Use Brief Summaries," *Medical Marketing and Media*, 39 (November 2004), 10.

12 See, for example, Babin, Barry J., J. C. Chebat, and Richard Michon, "Perceived Appropriateness and Its Effect on Quality, Affect and Behavior," *Journal of Retailing and Consumer Services*, 11 (September 2004), 287–298.

13 Sin, Leo Y. M., Alan C. B. Tse, Oliver H. M. Yau, Raymond P. M. Chow, Jenny S. Y. Lee, Lorett B. Y. Lau,"Relationship Marketing Orientation: Scale Development and Cross-Cultural Validation," *Journal of Business Research*, 58 (February 2005), 185–194; Nakata, Cheryl and K. Sivakumar, "Instituting the Marketing Concept in a Multinational Setting: The Role of National Culture," *Journal of the Academy of Marketing Science*, 29 (Summer 2001), 255–275; Day, George,"The Capabilities of Market-Driven Organizations," *Journal of Marketing*, 58 (October 1994), 37–52; Ward, James C., M.D. Hutt and Peter H. Reingen, "Evolving Patterns of Organizational Beliefs in the Formation of Strategy," *Journal of Marketing*, 58 (April 1994), 96–110.

14 Reyes, Sonia, "Ian Friendly: Groove Tube," *Brandweek* (October 16, 2000), M111–M116.

15 Stoll, J. D., "GM Weighs More Layoffs, Sale of Brands," *Wall Street Journal* (July 7, 2008), A1.

16 Gelb, Betsy D. and Gabriel M. Gelb,"What Research Inside the Organization Can Accomplish," *Marketing Research* (December 1991), 44.

17 *Marketing News*,"Burger King Opens Customer Hot Line" (May 28, 1990), 7.

18 *Professional Builder*, "David Weekley Homes Reign in Fort Worth Market," 69 (December, 2004), 31–34.

19 Sharman,G. K.,"Sessions Challenge Status Quo," *Marketing News* (November 10, 1997), p. 18.

20 Schwartz, David, *Concept Testing: How to Test Product Ideas Before You Go to Market* (New York: AMACOM, 1987), p. 91.

21 Wyner, Gordon A., "Biz Problems Can Get Solved With Research," *Marketing News* (September 15, 2005), 33–34.

22 Benezra, Karen, "Fritos Around theWorld," *Brandweek* (March 27, 1994), 32; "Cheetos Make Debut in China But Lose Cheese inTranslation" *USAToday* (September 2, 2004), B-1.

23 See Allenby, Greg M.,Thomas S. Shively,Yang Sha and Mark J. Garratt, "A Choice Model for Packaged Goods: Dealing with Discrete Quantities and Quantity Discounts," *Marketing Science*, 23 (Winter 2004), 14–21.

24 Mohn, N. Carroll, "Pricing Research for Decision Making," *Marketing Research* (Winter 1995), 11–12.

25 See Allenby, Greg M., Thomas S. Shively,Yang Sha and Mark J. Garratt, "A Choice Model for Packaged Goods: Dealing with Discrete Quantities and Quantity Discounts," *Marketing Science*, 23 (Winter 2004), 14–21. Mohn, N. Carroll, "Pricing Research for Decision Making," *Marketing Research* (Winter 1995), 11–12. Ofir, Chezy, "Reexamining Latitude of Price Acceptability and Price Thresholds: Predicting Basic Consumer Reaction to Price," *Journal of Consumer Research*, 30 (March 2004), 612–621.

26 Bonamici, Kate,"Big-Foot Dips Toe in Coffee," *Fortune*, 149 (January 26, 2004), 70.

27 Gardyn, Rebecca, "Same Name, New Number: AT&T's Brand Image Gets a Needed Boost from a Well-Rounded Hero," *American Demographics* (March 2001), 56.

28 Schneider, Lars-Peter and Bettina T. Cornwell, "Cashing in on Crashes via Brand Placement in Computer Games," *International Journal of Advertising*, 24, no. 3 (2005), 321–342.

29 Low, George S., "Correlates of Integrated Marketing Communications," *Journal of Advertising Research* (May 2000).

30 Hein, Kenneth, "Best Buy Calls the 'Odd' Squad: Group of Tech 'Geeks' gets Spotlight in National Branding Spot," *Brandweek*, 45 (October 18, 2004), 11; *DSN Retailing Today*, "Best Buy Turns On the Geek Appeal. (CE & Entertainment)," 42 (February 24, 2004), 22.

31 Garretson, Judith and Scot Burton, "The Role of Spokescharacters as Advertisement and Package Cues in Integrated Marketing Communications," *Journal of Marketing*, 69 (October, 2005), 118–132.

32 Clancy, Kevin J. and Randy L. Stone, "Don't Blame the Metrics," *Harvard Business Review*, 83 (June, 2005), 26–28.

33 Honomichl, Jack, "Growth Stunt," *Marketing News* (June 4, 2001), 144.

34 *Express Magazine*, "You Say Tomato, I say Tomahto," (Spring 2006), 19.

35 Kiley, D. "Jack Daniel's International Appeal," *Businessweek*, October 10, 2007, accessed at http://www.businessweek.com/innovate/content/oct2007/id20071010_651037.htm, September 14, 2008.

Chapter 2

1 Granados, N., A. Gupta and R. J. Kauffman, "Designing Online Selling Mechanisms: Transparency Levels and Prices," *Decision Support Systems*, (2008), forthcoming; Jackson, T. W., "Personalization and CRM," *Journal of Database Marketing & Customer Strategy Management*, 15, no. 1 (2007), 24–36; Beirne, M., "Southwest Airlines Delivers Fare Offers with DING!" *Brandweek* (2006), www.brandweek.com/bw/news/recent_cisplay-jsp?vnu_content_id=1002765480 accessed June 16, 2008.

2 See Albers, Brad, "Home Depot's Special Projects Support Team Powers Information Management for Business Needs," *Journal of Organizational Excellence*, 21 (Winter 2001), 3–15; Songini, Marc L., "Home Depot's Next IT Project: Data Warehouse," *Computerworld*, 36 (October 7, 2002), 1–2.

3 "SAS helps ImpactRX Provide Real Time Marketing Intelligence to Pharma Companies," *Business Wire*, (March 17, 2008). Retrieved July 14, 2008 from ABI/INFORM Dateline database (document ID: 1447327611).

4 Wells, H. G., "*The Brain: Organization of the Modern World*" (1940).

5 "Benefits of RFID Becoming More Visible" *DSN Retailing Today*, (August 8, 2005), 22.

6 Hall, Mark, "Seeding for Data Growth," *Computerworld*, 36 (April 15, 2002), 52.

7 Angwein, J. and K. J. Delaney, "Top Web Sites Build Up Ad Backlog, Raise Rates," *Wall Street Journal* (November 16, 2005), A1.

8 Sellers, J., "Teen Marketing 2.0," *Publishers' Weekly*, 254, no. 35 (2007), 27. www.compete.com, accessed Nov. 29, 2008.

9 *Gale Annual Directory of Databases*, Gale Research Inc.: Detroit.

10 Beasty, C., "Analytics Brought to Bear," *Customer Relationship Management*, 10 (December 2006), 26–29.

11 "A Better Web Through Higher Math," *Business Week Online*, (January 22, 2002), http://

www.businessweek.com (accessed November 12, 2005).

12 Jackson, T. W., "Personalisation and CRM," *Database Marketing & Customer Strategy Management*, 15, no. 1 (2007), 24–36.

13 Rangaswamy, Arvind and G. Lilien, "Software Tools for New Product Development," *Journal of Marketing Research*, 34 (February 1997), 177–184.

14 Desouza, Kevin and Yukika Awazu, "Maintaining Knowledge Management Systems: A Strategic Imperative," *Journal of the American Society for Information Science and Technology*, 56 (May 2005), 765–768.

15 Rangaswamy, Arvind and G. Lilien (1997).

16 Adopted with permission from deJony, Jennifer, "View from the Top," *Technology*, 1 (1995), downloaded from the Internet July 3, 1998.

Chapter 3

1 Haytko, D., "Message from the Guest Editor," *Marketing Education Review*, 18 (Spring 2008), 1; Anwar, A., M. Al-Shami and S. A. Ahmed, "Developing a Market-Oriented MBA Program: Practitioners' Views from GCC Countries," *Journal of International Marketing & Marketing Research*, 31 (October 2006), 129–139.

2 Zahay, Debra, Abbie Griffin and Elisa Fredericks, "Sources, Uses, and Forms of Data in the New Product Development Process," *Industrial Marketing Management*, 33 (October 2004), 658–666.

3 Hara, Yoshika, "New Industry Awaits Human-Friendly Bipeds—'Personal Robots' Get Ready to Walk on the Human Side," *Electronic Engineering Times* (September 16, 2002), 157–159.

4 Bocchi, Joe, Jacqueline K. Eastman, and Cathy Owens Swift, "Retaining the Online Learner: Profile of Students in an Online MBA Program and Implications for Teaching Them," *Journal of Education for Business* (March/April 2004), 245–253.

5 Janoff, Barry, "Brands of the Land," *BrandWeek* (April 20, 2001), 28.

6 Bocchi, Eastman and Swift (2004); Carr, S., "As Distance Education Comes of Age, the Challenge is Keeping the Students," *Chronicle of Higher Education* (2000) 23, A1.; Moskal and Dziuban, "Present and Future Directions for Assessing Cybereducation: The Changing Research Paradigm," in L. R. Vandervert, L. V. Chavinina and R. A. Cornell, Eds., *Cybereducation: The Future of Long-Distance Learning* (2001), New York: P. D. Moskal and C. G. Dziuban, Liebert, 157–184.

7 Thomas, Jerry W., "Skipping MR a Major Error," *Marketing News* (March 4, 2005), 50.

8 A. Einstein and L. Infeld, *The Evolution of Physics* (New York: Simon and Schuster, 1942), p. 95.

9 See Bhardwaj, S., I. Palaparthy and A. Agrawal, "Exploration of Environmental Dimensions of Servicescapes: A Literature Review," *The Icfai Journal of Marketing Management*, 7, no. 1 (2008), 37–48 for a relevant literature review.

10 Perdue, B. C. and J. O. Summers, "Checking the Success of Manipulations in Marketing Experiments," *Journal of Marketing Research*, 23 (November 1986), 317–326.

11 See, for example, Kwok, S. and M. Uncles, "Sales Promotion Effectiveness: The Impact of Consumer Differences at an Ethnic-Group Level," *Journal of Product and Brand Management*, 14, no. 3 (2005), 170–186.

12 Approximate currency rates as of August 2008.

13 Babin, B. J., D. M. Hardesty and T. A. Suter, "Color and Shopping Intentions: The Effect of Price Fairness and Perceived Affect," *Journal of Business Research*, 56 (July 2003), 541–551.

14 Crowley, Michael, "Conservatives (Finally) Rejoice," *New Republic*, 231, (2004) 13–14.

Chapter 4

1 Lanzoni, G. and N. Marcus, "Seeking Market Research/Competitive Intelligence," *LIMRA's Market Facts Quarterly*, 23 no. 1 (2004), 20–23.

2 Russell-Bennett, R., J. R. McColl-Kennedy and L.V. Coote, "Involvement, Satisfaction, and Brand Loyalty in a Small Business Services Setting," *Journal of Business Research*, 60 (December 2007), 1253–1262.

3 Kinnear, Thomas C. and Ann Root, Eds., *Survey of Marketing Research* (Chicago: American Marketing Association, 1994).

4 See Izzo, G. Martin and Scott J. Vitell, "Exploring the Effects of Professional Education on Salespeople: The Case of Autonomous Agents," *Journal of Marketing Theory & Practice*, 11 (Fall 2003), 26–38; Loe, Terry and William A. Weeks, "An Empirical Investigation of Efforts to Improve Sales Students' Moral Reasoning," *Journal of Personal Selling and Sales Management*, 20 (Fall 2000), 243–252.

5 Barnett, Tim and Sean Valentino, "Issue Contingencies and Marketers' Recognition of Ethical Issues, Ethical Judgments and Behavioral

Intentions," *Journal of Business Research*, 57 (April 2004), 338–346.

6 Robin, D. P., R. E. Reidenbach and B. J. Babin, "The Nature, Measurement and Stability of Ethical Judgements in the Workplace," *Psychological Reports*, 80, (1997), 563–580.

7 Gillin, Donna L., "The Evolution of Privacy Legislation: How Privacy Issues Are Changing Research," *Marketing Research*, 13 (Winter 2001), 6–7.

8 Jarvis, Steve, "CMOR Finds Survey Refusal Rate Still Rising," *Marketing News*, 36 (February 4, 2002), 4.

9 Gillin, Donna (2001).

10 Ahuja, R. D., M. Walker, and R. Tadepalli, "Paternalism, Limited Paternalism and the Pontius Pilate Plight When Researching Children," *Journal of Business Ethics*, 32 (July 2001), 81–92; Clegg, A., "Out of the Mouths of Babes," *Marketing Week*, (June 23, 2005), 43.

11 Spangenberg, E., B. Grohmann and D. E. Sprott, "It's Beginning to Smell (and Sound) a Lot Like Christmas: The Interactive Effects of Ambient Scent and Music in a Retail Setting," *The Journal of Business Research*, 58 (November 2005), 582–589; Michon, Richard, Jean-Charles Chebat and L. W. Turley, "Mall Atmospherics: The Interaction Effects of the Mall Environment on Shopping Behavior," *Journal of Business Research*, 58 (May 2005), 576–583.

12 Mack, Beth, "Online Privacy Critical to Research Success," *Marketing News*, 36 (November 25, 2002), 21.

13 Carrigan, M. and M. Kirkup, "The Ethical Responsibilities of Marketers in Retail Observational Research: Protecting Stakeholders through the 'Ethical Research' Covenant," *International Journal of Retail, Distribution and Consumer Research*, 11 (October 2001), 411–435.

14 Brennan, M., S. Benson and Z. Kearns, "The Effect of Introductions on Telephone Survey Participation Rates," *International Journal of Market Research*, 47, no. 1 (2005), 65–74.

15 *Marketing News*, "Marketers Value Honesty in Marketing Researchers," 29 (June 5, 1995), 27.

Chapter 5

1 Cassidy, Hilary, "Many Paths to Cool, But Big Gains for All," *Brandweek*, 46 (June 20, 2005), 53.

2 Niemi, Wayne, "Schoenfeld to Leave as Vans CEO; As Its Deal with VF Corp. Closes, The Skate Brand Gains a New President and A New Focus on Apparel," *Footwear News* (July 5, 2004), 2; Montgomery, T., "Vans' Second Life," *OC Metro*, (October 11, 2007), 24.

3 McLaughlin, Lisa, "The New Roll Model," *Time*, 164 (July 26, 2004), 74.

4   *Entertainment Newsweekly*, "Electronic Arts Inc.; EA Brings Entries' Fifth Annual Goofy versus Regular Skateboarding Competition to Skate," (September 26, 2008), 181.

5   Sayre, Shay, *Qualitative Methods for Marketplace Research* (Sage: Thousand Oaks, CA, 2001).

6   Sayre, Shay (2001); Morse, Janice M. and Lyn Richards, *Readme First for a User's Guide to Qualitative Methods* (Sage: Thousand Oaks, CA, 2002).

7   See, for example, May, Carl, "Methodological Pluralism: British Sociology and the Evidence-Based State: A Reply to Payne et al.," *Sociology*, 39 (July 2005), 519–528; Achenbaum, A. A., "When Good Research Goes Bad," *Marketing Research*, 13 (Winter 2001), 13–15; Wade, K. R., "We Have Come Upon the Enemy: And They are Us," *Marketing Research*, 14 (Summer 2002), 39.

8   Babin, Barry J., William R. Darden and Mitch Griffin, "Work and/or Fun: Measuring Hedonic and Utilitarian Shopping Value," *Journal of Consumer Research*, 20 (March 1994), 644–656.

9   Stengal, J. R., A. L. Dixon and C. T. Allen, "Listening Begins at Home," *Harvard Business Review* (November 2003), 106–116.

10 Semon, Thomas T., "You Get What You Pay For: It May be Bad MR," *Marketing News*, 36 (April 15, 2002), 7.

11 Hamel, G. and C. K. Prahalad, "Corporate Imagination and Expeditionary Marketing," *Harvard Business Review* (July–August 1991), 85.

12 Martens, Claire, "Sometimes a Great Notion Isn't Yet a Great Product," *Harvard Management Update* (March 2004), 3–4.

13 Thompson, Craig J., "Interpreting Consumers: A Hermeneutical Framework for Deriving Marketing Insights from the Tests of Consumers' Consumption Stories," *Journal of Marketing Research*, 34 (November 1997), 438–455 (see pp. 443–444 for quotation).

14 Thompson (1997). Craig J., "Interpreting Consumers: A Hermeneutical Framework for Deriving Marketing Insights from the Tests of Consumers' Consumption Stories," *Journal of Marketing Research*, 34 (November 1997), 438–455; Woodside, Arch G., H. M. Pattinson and K. E. Miller, "Advancing Hermeneutic Research for Interpreting Interfirm New Product Development," *Journal of Business and Industrial Marketing*, 20 (2005), 364–379.

15 While we refer to a hermeneutic unit as being text-based here for simplicity, they can actually also be developed using pictures, videotapes, or artifacts as well. Software such as ATLAS.ti will allow files containing pictures, videos, and text to be combined into a hermeneutic unit.

16 Morse, Janice M. and Lyn Richards (2002).

17 Winsome, S. J., and P. Johnson, "The Pros and Cons of Data Analysis Software for Qualitative Research," *Journal of Nursing Scholarship*, 32, no. 4 (2000), 393–397.

18 See Feldman, Stephen P., "Playing with the Pieces: Deconstruction and the Loss of Moral Culture," *Journal of Management Studies*, 35 (January 1998), 59–79.

19 Louella, Miles, "Living their Lives," *Marketing* (UK) (December 11, 2003), 27–28.

20 Reid, D. M., "Changes in Japan's Post-Bubble Business Environment: Implications for Foreign-Affiliated Companies," *Journal of International Marketing*, 7, no. 3 (1999), 38–63.

21 Cutler, I. S., "Avoid Instinktive Marketing," *Upholstery Manufacturing*, 19 (January 2006), 33.

22 Morse, Janice M. and Lyn Richards (2002).

23 Strauss, A. L. and J. Corbin, *Basics of Qualitative Research* (Sage Publications: Newbury Park, CA, 1990).

24 Geiger, S. and D. Turley, "Personal Selling as a Knowledge-Based Activity: Communities of Practice in the Sales Force," *Irish Journal of Management*, 26 (2005), 61–70.

25 Beverland, M., "The Components of Prestige Brands," *Journal of Business Research*, 59 (February 2006), 251–258. Beverland, M., "Brand Value, Convictions, Flexibility and New Zealand Wine," *Business Horizons*, 47 (September/October 2004), 53–61.

26 Harwood, Jonathan, "Philip Morris Develops Smokeless Cigarette," *Marketing Week*, 28 (March 31, 2005), 5.

27 See Palan, K. M. and R. E. Wilkes, "Adolescent-Parent Interaction in Family Decision Making," *Journal of Consumer Research*, 24 (September 1997), 159–170; Haytko, Diana L. and Julie Baker, "It's All at the Mall: Exploring Adolescent Girls' Experiences," *Journal of Retailing*, 80 (Spring 2004), 67–83.

28 Henderson, N. R., "The Power of Probing," *Marketing Research*, 19 (Winter 2007), 38.

29 Gibson, Lawrence D. (1988).

30 Godes, David and Dina Mayzlin, "Using On-Line Conversations to Study Word-of-Mouth Communications," *Marketing Science*, 23 (2004), 545–560.

31 Babin, Barry J., William R. Darden and James S. Boles, "Salesperson Stereotypes, Consumer Emotions, and Their Impact on Information Processing," *Journal of the Academy of Marketing Science*, 23 (Spring 1995), 94–105.

32 Murphy, Ian, "Aided by Research, Harley Goes Whole Hog," *Marketing News*, 30 (December 2, 1996), 16–17.

33 Heather, R. P., "Future Focus Groups," *American Demographics* (January 1, 1994), 6.

34 Creamer, Mathew, "Slowly, Marketers Learn How to Let Go and Let Blog," *Advertising Age*, 76 (October 31, 2005), 1–35.

35 Fass, Allison, "Collective Opinion," *Forbes*, 176 (November 28, 2005), 76–79.

36 Godes, David and Dina Mayzlin, "Using On-Line Conversations to Study Word-of-Mouth Communications," *Marketing Science*, 23 (2004), 545–560.

37 Smith, A., R. Bolton and J. Wagner, "A Model of Customer Satisfaction with Service Encounters Involving Failure and Recovery," *Journal of Marketing Research*, 36 (August 1999), 356–372. Bolton, R. and T. M. Bronkhorst, "Quantitative Analysis of Depth Interviews, Psychology & Marketing, 8 (Winter 1991), 275–297.

38 "SPSS Text Mining Reveals Customer Insights As Organizations Worldwide Tap into Unstructured Data," *Business Wire*, (June 16, 2008), accessed through ProQuest, document number 14956884601 on July 14, 2008.

39 Wooliscroft, B., R. D. Tamilia and S. J. Shapiro (2006), A Twenty-First Century Guide to Aldersonian Marketing Thought, Springer, New York, NY.

40 Klahr, S., "Getting' Buggy With It," *Advertising Age's Creativity*, 8 (May 2000), 9.

Chapter 6

1   "Licensed to Snoop," *Human Resources*, (June 2008), 57–58; Marks, P., "Pentagon Sets Its Sights on Social Networking Websites," *New Scientist* (June 9, 2006), http://www.newscientist.com/article/mg19025556.200, accessed August 6, 2008; Lowry, Tom, "Obama's Secret Weapon," *Business Week* (July 7, 2008), 56–57.

2   "Breakfast Sandwich Boom," *Restaurants & Institutions,* 116 (Jan 15, 2006), p. 39.

3   Grow, Brian, "Yes, Ma'am, That Part Is in Stock," *Business Week*, (August 1, 2005), p. 32 "Servigistics Pricing: Maximizing the Profitability of Your Service Network," Servigistics, http://www.servigistics.com, accessed February 7, 2006.

4   Prasso, Sheridan, "Battle for the Face of China," *Fortune*, 152 (December 12, 2005), p. 156–161.

5   Charles, Susan K., "Custom Content Delivery," *Online*, (March–April 2004), p. 24–29. Fleming, Lee, "Digital Delivery: Pushing Content to the Desktop," *Digital Information Group*, (January 31, 1997), p. 7; and "How Smart Agents Will Change Selling," *Forbes ASAP*, (August 28, 1995), p. 95.

6   "Seeking New Beer Drinkers in the High Andes," *Global Agenda*, (September 6, 2005), p. 1; and "China Ranked Largest Beer Consumer in 2004," *Kyodo News International*, (December 15, 2005), Knight Ridder Tribune Business News, p. 1.

7   This section is based on Levy, Michael and Barton Weitz, *Retail Management* (Homewood, IL: Richard D. Irwin, 1992), pp. 357–358.

8   Data from the "About Us" section of the Capital One Web site, http://www.capitalone.com, accessed February 9, 2006.

9   Rao, Srikumar S., "The Hot Zone," *Forbes*, (November 18, 1996).

10 Mehta, N., "Investigating Consumers' Purchase Incidence and Brand Choice Decisions Across Multiple Product Categories: A Theoretical and Empirical Analysis," *Marketing Science*, 26 (Mar/Apr 2007), 457–479.

11 Wasserman, Todd, Gerry Khermouch and Jeff Green, "Mining Everyone's Business," *BrandWeek*, (February 28, 2000), p. 34.

12 "Clients: Case Studies," DataMind, http://www.datamind.com, accessed February 6, 2006.

13 Totty, Michael, "Making Searches Work at Work," *Wall Street Journal*, (December 19, 2005), http://online.wsj.com, accessed February 10, 2006.

14 Weiss, A. M., N. H. Lurie and D. J. MacInnis, "Listening to Strangers: Whose Responses Are Valuable, How Valuable Are They, and Why?" *Journal of Marketing Research*, 45 (August 2008), 425–436.

15 "Hispanic-Owned Businesses: Growth Projections, 2004–2010," HispanicBusiness.com Store, http://www.hbinc.com, accessed February 7, 2006.

16 Neff, Jack, "Wal-Mart Takes Stock in RetailLink System," *Advertising Age*, (May 21, 2001), p. 6.

17 See Federal Grants Wire, "National Trade Data Bank (NTDB)," http://www.federalgrantswire.com, accessed February 6, 2006; and STATUSA, "What Information Is Available under GLOBUS and NTBD?" and "GLOBUS & NTDB," http://www.stat-usa.gov, accessed February 6, 2006.

18 Based on Brown, Warren, "Pain at the Pump Doesn't Faze New-Car Buyers," *Washington Post*, (January 29, 2006), http://www.washingtonpost.com, accessed, February 10, 2006; and Halliday, J., "Prius Prices Outrun Inventory," *Advertising Age,* 79 (June 2, 2008), pp. 3–4.

Chapter 7

1 Brady, D., "Showcase Covers Hot Topics," *Marketing Week*, 30 (November 1, 2007), 37–40; Callegaro, M., C. Steeh, T. D. Buskirk, V. Vehovar, V. Kuusela, and L. Piekarski, "Fitting Disposition Codes to Mobile Phone Surveys: Experiences from Studies in Finland, Slovenia and the USA," *Journal of the Royal Statistical Society*, 170, no. 3 (2007), 647–670; Tourangeau, R., "Survey Research and Social Change," *Annual Review of Psychology*, 55 (2004), 775–801.

2 Swientek, B., "Using Consumer Insights to Guide Package Design: Traditional Research Can Give You Answers. But…" *Brand Packaging*, (March 1, 2003), accessed at www.interbrand.com, June 30, 2008.

3 Vascellaro, Jessica E. "Who'll Give Me $50 for This Purse from Nana?" *Wall Street Journal*, (December 28, 2005), http://online.wsj.com; "Survey Reveals Majority of Americans Receive Unwanted Gifts," *Survey.com* news release, (December 19, 2005), http://www.survey.com.

4 Excerpts from Arlen, Michael J., *Thirty Seconds* (New York: Farrar, Straus and Giroux, Inc., 1979, 1980), pp. 185–186. This material first appeared in the *New Yorker*.

5 Tuckel, Peter and Harry O'Neill, "The Vanishing Respondent in Telephone Surveys," a paper presented at the 56th annual conference of the American Association of Public Opinion Research (AAPOR) in Montreal on May 17–20, 2001.

6 Cull, William L., Karen G. O'Connor, Sanford Sharp, and Suk-fong S. Tang, "Response Rates and Response Bias for 50 Surveys of Pediatricians," *Health Services Research*, 40 (February 2005), p. 213.

7 Lee, Eunkyu, Michael Y. Hu and Rex S. Toh, "Respondent Noncooperation in Surveys and Diaries: An Analysis of Item Non-response and Panel Attrition," *International Journal of Market Research*, 46 (Autumn 2004), p. 311.

8 Douglas Aircraft, Consumer Research (undated), p. 13.

9 For an interesting study of extremity bias, see Baumgartner, Hans and Jan-Benedict E. M. Steenkamp, "Response Styles in Marketing Research: A Cross-National Investigation," *Journal of Marketing Research*, (May 2001), pp. 143–156.

10 Raven, G., "Major Holocaust Polls Show Built-In Bias," *Journal of Historical Review*, 15, no. 1 (2008), accessed at http://www.ihr.org/jhr/v15/v15n1p25_Raven.html, August 12, 2008.

11 Turner, Charles F., Maria A. Villarroel, James R. Chromy, Elizabeth Eggleston and Susan M. Rogers, "Same-Gender Sex among U.S. Adults: Trends across the Twentieth Century and during the 1990s," 70 *Public Opinion Quarterly*, (Fall 2005), pp. 166–196.

12 Warwick, Donald T. and Charles A. Lininger, *The Sample Survey: Theory and Practice* (New York: McGraw-Hill, 1975), p. 2.

13 Lockley, L. C. "Notes on the History of Marketing Research," *Journal of Marketing* (April 1950), pp. 733–736.

14 Hof, Robert D. "The Power of Us," *BusinessWeek* (June 20, 2005), 74–82.

15 For a complete discussion of conducting surveys in Hispanic neighborhoods, see Hernandes, Sigfredo A. and Carol J. Kaufman, "Marketing Research in Hispanic Barrios: A Guide to Survey Research," *Marketing Research* (March 1990), pp. 11–27.

16 Lavrakas, P. J., C. D. Shuttles, C. Steeh and H. Fienberg, "The State of Surveying Cell Phone Numbers in the United States," *Public Opinion Quarterly*, 71, no. 5 (2007), 840–854.

17 Brick, J. M., P. D. Brick, S. Dipko, S. Presser, C. Tucker and Y. Yuan, "Cell Phone Survey Feasibility in the U.S.: Sampling and Calling Cell Numbers Versus Landline Numbers," *Public Opinion Quarterly*, 71 (Spring 2007), 23–39.

18 Curtin, Richard, Stanley Presser and Eleanor Singer,"Changes in Telephone Survey Nonresponse over the Past Quarter Century," *Public Opinion Quarterly* (Spring 2005), downloaded from InfoTrac at http://web3.infotrac.galegroup.com.

19 Cuneo, Alice Z., "Researchers Flail as Public Cuts the Cord," *Advertising Age* (November 15, 2004), 3–52.

20 Hembroff, Larry A. Debra Rusz, Ann Rafferty, Harry McGee and Nathaniel Ehrlich, "The Cost-Effectiveness of Alternative Advance Mailings in a Telephone Survey," *Public Opinion Quarterly*, 69 (Summer 2005), 232–245.

21 Brennan, Mike, Susan Benson and Zane Kearns, "The Effect of Introductions on Telephone Survey Participation Rates," *International Journal of Market Research*, 47, no. 1 (2005), 65–74.

22 Dillman, Don A., *Mail and Internet Surveys: The Tailored Design Method* (New York: John Wiley and Sons, 2000), p. 173.

23 Schaefer, David R. and Don A. Dillman, "Development of a Standard E-Mail Methodology: Results of an Experiment," *Public Opinion Quarterly*, 62, no. 3 (Fall 1998), p. 378.

24 Ibid.

25 For a complete discussion of fax surveys, see the excellent article by Dickson, John P. and Douglas L. Maclachlan, "Fax Surveys: Return Patterns and Comparison with Mail Surveys," *Journal of Marketing Research* (February 1996), pp. 108–113.

26 Merriman, Joyce A., "Your Feedback Is Requested," *American Family Physician* (October 1, 2005), downloaded from InfoTrac at http://web3.infotrac.galegroup.com.

27 Dillmann, Don A., *Mail and Internet Surveys, The Tailored Design Method* (New York: John Wiley and Sons, 2000), pp. 369–372.

28 Göritz, Anja S., "Recruitment for On-Line Access Panels," *International Journal of Market Research*, 46, no. 4 (2004), 411–425.

29 Fricker, Scott, Mirta Galesic, Roger Tourangeau and Ting Yan, "An Experimental Comparison of Web and Telephone Surveys," *Public Opinion Quarterly*, 69 (Fall 2005), 370–392.

30 See Nielsen, Jakob "Keep Online Surveys Short," Alertbox (February 2, 2004), http://www.useit.com; "About Jakob Nielsen," http://www.useit.com, accessed February 21, 2006; and "About Nielsen Norman Group," Nielsen Norman Group, http://www.nngroup.com, accessed February 21, 2006.

31 See Kilbourne, Lawrene, "Avoid the Field of Dreams Fallacy," *Quirk's Marketing Research Review* (January 2005), pp. 70, 72–73.

32 Porter, P. R. and M. E. Whitcomb, "Mixed-Mode Contacts in Internet Surveys: Paper Is Not Necessarily Better," *Public Opinion Quarterly*, 71 (Winter 2007), 635–648.

33 Gruen, T., T. Osmonbekov and A. J. Czaplewski, "eWOM: The Impact of Customer-to-Customer Online Know-How Exchange on Customer Value and Loyalty," *Journal of Business Research*, 59 (April, 2006), 449–456.

34 Mary Lisbeth D'Amico, "Call Security," *Wall Street Journal* (February 13, 2006), http://online.wsj.com.

35 Braunsberger, K., H. Wybenga and R. Gates, "A Comparison of Reliability between Telephone and Web-Based Surveys," *Journal of Business Research*, 60 (July 2007), 758–764.

36 For an interesting empirical study, see Akaah, Ishmael P. and Edward A. Riordan, "The Incidence of Unethical Practices in Marketing Research: An Empirical Investigation," *Journal of the Academy of Marketing Sciences* (Spring 1990), pp. 143–152.

37 Forelle, Charles, "Many Colleges Ignore New SAT Writing Test," *Wall Street Journal*, (December 7, 2005), http://online.wsj.com; "Kaplan's New SAT Survey Results," Kaplan Inc., College Admissions, Kaplan Web site, http://www.kaptest.com, accessed February 14, 2006.

38 Based on "Do-Not-Call List Reduces Telemarketing, Poll Finds," *Wall Street Journal* (January 12, 2006), http://online.wsj.com.

Chapter 8

1 Based on Thomas Mucha, "This Is Your Brain on Advertising," *Business 2.0* (August 2005), 8 (August), 47–49 and Peter Laybourne and David Lewis, "Neuromarketing: The Future of Consumer Research?" *Admap* (May 2005), pp. 28–30.

2 Abrams, Bill, *The Observational Research Handbook* (Chicago: NTC Business Books, 2000), pp. 2, 105.

3 Redmond, E. C. and C. J. Griffith, "A Comparison and Evaluation of Research Methods Used in Consumer Food Safety Studies," *International Journal of Consumer Studies*, 27 (January 2003), 17–33.

4 Adapted with permission from the April 30, 1980 issue of *Advertising Age*. Copyright © 1980 by Crain Communications, Inc.

5 "About Nielsen Media Research," Nielsen Media Research, http://www.nielsenmedia.com, accessed February 24, 2006.

6 "The Portable People Meter System," Arbitron, http://www.arbitron.com, accessed December 17, 2008.

7 "About the PreTesting Company" and "Television," PreTesting Company, http://www.pretesting.com, accessed February 24, 2006.

8 Conley, Lucas, "At 1600 Pennsylvania Avenue, Of Course, It's 'Rush Limbaugh,'" *Fast Company* (February 2005), 91, 29; Dina ElBoghdady, "Advertisers Tune In to New Radio Gauge," *Washington Post* (October 25, 2004), http://www.washingtonpost.com; "iBiquity and Mobiltrak: Bringing Radio into the Digital Age," Bear Stearns Equity Research, February 8, 2005, http://www.bearstearns.com.

9 "Losing Track," Direct, 17 (October 15, 2005), 50–51. See also Steve Johnson, "Who's in Charge of the Web Site Ratings Anyway?" *Chicago Tribune* (February 26, 2006), 1, 18.

10 Kiley, David "Google: Searching for an Edge in Ads," *Business Week* (January 30, 2006), 80–82. infotrac.galegroup.com. See also Pieter Sanders and Bram Lebo, "Click Tracking: A Fool's Paradise?" *Brandweek* 46 (June 6, 2005), 46. Klaassen, A., M. Creamer, A. Hampp and E. Tan "10 Lessons from the Ad Age Digital Marketing Conference," *Advertising Age*, (3/12/2007), 42.

11 Neff, Jack, "Aging Population Brushes Off Coloring," *Advertising Age*, 76 (July 25, 2005), 3–49.

12 Horovitz, B., "Marketers Take a Close Look at Your Daily Routines," *USA Today* (2007), www.usatoday.com/money/advertising/2007-04-29-watching-marketing_N.htm, accessed August 10, 2008.

13 Starr, R. G. and K. V. Fernandez, "The Mindcam Methodology:

Perceiving through the Native's Eye," *Qualitative Market Research: An International Journal*, 10, no. 2 (2007), 168–182.

14　Lee, N. and A. J. Broderick, "The Past, Present and Future of Observational Research in Marketing," *Qualitative Market Research: An International Journal*, 10, no. 2 (2007), 121–129.

15　Stringer, Kortney "Eye-Tracking Technology for Marketers," *Detroit Free Press* (August 1, 2005), downloaded from http://www.highbeam.com/doc/1G1-134701284.html, accessed December 18, 2008, Hill, D., "Face Value," *Marketing Research*, 19 (Fall 2007), 9–14.

16　Krugman's, Herbert B. statement as quoted in "Live, Simultaneous Study of Stimulus, Response Is Physiological Measurement's Great Virtue," *Marketing News* (May 15, 1981), pp. 1, 20.

17　Based on "Mazda Turns to Eye-Tracking to Assist Revamp of European Site," *New Media Age* (November 3, 2005), 8; and "Persuasion Is the New Focus," *Revolution* (February 21, 2006), downloaded from the Media Coverage page of the Syzygy Web site, http://www.syzygy.co.uk.

Chapter 9

1　See http://www.law.com and search key terms such as cigarettes, tobacco, Brown and Williamson, and so on for some examples.

2　Doward, J., "Cigarette Giant to Deny Cancer Link," *The Observer* (October 5, 2003), http://www.guardian.co.uk/society/2003/oct/05/smoking.cancercare, accessed August 24, 2008; Seenan, Gerard, "Smoker's Widow Loses Legal Fight," *The Observer* (June 1, 2005). http://www.guardian.co.uk/society/2005/jun/01/smoking.publichealth1, accessed August 24, 2008.

3　See for example, Bolton, L. E., J. B. Cohen and P. N. Bloom, "Does Marketing Products as Remedies Create "Get Out of Jail Free Cards'?" *Journal of Consumer Research* 33 (June 2006), 71–84; Smith, K. H. and M. A. Stutts, "The Influence of Individual Factors on the Effectiveness of Message Content in Antismoking Advertisements Aimed at Adolescents," *The Journal of Consumer Affairs* 40 (2006), 261–293; Zhao, G. and C. Pechmann, "The Impact of Regulatory Focus on Adolescents' Response to Antismoking Advertising Campaigns," *Journal of Marketing Research* 44 (November 2007), 671–687.

4　Babin, Barry J., David M. Hardesty and Tracy A. Suter, "Color and Shopping Intentions: The Intervening Effect of Price Fairness and Perceived Affect," *Journal of Business Research* 56 (July 2003), 541–551.

5　Christie, J., D. Fisher, J. Kozup, S. Smith, S. Burton, and E. Creyer, "The Effects of Bar-Sponsored Alcohol Beverage Promotions Across Binge and Nonbinge Drinkers," *Journal of Public Policy and Marketing* 20 (Fall 2001), 240–253.

6　Shadish, William R., Thomas D. Cook and Donald T. Campbell, *Experimental and Quasi Experimental Designs for Generalized Causal Inference* (Geneva, IL: Houghton Mifflin, 2002).

7　Like Dragnet, the story is true but the brand names are fictitious.

8　Reitter, Robert N., "Comment: American Media and the Smoking-Related Behaviors of Asian Adolescents," *Journal of Advertising Research* 43 (March 2003), 12–13.

9　Lach, Jennifer, "Up in Smoke," *American Demographics,* 22 (March 2000), 26.

10　Mitchell, Vincent-Wayne and Sarah Haggett, "Sun-Sign Astrology in Market Segmentation: An Empirical Investigation," *Journal of Consumer Marketing* 14, no. 2 (1997), 113–131.

11　Shiv, Baba, Ziv Carmon and Dan Aneley, "Placebo Effects of Marketing Actions: Consumers May Get What They Pay for," *Journal of Marketing Research* 42 (November 2005), 383–393.

12　Peterson, Robert A., "On the Use of Students in Social Science Research: Evidence from a Second Order Meta Analysis," *Journal of Consumer Research* 28 (December 2001), 450–461.

13　Tybout, Alice M. and Gerald Zaltman, "Ethics in Marketing Research: Their Practical Relevance," *Journal of Marketing Research* 21 (November 1974), 357–368.

14　Riell, H., "Getting Back to Beer," *Convenience Store Decisions* 19 (February 2008), 14.

15　*Market Testing Consumer Products* (New York: National Industrial Conference Board, 1967), p. 13.

16　Riste, Christine, "La suprématie contée des prospectus," *Libre Service Actualité-LSA* (January 17, 2002), 1751.

17　Babin, B. J. and Adilson Borges, "Product Category and Promotional Theme Congruency: Its Effect on Preference and Retail Store Image," in *Development in Marketing Science,* H. Spotts, Ed., (Academy of Marketing Science, Coral Gables, FL, 2005).

18　*Jackass 2.5* to Test Market for Online Film Release," CBC News, http://www.cbc.ca/arts/film/story/2007/12/13/jackass-online.html?ref=rss, accessed August 24, 2008.

19　Neff, Jack, "Millstone," *Advertising Age* (June 29, 1998), S16.

20　Cadbury, N. D., "When, Where, and How to Test Market," *Harvard Business Review* (May–June 1975), 96–105.

21　Neff, Jack, "Average City, USA," *Advertising Age* 72 (July 9, 2001), 12.

22　Ramage, Norma, "Testing, Testing 1, 2, 3," *Marketing Magazine* 110 (July 2005), 1196; CNW_Telbec, "Imperial Tobacco Canada Lives Up to Its Corporate Social Responsibility Promise," Groupe CNW (2007), http://www.newswire.ca/fr/releases/archive/September2007/12/c7976.html, accessed November 12, 2008.

23　"How to Open the Northern European Market," U.S. Commercial Service Denmark (2006), http://www.buyusa.gov/denmark, accessed January 22, 2006.

24　Reprinted with permission from Lee Martin, Geoffrey "Drinkers Get Court Call," *Advertising Age* (May 20, 1991). Copyright © 1991 Crain Communications, Inc.

Chapter 10

1　Reichheld, F. F., "The One Number You Need to Grow," *Harvard Business Review* 81 (2003), 46–54; Keiningham, T. L., B. Cooil, T. W. Andreassen and L. Aksoy, "A Longitudinal Examination of the Net Promoter and Firm Revenue Growth," *Journal of Marketing* 71 (2007), 39–51; Grisaffe, D. B., "Questions About the Ultimate Question: Conceptual Considerations in Evaluating Reichheld's Net Promoter Score (NPS)," *Journal of Consumer Satisfaction, Dissatisfaction and Complaining Behavior* 20 (2007), 36–53; Mitchell, A., "The Only Number You Need to Know Does Not Add Up to Much," *Marketing Week* (March 6, 2008), 22–23.

2　Babin, Barry J. and Jill Attaway, "Atmospheric Affect as a Tool for Creating Value and Gaining Share of Customer," *Journal of Business Research*, 49 (August 2000), 91–99; Verhoef, P. C., "Understanding the Effect of Customer Relationship Management Efforts on Customer Retention and Customer Share Development," *Journal of Marketing* 67 (October 2003), 30–45.

3　Periatt, J. A., S. A. LeMay and S. Chakrabarty, "The Selling Orientation-Customer Orientation (SOCO) Scale: Cross-Validation of the Revised Version," *Journal of Personal Selling and Sales Management*, 24 (Winter 2004), 49–54.

4　Anderson, Barry F., *The Psychology Experiment* (Monterey, CA: Brooks/Cole, 1971), p. 26.

5　Cohen, Jacob, "Things I Have Learned (So Far),"*American Psychologist*, 45 (December 1990), 1304–1312.

6　Arnold, Catherine, "Satisfaction's the Name of the Game," *Marketing News*, 38 (October 15, 2004), 39–45. Also, see http://www.theacsi.org.

7　In more advanced applications such as those involving structural equations analysis, a distinction can be made between reflective composites and formative indexes. See Hair, J. F., W. C. Black, B. J. Babin, R. Anderson and R.Tatham, *Multivariate Data Analysis*, 6th ed. (Upper Saddle River, NJ: Prentice Hall, 2006).

8　Bart,Yakov,Venkatesh Shankar, Fareena Sultan and Glen L. Urban, "Are the Drivers and Role of Online Trust the Same for All Web Sites and Consumers? A Large-Scale Exploratory Study," *Journal of Marketing*, 69 (October 2005), 133–152.

9　Cronbach, Lee J., "My Current Thoughts on Coefficient Alpha and Successor Procedures," *Center for the Study of Evaluation Report*, 64, no. 3 (2004), http://epm.sagepub.com/cgi/content/short/64/3/391, accessed October 25, 2008.

10　Hair et al. (2006).

11　Burke Marketing Research, "Rough Commercial Recall Testing," Cincinnati, OH (undated).

12　Hair et al. (2006).

13　Cox, Keith K. and Ben M. Enis, *The Marketing Research Process* (Pacific Palisades,CA: Goodyear, 1972); Kerlinger, Fred N., *Foundations of Behavioral Research,* 3rd ed. (Ft.Worth: Holt, Rinehart and Winston, 1986).

14　Howell, N., "Looking Deeper," *New Media Age* (December 1, 2005), 24–25.

15　Breeden, Richard, "Owners, Executives Cite Small Firms' Advantages," *Wall Street Journal* (January 3, 2006), http://online.wsj.com, accessed August 1, 2006; "Third Annual State of the Union Study for Small and Mid-Sized Business," AllBusiness.com (Winter 2008), News and Press page, http://www.allbusiness.com/economy-economic-indicators/economic-indicators/6598585-1.html, accessed November 14, 2008.

16　Osgood, Charles, George Suci and Percy Tannenbaum, *The Measurement of Meaning* (Urbana: University of Illinois Press, 1957). Seven-point scales were used in the original work; however, subsequent researchers have modified the scale to have five points, nine points, and so on.

17　Peterson, R. A. and W. Wilson, "Measuring Customer Satisfaction: Fact and Artifact," *Journal of the Academy of Marketing Science* 20 (Spring 1992), 61–71; Dawes, J., "Do Data Characteristics Change According to the Number of Scale Points Used? An Experiment Using 5-Point, 7-Point and 10-Point Scales," *International Journal of Market Research* 50, no. 1 (2008), 61–77.

18 See Muk, A., "Consumers' Intentions to Opt in to SMS Advertising," *International Journal of Advertising* 26, no. 2 (2007), 177–198; or Summers, T. A., "Predicting Purchase Intention of a Controversial Luxury Apparel Product," *Journal of Fashion Marketing & Management* 10, no. 4 (2006), 405–419, for examples.

Chapter 11

1 White, Joseph B. "The Price of Safety," *Wall Street Journal* (December 5, 2005), http://online.wsj.com; J.D. Power and Associates, "J.D. Power and Associates Reports: Premium Surround Sound Systems and HD Radio Garner High Consumer Interest Based on Their Market Price, while Consumers Prefer One-Time Fee over the Monthly Fee Associated with Satellite Radio," news release (August 18, 2005), http://www.jdpower.com.

2 Smith, Robert, David Olah, Bruce Hansen and Dan Cumbo, "The Effect of Questionnaire Length on Participant Response Rate: A Case Study in the U.S. Cabinet Industry," *Forest Products Journal* 53 (November–December 2003), 31.

3 "Insurers Question Methods in U.S. Treasury Survey on Terror Backstop," A. M. Best Newswire (April 12, 2005), downloaded from Business & Company Resource Center, http://galenet.galegroup.com.

4 "Mothers Misunderstand Questions on Feeding Questionnaire," Medical Letter on the CDC and FDA (September 5, 2004), downloaded from Business & Company Resource Center, http://galenet.galegroup.com.

5 Donahue, Amy K. and Joanne M. Miller, "Citizen Preferences and Paying for Police," *Journal of Urban Affairs* 27, no.4 (2005), 419–35.

6 Nathan Weber, "Research: A Survey Shows How Media Influence Our Decorating and Cooking Choices," *HFN, the Weekly Newspaper for the Home Furnishing Network* (December 5, 2005), downloaded from Business & Company Resource Center, http://galenet.galegroup.com.

7 Roll, Charles W., Jr. and Albert H. Cantril, *Polls: Their Use and Misuse in Politics* (New York: Basic Books, 1972), pp. 106–7.

8 Other product attributes are relative advantage, compatibility, complexity, and communicability.

9 Dawson, L., "Will Feminization Change the Image of the Sales Profession?" *Journal of Personal Selling and Sales Management* 12 (Winter 1992), 21–32.

10 Payne, Stanley L., *The Art of Asking Questions* (Princeton, NJ: Princeton University Press, 1951), pp. 102–3.

11 Dillman, Don A., *Mail and Internet Surveys: The Tailored Design Method* (New York: John Wiley and Sons, 2000), pp. 357–61.

12 Young, Sarah J. and Craig M. Ross, "Web Questionnaires: A Glimpse of Survey Research in the Future," *Parks & Recreation* 35, no. 6 (June 2000), p. 30.

13 Michel, Marr, "Controversy Redux," CASRO Journal, http://www.decisionanalyst.com/publ_art/contredux.htm, downloaded February 8, 2001.

14 Ghaleb Almekhlafi, Abdurrahman, "Preservice Teachers' Attitudes and Perceptions of the Utility of Web-Based Instruction in the United Arab Emirates," *International Journal of Instructional Media* 32, no. 3 (2005): 269–84.

15 Harzing, Anne-Wil, "Does the Use of English-Language Questionnaires in Cross-National Research Obscure National Differences?" *International Journal of Cross Cultural Management* 5, no. 2 (2005): 213–24.

16 Cateora, Philip R., *International Marketing* (Homewood, IL: Richard D. Irwin, 1990), pp. 387–89.

Chapter 12

1 Based on Deborah Ball, "As Chocolate Sags, Cadbury Gambles on a Piece of Gum," *Wall Street Journal* (January 12, 2006), A1; Cadbury Schweppes, "Products: Trident Splash," Gumopolis, http://www.tridentgum.com, accessed March 16, 2006; Cadbury Schweppes, "New Cadbury Schweppes Americas Confectionary Facility Holds Future Gum Innovation: New Jersey Based Science & Technology Center to Meet Demands of Growing Gum Market," news release, http://www.cadburyschweppes.com (February 6, 2006).

2 Kinne, Susan and Tari D. Topolski, "Inclusion of People with Disabilities in Telephone Health Surveillance Surveys," *American Journal of Public Health* 95, no. 3 (March 2005): 512–517.

3 Brock, Sabra E. "Marketing Research in Asia: Problems, Opportunities, and Lessons," *Marketing Research* (September 1989), p. 47.

4 Rideout, Bruce E., Katherine Hushen, Dawn McGinty, Stephanie Perkins and Jennifer Tate, "Endorsement of the New Ecological Paradigm in Systematic and E-Mail Samples of College Students," *Journal of Environmental Education* 37 (Winter 2005), 3–11.

5 SurveySite, "What We Do: Quantitative Research," http://www.surveysite.com, accessed March 15, 2006.

6 Council of American Survey Research Organizations (CASRO), "Frequently Asked Questions about Conducting Online Research: New Methodologies for Traditional Techniques," (1998), http://www.casro.org.

7 Krosnick, J., "The Distinguishing Characteristics of Frequent Survey Participants," *Proceedings of Midwestern Political Science Association* 1 (2006).

8 Krosnick, J., D. Rivers and N. Norman, "Web Survey Methodologies: A Comparison of Survey Accuracy," *Proceedings of the American Association for Public Opinion Research* 1 (2005).

9 Mellinger, Gloria, "Harris Interactive Inc.," *World Opinion Research Profiles* (July 18, 2000).

10 Ibid.

11 Survey Sampling International, "Internet Sampling Solutions," http://www.ssisamples.com, accessed March 15, 2006.

12 Yeganeh, Hamid, Zhan Su, Elie Virgile and M. Chrysostome, "A Critical Review of Epistemological and Methodological Issues in Cross-Cultural Research," *Journal of Comparative International Management* (December 2004), downloaded from InfoTrac at http://web2.infotrac.galegroup.com.

13 Sigenman, Lee, Steven A.Tuch and Jack K. Martin, "What's in a Name? Preference for 'Black' versus 'African-American' among Americans of African Descent," *Public Opinion Quarterly* 69 (Fall 2005), 429–438.

14 Based on Gene Mueller, "It's Hard to Figure Number of Anglers," *Washington Times* (March 20, 2005), downloaded from InfoTrac at http://web3.infotrac.galegroup.com; Atlantic Coastal Cooperative Statistics Program, "About Us: Committees," http://www.accsp.org, accessed March 16, 2006; Atlantic States Marine Fisheries Commission, "About Us," http://www.asmfc.org, accessed March 16, 2006.

Chapter 13

1 "Gaming News," *Marketing News*, 42 (February 1, 2008), 39; Hellebusch, S J., "Know Sample Quantity for Clearer Results," *Marketing News* 40 (September 15, 2006), 23–26; Sheth-Voss, P., "How Big Should Your Sample Be?" *Marketing Research* 20 (Summer 2008), 25–29.

2 Most of the statistical material in this book assumes that the population parameters are unknown, which is the typical situation in most applied research projects.

3 See Jurik, R., M. Moody and J. Seal, "The Mean vs. the Top Box(es) Scores," *Marketing Research* 20 (Summer 2008), 41–42.

4 The reasons for this are related to the concept of degrees of freedom, which will be explained later. At this point, disregard the intuitive notion of division by n, because it produces a biased estimate of the population variance.

5 In practice, most survey researchers will not use this exact formula. A modification of the formula, $Z = (X - \mu)/S$, using the sample standard deviation in an adjusted form, is frequently used.

6 Hayes, William L. *Statistics* (New York: Holt, Rinehart and Winston, 1963), p. 193.

7 Wonnacott, Thomas H. and Ronald J. Wonnacott, *Introductory Statistics* 2nd ed. (New York: Wiley, 1972), p. 125.

8 Note that the derivation of this formula is (1) $E = ZSX$; (2) $E = ZS/\sqrt{n}$; (3) $\sqrt{n}\, ZS/E$; (4) $(n) = (ZS/E)2$.

Chapter 14

1 Gale Research Database, http://www.gale.cengage.com/.

2 Ziobro, P., "At Domino's, Dough Gets Tighter," *Wall Street Journal* (October 15, 2008), B1.

3 Corso, R. A., "The Harris Poll #6," (January 14, 2008), www.harrisinteractive.com, accessed October 6, 2008.

4 Ricklefs, Roger, "Ethics in America," *Wall Street Journal* (October 31–November 3, 1983), 33.

5 See Dubinsky, Alan J., Rajan Nataraajan and Wen-Yeh Huang, "Consumers' Moral Philosophies: Identifying the Idealist and the Relativist," *Journal of Business Research* 58 (December 2005), 1690–1701; Deal, Ken, "Deeper into the Trees," *Marketing Research* 17 (Summer 2005), 38–40.

6 http://www.wineinstitute.org/resources/statistics, accessed December 30, 2008; http://winemarketcouncil.com, accessed December 30, 2008.

7 The data analysis tool must be added to the conventional Excel install by unpacking the data tool. This can be done by clicking on tools and then clicking on ad-ins and following the instructions. See http://www.microsoft.com for more instructions on how to accomplish this.

8 Iuso, Bill, "Concept Testing: An Appropriate Approach," *Journal of Marketing Research* 12 (May 1975), 230.

9 See a comprehensive statistics text for a more detailed explanation.

10 Diamon, Sidney, "Market Research Latest Target in Ad Claim," *Advertising Age* (January 25, 1982), 52. Reprinted with permission by Crain Communications, Inc.

Chapter 15

1 Murphy, Victoria, "The Revolution That Wasn't," *Chain Store Age* 172 (October 27, 2003), 210.

2   Tang, F. F. and X. Xing, "Will the Growth of Multi-Channel Retailing Diminish the Pricing Efficiency of the Web?" *Journal of Retailing* 77 (2001), 319–333.

3   Three nonparametric tests—the Wilcoxon matched-pairs signed ranks test, the Kruskal-Wallis test, and the Mann-Whitney U test can also be used but are not described here.

4   The formula is not shown here but it can be found in most basic statistics books.

5   See, for example, Armstrong-Stassen, M., "Designated Redundant but Escaping Lay-Off: A Special Group of Lay-Off Survivors," *Journal of Occupational and Organizational Psychology* 75 (March 2002), 1–13.

6   This is the "statistical alternative" hypothesis.

7   Sukhdial, Ajay, Damon Aiken and Lynn Kahle, "Are You Old School? A Scale for Measuring Sports Fans' Old-School Orientation," *Journal of Advertising Research* 42 (July/August 2002), 71–81.

Chapter 16

1   Dowling, Mike, "Mr. Dowling's Rosetta Stone Page," http://www.mrdowling.com/604-rosettastone.html, accessed November 2, 2008; "Rosetta Stone," Microsoft Encarta Online Encyclopedia (2008), http://encarta.msn.com, accessed November 2, 2008.

2   Yore, L. D., M. K. Florence, T. W. Pearson and A. J. Weaver, "Written Discourse in Scientific Communities: A Conversation with Two Scientists about Their Views of Science, Use of Language, Role of Writing in Doing Science, and Compatibility between Their Epistemic Views and Language," *International Journal of Science Education* 28 (February 2006), 109–141.

3   Sullivan, E. A., "Twitterpated: Marketers Enamored of Online Communication System," *Marketing News* (October 15, 2008), 8.

4   The original version of this chapter was written by John Bush, Oklahoma State University, and appeared in William G. Zikmund, *Business Research Methods* (Hinsdale, IL: Dryden Press, 1984).

5   Keating, M., "Research Reports: A Valuable Tool for Getting Up to Speed in the Marketplace," *Occupational Hazards* (August 2008), 56D–56F.

6   "A Speech Tip," *Communication Briefings* 14, no. 2 (1995), p. 3.

7   These guidelines, adapted with permission from Marjorie Brody (President, Brody Communications, 1200 Melrose Ave., Melrose Park, PA 19126), appeared in "How to Gesture When Speaking," *Communication Briefings* 14, no. 11 (1995), p. 4.

8   "Tips of the Month," *Communication Briefings* 24, no. 7 (May 2005), p. 1.

9   Based on Bridis, Ted, "Study: Shoppers Naïve about Online Pricing," *Information Week* (June 1, 2005), downloaded from InfoTrac at http://web2.infotrac.galegroup.com; Annenberg Public Policy Center (APPC), "Annenberg Study Shows Americans Vulnerable to Exploitation in the Online and Offline Marketplace," news release (June 1, 2005), http://www.annenbergpublicpolicycenter.org; and Joseph Turow, Lauren Feldman and Kimberly Meltzer, "Open to Exploitation: American Shoppers Online and Offline," APPC report (June 2005), downloaded at http://www.annenbergpublicpolicycenter.org.

INDEX

INDEX

A

Absolute zero, ratio/interval scale characteristic, 244–245
A.C. Nielsen Company
  data, 340
  data storage/retrieval, 197
  information collection, 69
  television ratings, estimates, 345
Accuracy, 270. See also Questionnaires
Acquiescence bias, 152
Active research, 76
Administrative error, 153–154
Advertisements, viewing data, 197
Advertising research, 139
Advocacy research, 80–81
Aided recall, 281
Ambiguity, avoidance, 278–279
Analysis
  computer programs, 362–365
  definition, 358–359
  interpretation, contrast, 364–365
Analysis of variance (ANOVA), 384
  display, 388
  illustration, 385–386
  interpretation, 387e
  logic, illustration, 385e
  variance, partitioning, 386–387
Answers, falsification (deliberateness), 151
Appendix, 404
Applied marketing research, 7–8
Arbitron, 340
Artifacts, 194–195
Assumptions, making (avoidance), 280
At-home scanning systems, 199
Attitudes
  defining, 252
  face, matching (example), 258e
  intention, relationship, 263–265
Attitude scaling, 237
Attitudinal rating scales, 252–263
Attributes, 246
Authorization letter, 403
Axes values, impact, 408e

B

Back translation, 293–294
Balanced rating scale, 261–262
Bannerheads, usage, 405
Bar charts, 409–410
  example, 410e
Basic experimental designs, factorial experimental designs (contrast), 220
Basic marketing research, 7–8
Beer markets, market potential, 129e
Behavioral intention, 264–265
Behavioral tracking, 31–32
Benchmark value, 366
Best Buy, sales/service integration (success), 17–18
Between-groups variance, 386

Between-subjects designs, advantages, 222
Bias. See Order bias
  sources, 313
Bimodal distribution, 360
  consistency, 360e
Bivariate χ^2 test value, calculation, 377
Bivariate hypothesis, 374e
Bivariate statistical analysis, 365
Blind experimental administrator, usage, 219
Blocking variables, 210
Books, information, 137
Boolean search, 37
Business, information problem, 5
Business research, 5
Buyer/seller, ethical behavior, 79

C

χ^2 test, 375–378
Callbacks, 159, 165
Camera surveillance, 199–200
Case studies, 97
  defining, 101
  usage process, 101
Category labels, 261
Category scales, 253–254
  selection, 254e
CATI. See Computer-assisted telephone interviewing
Causal evidence, establishment, 233
Causal inference, 47
Causality, 47–48
  direct evidence, absence, 46
Causal marketing research, 44
Causal research, 47–49
  focus, 50
Cell, term (usage), 214
Census, 301
  requirement, absence, 321
  updates, 139
Central-limit theorem, 337–339
Central location interviewing, 165
Central tendency, measures, 328–329
  usage, 347
Channel power, 240
Charts, usage (effectiveness), 407–410
Check boxes, 289
Checklist questions, 274, 289
Cheetos, taste tests, 15
Children, spending (research), 77–78
Chi-square automatic interaction detection (CHAID), 359
Chi-square calculator, 377–378
Chi-square test, 375-378
Choice, 253
  technique, 260
Click-through rates (CTRs), 198
  online advertising, relationship, 198
Click-through sequence, 382
Click-through tracking, 32
Client sponsor (user), rights/obligations, 79–81

Closed questions, 272
Close-ended statements, usage, 272–276
Clusters
  examples, 318e
  sampling, 318–319
Codes, 353
Coding, 353
Coefficient alpha, 249
Coffee
  industry, sales (increase), 3–4
  statistics, 4
Cohort effect, 223
Collages, 110–111
Color/lighting, experimental conditions (example), 210e
Commercial information sources, 138–139
Communication
  content, study, 196
  technologies, usage, 20
Company
  consumer perspective, 5
  efforts, integration (importance), 12
  meaning, 5
Comparative rating scale, 260
Comparative scale, selection, 260–261
Competitive business firm, marketing research, 4
Competitive environment, reading, 228–229
Complementary evidence, 190–191
Complexity, avoidance, 276
Composite measures, 247
Composite scale, computation, 247e
Computer-assisted telephone interviewing (CATI), 165–166
Computerized data archives, 32–35
Computerized voice-activated telephone interview, 166
Computer programs, analysis, 362–365
Computer software, usage, 380–382
Computer technology, changes, 20
Concept, 240
  testing, 96–97
Concerned parties, rights/obligations, 74–75
Conclusions, 60
  reporting, relationship, 50
Concomitant variation, 47
Conditions. See Experimental conditions
  constancy, 220
Confidence expression, 341
Confidence intervals, 340–342
  estimate, 340–341
  estimation, 339–342
Confidence level, 341
  estimation, 346
  factor, 344
Confidentiality, 75, 84–85
Confounds, 216. See also Experimental confounds
Constant-sum scale, 257–258

Constructs, 241
  validity, 251
Consumers
  attitude, 139
    direct assessment, 260
  average patronage scores, 211e
  behavior
    cross-cultural differences, 312
  behavior, identification, 127–128
  desire, 5
  needs, marketing department focus, 10
  perspective. See Company
  problems, 230
  quality perceptions, pricing research (usage), 15
Consumption data, 139
Content
  analysis, 196
  observation, 187–188
  providers, 36
  validity, 250
Contingency tables, 356–358, 368
  frequencies, involvement, 375
  variables, 358
Continuous measures, 246
Continuous variable, 368
Contrived observation, 191, 192–193
Control establishment, 219–220
Control groups, 213
Convenience samples, 321
Convenience sampling, 312
Convergent validity, 251
Conversations, 109–110
Cookies, 38
Corporate culture, 240
Correspondence rules, 240
Cost per click, 198
Counterbalancing, 220
Counterbiasing statement, 277–278
Covariate, 210
Cover letter, 169
  request, 170e
Criterion validity, 250–251
CRM. See Customer relationship management
Cross-cultural differences, research, 312
Cross-functional effort, 10–11
Cross-functional teams, 73
Cross-tabulation, 356–359. See also Percentage cross-tabulations
  application, 393
  depiction, 357e
  inclusion, 406e
  number, determination, 359
  result, 378e
  SPSS output, examples, 364e
  tables, 357e, 368, 375–378
Customer relationship management (CRM), 38
  database marketing, relationship, 132–133

Customers
  behavior, casino tracking, 29
  chain, marketing-oriented firm
      visualization, 11
  discovery, 132
  information, competitor information
      (integration), 67
  orientation, 8–9
  relationships, building, 67
  retention, 11
  satisfaction, 240
Custom research, 69

D

Data
  availability, 19
  characteristics, 26–27
  collection
      ease, 20
      technology, impact, 77
  completeness, 27
  conversion, 125, 359–360
  display, tabular/graphic methods, 362
  editing/coding, 59
  gathering, 59
      advantage, 189
      impact, 280
  mining, 131–132
      blogs, usage, 133
  obtaining, 192
  processing, 59
      error, 153
  qualitative meaning, 365
  relevance, 27
  term, usage, 25
  transformation, 359–362
      problems, 361–362
  value, 25–26
  warehouse, 29
  warehousing, 29
  wholesalers, 33
Data analysis, 59, 352
  ease, 20
  Excel, usage, 363e
  marketing research form, 12
Databases, 29
  marketing, CRM (relationship),
      132–133
Debriefing, 78, 225
Deception, impact, 78
Decision
  encounters, 65–67
Decision risk, reduction, 13e
Decision statements, 56e
Decision support system (DSS), 28–35
  illustration, 29e
  manager, 71
  marketing input sources, 30e
  usage, 28
Deliberate falsification, 151
Deliverables, 51
Delivery information acquisition devices
      (DIADs), 27
Demand characteristics, 217–225
  reduction, 218–219
  reference, 217–218
Demand effect, 218
  experimenter bias, relationship, 218
Demographic characteristics, 232e
Demographic updates, 139
Dependent variable, selection/
      measurement, 214
Deposits
  frequency distribution, 326e

  probability distribution, 327e
Depth interviews, 91–92, 107–108
  procedure, 108
  results, example, 107
Descriptive analysis, 354–355
Descriptive marketing research, 44
Descriptive research, 45–46
  accuracy, importance, 46
  focus, 50
Descriptive statistics, 325–332, 354
  illustration, 355e
  SAS computer output, 364e
Determinant-choice question, 274
Deviation scores, 331
Diagnostic analysis, 46
Dichotomous-alternative question, 274
Differences, test, 373
Ding, usage, 24–25
Direct observation, 191–193
  errors, 192
  Research Snapshot discussion, 193
  usage, 192
Discrete measures, 245–246
  statistics, appropriateness, 245
Discrete scales, values (assignation), 246
Discriminant validity, 251
Discussion guide, 112
Dispersion
  contrast, 330e
  measures, 329–332
      purpose, 332
Disproportional sampling
  example, 317e
  proportional sampling, contrast, 317–318
Disproportional stratified sample, 317
Distribution
  channel, 227
  research, 16
Do-not-call legislation, 76
Door-to-door interviews, 159
Double-barreled questions, avoidance, 279
Drop-down box, 289
Drop-off method, 172
DSS. See Decision support system
Dummy coding, 353
Dummy variables, 353–354

E

Effects, 210–212
Effects coding, 353–354
Efficiency, improvement, 12
Elaboration, 358–359
  analysis, 359
Electronic data interchange (EDI), 35
Electronic indexing, vendors, 34e
E-mail
  advantages/disadvantages, 173–174
  questionnaire, 172–173
  sampling, relationship, 173
  surveys, 172–174
  usage, 172–173
Environmental conditions, 107
Environmental scanning, 37–38, 128–129
Errors. See Within-group error
  magnitude, 344
  range, doubling, 345
  reporting, honesty, 84
Error trapping, 291
Ethical dilemmas, 74
Ethical questions, philosophical
      questions, 74
Ethnography, 97, 99–100
  observation, 99–100
Executive summary, 403

Experimental administrator, usage. See
      Blind experimental administrator
Experimental characteristics, summary, 212
Experimental conditions, 209–210
  administration, 219
  example, 210e
Experimental confounds, 216–217
Experimental designs
  contrast, 220
  issues, 212–217
Experimental disguise, 218–219
Experimental graphs
  example, 211e
  usefulness, 233
Experimental groups, 213
Experimental research, descriptive
      research (contrast), 219–220
Experimental subjects
  debriefing, 225
  isolation, 219
Experimental treatment, 212–213
  levels, 213
Experimental validity, 217–225
Experimental variable, 48
Experimentation, ethical issues, 225
Experimenter bias, demand effects
      (contrast), 218
Experiments, 48–49. See also Marketing
  causes, testing, 49e
  characteristics, 208–212
Explanatory legends, 407
Exploratory marketing research, 44
Exploratory qualitative research, misuses,
      117–119
Exploratory research, 44, 53
  designs, qualitative research
      (relationship), 95–97
  practice, 117–119
  problem solving, relationship, 44
External distributors, information
      marketing, 32
External secondary data sources, 134–139
External validity, 224–225
  increase, field experiments (usage), 233
  internal validity, trade-offs, 225
Extraneous variables, 216–217
  identification, 217
Extremity bias, 152
Eye-tracking monitor, 201

F

Face-to-face contact, absence, 163–165
Face-to-face focus group techniques,
      online group techniques
      (contrast), 115
Face validity, 250
Fact-finding, 127–129
Factorial experimental designs, basic
      experimental designs (contrast), 220
Fax surveys, 172
Feedback, opportunity, 156
Field experiments, 221–222
  laboratory experiments, artificiality, 221e
  usage, 233
Field notes, 110
Figure number, usage, 407
Filter question, 282
Financial databases, 34
Fireclicks (software), 412e
Firms
  marketing, isolation/cross-functionality
      (contrast), 10e
  organizational procedures, absence,
      10–11

Fixed-alternative questions
  limited-alternative responses, 272
  open-ended response questions,
      contrast, 272–273
  types, 274–275
  usage, 273
Focus blog, 115
Focus group, 54–55
  composition, 105–106
  diagnostic tools, 106–107
  disadvantages, 113–114
  discussion guide, conducting, 113
  emotion, impact, 119
  flexibility, 103–104
  illustration, 104
  interview, 102–107
      advantages, 103–104
      conducting, 112–113
  moderator, 106
  outline, preparation, 112–114
  piggybacking, 103
  respondents, 104–106
  scrutiny, 104
  session, 107
  speed/ease, 103
  time, impact, 118
Footnotes, usage, 407
Forced answering software, 291
Forced-choice rating scale, 262
Ford Motor Company
  quality advertisement, 11
  research, importance, 13
Forecast analyst, 71
For-profit business organizations,
      functions, 6
F-ratios, variance components (usage), 388
Free-association techniques, 110–111
Frequency
  distribution, 326–327
  table, 355–356, 368
Frequency-determination question, 274
F-test, 387–388
  examination, 391
Funnel technique, 282

G

Gallup, George, 306
General linear model (GLM), 390–393
  equation, 390
Geo-demographics, 14
Geographic areas, market potential
      (estimation), 129–130
Global information system, 27
Global marketing information, sources
      (examples), 141e
Global markets, questionnaires (design),
      293–294
Global research data, 140–142
Golden Books, distribution efforts, 16
Goodness of fit, χ^2 test, 375–378
Google, customer click-through
      tracking, 32
Government agencies, 140–141
Government information sources, 137
Grand mean, 386
Graphic aids, 405
Graphical tools, advantage, 393
Graphical user interface (GUI) software, 288
Graphic rating scales, 258–259
Grounded theory, 97, 100–101
  defining, 100
  usage process, 101
Groups, differences (testing), 372

H

Häagen-Dazs, China appearance, 68
Harley-Davidson, overseas operation, 12
Harm, protection, 78–79
Harris Interactive, Inc., 310
    poll, responses, 340
Hermeneutics, 98–99
Hermeneutic unit, 98
Heterogeneity, 343
Hidden observation, 189
Hidden Valley Ranch (HVR), field
        market experiment, 231
High dispersion, low dispersion
        (contrast), 330e
Histogram, 355
History effect, 223
Humans
    behavior, observation, 189–190
    observation, ethical issues, 193–194
Human subjects review committee, 79
Hypothesis, 55–56
    testing, 226
        procedure, 365–366
        statistics, usage, 365–368

I

Idealism, 74
Ideas, generation, 96
Independent samples *t*-test, 378
    appropriateness, 381
    calculation, 378–380
    one-way ANOVA, special case, 389
    results, 380e
Independent variable (IV)
    manipulation, 212–214
    multiple usage, 213–214
    number, 373
Indexes, 247
Index measures, 246–249
Index numbers, 362
Inferential statistics, 325–332
Information
    characteristics, 26–27
    completeness, 27
    distribution channels, 134–139
    FDA concern, 6
    gathering, 36
        survey, usage, 146–147
    marketing, 32
    problem, 5
    product, 134–139
    services, vendors, 34e
    systems, 24. *See also* Global
        information system
    technology, 38
    term, usage, 25
    value, 25–26
Informed consent, 75
    right, 78
In-home phone surveys, 161
In-house research, 65
    attractiveness, 66–67
Innovation, exploratory research
        (relationship), 44
Input management, 29–32
Institutional Review Board, 79
Instrumentation effect, 223–224
Integrated marketing communication, 17
Integrated marketing mix, 17–18
Intelligence, value, 25–26
Intelligent quotient (IQ) scores,
        distribution, 333e

Interaction effects, 211
Interactive help desk, 291
Interactive media, online focus groups
        (relationship), 114–115
Interactive surveys, approaches, 155
Internal consistency, 248–249
Internal data, 133–134
Internal records, 30–31
Internal secondary data, sources, 133–134
Internal validity, 222–224
    external validity, trade-offs, 225
    maximization, laboratory experiments
        (usage), 233
    researcher concern, 321
International audience, counting, 293
International marketing research,
        sampling frames, 307
International marketing researchers,
        questionnaires, 293
Internet
    callbacks, 175–176
    information, 135
    navigation, 36–37
    personalized/flexible questioning, 176
    privacy, 81
    questionnaires, 287–291
    questions, display, 290e
    reports, 412
    response
        quality, 178
        rates, improvement, 176–177
    secondary data sites, 136e
    security, concerns, 177
    software, usage, 291
    survey, ease/cost, 309
Internet Service Provider (ISP),
        complaints, 310
Internet surveys, 174–178
    mail surveys, contrast, 177
    real-time data capture, 175
    respondent participation/
        cooperation, 175
    speed/cost-effectiveness, 174
    visual appeal/interactivity, 174–175
Interpretation, 364–365
    axes values, impact, 408e
Interpretive software, 116
Interquartile range, 331
Interval scales, 244
    information, providing, 243e
Interviewer
    absence, 168
    bias, 152–153
    cheating, 151
    error, 154
    influence, 158
Interviewing, facilitation, 114–116
Intranets, 38–39
Inventories, 195–196
Isolation, cross-functionality (contrast), 10e
Item quality, assessment, 256

J

Jelly Belly
    marketing research, 3
    Sports Beans, introduction, 3
Judgment sampling, 312

K

Keyword search, usage, 37
Knowledge management, 24
Krispy Kreme, product offering (change), 27

L

Laboratory experiments, 220–221
    field experiments, artificiality, 221e
    usage, 233
Laddering, 107–108
Landline phones, 160–161
    interviews, pros/cons, 162e
    results, mobile phone results
        (contrast), 163
Language
    simplicity, 276
    specificity, 278–279
Large research firms, 71
Law of diminishing returns, 343
Layout
    decisions, 288
    determination, 284–291
    importance, 287
    issues, 288–289
Leading questions, avoidance, 276–278
Libraries, information, 134–135
Likert scale, 255
    items, selection, 255
Limited research service companies, 69
Line graphs, 408
List, systematic sampling, 316e
List brokers, 306
Literature review, 53–54
Loaded questions, avoidance, 276–278
Local project, national project (contrast), 320
Long-run profitability, 9–10
    emphasis, 8
    illustration, 9e
Low dispersion, high dispersion
        (contrast), 330e
Loyalty, concept, 240

M

Magnitude of error, 344
Mail notification, advantages, 177
Mail questionnaires, 166–168
    cost, 167
    geographic flexibility, 167
    keying, codes (usage), 171–172
    length, 168
    respondent convenience, 167
Mail surveys, 166–167
    advance notification, 171
    follow-ups, 171
    Internet surveys, contrast, 177
    money, impact, 169–170
    response rates, increase, 169–172
    return rate, problem, 281
Main effects, 210
Managerial decision situation, defining,
        52–53
Manipulation, 48
    checks, 222–223
Marginal tabulation, 355
Market
    intelligence, 25
    opportunities, identification/
        evaluation, 14
    potential, estimation, 129–130
    research reports, 373
    segment, catering, 305e
    tracking, 128
Market-basket analysis, 132
Market-driven design processes,
        implementation, 11
Marketing
    channel, 16

communication. *See* Integrated
        marketing communication
concept, 8
    aspects, 9–10
    implementation, 11–12
    ethics, 74
experiments
    conducting, 207
    effects, 210–212
input sources. *See* Decision
        support system
isolation, cross-functionality
        (contrast), 10e
knowledge, increase, 28
metrics, 18
    application, 259
    orientation, 8
    performance, analysis, 18
    problems, 46
    researchers
        observation, 188e
        surveys, conducting, 154–155
    strategy
        elements, 15
        stages, development/
            implementation, 13
        weaknesses, identification, 226
    term, reservation, 7
Marketing mix. *See* Integrated marketing mix
    elements, 226
    planning/implementing, 14–18
    testing, 226–227
Marketing-oriented firms, customer chain
        visualization, 11
Marketing research, 11–12. *See also*
        Applied marketing research; Basic
        marketing research
    advantages, 123
    benefits, costs (contrast), 19
    census, requirement (absence), 321
    classification, 43–44
    conducting, timing
        (determination), 20e
    data, availability, 19
    decision, nature, 19
    defining, 5–6
    department, organization, 72e
    director, 71
        managerial role, 71–72
    disadvantages, 124–125
    ethical issues, 74–85
    experimental manipulations, 233
    field, usage, 67–73
    firm, size, 69–71
    future, 20–21
    human side, 64
    impact, 13e. *See also* Product
    jobs, range, 72
    necessity, 18–20
    observation, 187–191
    organizational/ethical issues, 64
    payment, 73
    process, 42
        flowchart, 52e
    questions, 5
    report, 400–405
        basics, 405
    role, 2
    secondary data, usage, 123–126
    strategic marketing management,
        relationship, 13–14
    time research, 18
    types, 43–50
        characteristics, 49e

Market-share data, 138–139
Matching, 216
Maturation effect, 223
McDonald's digital archive maintenance, 34–35
Mean, 328–329. *See also* Grand mean
    comparison, *t*-test, 378–383
    distribution, 338e
    involvement, 344–345
    standard error, 337
    usage, commonness, 347
Meaning, semantic differentials (relationship), 257
Measurement, 237
    process, 238–241
    system, error (existence), 240
    units, 125
    validity issues, 239e
Mechanical observation, 196–200
Media
    information sources, 137–138
    representatives, demographic/lifestyle data, 32
Media research, assistance, 17
Median, 329
    appropriateness, 347
    split, 361
        problem, 361e
Medina's Kicks, Wal-Mart testing, 16
Metropolitan Statistical Area (MSA), 364
Mid-sized research firms, 71
Mindcam, usage, 200
MINITAB, 363
Misrepresentation, 151
Mistakes, avoidance, 276–281
Mobile phone interviews, 161
    pros/cons, 162e
        results, landline phone results (contrast), 163
Mobiltrak, content observation, 197
Mode, 329
Model building, 129–133
Moderator variable, 359
Monadic rating scale, 260
Monadic scale, selection, 260–261
Moral standards, 74
Mortality effect, 224
Moving averages, usage, 130e
Multi-attribute attitude score, 263–264
Multicollinearity, diagnosis, 392
Multiple-bar chart, 410e
Multiple-grid question, 284
Multiple items, usage, 262–263
Multiple regression
    analysis, interpretation, 390
    model, interpretation (steps), 391–392
    results, interpretation, 392e
Multistage area sampling, 319
Multivariate statistical analysis, 365
MySpace, data, 33
Mystery shoppers, 78, 192
    research, 78

N

National project, local project (contrast), 320
Networks, EDI (relationship), 35
Neural network, 132
Neurological devices, 200
New product success, forecasting, 226
No-call legislation, 161
No contacts, number, 150
Nominal numbering systems, usage, 242
Nominal scale, 241–242
    information, providing, 243e

Nominal scaling, arbitrariness, 242
Non-forced-choice scale, 262
Noninteractive media, 155
Noninteractive surveys, approaches, 155
Nonprobability sampling, 311
    probability sampling, contrast, 311–314
Nonrespondents, 150
Nonresponse error, 149–150
Nonsampling error, 308–311
    occurrence, 215
Nonspurious association, 47–48
Nonspuriousness, evidence (establishment), 48
Nonverbal behavior, recognition, 190
Nonverbal communication, observation/interpretation, 190e
Normal curve, representation, 333
Normal distribution, 333–336
    example, 333e
Null hypothesis, 366

O

Observation, 110, 186–191. *See also* Content; Contrived observation; Direct observation; Hidden observation
    studies
        design, 195
        nature, 188–189
Observer bias, 192
One-way analysis of variance, 384–389
    special case, 389
Online advertising, CTRs (relationship), 198
Online focus groups, interactive media (relationship), 114–115
Online focus group techniques, face-to-face focus group techniques (contrast), 115
Online panels, 307
Online reports, 411
Online screening survey, questions, 289e
Open-ended boxes, 289
Open-ended response questions
    fixed-alternative questions, contrast, 272–273
    problem/topic, posing, 272
    usage, 273
Open-ended statements, usage, 272–276
Operational definitions, 240–241
Operationalization, 240
Opportunities. *See* Market opportunities
Opt in, 310
Oral presentation, 410–412
    example, 410e
    gestures, usage, 412
    preparation, importance, 411
Order bias, 281–282
Ordinal scales, 242, 244
    information, providing, 243e
Organizational behavior, cross-cultural differences, 312
Organizational culture, ethnography study relevance, 99
Outside agency, 65
Outside vendors, information marketing, 32
Overattention, 228

P

Paired comparisons, 259–260
Paired-samples *t*-test, 382–383
    management researcher usage, 382
    results, example, 383e
Paired values, 382
Panel members, compensation, 310

Panel samples, 309–310
Parameter estimate choices, 391
Parameters, estimation, 339–342
Participant-observation, 99
Participation rate, 157–158
Passive research, 76–77
Percentage cross-tabulations, 358
Percentage distribution, 327
Percentages, direction (determination), 358
Performance
    analysis. *See* Marketing
    criteria, usage, 14
Performance-monitoring research, 18
Periodicals, information, 137
Personal interviews
    advantages, 156–158
    complex answers, examination, 157
    conducting, 155–166
    cost, 159
    disadvantages, 158–159
    feedback, opportunity, 156
    global considerations, 160
    length, 157
    participation rate, 157–158
    props, 157
    questionnaire, 286e–287e
        completeness, 157
    surveys, question phrasing, 275–276
    visual aids, 157
Personality, concept, 240
Phenomenology, 97–99
Physical objects, observation, 194–196
Physical-trace data, recording, 195
Physiological reactions, measurement, 200–202
Picture frustration, 111
Pie charts, 408
Piggybacking, 103
Pilot studies, 54–55
Pivot question, 283
Placebo, 78
    effect, 219
Point estimates, 340
Polling, experiment, 277
Pooled estimate, 379
Population (universe), 301. *See also* Target population
    advance knowledge, 320
    defining, 304–305
    distribution, 336
        example, 338e
    element, 301
        frequency distribution, 336
    heterogeneity, 343
    identification, 304–307
    investigation, 302
    mean, calculation, 339e
    members, exclusion, 306
    parameters, 326
        characteristics, 325–327
    size, sample size (relationship), 345
    standard deviation, 343
        formula, 332
    variance, 343
Pop-ups, usage, 309
Predictive analytics, 35–39
Predictive validity
    example, 251
Preliminary tabulation, 292–293
Prescription drugs, Internet purchase, 16
Presentation, results (misrepresentation), 85e
Pretest, 54–55
    conducting, 293
    results, tabulation, 292–293
Pretesting, 178–180

Pricing
    definition, 15
    research, 15–16
    usage. *See* Consumers
Primary sampling unit (PSU), 307
Privacy, 81. *See also* Internet
    participant right, 76–78
Probability, 327
    distribution, 334
    sampling, 311, 314–319
        nonprobability sampling, contrast, 311–314
Probing, 108
Problem, formulation (importance), 52
Procter & Gamble (P&G), product management, 95
Producers, information, 136–139
Product
    category, consumer behavior (identification), 127–128
    commercialization (prevention), marketing research (impact), 12
    concepts, testing, 97e
    content, sale, 5
    designs, weaknesses (identification), 226
    meaning, 5
    research, 15
    success, forecasting, 226. *See also* New product success
    weaknesses, identification, 227–228
Production-oriented firm, 8
Product-oriented firm, 8
Project, report format (tailoring), 402
Projective research techniques, 111
Promotion
    definition, 16
    experiments, results, 212e
    research, 16–17
Proportional sampling, disproportional sampling (contrast), 317–318
Proportional stratified sample, 317
Proportions, 327
    comparison, Z-test (usage), 383–384
    sample size, determination, 345–346
Proprietary data, 133–134
Proprietary marketing research, 31
Pseudo-research, 82
Psychogalvanometer, 201
Public opinion research, 139
Pull technology, 38
Pupilometer, 201
Purchase behavior data, 139
Purposive sampling, 312
Push button, 288
Push polls, 83
Push technology, 38
Puzzle, sample, 303e
P-value, 366
    statistical tests, relationship, 367e

Q

Qualitative data, 96
Qualitative marketing research, 92
Qualitative methods, quantitative methods (contrast), 94–95
Qualitative research, 91
    defining, 92–94
    description, 92–93
    exploratory research designs, relationship, 95–97
    orientations, 97–101
    quantitative research, contrast, 93–94
        illustration, 94e
    researcher dependence, 92

technology, impact, 114–116
tools, 102e
uses, 92–93
Qualitative responses. *See* Structured
    qualitative responses
    coding, 353–354
Qualtrics, 288
Quantitative data, 96
Quantitative marketing research, 94
Questioning phrasing, 272–276
Questionnaires. *See* Internet;
    Traditional questionnaires
    accuracy, 271
    ambiguity, avoidance, 278–279
    assumptions, making (avoidance), 280
    completeness, 157
    complexity, avoidance, 276
    content, 271
    design, 269, 284
        consideration, 270–271
    distribution, 173
    interactivity, software (usage), 289–291
    items, design, 294
    language, simplicity, 276
    open-ended/closed questions,
        mixture, 273
    pretesting/revising, 291–294
    relevancy, 271
    specificity, 278–279
Questions. *See* Filter-question;
    Pivot question
    answers, 305
    asking
        order bias, 281–282
        variety, 302
    avoidance, 280–281
    complexity, reduction, 275
    criteria, 270
    flow, 283e
    means, involvement, 344–345
    phrasing, 275–276
    sequence, 281–284
Quota sampling, 312–314
    advantages, 313
    purpose, 313

R

R^2, examination, 391
Radio button, 289
Radio frequency identification (RFID),
    usage, 27–28
Radio monitoring, 196–197
Random assignment. *See* Subjects
Random digit dialing, 162–163
Random error, sample size (relationship),
    342–343
Randomization, 215–216
Random number tables, 314e
Random sampling. *See* Simple
    random sampling
    error, 214–215, 308–311
        systematic sampling error, contrast,
        148–154
Range, 330–331
Ranking, 253, 259
    technique, 260
Rank order, 259
Rating, 253
    technique, 260
Ratio scales, 244–245
    information, providing, 243e
Recall stimulation, requirement, 283e
Recoding, usage, 248
Refinement, 358–359

Refusals, 150
Regression analysis, 390–392
Regression weight, 391
Relationship marketing, 11
Relationships, building, 11
Relativism, 74
Relevance, 27, 270
Relevancy. *See* Questionnaires
Reliability, 248–249
    necessity, 249
    validity, construct, 251
Repeated measures, 216
Replicable, term (usage), 117
Report. *See* Internet; Marketing research
    appendix, 404
    body, 404
    components, 402–404
    conclusions/recommendations
        section, 404
    format, 400–401
        flowchart, 401e
    introduction section, 404
    preparation, 60
Research. *See* Customer research;
    Marketing research
    absence, 82–83
    action, 50e
    analyst, 71
    assistants, 71
    best design, 57–58
    conducting, questions, 19
    contractors, 67–69
    definition, 6
    departments, staff function, 67
    design, 56
        planning, 56–58
    essence, 7
    firms, size (ranking), 70e
    follow-up, 412
    harm, protection, 78–79
    hypotheses, 56e
    information, value, 19
    Internet, usefulness, 36–37
    method, selection, 57
    methodology section, 404
    misrepresentation, 84
    objectives, 51
        defining, 50–56
        example, 56e
        stating, 55
    participant, rights/obligations, 75–79
    phenomenological approach, 98
    process
        alternatives, 50–51
        stages, 50–60
        stages, illustration, 51e
    program, 61
        strategy, 60–61
    project, 60
    purpose, 82–83
    report, 400, 413
        components, 402–404
    results
        communication, 399
        production, 49–50
    service. *See* Standardized research service
    suppliers, 67–69
        open relationship, 79
    type, uncertainty (impact), 49–50
    users, 312
    vague questions, impact, 60
Researchers
    conflicts of interest, 85–86
    identification, 65–67
    rights/obligations, 81–85

Respondents, 146
    anonymity, 167–168, 176
        absence, 159
    attitude, 264
    errors, 149–153
    memory, taxing, 280–281
    participation/cooperation, 175
    questionnaire convenience, 167
    research investigator selection, 57
Response bias, 151
    types, 152–153
Response rates, 168–169
    improvement, 176–177
Responses
    categories, number, 261
    incentives, 164–165
    latency, 191
    number, existence, 362–363
    positions, 261
Results
    misrepresentation, 85e
    presentation, honesty, 84
    production. *See* Research
    section, 404
Retail saturation, index, 131
    calculation, secondary data (usage), 131e
Reverse coding, 248
Reverse directory, 307
Rights/obligations. *See* Client sponsor;
    Concerned parties; Research
    interaction, 75e

S

Sales
    calls, number, 328e, 332e
    forecast, secondary data/moving
        averages (usage), 130e
    forecasting, 130–131
    levels, example, 330e
    research, mixing, 82
    volume
        emphasis, absence, 8
        estimation, 228–229
Salesperson input, 31
Sample, 301
    accuracy, degree, 320
    attrition, 224
    bias, 149
    design, selection, 319–321
    distribution, 336
    imperfections, 311
    mean, sampling distribution, 336
    reasons, 301–303
    resources, 320
    sample distribution, contrast, 333–337
    selection
        error, 153–154, 214–215
        stages, 304e
    statistics, 326
        characteristics, 325–327
    survey, 146
    time, allotment, 320
Sample size, 342–347
    determination, 324, 345–346
    factors, 343–344
    judgment basis, 346–347
    estimation, 344–345
    population size, relationship, 345
    random error, relationship, 342–343
Sampling, 58–59. *See also* Probability
    designs, 300
    distribution, 336–337
        formal definition, 337
    e-mail, relationship, 173

errors, 311e
    frame, 306–307. *See also* International
        marketing research
        error, 306
        identification, 304–307
    procedures, 300
    results, accuracy/reliability, 302–303
    services, 306–307
    units, 307
    selection, 58–59
SAS, 363–364
    ANOVA display, 388e
    computer output, 364e
    cross-tabulation result, 378e
Scales, 240
    categories, number, 261
    levels, facts, 243e
    mathematical/statistical analysis,
        245–246
    measurements, levels/types, 241–246
        illustration, 355e
    quality, assessment, 256
    values
        computation, 247–248
        selection, 408
Scanner-based consumer panel, 199
Scanner-based research, 199
Scanner data, 32
    weakness, 34
Scanner research parallel data, 199
Science, exploratory research, 117–119
Scientific decision processes, 118
Scientific investigation, objectivity, 84
Scientific method, 7
    summary, 8e
Scrolling layout, 288
Search engine
    Google revolution, 37
    usage, 37
Secondary data
    collection, 124
    evaluation, 126e
    fact-finding, 127–129
    Internet sites, 136e
    measurement units, 125
    reliability/validity, 125–126
    research, 122
    research designs, objectives, 127–133
    source, providing, 356
    studies, research objectives, 127e
    usage, 130e
Secondary sampling unit, 307
Secrecy, loss, 231
Selection effect, 224
Self-administered questionnaires, 166–178
    distribution forms, usage, 172
    print/electronic form, 167e
Self-administered surveys, question
    phrasing, 275–276
Self-selection bias, 150
Semantic differential, 256–258
    meaning, relationship, 257
    scale, example, 256e
    scoring, 257
Semi-structured interviews, 109–110
Sentence completion methods, 110–111
Sequential sampling, 344
Service monitoring, 83
Shopping mall intercepts, 159, 160
Short-term profits, emphasis (absence), 8
Significance levels, 366
Simple bar chart, 410e
Simple-dichotomy questions, 274
Simple line graph, 408
    sales frequency, representation, 409e

Simple random sampling, 314–315
Simple transformations, 359–360
Single items, usage, 262–263
Single-source data, 32, 140–142
Single-source databases, examples, 140e
Single-source data-integrated
    information, 140
Site analysis techniques, 131
Skip questions
    example, 287e
    usage, 285e
Small research firms, 70–71
Smart agent software, 38
Snowball sampling, 313–314
Social desirability bias, 153
Social networking, 115
Software development, 116
Sorting, 253
    technique, 260
Source notes, usage, 405, 407
Southwest Airlines, examination, 24
Special-interest topics, availability, 138
Split-ballot technique, 278
Split-half method, 249
SPSS, 363–364
    ANOVA display, 388e
    cross-tabulation, 364
    cross-tab window, 377
    output, 364
Spurious association. See
    Nonspurious association
    example, 48e
Spyware, 77
SSB, 388
SSE, 388
SST, 388
Standard deviation
    calculation, 332e
    definition, 332
    usage, reasons, 331–332
Standard error, pooled estimate, 379
Standardized distribution curve, 336e
Standardized normal distribution, 333
    example, 334e
Standardized normal table, example, 334e
Standardized regression coefficient
    (β), 391
Standardized research service, 68–69
Standardized values, computation,
    335–336
    example, 335e
Statistical base, 358
Statistical databases, 33–34
Statistical error, 308
Statistical packages, 362–364
Statistical tests
    examination, 391
    p-values, relationship, 367e
Statistical theory, review, 324
Statistics
    selection, 375e
    usage, 365–368
Status bar, 288–289
Store conditions, problems, 228
Strategic marketing management,
    marketing research (relationship),
    13–14
Stratified sampling, 315–317
    selection, 316
Streaming media, 114
Structured qualitative responses, 353–354
Stubheads
    format, usage, 406e
    usage, 405

Student surrogates, 224–225
Subjective results, 95
Subjects, 209
    experimental condition,
        administration, 219
    isolation. See Experimental subjects
    random assignment, 216
    referral, 209
Summary. See Executive summary
Summated scale, 247
Supply chain, 16
Survey Monkey, 288
Surveys, 56, 146
    advantages/disadvantages, 147–148
    approach, selection, 178
    conducting, 154–155
    cross-tabulation tables, 357e
    errors
        categories, 149e
        reduction, 154
        sources, 148–154
    instruments, pretesting, 178–180
    methods, advantages/
        disadvantages, 179e
    participation, cover letter (usage), 170e
    research, 145
        advantages, 147
        disadvantages, 148
        ethical issues, 180
        responses, 292
    results
        distortion, order bias (impact), 281
        representation, 310
    sample, 146
    self-administered questionnaires, usage,
        166–178
    sponsorship, 171
Survey Sampling International, 310e
Symptoms, 44
Syndicated service, 68
Systematic error
    occurrence, 215
    rule-of-thumb estimates, 154
Systematic sampling, 315–316
    error, 308–310
        random sampling error, contrast,
        148–154

T

Table of contents, 403
Tables
    components, 406e
    creation, 405–406
    elements, 405
    numbers, usage, 405
    usage, effectiveness, 405–406
Tabulation. See Cross-tabulation;
    Marginal tabulation
    creation/interpretation, 355–356
Tachistoscope, 221
Target, shoppers (differences), 343
Target markets, analysis/selection, 14
Target population
    defining, 304–305
    identification, 58
Technology, qualitative research
    (relationship), 114–116
Telephone interviewing. See Computer-
    assisted telephone interviewing
Telephone interviews, 160–161. See also
    Computerized voice-activated
    telephone interview
    characteristics, 162–165

    cooperation, 164
    global considerations, 166
    representative samples, 162–163
    response incentives, 164–165
    speed/cost, 163
Telephone questionnaire, skip questions
    (usage), 285e
Telephone surveys, question phrasing,
    275–276
Television monitoring, 196–197
Temporal sequence, 47
Tertiary sampling unit, 307
Testing effects, 223
Test-marketing
    advantages, 229
    cost, 229–230
    disadvantages, 229–231
    secrecy, loss, 231
    time, problem, 230
    usage, 226
Test-markets
    demographic characteristics, 232e
    research, 226
    results, projection, 228
    sabotage, 228–229
    site, selection, 231–233
    usage, 226
Test of differences, 373
Test-retest method, 249
Test-retest reliability, 249
Test statistic, appropriateness, 373–375
Test units, 214
    destruction, 303
    selection/assignments, 214–217
Text-message surveys, 178
Text mining, 116
Thematic apperception test (TAT), 111
Themes, 101
Theory, 55
Time constraints, 18
Time lapse, 229
Title, usage, 407
Title page, 403
Top-box scores, 327
Total quality management, 11
Total value management, 18
Total variability, 386–387
Trade areas/sites, analysis, 131
Trade association information
    sources, 138
Traditional questionnaires, 284, 287
Transformations, bimodal distributions
    (consistency), 360e
Transmittal letter, 403
Trends
    analysis, 128
    spotting, 35
Trust, concept, 240
Truth, obligation, 75
t-statistic, calculation, 379–381
t-test, 378–383. See also Independent
    samples t-test; Paired-samples
    t-test
    interpretation, 381
    results, computation, 380–382
    usage, 382
Two-variable cross-tabulations,
    usage, 375
Type I errors, 366–368
Type II errors, 366, 368

U

Unaided recall, 281

Unbalanced rating scale, 261–262
Uncertainty, impact. See Research
Unconscious misrepresentation, 151
Unequal intervals, usage, 407e
Uniform Resource Locator (URL),
    36–37
Unimodal data, problems, 361e
Unique visitors, number, 198
Univariate hypothesis, 366
Univariate statistical analysis, 365
Universal Product Code (UPC),
    information, 34
Universe (population), 301
Unobtrusive methods, 59
Unobtrusive observation, 189
U.S. Food and Drug Administration
    (FDA), function, 6

V

Validity, 250–251
    establishment, 250–251
    reliability, contrast, 251
Value
    concept, 240
    input, decision risk (reduction), 13e
Variable piping software, 291
Variables, 240–241. See also
    Extraneous variables
    categories, collapsing/combining, 360
    differences, testing, 372
Variance, 331–332, 343. See also
    Between-groups variance;
    Within-groups variance
    components, usage, 388
Vendors
    information, 135–136
    working relationships,
        improvement, 67
Videoconferencing, 114
Video databases, 34–35
Viewership, measurement, 340
Visible observation, 189
    personal interviews, combination, 191
Visual medium, absence, 165
Voice-pitch analysis, 201

W

Wal-Mart shoppers, differences, 343
Web sites
    secondary data source,
        providing, 356
    traffic, monitoring, 198
    visitors, 309
Web surveys, page-by-page/scrolling
    format, 288
Web tracking, 32
Weighting factor, 386
Within-group error, 387
Within-group variance, 387
Within-subjects design, 222

Y

Yoplait Go-Gurt, consumer research, 9

Z

Zales, marketing research findings,
    16–17
Zoomerang, 288
Z-test, usage, 383–384